GRANT
LEE
AND

D1590381

VICTORIOUS AMERICAN AND VANQUISHED VIRGINIAN

EDWARD H. BONEKEMPER III

REGNERY
HISTORY

Copyright © 2012 by Edward H. Bonekemper III

All rights reserved. No part of this publication may be reproduced or transmitted in any form or by any means electronic or mechanical, including photocopy, recording, or any information storage and retrieval system now known or to be invented, without permission in writing from the publisher, except by a reviewer who wishes to quote brief passages in connection with a review written for inclusion in a magazine, newspaper, broadcast, or on a website.

Cataloging-in-Publication data on file with the Library of Congress
ISBN 978-1-62157-010-3

Published in the United States by
Regnery History
An imprint of Regnery Publishing, Inc.
One Massachusetts Avenue NW
Washington, DC 20001
www.RegneryHistory.com

Originally published in 2008 by
Praeger Publishers, 88 Post Road West, Westport, CT 06881
An imprint of Greenwood Publishing Group, Inc.
www.praeger.com

This is the first Regnery edition published in 2012

Manufactured in the United States of America

10 9 8 7 6 5 4 3 2 1

Books are available in quantity for promotional or premium use. Write to Director of Special Sales, Regnery Publishing, Inc., One Massachusetts Avenue NW, Washington, DC 20001, for information on discounts and terms or call (202) 216-0600.

Distributed to the trade by
Perseus Distribution
250 West 57th Street
New York, NY 10107

*This book is dedicated to the faculty,
past and present, of Muhlenberg College,
a small but great liberal arts institution
in eastern Pennsylvania.*

CONTENTS

List of Maps ix

Preface xi

Introduction

Why Grant Won and Lee Lost xiii

Civil War Timeline xxv

Chapter 1

Tough Beginnings and Mexican War Experiences 1

Chapter 2

1861: Open and Closed Doors to Civil War Command 17

Chapter 3

Late 1861/Early 1862: Lee's First Loss and Grant's Early

Victories 27

Chapter 4

March–June 1862: Grant Wins at Shiloh while Lee Stymies

McClellan 47

Chapter 5

1862–63: Lee Conducts a Costly Offensive while Grant Aims
for Vicksburg 97

Chapter 6

May–July 1863: Lee Loses Gettysburg as Grant Captures
Vicksburg 155

Chapter 7

Autumn 1863: Lee Lends an Assist as Grant Saves Chattanooga
and a Union Army 247

Chapter 8

Early 1864: Both Generals Prepare for Confrontation. 269

Chapter 9

Spring 1864: Grant Attacks and Besieges Lee 285

Chapter 10

Late 1864: Grant and Sherman Move toward Victory 321

Chapter 11

Early 1865: Lee Surrenders to Grant 349

Chapter 12

A Comparison of Grant and Lee 379

Appendix I

Casualties in Grant's Battles and Campaigns 435

Appendix II

Casualties in Lee's Battles and Campaigns 479

Acknowledgments 503

Notes 505

Selected Bibliography

Memoirs, Letters, Papers, and Other Primary Documents 625

Index 659

MAPS

Grant's Early Western Battles and Campaigns (1861–62) 34

The First Day of Shiloh (April 6, 1862) 54

The Peninsula Campaign (April–June 1862) .69

Battle of Seven Pines (May 31–June 1, 1862) 72

Seven Days' Battle (June 25–July 1, 1862) 78

McClellan's Slow Movement from the Peninsula
    to Second Manassas (August 1862) 102

Maryland Campaign (September 3–13, 1862) 108

Maryland Campaign (September 14–16, 1862) 111

The Battle of Antietam (September 17, 1862). 115

McClellan's Failure to Promptly Pursue Lee after Antietam
    (September 18–November 6, 1862). 126

Highlights of the Battle of Chancellorsville (May 2–4, 1863) 162

Armies' Movements to Gettysburg (June–July 1863). 178

The Battle of Gettysburg (July 1–3, 1863) 182

Grant's Vicksburg Campaign (March–July 1863). 220

x

Maps

Grant's Breakout at Chattanooga (Oct.–Nov. 1863)..............256
Grant's and Sherman's Pincers Movements (1864–65)...........276
The Overland Campaign (May–June 1864) 292
The Appomattox Campaign (April 2–9, 1865)..................368

PREFACE

While researching my first two books, *How Robert E. Lee Lost the Civil War* and *A Victor, Not a Butcher: Ulysses S. Grant's Overlooked Military Genius*, I became convinced that Lee often has been overrated and, moreover, that the deification of Lee frequently led to the unfair denigration of Grant. My work on *McClellan and Defeat: A Civil War Study of Fear, Incompetence and Worse* reinforced my view that Lee has been given more credit than he deserves.

In the course of discussing those books with thousands of Civil War Round-table members and others interested in the Civil War, I detected both a need and a desire for a fresh, sharp, and comprehensive comparison of Lee and Grant. That comparison would necessarily include a discussion of the interrelationship of their seemingly separate 1861–63 campaigns as well as their more familiar head-to-head contests in 1864–65. This book contains my subjective analysis of their intertwined campaigns, relationships, and impacts during the Civil War, as well as exhaustive statistics on both sides' casualties in all the Civil War battles and campaigns of both generals.

WHY GRANT WON
AND LEE LOST

Ulysses S. Grant and Robert E. Lee were the generals primarily responsible for the outcome of America's great Civil War. Superseded in overall importance only by their respective presidents, Abraham Lincoln and Jefferson Davis, Grant and Lee were the key players on the war's battlefields.

Because Southerners were more greatly affected by the war and had a need to rationalize its origins and results, Southern-oriented historians dominated Civil War historiography for the first century after the war. They created the "Myth of the Lost Cause" and designated Lee as the god of this mini-religion. Their creation was so effective that many Americans have perceived Lee as the greatest general of the war (and perhaps in "American" history) while Grant often was denigrated and rebuked as a butcher, a drunk, and a victor by brute force alone.

This book presents a different view of the performances of Grant and Lee as Civil War generals. Grant, a national general, was the most successful Union or Confederate general of the war. He drove the Confederates from the Mississippi Valley, the primary "western" theater of the war, through a series of brilliant battles and campaigns—from the early capture of Forts Henry and Donelson through the unparalleled Vicksburg campaign. Then it took him a mere month to save a Union Army trapped in Chattanooga and drive the Rebels there back into Georgia—with a giant assist from Lee. Finally, Grant was brought to the East to face Lee's army, which he defeated within a year to effectively bring the war to a close.

Although Lee has been praised for his offensives against the Union Army of the Potomac, he was carrying out an aggressive strategy with aggressive tactics that were inconsistent with what should have been a Confederate grand defensive strategy. The Union, not the Confederacy, had the burden of winning the war, and the South, outnumbered about four-to-one in white men of fighting age, had a severe manpower short-age. Nevertheless, Lee acted as though he were a Union general and attacked again and again as though his side had the burden of winning and also had an unlimited supply of soldiers. Lee's aggressiveness resulted in a single general's record 209,000 casualties for his army (55,000 more than Grant's)[*]; those were casualties the South could not afford. After Lee's first fourteen months of command, the Confederate Army of Northern Virginia had incurred an intolerable 98,000+ casual-ties by the close of the Gettysburg Campaign. These losses left Lee's army too weak to effectively stymie Grant's Overland Campaign to Richmond and Petersburg in 1864 and eventually resulted in Lee's surrender on April 9, 1865.

Ironically, Grant, who could not even obtain a command at the beginning of the war, rose to the top of the Union armies and oversaw victories in three theaters of war. Lee, on the other hand, started near the top in the Confederate hierarchy of generals and oversaw the

---

[*] See Appendices I and II for detailed listings of the casualties incurred and imposed by the armies of Grant and Lee.

slaughter, decline, and surrender of his army—despite the fact that the rest of the Confederacy was drained of soldiers to replace those killed and wounded under Lee's command. A study of the roles and actions of Grant and Lee, and the interplay between their activities throughout the war, is critical to an understanding of their positive and negative influences on the war's outcome.

The antebellum experiences of these two generals affected their Civil War careers. Grant's small-town childhood was unremarkable, his first military career ended in an alcohol-related resignation and disgrace, and his seven years of civilian jobs immediately prior to the Civil War were marked by uninterrupted failure. Although Lee's childhood was marred by his father's abandonment of the family, their survival on intra-family charity, and his father's and brother's scandalous behavior, he married into the wealthy Washington/Custis family, had a successful 32-year antebellum military career, and was recognized as one of the nation's leading military officers when the Civil War erupted.

Grant and Lee's Mexican War experiences were marked by both similarities and differences. Both of them performed heroically and were awarded multiple brevet (temporary and honorary) promotions as they played key roles in General Winfield Scott's war-winning campaign from Vera Cruz to Mexico City. Grant, however, had the advantage of also serving under Zachary Taylor, a less formal and more communicative officer than Scott, in the similarly successful early Mexican War campaigns in Texas and northern Mexico.

Because of his disastrous, alcohol-related exodus from the army in 1854, Grant was unable to interest George B. McClellan, John C. Frémont, or anyone else in the Union Army in offering him a commission when the Civil War began. Only by training novice Illinois volunteer regiments was Grant able to earn the attention and respect of Illinois' governor and thereby obtain a colonelcy in the Union Army. Lee, on the other hand, had his choice of plum assignments for either side in the Civil War. His mentor, Union General-in-Chief Winfield Scott, offered him command of all Union armies, but then-Colonel Lee declined the offer, resigned his United States commission, immediately took command of Virginia's military forces, and soon was appointed the second-highest-ranking operational full general in the Confederate Army. In the opening months of the Civil War, therefore, Grant started at the bottom while Lee started at the top.

In Richmond, a desk-bound and frustrated Lee effectively supervised Virginia operations of other Confederate generals in the early stages of the war. He was particularly disappointed about missing the field action during the Rebels' initial victory at First Manassas (First Bull Run) in July 1861. When at last he was given a field command in northwestern Virginia, Lee failed dismally. At Cheat Mountain in September, he devised a complicated battle plan that resulted in Rebel defeat. After other failures and final loss of control in the mountains that would become the new state of West Virginia, Lee was withdrawn to Richmond and then assigned to improving Confederate defenses in the southeast.

Grant, meanwhile, was on a roll. In September 1861, just after the Rebels violated Kentucky's neutrality, Grant's troops seized the crucial Kentucky towns of Paducah and Smithland, where the Tennessee and Cumberland rivers respectively meet the Ohio. Two months later, Grant commanded his first battle at Belmont, Missouri. As he conducted a raid, he relied on diversionary feints to keep the enemy guessing about his intent.

When Grant suggested to Major General Henry Halleck that a joint navy/army force capture Confederate Forts Henry and Donelson on the Tennessee and Cumberland rivers, Halleck told him such a campaign was none of his business. After Lincoln tired of Major General George B. McClellan's "slows" in the East, however, and ordered all Union forces forward, Halleck authorized the attack on Fort Henry. Within hours, Grant and Navy Flag Officer Andrew Foote launched an upriver assault and quickly captured the fort. On his own initiative, Grant then moved on to Fort Donelson. Within two weeks he captured that better-defended fort and a 14,000-man army in a manner that earned him the nickname "Unconditional Surrender" Grant. The February 1862 capture of Forts Henry and Donelson was a major blow to the left flank of the Confederacy and ranks among the most significant actions of the Civil War. It earned Grant a promotion to Major General of Volunteers.

After advancing his Army of the Tennessee deep into the Confederacy—to Pittsburg Landing, or Shiloh, in far southwestern Tennessee—Grant was so focused on moving on to capture Corinth, Mississippi, that he became careless. His army was surprised at Shiloh in April by a massive attack by Rebel forces that had been gathered from around the Confederacy. On the first day of "Bloody Shiloh," Grant saved his army, and on the second he daringly counterattacked and drove the enemy forces from the battlefield and back toward Corinth. Despite its disastrous start, Shiloh was a major strategic and tactical victory for Grant.

Adverse public reaction to the numerous casualties at Shiloh led Halleck to take command of the combined armies of Grant, John Pope, and Don Carlos Buell; relieve Grant of his army command; elevate Grant to a meaningless deputy position under Halleck; and almost cause Grant to resign his commission. Halleck went on to win a hollow victory at Corinth but then dispersed his huge armies. After Halleck was promoted to general-in-chief and left for Washington, Grant resumed command of the Army of the Tennessee. He spent most of 1862 protecting his hard-earned territorial gains with the forces left to him in the Mississippi Valley. While the bulk of "western" Union troops moved to the middle theater (between the Mississippi Valley and Eastern/Virginia theaters) to repel a Rebel invasion of eastern Tennessee and Kentucky, Grant won victories at Iuka and Corinth, Mississippi, with his limited number of troops.

While Grant had won significant victories that weakened the Confederate left flank, Lee remained in the background building defenses in the Southeast and then (beginning in March 1862) serving as Jefferson Davis' military advisor in Richmond. Lee's opportunity for major field command came with Joseph Johnston's wounding on May 31, 1862, at the Battle of Seven Pines (Fair Oaks) just outside Richmond. That battle marked the first serious fighting during McClellan's slow and deliberate Peninsula Campaign from Fort Monroe in Hampton up the Virginia Peninsula toward Richmond.

After assuming command of the Army of Northern Virginia on June 1, 1862, Lee achieved fame and success through victories over McClellan and Major General John Pope. With high casualties, Lee drove McClellan away from Richmond during the Seven Days' Battle and then moved into central and northern Virginia to sweep Pope's army, undermined by McClellan, off the battlefield at Second Manassas (Second Bull Run). On his own volition, Lee then overextended his army by invading Maryland, splitting his army into five segments, incurring almost 14,000 casualties on a single day at the Battle of Antietam, and retreating back to Virginia. That Maryland (Antietam) Campaign cost Lee irreplaceable losses and also lost the Confederacy its last real chance for European intervention on its behalf. But for McClellan's cowardly and incompetent conduct, Lee would have lost his army at Antietam.

Lee's good fortune in the Union's selection of commanders of the Army of the Potomac continued when Ambrose Burnside replaced McClellan and then was replaced by Joseph Hooker. In December 1862, Burnside ordered suicidal Union attacks at Fredericksburg, Virginia, that gave Lee a major defensive victory.

By the end of 1862, therefore, both Lee and Grant had won significant victories, but the results of those victories were quite different. Grant's victories at Belmont, Fort Henry, Fort Donelson, Shiloh, Iuka, and Corinth greatly expanded Union control in western Kentucky and Tennessee, as well as northern Mississippi. Grant's successes had been achieved with a little over 20,000 casualties while he imposed more than 35,000 casualties on his opponents. Meanwhile, Lee's victories at the Seven Days', Cedar Mountain, Second Manassas, and Fredericksburg engagements had foiled Union strategic offensives, but his embarrassing Maryland Campaign had lost the possibility of European intervention and nearly cost Lee his army. Lee's constant demand for reinforcements and his 50,000 casualties had drained other areas of the South of many of their soldiers. That drainage made Grant's and other "western" generals' jobs easier.

In late 1862 and early 1863, Grant undertook a number of initiatives aimed at capturing Vicksburg, Mississippi, the last significant Rebel bastion on the Mississippi River. Although stymied at first, he persisted in his efforts and ultimately carried out one of the greatest military campaigns in history. While employing three major diversionary feints, Grant moved the bulk of his army down the west bank of the river, conducted a huge amphibious crossing of the river to the Mississippi shore, and headed inland. Although they initially outnumbered Grant in the theater, the befuddled Rebels could not ascertain his movements and whereabouts. Thus, he outnumbered and defeated them in each of five battles fought in the eighteen days following his troops' landing. After two unsuccessful assaults on Vicksburg itself, Grant settled into a siege. Six weeks later he accepted the surrender of the city and a 28,000-man army—a surrender regarded by many as the most important of the war.

Grant's Vicksburg Campaign, which gave the Union control of the entire Mississippi Valley, was greatly assisted by Lee. In early May 1863, Lee had repelled a Union offensive commanded by Hooker at Chancellorsville, but Rebel frontal assaults on the final days of that battle (often ignored by historians) cost Lee many casualties. Riding the crest of his influence following Chancellorsville, Lee convinced Jefferson Davis to allow him to keep Lieutenant General James Longstreet's First Corps with him in the East for what became his Gettysburg Campaign. Longstreet had been seeking new opportunities in other theaters, but Lee argued that Longstreet's corps was needed for an offensive in the East and that the semi-tropical Mississippi climate would defeat the Vicksburg Campaign of Grant, who was sweeping through Mississippi at that very moment.

Instead of sending the 1st Corps to oppose Grant in Mississippi or even to aid the outnumbered General Braxton Bragg's Army of Tennessee, Lee retained that corps for his own offensive campaign in the East. Early in June 1863, while Grant besieged Vicksburg, Lee began troop movements toward Pennsylvania. In the ensuing Gettysburg Campaign, Lee committed a series of costly errors, and his army suffered 28,000 casualties before retreating back to Virginia once again. By the close of the Gettysburg Campaign, Lee's cumulative casualties had reached more than 80,000 while he had imposed about 75,000 on his Union opponents, who could afford the losses much more than he. Lee's army thereafter would remain relatively inactive until it faced Grant in 1864.

With Lee's assistance in ensuring that his Mississippi Valley foes received no help from the East, Grant completed his Vicksburg Campaign with little difficulty. As he had done at Fort Donelson, Grant maneuvered so that he would capture a Confederate army as well as a critical place. Those two armies who surrendered to Grant were the only

Civil War armies that surrendered to their opponents before Lee surrendered to Grant at Appomattox. Their surrenders demonstrate Grant's focus on going after enemy armies as well as places—a focus shared by Lincoln and critical to Union victory. After Vicksburg, Grant's cumulative casualties were about 31,000 while he had imposed over 77,000 on his foes. So Grant had gained control over a wide swath of the western Confederacy and made Confederate armies pay the price for opposing him, while Lee had decimated his own army in a series of strategic and tactical offensives that were unnecessary to the stalemate the Confederacy needed.

In late 1863, these two generals' activities became even more intertwined. After the Gettysburg defeat, Lee's political capital ebbed and he could not prevent the transfer of Longstreet and most of his corps to another theater—the Confederates' one significant inter-theater transfer. Lee's opposition, however, resulted in those troops' transfer from Virginia to northern Georgia being delayed from August 20 to September 7. That delay proved devastating because Union General Burnside's capture of Knoxville, Tennessee, on September 2 converted a two-day rail journey to a ten-day one and kept Longstreet's artillery and many of his troops from arriving in time for the two-day Battle of Chickamauga in northern Georgia. Those missing troops and guns probably allowed the escape, rather than the destruction of, Union Major General William Rosecrans' army, which fled back to Chattanooga, Tennessee.

But Lee did even more damage. Within days after Longstreet started his ten-day trek, Lee began a series of letters to Davis and Longstreet urging that Longstreet be sent to clear Burnside out of Knoxville and then be promptly returned to Lee. Amazingly, Davis carried this suggestion to Bragg and Longstreet during a trip to Bragg's headquarters to resolve a dispute between Bragg and all his subordinate generals (including the borrowed Longstreet). Because Bragg and Longstreet wanted to be rid of each other, they agreed to Lee's proposal and Longstreet and 15,000 troops were sent away from Chattanooga on November 5.

The Lee-generated departure of Longstreet played into the hands of Grant, who had been brought to Chattanooga to save the nearly besieged Army of the Cumberland. Grant arrived there on October 23, created a life-saving supply line within five days, and began gathering Union troops from around the country (including two corps from Lee's theater) for a breakout from Chattanooga. While Grant thus built his forces up to perhaps 75,000, the Lee-inspired exodus of Longstreet's 15,000 troops simultaneously reduced Rebel strength in the area to a mere 36,000. Thus, when Grant's troops successfully charged up Missionary Ridge, the spread-thin Confederates fled in considerable disarray into northern Georgia.

Grant's victory at Chattanooga, with the unintended assist from Lee, ended any semblance of Rebel control in Tennessee and set the stage for Sherman's 1864 Atlanta Campaign. Having won the Mississippi Valley and saved the trapped Union army in the middle theater, Grant was the obvious choice to be brought east and promoted to general-in-chief. His troops' total western and middle theater casualties were 37,000, and they imposed 84,000 casualties on their opponents. He had won the West and was expected to win the East, the middle theater, and the war. With Sherman's help, he lived up to those expectations.

In their well-known head-to-head confrontation in 1864–65, Grant achieved complete success in less than a year after launching his Overland Campaign on May 4, 1864. Expected to produce results in time to aid Lincoln's critical bid for reelection in November 1864, Grant took his aggressiveness and persistence beyond the levels he had demonstrated in the Western and Middle Theaters. But he also continued to demonstrate his dexterity and cunning. After bloody conflicts at the Wilderness, Spotsylvania Court House, the North Anna River, and Cold Harbor, Grant disengaged his entire army from Lee's without Lee's knowledge, sent it across the James River, and attacked Petersburg, the key to Richmond, before Lee could reinforce it. Because Grant's subordinates failed miserably, Petersburg held. Thus, Grant won the war in the East in eleven months instead of two.

While Grant and Lee fought in Virginia, Sherman advanced three armies toward Atlanta. Although Lee had succeeded in getting Longstreet's troops back to Virginia, the Union 11th and 12th Corps, which had been transferred from Virginia to Chattanooga as part of Grant's buildup there, remained in the middle theater as the new Army of the Ohio. Sherman's armies thus outnumbered Joseph Johnston's Army of Tennessee and continually moved around its flanks toward Atlanta. While all those armies were in the Atlanta environs, Davis (with Lee's blessing) replaced Johnston with John Bell Hood—one of the major mistakes of the war. A protégé of Lee's, Hood wanted to attack whether or not circumstances justified attacking. Hood proceeded to go on the offensive, weaken his army, lose Atlanta, and virtually destroy his army in a quixotic foray into Tennessee late in 1864.

The fall of Atlanta virtually ensured Lincoln's reelection, which doomed the Confederacy. Lee had facilitated Atlanta's fall by vouching for Hood's fighting capabilities and also by not reinforcing the outnumbered opponents of Sherman. Such an inter-theater transfer was the worst nightmare of Grant and Sherman as they planned and executed their simultaneous 1864 campaigns. But Lee, first a Virginian and second a Confederate, never considered that option. Proof of its feasibility is that Lee sent Lieutenant General Jubal Early on a "long-shot" mission against Washington instead of proposing to send his 14,000 to 18,000 troops south to oppose Sherman and at least keep Union forces from capturing Atlanta before the crucial presidential election. Lee's failure to reinforce the Confederates in Georgia demonstrated that Lee was a one-theater general (while Grant was a national general).

Grant's performance outshone that of Lee. Grant, a national general, won the Mississippi Valley theater, saved a trapped Union army in the middle theater, and won the eastern theater (with fewer casualties than incurred there by his Union predecessors). The North had the burden of winning the war to end Southern independence, and Grant's aggressive actions were consistent with achieving victory. Grant won the war and was the greatest general of the war. On the other hand, Lee was a one-theater general who adversely influenced Confederate prospects in his own and other theaters. Although the South needed only a stalemate to maintain its independence and was badly outnumbered, Lee gambled for victory, initiated the disastrous Maryland and Gettysburg strategic campaigns, used overly aggressive tactics that decimated his army, and placed the Confederacy in a weakened condition that assured the reelection of Lincoln, whose defeat had become the South's best hope for victory. Finally, as the appendices to this book demonstrate in detail, the respective casualty figures of these two generals contradict the myth about who, if either, was a butcher. For the entire war, Grant's soldiers incurred about 154,000 casualties (killed, wounded, missing, captured) while imposing about 191,000 casualties on their foes. In all their battles, Lee's troops incurred about 209,000 casualties while imposing about 240,000 casualties on their opponents. Thus, both generals' armies imposed almost 40,000 more casualties than they incurred. Lee, however, who should have been fighting defensively and preserving his precious manpower, instead exceeded Grant's understandable aggressiveness and incurred 55,000 more casualties than Grant.

In summary, Grant's aggressiveness in three theaters was consistent with the Union need for victory and resulted in success at a militarily reasonable cost.

CIVIL WAR TIMELINE
Selected campaigns and battles

	1861	1862	1863	1864	1865
WESTERN THEATER	Belmont (Nov. 7)	Forts Henry and Donelson (Feb. 6–16) Shiloh (April 6–7) Iuka (Sept. 19) Corinth (Oct. 3–4)	Vicksburg Campaign (March 31–July 4)		
MIDDLE THEATER		Perryville (Oct. 8) Stones River (Murfreesboro) (Dec. 31, 1862–Jan. 2, 1863)	Tullahoma Campaign (June 23–July 3) Chickamauga (Sept. 19–20) Chattanooga Campaign (Oct. 24–Nov. 25)	Atlanta Campaign (May 1–Sept. 2) Battles of Atlanta (July 20–Sept. 1) Sherman's March to the Sea (Nov. 15–Dec. 21) Hood's Tennessee Campaign (Nov. 29–Dec. 27)	Sherman's March through the Carolinas (Jan. 19–April 26) Bentonville (March 19–21)
EASTERN THEATER	First Bull Run (Manassas) (July 21) Ball's Bluff (Oct. 21)	Peninsula Campaign (March 17–July 1) Seven Days' (June 25–July 1) Second Bull Run (Manassas) (Aug. 28–30) Antietam (Sept. 17) Fredericksburg (Dec. 13)	Chancellorsville (May 1–5) Gettysburg (July 1–3)	Overland Campaign (Wilderness, Spotsylvania Court House, North Anna River, Cold Harbor (May 4–June 12) Petersburg Campaign (June 15, 1864–April 3, 1865)	Appomattox Campaign (April 1–9)

CHAPTER ONE

TOUGH BEGINNINGS AND MEXICAN WAR EXPERIENCES

*Grant and Lee work their way through challenging boyhoods,
have different West Point experiences, and follow
up their disparate Mexican War actions with
radically different life experiences*

Neither Grant nor Lee had an easy childhood. Grant was born into a lower-class family, and Lee's immediate family lived a hard life after being abandoned by his father. Although they both went to West Point, Lee emerged the clear favorite to succeed in a military career.

GRANT'S FORMATIVE YEARS

Grant was born as Hiram Ulysses Grant in the Ohio River town of Point Pleasant, Ohio, on April 27, 1822. Young "Ulysses" or "Ulyss" loved working with horses but detested his father's tannery. By the age of nine or ten, he was earning money breaking horses and driving passengers all over Ohio. In his memoirs, Grant described his childhood as a pleasant one: "I did not like to work; but I did as much of it, while young, as grown men can be hired to do in these days, and attended school at the same time. I had as many privileges as any boy in the village, and probably more than most of them."[1]

Unknown to Ulysses, his father arranged for his appointment to West Point through their local congressman, who submitted Grant's name as Ulysses Simpson (his mother's maiden name) Grant. Although Grant signed some Academy documents as U. H. Grant, he signed his eight-year enlistment oath as "U. S. Grant" and was on his way to being known to history as Ulysses S. (or U.S.) Grant. William T. Sherman, a cadet three years ahead of Grant, saw his name appearing on a list of new cadets as "U.S. Grant." He and other cadets made up the names "United States" and "Uncle Sam" to fit the initials, and then finally settled on the moniker "Sam," which became his nickname for life.[2]

At West Point from 1839 to 1843, Grant made many lifelong friends, including James Longstreet, who later commanded the 1st Corps in Lee's Army of Northern Virginia, and Rufus Ingalls, who would serve as Quartermaster of the Army of the Potomac. He knew all of the cadets in the classes that graduated between 1840 and 1846; those classes included over fifty men who were generals in the Civil War.[3] Grant's great horse riding, middling grades, and below-average conduct marks resulted in his graduating 21st in his 1843 class of 39.[4] Perhaps the highlight of his West Point years was his graduation ceremony, during which he rode a large, unmanageable horse and jumped a bar higher than a man's head. Grant was the only cadet who could ride that horse well, and their jump astounded the crowd at the ceremony.[5]

During his post-graduation leave of absence in Ohio, Grant twice was mocked about his new military uniform, and the incidents, in

Grant's own words, "gave me a distaste for military uniform that I never recovered from." Thereafter, he never wore a sword unless ordered to do so, and during the Civil War was notorious for his rumpled, informal, and plain uniforms.[6] He generally wore a private's blouse with his indicia of rank stitched on the shoulders.

As a junior officer, Grant was assigned to Jefferson Barracks outside St. Louis. He visited the nearby home of an Academy roommate, Frederick T. Dent, and met Dent's slave-holder father, Frederick F. Dent, and young Dent's sister, Julia Boggs Dent. Ulysses courted and became engaged to Julia before the Mexican War intervened. Her father, however, gave only lukewarm approval to the match.[7]

LEE'S FORMATIVE YEARS

Robert E. Lee carried the burden of a respected family name that had been stained by the behavior of his father and half-brother. One simple phrase, "The Lees of Virginia," conveyed that historical burden. Most of his ancestors had been rich, famous, and, most importantly, respected.

But despite his fame as a Revolutionary War general, Lee's father, Henry Lee III, had disgraced the family name. "Light-Horse Harry's" war record was tainted by two courts-martial and other antics. He had ordered a deserter hanged and then thoughtlessly had the man's severed head sent to Commanding General George Washington. Finally, he had resigned from the army in 1782—apparently as the result of an illicit affair.

It was primarily Henry Lee's profligate spending of his two wives' fortunes that brought dishonor and disgrace to him and the family. In 1782, he married his cousin, Matilda Lee, and spent their (her) money so foolishly that she hired an attorney to put the remaining assets in trust for their two sons. After her sudden death, Henry married Ann Hill

Carter of the famous and wealthy Carters of Virginia—over the strong
and wise opposition of Ann's father. That 1793 marriage resulted in the
birth of five children, including Robert E. Lee (the fourth child) on
January 19, 1807, but ended in another financial disaster. The grand
Stratford Hall plantation, Robert E. Lee's birthplace, was reduced from
6,600 acres to 236 acres and then finally lost under the profligate management of Light-Horse Harry.[8]

In addition to squandering a second fortune, Harry passed bad
checks (including one to Washington), fraudulently sold to his brother
land that he no longer owned, and served two jail terms totaling a year
for failure to pay debts. Four relatives cut him out of their wills. In 1813,
Lee's father, desperate to escape his debtors, fled the country. Five years
later, the mortally ill Harry tried to return to Virginia to die, but instead
perished on Cumberland Island off the Georgia coast.[9]

As if that disgrace were not enough, Light-Horse Harry's son, Henry
IV (Robert E. Lee's half-brother), earned the sobriquet "Black-Horse
Harry" by impregnating his wife's younger sister, who also was his legal
ward. That 1820 indiscretion became public the next year when she
obtained a court order ending the guardianship. The court said, "Henry
Lee hath been guilty of a flagrant abuse of his trust in the guardianship
of his ward...." The scandal reached national proportions a decade later
when President Andrew Jackson in 1829 attempted to name Black-Horse
Harry consul to Algiers. Because of his prior misconduct, the Senate
unanimously rejected his nomination—in the same year Robert graduated from West Point. By then, Black-Horse Harry, like his father before
him, had fled the country. He never returned.[10]

The notoriety and prodigality of Robert's father and half-brother
brought shame and humble circumstances to the small family of Robert
and his mother and siblings. After his 1807 birth at stately Stratford Hall
on Virginia's Northern Neck (east of Fredericksburg), Robert and his

immediate family moved to Alexandria in 1810. This forced move followed the 1809 imprisonment of Light-Horse Harry because of unpaid debts. Thereafter, Robert and his mother and siblings lived in borrowed homes courtesy of well-to-do relatives.

From a very early age, Robert cared for his frail mother, Ann Carter Lee, and his two sisters until he left their Alexandria home to go to West Point in 1825. When he departed Alexandria, his mother reportedly said, "How can I live without Robert? He is both son and daughter to me."[11] Having struggled to live until Robert's return, she died in 1829, about a month after he had returned to Alexandria as a graduate of West Point and an officer in the United States Army.

Given the tarnishing of the Lee name caused by his father and half-brother, it is not far-fetched to surmise that restoration of his family's honor became a driving force in the life of Robert E. Lee. At West Point, where he and five of his peers graduated without receiving a single demerit, Lee's classmates tagged him "the Marble Model." Lee finished second in the class of 1829.[12]

Upon his mother's death, Lee inherited ten slaves. Two years later, in July 1831, Lee married Mary Anne Randolph Custis, the only child of George Washington's adopted son, and thereby took a giant step toward establishing his aristocratic credentials. His marriage also gained him access to the grand, 1,100-acre Arlington House plantation, which he made his permanent home until the Civil War. Between 1832 and 1846, the Lees had seven children, two of whom became Civil War major generals; another became a captain in Lee's army.

Lee served in a variety of engineering posts in Virginia (Fort Monroe), New York (Fort Totten), Maryland, Georgia, and Missouri. While Lee was on duty around the country, his wife and children usually remained at the Custis family estate in Arlington, across the Potomac River from Washington and just north of Alexandria. Mary had been a

pampered child and could not tear herself away physically or emotion-
ally from her doting parents and the luxurious estate.

MEXICAN WAR EXPERIENCES

The military highlight of the pre-Civil War careers of both Grant and
Lee was the Mexican War. Grant had a longer and more varied experience than Lee in that war. Grant entered it earlier and fought in two
theaters under two very different commanding officers. Lee entered later
and fought only under Grant's second commander.

After proposing to Julia Dent, Grant left almost immediately for
Louisiana and four years of separation for the growing dispute and
ultimate war with Mexico.[13] The Mexican War was a preemptive war of
aggression initiated by President James K. Polk to expand the slavehold-
ing territory of the United States. Grant later wrote in his memoirs that
he had no romantic illusions about the nature of the U.S. conduct that
led to the annexation of Texas and war with Mexico:

> For myself, I was bitterly opposed to [the annexation of
> Texas], and to this day regard the war, which resulted, as one
> of the most unjust ever waged by a stronger against a weaker
> nation. * * * * * Even if the annexation itself could be justified,
> the manner in which the subsequent war was forced upon
> Mexico cannot. The fact is, annexationists wanted more ter-
> ritory than they could possibly lay any claim to * * * * * The
> Southern rebellion was largely the outgrowth of the Mexican
> war. Nations, like individuals, are punished for their trans-
> gressions. We got our punishment in the most sanguinary
> and expensive war of modern times.[14]

During that war, Grant served under both Winfield ("Old Fuss and Feathers") Scott and Zachary ("Old Rough and Ready") Taylor. He clearly preferred Taylor. Historians McWhiney and Jamieson concluded that Grant and Taylor shared several characteristics: opposition to plundering, willingness to work with available resources, informality of uniform, attention to detail on the battlefield, reticence in conversation, ability to quickly compose clear and concise written orders, and calmness in the face of danger and responsibility.[15] Grant retrospectively praised the quality of Taylor's army: "A more efficient army for its number and armament, I do not believe ever fought a battle than the one commanded by General Taylor in his first two engagements on Mexican—or Texan soil."[16]

Perhaps in part because of a famous incident in which Grant rode a wild horse for three hours and thereby tamed it, Taylor selected Grant as a regimental quartermaster and commissary officer. Grant protested the appointment because he feared it would remove him from combat. The military logistics experience, however, proved invaluable. "During the Civil War Grant's armies might occasionally have straggled, discipline might sometimes have been lax, but food and ammunition trains were always expertly handled. [Grant's victories] depended in no small measure on his skill as a quartermaster," said historian Jean Edward Smith.[17]

Grant's 1846 service with Taylor's high-quality army gave Grant an opportunity to perform well in battles at Palo Alto and Resaca de Palma, and even heroically as the Americans captured Monterey. After the first two battles, he wrote to Julia, "There is no great sport in having bullets flying about one in every direction but I find they have less horror when among them than when in anticipation."[18] In the latter battle, he volunteered to ride through the city streets under enemy fire to carry a message requesting a resupply of ammunition.[19]

In his memoirs, Grant described his admiration for Zachary Taylor in words that may just as well have applied to Grant himself:[20]

> General Taylor was not an officer to trouble the administra-
> tion much with his demands, but was inclined to do the best
> he could with the means given him. He felt his responsibility
> as going no further. If he had thought that he was sent to
> perform an impossibility with the means given him, he would
> probably have informed the authorities of his opinion and
> left them to determine what should be done. If the judgment
> was against him he would have gone on and done the best he
> could with the means at hand without parading his grievance
> before the public. No soldier could face either danger or
> responsibility more calmly than he. These are qualities more
> rarely found than genius or physical courage.
>
> General Taylor never made any great show or parade,
> either of uniform or retinue. In dress he was possibly too
> plain…; but he was known to every soldier in his army, and
> was respected by all.[21]

Historian Brian John Murphy concluded that the no-nonsense leadership style of the "direct, aggressive, methodical, and unflappable" Taylor
deeply impressed the young Grant.[22]

Because President Polk feared that Taylor would capitalize on battlefield victories to win the Presidency as a Whig candidate in 1848, Polk
decided to spread out the laurels and shifted most of Taylor's force,
including Grant's regiment, to another Whig general, Major General
Scott.[23] Early in 1847, therefore, Grant's regiment joined Scott's famous
campaign from Vera Cruz, on the coast, to Mexico City. After Vera Cruz
surrendered, Grant fought in the major campaign battles of Cerro

Gordo, Churubusco, Molino del Rey, Chapultepec, and Mexico City. Just outside Mexico City, Grant outflanked causeway-blocking Mexican artillery with a small detachment, hauled a disassembled mountain howitzer to the top of a church, enfiladed the Mexican position, and thereby opened the way into the city.[24] His heroism, about which he wrote nothing in his correspondence to Julia, earned him two brevet (temporary) promotions.

As was the case with Grant, the Mexican War was the pre-Civil War highlight of Lee's career. In that war, he garnered experience and exposure as a member of Scott's staff. In the same Vera Cruz-to-Mexico City campaign as Grant, Lee demonstrated initiative, intelligence, and bravery. He was a hero in several battles, particularly Cerro Gordo, Contreras, Churubusco, and Chapultepec, and received three brevet promotions in recognition of his sterling performance. Lee emerged from the war with the brevet rank of colonel. Scott even talked of insuring Lee for five million dollars if the nation ever went to war.[25]

On the down side, however, his Mexican War experiences may have given Lee an erroneous impression of what could be accomplished by daring, perhaps rash, frontal assaults. He actively participated in a series of successful assaults against positions defended by poorly trained infantry armed with unrifled, inaccurate, short-range, muzzle-loading muskets. At Cerro Gordo, for example, the Americans attacked successfully, even against some field works, and emerged victorious with losses of only five percent. Similarly, they incurred insignificant casualties in their successful, war-winning assault on the Mexican fortress of Chapultepec, just outside Mexico City. There was to be little resemblance between those heroic and victorious charges of the Mexican War and the deadly, disastrous frontal assaults of the Civil War.[26]

Lee's heroic Mexican War experience probably gave rise to an unrealistic confidence in the success that could be achieved through offensive warfare. For example, the capture of Mexico City by an army of 9,000 opposed by 30,000 defenders and a hostile populace may have been misleadingly easy. Any confidence gained by this experience was misplaced because of the basic incompetence of Santa Anna's Mexican Army and the soon-to-be-outmoded weaponry used by Mexican defenders against American assaults.

The relatively small number of troops on both sides also distinguished that struggle from the Civil War. The Americans invading Mexico could be managed by a commanding general with a small staff. Lee later would make the mistake of attempting to manage a force many times as large as Scott's with the same small staff. In addition, Scott's strategic position in Mexico was similar to the North's position, not the South's, in the Civil War. Unlike the Confederacy fifteen years later, Scott had to conquer the Mexicans and win the war and therefore was compelled to take the offensive. Also, as Scott moved farther from Vera Cruz, retreat became a less viable option and attack became increasingly necessary. Scott at Mexico City, unlike Lee at Antietam, Chancellorsville, and Gettysburg, was compelled to engage the enemy directly. These strategic and tactical distinctions seem to have escaped Lee in the 1860s.

What military lessons did Grant learn from his experiences in the Mexican War? From both Taylor and Scott, he learned that aggressiveness on the offensive could lead to victory. This was a useful lesson for Grant, whose side in the Civil War would have the same strategic burden of going on the offensive to win as the U.S. had in the Mexican War. According to Jean Edward Smith, Grant "saw how time and again Taylor and Scott moved against a numerically superior foe occupying a fortified position, and how important it was to maintain the momentum of the attack."[27] Particularly from Taylor, he learned that speed and maneuver were real assets. From both, he learned the value of being cunning and deceptive about planned offensives. From Scott's abandoning his supply line midway through his march on Mexico City, Grant learned that an army could live off the countryside—a lesson that he applied during his 1863 Vicksburg Campaign.[28]

Grant and Lee both learned that death was a normal occurrence among soldiers at war. Of the 78,718 American soldiers engaged in the war, 13,283 (16.8 percent) perished—the highest percentage of any war the United States Army has fought (including the Civil War and both World Wars). They may have noted, however, that most deaths resulted from causes other than battle; only 1,721 of the dead Americans were killed in action. Grant's personal experience with death was quite real; only four of the twenty-one officers originally assigned to his regiment survived the war.[29]

Americans' experience in Mexico confirmed many military theorists' idea that an aggressive attack would usually overcome fortified defenders.[30] Grant, however, noted the inadequacy of Mexican War muskets that were used by such defenders; he said that a man with a musket at a distance of a few hundred yards "might fire at you all day without you finding it out."[31] His somewhat facetious observation was confirmed by Illinois infantry soldiers who fired 160 shots at a flour barrel 180 yards away with their smoothbore muskets and hit the barrel four times. But the development of the rifled musket (the rifle) had changed things by 1861, when a Union soldier wrote, "We went out the other day to try [our rifles]. We fired [from a distance of] 600 yards and we put 360 balls into a mark the size of old Jeff [Confederate President Jefferson Davis]."[32]

POST-MEXICAN WAR DIFFERENCES

Although Grant's wartime experience had been more extensive than Lee's, the latter's seniority and closeness to Scott enabled him to achieve far more than Grant during the succeeding decade. In fact, Lee rose to his profession's highest levels. During the early 1850s, Lee served as Superintendent of West Point. In 1855, he became the lieutenant colonel of the just-formed 2nd Cavalry Regiment and embarked on a western tour of duty. His colonel was Albert Sidney Johnston, and they later joined John Bell Hood and Edmund Kirby Smith of the same famed regiment as four of the Confederacy's eight four-star generals. In fact, the 2nd Regiment furnished eleven generals to the Confederacy and eight to the Union.

In 1857, Lee deplored the growing national discord and expressed his concern about certain Northerners who seemed dedicated to "interfere with & change the domestic institutions of the South."[33] Two years later Lee had the opportunity to suppress John Brown's poorly planned slave insurrection and raid on the federal armory at Harper's Ferry, Virginia. Lee's men captured Brown and freed his hostages. The efficiency of Lee's actions at Harper's Ferry enhanced Lee's military reputation in Washington and Virginia.

In 1860, Lee returned to duty in Texas, where he watched with interest and apprehension the accelerating rift between the North and South. His correspondence made it clear that he would cast his lot with the Commonwealth of Virginia. In December 1860, he tellingly wrote, "As an American citizen, I prize the Union very highly & know of no personal sacrifice that I would not make to preserve it, save that of honour."[34] By January, he made it clear in other letters that his honor compelled him to side with Virginia: "If the Union is dissolved, I shall return to Virginia & share the fortune of my people," and "If the Union is dissolved, I shall return to Virginia and share the misery of my native state...."[35]

On the eve of the Civil War, Robert E. Lee was one of the finest officers of the United States Army, a military hero of the nation's last war, an officer convinced of the advantages of offensive warfare, and a man obsessed with a need to prove himself and to uphold the honor of the Lee name.

Meanwhile, Grant's career and life ultimately went into a downward spiral in the years between the two wars. Grant married Julia Dent on August 22, 1848, with James Longstreet at the ceremony as his best man. Grant and his wife lived at duty stations in Sackets Harbor, New York (on Lake Ontario), and Detroit, Michigan. They lived together until mid-1852 except when one or the other went to visit family, such as Julia's giving birth to their first child back in Missouri. Their time together ended when he received orders to the Pacific Northwest and decided against taking his pregnant wife and infant son on the dangerous journey to frontier country.[36]

Crossing Panama during the journey to the Pacific, Grant helped fight a cholera epidemic and was depressed by the death of a hundred persons, including friends and their children.[37] After staying at the Presidio in San Francisco, he traveled north and assumed his duties as commissary officer at Columbia Barracks (renamed Fort Vancouver), where he invested in a store, cattle, hogs, and a farm. These investments, a common practice in those days, brought only losses to Grant. He sold firewood to steamers and rented horses, but his farm was flooded by the Columbia River. Separated from his family, Grant joined many of his fellow officers in off-duty drinking. His small size and apparent sensitivity to alcohol made him more likely to become intoxicated, and his behavior was observed by visiting officers, including future general George B. McClellan.[38]

Then he received orders to move to Fort Humboldt in northern California, where he reported on January 5, 1854. As a company commander at Fort Humboldt in 1854, Grant served under Lieutenant Colonel Robert Buchanan, an officer with whom he had feuded in Missouri. Buchanan made life miserable for Grant. Receiving little mail and anxious to return east, Grant was lonely and depressed, and appeared to drink heavily.[39]

Separated from his wife and family, Grant reflected his depression in his letters to Julia. On February 2, 1854, he wrote to her, "You do not know how forsaken I feel here…. I got one letter from you since I have been here but it was some three months old."[40] Four days later he voiced greater concern and frustration:

> A mail come in this evening but brought me no news from you nor nothing in reply to my application for orders to go home. I cannot conceive what is the cause of the delay. The state of suspense that I am in is scarsely bearable. I think I have been from my family quite long enough and sometimes I feel as though I could almost go home "nolens volens." I presume, under ordinary circumstances, Humboldt would be a good enough place but the suspense I am in would make paradice form a bad picture. [*sic*][41]

In a March 6 letter, he said he was "almost tempted to resign," and on March 25 he said that he had received only one letter from Julia at Fort Humboldt (written the prior October) and added, "How very anxious I am to get home once again. I do not feel as if it was possible to endure this separation much longer."[42]

By April 11, 1854, Grant had reached his breaking point. Upon receiving notice of his promotion to captain and possibly a threat from Buchanan of a court-martial for being intoxicated while on duty, Grant acknowledged receipt of his new commission, resigned his army commission (effective July 31, 1854), and requested a leave of absence.[43] His financial situation deteriorated as he was unable to collect a $1,750 debt owed him in San Francisco and $800 owed him by an army sutler. To return home, he borrowed money from a friend, Captain Simon Bolivar Buckner.[44] The circumstances surrounding his resignation and his public drinking throughout much of his 15-year army career had tarred him with a reputation as a heavy drinker.[45]

After reentering civilian life, Grant endured the most trying and frustrating years of his life. For several years his primary source of income was sales in St. Louis of firewood that he cut on land that had been given to Julia by her father. Grant was an unsuccessful farmer and rent collector. He built a ramshackle house—appropriately named Hardscrabble—that Julia despised. He tried to borrow money from his father. A particularly low point occurred in the midst of the 1857 depression when he pawned his gold watch for $22. Throughout this period, Grant was quite dependent upon Julia's father, with whom Grant had an acrimonious relationship. After giving up farming in 1858, Grant dabbled in real estate sales until 1860. Finally, he twice applied unsuccessfully for the position of St. Louis County engineer. All in all, these were depressing times.[46]

Although it was difficult for him to do, Grant went to his father for help and finally escaped the clutches of Frederick Dent. In May 1860, Ulysses began working under his younger brothers, Simpson and Orvil, in the Grant family's leather-goods store in Galena, Illinois. He moved his family into a rented house, led a sober life, and apparently began rebuilding his self-respect.[47]

On the eve of the Civil War, therefore, Grant had a less-than-successful record as a peacetime army officer, a distant history of Mexican War heroism, and a well-known drinking problem. While Lee had reached the pinnacle of the antebellum army, Grant had given no indication of the military greatness he would demonstrate during the coming conflict.

CHAPTER TWO

1861:

OPEN AND CLOSED DOORS
TO CIVIL WAR COMMAND

*As the Civil War breaks out, Grant desperately
seeks a command while Lee immediately ascends
to the top echelon of the Confederate military*

After Confederates initiated hostilities by firing on Fort Sumter on April 12, 1861, Grant was anxious to enter the fray in response to Lincoln's call for 75,000 volunteers. He presided over a public meeting in Galena on April 16 and chaired a recruiting rally two days later. After refusing to become a mere captain of the company of Galena volunteers, he drilled them in Galena and at Camp Yates near Springfield. Although Grant initially declined to seek political intervention in order to obtain a senior military position, he did not refuse an offer of assistance from the local, powerful Congressman Elihu B. Washburne, the senior Republican in the House of Representatives. With Washburne's help, Grant became a military aide to Illinois Governor

Richard Yates on April 29. That position had high-level promotion potential. Grant took charge of mustering ten regiments into Illinois service.[1]

When that assignment was completed, Grant still had no military command or position. Grant hoped that his fifteen years of army service would quickly earn him a position of leadership and responsibility in the United States Army. His hopes were soon dashed. First, he wrote a May 24 letter, to the Adjutant General in Washington, offering his services for the duration of the war and stating his competence to command a regiment. Next, he personally applied in Cincinnati for a position with Major General McClellan, who commanded Ohio's militia and may have remembered Grant as a heavy drinker. Hearing nothing from McClellan, Grant next applied to Brigadier General Nathaniel Lyon in St. Louis. Again, he received no response.[2]

While Grant desperately sought a position, Confederate Brigadier General Richard S. Ewell in Richmond warned a friend, "There is one West Pointer, I think in Missouri, little known, and whom I hope the Northern people will not find out. I mean Sam Grant. I knew him well at the Academy and in Mexico. I should fear him more than any of their officers I have yet heard of. He is not a man of genius, but he is clear-headed, quick and daring."[3]

Grant resigned himself to returning home and somehow creating his own opportunity. However, his mustering-in work had caught the attention of Congressman Washburne, who would prove to be a dependable sponsor and protector of Grant throughout the war. Washburne had seen Grant's performance, realized his possible military potential, and helped convince Governor Yates to name Grant a colonel and regimental militia commander. Perhaps even more significant was the request to Yates from the officers of the 21st Illinois Volunteers that Grant replace their commander. Their colonel had lost control of the volunteers; the men had become notorious for their drunken rowdiness, petty thefts, and lack of any military discipline. Yates consulted his aides, who had been impressed by Grant's professional "mustering in" of that and other regiments, and then offered the command to Grant. After his appointment, Grant quickly brought discipline to the previously unruly regiment, which was then mustered into national service on June 28. To successfully convince his troops to extend their 90-day enlistments to three years as a condition of undertaking national service, Grant had them addressed by two Illinois members of Congress, John A. McClernand and John A. Logan, both of whom later would become Union generals.[4]

In taking command of his regiment, Grant recognized that lack of leadership was its fundamental problem. He addressed that issue in his first order of the war: "In accepting this command, your Commander will require the cooperation of all the commissioned and non-commissioned Officers in instructing the command, and in maintaining discipline, and hopes to receive also the hearty support of every enlisted man."[5] Jean Edward Smith perceptively analyzed the significance of this order and what it represented in Grant's approach to commanding units primarily consisting of volunteers:

> The phraseology is vintage Grant. The cooperation of officers and noncommissioned officers was *required*; the support of the enlisted men was something to be *hoped for*. That distinction became a hallmark of Grant's leadership. No West Point-trained officer understood the nature of the Union's volunteer army better than Grant. Having survived a number of years on the bottom rung in civil life, he had developed an instinctive feel for how civilians behaved. He recognized that volunteer soldiers were not regulars and never tried to impose the spartan discipline of the old army.[6]

Grant used his experience and common sense to establish his credibil-
ity in numerous ways. When ordered to move his men one hundred
sixteen miles to the Mississippi River, Grant declined rail transportation
and had his men march the distance. He told Yates, "The men are going
to do a lot of marching before the war is over and I prefer to train them
in friendly country, not in the enemy's." Based on his Mexican War
experience, his supply requisitions were complete and required no
changes.[7]

In July 1861, Grant's regiment was ordered to Missouri, where he
was to dislodge reported Confederate forces. There Grant first experienced the pre-battle anxiety of a Civil War commander. In his memoirs,
he described his emotional experience:

> My sensations as we approached what I supposed might be
> "a field of battle" were anything but agreeable. I had been in
> all the engagements in Mexico that it was possible for one
> person to be in; but not in command. If some one else had
> been colonel and I had been lieutenant-colonel I do not think
> I would have felt any trepidation. * * * * * As we approached
> the brow of the hill from which it was expected we could see
> Harris' camp, and possibly find his men ready formed to
> meet us, my heart kept getting higher and higher until it felt
> to me it was in my throat. [After finding the enemy camp
> abandoned,] [m]y heart resumed its place. It occurred to me
> at once that Harris had been as much afraid of me as I had
> been of him. This was a view of the question I had never
> taken before; but it was one I never forgot afterwards. From
> that event to the close of the war, I never experienced trepida-
> tion upon confronting an enemy, though I always felt more
> or less anxiety.[8]

Grant was appointed brigadier general of volunteers on August 5 (based on Washburne's recommendation) and named his Galena friend, John Rawlins, his adjutant.[9] While in Missouri, Grant told his headquarters he was, contrary to orders, not building fortifications for his troops. He wrote, "I am not fortifying here at all. . . . Drill and discipline is more necessary for the men than fortifications. . . . I have . . . very little disposition to gain a 'Pillow notoriety' for a branch of service that I have forgotten all about."[10] As Jean Edward Smith noted, "Fortifications reflected a defensive mentality alien to his nature."[11]

Major General John C. Frémont, Union commander in the West, then passed over more senior generals and appointed Grant Commander of the District of Southeast Missouri. This appointment put Grant in charge of the critical Mississippi River region that included Missouri on the west and Kentucky and Illinois on the east. He established his headquarters in Cairo, Illinois, where the Mississippi and Ohio rivers intersect.[12]

Grant immediately faced a crisis and converted it into a strategic success. He learned that Confederate soldiers under Major General Leonidas Polk had breached Kentucky's neutrality and had occupied and were fortifying Columbus, Kentucky, a strong position on the Mississippi a mere twenty miles south of Cairo. More critically, Grant heard from a supposedly reliable spy that Confederates were marching on Paducah, a key Kentucky town at the junction of the Ohio and Tennessee rivers. As soon as he learned of the Confederate occupation of Columbus and the apparent threat to Paducah, Grant wired Frémont of the developments and his intent to move on Paducah unless instructed otherwise. Within a day, Grant organized an expedition and on September 6, 1861, took possession of Paducah with troops and gunboats. Grant seized Paducah without any orders to do so.[13] Grant did not wait for an answer to his wire to Frémont; Frémont's orders to take Paducah were awaiting Grant at Cairo when he returned from Paducah.[14] Although Confederate troops had not actually been marching on Paducah, Grant's initiative in quickly seizing the town reflected his concern about the damage its loss could impose and his belief in its utility to the Union.[15]

Shortly thereafter, Brigadier General Charles F. Smith's troops occupied Smithland, Kentucky, where the Cumberland meets the Ohio. Thus, the scene was set for Grant's early 1862 thrust into Kentucky and Tennessee via the two riverine highways, the Tennessee and the Cumberland.

Although Grant had found it difficult to obtain a commission and a command, he eventually earned both and quickly began to work his way up the Union command structure through outstanding performance. Lee, on the contrary, found the path to the top already open.

While the first seven states were seceding, Lee was on duty in Texas. On February 13, 1861, the same day Virginia's Constitutional Convention initially voted against secession, Lee was ordered to report to Washington. He made the long trek from Texas to Virginia and arrived at his Arlington home on March 1. It is clear from Lee's Texas correspondence and letters he wrote while journeying to Virginia that he intended to cast his lot with the Commonwealth of Virginia. Critical to Lee's determination of his future, therefore, was Virginia's decision whether to secede. That decision awaited military developments.

After the fall of Fort Sumter, Lincoln issued an April 15 public proclamation seeking 75,000 volunteers to suppress the rebellion in South Carolina. Two days later Virginia's Convention reversed its earlier vote and decided to secede—subject to later confirmation by popular vote. On April 18, Scott, through Francis Blair, Sr., offered Lee command of the Union Army, but he declined. Lee immediately went to pay his respects to Scott, his 75-year-old mentor, who told Lee he was making the biggest mistake of his life.[16]

That night Lee drafted and signed his resignation from the United States Army. Immediately after signing his resignation, Lee penned a letter to his brother in which he tellingly said, "*Save in defense of my native State*, I have no desire ever again to draw my sword."[17] The emphasized words reflected Lee's primary allegiance to Virginia rather than the Confederacy and augured ill for the latter.

On April 22, Lee traveled to Richmond, where Governor John Letcher formally offered him a commission as a major general in the Virginia Militia and command of the "military and naval forces of Virginia."[18] Lee promptly accepted the Virginia command. On April 23, Virginia's Constitutional Convention gave Lee a hero's welcome. Unfortunately for the Confederacy, Lee would forever be committed to promoting the military interests of the Old Dominion—with little regard to the impact on other theaters of battle.

On May 10, Lee was commissioned a brigadier general in the Provisional Army of the Confederate States. For one month, until Davis took charge, Lee was Commander-in-Chief of the Confederate forces. He spent several months recruiting, training, and provisioning the Virginia Militia; building a unified force of 40,000 from numerous disparate units of 18,000 men; integrating them into the Provisional Army of the Confederate States; and serving as the primary military advisor to President Davis. Lee, who effectively mobilized an army from scratch in eight weeks,[19] remained in Richmond until late July.[20]

After Union successes in western Virginia exposed that area's vulnerability, Lee sent his own adjutant Brigadier General Robert S. Garnett to take command there. With ominous prescience, Garnett complained, "They have not given me an adequate force. I can do nothing. They have sent me to my death."[21] Between July 10 and 13, Union troops swept over the remaining Confederates in the area with victories at Rich Mountain,

Laurel Hill, and Carrick's Ford. Garnett, the first general officer to die in Civil War combat, was killed at Carrick's Ford.

Although McClellan was in command of the Union troops who won all these battles, he was present at none of them.[22]

On the northern Virginia front, the Confederates abandoned Harper's Ferry on June 14 as Union Generals McClellan and Robert Patterson advanced toward them from the west and north. Lee, as the de facto chief of staff, ordered a concentration of Confederate forces near Manassas Junction, an obvious Union target if the Northerners were to move toward Richmond. Pressure built toward a major battle. To maintain public support in the North and to utilize the original 90-day enlistees, Lincoln and his cabinet met with Generals Scott and McDowell on June 29 to discuss plans for military action. The drumbeat for action continued as Congress convened on July 4 at the president's request. Lincoln sent Congress a message blaming the war on the South, urging a declaration of war, and requesting an additional 400,000 troops.

Northern pressure for battle resulted in the First Battle of Bull Run, or Manassas, on July 21. Union forces took the offensive, attacked the Rebel left flank, and met with initial success. But the tide of battle turned, and the Union attackers were repulsed and routed— primarily due to the undetected movement of Brigadier General Joseph E. Johnston's (including Brigadier General Thomas Jackson's) forces from the Shenandoah Valley to the Manassas battlefield. Jackson's stalwart performance on the Confederate left earned him the name "Stonewall" and promotion to major general that October. While Davis rushed to the scene of the battle (and thus became involved in a dispute about who was responsible for the victorious Rebels not immediately taking Washington), a frustrated Lee remained in Richmond to work on administrative matters.

A major impact of the Confederate victory at Manassas was the feeling of superiority and overconfidence throughout the South. A September 27, 1861, *Richmond Examiner* editorial expressed these feelings:

> The battle of Manassas demonstrated, at once and forever, the superiority of the Southern soldiers, and there is not a man in the army, from the humblest private to the highest officer, who does not feel it.... The enemy... know now that when they go forth to the field they will encounter a master race. The consciousness of this fact will cause their knees to tremble beneath them on the day of battle.[23]

In the early months of the war, ironically, it was Grant who overcame the lack of interest in his receiving a commission or a command, obtained both at the regimental and brigade level, and moved his troops to occupy key positions on the Ohio River and two of its major tributaries. On the other hand, Lee had been welcomed with open arms at the highest level of the Confederacy but was tied to a desk in Richmond. The pace would soon quicken for both of them.

CHAPTER THREE

LATE 1861/ EARLY 1862:

LEE'S FIRST LOSS AND GRANT'S EARLY VICTORIES

Lee takes to the field unsuccessfully in northwestern Virginia while Grant achieves major success in the Mississippi Valley

In late 1861 and early 1862, Lee and Grant's combat records moved in opposite directions. Lee found nothing but failure in his first field command in northwestern Virginia. At the same time, Grant achieved a number of victories—victories that seriously impaired Confederate prospects in the vital Mississippi Valley.

LEE FAILS IN NORTHWESTERN VIRGINIA

Lee's first opportunity to command Southern forces in the field resulted in disaster. While tied to his desk in Richmond, he watched in dismay as Union troops occupied the western and northwestern counties of

Virginia, which then seceded from the Confederacy and later became the State of West Virginia. The outnumbered northwestern Virginia forces interspersed defeats at Philippi, Rich Mountain, and elsewhere with consistent retreats. By July 2, a legislature for western Virginia convened at Wheeling and received U.S. recognition. On July 24, Union forces under Brigadier General Jacob D. Cox forced the retreat of Confederates from Charleston to Gauley Bridge in the southern part of the area that was to become West Virginia.[1]

After those defeats and the death of Garnett, Lee in July named Brigadier General William W. Loring to command the Army of the Northwest. Not realizing that the Federals already held the key position of Cheat Mountain, northwest of Staunton and Monterey, Lee ordered Loring to hold that position. Although Loring had only arrived in the area on July 22, Lee left Richmond for northwest Virginia on July 28. Lee was under orders from Jefferson Davis to inspect and consult on the campaign plan.[2]

Lee's unannounced arrival at Loring's headquarters probably disconcerted Loring, who only recently had assumed command and had discretionary orders on how to handle the situation. Nonetheless, Lee's arrival was less troubling than the inadequate supplies, widespread illness, and terrible weather—all of which hampered Loring's ability to push the Yankees back over the Alleghenies. Because Lee failed to compel or cajole Loring into attacking the enemy before it increased its strength and fortified its position, Lee has been criticized for being too much the gentleman and too little the general.[3]

The cold mountain weather caused Lee to grow his famous beard, and on August 31 he was promoted to general retroactive to June 14—the third senior general in the Confederacy (junior only to Adjutant General Samuel Cooper and Albert Sidney Johnston). With this additional encouragement, Lee replaced Loring as commander-in-fact. Lee became personally involved in scouting for attack routes on the Union stronghold, the Cheat Mountain Summit Fort, and allowed Colonel Albert Rust of the 3rd Arkansas Infantry to convince him of the utility of a rugged route to a vantage point that commanded the Union position.

In his perceptive analysis of this northwest Virginia campaign, historian Martin Fleming comments on that decision and its reflection of a weakness on the part of Lee:

> Rust was very confident that he could lead his men to this vantage point without losing the important element of surprise and argued his point. Lee acquiesced, revealing his weakness of sometimes being more of a gentleman than a forceful leader.
>
> Lee was not a stern commander. He tended to avoid personal controversy and worked best with commanders with whom he was familiar, giving them broad discretion in carrying out their orders. These qualities, and other manly traits for which history remembers him, earned Lee great respect and loyalty in the rank and file of the Army of Northern Virginia. However, such traits sometimes caused problems, and during the campaign in northwestern Virginia problems arose with Loring, and later with Generals [Henry Alexander] Wise and [John Buchanan] Floyd in the Kanawha Valley. But none were as costly as Lee's decision to allow Rust to embark on his risky mission.[4]

Forecasting the mistake-prone approach he would take in the Seven Days' Battle the following year, Lee devised a complicated battle plan calling for a coordinated six-column assault on Cheat Mountain and nearby Camp Elkwater. After marches of up to two and a half days, three columns were to converge on each of the two Union positions, and the attack on Cheat Mountain was to serve as the signal for the companion assault. To succeed, everything had to go well; not surprisingly, it did not, and the Battle of Cheat Mountain (September 10-14, 1861) resulted in Rebel defeat.

Early on September 12, the incompetent Colonel Rust's 1,500-man force was routed by 200 Yankee skirmishers. The small amount of noise made by this farce of a battle failed to alert the other Rebel columns—including the three commanded by Lee at Camp Elkwater—that the time for fighting had arrived. Long after Lee's attacks were to have started in earnest, Union scouts discovered the Rebel threat and prepared their defenses. No serious attack ever took place. Lee, with 10,000 troops, had failed to dislodge 3,000 Yankees. The next day, Lee sent his aide-de-camp, Lieutenant Colonel John A. Washington, and his son, William Henry Fitzhugh "Rooney" Lee, to scout Union positions for an opportunity to salvage something from all these efforts. The result was that Washington was killed by Union pickets. After two days of skirmishes, Lee withdrew his forces from the Cheat Mountain area. A few weeks later, Union troops moved from Cheat Mountain and defeated a Rebel force at Greenbriar, Virginia, thereby completing the rout of Lee's Confederates in the midst of Virginia's Allegheny Mountains.

During August and September 1861, Lee switched his attention to the Kanawha Valley in southern West Virginia. There he failed to exercise his authority and resolve a blood feud between two subordinate generals, Brigadiers Floyd and Wise. They spent more time bickering with each other than fighting Yankees. Lee allowed this intolerable situation to continue by declining their specific requests that he issue orders to straighten out the mess and instead referring the matter to Richmond.[5]

In the Kanawha Valley, Lee faced Brigadier General William S. Rosecrans. But Lee arrived there too late to accomplish anything. Union forces under General Jacob Cox had moved up (southeasterly) the Kanawha River from below Charleston in July. After losing a skirmish at Cross Lanes on August 26, Cox's outnumbered forces had been rein- forced by Rosecrans. On September 10, Rosecrans' troops had defeated 2,000 Confederates at Carnifax Ferry, and the losers had retreated to Meadow Bluff, where Lee found them when he arrived. After an October 3 battle at Camp Bartow, the opposing armies fought again in early November and eventually went into winter quarters. On October 30, Lee left western Virginia for the last time—his efforts there having been less than noteworthy.[6]

In western Virginia, Lee had demonstrated two of his common tactical mistakes: he had failed to take charge of the battlefield, and he had issued overly complex, ineffective, and often ambiguous orders. The press and the public criticized Lee's performance as weak and vacillating.

Nevertheless, at an 1870 Lee memorial meeting, a sympathetic Jef- ferson Davis found Lee blameless for the western Virginia failures:

> ... if his plans and orders had been carried out, the result would have been victory rather than retreat.... Yet, through all this, with a magnanimity rarely equalled, he stood in silence, without defending himself or allowing others to defend him, for he was unwilling to offend anyone who was wearing a sword and striking blows for the Confederacy.[7]

GRANT GOES ON THE OFFENSIVE

While Lee was struggling in the Virginia mountains, Grant was achiev- ing success in the Mississippi Valley. On November 2, Grant received orders to proceed to the vicinity of Columbus, Kentucky. His assignment was to "demonstrate" against the enemy in order to discourage a westward movement of Confederate troops from Columbus into Missouri. Grant's idea of a demonstration was an attack—even though his orders specifically said he was not to attack. Therefore, he planned to assault the Confederate position across the river from Columbus at Belmont, Missouri. His decision to attack in violation of orders was based on two months of intelligence-gathering, his reading of enemy intentions, and his increasing willingness to take the initiative, which was reinforced by his earlier success in seizing Paducah and Smithland without orders to do so.[8]

Although Grant would be attacking with only 3,100 troops and the Columbus citadel had 17,000 defenders and 140 artillery pieces, Grant kept General ("Bishop") Leonidas Polk, the Confederate commander, guessing about his intentions by use of several deceptions. Grant did this by ordering three diversionary columns to move south in Kentucky and two more to do so in Missouri. With his multiple diversionary columns on the move, Grant embarked his 3,100 attackers on steamboats on November 6 and moved south from Cairo. That night he tied up his vessels on the Kentucky (eastern) shore, an action that threatened Columbus. The next morning, however, Grant's men landed at Belmont on the Missouri (western) shore. They came under fire from Columbus artillery and Belmont infantry. Under Grant's personal direction, his men successfully drove the Confederate defenders back to and ultimately through their camp. Grant lost control of his neophyte troops, however, as they looted the abandoned camp.[9]

Grant's officers and men were shocked and frightened by Confederate shells that began falling among them. They were cut off from their transports by the Rebels who had fled, moved upstream, and then been reinforced by troops from the Kentucky shore. Suddenly the Union troops realized they had to quickly get back to their transports. Grant restored them to order, and they fought through the Confederates again—just in time to get back to their steamboats before being overwhelmed by a superior Confederate force sent across in two more steamers from Columbus. Grant was the last man aboard the departing Union transports as his horse leaped over the riverbank edge, slid down the bank, and trotted aboard the boat on a single gangplank.[10] As Major General Lewis ("Lew") Wallace later wrote, Grant's actions at Belmont were noteworthy, and "the addendum that he had lingered in face of the enemy until he was hauled aboard with the last gangplank, did him great good."[11]

Grant's foray had created quite a stir among Polk and the Confederates at Columbus. Polk telegraphed President Davis that he had driven away 8,000 attackers and that Grant was reported to have been killed. Three days later, Polk wrote in his official report that "the battle was fought against great odds" and that the Union attackers had lost at least 1,500 men. Confederate dead and wounded poured into Memphis, however, and Grant miraculously reappeared. As soon as it became known that Grant had attacked with only 3,100 troops, an embarrassed Polk ceased claiming victory. He called in his outlying troops and hunkered down in Columbus. The momentum was with Grant—as it would be throughout the war.[12]

On the down side, Grant had underestimated the Rebels' ability to counterattack his men; this tendency to overlook the potential for enemy attacks would create problems for him again at Fort Donelson and Shiloh. But Grant's deceptive hit-and-run attack kept Polk from effectively using his superior numbers and amazingly resulted in slightly more casualties for the defenders than the attackers—an unusual occurrence in the Civil War. Of the 3,100 men engaged by Grant, only about 500 were killed, wounded, or missing. The Confederate force of 7,000, including reinforcements from Columbus, reported about 640 men killed, wounded, or missing.[13] Grant was pleased with the results: his

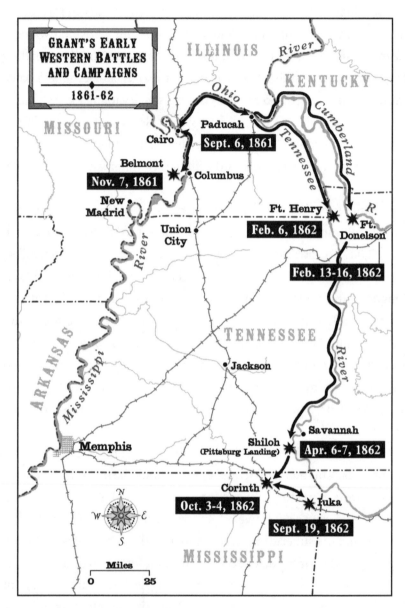

Grant's Early Western Battles and Campaigns (1861–62)
Map by David Deis, Dreamline Cartography, Northridge, CA

soldiers gained self-confidence, the Rebel forces at Columbus were at least disconcerted, and the Confederates canceled any plans to move troops across the Mississippi to assist their comrades in Missouri. Even more importantly for the North, Belmont brought Ulysses Grant's name to the attention of President Lincoln, who was desperate for any kind of action by a Union general.[14]

But Grant was just getting started. From his headquarters at Cairo, he conceived a brilliant strategy to bypass the Confederate stronghold at Columbus and use more easterly rivers to take the war deep into Tennessee. His plan was to coordinate waterborne and overland troop movements with naval gunboats to capture Confederate Fort Henry on the Tennessee River and Fort Donelson on the Cumberland River. If successful, this campaign would not only force Polk to abandon Columbus on the Mississippi, but would open the way for Union capture of Nashville, the Tennessee capital; sever the major east-west Memphis-to-Charleston (South Carolina) railroad; open western Tennessee to occupation; and enable Union gunboats to reach as far south as northern Mississippi and Alabama.[15]

Grant's major problem was the reluctant Major General Henry W. Halleck, the new Commander of the Department of the Missouri. Halleck spent his first two months probing the enemy and discouraging any offensive action. When Grant went to St. Louis on January 23, 1862, to propose his offensive, Halleck abruptly cut off Grant's discussion of an upriver campaign and told him that such a matter was Halleck's, not Grant's, business. After returning to Cairo, Grant persisted and won support from his Navy counterpart, Navy Flag Officer Andrew H. Foote. Therefore, he was prepared to act when a frustrated President Lincoln issued his famous January 27 General Orders No. 1 calling for a general advance by all U.S. forces, including "the Army and Flotilla at Cairo," by not later than February 22. The next day Grant sent Halleck a telegram—

endorsed by Foote—requesting permission to initiate the assault jointly with Foote's riverboat flotilla. The following day Grant sent a follow-up message telling Halleck, "The advantages of this move are as perceptible to the General Commanding the Department as to myself therefore further statements are unnecessary [*sic*]."[16]

Seeing that he had no other course of action, Halleck sent a January 30 telegram and letter to Grant directing him to "move with the least possible delay" to take and hold Fort Henry. In the words of Jean Smith, "In three days Grant organized his command for battle, issued rations and ammunition, provided for resupply, procured river transportation, and coordinated the movement of seven Union gunboats...."[17] Therefore, Grant was in a position to sail up the Tennessee from Paducah early on the morning of February 3. Foote's fleet consisted of four ironclad and three timber-clad gunboats, as well as nine transports carrying Grant's 15,000 troops, animals, supplies, and artillery. As the fleet left Paducah, Grant told his aide Rawlins how relieved he was that they were now beyond recall by Halleck.[18]

As General C. F. Smith had advised Grant, Fort Henry was so poorly situated on the Tennessee that much of it was under high water when its defenders learned of the impending attack. Its guns, however, posed a meaningful threat and almost killed Grant when he ordered the gunboat *Essex* to move within two miles of the fort to test the range of those guns. After that, he ordered McClernand's troops to disembark three miles north of the fort.

Shortly after noon on February 6, Foote's fleet began its bombardment of the fort. His fifty-four guns out-dueled the seventeen heavy guns inside the flooded fort. The bombardment was so horrific that the 3,400-man garrison panicked and fled east toward Fort Donelson, about eleven miles away on the Cumberland River. Within two hours, Brigadier General Lloyd Tilghman hoisted the white flag of surrender. Foote's sailors actually rowed into the fort to accept its surrender. Embarrassed by the flight of his soldiers, Tilghman formally reported that he had transferred them to Fort Donelson the previous day. Frustrated by McClernand's mud-marching soldiers' inability to cut off the Rebels' escape, Grant never contested Tilghman's lie, which has become the commonly accepted version of what occurred at Fort Henry.[19]

Grant had to be thrilled at the quickness of the victory but disappointed that his soldiers, who had been disembarked miles downstream and encountered swampy marching conditions, had not had time to reach the scene before the surrender or to intercept the fleeing Confederates. Nevertheless, Grant sent out patrols and then decided on his next step.

Although he had no orders from Halleck authorizing his action, Grant ordered his troops to follow the retreating Confederates to Fort Donelson. "In doing so," in Jean Edward Smith's words, "he disregarded explicit instructions to entrench at Fort Henry, ignored Halleck's order to prepare to receive a Confederate attack, and took virtually all of his command with him."[20] Heavy rains and flooded roads, however, hindered the movement of Grant's troops to Fort Donelson. Finally, they marched on February 11 and reached Donelson on February 12. The delay was fortuitous because it provided time for Foote to reach Donelson by a circuitous riverine route and transport reinforcements to Grant at Donelson.[21]

In the interim, Grant and Foote took advantage of their control of the Tennessee River by sending three wooden gunboats twenty-five miles upriver to destroy the Memphis and Ohio Railroad bridge (linking Memphis with Bowling Green, Kentucky) and a total of one hundred and fifty miles south—all the way to the head of navigation at Muscle Shoals, Alabama. The mini-fleet captured a fast steamboat, destroyed or captured five other vessels, destroyed a wealth of shipbuilding supplies, revived Union sentiment along the river, and spread discontent among Confederate supporters.[22] Meanwhile Foote's fleet had to steam northward down the Tennessee to the Ohio, eastward up the Ohio to the Cumberland, and southward up the Cumberland to threaten Fort Donelson from the north. On the way, they diverted down the Ohio for repairs at Cairo.[23]

General Albert S. Johnston, the Confederate Departmental Commander, played into Grant's hands by neither withdrawing from Fort Donelson to enable his troops to fight another day nor forcefully reinforcing that position with all his available troops. Instead, he temporized and sent three brigades to boost the Confederate force there to 17,000. Perhaps shocked by the unexpectedly sudden loss of Fort Henry, Johnston, said Jean Edward Smith, had committed "an error of catastrophic proportions."[24]

Grant's troops laid siege to Fort Donelson on February 12. They were reinforced and resupplied by General William T. Sherman from Smithland and from other commands throughout the Midwest. Although as soon as Fort Henry had fallen, Grant had advised Halleck of his intention to take Fort Donelson and Halleck had ordered reinforcements to his command, Halleck sent no communication to Grant either approving or disapproving his plans. Grant was on his own.[25]

The Battle of Fort Donelson ensued.[26] February 13 brought fighting on land and water. Despite Grant's orders not to start a battle until they had received reinforcements, both Smith and McClernand sent some troops on senseless and unsuccessful assaults of the Confederate line. Meanwhile, Foote initiated an exchange of long-range fire between his ships and the fort's batteries. The unimpressive Union efforts that day were followed that night by the arrival of bitterly cold weather, including snow, sleet, and freezing rain, that brought suffering to the men of both armies.[27]

In recognition of the new situation created by the fall of Fort Henry, Grant on February 14 was appointed Commander of the District of West Tennessee, and his troops became the Army of the Tennessee. Valentine's Day also brought Grant more reinforcements, which he formed into a third division and placed under the command of Lew Wallace between Smith on the left and McClernand on the right. That same busy day, Foote unsuccessfully launched his major gunboat assault on Fort Donelson. He learned to his dismay that, unlike Fort Henry, Donelson had been built on high ground and had an artillery advantage over attacking gunboats. The thirty-two-pounder guns of the fort raked the Union vessels, which had ventured too close. Fifty-four men on the ships were killed. The Confederate defenders were heartened by the sight of Union vessels falling back down the river—several of them badly damaged and clearly out of control.[28]

The next morning Grant was miles downriver from Donelson with the wounded Foote on his flagship planning their next actions when the Confederates successfully attacked from Donelson and pushed back McClernand's troops on Grant's right flank. Wallace eventually sent help from the center of Grant's line, and the Confederate attack was halted by fifty-five rounds of shot and shell from Wallace's guns. By pushing back McClernand's division, the Confederates had created an opportunity to flee south along the Cumberland toward Nashville away from the Fort Donelson trap. They failed to do so, and their hesitation provided Grant with the opportunity to regroup, counterattack, and seal off their escape route.[29]

When Grant first arrived on the deadlocked scene after a seven-mile ride from Foote's vessel, he saw that the battle hung in the balance and took the initiative to win it. When informed that the enemy had an open escape route, he ordered the position on the Union right retaken.[30] He told his subordinates that the enemy must be demoralized and that victory belonged to the aggressor. Grant's own description of the events demonstrates his quick grasp of the situation and his hands-on battlefield tactics:

> I turned to Colonel J[oseph].D. Webster, of my staff, who was with me, and said: "Some of our men are pretty badly demoralized, but the enemy must be more so, for he has attempted to force his way out, but has fallen back: the one who attacks first now will be victorious and the enemy will have to be in a hurry if he gets ahead of me."… I directed Colonel Webster to ride with me and call out to the men as we passed: "Fill your cartridge-boxes, quick, and get into line; the enemy is trying to escape and he must not be permitted to do so." This acted like a charm. The men only wanted some one to give them a command.[31]

Grant reasoned that the Donelson troops had been seeking to break out to the south and probably had left a thin line of defenders on the northern portion of their defensive line. Therefore, he ordered Smith to attack that weakened quarter while Wallace and McClernand recovered the lost ground on the Union right (south). Smith forced his way into the north end of the Confederate lines and bivouacked there in a threatening position that night, while the other two division commanders drove the Rebels back into their entrenchments. The Confederate escape route to Nashville appeared to be blocked.[32]

Late that afternoon Grant demonstrated his sympathy for the wounded of both sides. He discovered a wounded Union officer trying to give a drink to a wounded Confederate soldier. Grant dismounted, gave each of them a swig of brandy, ordered corpsmen to remove them on stretchers, and told the reluctant stretcher-bearers to "Take the Confederate too. The war is over between them." Continuing his ride among the wounded, Grant told his aide, Colonel Webster, "Let's get away from this dreadful place. I suppose this work is part of the devil that is left in us all." He then quietly recited the words of poet Robert Burns: "Man's inhumanity to man/Makes countless thousands mourn."[33]

Confederate Brigadier Generals Floyd, Gideon J. Pillow, and Simon Buckner (Grant's old friend) debated whether to attempt another breakout, maintain and defend their position, or surrender. Deciding that surrender was probably the wisest course in light of the dominance of Smith's guns, the incompetent and fearful Floyd and Pillow fled upriver in transports with 1,500 to 2,000 troops and left Buckner to negotiate terms of surrender. Donelson's cavalry commander, Lieutenant Colonel Nathan Bedford Forrest, escaped along the river with 700 to 1,000 Confederate riders.[34]

When, on February 16, Buckner requested negotiation of terms for yielding Fort Donelson, Grant (following Smith's advice) succinctly replied, "No terms except an unconditional and immediate surrender can be accepted. I propose to move immediately upon your works." As a result of this response and the Confederate capitulation on Grant's "ungenerous and unchivalrous terms" (in the words of Buckner in his response to Grant), Grant's West Point-imposed initials suddenly stood for "Unconditional Surrender" Grant.[35] Despite his use of "unconditional surrender" language, Grant, in fact, conducted two days of friendly and almost compassionate surrender negotiations with Buckner.[36]

From Fort Donelson, Grant took away an important lesson. He realized that in every battle there comes a critical time when the issue hangs in the balance, when both sides are exhausted, and that is the time when the outcome is decided. He realized, said historian T. Harry Williams, that "the general who had the moral courage to continue fighting would win."[37] Fellow historian Benjamin Franklin Cooling concurred with that analysis: "A crisis had been reached in the battle—in Grant's very career, in fact. Calling upon every resource at his command, the general did not waver or vacillate. Here was an opportunity to counterattack, and Grant seized it."[38]

Between Fort Sumter and Appomattox Court House, three Civil War armies surrendered to their foes. All three were Confederate armies that surrendered to Grant. Buckner's remaining army of 14,000 at Donelson was the first. Those soldiers were soon on their way to Union prison camps in the North.[39] Although Grant wired the good news to Halleck's chief of staff in St. Louis,[40] Halleck ominously never acknowledged Grant's telegram nor congratulated him on his victories.

The Northern press hailed "Unconditional Surrender" Grant and his twin victories. President Lincoln immediately rewarded Grant's success by promoting him to major general of volunteers (a temporary wartime position). In his brilliant, flowing prose, Southern historian Shelby Foote described how the Northern public, so desperate for victory, ignored all the mistakes Grant had made:

> They saw rather, the sweep and slam-bang power of a leader who marched on Wednesday, skirmished on Thursday, imperturbably watched the fleet's repulse on Friday, fought desperately on Saturday, and received the fort's unconditional surrender on Sunday. Undeterred by wretched weather, the advice of the tactics manuals, or the reported strength of the enemy position, he had inflicted about 2000 casualties and suffered about 3000 himself—which was as it should have been, considering his role as the attacker—and now there were something more than 12,000 rebel soldiers, the cream of Confederate volunteers, on their way to northern prison

camps to await exchange for as many Union boys, who otherwise would have languished in southern prisons under the coming summer sun. People saw Grant as the author of this deliverance, the embodiment of the offensive spirit, the man who would strike and keep on striking until this war was won.[41]

The news of the fall of Forts Henry and Donelson hit newly inaugurated Confederate President Davis "like an earthquake," and the impact grew worse as he realized that his armies were thereby being compelled to abandon all of Kentucky and much of Tennessee.[42] Confederate War Department clerk J. B. Jones tried to put a brave face on the Confederate calamity: "At last we have the astounding tidings that Donelson has fallen, and Buckner, and 9000 men, arms, stores, everything are in possession of the enemy! Did the President know it yesterday [the inauguration]? Or did the Secretary keep it back until the new government (permanent) was launched into existence? Wherefore? The Southern *people* cannot be daunted by calamity!"[43]

A harbinger of troubles to come was Halleck's wide dispersal of praise for the victories on the rivers—even to generals subordinate to Grant or barely involved in the fighting— coupled with his simultaneous failure to send Grant a message of congratulations. Even while Grant was campaigning against the twin forts, Halleck had tried to replace Grant with three other generals: Sherman, who declined; Major General Ethan Allen Hitchcock, an elderly Mexican War veteran who also declined, and Brigadier General Don Carlos Buell, a rival of Halleck's who did not even respond to Halleck. After Donelson, Halleck had the gall to wire McClellan: "Make Buell, Grant, and [John] Pope major generals of volunteers and give me command of the West. I ask this in return for Forts Henry and Donelson." Stanton and Lincoln, aware of who deserved credit, agreed to promote only Grant, who then ranked tenth among Union generals. Halleck, however, had clearly demonstrated that he was jealous of Grant.[44]

Not resting on his laurels nor dismayed by Halleck's snub, Grant moved his soldiers southward up both rivers, and they occupied Clarksville, Tennessee, on February 19 and the capital, Nashville, on February 25. Halleck delayed Grant's occupation of Nashville and thereby enabled Confederate cavalryman Forrest to remove commissary and quartermaster stores there.[45] Grant's swift movements, however, angered the slow-footed Buell, whose Army of the Ohio had targeted Nashville as its own goal. On March 1, Halleck belatedly ordered Grant to proceed south on the Tennessee to disrupt Confederate railroads.

Grant's quick thrust against and capture of Forts Henry and Donelson achieved his goals of forcing Polk from Columbus and the Confederates from most of Kentucky, capturing Nashville, seriously disrupting Confederate rail communications, opening western Tennessee to Union occupation, and threatening northern Mississippi and Alabama. He had thrust a dagger into the Confederate left flank.

Civil War historians Herman Hattaway and Archer Jones went so far as to say, "We suggest that Grant's capture of the forts, early in 1862, might justly be regarded as the major turning point [of the war]...."[46] Similar judgments were made by Benjamin Franklin Cooling in his *Forts Henry and Donelson: The Key to the Confederate Heartland* and Kendall D. Gott in his *Where the South Lost the War: An Analysis of the Fort Henry-Fort Donelson Campaign, February 1862*. Most impressively, Grant had accomplished all of this while incurring minimal casualties. Of his 27,000 troops, only 2,608 were killed or wounded while another 224 were missing or captured. His troops killed or wounded 2,000 Confederates and captured another 14,000.[47] Grant's first major victory was a harbinger of many future victories that he would achieve with no more than a reasonable loss of manpower.

LEE BIDES HIS TIME IN THE SOUTHEAST

While Grant was winning successive victories in the Mississippi Valley, Lee was availing himself of an opportunity for redemption. His next assignment came on November 6, when Davis dispatched him to the Southeast. There Lee was responsible for improving the coastal defenses of South Carolina, Georgia, and Florida. The fact that Davis found it necessary to write letters on Lee's behalf to the governors of South Carolina and Georgia indicates the low esteem in which Lee was held at that time.[48]

Shortly after receiving his new orders, Lee arrived farther south at Fort Pulaski on the Savannah River, fifteen miles east of the vital port city of Savannah. As a second lieutenant, he had been one of the engineers involved in the start of the fort's construction in 1829. Lee pronounced the 25-million-brick, 7-1/2-foot-thick walled fort impervious to artillery fire. A 30-hour Union bombardment on April 10–11, 1862, however, proved him wrong. Rifled artillery destroyed the walls, exposed the powder magazine, and brought about the surrender of three hundred eighty-five men and the fort. The early 1862 fall of Fort Pulaski ended virtually all Confederate blockade-running through Savannah.[49]

Lee found a deteriorating situation throughout the Southeast. A Union expeditionary force had captured Forts Clark and Hatteras on the North Carolina coast and gained control of strategically located Hatteras Inlet at the southern end of that state's Outer Banks. In lower South Carolina, an expeditionary force compelled the evacuation of Forts Beauregard and Walker and then occupied Port Royal, an ideal harbor for Union blockade vessels between Charleston and Savannah.

During his four months in South Carolina, Georgia, and Florida, Lee realized that, with the exception of a few strongholds, it was impossible to defend the coast against combined Union naval and army forces. Therefore, he concentrated his efforts on building defenses inland at points unreachable by the Union navy.[50]

As the spring campaigning season of 1862 approached, Lee was building defenses in the Southeast while Grant was moving deeper into Tennessee with his victorious army. Lee had failed in his western Virginia field command while Grant had capitalized on his hard-earned opportunities to win his first three battles, the latter being the first major Union victory of the war.

CHAPTER FOUR

MARCH–JUNE 1862:
GRANT WINS AT SHILOH WHILE LEE STYMIES McCLELLAN

Grant salvages a victory after his unprepared army is attacked at "Bloody Shiloh," and Lee uses costly frontal assaults to drive McClellan away from Richmond

In April and June 1862, Grant and Lee were involved in two separate but deadly battles that awakened the eyes of the public—both North and South—to the nightmarish fury the war would bring. Grant moved farther south in Tennessee and then saved his army from a surprise attack and drove the enemy from the field at "Bloody Shiloh," where the two sides incurred almost 24,000 casualties in a two-day bloodbath. Two months later Lee fought the Seven Days' Battle against McClellan on the Virginia Peninsula and saw his troops suffer 20,000 casualties while imposing 16,000 on their opponents.

GRANT SAVES HIS ARMY AT SHILOH

While Lee was hoping for another field command, Grant was fully utilizing his. He moved his Army of the Tennessee deeper into the Confederate left flank. Grant wanted to follow up his successes at Forts Henry
and Donelson with an immediate move up the Cumberland to seize the
Tennessee capital of Nashville. Instead, Halleck ordered him and Foote
to stay at Fort Donelson and neighboring Clarksville and not move on
Nashville. Halleck told them he was awaiting instructions from Washington. Actually, Halleck was pressuring General-in-Chief McClellan
and Secretary of War Edwin M. Stanton to put him (Halleck) in charge
of all the western Union armies and was holding Grant and Foote's
forward movement hostage to his ambitions. The Nashville situation
was resolved when the Confederates abandoned the city and Grant sent
a division of Buell's troops, which had arrived at Fort Donelson, upriver
to occupy Nashville.[1]

After Washington's brusque rejections of his self-promotion efforts,
Halleck took out his frustrations on Grant. As William S. McFeely
observed, "Halleck wanted Grant pushed aside; once a victor, Grant
became a rival." A Confederate-sympathizing telegraph operator apparently sabotaged Grant's communications to Halleck and thereby provided Halleck with a partial excuse to take radical action. On March 3,
Halleck wired McClellan that Grant was non-communicative, negligent,
and inefficient and that his army was demoralized. As Grant was moving
forces deeper into western Tennessee, Halleck tried to push Grant aside,
substituted General Smith as commander of an expedition up the Tennessee, and accused Grant of failing to report his strength and positions.
On March 4, he sent Grant a blunt and accusatory telegram that read:
"You will place Major Gen. C.F. Smith in command of expedition [up
the Tennessee], & remain yourself at Fort Henry. Why do you not obey
my orders to report strength & positions of your command?" For about

a week thereafter, Grant was on board a steamer in virtual, but unguarded, arrest.[2]

Halleck's March 4 telegram was the first indication to Grant that Halleck had not been receiving his reports. Grant stayed at Fort Henry to direct operations and denied Halleck's charges. In a March 6 telegram to Grant, Halleck repeated his allegations and expanded them to include a claim that Grant had exceeded his authority by advancing to Nashville. Not only was the latter claim false, but it was also a ludicrous complaint because the occupation of Nashville was a huge military and political success. The next two days Grant sent further denials and requested that he be relieved from serving under Halleck's command.[3]

Meanwhile, Halleck had also complained to McClellan that Grant's army lacked discipline and order. Of Grant himself, Halleck stated, "I never saw a man more deficient in… organization. Brave & able on the field, he has no idea of how to regulate & organize his forces before a battle or to conduct the operation of a campaign." McClellan, with Stanton's approval, authorized Halleck to remove Grant from command. Later Halleck wrote to McClellan of a rumor that Grant "has resumed his former bad habits." In light of Grant's victories and Lincoln's apparent opposition (aided by Congressman Washburne's intervention) to Halleck's anti-Grant actions, however, Halleck backed down. Halleck duplicitously explained to Grant that he (Halleck) had been getting pressure from General-in-Chief McClellan, who had received reports of Grant's misbehavior and wanted a full investigation. Halleck advised Grant that, instead of conducting an investigation, he was restoring Grant to his command. It was almost two decades after the war until Grant learned that Halleck himself had initiated the reports to Washington of Grant's alleged misbehavior and had backed down when told to either submit formal charges or reinstate Grant to command.[4]

On March 17, Grant headed south up the Tennessee to Savannah, Tennessee, in the far southwestern section of that state. From Savannah Grant sent reinforcements farther south on the river to Crump's Landing and Pittsburg Landing, where Sherman was organizing them for an offensive against Corinth, a crossroads of north-south and east-west railroads that was critical to transportation in the southwestern Confederacy. Grant delayed the offensive until he could be joined by Buell's Army of the Ohio, which was advancing slowly from Nashville. Most of Grant's troops camped between Pittsburg Landing and a small church at a place called Shiloh.[5]

Grant's Henry/Donelson campaign had succeeded despite the reluctance of Halleck and the lukewarm support of Buell. Furthermore, Grant's southward move toward Mississippi was delayed by Halleck's jealous interference and Buell's continuing dalliance. Without these hindrances, Grant might have been able to face a disjointed enemy before A.S. Johnston had time to assemble a Confederate army with reinforcements from much of the Confederacy. Halleck and Buell had provided Johnston with seven weeks to get organized.[6]

Meanwhile, the Confederates were planning an offensive of their own. Johnston was assembling an impressive force at Corinth by gathering troops from the Gulf Coast, the southeastern Atlantic Coast (including Beauregard and many troops from Charleston, South Carolina), and the Mississippi Valley (including Polk's forces that had abandoned Columbus, Kentucky). On April 2, Johnston began moving his 44,000 troops the twenty miles towards Pittsburg Landing. In the first few days of April, Johnston's cavalry sporadically encountered Grant's pickets, but Grant did not expect a Confederate offensive. The day before the surprise Confederate attack, Grant told a fellow officer, "There will be no fight at Pittsburg Landing; we will have to go to Corinth, where the rebels are fortified." In his memoirs, he explained: "The fact is, I regarded the campaign we were engaged in as an offensive one and had no idea that the enemy would leave strong intrenchments [*sic*] to take the initiative when he knew he would be attacked where he was if he remained."[7]

Skirmishes increased on April 4, and Grant was injured when his horse fell on his leg in the dark as he returned to his headquarters from a meeting with officers who had been at the front lines. He was unable to walk without crutches for two or three days. Grant was spending his nights downriver from Crump's and Pittsburg Landings at Savannah, Tennessee, where Buell's army was expected to arrive. On April 5, Brigadier General William ("Bull") Nelson and the lead division of Buell's army arrived at Savannah. Grant ordered Nelson to proceed down the east bank of the Tennessee so that he could be ferried across to Crump's or Pittsburg Landing.[8]

Grant was still at Savannah early on Sunday, April 6, 1862, when Johnston launched a massive surprise attack on the troops of Brigadier Generals Sherman and Benjamin M. Prentiss at Shiloh, just west of Pittsburg Landing.[9] Sherman and other Union generals had ignored reports from skirmishers and cavalry patrols that Confederates were present in large numbers. On April 5, Sherman had advised Grant, "I do not apprehend anything like an attack on our position." That same day Grant sent messages to Halleck stating, "The Main force of the enemy is at Corinth.... and "I have scarsely [*sic*] the faintest idea of an attack, (general one), being made upon us but will be prepared should such a thing take place."[10]

Grant and Sherman were caught by surprise, and accordingly their troops were not prepared for the Confederate assault. The Union troops had not dug defensive trenches, and Prentiss' troops were initially swept backward by the early morning onslaught. The initial attack was so successful that Union soldiers abandoned their personal belongings and breakfast campfires. The Confederate attack was delayed as hungry and poorly clad soldiers plundered the Union camp.[11] Grant had hurried downriver from Savannah as soon as he heard artillery. Before departing, he again ordered Nelson to move with his division south along the east bank of the Tennessee to a point opposite Pittsburg Landing. He also sent couriers urging Buell to hurry the rest of his army to the scene. After a brief stop at Crump's Landing, Grant hastened on to Pittsburg Landing and spent a long and desperate day keeping the Union forces from being driven into the Tennessee River.[12]

One problem arose early in the day that could have had disastrous consequences. As soon as Grant arrived at Pittsburg Landing and determined the serious nature of the situation inland there, he sent his quartermaster back to Crump's Landing with an order for General Lew Wallace to immediately march his division to the battlefield. Wallace's and other troops had previously built an inland bridge on the Shunpike Road across Snake Creek for that very purpose. Wallace, therefore, tried to use that inland road instead of the road along the river.[13]

After hearing nothing from Wallace by midday, Grant sent two more officers to hasten Wallace's arrival. When Wallace had not arrived by 2:30 p.m., Grant sent two more staff officers to bring Wallace to Pittsburg Landing. Also at 2:30, Wallace was contacted while at the head of his column miles inland in what had been an unsuccessful attempt by Wallace to enter the fray on the enemy's left (northwest) flank. Even though he was then made aware that Grant's army was in extreme jeopardy, Wallace proceeded to delay his division's march almost another hour by ordering a countermarch (the head of his misdirected column passing back through the entire column) rather than a simple about-face. During the march, Wallace caused additional delay by ordering his lead soldiers to await slower troops in order to keep the column closed up. Thus, Wallace crossed Snake Creek and reached the battlefield on Grant's right at 7:00 p.m. By arriving after the fighting had ceased that day, Wallace had unintentionally deprived Grant of the use of one of his six divisions at the most critical time and place of what was to become a two-day battle.[14]

It appears that Grant erred in relying on oral orders that failed to specify the road Wallace was to take. The use of oral—let alone vague—orders was something Grant tried to avoid for the rest of the war. In an 1885 note written shortly before his death, Grant admitted that he had relied on oral orders to first specify Wallace's route and that "If the position of our front had not changed, the road which Wallace took would have been somewhat shorter to our right than the River road." As historian Stacy Allen concluded, "One fact is known: A 6-mile march which might have been made in just over two hours had required seven hours and fifteen miles. This undeniable fact would haunt Lew Wallace for the rest of his life."[15]

With Wallace's division out of the battle for its first day, Grant's 40,000 remaining defenders consisted of five other divisions:

- Sherman's on the right near Shiloh Church,
- McClernand's on Sherman's rear and later his left,
- Prentiss' on Sherman's and then McClernand's left,
- Brigadier General Stephen A. Hurlbut's in reserve behind Prentiss, and
- C.F. Smith's (under Brigadier General William H.L. Wallace) in reserve behind all the other divisions.

Three of Grant's division commanders were Illinois lawyer-politicians who were new to their commands; Hurlbut had commanded his division for six weeks, Prentiss for eleven days, and William Wallace for all of two days.[16]

Immediately upon arriving at Pittsburg Landing, the injured Grant was assisted onto his horse and rode into the battle with crutches strapped to his saddle. Upon learning from General William Wallace that his army faced a full-scale attack, Grant sent appeals for reinforcements to Lew Wallace and Bull Nelson and issued an order for

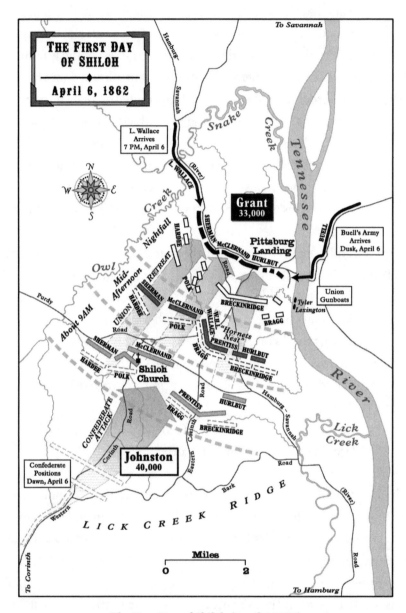

The First Day of Shiloh (April 6,1862)
Map by David Deis, Dreamline Cartography, Northridge, CA

ammunition wagons to be moved inland. He then visited his division commanders in the field, told them to hold their ground, and advised them that reinforcements were on the way.[17] To the west of the attack on Prentiss, several Confederate brigades attacked Sherman's line of green recruits. For hours, Sherman's men inflicted severe casualties on the Rebel attackers. The defenders finally gave way to the attackers, who swept into Sherman's abandoned camp and then spent valuable time looting it. Sherman ordered a fighting retreat and told Grant, "we are holding them pretty well just now—but it's hot as hell."[18]

After the initial shock of, and retreat from, the surprise attack, Grant's army carried out a desperate, daylong fighting retreat and established a series of defensive positions that were protected on the flanks by Lick Creek and the Tennessee River on its left and Snake Creek and its Owl Creek tributary on its right. Grant later summarized the strength of his position: "The water in all these streams was very high at the time and contributed to protect our flanks. The enemy was compelled, therefore, to attack directly in our front. This he did with great vigor, inflicting heavy losses on the National side, but suffering much heavier on his own."[19]

A major problem plaguing the Confederates was their disorganization. They had approached the battlefield division by division up the Corinth Road, but then each brigade and regiment had been sent haphazardly to the place of greatest immediate need without regard to their divisions. By 10:30 that morning, the senior Confederate generals addressed this problem of intermingled units by informally dividing the battlefield into sectors commanded, from their left to right (north to south), by Generals William J. ("Old Reliable") Hardee, Polk, Bragg, and Breckinridge.[20]

By the same time, two-thirds of the Confederates had drifted to their left and, with heavy casualties, pushed back Sherman and McClernand.

Their positions and actions were inconsistent, however, with General Johnston's plan to have the Confederate right turn the Federal left, which was putting up fierce resistance. In fact, throughout the late morning and early afternoon, Johnston personally directed the efforts on the Confederate right flank to turn the Union line. He made a fatal mistake by sending his surgeon away to help wounded troops. Thus, when Johnston was shot in the leg, no one realized the gravity of his wound. By the time its seriousness became apparent, it was too late to save Johnston, who apparently bled to death from a severed artery. Johnston, who was possibly shot by his own men, may not have realized that he had been shot because his leg was numb from an 1837 dueling wound. An unused field tourniquet was in his coat pocket when he died. General Beauregard assumed the Confederate command.[21]

At the other end of the lines, Sherman and McClernand, having received fresh ammunition and reinforcements, successfully counterattacked and drove back and inflicted many casualties on the Confederates in their front. While the Confederates were themselves regrouping and getting ammunition, Sherman and McClernand, realizing that they were overextended, drew back to strong defensive positions they would hold the rest of the day.[22]

The major fighting, however, would occur in an area that started as the center of the Union line and became the left of that line as the battle progressed. As the Confederates overran Sherman's and then McClernand's camps, they stopped to loot and eat; this delay gave Prentiss and other Union leaders valuable time to organize a defense. While his troops were being flanked or overpowered, Prentiss reorganized them, obtained reinforcements from other divisions, and finally put together an extremely effective defensive position, which achieved lasting fame as "the Hornets' Nest."[23] In that location, the divisions of Hurlbut, William Wallace, and Prentiss formed a semicircle facing south and west in the area of an old wagon-road on the southern (left) end of Grant's line. These 5,500 infantrymen and twenty-seven guns formed the anchor of Grant's critical mid-day defense against the Confederate attackers.[24]

The first Confederates to feel the sting of the Hornets' Nest were Tennessee and Kentucky troops. Around 11:00 a.m. they moved through thick underbrush toward the Union position, but they were devastated by masked (camouflaged) Union firepower at eighty paces. 6th Tennessee Private R. W. Hurdle described the effects of the vicious firestorm:

> Then came an incessant hail of lead and iron until our line was strewn with the dying and the wounded. The remainder had to lie down for protection. In a few minutes a Mississippi Regiment dashed up and they passed over our line, and called out: "get out of the way, Tennessee, and let Mississippi in!" They passed on a short distance and returned on the double quick, and as they passed a Tennessee fellow said "get out of the way, Tennessee, and let Mississippi out!"[25]

Shortly thereafter, Grant arrived to check out the Hornets' Nest. After observing that the position was a strong one and that Prentiss had deployed the troops effectively, Grant told Prentiss to "maintain that position at all hazards." For the next several hours, that is exactly what the men in the Hornets' Nest did. Between 11:30 a.m. and noon, Prentiss' troops repelled a 3,600-man, four-brigade attack led by Brigadier General Alexander P. Stewart. The attackers were stopped by blistering fire after advancing only one hundred yards. Next, Bragg ordered a series of four suicidal charges that came no closer than sixty yards to the inaccessible position of the Blue troops, and the attackers fell like leaves. Although Confederate bullets took their toll on Iowa infantry defending the Union guns, two more Confederate brigades made mid-afternoon assaults and were bloodily repulsed. Grant recalled being with Prentiss late that afternoon, and described him "as cool as if expecting victory."[26]

When it became clear that the Confederates were not about to go through the Hornets' Nest with infantry, they changed their tactics. Brigadier General Daniel Ruggles assembled fifty-two pieces of artillery that bombarded the Yankee stronghold, destroyed or drove off many federal batteries, and convinced many infantrymen to flee to the rear. Simultaneously, Confederate infantry flanked the left end of the Union line and caused Hurlbut's division to retreat toward Pittsburg Landing. The final Confederate assault on the Hornets' Nest involved parts of fourteen of the sixteen Rebel brigades on the field.[27] Military historian Herman Hattaway calculated that the final assault on the Hornets' Nest involved 10,000 Confederate troops, who incurred about 2,400 casualties.[28]

Finally, Grant's line north of the Hornets' Nest gave way, permitting Confederates to outflank Prentiss' left as well as his right. Soon the Hornets' Nest was surrounded. Some of the Union troops fought their way out of the trap, but finally Prentiss and 2,200 troops surrendered at about 5:30 p.m. As the Confederates cheered the mass surrender, a proud Prentiss exclaimed to his captors, "Yell, boys, you have a right to shout for you have this day captured the bravest brigade in the United States Army." The men he commanded, most from other commands, had done their job and held that position "at all hazards" for six hours—and stymied the Confederate attack for over twelve hours since the 5:00 a.m. initiation of hostilities.[29]

Having finally bypassed the Hornets' Nest, the Confederates made a final attempt to break Grant's left wing and capture Pittsburg Landing. But Grant himself had long before prepared a warm reception for them. At 2:30 that afternoon, he had directed his chief of staff Colonel Webster to create a line of defense for the Landing. For the next three hours,

Webster assembled artillery pieces along the Dill Branch of Lick Creek near Pittsburg Landing in a successful attempt to stem the Confederate tide. Using every gun in the reserve artillery and in the retreating units that approached the Landing, Webster assembled a seventy-gun line, which included five 24-pounder siege guns that had been hauled up from the Landing.[30]

By 5:30 p.m., 20,000 Union troops had joined those guns in "Grant's Last Line." The assembled defenders repelled a six-gun Alabama battery and a final assault by 4,000 of the 8,000 Confederates poised to capture the Landing. As a result, Grant's army held the Landing, maintained a strong and compact defensive position as night fell, and began receiving "Bull" Nelson's reinforcements at the Landing from Buell across the Tennessee.[31]

Grant had continually moved about the battlefield and visited each of his division commanders several times during the day.[32] He creatively used all of his forces, his cavalry, his artillery, his infantry—and even two naval gunboats. During the battle, Grant found a crucial use for his cavalry. He stationed them behind his infantry to discourage straggling and desertion by troops fleeing the heat of battle. He later wrote:

> The nature of this battle was such that cavalry could not be used in front; I therefore formed ours into line, in rear, to stop stragglers—of whom there were many. When there would be enough of them to make a show, and after they had recovered from their fright, they would be sent to reinforce some part of the line which needed support, without regard to their companies, regiments or brigades.[33]

Beauregard accurately believed that Grant's use of massed artillery at the close of the day was a significant factor in the Rebels' failure to force

Grant's army to surrender. Those artillery pieces were assisted by the firing of 32-pounder cannonballs and 8-inch shells from the two Union gunboats, *Tyler* and *Lexington*, at the mouth of Dill Branch. Those same vessels provided moderately effective support earlier in the day and intermittent shelling during the night after the first day of battle. They were constantly hindered, however, by an inability to determine the Confederates' position because of the nature of the terrain (including woods, hills, and high riverbanks).[34]

Grant's infantry had provided the bulk of resistance to the Confederate onslaught. Again and again during the long day, determined collections of Union infantrymen halted the Confederate advance until they either ran out of ammunition or were surrounded by the enemy. Most of them retreated from one defensive position to another and imposed severe casualties on the attacking Confederates. In fact, the Confederates suffered between 8,000 and 8,500 casualties in the day's fighting.[35]

The battle had taken its toll on the Union forces as well. Prentiss' Division was gone—mostly surrendered along with the division commander. General William Wallace had been mortally wounded, and his division was scattered among others. Union forces had suffered a remarkably similar 8,500 casualties. The three "intact" divisions in the Union line at dusk were those of Hurlbut on the left, McClernand in the center, and Sherman on the right. As Grant stated in his memoirs, however, "All three divisions were, as a matter of course, more or less shattered and depleted in numbers from the terrible battle of the day." He also described the relative losses of the two sides:

> The reports of the enemy show that their condition at the
> end of the first day was deplorable; their losses in killed and
> wounded had been very heavy, and their stragglers had been

quite as numerous as on the National side, with the difference that those of the enemy left the field entirely and were not brought back to their respective commands for many days. On the Union side but few of the stragglers fell back further than the landing on the river, and many of these were in line for duty on the second day.[36]

By nightfall, Grant's army was backed up more than a mile closer to the Tennessee than it had been at dawn. But it had survived a ferocious and unexpected attack and lived to fight another day. There were even reasons to be optimistic. By dusk, Buell's first 5,000 troops (specifically, Nelson's Division) had begun to arrive, and Grant hurried them toward the front. On the right, Lew Wallace at long last arrived with his 5,000 unscarred troops. By the next morning, Alexander M. McCook's and Thomas L. Crittenden's divisions of Buell's army had come upriver from Savannah and joined Grant's troops.[37]

Not content with surviving the ferocious daylong attack, Grant decided to launch a massive counterattack of his own the next day. In his own words:

> So confident was I before firing had ceased on the 6th that the next day would bring victory to our arms if we could only take the initiative, that I visited each division commander in person before any reinforcements had reached the field. I directed them to throw out heavy lines of skirmishers in the morning as soon as they could see, and push them forward until they found the enemy, following with their entire divisions in supporting distance, and to engage the enemy as soon as found.[38]

During the night following that first day at Shiloh, Grant had an experience that brought home to him the extent of the only truly significant number of casualties his troops would suffer in any of his western campaigns in the first three years of the Civil War:

> During the night rain fell in torrents and our troops were exposed to the storm without shelter. I made my headquarters under a tree a few hundred yards back from the river bank. My ankle was so much swollen from the fall of my horse the Friday night preceding, and the bruise was so painful that I could get no rest.... Some time after midnight, growing restive under the storm and the continuous pain, I moved back to the loghouse under the bank. This had been taken as a hospital, and all night wounded men were being brought in, their wounds dressed, a leg or an arm amputated as the case might require, and everything being done to save life or alleviate suffering. The sight was more unendurable than encountering the enemy's fire, and I returned to my tree in the rain.[39]

That same night Beauregard wired Richmond the news of what he perceived to be his glorious victory:

> We this morning attacked the enemy in strong position in front of Pittsburg, and after a severe battle of ten hours, thanks be to the Almighty, gained a complete victory, driving the enemy from every position. Loss on both sides heavy, including our commander-in-chief, General A.S. Johnston, who fell gallantly leading his troops into the thickest of the fight.[40]

But the reality was that the Confederates had suffered debilitating casualties and were, as Bragg wrote to his wife two days later, "disorganized, demoralized, and exhausted." Assured by an incorrect dispatch that Buell was not coming to join Grant, the Confederate commanders were satisfied to let their exhausted troops get some sleep and to reorganize in the morning.

Instead of being shocked into inaction by the massive attack that he had failed to anticipate and that his army had barely survived, Grant resolved to go on the offensive the next morning. Grant was heard to mutter, "Not beaten by a damn sight."[41] When asked by Lieutenant Colonel McPherson whether the army should retreat across the Tennessee, Grant responded, "Retreat? No, I propose to attack at daylight and whip them." A little later Sherman approached Grant and said, "Well, Grant, we've had the devil's own day, haven't we?" and Grant replied, "Yes. Yes. Lick 'em tomorrow though."[42] In the words of historian Jean Edward Smith, "If anyone other than Grant had been in command Sunday night [between the two days at Shiloh], the Union army certainly would have retreated."[43]

Soldiers of both armies spent a restless night as the Union gunboats fired shells inland, the rain fell, and cries of the wounded came from the battlefield and the makeshift hospitals. But Grant had been reinforced by Wallace's 5,000 troops and another 13,000 from Buell's three divisions. Confederate cavalryman Colonel Forrest observed thousands of reinforcements arriving by ferry across the river and from downstream, but his warnings to General Hardee were ignored.[44] Ignoring the possibility of reinforcements from Buell and expecting to conduct mopping-up operations in the morning, Beauregard and his fellow Confederate generals were shocked when Grant's artillery opened the Union counterattack before six o'clock the next morning. The Union goal was to drive the enemy from the ground they had fought so hard to gain the prior day. Casualties and desertions had reduced the Rebel force from 44,000 to 28,000. It was 10:00 a.m. before the disorganized and scattered Confederate units formed a respectable defensive line. While John C. Breckinridge commanded all units of his corps, Hardee, Bragg, and Polk commanded "mixed-bag" contingents that contained virtually no one from their own corps.[45]

Before the unexpected and overwhelming onslaught by four of Grant's divisions and three of Buell's, the disorganized Confederates conducted a fighting retreat much more chaotic than their Union counterparts had done the prior day. The Confederates kept moving back all day (except for periodic costly counterattacks), fell back on the Corinth Road, and halted there for the night five miles from Pittsburg Landing. While overseeing the progress of the battle, Grant came under fire and had a bullet hit and break the scabbard of his sword.[46]

The next day Grant conducted a reconnaissance-in-force down the Corinth Road. Although some critics have contended that he should have aggressively pursued and destroyed Beauregard's army, doing so was not a realistic possibility. Grant was under orders from Halleck to stay on the defensive, there were good defensive positions for the Rebels along the Corinth Road, Grant lacked sufficient cavalry and horses for rapid pursuit, and Grant's troops were totally exhausted. Thus, Beauregard and his survivors retreated all the way to Corinth. But Grant's "stubborn pugnacity," in the words of military historian Russell F. Weigley, had turned defeat into victory.[47]

LEE REBUFFS McCLELLAN— AT A TERRIBLE PRICE

Back East, meanwhile, Lee also was soon to be involved in major combat. While Lee worked on defenses in the Southeast in 1861–62, Lincoln grew increasingly impatient about inaction on the part of McClellan in the East and Halleck and Buell in the western theaters. This led him to issue his previously mentioned General War Order Number One directing a February 22, 1862, general movement of Union forces against the "insurgent forces."[48] In the same vein, Lincoln issued a January 31, 1862, Special War Order Number One directing seizure of a railroad position southwest of Manassas Junction. In early February, Lincoln and McClellan debated whether to move on Richmond overland or by water—with McClellan favoring the latter approach.

On March 4, Lee was replaced by Major General John C. Pemberton as commander of the Confederate Department of South Carolina, Georgia, and East Florida. Although he thus far had failed to achieve any operational success, Lee became military advisor to President Jefferson Davis. On March 13, Davis designated Lee to be in charge of "the conduct of military operations in the armies of the Confederacy." By making Lee his advisory chief of staff, Davis thwarted his congressional opponents who had tried to force Davis to formally appoint Lee secretary of war. In Lee's new advisory position, his only responsibility until June 1, he did little to bring about the national unity of command so necessary to Confederate defense and success. Instead, Lee focused on the East while Grant continued to roll in the West.

Yielding to the supposed military expertise of McClellan, Lincoln, on March 8, approved his plan for a campaign against Richmond via the Virginia Peninsula between the James and York rivers. In his second general war order, however, Lincoln required that sufficient troops be kept near Washington to defend the Union capital. That same day the Southern ironclad CSS *Virginia* (formerly the USS *Merrimack*) wreaked havoc on the Union fleet in Hampton Roads. That evening, however, the just-completed Union ironclad USS *Monitor* arrived on the scene after its hasty maiden voyage from the Brooklyn Navy Yard. The next day the two vessels fought to a draw in the first battle between ironclad ships, and the perceived threat of the *Virginia* to Washington and the entire northeast coast came to an end.

Also on March 9, McClellan's troops finally moved out of Alexandria and toward Manassas after reports of a Rebel retreat. To McClellan's embarrassment, they found only log "Quaker cannons," which had played a role in causing McClellan to overestimate enemy strength. It was only two days later that Lincoln removed McClellan from his General-in-Chief position and put Secretary of War Stanton in charge of overall coordination of military activities. As Commander of the Army of the Potomac, McClellan continued planning his Peninsula Campaign. On March 13 Stanton advised him to get on with it but to ensure that Washington and Manassas Junction were protected.

At long last, McClellan moved out, by water, for the Peninsula on March 17. He suffered a severe setback four days later and many miles away. At Kernstown, Virginia, in the northern Shenandoah Valley, Stonewall Jackson's 4,000 troops unwittingly attacked a vastly superior force of over 9,000 Union infantry. Although Jackson suffered a tactical defeat and retreated, he won a major strategic victory. As Lee had astutely observed, Lincoln and Stanton perceived Jackson as a threat to Washington or Harper's Ferry and took preventive action. They had Major General McDowell's troops remain at Fredericksburg and deprived McClellan of tens of thousands of additional troops for his campaign against Richmond. The following month Lee would unleash Jackson to continue this diversion of troops away from McClellan.

By April 1, McClellan had moved twelve divisions of the Army of the Potomac to the Peninsula. These joined Major General John E. Wool's 12,000 troops at Fort Monroe and began a long, deliberate trek up the Peninsula. On April 3, however, Lincoln discovered that McClellan had planned on leaving fewer than 20,000 untrained troops to guard

Washington—although he had deceptively claimed that 70,000 were handling that responsibility. Having been disconcerted by Jackson, Lincoln ordered retention of an additional corps at the capital. Nevertheless, McClellan had about 110,000 Union troops to begin his siege of Yorktown the next day. General Joseph Johnston had only 17,000 Confederates to defend Yorktown and an eight-mile line across the Peninsula from the York River on the northeast to the James River on the southwest. Although Johnston wanted to retreat immediately to the Richmond area, Lee convinced Davis that Johnston must be ordered to contest McClellan's advance up the Peninsula.

On April 10, immediately following Shiloh, Lee advised his southeastern successor, Pemberton, of the critical need for troops in the "West": "Beauregard is pressed for troops. Send, if possible [certain troops] ... If Mississippi Valley is lost Atlantic states will be ruined."[49] For once, Lee recognized the critical importance of the Mississippi Valley theater, but the reinforcements he recommended were not coming from Virginia. More typically, ten days later Lee requested Pemberton to send troops to Virginia—not to the Mississippi Valley or middle theaters.[50]

Realizing the serious threat that McClellan on the Peninsula and McDowell at Fredericksburg posed to Richmond and Johnston's army, Lee wrote to Stonewall Jackson on April 21.[51] In that letter and another on April 25,[52] Lee turned Jackson loose (with reinforcements under Major General Richard S. "Old Baldy" Ewell) on a brilliant diversionary campaign, the Shenandoah Valley Campaign, which prevented the Union forces in Virginia from uniting against Johnston. Reflecting the essence of their relationship, Lee only had to advise Jackson of the goals and options and then left the execution to Jackson: "I cannot pretend at this distance to direct operations depending on circumstances unknown to me and requiring the exercise of discretion and judgment as to time and execution, but submit these suggestions for your consideration."[53]

Lee's strategy would bear fruit through Jackson's execution of it during the following several weeks. Lee and Jackson were an excellent match because Jackson—unlike many of Lee's other subordinates—generally[54] thrived under Lee's hands-off approach.

Back on the Virginia Peninsula, Johnston, outnumbered by as much as six to one and having held out as long as possible by bluffing McClellan into grossly overestimating the Confederate "strength," finally evacuated Yorktown on May 3. The next day Union troops moved in and once again found a collection of "Quaker cannons." On May 5, however, the Yankees finally had a successful day on the Peninsula. In a battle at Williamsburg, they took advantage of Brigadier General Jubal A. Early's excessive aggressiveness, decimated Confederate troops, and inflicted 1,700 casualties, while suffering fewer than 500 themselves.[55]

Frustrated by McClellan's slow progress on the Peninsula, Lincoln, with some of his cabinet, came to Fort Monroe on May 7. Perplexed that McClellan had not driven the Rebels from Norfolk and its vital shipyard, Lincoln cobbled together an attack against it. As a result, Confederate forces abandoned Norfolk and its valuable shipyard and naval facilities on May 9. Lincoln personally oversaw the May 10 occupation of Norfolk and prodded McClellan to move promptly on Richmond. Over the course of the next week, McClellan at last made some real progress advancing on Richmond. President Davis' wife and many others fled the city, and Johnston retreated toward the city by crossing the nearby Chickahominy River.

Although accompanying Union naval forces, including the *Monitor*, were repelled on May 15 at Drewry's Bluff seven miles below Richmond on the James River, a coordinated land assault on the Confederate capital appeared to be shaping up nicely. On May 17, McDowell at Fredericksburg was ordered to head south with his 20,000 men to connect with McClellan's right flank. Three days later, McClellan, still awaiting

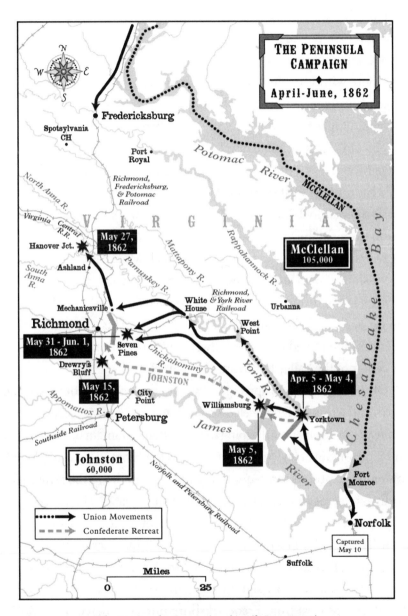

The Peninsula Campaign (April–June 1862)
Map by David Deis, Dreamline Cartography, Northridge, CA

McDowell, had troops as close as eight miles from Richmond and appeared to be poised for attack. McDowell, however, was not advancing to McClellan's side and was still in Fredericksburg on May 23, when he met there with Lincoln. As Lee had accurately presumed because of Lincoln's omnipresent fears for the security of Washington, the president prevented McDowell's merger with McClellan.

Lincoln's fears reflected developments on the other side of the Blue Ridge Mountains. With a force of 10,000 moving secretly into the Virginia mountains west of Staunton, Stonewall Jackson had begun his classic Shenandoah Valley Campaign with a May 8 victory over 6,000 Union troops at the mountain town of McDowell, Virginia. After climbing twenty miles over the rugged Shenandoah Mountains in less than a day, pushing those Union forces back to Franklin, and blocking the road between Franklin and Staunton, Jackson's men quickly slipped back into the Valley for their brilliant general's next move. This came on May 20 when Jackson joined forces with Ewell and moved to the Luray area in the center of the Valley to threaten Nathaniel Banks' army.

On May 23, Jackson sprung the surprise attack that convulsed the North and temporarily canceled attempts to reinforce McClellan on the Peninsula. Jackson's men, keeping Massanutten Mountain between them and Banks' main army, struck 1,400 Yankees at Front Royal. They killed, injured or captured three-quarters of them and drove the remainder northward across both branches of the Shenandoah.[56] This success put Jackson and Ewell's 16,000 troops in a position to cut off Banks' entire army. The next day Lincoln reacted predictably by ordering Major General John C. Frémont to close in on Jackson's rear by moving east from Franklin and, even more significantly, ordering McDowell to send his 20,000 troops west from Fredericksburg into the Shenandoah Valley instead of south toward Richmond.

On May 25, Jackson pressed his forces northward and forced Banks to retreat all the way to Williamsport, Maryland, on the Potomac River. It was now clear to Lincoln that he was not going to be able to send any additional troops to McClellan, who had an insatiable appetite for reinforcements. Realizing that and concerned about Jackson's forceful foray, Lincoln, also on May 25, ordered McClellan to get on with his attack on Richmond or to return and defend Washington. Possibly in response, McClellan initiated minor offensive actions north of Richmond at Hanover Station on May 27 and Ashland on May 29. Richmonders breathed a sigh of relief when they learned on May 28 that McDowell was heading to the Shenandoah Valley instead of Richmond. Lee's strategy had worked.

Jackson's 16,000 men were keeping 60,000 Union troops occupied in the Shenandoah. After chasing Banks across the Potomac, Jackson threatened Harper's Ferry before finally retreating. With Union armies closing in from the north (Banks), east (McDowell), and west (Frémont), Jackson's foot-soldiers conducted one of their patented marches southward "up" the Valley on the last two days of May and eluded their pursuers with minimal conflict and casualties. Jackson had done his job.[57]

A few days earlier on the Peninsula it was Joseph Johnston, not McClellan, who launched a major attack. On May 31, in the Battle of Fair Oaks (Seven Pines), Johnston assaulted 30,000 Union troops isolated on one side of the Chickahominy River. The plan of attack proved too complicated. Uncoordinated marches and attacks resulted in high Confederate casualties and Union retreats but in no Confederate breakthrough or capture of large numbers of Union soldiers. Committing errors that Lee would often repeat, Johnston had given his generals verbal orders, failed to ensure that Major General James Longstreet understood his orders, and failed to oversee execution of his orders.

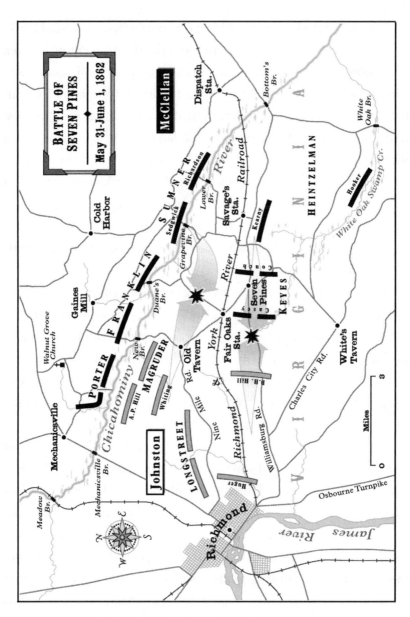

Battle of Seven Pines (May 31–June 1, 1862)
Map by David Deis, Dreamline Cartography, Northridge, CA

Either by mistake or with the intent to seek a more glorious role, Longstreet took the wrong road and destroyed the coordination of the Rebel attack.

Late on May 31, however, an event occurred that changed the character of the war. Johnston was seriously wounded by flying shell fragments and succeeded by Major General Gustavus W. Smith. Within hours Smith suffered a breakdown, and that night Davis replaced him with Lee. To avoid naming another general-in-chief who might interfere with his playing that role, Davis kept Lee in that position and simply added an army command to Lee's duties. The next day Lee issued Special Orders No. 22 referring for the first time to the Army of Northern Virginia. From June 1, 1862, until April 9, 1865, Lee would command that army.

The Battle of Fair Oaks continued the next day with a disastrous Confederate assault and retreat. Although ordered from Richmond to the battlefield at 8:00 a.m., Lee mysteriously delayed until 2:00 p.m. his arrival on the battlefield, which was only six miles from Richmond. The two days of Rebel frontal assaults at Fair Oaks resulted in 4,400 Union casualties but a total of 5,700 for the attacking Confederates.[58]

By the beginning of June, Jackson was requesting reinforcements so that he could extend his Valley Campaign into the North and thereby draw McClellan away from Richmond. Lee, however, convinced Davis that an assault on McClellan's army was the preferred option. In the words of historian Bevin Alexander, "The difference between Lee and Jackson as generals can be seen most cogently in this context. Jackson wanted to move *away* from the Union armies and win indirectly and with little bloodshed by deception, surprise, and distraction. Lee sought to destroy McClellan's army *in place* by frontal attack, main force, and direct blows into the heart of Union strength."[59]

When McClellan learned that Lee had replaced Joe Johnston as commander of the Confederate forces defending Richmond, he must have been pleased. Less than two months before, he had written to Lincoln: "I prefer Lee to Johnston—the former is too cautious and weak under grave responsibility—personally brave and energetic to a fault, yet he is wanting in moral firmness when pressed by heavy responsibility and is likely to be timid and irresolute in action."[60] Not only had McClellan failed to detect Lee's propensity for aggressiveness, but in fact he attributed to Lee the very traits that made McClellan a failure as a Civil War general.[61] McClellan was not alone in his judgment of Lee at the time Lee replaced Johnston. Because of Lee's lack of prior battlefield success, many Southerners were not pleased by his appointment. The *Richmond Examiner* commented: "Evacuating Lee, who has never yet risked a single battle with the invader, is commanding general."[62]

Some insight into how badly McClellan had misjudged Lee comes from a conversation that June between Longstreet's chief of artillery, Colonel E. Porter Alexander, and Captain Joseph C. Ives of Jefferson Davis' staff. To Alexander's question whether Lee would be sufficiently audacious, Ives responded: "Alexander, if there is one man in either army, Federal or Confederate, who is, head and shoulders, far above every other one in either army in audacity, that man is General Lee, and you will very soon have lived to see it. Lee is audacity personified. His name is audacity, and you need not be afraid of not seeing all of it that you will want to see."[63]

Jackson and Ewell meanwhile kept the troops of Union generals Frémont and Shields separated by the South Fork of the Shenandoah River and defeated each of them, respectively, in engagements at Cross Keys on June 8 and Port Republic on June 9. Total casualties were nine hundred for Jackson and 1,600 for the Yankees. Those battles brought an end to Jackson's Valley Campaign. At the cost of 3,100 casualties, he had inflicted 7,500 casualties. More significantly, Jackson had carried out Lee's strategy and performed his primary mission of preventing a massive coalition of Union armies against Richmond and its defenders. Now Lee had other plans for Jackson and his exhausted men.

Lee realized that he needed to maximize his forces in the Richmond area without letting Lincoln and his generals comprehend what was happening. Therefore, on June 15, he sent 10,000 troops west from Richmond in what appeared to be an effort to reinforce Jackson. Lee made sure that this activity appeared surreptitious but was in fact known to the enemy. At the same time, Lee executed his "real" plan and on June 16 ordered Jackson to proceed east expeditiously to join the Army of Northern Virginia. Barely a week after the end of his Valley campaign, an exhausted Jackson moved his tired army, on June 17, toward the Chickahominy River northeast of Richmond.

Lincoln, who Lee expected to reinforce the Valley, reacted differently to news of the apparent 10,000-troop transfer to the Valley. On June 18, he wrote to McClellan and urged him to attack the opposing Confederate lines, which had been weakened by the movement of 10,000 troops. McClellan, of course, saw this deployment as proof of his position that the Rebels greatly outnumbered his and could spare those troops. So he continued to do nothing. Meanwhile, between June 12 and 15, Brigadier General Jeb Stuart embarrassed him by leading a cavalry ride completely around the Union army, capturing 165 prisoners and 300 horses, and exposing the inadequacy of Union communications.[64] Lincoln's frustrations concerning recent developments, or the lack of them, led him, on June 17, to create the Army of Virginia and bring Major General John Pope in from the West to head it.

On June 25, McClellan at long last launched a feeble assault at the Battle of Oak Grove. With his army still divided by the Chickahominy, he ordered an advance by the picket lines on his left (southern) flank near the James River. A furious but minor fight ensued with the Rebel defenders prevailing. They suffered only half of the Union's 500-plus casualties. This small struggle nevertheless was significant enough to rattle McClellan. That evening he sent Stanton a bizarre, panic-driven cable stating that Jackson was at Hanover Station (he was), Beauregard's army (actually in Alabama) was in Richmond, the Confederates had more than 200,000 men (more than double their true strength), he expected to be attacked the next day (he was), he could at least die with his army if it was destroyed by the overwhelming numbers, any disaster would not be his fault, and he could not get reinforcements even if he wanted them.[65]

Even though Lee and McClellan's armies were of about even strength (85,000 to 100,000),[66] Lee planned to go on the offensive to save Richmond. Therefore, he devised a series of complicated, frontal-assault battle plans that resulted in severe casualties on both sides, especially the Confederate side, and the retreat of the Union forces in the Seven Days' Battle. For his offensive, Lee organized his army into divisions, including those under Major Generals Jackson, Longstreet, Ambrose Powell "A.P." Hill, and Daniel Harvey ("D.H." or "Harvey") Hill. By eliminating the two-wing concept of army organization Johnston had created to avoid Davis' prohibition of the use of corps, Lee undercut his own ability to effectively manage his large army.

Lee's problems began in the weeks and days preceding the offensive. Although Lee planned to cut off McClellan's army from its supply base to the north at White House Landing on the Pamunkey River (a tributary of the York River), Union capture of Norfolk had enabled McClellan to begin shifting his base to Harrison's Landing on the James River to his south. Jeb Stuart's grandiose ride around McClellan's army revealed the vulnerability of White House Landing (miles from the bulk of McClellan's troops). Thus, it should have confirmed for Lee McClellan's existing plans to move his base from the Pamunkey to the James (which could be viewed as planning for retreat before the Seven Days' Battle even started), rendered Lee's plan for cutting off McClellan moot, and exposed McClellan's vulnerability to a wide sweeping movement to the east around his northern flank.

Lee also underestimated the easily discernible exhaustion of both Jackson and his "foot cavalry." Between March 22 and June 9, at Lee's suggestion and with his full knowledge, Jackson's men had marched 676 miles; in their May 30–June 5 retreat from the Potomac alone, they had rapidly marched 104 miles. It therefore should not have surprised Lee when Jackson's tired troops took longer than originally contemplated to move once again, by marching and using limited rail facilities, from the Valley to the Peninsula.

At Lee's critical pre-battle conference on June 23, an exhausted and overly optimistic Jackson said he would be on Lee's army's left, or north flank, early on June 25. Even though the offensive was delayed until June 26, Jackson would fail to arrive in time for the assault that day. After the conference, Jackson rode in the rain all night to return to his exhausted men northwest of Richmond. Often in rainy weather, Jackson's men took three days to march the final forty miles to their assigned position on the Confederate left. Lee, however, had sufficient information about the whereabouts of Jackson's troops to know that the timing of the offensive for early on June 26 was—at the least—a real gamble. But Lee was anxious to get on with it.

Thus, in his General Orders Number 75 on June 24, 1862, Lee set his complex, coordinated Mechanicsville attack for early on June 26 against Union Brigadier General Fitz John Porter's isolated corps north of the Chickahominy. Lee hoped to drive it back, break the Union supply-line from White House on the York River south to the Union army, and capture that supply base, as well as the Union supply trains at Cold

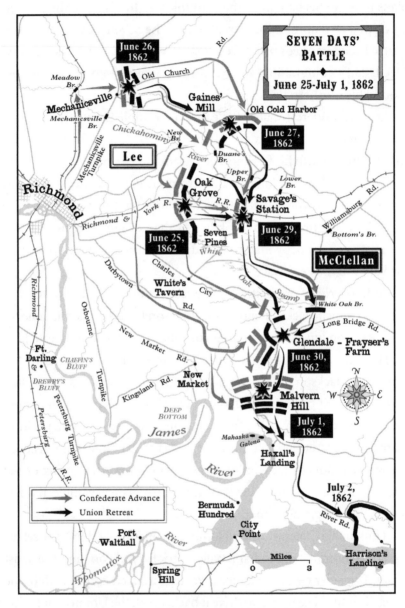

Seven Days' Battle (June 25–July 1, 1862)
Map by David Deis, Dreamline Cartography, Northridge, CA

Harbor. Those goals might have been achieved more efficiently and simply by going around the north flank of McClellan's army instead of launching a complicated frontal assault. In any event, Lee ordered Magruder to create a diversion south of the Chickahominy and Jackson, A. P. Hill, Longstreet, and D. H. Hill, in that order from north to south, to attack Porter with their respective divisions.

Lee's complicated order was reminiscent of Cheat Mountain. Specifically, Jackson was to march from Ashland to the Slash Church on June 25, camp west of the Virginia Central Railroad, march at 3:00 a.m. on June 26, and capture Beaver Dam on the Yankee right flank and rear. When A. P. Hill heard Jackson's cannon, he was to cross the Chickahominy at Meadow Bridge and take Mechanicsville. As soon as Hill had moved sufficiently east to control the Mechanicsville Bridge across the Chickahominy, Longstreet and D. H. Hill were to cross that bridge and go to the support of Jackson and A. P. Hill respectively. The major problem with this battle plan was that, with a single error, the entire enterprise would collapse.[67] Failure or disaster was likely, and both occurred.

Not surprisingly, Jackson failed to appear. Fatigued by their just-completed Valley Campaign, Jackson's men arrived at Ashland late on June 25—one day later than planned. Then, exhausted by their twenty-mile, mud-encased march that day, they failed to march at the ordered time of 3:00 a.m. on June 26 and did not begin leaving Ashland until 8:00 that morning. Not arriving at Hundley's Corner near Mechanicsville on the Confederate left flank until 5:00 p.m. that afternoon, Jackson, of course, was unable to carry out the planned June 26 assault that was to have initiated the entire Confederate offensive. Jackson himself had gotten only eight to ten hours of sleep in four days and was physically ill for the next several days; Jackson's primary biographer James Robertson described him as in a stupor while trying to understand Lee's battle plan and move his troops toward Richmond.[68] Inexplicably, Lee apparently had taken no steps to stay informed of Jackson's location and simply waited for the battle plan to unfold. Instead it unraveled.

A. P. Hill grew impatient waiting for the sound of Jackson's nonexistent attack and decided to go ahead on his own. His men crossed the Chickahominy and entered Mechanicsville at 3:00 p.m. on June 26, had some initial success, and then were decimated by massed Union artillery and rifles. About 1,500 Rebels attacked 20,000 entrenched Northerners at Beaver Dam and were slaughtered. Instead of halting the ill-advised offensive, Lee allowed D. H. Hill to enter the fray on A. P. Hill's right and come under the same deadly fire.

When Jackson finally arrived at Hundley's Corner near the Rebel left flank at 5:00 p.m., he decided his 20,000 men were not fit for fighting. He went into camp before sundown while the fighting raged three miles away and he was in a position to flank, or cut off the possible retreat of, the entrenched Union forces of Fitz John Porter. Jackson biographer Robertson stated that Jackson had done all that Lee had required him to do because of Lee's ambiguous orders.[69] That evening Lee withdrew A. P. Hill's troops and prepared to attack again the next day. Porter retreated to another strong defensive position still north of the Chickahominy, and McClellan decided to move his entire army toward Harrison's Landing—thereby forfeiting the supposedly offensive nature of his entire campaign.

Although it was a strategic success, the complex, intricately timed offensive Lee planned had proven to be a tactical disaster. Lee had managed to get only 30 percent of his army involved in the assault. Of about 20,000 Union troops, only about two hundred fifty were killed or wounded. On the other hand, about 16,000 Confederates suffered 1,500 to 2,000 casualties.[70]

Jackson's failure to enter the fray on this second of the Seven Days' presaged his disastrous noninvolvement throughout the entire series of battles. Again and again in these consecutive days of bitter fighting, Jackson's men were late participants or nonparticipants —due primarily to their commanding officer being in a stupor. Jackson slept for most of one afternoon of battle and fell asleep that night with food still in his mouth. Jackson's collapse probably resulted from extreme exhaustion brought on by his brilliant but fatiguing Valley campaign and his lack of sleep while he oversaw his army's movement to the Peninsula. Between June 22 and 30, Jackson had very little sleep.[71]

Jackson's condition was so evident and debilitating that Lee should have been aware of it and taken corrective action. Lee may have been victimized by his practices of having a small staff and exercising lax battlefield oversight of his commanders. In any event, Lee either was or should have been aware of Jackson's incredible battlefield lapses from the very first day and should either have placed him on sick leave, temporarily relieved him of command, or personally supervised Jackson's operations after the first day. He did none of these. The situation was aggravated by Lee's issuance of such vague orders throughout the campaign that Jackson may have believed he was complying with them and not have realized he was failing to carry out his commander's desires.[72]

Although a tactical failure, the Battle of Mechanicsville was a major strategic success for Lee because it caused McClellan to panic and order the withdrawal of Porter—over his objections—across the Chickahominy, final abandonment of the White House Landing supply base, and then withdrawal of the Union army from the siege lines. Although he did not know it that night, Lee already had achieved his primary strategic objective—relieving the siege of Richmond. While ordering frontal attacks during the next several days, Lee ignored cavalry-obtained information indicating that McClellan's forces were retreating and were vulnerable to a flank attack on their James River base. Instead of going around McClellan's right flank, Lee directed frontal assaults again and again.

Therefore, the next day (June 27) A. P. Hill went on the offensive again, carried out a direct assault at Gaines' Mill (east of Mechanicsville and north of the Chickahominy) for much of the day, and fought his division until it was no longer an effective fighting unit. Hill's problems were that Porter's forces had retreated during the night from Beaver Dam to another strong position east of Powhite Creek and that Jackson this time barely entered the fray. That morning Lee had met with Hill and an exhausted Jackson to discuss a coordinated attack on the Union troops, which were being withdrawn from Mechanicsville for an ultimate retreat across the Chickahominy. It should have been apparent to Lee that Jackson was too exhausted to be relied upon.

Because of Jackson's failure to bring his men a few miles to the Confederate left flank, Hill once again fought alone for many long, bloody hours. The battle began at 11:00 a.m. and continued till dark. When Hill was suffering from withering artillery and small arms fire at Boatswain's Swamp, Lee finally sent his adjutant Major Walter H. Taylor at about 1:00 p.m. to prod the missing Jackson into action. Jackson was hampered by the absence of Jedediah Hotchkiss (his expert cartographer), his "fatigued-muddled mind," and his usual obsession with secrecy. His failure to explain his desires to a local guide cost hours in getting his troops into battle.[73] It was another five hours until Jackson finally appeared and deployed.

Jackson, whose absence Ewell was unable to explain to Lee, finally entered the battle on the Confederate left at six o'clock. Lee's at-long-last-combined forces broke Porter's line with a costly and desperate charge. They compelled Porter to retreat across the river at dusk. If Jackson had arrived and attacked Porter's right flank during the afternoon, Porter's retreat route across the Chickahominy could have been cut off and his forces isolated. Jackson's failure to promptly engage on the Union flank was due to his fatigue, his usual failure to share information, his use of vague oral orders to his subordinates, his failure to seek additional guidance from Lee, and Lee's misguided battle plan and failure to adequately supervise the ongoing conflict.[74]

Lee's second offensive had again proven devastating to his own army. At Gaines' Mill (Boatswain's Swamp), the 39,000 Union troops had a total of 4,000 killed or wounded and 2,800 missing, while the 33,000 Confederates had 8,800 killed or wounded.[75] Porter later wrote, " Nor… did we fear the combined attack of Lee and Jackson at Gaines's Mill. Defeat to us was necessarily great damage to them. Our flanks were secure and could not be turned; though fewer in numbers, the advantages of our position, combined with the firm discipline of our own brave men, overcame the odds."[76]

James Robertson explained Lee's responsibilities for the disasters at Mechanicsville and Gaines' Mill:

> The absence of a tight chain of command was the root of the June 26–27 Confederate failures. Lee commanded an army, but it was fighting like a group of disconnected divisions. The general's most respected biographer, Douglas Southall Freeman, blamed the division commanders rather than Lee for the disorganization. Each seemed "under no necessity of coordinating his movements with the other." That is somewhat far-fetched. The captain of a ship, not the mates, is responsible for the continuing progress of the vessel on its journey. Worst of all, the lack of a competent general staff left Lee out of touch with the pieces—and the pieces ignorant of exactly what the commander wanted of them in the strange country where they were supposed to be on the offensive. Basic communication and coordination were sadly missing….[77]

On June 28, the Federals destroyed most of their huge stockpile of supplies at White House Landing, and moved toward the James. Having escaped disaster, McClellan's forces were in full retreat, and Lee's eagerness to assault continued unabated. Lee chose to continue attacking them directly instead of sweeping well around the east of them and cutting them off from embarking on vessels on the James River or escaping down the Peninsula.[78] Meanwhile, Lee was fortunate that McClellan's defensive mentality prevented him from exploiting Richmond's vulnerable position while Lee attacked north of the Chickahominy. At that time, in the words of General D. H. Hill, "Richmond was at the mercy of McClellan.... The fortifications around Richmond at that time were very slight. McClellan could have captured the city with very little loss of life" and compelled Lee to attack him there.[79]

On June 29, Lee resumed his offensive against the retreating enemy. Once again he had a complicated plan of attack requiring coordination among many of his generals. Not only was this plan complicated, it also was unwritten. Jackson was to cross the Grapevine Bridge over the Chickahominy and get on the flank and rear (north and east) of the Union forces at Savage's Station. Magruder and Benjamin Huger were to attack those forces from the west. Holmes was to seize Malvern Hill in front of the retreating Yankees.

Due to a lackadaisical effort to rebuild or bypass the destroyed Grapevine Bridge, Jackson took all day to cross the river and never engaged the enemy. Jackson apparently had received unclear and conflicting orders from Lee (to guard the Chickahominy crossings and pursue the enemy) and therefore concluded there was no urgency about pursuing or attacking the retreating Union army.[80] Meanwhile, Magruder delayed his attack on particularly vulnerable troops of Brigadier General Edwin V. Sumner's 2nd Corps because Magruder mistakenly believed that Lee's orders required him to wait for Huger's arrival on his right flank. Magruder finally got Lee to order Huger to Magruder's flank. But, after his arrival on that flank, Huger departed without advising Magruder. The latter general then went ahead with his unsupported attack at Savage's Station, and two brigades of his division were decimated by Sumner's corps before the latter retreated toward White Oak Swamp. The Union army left behind 2,500 wounded and sick. Due to lack of close on-scene coordination by Lee, lack of communication between Lee and his generals, and poor performance by all those generals,[81] Savage's Station became a major lost opportunity to strike the Bluecoats on the move. Freeman said, "The day's operations had been a failure, not to say a fiasco."[82]

More of the same occurred the next day. The June 30 Battle of Glendale (Frayser's [Frazier's] Farm) was a classic example of the difficulty of coordinating a multi-divisional attack and the disastrous results of failure to do so. In Lee's mind, Jackson was to attack the Union army from the north as it retreated southward, while the other Rebel divisions were to attack that army from the west. Those other divisions were (from north to south) those of Major Generals Huger, Longstreet, A. P. Hill, and (Theophilus) Hunter Holmes.

After an early morning meeting with Lee, the totally fatigued Jackson failed until late in the day to get across White Oak Creek and Swamp, where the bridges (like Grapevine before them) not surprisingly had been destroyed. During an early afternoon artillery battle, Jackson slept under a tree and seemed unable to comprehend the news that his scouts had found a way through the swamp. Off on the far right, Huger delayed opening the attack and then inexplicably stopped firing. Jackson and Huger's reticence allowed 14,000 Union troops to reinforce the Frayser's farm area. Once again Lee sent no couriers to the flanks to see what was amiss. He waited for his generals to carry out his grand plan. Two of them did. Longstreet and A. P. Hill slugged it out with the Federals whom they attacked at Frayser's Farm. Unsupported on either flank, these 20,000 Rebels took significant losses at the hands of 40,000 Yankees; they suffered 3,500 casualties while the basically uninvolved Jackson lost a mere fifteen.[83]

Porter Alexander thought that June 30, 1862, may have been the Confederates' best opportunity to win the war because the Confederacy was at its prime, especially in manpower, and had a chance to shock the North by capturing McClellan's army. He blamed Jackson for the lost opportunity but did not discount Lee's role:

> Yet it is hardly correct either to say that the failure to reap the greatest result was in no way Gen. Lee's fault. No commander of any army does his whole duty who simply gives orders, however well considered. He should supervise their execution, in person or by staff officers, constantly, day & night, so that if the machine balks at any point, he may be most promptly informed & may most promptly start it to work. For instance on Jun. 30 I think he should have been in person with Huger, & have had reliable members of his staff with Jackson on his left & Longstreet & others on his right, receiving reports every half hour or oftener, & giving fresh orders as needed.[84]

When confronted with the opinion that McClellan was about to escape, the frustrated Lee exclaimed, "Yes, he will get away because I cannot have my orders carried out."[85] Actually, the problem was with Lee's failure to communicate and oversee. For the fourth consecutive battle, Lee failed to adequately communicate his offensive plans to Jackson—either before or during the battle—even though Lee was a mere forty minutes away from Jackson.[86] In his official report on the battle, Lee claimed, "The extent of the fields of battle, the nature of the ground, and the denseness of the forests rendered more than general directions impracticable." Historian Thomas Buell explained that these words meant that "Lee had removed himself from the battlefield. The plan had been his. The execution of his plan, for better or worse, had not been his responsibility."[87] It is enlightening to compare Lee's hands-off approach through most of the Seven Days' Campaign to Grant's direct battlefield involvement at both Donelson and Shiloh during the preceding months.

The Rebels' delay on June 30 allowed McClellan to consolidate his forces in a dominating position on Malvern Hill near the James River. Malvern Hill became the scene of the most disastrous and unnecessary of Lee's frontal attacks during the Seven Days' Battle. After observing that Malvern Hill was a magnificent defensive position on which the Union infantry and artillery, including its siege and reserve train of 100 guns, could be assembled and that it had protected positions for 300 guns that could sweep the narrow and obstructed approaches below, General Alexander offered a personal insight on the situation there:

> I don't think any military engineer can read this description of this ground without asking in surprise, & almost in indignation, how on God's earth it happened that our army was put to assault such a position. The whole country was but a gently rolling one with no great natural obstacles anywhere, fairly well cultivated & with farm roads going in every direction. Why was not half our army simply turned to the left & marched by the nearest roads out of the enemy's view & fire to strike his road of retreat, & his long, slow & cumbersome trains, a few miles below, while the rest in front could threaten & hold his battle array without attacking it.
>
> I have myself, on the ground afterward, discussed the feasibility of this in company with Gen. Wade Hampton, & [Major] Gen. J[eremy] F[rancis] Gilmer, chf. engineer, & we

examined & found short, easy, & covered roads in every way favorable.

But Gen. Lee, though himself distinguished as an engineer, & for engineer work, in Mexico, had but few engineer officers close to him, & seemed to have such supreme confidence that his infantry could go anywhere, that he took comparatively little pains to study out the easier roads.

In the Mexican War fought with smooth bore, short range muskets, in fact, the character of the ground cut comparatively little figure. But with the rifled muskets & cannon of this war the affair was very different as was proven both at Malvern Hill, & at Gettysburg.... [88]

Having long since achieved his strategic goal of protecting Richmond but not satisfied with the Union retreat to the James River, Lee ignored the nearly unanimous advice of his corps commanders and, on July 1, launched a daylong series of suicidal attacks by valuable veteran forces on strong Union positions. D. H. Hill had personally advised Lee of the height, vulnerable approaches, and size and strength of Malvern Hill, and he added, "If General McClellan is there in force, we had better let him alone."[89]

Lee's battle plan, said Robertson, was "reflective more of [his] fatigue and frustration than of any strategic soundness."[90] In addition, Lee's usual lack of battlefield control and coordination resulted in the troops of Longstreet, A. P. Hill, and Jackson being barely involved in the assault. A four-hour artillery duel resulted in the serial elimination of Southern batteries when never more than sixteen Rebel guns were placed in action at one time and ninety of their guns were kept in reserve all day. Jackson personally ordered the exposure of sixteen guns to the fire of over a hundred Yankee guns; the guns and their crews were immediately destroyed.[91]

After that artillery debacle, Union cannons and rifles slaughtered Rebel infantry attackers from D. H. Hill's, Lafayette McLaws', and Huger's divisions. Their piecemeal attacks were brought about by a vague and flawed order Lee issued to his generals: "Batteries have been established to rake the enemy's lines. If it is broken as is probable, [Brigadier General Lewis Addison] Armistead, who can witness the effect of the fire, has been ordered to charge with a yell. Do the same."[92] The infantry attacks continued even after the first ones had demonstrated the correctness of the advice of Lee's subordinates and the folly of continued assaults on Union artillery and infantry firing down on the Confederates.

After the first failed attacks by five of D. H. Hill's brigades with a loss of 2,000 men, Lee himself ordered Magruder to attack. This led to the slaughter of additional thousands in the nine brigades of Huger and McLaws as each one emerged from the woods separately and was eliminated. The disjointed attacks, spread out over several hours, were marked by what Union General Porter called "a reckless disregard of life."[93] He described how fourteen Rebel brigades successively charged the Union stronghold and "the artillery… mowed them down with shrapnel, grape, and canister; while our infantry, withholding their fire until the enemy were within short range, scattered the remnants of their columns."[94] The waves of attackers achieved nothing but self-destruction at the hands of Union artillery and infantry.

Historian Freeman concluded that Lee realized that evening that he had made a mistake in allowing his army's right wing to assault a position of unknown strength. That same evening Lee approached Magruder and asked him why he had undertaken such an attack; Magruder responded, "In obedience to your orders, twice repeated."[95] Historian Angus Konstam later concluded, "Lee had lost control of the battle from the start, and consequently his army was led piecemeal into a perfect killing ground to be slaughtered."[96]

In all, Lee had 6,000 men killed or wounded in that single day of slaughter. Fifty percent of the Confederate casualties may have been attributable to artillery.[97] D. H. Hill himself said that Lee's assault at Malvern Hill "… was not war—it was murder."[98] As a result of this ill-conceived assault, the Confederates were in complete disarray and could have been swept from the field by a Union assault, which most generals other than McClellan would have launched. Fortunately for Lee, while McClellan was absent at Harrison's Landing and on the James River most of that day, Porter was left in charge of the Army of the Potomac without authority to initiate a counterattack. In addition, when McClellan returned to the field, he rejected the advice of many of his generals to counterattack the vulnerable Rebels. Thereby, he missed perhaps his finest opportunity to capture Richmond and one of his better chances to decimate Lee's army. Lee was most fortunate to have McClellan as his foe.

As Confederate Porter Alexander indicated, Malvern Hill was the first, but certainly not the last, instance in which Lee gave insufficient weight to the Civil War's new weaponry. With increasing frequency throughout the war, the combatants, especially the Yankees, used rifled muskets. They propelled inch-long Minié balls, which were accurate at up to 200 yards and could kill at over half a mile. These weapons were ahead of Lee's tactics. Although Lee was not alone in making this miscalculation, he lost far more soldiers than any other Confederate general—losses that the outmanned Confederates simply could not absorb. His experience supported the later conclusion of military historian Russell Weigley: "So destructive did rifled muskets and cannons prove themselves to be against attacking infantry in the American Civil War that attackers could win battlefield decisions if at all only through immense sacrifices of their own manpower."[99]

With McClellan slinking away downstream to Harrison's Landing, the Seven Days' Battle had ended. What were its results and impacts?

Although, in Michael C. C. Adams' words, McClellan had proven "incapable as ever of bold, aggressive action,"[100] Lee had inflicted grievous wounds on his own army. One Northern postwar analyst commented, "That Lee defeated McClellan is clear enough, but can it be claimed in any sense, except technically, the Army of the Potomac was defeated by him during these seven bloody days, a continuous battle in six separate but related actions, in four of which parts of his army were repulsed by parts of the opposing army, and on the sole occasion when all of the forces of each were opposed, the Army of Northern Virginia met with a decisive defeat?"[101]

That battle had terminated the threat to Richmond but had done so at an unnecessarily high cost. The threat had disappeared after the first day of battle and was known by Lee to be gone after the second day. Lee's abysmal control of his forces, insistence on continual frontal attacks, poor oversight of Jackson, and persistent attempts to carry out difficult coordinated attacks resulted in dreadful Southern casualties. As Lee was to learn to his regret, the Confederacy could not afford many such "victories."

Alexander summarized Lee's first series of offensive thrusts:

> Very few of the reports distinguish between the casualties of the different battles, of which there were four, beside a sharp affair of Magruder's at Savage Station on Sunday the 29th, about which I have never known the particulars except that it was an isolated attack on a strong rear guard by 2–1/2 brigades & it was repulsed, as might have been expected. No small force of ours could have hoped for any real success, & all such inadequate attacks were mistakes.
>
> Of the other four actions, three were assaults by main force right where the enemy wanted us to make them. The

first, Ellison's Mill [Mechanicsville], was an entire failure &
very bloody—but fortunately was in a small scale. The second, Cold Harbor or Gaines's Mill, was also a bloody failure
at first—being made piecemeal. Finally made in force it was
a success. The third, Malvern Hill, was an utter & bloody
failure. Ellison's Mill & Malvern Hill could both have been
turned [flanked], & Gen. D. H. Hill asserts that the enemy's
right at Cold Harbor could have better [*sic*] assaulted than
the centre or left where our attack was made.[102]

The just-mentioned Confederate General Hill further criticized his own
army's efforts: "Owing to our ignorance of the country and lack of
reconnaissance of the successive battlefields, throughout this campaign
we attacked just when and where the enemy wished us to attack."[103]
These Confederate military critics of Lee were not asserting that he
should have done nothing but rather that he should have done things
differently. These possibilities included going around McClellan's right
flank and cutting off his access to Harrison's Landing on the James River.
What they did oppose was uncoordinated frontal assaults. Of this week-
long struggle, Freeman said, "Lee displayed no tactical genius in combat-
ing a fine, well-led Federal army."[104] Another historian pointed to Lee's
loss of control over his subordinates and his army[105]—a problem that
would occur again at Gettysburg.

As a result of Lee's aggressively offensive strategy and tactics during
the Seven Days' Battle, the Confederates suffered 20,000 casualties to the
Union's 16,000. Lincoln perceptively noted, "in men and material, the
enemy suffered more than we, in that series of conflicts; while it is certain
that he is less able to bear it."[106] Distilled to their essence, these figures
show that McClellan had lost one in eight of his men while Lee was
losing close to one in four. Victories at that cost would lose the war—and
they did. As military historian Bevin Alexander said, "With the

direct-assault kind of war Robert E. Lee unveiled in the Seven Days, the South might win battles, but it would bleed to death long before it could achieve victory."[107]

Throughout the Seven Days' Battle, Lee's strategy and tactics were excessively aggressive. His strategy was totally offensive. Incredibly, Lee watched thousands of his fine troops slaughtered while charging usually fortified Union forces but did not seem to realize the foolhardiness of such tactics. Lee's Seven Days' battle-plans were overly complex; he frequently issued vague and discretionary orders to his generals, and then he failed to supervise their execution through adequate on-the-field command and control.[108] He repeated these mistakes on several later occasions and thereby squandered the Confederacy's chances of winning the war.

COMPARISON OF SHILOH AND SEVEN DAYS'

As the result of two days of ferocious fighting at Shiloh, the two armies suffered a total of 19,900 killed and wounded. Another 4,000 were missing. Grant described the battle's ferocity:

> Shiloh was the severest battle fought at the West during the war, and but few in the East equaled it for hard, determined fighting. I saw an open field, in our possession on the second day, over which the Confederates had made repeated charges the day before, so covered with dead that it would have been possible to walk across the clearing, in any direction, stepping on dead bodies, without a foot touching the ground.[109]

Grant, fighting on the defensive on the first day and on the counteroffensive on the second, had about 1,750 men killed and another 8,500 wounded (15–16 percent) among his 63,000–65,000 troops. At the same time, his troops killed 1,730 and wounded 8,000 (22–24 percent) of the 40,000–45,000 Rebels. There were 2,900 missing or captured Union troops and almost 1,000 missing or captured Rebels. Thus, Grant's casualties at Shiloh were 13,100 to his enemies' 10,700.[110]

Grant had not brought on the Battle of Shiloh. In fact, his aggressive concentration on attacking Confederates, perhaps augmented by frustration over the faint support of Halleck and Buell, caused him to overlook the possibility of a Confederate attack and to be less than fully prepared for the Rebel assault.[111] He had survived the shock of the surprise attack and repelled that assault in a way that caused his enemy to suffer casualties at a rate almost fifty percent in excess of his own. Because the Confederate armies had less than half the manpower of Union armies, the Confederates could not afford to take such high casualties—especially at a one-to-one ratio with their counterparts. Historians Jean Smith and Stacy Allen summarized the impact of Shiloh's casualties: "The difference was the Union could replenish its men and equipment, the Confederacy could not,"[112] and "Therefore, the Confederacy suffered a substantial, even decisive defeat in the war of attrition."[113]

After Shiloh, the Northern press was filled with venomous, inflated, and inaccurate criticisms of Grant—including claims that he was drunk when Johnston launched his surprise attack. Many newspapers called for his resignation or dismissal. Perhaps realizing the value of Grant but more likely saving his own hide, Halleck falsely claimed that Grant had not been surprised and thus helped shut down the calls for his removal. Grant's critics were reacting to the unprecedented number of casualties at Shiloh (more than any four other Civil War battles fought thus far and more than in all of the nation's preceding wars combined). They also were responding to false reports from ill-informed reporters and vicious rumors spread by officers jealous of Grant's ascension and success.

Lincoln, however, stood behind Grant and said, "I can't spare this man; he fights."[114] Few other senior Union generals met that basic standard.

Three months after Shiloh, Grant's casualties at that battle were exceeded by almost 50 percent by Lee, who incurred 19,700 killed and injured (21 percent) during the Seven Days' Battle—while killing and wounding "only" 9,800 (11 percent) of his enemy.[115] Lee's total casualties (including missing and captured) were about 20,000, and his total foes' casualties were about 16,000.[116] With the Confederates outnumbered almost four to one in white men of fighting age, it could not afford many such victories.

As for Lee, however, his strategic success in driving McClellan away from Richmond caused a major shift in Southerners' perception of him. Overnight, he became a Confederate national hero. The three Richmond newspapers vied with each other in their praise for Lee. The *Dispatch* said Lee's operations "were certainly those of a master;" the *Enquirer* questionably claimed, "Never has such a result been achieved in so short a time and with so small cost to the victors;" and the *Whig* said that Lee "has amazed and confounded his detractors by the brilliancy of his genius, the fertility of his resources, his energy and daring. He has established his reputation forever, and has entitled himself to the lasting gratitude of his country."[117]

After his success defending Richmond with a tactical offensive, Lee would go on the strategic offensive in the following months—with drastic consequences for the Confederacy.

CHAPTER FIVE

1862–63:
LEE CONDUCTS A COSTLY OFFENSIVE WHILE GRANT AIMS FOR VICKSBURG

Lee moves into northern Virginia and wins at Second Manassas before entering Maryland and almost losing his army at Antietam. Meanwhile Grant resumes his winning ways and initiates his first efforts to capture Vicksburg

July 2, 1862, marked the beginning of a new phase of the war. It was now clear that, at least under the weak-willed McClellan, the Army of the Potomac was not about to capture Richmond or aggressively pursue Lee, let alone put a quick end to the war. On that day, McClellan's army began arriving at Harrison's Landing on the James River. From there its pouting commanding general eventually would send it back north. Also on July 2, Lincoln, realizing that he would have to make greater use of the Union's numerical superiority, issued a call for an additional 300,000 men to enlist for three-year terms.

While fortifying his do-nothing position at Harrison's Landing, McClellan, on July 3, wrote one of his usual complaining and requisitioning letters to Secretary of War Stanton. He told Stanton that he needed at least 100,000 reinforcements in order to capture Richmond and end the rebellion.[1] McClellan was unaware that Lee had started withdrawing his troops back toward Richmond—a movement hidden from McClellan for days by a cavalry screen. On July 13, Lincoln urged McClellan to resume the assault on Richmond, but another request for reinforcements was the only response.

The scene of battle was about to move north. On July 10, John Pope, the bombastic newly appointed Federal Army of Virginia Commander, announced his intention to deal harshly with Confederate sympathizers. The next day Lincoln, having lost confidence in McClellan, named Major General Henry Halleck General-in-Chief of the Federal Armies.

On July 12, Lee learned that Pope had occupied Culpeper, thereby threatening the Virginia Central Railroad connection between Richmond and its Shenandoah Valley breadbasket. Therefore, the next day Lee dispatched Jackson's two divisions to the critical railroad junction town of Gordonsville. Jackson arrived there on July 19. Bevin Alexander contended that "Jackson, not Lee, developed the strategy to defeat Pope before his army could be consolidated and before McClellan's troops could join him."[2] On July 14, the boastful Pope moved southward toward Gordonsville with his Army of Virginia. Pope ordered Banks' cavalry to seize Gordonsville, but Lee had precluded that maneuver with his Jackson gambit.

Two significant political events occurred on July 22. Lincoln advised his Cabinet that he had drafted an Emancipation Proclamation to free slaves in Confederate-controlled areas. He admitted that he could not publicly announce it until the North had some battlefield success; otherwise, it would appear to be an act of desperation. That day also saw the signing of an agreement for an exchange of prisoners between the warring sides; Lincoln and his generals had not yet realized how significantly these exchanges primarily aided the manpower-deficient Confederacy.

Lee was concerned about protecting Richmond and points to the north from Pope. He also wanted, however, to take advantage of the division of the Union forces under Pope and McClellan. Lee did an excellent job speculating on McClellan's inactivity, the decreasing threat he posed to Richmond, and his eventual movement back north via the Chesapeake Bay. In light of the reduced threat to Richmond and the increased threat posed by Pope near Gordonsville, Lee sent A. P. Hill's Division toward Gordonsville on July 27. Hill joined Jackson there on June 29. Hoping to head off the type of problem Jackson had previously had with his subordinates, Lee on June 27 wrote to Jackson, "A. P. Hill you will find I think a good officer with whom you can consult and by advising with your division commanders as to your movements much trouble will be saved by you in arranging details, as they can act more intelligently."[3] Lee's advice went unheeded, and Jackson continued to consult with no one but Lee.

Jackson and Hill's respective departures had left 69,000 and then 56,000 Confederate troops in the Richmond area to monitor McClellan. On July 31, McClellan's army at Harrison's Landing was bombarded by a thousand of D. H. Hill's artillery shells from the south side of the James River. Although the Union soldiers suffered only twenty-five casualties, they were reminded of the continuing Confederate presence near Richmond.

Developments in early August indicated that action and control on the Union side were shifting from McClellan's army north to Pope's. On August 2, Pope's men crossed the Rapidan and seized Orange Court House, a key central Virginia crossroads town. The next day new General-in-Chief Halleck ordered McClellan to bring his Army of the Potomac immediately back to northern Virginia. McClellan ineffectively protested that his army was more useful threatening Richmond than defending Washington. He, of course, could not resist requesting more troops.[4]

With discretionary orders from Lee, Jackson moved out from Gordonsville on August 7.[5] That night his troops camped at Orange Court House, from which Pope had withdrawn, and Jackson issued the order of battle for the next day. Overnight he changed the order but failed to inform A. P. Hill. This oversight resulted in Hill's barely moving on August 8 and initiated a serious rift between Jackson and Hill. In his over-eagerness to exploit the division of the Union armies and circle Pope's left flank, Jackson advanced carelessly toward Culpeper without scouting the area to his west. As a result, at Cedar Mountain, Banks' Federal corps hit Jackson's division hard in the left flank. Two divisions of Banks' soldiers smashed into Jackson's men and almost flanked their quickly formed line. Three of Jackson's brigades broke and fled. Only a brave stand by Jubal Early's brigade saved the day until the arrival of A. P. Hill's division. Banks, however, had made the mistakes of attacking without keeping some troops in reserve and failing to send for reinforcements. After the Confederate line held and Hill came to the rescue, therefore, the Rebels counterattacked and drove the Bluecoats from the field.[6] Although the Confederates held the field after the battle, they suffered 1,300 casualties to the Union troops' 2,400.[7]

By August 13, Lee accurately calculated that McClellan's force at Harrison's Landing, only twenty-five miles from Richmond, no longer represented a viable threat. Therefore, he moved Longstreet with the bulk of Lee's remaining forces toward Gordonsville to counter the threat posed by Pope. The move was prescient because, on August 16, McClellan at long last began moving out of Harrison's Landing to return to Alexandria for the purpose of backing up Pope—thirteen days after being ordered to do so immediately.

By August 17, Lee appeared to have Pope's army trapped between the Rapidan on its southern front and the Rappahannock in its rear. Before Lee could take advantage of Pope's incautious movement, however, Pope retired across the Rappahannock to await reinforcements from McClellan. By August 20, Lee had his army across the Rapidan, controlled the west bank of the Rappahannock, and was desperately attempting to cross the latter river to get between Washington and Pope's temporarily outnumbered forces.

On the night of August 22, Jeb Stuart led the 6th Virginia Cavalry on a successful raid on Pope's headquarters at Catlett's Station. Stuart and his men captured some Union officers and, most significantly, Pope's dispatch book. That book revealed the exact position of Pope's army, his need for reinforcements, and the expected arrival times of those reinforcements.

After massive rainfall the next night made the Rappahannock impassable and wiped out offensives planned by both Lee and Pope, Lee used the information obtained by Stuart to devise his next course of action. Lee intended to hold Pope in place along the Rappahannock while he slipped his army piecemeal to the northwest, moved around Pope's right (west) flank, and finally got between Pope and Washington. Lee hoped to cut off Pope from his supplies and defeat him with his momentarily stronger force. To accomplish this, Lee relied heavily on Stonewall Jackson, the only one of Lee's generals who usually thrived when given independence and daring assignments. Early on August 25, Jackson moved away from the Rappahannock to the northwest and launched one of his patented flanking marches around the right flank and rear of Pope's Army of Virginia.

On the first day of his march, Jackson moved twenty-five miles between the Blue Ridge and Bull Run mountains all the way to Salem, from where he planned to move through Thoroughfare Gap onto Pope's

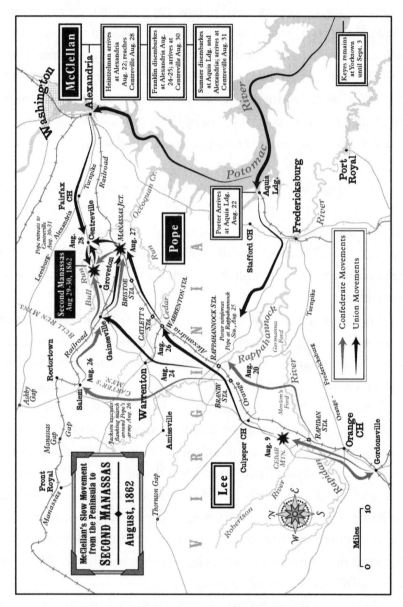

*McClellan's Slow Movement from the Peninsula
to Second Manassas (August 1862)*
Map by David Deis, Dreamline Cartography, Northridge, CA

rear. Pope thought he had things in hand because Jackson's movements were being tracked by Union cavalry. That cavalry reported that Jackson had thirty regiments and significant cavalry when, in fact, he had sixty-six regiments and all of Lee's cavalry. Jackson's huge force moved through Thoroughfare Gap on August 26. Early on August 27, Stuart seized Bristoe Station on Pope's railroad supply line, and Jackson's men next destroyed hundreds of boxcars and huge amounts of Union supplies at Manassas Junction four miles to the northeast. Although Jackson's men were allowed to fill their knapsacks with canned lobster and other delicacies, he ordered the destruction of barrels of whiskey to preserve their fighting capacity. In order to carry out this remarkable end run on Pope's army, Stuart's men had ridden, and Jackson's foot infantry had incredibly marched, over fifty miles in forty-eight hours.

On the same day of the Manassas Junction debacle, Longstreet, who had been holding Pope in place along the Rappahannock, moved away to the northwest to go to Jackson's assistance. Advised of the disaster in his rear, Pope marched hard toward Manassas in hopes of destroying Jackson before Longstreet could come to his rescue. The resultant clash would be known as the Second Battle of Bull Run (Second Manassas).[8]

After repelling the first Union forces responding to his attack at Bristoe Station and Manassas Junction, Jackson withdrew to a strong defensive position at Groveton, just northwest of the 1861 Bull Run battlefield. Although vulnerable until Longstreet could come to his aid, Jackson revealed his position by attacking a portion of thirty-four passing Union regiments, including the famous Iron Brigade, near dusk on August 28. In two hours of vicious fighting, both sides suffered heavy casualties until darkness halted the battle.

On the morning of August 29, Jackson's exhausted 23,000 men had moved to a strong position in an unfinished railroad cut between Groveton and Sudley Springs but faced 50,000 Union attackers. Jackson's three divisions withstood a full day of uncoordinated assaults by ten Union divisions. Jackson sent Stuart in search of the marching Longstreet, and he returned with Lee and Longstreet themselves by midmorning. Pope had failed to isolate Jackson by blocking Thoroughfare Gap in strength, and Lee therefore had little difficulty transiting the gap and merging his forces. It was early afternoon, however, until Longstreet's men began arriving and digging in on Jackson's right.

That afternoon Lee wanted to attack immediately with the troops on hand. Longstreet, however, advised Lee against doing so because they did not know the strength of the opposing forces, they knew that McClellan was reinforcing Pope, and Longstreet believed there were Union forces free to attack his right flank in the event of a Confederate assault. Lee took Longstreet's advice.[9]

On the morning of August 30, Lee and his generals watched in puzzlement as Pope's forces did nothing. Starting around noon, the Union forces resumed their assaults on Jackson's position. While Lee and Longstreet waited for the perfect moment to counterattack, Jackson's line was almost broken. Some of his men ran out of ammunition and repelled their attackers by throwing rocks and using their rifles as clubs. They were greatly assisted by oblique and devastating artillery fire on the Federals from twenty-two guns of a large artillery battalion under Longstreet.

Finally, at 4:00 p.m., Longstreet launched a devastating counterattack; Jackson much later sent his forces on the offensive, and between them they drove the panicked and disorganized Union troops from the field. In three hours on the offensive, however, Longstreet lost more men than Jackson had lost in three days on the defensive.[10] British General Fuller described Jackson's maneuver around Pope's army as sound strategy and Lee's maneuver [Longstreet's attack] as unsound and "not strategically remunerative."[11]

Aggressive Confederate pursuit toward Fairfax Court House the next day was hampered by heavy rain. That same day Lee fell while trying to grab his spooked horse and broke his right wrist. For the next two weeks he traveled by ambulance. Near evening and in a torrential downpour, the two sides clashed again on September 1 at Ox Hill near Chantilly. Both sides suffered heavy losses in the brief but bloody Battle of Chantilly, and the Union forces lost two outstanding generals.

Although Lee's forces clearly had won a major battlefield victory at Second Manassas, once again they paid a dear price. His 49,000 men engaged suffered 9,500 casualties (19 percent), while Pope's forces lost 14,400 out of 75,000 (19 percent). At Chantilly, the Confederate casualties were 800 while the Union suffered 1,300 casualties. Lee was continuing his pattern of aggressive attrition through offensive strategy and tactics. He had assumed command, on June 1, of an army of 95,000; within exactly three months, that now-outnumbered army had suffered almost 32,000 casualties. Although he had moved the scene of conflict from the environs of Richmond to the outskirts of Washington, Lee's offensives were seriously weakening his army.[12]

So far, Lee's summer may have appeared successful. He had driven the Yankees from the Peninsula, swept them from the field at Manassas, and beaten them at Chantilly. Although these victories had taken their toll on his army, Lee decided to take a daring gamble and carry the war to the North. On September 3 and 4, Lee wrote to Davis that he planned to move north into Maryland to take advantage of Confederate sympathies there and perhaps to move on to destroy the critical railroad bridge across the Susquehanna River at Harrisburg, Pennsylvania. In his first letter, Lee admitted that the proposed effort was risky and had little chance of success: "I am aware that the movement is attended with much risk, yet I do not consider success impossible...."[13] Consistent with his eastern theater focus, Lee suggested to President Davis that Bragg's Army of Tennessee, outnumbered more than 3 to 1 and struggling to defend eastern Tennessee and Chattanooga, be brought east to protect Richmond while Lee went north.[14] Specifically, according to Thomas Connelly, "At the time of Lee's request, Bragg was outnumbered 124,000 to 35,000, and the Union Army of the Ohio was maneuvering within twenty miles of Chattanooga."[15] Lee's suggestion, which was wisely ignored, demonstrated that he either did not know or did not care what was occurring in the middle theater.

On September 4, Lee's 53,000 battered troops left Manassas. The next day they crossed the Potomac into Maryland at White's Ferry, just east of Leesburg, with false expectations that many Marylanders would increase their dwindling numbers. Although some have claimed that Lee was seeking food for his army in Maryland, his army would have found adequate food in Virginia.[16] Crossing the Potomac was a fateful step because eventually Lee would have to return to Virginia, that return would be interpreted as a retreat and defeat, and Lincoln was desperately waiting for anything that could be construed as a Confederate defeat. Then he could announce his Emancipation Proclamation and thereby change the nature of the war.[17] As summarized by Thomas Buell, "No good reason existed to warrant an invasion of Maryland at that time and under those circumstances. Lee's soldiers certainly knew this, for they abandoned his army in wholesale numbers."[18]

While underway in Maryland on September 8, Lee optimistically wrote to Davis that this might be a propitious time for the Confederacy, in a perceived position of strength, to propose to the Union a negotiated settlement that included recognition of the Confederacy's independence.[19] Unknown to Lee, English and French leaders had tentatively decided to intervene through arbitration in the American war—a step that would have greatly aided the Confederacy. When, however, they learned of Lee's invasion of the North, they decided to await its outcome.

That delay matured into a European refusal to become involved when they learned of the unsuccessful outcome of Lee's Maryland campaign and Lincoln's consequent issuance of his preliminary Emancipation Proclamation.[20]

The reality of the Maryland incursion sharply contrasted with Lee's hopes for success. By the time Lee reached Frederick, Maryland, his soldiers were but a shadow of the army Lee had inherited only three months before. Lee's aggressiveness had resulted in over 30,000 casualties, and straggling became a significant problem throughout Lee's exhausted forces.[21] On August 20, Jackson had ordered that deserters be shot without the nicety of a court-martial to determine their guilt.[22]

Contributing to the straggling problem were the scarcity of provisions and the resulting sickness of many men when they satisfied their hunger by eating raw corn and green apples.[23] In his September 3 letter to Davis, Lee himself admitted that the army had its problems: "The army is not properly equipped for an invasion of an enemy's territory. It lacks much of the material of war, is feeble in transportation, the animals being much reduced, and the men are poorly provided with clothes, and in thousands of instances are destitute of shoes."[24]

According to Alexander, divisions had been nearly reduced to brigades, and brigades were only slightly larger than regiments.[25] By September 13, Lee was telling Davis that one-third to one-half of his original number of soldiers had deserted.[26] In addition, the army's leadership had been devastated by the months of battle; eight of Jackson's nineteen brigades were led by colonels in place of dead or wounded brigadier generals.

On September 9, Lee took a potentially fatal gamble and separated his army into four, and eventually five, vulnerable segments—against the advice of both Longstreet and Jackson.[27] He issued his famous Special Orders No. 191,[28] calling for:

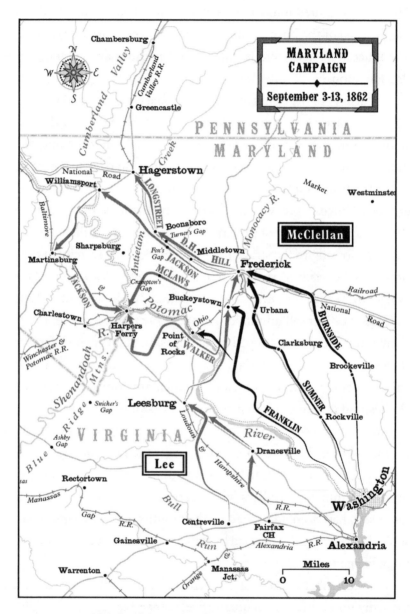

Maryland Campaign (September 3–13, 1862)
Map by David Deis, Dreamline Cartography, Northridge, CA

- Jackson's large corps to seize Bolivar Heights between the Shenandoah and Potomac Rivers (thereby cutting off Harper's Ferry located southeast of Bolivar Heights at the junction of those rivers);
- Brigadier General John George Walker's small division to occupy Loudon Heights south of those rivers and across from Harper's Ferry;
- McLaws' division to close the noose on that town by occupying Maryland Heights northeast of the rivers' junction; and
- Longstreet's and D. H. Hill's divisions to proceed over South Mountain to Boonsboro, north of Harper's Ferry and west of Frederick.

Subsequently, Lee (apparently anxious to continue northward) aggravated the situation by taking his headquarters and Longstreet's Division farther northwest to Hagerstown, advancing pickets to Middleburg on the Pennsylvania border, and leaving Harvey Hill with less than 6,000 troops thirteen miles behind at Boonsboro. Longstreet so opposed Lee's splintering of his army that he even cursed in Lee's presence as they traveled to Hagerstown: "General, I wish we could stand still and let the damned Yankees come to us!"[29]

A strange occurrence increased Lee's army's vulnerability. His division of his forces was revealed to McClellan when a copy of Lee's Special Orders No. 191, having been used to wrap three cigars, was discovered by a Union enlisted man on the morning of September 13 in a field outside Frederick, Maryland. The order fairly flew up the chain of command and reached McClellan himself by early afternoon. He was obviously elated and openly remarked, in the presence of unfriendly Marylanders' ears, that he now had Lee where he wanted him.

McClellan's foolish revelation of the order's discovery apparently resulted in Jeb Stuart's learning of some unusual occurrence in the Union camp just after midnight on September 14.

Lee was alerted by reports of McClellan's quasi-aggression that something significant had happened.[30] Nevertheless, Lee continued to risk his entire army by remaining in Maryland long enough to bring about a major battle. Lee inexplicably either failed to realize that "the jig was up" or hesitated to admit the vulnerable position in which he had placed his army. The possible temporary capture of Harper's Ferry was insufficient reason for Lee to remain in Maryland with the bulk of his army vulnerable to being trapped north of the Potomac River. Except for the plodding response of McClellan, Lee's forces would have been destroyed in piecemeal fashion.[31] McClellan waited until evening to issue orders responsive to the new opportunity he had been handed and ordered his troops to begin moving early the next morning—eighteen hours after he could and should have. As Bevin Alexander concluded, "This incredible delay saved the Army of Northern Virginia."[32]

From Frederick, McClellan sent two of his seven corps southwest toward Crampton's Gap in South Mountain to trap McLaws against the Potomac. He directed his other five corps northwest toward Turner's and Fox's gaps, also in South Mountain, to deal with the isolated and separated divisions of Hill and Longstreet. After learning from Jeb Stuart of McClellan's atypical movement, Lee ordered Longstreet to move Law and Hood's brigades from Hagerstown to Turner's Gap to fend off disaster.

The march of one of Hood's brigades presented Lee with a problem. Its Texas soldiers were angered about the possibility of going into battle without their division commander, whom Longstreet had placed in arrest status as the result of a dispute at Manassas over disposition of seized Federal ambulances. As they neared South Mountain and passed

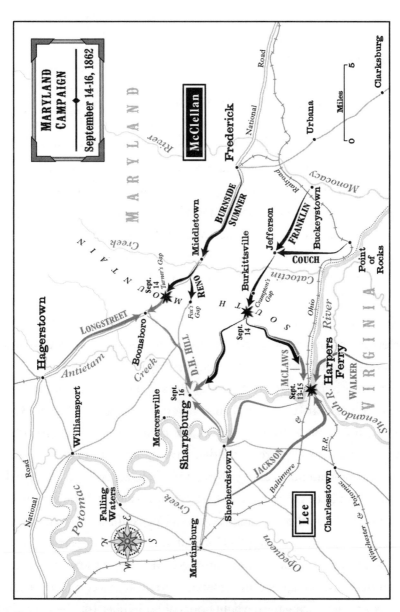

Maryland Campaign (September 14–16, 1862)
Map by David Deis, Dreamline Cartography, Northridge, CA

Lee, the Texans repeatedly shouted, "Give us Hood!" Lee replied, "You shall have him, gentlemen," and then sought out Hood.[33] Hood later wrote of that encounter:

> I found General Lee standing by the fence, very near the pike, in company with his chief of staff, Colonel [Robert] Chilton. The latter accosted me, bearing a message from the General, that he desired to speak to me. I dismounted, and stood in his presence, when he said, "General, here I am just upon the eve of entering into battle, and with one of my best officers under arrest. If you will merely say that you regret this occurrence [the Manassas incident], I will release you and restore you to the command of your division."[34]

When Hood tried to explain the injustice of his arrest, a frustrated Lee interrupted him and suspended the arrest for the duration of the battle. After Antietam, the issue was never raised again.[35]

Reinforced by Longstreet, Harvey Hill's desperate and valiant all-day holding action at Turner's and Fox's gaps on September 14 kept McClellan's army from destroying Lee's scattered forces one after the other. Although the Rebels were on the defensive and held the higher position, they were spread thinly along a three-mile front accessible by five roads. As a result of Lee's dispersion of his forces, they also were outnumbered (28,000 to 18,000) by the aggressive 6th Corps of Major General Jesse Lee Reno and the dawdling 1st Corps of Major General Joseph Hooker.

Because of the Confederates' on-the-field leadership and bravery and their defensive advantage, they managed to prevent a complete Federal breakthrough during the daylight hours of September 14. Their position at nightfall, however, was untenable because they had been flanked at both gaps, had taken heavy casualties, and were about to be overrun by the enemy's sheer mass. This situation left Lee with no choice but to retreat. He ordered Hill and Longstreet to move toward Sharpsburg.

As a result of inadequate forces being in place at South Mountain and at Crampton's Gap a few miles to the south, the Rebels lost over 3,400 troops while the attacking Yankees lost only about 2,350.[36] Lee's disproportionate losses in the one day at South Mountain and Crampton's Gap were a mere prelude to the devastating casualties his army was to suffer three days later at Antietam.

Because of the Union corps' delays in crossing South Mountain at Turner's and Fox's gaps and in breaking through McLaws' troops at Crampton's Gap, Walker and McLaws had enough time to bombard Harper's Ferry from the commanding heights while Jackson moved on the town from the northwest. The trapped 12,000-man garrison, under the ineffective leadership of Colonel Dixon S. Miles, put up only a feeble fight and quickly surrendered to Jackson on the morning of September 15. Two thousand Union cavalry had escaped under the cover of darkness.

Meanwhile, Lee oversaw the retreat, on the night of September 14, of Harvey Hill southwest from South Mountain and Longstreet south from Boonsboro toward Sharpsburg, which brought them both closer to Jackson's troops at Harper's Ferry. About noon on September 15, Lee gathered those outnumbered retreating forces of Longstreet and Hill at the small town of Sharpsburg. There, behind Antietam Creek and with the Potomac River at his back, Lee arrayed his troops awaiting both an attack by the ever-cautious McClellan and the hoped-for arrival of assistance from the victorious Rebel troops at Harper's Ferry. Union troops arrived east of the creek on the afternoon of September 15 and kept arriving for the next twenty-four hours.

On the night of September 15, Lee learned of the capture of Harper's Ferry. Instead of declaring the campaign a success and safely returning to Virginia, he stayed in his vulnerable position with his meager two divisions. On that night, McClellan outnumbered Lee by four to one and was in a position to destroy Lee's Sharpsburg defenders. But he did not attack—either that night or early the next morning, when Lee had a mere 18,000 troops.[37]

Although three additional Confederate divisions arrived from Harper's Ferry on September 16, McClellan was acquiring troops even faster than Lee. By midday, McClellan had accumulated an overwhelming force east of Antietam Creek, was aware that Lee still had a significant part of his army at Harper's Ferry, and continued to be in a position to launch a devastating attack on Lee's depleted forces. Late that afternoon, the Union commander had 72,000 troops and 300 pieces of artillery with which to attack Lee's 27,000 men and 200 guns spread out along a four-mile front. McClellan passed up this glorious opportunity to destroy Lee's army, did not attack at all on September 16, and instead went about deliberately making arrangements for an attack the next day.[38] Although Lee therefore had over a day to prepare for battle, he did not order his men to entrench—perhaps because they were too weak and had no specific trenching tools.[39]

During the bloodiest single day of the war, September 17, 1862, the blundering McClellan once again saved Lee's army from destruction by committing his overwhelmingly superior 75,000 Union troops in serial fashion from north to south along Antietam Creek. This method of attack enabled Lee, as the daylong battle progressed, to move his outnumbered defenders first to the North and West woods and Miller's cornfield in the north of the battlefield and later to Bloody Lane and the Mumma Farm in the center of the battlefield to contest a series of separate and uncoordinated Union attacks.[40]

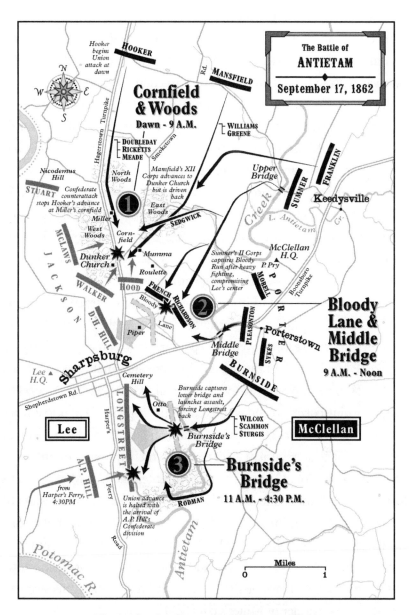

The Battle of Antietam (September 17, 1862)
Map by David Deis, Dreamline Cartography, Northridge, CA

Following hours of pre-dawn artillery exchanges, Hooker's 1st Corps launched a dawn attack from the East Woods against Jackson's three divisions on the Confederate left (north). Like most attacks that day, this one was repulsed and then followed by an enemy counterattack. Wrote historian David Lowe, "At Antietam, Lee had the perfect rationale to entrench but chose not to, relying instead on the tactical counterattack."[41] When Major General Richard Anderson's counterattack was failing, the ever-aggressive Hood reinforced him. The men of Hood's Texan-dominated division charged into the never-to-be-forgotten thirty-acre cornfield, were slaughtered (60 percent killed or wounded in thirty minutes), and were compelled to retreat. Harvey Hill led another Rebel counterattack, and Brigadier General Joseph Mansfield's Union 12th Corps drove them back with a counterattack of their own.

When Jackson tried to impede this Federal movement, he lost 50 percent of one brigade and 30 percent of another in the cornfield. Hooker's and Mansfield's forces were sweeping the field and approaching the Dunker Church south of the cornfield. There they finally were repulsed by the combined forces of Hood, Early, Hill, Walker, and McLaws. The early morning cornfield and woods casualties—incurred in under three hours—were horrific: Hooker lost 2,600 of 8,600, Hood lost 1,400 of 2,300, the 1st Texas regiment lost 186 of 226 men in twenty minutes, the Louisiana Tigers lost 323 men in fifteen minutes, the 12th Massachusetts lost 224 of 334 men, and on and on.[42] These were not the results of anyone standing on the defensive. The annihilation consisted of one fearless, perhaps mindless, assault after another by the officers and men of both armies as they swept back and forth across the cornfield a total of fifteen times. As Lowe observed, Lee "had fed much of his strength into the meat-grinder of Miller's cornfield."[43]

Lee had stripped the middle and southern segments of his lines to prevent a disaster on the north end of the Antietam battlefield, and

McClellan had achieved an almost inconceivable numerical superiority over those other un-entrenched segments of Lee's lines. But McClellan did nothing about it until the fighting had died down in the north. He moved the fighting southward after Jackson had committed his last troops to defense of the north sector.[44]

From 9:00 a.m. to noon, the fighting moved south of the cornfield to the Dunker (Dunkard) Church and the Sunken Road, known ever since as Bloody Lane. The church was the scene of more back-and-forth suicidal charges as both sides took the same type of grotesquely massive casualties as they had just to the north. The Confederates under Harvey Hill initially had the better of it for about two hours at Bloody Lane, where they stood on the defensive in the shelter of the depressed road and slaughtered a series of Yankee attackers. Ten thousand Union attackers, two full divisions, were halted as their front ranks were cut down man by man, brigade by brigade, as they frontally assaulted the out-of-sight defenders. Thousands of Union survivors found safety by lying prone on the ground and waiting for others to break the seemingly impregnable Confederate line. By midday, the attackers, spurred on by courageous if foolhardy assaults by New York's Irish Brigade, managed to flank Bloody Lane, enfilade the suddenly helpless defenders, and then overrun the position. Fighting at Bloody Lane resulted in the wounding and killing of 3,000 Blue attackers and 2,600 Gray defenders.

As the Rebel line was being broken there, Longstreet launched a fortunately timed counterattack back at the Dunker Church, and more vicious fighting broke out on the Mumma Farm between the church and Bloody Lane. Vicious fighting continued to cut down hundreds more on both sides, but the momentum was clearly with the Union forces. They were about to break through the entire center of the battlefield, isolate Lee's flanks, and virtually end the war in the East. Lee had no more reserves. But Longstreet saved the day by personally leading an advance of the Rebel artillery and a devastating assault on startled New Yorkers in the center of the cauldron. Seeing this repulse, the weak-kneed McClellan twice refused to launch additional attacks by his reserve troops in the center of the field just when another assault could have broken Lee's army.[45]

To the south, where Lee had been removing troops all day to protect his left and center, McClellan was compounding all of his other errors of that fateful day. On that end of the battlefield, the road to Sharpsburg crossed the Rohrbach Bridge, destined to be known as Burnside's Bridge in mocking tribute to General Burnside, who took so long to get his troops across it. Ineffectively superintended and perhaps cut out of the chain of command by McClellan, Burnside had over 9,000 troops to assault the Confederate right flank of about 3,000 defenders.

Of those 3,000 Confederates, only 400 were assigned to defend the bridge itself.[46] The bridge rested in a valley under a steep hill on the west bank, an ideal defensive position that made crossing very difficult. Even so, given Burnside's overwhelming manpower advantage, the shallowness of the Antietam, and the presence of a downstream ford, there was no excuse for the fatally gross tardiness of the Union attack in that sector, a tardiness that cost the Union a battlefield victory.[47]

Although the artillery fire had started at 3:00 a.m. and the Union assault to the north at dawn, Burnside received no attack orders from McClellan until 10:00 a.m. Therefore, Burnside's first assault on the bridge did not occur until shortly after that hour. Unprepared for the intense fire it would receive in attacking across the bridge, the 11th Connecticut Regiment was repulsed in that assault. It was another two hours until the 2nd Maryland was bloodily thrown back in a virtually identical attack. Belatedly realizing that other avenues of approach were available, Burnside sent a fourth of his troops to cross Snavely Ford less than a mile south of the bridge.

Shortly after 1:00 p.m., Burnside's men finally made it across Burnside's Bridge. An additional two-hour delay unbelievably ensued, however, while Burnside properly positioned his troops and provided them with adequate ammunition. It was not until 3:00 p.m., therefore, that the bulk of his 9th Corps finally began driving up the hills above the creek and threatened Sharpsburg itself. Meanwhile the rest of Burnside's corps fought across Snavely Ford and drove two miles inland on the far southern end of the Antietam battlefield. Burnside's numbers had overcome his slowness, and he finally posed a deadly threat to Lee's right flank.

It looked as though Lee's mistakes in entering Maryland, dividing his forces, and choosing to fight at Sharpsburg were about to cost him his army. Even though McClellan had halted the northern and middle assaults, Lee's forces there were effectively tied down and unable to help the 2,000 Rebels remaining on the right flank or the 2,800 in Sharpsburg itself defend against Burnside's finally swarming 15,000 troops. Those Blue attackers on the south were within a half-mile of Lee's only line of retreat to the Potomac, and all seemed lost.

An hour after A. P. Hill had arrived at 2:30 p.m. in advance of his men, Lee observed a dust cloud to the south with a mixture of fear and hope. It meant either complete Union encirclement or the arrival of help from Harper's Ferry. Fortunately for Lee, the cloud of dust signified the 3:30 p.m. arrival of Hill's 3,300 men, exhausted from their seventeen-mile, eight-hour march but excited by the desperateness of the situation they found. Unbelievably, these few soldiers, clad in captured Union uniforms, plowed into the flank of Burnside's 15,000 attackers and drove them from the Sharpsburg heights with the surprise and ferocity of their assault. Lee's army was saved, and the Battle of Antietam was over.[48]

Lee could thank McClellan's incompetence and Burnside's sluggishness, as well as the good fortune of Hill's timely arrival, for sparing the

Army of Northern Virginia from destruction. The overly cautious Union commander had compounded his error of making consecutive attacks by holding one-third of his forces in reserve and unused throughout the entire battle (primarily Porter's 5th Corps in the center of the battlefield). He also failed to use Major General Darius N. Couch's Division, which he had left near Harper's Ferry. In addition, even before Hill's troops arrived, McClellan actually recalled a division of regulars, who had been attacking alongside Burnside.[49]

Given the forces at his disposal since the night of September 15, McClellan's attacks were too late, too short, too uncoordinated, and too weak. As usual, he was concerned about not losing instead of about winning.[50] McClellan also erred by keeping his cavalry in the center of his lines rather than on the flanks, where they could have expedited Burnside's crossing of the Antietam and precluded, or at least minimized, the surprise and impact of A. P. Hill's last-minute arrival. He further erred by sending Couch's division toward Harper's Ferry and not bringing them back to Sharpsburg when A. P. Hill's troops marched from Harper's Ferry to turn the tide of battle.[51] According to General Cox, McClellan acted with his usual disastrous caution because of his incessant fear that he was greatly outnumbered.[52] All these mistakes by McClellan enabled the Confederates to barely hold throughout the day and luckily escape defeat. Had McClellan used all of his forces and attacked simultaneously along the entire front, there would have been no Army of Northern Virginia by the time Hill reached Sharpsburg.

That night the bloodied and ravaged Confederate army had no sane course of action available except retreat. At their Sharpsburg war council that night, Lee's generals responded to his inquiries and reported their abysmal condition to him. Stephen Lee described Hood's shocking report:

[Hood] displayed great emotion, seemed completely unmanned, and replied that he had no division. General Lee, with more excitement than I ever witnessed him exhibit, exclaimed, "Great God, General Hood, where is the splendid division you had this morning?" Hood replied, "They are lying on the field where you sent them, sir; but few have straggled. My division has been almost wiped out."[53]

East of Sharpsburg, the Union forces still posed a significant threat. Porter's 20,000-man corps was unsullied, Burnside's 9th was fairly fresh, and McClellan had reinforcements on the way. The unused Federal reserves at Antietam outnumbered Lee's remaining forces. Instead of retreat, however, Lee discussed with his generals whether they should stand in place or attack.

When his generals urged him to retreat because of their severe losses, he rejected their advice and added, "If McClellan wants to fight in the morning, I will give him battle again."[54] Lee thus chose to remain at Sharpsburg through September 18. Given the inequality of the armies' numbers and fighting conditions, as well as Lee's inability to retreat under fire during daylight, McClellan committed another egregious error by failing to attack that day and thus end the struggle in the East in one fell swoop. He issued incredible orders not to precipitate hostilities because he wanted to await expected reinforcements.

General Alexander provided a terse summary of what he judged to be Lee's greatest military blunder—his excessive audacity at Antietam:

> He gave battle unnecessarily at Sharpsburg Sep. 17th, 1862. The odds against him were so immense that the utmost he could have hoped to do was what he did do—to repel all assaults & finally to withdraw safely across the Potomac. And he probably only succeeded in this because McClellan kept about 20,000 men, all of Fitz John Porter's corps, entirely out of the fight so that they did not pull a trigger. And Lee's

position was such, with a great river at his back, without a bridge & with but one difficult ford, that defeat would have meant the utter destruction of his army. So he fought where he could have avoided it, & where he had nothing to make & everything to lose—which a general should not do.[55]

In summary, even though McClellan had fumbled away his glorious opportunity to destroy Lee's entire army, Lee himself had blundered just as badly. First, he went on the offensive with a weakened army into Maryland, from which he would have to retreat. Second, he badly divided his forces. Third, he failed to reunite them quickly or to return to the South when he realized that his divided condition was known and after he already had won a significant victory at Harper's Ferry. Fourth, he selected a battlefield which jeopardized his entire army by having no ready means of retreat. Fifth, instead of entrenching and remaining on the defensive at Sharpsburg, Lee counterattacked frequently throughout the day, and in those suicidal charges the attacking forces were decimated. Sixth, he selected a defensive location where he had no space to launch a flanking counterattack.[56] Finally, he stayed at Sharpsburg an additional day and defied McClellan to attack when such an attack could have destroyed Lee's army.

Each of these errors deserves separate examination. Following Seven Days', Cedar Mountain, Second Manassas, and Chantilly, Lee's army was exhausted and badly depleted. His men were in no condition to launch a campaign into the North; they were exhausted and sick. Freeman stated, "There can be no sort of doubt that Lee underestimated the exhaustion of his army after Second Manassas. That is, in reality, the major criticism of the Maryland operation: he carried worn-out men across the Potomac."[57] Instead of savoring his army's series of victories and rebuilding their strength, Lee took them on a mission which could only result in a damaging retreat back to Virginia.[58]

Against the advice of both Longstreet and Jackson, Lee inexplicably divided his small forces so badly that even a general as incompetent on the offensive as McClellan could have overwhelmed them separately and almost did destroy them. Dividing his forces to surround Harper's Ferry from three directions is understandable, but allowing Hill's and Longstreet's divisions to float to the north and then splitting them up, instead of using them to screen the Harper's Ferry operation and possibly capture the fleeing 2,000 cavalrymen, is inexplicable. Lee's multiple division of his forces was daring but foolish.[59]

After he was aware of the Union discovery of his order, Lee failed to quickly reunite his forces and to return to Virginia. Even worse, he failed to cross the Potomac at Sharpsburg with D. H. Hill's and Longstreet's divisions on the night of September 15 when he learned of the capture of Harper's Ferry.[60] On this point, historian Archer Jones concluded, "So politically and strategically Lee's Antietam campaign was a fiasco. It was really doomed to fail, but Lee could have mitigated the political damage by ending his raid without a battle."[61] He could have avoided perhaps 10,000 casualties by withdrawing into Virginia after the Battle of South Mountain.[62]

Lee gravely erred in selecting the Sharpsburg battlefield. His army was backed up against the Potomac River and had a marginal avenue of retreat. There was no bridge, and the road to the only ford was barely wide enough for a wagon and would have been totally unusable under fire. In addition, Lee's position was vulnerable to Federal artillery on the hills east of the Antietam and provided little or no opportunity for a counterattack on the Union flanks.[63] Lee himself admitted his poor battlefield selection in a September 20 letter to Davis: "Since my last letter to you of the 18th, finding the enemy indisposed to make an attack on that day, and our position being a bad one to hold with the river in rear, I determined to cross the army to the Virginia side."[64]

During the opening portion of the battle, the opposing forces swept back and forth across the infamous Miller cornfield fifteen times. Instead of staying on the defensive, the un-entrenched[65] Gray forces frontally counterattacked again and again—and as a result suffered extremely heavy casualties. Finally, his army having barely survived the all-day battle on September 17, Lee further jeopardized the very existence of that army by remaining on the field in the same vulnerable, difficult-to-retreat-from position for an additional day. He offered McClellan one more chance to crush the Rebel army with his increasingly superior forces. Although Lee had accurately gauged the timidity of the Union commander, there was nothing to be gained by so jeopardizing his decimated force. The safe, sensible course of action would have been to retreat during the night of September 17 rather than to throw down the gauntlet for one more day.

Through his combination of errors, Lee managed to lose an irre-placeable twenty-seven percent of his veteran fighters in a single day. 11,500 of his 52,000 men were casualties, while McClellan lost a similar but militarily tolerable 12,400 of his 75,000.[66] These respective casualties of twenty-two and seventeen percent demonstrate that this was a battle Lee should never have fought, one he fought poorly, or both. The latter appears to have been the case. Antietam was an unmitigated disaster for the Confederacy. In fact, Weigley said, "there is much to be said for the view that counts the Maryland campaign and the battle of Antietam as the turning point of the war—in favor of the Union."[67] Buell added, "Lee's Maryland campaign was a calamity for the Confederacy that would forever cripple its war aims…. With no credit to Lee, the valor of his soldiers allowed two-thirds of them to survive the catastrophe."[68] Antietam's greatest impact may have been that it enabled Lincoln to claim victory and, on September 22, issue his Emancipation Proclamation. That declaration changed the war from one just to save the Union to one both to save the Union and to end slavery. Lincoln's shrewd maneuver foreclosed European intervention.[69]

Through the Seven Days' Battle, Cedar Mountain, Second Manassas, Chantilly, South Mountain, Harper's Ferry, and Antietam, Lee's army had suffered an intolerable 45,000 casualties during his first four months in command.[70] His army was exhausted, and straggling again became a problem. Sent to retrieve absentees from the army, Brigadier General John R. Jones wrote, "It is disgusting and heartsickening to witness this army of stragglers."[71] Historian Weigley contended that the troops' unprecedented straggling was partially due to their prolonged campaigning and also to their reluctance to invade enemy territory in what was supposed to be a defensive war.[72]

Two days after the bloody battle at Antietam, Lee's army began its retreat across the Potomac. Still hoping to salvage a major victory from his northern trek, Lee sent his army on a march north toward Williamsport and Hagerstown but had to give up that dream when problems developed back at the Sharpsburg crossing. At midnight, Lee's incompetent chief of artillery, Brigadier General William Nelson Pendleton, reported to Lee that he had lost all the reserve artillery to the enemy, but A. P. Hill counterattacked and discovered that only four pieces of artillery had been lost. Lee's decimated army then headed south toward the Shenandoah.[73] Lee still preferred an offensive, however, as he wrote on September 21, "… it is still my desire to threaten a passage into Maryland, to occupy the enemy on this frontier, and, if my purpose cannot be accomplished, to draw them into the Valley, where I can attack them to advantage."[74]

When McClellan failed to follow Lee into Virginia, Lincoln made a personal visit to McClellan at the Antietam battlefield with the specific purpose of prodding him into action. While there, Lincoln corrected

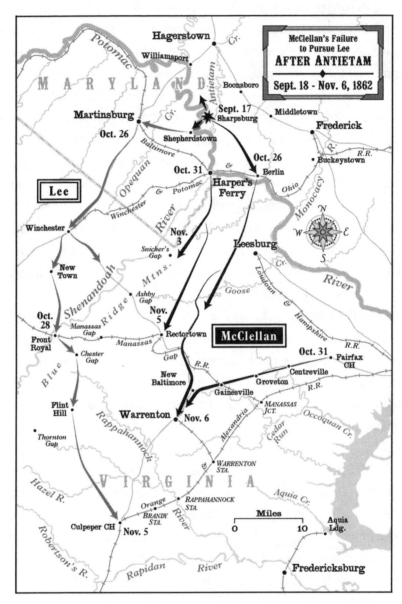

McClellan's Failure to Promptly Pursue Lee after Antietam
(September 18–November 6, 1862)
Map by David Deis, Dreamline Cartography, Northridge, CA

Illinois Senator Ozias M. Hatch when he identified the Union army there as the Army of the Potomac. Lincoln explained, "So it is called, but that is a mistake; it is only McClellan's body-guard."[75] Despite the president's visit and clear intent that McClellan pursue Lee, the Union Army commander continued for several weeks more to make excuses instead of war.

Lincoln's exasperation with McClellan was reflected in his response to one of the general's excuses for his inertia: "I have just read your dispatch about sore-tongued and fatigued horses. Will you pardon me for asking what the horses of your army have done since the battle of Antietam that fatigues anything?"[76] As October turned into November, McClellan finally crossed the Potomac in "pursuit" of Lee. Little Mac's army took nine days to cross the Potomac. A frustrated Lincoln finally removed McClellan from command just after the 1862 congressional elections. Burnside, who initially refused the army command, accepted it in order to keep the honor from going to Joe Hooker, whom he despised. Lee regretted the change and commented to Longstreet about McClellan: "We always understood each other so well. I fear they may continue to make these changes till they find someone I don't understand."[77] Lee understandably regretted McClellan's departure because the latter's reticence to fight against imaginary superior forces made life easier for Lee and morally weakened the Army of the Potomac.[78] That weakness continued until after Grant was brought to the East in 1864.[79]

As a result of Lee's strategy and tactics, the Confederates in the fall of 1862 suffered from a severe shortage of soldiers. In addition to the 47,000 casualties, Lee's army was missing 20,000 deserters and stragglers.[80] Only a few days after Antietam, therefore, the Confederate Congress raised the draft age to 45 and thus impacted small farm families across the South.[81]

Reacting to his extensive losses of experienced officers, Lee, on November 6, formally reorganized his army into two corps under two newly promoted lieutenant generals. Longstreet's 1st Corps consisted of 31,000 men in five divisions, and Jackson's 2nd Corps was made up of 34,000 men in four large divisions. On the basis of Lee's recommendations, Longstreet had been made the senior lieutenant general in the Confederacy on October 10, and Jackson had been the junior of six lieutenant generals named the following day.[82]

Lee meanwhile continued to demonstrate his Virginian myopia. That November he still had a reinforced army of 90,000 to face about 216,000 Union troops in the East, while the western Confederates had only 55,000 soldiers against Union forces of 180,000. Nevertheless, in December he suggested that Bragg's army might be moved from Tennessee to Virginia.[83] Lee's actions reflected his concern about a new Union offensive. Realizing that Lincoln wanted action, Burnside initiated a course of action that ultimately should have convinced Lee of the foolhardiness of frontal assaults against modern weaponry. Burnside decided to take the direct road to Richmond by bridging across the Rappahannock at Fredericksburg.

On November 17, Burnside's army began arriving at Falmouth, across the Rappahannock from Fredericksburg. Unfortunately for him, the bridging equipment arrived many days later. Although Burnside later blamed Washington authorities for this lapse, General Jacob Cox provided another view: "... I could easily see that if his supervision of business had been more rigidly systematic, he would have made sure that he was not to be disappointed in his means of crossing the Rappahannock promptly."[84] With a little initiative and creativity, Burnside could have at least ferried most of his men across before the arrival of Longstreet on November 20. This possibility was demonstrated three weeks later when Burnside rowed infantry across the river to gain a foothold. By crossing the river earlier and unopposed, the Union forces could have occupied Fredericksburg and the heights beyond and thereby avoided the disaster that was to follow.

Because Burnside stayed north of the river too long, Lee had sufficient time to move his army to Fredericksburg and the high ground overlooking the town and the river. The extent of Burnside's error in not promptly crossing the Rappahannock is demonstrated by the fact that Jackson's four divisions did not arrive at Fredericksburg from the Shenandoah Valley until December 3. Lee, who had belatedly realized and responded to the threat at Fredericksburg, then made his suggestion that the Army of Tennessee (again facing a threat to Chattanooga) be brought to Virginia.[85]

Burnside pressed his offensive even though he had badly lost the element of surprise. Realizing that Lincoln had fired McClellan for his timidity and wanted offensive progress, Burnside foolishly initiated and persisted in a suicidal frontal assault on an enemy occupying the high ground directly in his front. The persistence and bravery of the Union soldiers could not overcome the advantages held by the defenders.

On December 11, Burnside's engineers attempted to cross the Rappahannock, but Mississippi sharpshooters kept them from building their pontoon bridges even when the sharpshooters were fired on by Union artillery from the Falmouth hills to the north and east. That night, under cover of fog and darkness, the Yankees at long last crossed the river in boats and then drove the Confederates from the town itself. On December 12, Burnside's forces established footholds on the southwest bank of the river and prepared to launch their long-delayed assaults. Having delayed his boat crossing for three weeks, Burnside now faced Confederates entrenched along miles of hills overlooking Fredericksburg and the Rappahannock River valley.

Early on December 13, the Union left wing attacked Jackson's unentrenched troops and achieved initial success because of a flaw in A. P. Hill's alignment that left a gap in the Rebel line. The Union breakthrough, however, was thwarted, and the attackers were driven back by the second line of Rebel defenders. Hill's mistake, however, resulted in the Rebels having 3,000 killed and wounded while they killed and wounded 3,200 of their attackers on the eastern end of the armies' lines.[86]

Meanwhile a Union disaster was developing in the town. Burnside's plans for a flanking assault had gone awry because of his failure to clearly convey his intentions and his subordinate generals' halfhearted efforts. Against the advice of his commanders after the slaughter became obvious, Burnside ordered attack after attack up Marye's Heights. All told, from 11:00 a.m. to 5:00 p.m., there were fourteen suicidal charges up the hill. The result was the massacre of brigade after brigade as fourteen Confederate guns and six or seven thousand Confederate infantrymen, often four deep, fired from the heights and a sunken road behind a stone wall and eliminated anything that moved on the hillside.

From a nearby location, Rhode Island Lieutenant Elisha Hunt Rhodes "could see the long lines of Union troops move up the hill and melt away before the Rebel fire."[87] General Humphreys wrote to his wife,

> I led my division into a desperate fight and tried to take at
> the point of a bayonet a stone wall behind which a heavy line
> of the enemy lay. The heights just above were lined with artil-
> lery that poured upon us round shot, shell, and shrapnel; the
> musketry from the stone wall made a continuous sheet of
> flame. We charged within 50 yards of it each time but the men
> could not stand it.[88]

There were at least 7,700 Union soldiers killed or wounded on the slaughtering ground in front of Marye's Heights while their Rebel foes suffered only 1,750 similar casualties.[89]

That night and early the next morning Lee missed an opportunity to annihilate the Union troops massed below his army in Fredericksburg.

The Union soldiers were shocked and dispirited, and they were trapped against the river with limited means of retreat. Their artillery across the river could provide them no protection either at night, in the early morning mist, or during an attack at close quarters. Lee, however, rejected advice to assault his vulnerable foe in the town—apparently with the hope that the Union forces would resume their suicidal attacks the next day. Lee apparently was misled by a captured Burnside order for such an attack—an order that was cancelled.[90] Lee thus returned the favor McClellan had given him by not attacking when Lee kept his own vulnerable army at Sharpsburg an extra day.[91] Although Burnside may have been relatively stronger at Fredericksburg than Lee at Antietam after the primary day of fighting, Lee would have been attacking downhill against only a portion of a completely demoralized Union force that straddled the Rappahannock River and could not have utilized its artillery against a close-quarters attack.[92]

Lee almost got his wish for another Union attack. While the wounded, the dead, and a few unscathed survivors spent the night on Marye's Heights, Burnside gave the order for renewed attacks in the morning. This notion, however, so enraged his division commanders, who had witnessed the day's massacre, that they threatened to resign en masse. Burnside took the hint, called off the attack, and ordered a retreat back across the river before Lee could pounce upon the Union Army straddling the Rappahannock. The next month Burnside resigned from a job he never wanted when Lincoln refused to approve Burnside's plan to replace most of his subordinate generals.[93]

It is intriguing to analyze Lee's observation of the events that cold December day at Fredericksburg. Overlooking the decimation of the Union forces charging up Marye's Heights, Lee observed of the thousands of dead and wounded bodies, "It is well that war is so terrible; we should grow too fond of it."[94] Once again the attackers' casualties far exceeded those of the defenders; while the Union lost about 12,700 killed and wounded, the Confederates lost only about 4,200.[95]

As 1862 came to a close and the war entered its third year, Lee had reason for concern despite his recent Fredericksburg victory. In a January 1863 letter to Secretary of War James A. Seddon, Lee expressed his concern about his loss of manpower and the need for additional troops:

> While the spirit of our soldiers is unabated, their ranks have been greatly thinned by the casualties of battle and the diseases of the camp....
>
> More than once have most promising opportunities been lost for want of men to take advantage of them, and victory itself has been made to put on the appearance of defeat, because our diminished and exhausted troops have been unable to renew a successful struggle against fresh numbers of the enemy. The lives of our soldiers are too precious to be sacrificed in the attainment of successes that inflict no loss upon the enemy beyond the actual loss in battle. Every victory should bring us nearer to the great end which is the object of this war to reach.[96]

This letter reflects Lee's proclivity for offense rather than defense because the latter would involve only the mutual exchange of casualties. His concern about casualties and declining manpower was well-founded. In Lee's first seven months of command, his army had inflicted 50,000 casualties on the enemy, but it had done so at a cost it could not afford: about 45,000 casualties of its own. Given the Union's 4:1 manpower advantage, this was a pace that could not be sustained without fatally weakening the Army of Northern Virginia and eventually subjecting it to a war of attrition, regardless of its commander's strategy in subsequent years.

What had Lee learned from Seven Days', Second Manassas, Antietam, and Fredericksburg? Had he yet learned the folly of frontal assaults in this first of modern wars? Did he comprehend the newfound power of the defense that resulted from rifled guns and artillery, Minié balls, repeaters, and breechloaders? Did he recognize the similar results that occurred when his troops assaulted Malvern Hill, when Pope tried to drive Jackson out of the unfinished railroad cut at Manassas, when both armies charged the other again and again across the cornfield at Antietam, or when Burnside ordered fourteen assaults at Marye's Heights? Did Lee, with his steadily declining personnel, understand the strategies and tactics that were making this war "so terrible"? The year 1863 would tell.

GRANT RESUMES WINNING AND TAKES AIM AT VICKSBURG

While Lee was going on the offensive whenever he could, costing his army severe quantitative and qualitative losses, and being handed a great defensive victory at Fredericksburg, Grant had his hands full in the "West." After Halleck was promoted and assigned to Washington and while the Confederates launched offensives in the summer and fall of 1862, Grant, with a minimum number of troops, fought to hold on to the territory he had conquered. He not only did that, but he also won minor victories and began laying the groundwork for his brilliant Vicksburg Campaign of 1863.

A year of frustrations for Grant began on April 11, 1862, when Halleck arrived at Pittsburg Landing to take command of Grant's and Buell's armies. Pilloried by the press for "Bloody Shiloh" and mourning the recent death of his friend and mentor, General Charles Smith, Grant was disconsolate. Halleck added to his woes with an April 14 letter stating that Grant's "army is not now in condition to resist an attack" and directing him to achieve that condition, as well as a petty directive that same day relating to the content, routing, folding, and endorsement of official communications. Looking back on those mid-April days, Grant recalled: "Although next to [Halleck] in rank, and nominally in command of my old district and army, I was ignored as much as if I had been at the most distant point of territory within my jurisdiction...."[97]

Grant's morale soon hit a new wartime low. On April 30, Halleck relieved Grant of his army command, named him his (Halleck's) deputy, and replaced him with newly promoted Major General George II. Thomas as commander of the Army of the Tennessee. In Russell Weigley's words, "Halleck appears to have been jealous of [Grant] for his early successes ... and he did all that he could to deny Grant full credit for his achievements at Henry, Donelson, and Shiloh and kept him under a shadow as second in command in the West, practically a supernumerary, through the Corinth campaign."[98]

Having thrived as a commander of troops, Grant was extremely frustrated by what he regarded as a demotion to a meaningless and powerless position under Halleck. His frustration was aggravated by Halleck's overly cautious, excruciatingly slow "march" on Corinth, Mississippi, to which Beauregard's Confederates had retreated after Shiloh. Corinth, where the east-west Memphis & Charleston Railroad intersected with the north-south Mobile & Ohio Railroad, was so critical that it has been called "The Crossroads of the Western Confederacy."[99]

Beginning on April 30, it took four weeks for the 120,000 Union troops to advance twenty-two miles to Corinth as they entrenched daily and none of the three constituent armies (those of the Tennessee, the Ohio, and the Mississippi) was permitted to edge ahead of the others. On May 11, Grant wrote to Halleck requesting either a field command or relief from duty. Halleck denied the request. Grant told a fellow officer from Galena that he felt like "a fifth wheel to a coach."[100]

During May, the Federal armies, with deliberate and frustrating slowness, arrived near Corinth, partially invested the town, cut off the railroads north and east of town, and engaged in some minor fighting with Beauregard's troops. Meanwhile, Beauregard was facing greater challenges: bad water, typhoid fever, dysentery, and desertions. Army of Tennessee Private Sam R. Watkins reported, "We became starved skeletons; naked and ragged rebels. The chronic diarrhoea [*sic*] became the scourge of the army. Corinth became one vast hospital. Almost the whole army attended the sick call every morning. All the water courses went dry, and we used water out of filthy pools." Apparently in shock from Shiloh, neither Halleck nor Beauregard seemed anxious to engage in combat. Finally, Beauregard ended the standoff with a cleverly executed retreat from Corinth.[101]

The strategic ineffectiveness of Halleck's slow-motion movement against, and partial encirclement of, Corinth became obvious when the 50,000 Confederates escaped by abandoning the city on May 29 and 30. In executing their retreat, the Confederates made Halleck appear even more foolish by running their evacuation trains in a manner that caused Halleck to fear they were reinforcing, not evacuating, Corinth. They did this by cheering the arrival of empty evacuation trains as though they were bringing reinforcements. In fact, on the morning of May 30, Halleck had his entire army prepared for defensive battle and issued orders indicating that the Union left was likely to be attacked.

Instead, the Confederates' movement fifty miles south to Tupelo, Mississippi, left Corinth in Union hands and forced the Confederate military abandonment of the now uncovered city of Memphis. But their retreat also allowed Beauregard's soldiers to fight future battles. With a war-high 137,000 troops at Corinth, Halleck failed to pursue the 50,000 Confederates to Tupelo or to move on significant locations such as

Vicksburg, Chattanooga, or Atlanta. Instead, he had his troops dig even more extensive fortifications than the Rebels had abandoned.[102] Unlike Lincoln and Grant, Halleck did not realize that the Union had to destroy enemy armies in order to win the war.

Halleck's month-long "movement" to cover a distance Grant believed should have taken two days frustrated and disgusted Grant. These feelings were reinforced by the Rebels' successful evacuation from Corinth of all their healthy troops, their wounded, and their supplies—with only a few log "Quaker guns" left behind for Halleck's army. The 50,000 Rebel troops who escaped to Tupelo would be the nucleus of the Confederate invasion of eastern Tennessee and Kentucky in the fall of 1862. With 130,000 troops under his command, Halleck, not comprehending the need to break up Rebel armies, had let them escape to fight again another day. As a *Chicago Tribune* correspondent commented, "General Halleck has thus far achieved one of the most barren triumphs of the war. In fact, it was tantamount to a defeat." During the cautious siege, Halleck had sent orders directly to Grant's wing of the army without going through Grant. Believing that he was nothing more than an observer and embarrassed by his position, Grant made several applications to be relieved. Halleck abruptly rejected a suggestion from Grant about how to attack and trap the enemy.[103]

But Grant's concerns went deeper. He realized that the Army of the Tennessee believed the capture of Corinth was hollow: "They could not see how the mere occupation of places was to close the war while large and effective rebel armies existed. They believed that a well-directed attack would at least have partially destroyed the army defending Corinth." As he wrote in his memoirs, Grant also was disappointed in Halleck's tepid pursuit of the enemy after Corinth and his failure to pursue other opportunities with his large army:

After the capture of Corinth a movable force of 80,000 men, besides enough to hold all the territory acquired, could have been set in motion for the accomplishment of any great campaign for the suppression of the rebellion… If [Buell] had been sent directly to Chattanooga as rapidly as he could march,… he could have arrived with but little fighting, and would have saved much of the loss of life which was afterwards incurred in gaining Chattanooga. Bragg would then not have had time to raise an army to contest the possession of middle and east Tennessee and Kentucky; the battles of Stones River and Chickamauga would not necessarily have been fought; Burnside would not have been besieged in Knoxville without the power of helping himself or escaping; the battle of Chattanooga would not have been fought. These are the negative advantages, if the term negative is applicable, which would probably have resulted from prompt movements after Corinth fell into the possession of the National forces. The positive results might have been: a bloodless advance to Atlanta, to Vicksburg, or to any other desired point south of Corinth in the interior of Mississippi.[104]

Halleck's intervention after Shiloh stopped the momentum of Grant's offensive into the western Confederacy and threat to the Mississippi Valley. After Shiloh, said Weigley, "Halleck dispersed the western armies on garrison and railroad-building work… it was Halleck who sneered at Lincoln for wanting to violate the principle of concentration by maintaining pressure against the Confederacy everywhere."[105] A disgusted Grant took leave to visit his family and perhaps seek transfer to another theater. His friend Sherman told him to be patient and hope for reinstatement. That is exactly what happened when Halleck restored him to command of the Army of the Tennessee on June 10.

Grant established his headquarters—independent of Halleck—at Memphis on June 23. Even more significantly, Halleck headed for Washington and left the western theater for good after being appointed general-in-chief on July 11. Historian T. Harry Williams commented on Halleck's legacy to the western theater:

> Before he left he split the Western Department into two commands under Buell and Grant. Characteristically, he assigned to Buell, who had done practically no fighting, a fighting mission—the seizure of well-guarded Chattanooga. To Grant, who had done much hard and victorious fighting, he gave the relatively inactive mission of protecting communications along the Mississippi River.[106]

With Halleck gone, Grant commanded about 64,000 scattered troops of the Armies of the Tennessee (commanded by Grant) and the Mississippi (commanded by Rosecrans). They were tasked with defending a one hundred fifteen-mile front and over three hundred sixty miles of railroad track.[107] Then Grant's scattered force was weakened by the transfer of troops to another theater. Not only had Halleck stopped Grant's momentum, but his wait-and-see approach had left the North vulnerable to Confederate offensives. In the fall of 1862, Confederates took advantage. While Lee moved into Maryland on his Antietam Campaign, Bragg and [Edmund] Kirby Smith moved northward into central Tennessee and eastern Kentucky. As Buell moved north to intercept them in Kentucky, Grant was directed to send three of Rosecrans' divisions as reinforcements to Buell. Grant then faced the challenge of defending his assigned territory with reduced forces and simultaneously keeping the Rebels in the area from reinforcing Bragg and Smith in Kentucky.[108]

Taking advantage of this situation, Confederate Major Generals Sterling Price (Army of the West) and Earl Van Dorn (Army of Mississippi) posed a threat to Grant's remaining and scattered 50,000 troops. The Confederates were east and south of Grant, who was headquartered at Corinth. Price had conflicting orders from Bragg, who wanted him to threaten Nashville and thus protect Bragg's invasion flank, and from Van Dorn, who wanted him to join Van Dorn in a western Tennessee offensive. On September 14, the hesitant Price and his 12,000 to 14,000 Confederate troops occupied Iuka, about twenty miles east of Corinth on the Memphis & Charleston Railroad. Grant characteristically saw the situation as an opportunity and went on the offensive.[109]

Halleck had ordered Grant to keep Price from crossing the Tennessee River to join Bragg and Smith in Tennessee. Grant's plan was to trap Price in Iuka before Van Dorn could come to his aid from the south. From Corinth, Grant accompanied Major General Ord with 8,000 men along the Memphis & Charleston Railroad to attack from the west and directed William Rosecrans with 9,000 troops to attack from the southwest and southeast. Rosecrans, who had been slow in reaching Iuka, was under orders to block the southern roads out of Iuka. Ord was under orders to engage the enemy when he heard the guns from Rosecrans' direction. Rosecrans drove in the Confederate pickets southwest of Iuka starting at about 2:00 p.m. on September 19. After Rosecrans' initial success, Price's troops counterattacked and drove the Federals back. A fierce battle raged for several hours, and both sides incurred hundreds of casualties. Ord, however, did not simultaneously attack from the northwest because he never heard the sounds of fighting between Price and Rosecrans. The wind and weather conditions had created an "acoustic shadow" that prevented both Ord and Grant from hearing the sounds of battle.[110]

Price intended to resume his attack the next morning. However, the death of his best division commander and the advice of his other generals about the threat from Ord caused him to reconsider. Instead he decided to retreat and join up with Van Dorn. Fortunately for Price, Rosecrans had left open the road to the southeast—thereby allowing Price to escape Grant's planned pincers attack. Grant came up after the battle and had to direct Rosecrans to pursue the retreating enemy.[111]

Unlike Halleck, when Grant saw an opportunity to attack he did so—and did so promptly. Grant aggressively sought a fight at Iuka, and the battle was a strategic and tactical victory. Although Rosecrans' dilatoriness and the acoustic shadow had squandered an opportunity to even more seriously damage Price's force, Rosecrans' men suffered only eight hundred casualties while imposing about 1,600 on the enemy. Grant also had succeeded in defending his territory without any need to recall the three divisions that had been sent to Buell in Kentucky—and meanwhile preventing the Rebels he faced from heading north to oppose Buell.[112]

After Iuka, Grant moved his headquarters from Corinth, back to Jackson, Tennessee. Meanwhile, Van Dorn compelled a reluctant Price to join him in an attack on Rosecrans at Corinth. Under the command of Van Dorn, 22,000 Confederates with sixty-four guns moved fourteen miles northwest of Corinth and then turned to march east and south on the key rail hub. Realizing the threat, Grant ordered reinforcements to Corinth from Jackson and Bolivar. The 23,000 Union defenders also would be aided by an effective new series of fortifications—batteries and redoubts—that Rosecrans had recommended and Grant had approved. Those facilities constituted a final defensive line, the College Hill Line, which was inside the middle "Halleck Line" from earlier days and the outer line of fortifications constructed by the Confederates when they had been defending Corinth against Halleck after Shiloh.[113]

On October 3, Van Dorn pressed a three-division attack against Corinth. In ferocious fighting that lasted all day, the Confederates drove Rosecrans' defenders back almost two miles. That advance proved to be pyrrhic, however, as it enabled Rosecrans to effectively deploy his four divisions in shortened and extremely strong defensive positions for the next day's battle. With a terrible loss of life, Van Dorn's divisions attacked again the next day, overran Union batteries, entered the town itself, and then were driven out by a fierce counterattack. Van Dorn withdrew, and Price wept as he saw the scant remnants of his troops retreat. One of his divisions lost 2,500 of its 3,900 men at Corinth and then another six hundred to desertion during the retreat. The bloody, vicious Battle of Corinth was a decisive Union victory.[114]

Grant tried to follow up that victory by trapping and destroying Van Dorn's retreating army. He sent Major General Hurlbut with 8,000 men from Bolivar to the Davis Bridge on the Hatchie River to block the retreat. In addition, Grant ordered Rosecrans to pursue Van Dorn hastily because of danger to Hurlbut's force. Instead of immediately pursuing the enemy fleeing Corinth on the afternoon of battle, Rosecrans merely rode along his lines assuring his men that the report of his death was wrong. Even the arrival of McPherson with five regiments of reinforcements that Grant had sent from Jackson could not convince Rosecrans to initiate the chase until the next morning. Understandably, Grant was disappointed by Rosecrans' effort.[115] As Grant later recalled:

> General Rosecrans, however, failed to follow up the victory, although I had given specific orders in advance of the battle for him to pursue the moment the enemy was repelled. He did not do so, and I repeated the order after the battle. In the

first order he was notified that the force of 4,000 men which was going to his assistance would be in great peril if the enemy was not pursued.[116]

General Ord arrived to command Hurlbut's force and kept Van Dorn's forces from retreating across the Hatchie River at the bloody Battle of Davis' Bridge.[117] The Confederates might have been trapped in the Mississippi swamps if Rosecrans had followed his orders. Instead he delayed pursuit until the next day, took the wrong road, and allowed Van Dorn to escape the trap by another crossing of the Hatchie and to retreat to Holly Springs, Mississippi. In the river-crossing battles, Ord's men attacked a strong Rebel position and incurred about five hundred casualties.[118] Rosecrans' failure to immediately and aggressively pursue Van Dorn after the Battle of Corinth led to a permanent coolness between Grant and Rosecrans.[119]

Ironically, Rosecrans later decided he wanted to aggressively pursue and ignored Grant's new orders to halt the pursuit. Grant raised the issue to Halleck, who allowed Grant to decide. Grant, again ordering Rosecrans back, reasoned that "Had he gone much farther he would have met a greater force than Van Dorn had at Corinth and behind intrenchments or on chosen ground, and the probabilities are he would have lost his army." It appears that Grant and Rosecrans were seriously miscommunicating and that Grant may have erred in not allowing Rosecrans to continue after Van Dorn—an atypical lack of aggressiveness on Grant's part. By this time, Grant apparently had lost confidence in Rosecrans and doubted that he could effectively pursue and engage Van Dorn.[120]

At Corinth, Grant (as Rosecrans' commander) once again had achieved a significant victory while incurring few casualties. His troops had 355 killed, 1,841 wounded and 324 missing, and the Confederates suffered 505 killed, 2,150 wounded, and 2,183 missing or captured.[121] The defeat cost Van Dorn his command, and he was replaced by Lieutenant General John C. Pemberton as Commander of the Department of Mississippi and East Louisiana. The twin victories at Iuka and Corinth fulfilled Grant's dual mission of protecting his previous gains in the Mississippi Valley and preventing Rebel reinforcements from moving to Kentucky.

Disappointed with Rosecrans' failure at Iuka and his off-and-on pursuit at odds with Grant's orders after Corinth, Grant was ready to remove him from command. On October 23, 1862, however, Rosecrans was transferred eastward to relieve Buell as commander of the Army of the Ohio, which then became the Army of the Cumberland. On October 25, Grant was given command of the newly formed Department of Tennessee (Tennessee and Kentucky west of the Tennessee River and northern Mississippi) with headquarters at Jackson, Tennessee.[122]

Grant's numerous victories and the September 22 announcement of President Lincoln's preliminary Emancipation Proclamation induced many African-American slaves to flee and seek refuge behind Union lines. In December 1862, Grant reported that 20,000 Black refugees were being housed, fed, and protected in his Department. Men among the former slaves, joined by free Blacks, began to play significant support, and then active military, roles in Grant's Department.[123]

FIRST ATTEMPTS TO CAPTURE VICKSBURG

That November, bolstered by reinforcements, Grant began an undertaking that would consume him and require his dominating trait—perseverance—more than ever before. He began organizing his first attempt to capture Vicksburg, the citadel city that, along with Port Hudson, Louisiana, to its south, blocked Union control of the Mississippi River.

Vicksburg occupied the first high ground adjacent to the river south of Memphis and was a railroad junction that allowed food, fodder, and imports to move from Mexico and the Trans-Mississippi to the eastern portions of the Confederacy.[124] Grant's next six months would be filled with frustration upon frustration as he struggled to find a way to seize Vicksburg.

Weigley put Grant's long-term focus on Vicksburg and the Mississippi in perspective:

> [Grant's] Vicksburg campaign, which extended from the autumn of 1862 into the summer of 1863, was a model of persistent long-range planning. He did not draw inflexible plans, because war is too unpredictable for that, and his progress toward Vicksburg did suffer many reverses. But while always retaining a variety of options in preparation for the unexpected, nevertheless Grant kept pursuing consistently a well-defined strategic goal, the opening of the Mississippi; and viewing battles as means rather than as ends, he refused to be diverted from his goal by the temporary fortunes of any given battle.[125]

Grant's first thrust toward Vicksburg was a two-pronged assault from the north. He led troops overland along the Mississippi Central Railroad from Grand Junction, Tennessee, while Sherman took others down the Mississippi for an amphibious attack. Wasting no time after assuming his departmental command, Grant began the Vicksburg campaign on November 2, when he wired Halleck from Jackson, Tennessee, "I have commenced a movement on Grand Junction with three 3 [sic] divisions from Corinth and two from Bolivar. Will leave here tomorrow evening and take command in person. If found practicable I will go on to Holly

Springs and may be [*sic*] Grenada completing Railroad & Telegraph as I go."[126]

Back in Washington, meanwhile, McClernand was lobbying Lincoln and Stanton for an independent command on the Mississippi that would overlap with Grant's area of responsibility. From newspaper stories, Grant learned of McClernand's efforts. Realizing the chaotic effects such an arrangement would create, Grant was relieved to receive, on November 12, a dispatch from Halleck giving him command over all troops in his department and the freedom to fight them where he chose. A few weeks earlier, on October 21, Stanton had given McClernand a confidential order authorizing him to raise troops in the Midwest for a campaign against Vicksburg that McClernand would command. Only later, to his chagrin, did McClernand realize that the fine print in that order made his actions subject to approval by both Grant and General-in-Chief Halleck.[127]

After Grant's cavalry occupied Holly Springs, Mississippi, on the Mississippi Central, Grant chose that location for a supply depot, from which he planned to move across the Tallahatchie River toward Vicksburg. To do so, Grant ordered Sherman to bring most of his troops southeast from Memphis so that he had a sufficient force to challenge Pemberton, who was fortified on the south side of the Tallahatchie. Grant's cavalry crossed upstream to the east of Pemberton, who then retreated south beyond Oxford. Delaying at Oxford to repair the railroad, Grant learned that Halleck had approved a waterborne movement from Memphis to Vicksburg.[128]

Wanting to ensure that this expedition was not led by the conniving McClernand and having been authorized by Halleck to go himself or send Sherman, Grant gave the command to Sherman. Sherman would proceed south on the Mississippi while Grant continued his inland trek in the same direction—separated from Sherman by massive bayous.

Thus, on December 8, from Oxford, Mississippi, Grant issued orders directing his right-wing commander to move south from Memphis and attack Vicksburg.[129]

Grant's plan was to maintain contact with Pemberton's main body of troops—either keeping them away from Vicksburg or following them to Vicksburg if they retreated to that city. In his memoirs, Grant reflected back to that time:

> It was my intention, and so understood by Sherman and his command, that if the enemy should fall back I would follow him even to the gates of Vicksburg. I intended in such an event to hold the [rail]road to Grenada on the Yallabusha [River] and cut loose from there, expecting to establish a new base of supplies on the Yazoo, or at Vicksburg itself, with Grenada to fall back upon in case of failure. It should be remembered that at the time I speak of it had not been demonstrated that an army could operate in an enemy's territory depending upon the country for supplies.[130]

On December 18, Grant received orders to divide his command into four corps and assign one of them to McClernand as part of the Mississippi River assault force. Grant obeyed those orders and sent dispatches to McClernand, who was back in Springfield, Illinois. No doubt anxious to depart for Vicksburg before the arrival of McClernand, who was senior to him, Sherman left Memphis on December 19 with 20,000 men. Later he picked up 12,000 reinforcements at Helena, Arkansas.[131]

Disaster, however, struck Grant's wing one day after Sherman left Memphis. Confederate cavalry under Van Dorn destroyed Grant's supply depot back at Holly Springs. The 1,500-man garrison there had been forewarned, but it fought incompetently and surrendered. The Rebel cavalry destroyed massive supplies of munitions, food, and forage. Grant was further isolated by a concurrent, more northern, cavalry raid, led by Forrest, on Grant's rail connection between Columbus, Kentucky, and Jackson, Tennessee. Therefore, Grant had to retrace his steps northward along the railroad but was unable to contact Sherman about the collapse of the eastern prong of the campaign.[132] Grant found a silver lining behind this cloud of disaster. From Oxford back to Grand Junction, Grant had his troops bring in supplies of food and forage for fifteen miles on each side of the railroad and was surprised at the successful results:

> I was amazed at the quantity of supplies the country afforded. It showed that we could have subsisted off the country for two months instead of two weeks without going beyond the limits designated. This taught me a lesson which was taken advantage of later in the campaign when our army lived twenty days with the issue of only five days' rations by the commissary. Our loss of supplies was great at Holly Springs, but it was more than compensated for by those taken from the country and by the lesson taught.[133]

On the downside for his campaign, however, Grant's retreat north left Pemberton free to return to Vicksburg. Thus, Pemberton was there when Sherman arrived. During the last week of the year, Sherman carried out an assault on Confederate forces between the Yazoo River and Vicksburg. The Confederates held the high ground on bluffs, and high water flooded the bottom lands and forced the attackers into narrow corridors that were well-defended. Perhaps hoping that Grant was about to come to his aid, Sherman continued attacking until his heavy casualties revealed the hopelessness of the situation. In this Battle of Chickasaw Bluffs,

Sherman incurred 1,780 casualties while the well-entrenched Confederates lost a mere 190. He then retreated back up the Mississippi. Grant's
first grasp at Vicksburg had failed ignominiously.[134]

Grant returned to Holly Springs by December 23, and, after railroad
repairs had been made, moved his command to Memphis on January
10. From then on, he would stay on or near the Mississippi until he succeeded in capturing Vicksburg. Meanwhile McClernand had gone downriver, assumed command of Sherman's and his own troops, and led a
successful expedition up the Arkansas River to capture Fort Hindman
at Arkansas Post, along with about 5,000 prisoners. When Grant complained to Halleck that McClernand was on "a wild goose chase," Halleck
authorized Grant to remove McClernand from command; Grant wrote
an order doing so but inexplicably did not send it. McClernand would
remain a thorn in his side for several more months.[135]

After McClernand returned to the mouth of the Arkansas River, both
Sherman and Admiral David Dixon Porter sent messages to Grant urging him to join them and take personal command because of their
doubts about McClernand's competence. On January 17, Grant jour-
neyed downriver, met with McClernand and others, and realized he
would have to assume personal command. Grant could not put Sherman
in command of the expedition because he was junior to McClernand,
and Grant chose not to exercise the authority recently given to him by
Halleck to relieve McClernand. Even when McClernand responded
disrespectfully upon Grant's assuming personal command on January
29 at Young's Point near Vicksburg, Grant chose not to relieve him
because of his political value as a strong, pro-Union Democrat from
President Lincoln's home state.[136]

Although the safe thing to do would have been to return to Memphis
and Holly Springs and launch another overland campaign against

Vicksburg, Grant was concerned that doing so would be demoralizing for the North:

> It was my judgment at the time that to make a backward movement as long as that from Vicksburg to Memphis, would be interpreted, by many of those yet full of hope for the preservation of the Union, as a defeat, and that the draft would be resisted, desertions ensue and the power to capture and punish deserters lost. There was nothing left to be done but to *go forward to a decisive victory.* This was in my mind from the moment I took command in person at Young's Point.[137]

Rather than be seen as retreating northward, Grant initiated a series of experiments intended to secure a base on the east bank of the Mississippi for an attack on Vicksburg. Geography made the chore difficult. The city was protected on the north by the Yazoo River and associated swamps, as well as heavily-fortified Haines' Bluff. Its western edge consisted of high bluffs overlooking the Mississippi. Grant saw the experiments as diverting the attention of his troops, the enemy, and the public; he had doubts about their success but was prepared to take advantage if any succeeded.[138]

The first of these experiments was the digging of a canal that was intended to divert the river in a straight north-south path across a peninsula and away from the bend below Vicksburg. Four thousand soldiers struggled to dig this canal between late January and March 8, when the river broke through a dam that had been built on the north end of the canal to protect the excavation. Even had the canal been completed, its effectiveness would have been reduced by the fact that it was within range of Confederate guns about a mile away.[139] Slightly farther to the west, Grant ordered General McPherson and his troops to flood Lake Providence and attempt to clear a waterway through bayous and rivers all the way back to the Mississippi south of Port Hudson. This project began January 30 and was discontinued at the same time as the failed canal project.[140]

Those two projects west of the Mississippi were matched in futility by two others on the east side of the river. First, Grant sought backdoor access to the Yazoo River by destroying a levee across from Helena, Arkansas, far north of Vicksburg. The plan was to restore a previously navigable waterway through the bayous to the Yazoo River. A Union expedition of 4,500 troops on transports made it all the way to Confederate Fort Pemberton at the juncture where the Tallahatchie and Yallabusha rivers formed the Yazoo. They, however, were repelled by Confederate fire from the fort. After destroying another levee on the Mississippi in an unsuccessful effort to flood Fort Pemberton, the Union fleet retreated.[141]

Grant's second effort on the east side of the Mississippi consisted of an Admiral Porter-led fleet of five gunboats, four mortar-boats, and troop-carrying river steamers trying to wend their way through another series of waterways to the Yazoo River about ten air miles above Haines' Bluff. Grant himself accompanied the fleet at the start of the mission but went back to hurry up reinforcements under Sherman. The smaller gunboats got too far ahead of the steamers, which were impeded by the heavy, overhanging swamp trees and the sharp turns in the bayous. Just as the lead vessels were about to break into open water, they ran into more obstructions and a 4,000-man contingent of Confederates. The gunboats were no match for the Rebel sharpshooters. Sherman's infantry left their hung-up ships and marched along the riverbanks to rescue the gunboats and their crews, and the Union vessels were lucky to be able to back out of the hazardous waterways. As Edwin Bearss concluded, "thus ended in failure the fourth attempt to get in rear of Vicksburg."[142]

In fact, Grant made one final effort—back on the west bank—to use waterways to bypass Vicksburg. He had his men dredging and widening natural bayou channels from Milliken's Bend, northwest of Vicksburg, through Richmond, Louisiana, and back to the Mississippi at Carthage, twenty-five or more miles above Grand Gulf, Mississippi, and a few miles below Vicksburg. He halted the work when it became clear that a useable channel could not be developed. Deteriorating levees and abnormally high water in the river caused excessive water everywhere and made dry land a rarity. As a result, Union soldiers were afflicted with malaria—in addition to the usual measles and chickenpox.[143]

Reports of these conditions—and the several failed projects—caused grumbling back home and new calls for Grant's replacement. Many Northern newspapers called for Grant's removal and suggested that he be replaced with McClernand, Frémont, McClellan, or Major General David Hunter. The *New York Times* reported on March 12 that "There is no symptom of any plan of attack on Vicksburgh [*sic*]." and later that month that "Nothing visible... has been done lately toward the reduction of Vicksburgh [*sic*]."[144] On March 15, McClernand launched a personal campaign against Grant by writing to Lincoln. McClernand told the president that Grant had been "gloriously drunk" on March 13 and sick in bed all the next day. If the president had decided to remove Grant, McClernand, the next senior officer, would have succeeded him.[145] Lincoln had other ideas.

Others were critical too. Congressman Washburne's brother, Cadwallader C. Washburn,[146] a brigadier general in McPherson's corps, wrote that "All Grant's schemes [against Vicksburg] have failed. He is frittering away time and strength to no purpose. The truth must be told even if it hurts. You cannot make a silk purse out of a sow's ear." A Cincinnati newspaper editor wrote to Secretary of the Treasury Salmon P. Chase that Grant was "a jackass in the original package. He is a poor drunken imbecile. He is a poor stick sober, and he is most of the time more than half drunk, and much of the time idiotically drunk." But Lincoln had the final word: "What I want, and what the people want, is generals who will fight battles and win victories. Grant has done this and I propose to stand by him."[147]

Regardless of what his critics had to say, Grant had a purpose in having his men undertake these operations—in addition to the possibility they just might succeed. As General Fuller explained, "All were extremely difficult, entailed immense labor on the part of the army and the fleet; and though all failed in their object, they undoubtedly formed admirable training for Grant's army, hardening and disciplining the men, in fact turning them into salted soldiers."[148]

By early 1863, Grant had endured a year of frustration, which had begun with Halleck's assumption of command and demonstration of what not to do with a 120,000-man army. Halleck's breakup of the huge Union force preceded his promotion to Washington and left Grant with decreasing numbers of troops to hold the gains he previously had made. Grant's victories at Iuka and Corinth were undercut by the less-than-stellar performances there by Rosecrans. Then Grant launched his first campaign against Vicksburg—only to be thwarted by aggressive Confederate cavalry and a faint-hearted Union commander at Holly Springs. That episode led to Sherman unsuccessfully attacking near Vicksburg without the expected support from Grant's stymied overland march. Grant next endured a series of frustratingly unsuccessful efforts to get at the Confederates in Vicksburg.

Grant kept his troops active, kept pressure on his adversaries, and did so with minimal casualties as he preserved his resources for opportunities for significant victory. With each disheartening experience, however, Grant demonstrated his characteristic tenacity and even seemed to draw lessons from each setback. His persistence and experience would soon reap huge dividends.

On the other hand, Lee's army had incurred numerous casualties in a series of unnecessarily offensive battles since June 1, 1862—casualties that severely worsened the Confederacy's long-term prospects. At the close of 1862, Lee had been handed a substantial victory by Burnside's suicidal assaults at Fredericksburg, but Lee had not learned the lessons of Fredericksburg and was to repeat them at Chancellorsville and Gettysburg in 1863.

CHAPTER SIX

MAY–JULY 1863:
LEE LOSES GETTYSBURG
AS GRANT CAPTURES
VICKSBURG

*As Grant rampages toward Vicksburg, Lee prevents
reinforcements against him, marches into Pennsylvania, and
incurs disastrous defeat, all the while allowing Grant to capture
Vicksburg and a 28,000-man Rebel army*

OVERVIEW

In early 1863, Lee's aggressive strategy and tactics in the Virginia theater significantly affected Grant's prospects for success in the Mississippi Valley. Emboldened by his apparent victories in mid- to late 1862, Lee resisted suggestions in April that he transfer troops elsewhere and went on the offensive tactically in early May at Chancellorsville. That battle became a costly strategic victory.

Within two weeks after Chancellorsville, Lee pushed Jefferson Davis into making a crucial mistake that cost the Confederacy major defeats in the three primary theaters of the war. Lee strongly opposed the transfer of Longstreet and any of his 1st Corps outside the Virginia theater, and he convinced Davis and most of his cabinet to leave Longstreet with Lee for an offensive into the North, which became the disastrous Gettysburg Campaign.

The alternative uses for Longstreet's troops would have been (1) to reinforce, directly or indirectly, the Rebels in Mississippi who were opposing Grant's campaign against Vicksburg, or (2) to reinforce the outmanned Confederate forces under Bragg in east central Tennessee and thereby prevent them from being driven out of Tennessee by the numerically superior Union Army of the Cumberland commanded by Rosecrans. Because Lee kept Longstreet from going west, he coupled his Gettysburg disaster with twin defeats in other theaters. He helped ensure that Grant would not face insuperable opposition in Mississippi—and Vicksburg and the Mississippi Valley fell to the Union. And he kept Bragg so shorthanded that his army indeed was maneuvered back into Georgia from Tennessee in the virtually bloodless Tullahoma Campaign.

Therefore, Lee was responsible for a demoralizing Confederate triple disaster in the summer of 1863—Gettysburg, Vicksburg, and Tullahoma. Confederate morale and prospects fell to new lows and never recovered.

DEBATING THE USE OF LONGSTREET'S CORPS

After the Fredericksburg fiasco, Lincoln, on January 25, 1863, named "Fighting Joe"[1] Hooker to replace Burnside as Commander of the Army of the Potomac. Hooker got off to a great start. He restored the Union troops' morale by straightening out the supply mess, getting them up to six months' back pay, and ensuring that they were provided with abundant food, clothing, and other necessities.

Hooker then went about planning the next Union offensive. By this time, Lincoln had decided that the best strategy in the East was to go after Lee's army, not Richmond. Lee's continued aggressiveness in 1863 played into Union hands. For his spring offensive, Hooker would have seven infantry corps of over 15,000 each and about 10,000 cavalry for a total force of about 130,000. His opponent, weakened by the interminable battles of 1862, would have a mere six infantry divisions totaling about 50,000 and about 6,000 cavalry.[2] In addition, Lee was hampered by the absence of Longstreet's corps, which was in southeastern Virginia and northeastern North Carolina originally defending against the threat posed to Richmond and Petersburg by Burnside's 9th Corps and later foraging for food and fodder for Lee's troops and animals.

At this critical juncture in April 1863, Lee demonstrated his one-theater mindset and stoutly resisted the use of any of his army to help in the West. The Union in March moved Burnside's 9th Corps to the middle theater from the vicinity of Longstreet in southeastern Virginia,[3] and Lee was content to leave Longstreet far away from Lee's Fredericksburg position. Lee received a report of Burnside's movement on March 28 and was convinced of the report's validity by April 1.[4] Nevertheless, Lee resisted requests and suggestions by western Confederates, President Davis, Secretary Seddon, and Longstreet that Longstreet's corps should be sent to the West to counter the increased Union strength there.[5]

In early April, Confederate western generals John C. Pemberton and the recovered Joseph E. Johnston mistakenly advised Richmond that Grant apparently was moving troops from Mississippi to Tennessee to join Burnside and Rosecrans. They responded by sending 8,000 troops from Alabama and Mississippi to Bragg in Tennessee and requesting reinforcements from Lee.

On April 6, ironically the same day that Lee himself observed that the Union apparently "had a general plan to deceive us while reinforcing the western armies,"[6] Secretary Seddon requested him to acquiesce in the transfer westward of two or three of Longstreet's brigades.[7] Lee strongly opposed the request and argued, contrary to his usual advocacy of concentration of forces,[8] that separate Confederate forces should launch separate offensives from Mississippi to Maryland—reminiscent of the failed offensives of the prior autumn.[9] He minimized the threat to Vicksburg by stating it only needed enough troops to man the batteries because, "If the statements which I see in the papers are true, Genl Grant is withdrawing from Vicksburg, and will hardly return to his former position there this summer."[10] Lee wanted to move north and did not want to give up any of his troops; weeks before he had ordered the preparation of maps from the Shenandoah through Harrisburg to Philadelphia.[11]

When Seddon came back with a renewed and expanded request for some of Longstreet's forces, Lee created a new set of objections. Lee claimed that the forage Longstreet was gathering was critical to an imminent move north by Lee to test Hooker's strength, to ascertain the distribution of Union troops between the East and West, and to attempt to drive Hooker north of the Potomac. He suggested that Tennessee be strengthened by moving troops from Charleston, Savannah, Mobile, and Vicksburg—anywhere but from Virginia.[12] Learning that Grant actually had not moved forces to Tennessee and yielding to Lee, Davis and Seddon sent reinforcements to Bragg in Tennessee only from Beauregard in the southeast.

As soon as he was assured that he was not going to lose any troops, Lee's plans for an early northern offensive disappeared and he left Longstreet where he was. Lee remained concerned about his supplies, but he remained optimistic that the Northern will to win could be destroyed:

> I do not think our enemies are so confident of success as they
> used to be. If we can baffle them in their various designs this
> year & our people are true to our cause & not so devoted to

themselves & their own aggrandisement, I think our success
will be certain. We will have to suffer & must suffer to the end.
But it will all come right. This year I hope will establish our
supplies on a firm basis. On every other point we are strong.
If successful this year, next fall [1864] there will be a great
change in public opinion at the North. The Republicans will
be destroyed & I think the friends of peace will become so
strong as that the next administration will go in on that basis.
We have only therefore to resist manfully.[13]

But resisting manfully was not what Lee had in mind. Not only did Lee
want to go on the offensive in the East, but his refusal to part with any
of his men left the "western" Confederates shorthanded in two geographic areas. Johnston (the western theater commander) and Pemberton would be unable to deal with the imminent movement by Grant on
Vicksburg, and the fall of that Mississippi River citadel within three
months would be an ill omen for Lee's hopes about the 1864 presidential
election. Just as ominously, Bragg's army in Tennessee also went unre-
inforced against a stronger opponent; it ran out of meat and was short
on rations as it occupied an area from which most crops and livestock
were being shipped to Lee.[14]

Back on the eastern front, beginning on April 26, Hooker made a
major feint by crossing the Rappahannock with two corps below Fredericksburg. But he made his major effort surreptitiously west of the
town. On April 29, three entire corps crossed the Rappahannock far
upstream at Kelly's Ford and then pushed southward toward the fords
of the Rapidan River. That same evening they reached the Rapidan,
secured Ely's Ford and crossed Germanna Ford to the west. By April 30,
the brilliant and undetected move was completed with the securing of
the U.S. Ford across the Rappahannock downstream of its merger with

the Rapidan, the crossing of that ford by two more corps, and the resultant reuniting of the bulk of Hooker's army at the key Chancellorsville crossroads on the left flank of Lee.[15] Hooker had stolen a march on Lee.

Hooker issued a blustering general order bragging that "the operations of the last three days have determined that our enemy must either ingloriously fly or come out from behind his defenses and give us battle on our own ground, where certain destruction awaits him."[16] Even Union Major General George Meade, no friend of Hooker, exclaimed that day, "Hurrah for old Joe! We're on Lee's flank and he doesn't know it."[17] Hooker was now in a position to march south out of the Wilderness and interpose the bulk of his army between Lee and Richmond—unless Lee hastily retreated south, which is what Hooker expected. At worst, Hooker presumed, Lee would attack the Union forces in a way that Hooker could fight with superior numbers from a strong defensive position.

In deploying his forces, Hooker had made one major error; he had sent his cavalry, under Major General George Stoneman, on a raid far to the south. Hooker intended that Stoneman would cut Lee's supply line and prevent him from retreating to Richmond. These intentions were not realized because of bad weather, Stoneman's incompetence, and Hooker's confusing orders. Not only was Stoneman's cavalry held in check by part of Jeb Stuart's Rebel cavalry, this cavalry deployment left Hooker blind. Without the eyes of his cavalry, Hooker had no idea of the whereabouts of his opponent. As long as Jackson was alive, that was a fatal mistake.

Having been caught napping by Hooker's fleet's flanking thrust, an unhealthy Lee[18] responded quickly and effectively. On April 30 and May 1, Lee left Jubal Early with a small force to defend Fredericksburg and moved the divisions of Richard Anderson, McLaws, and Jackson westward to stop the Yankees from escaping the Wilderness. Despite

Hooker's overwhelming superiority of forces, especially at the beginning of the battle, he lost his self-confidence and retreated back into the Wilderness on May 1 at the first sign of opposition.[19]

Aggressive, Jackson-led Confederate attacks drove the Union forces back along two roads and an unfinished railroad running west from Fredericksburg to the Wilderness. Instead of capitalizing on his advantageous position threatening the rear of Fredericksburg and the road to Richmond, Hooker failed to move east and south and instead simply consolidated the bulk of his huge army in the Wilderness.

Unlike Hooker, Lee had retained some cavalry, under Jeb Stuart, in the vicinity. This action quickly bore fruit. On the afternoon and evening of May 1, Stuart and Brigadier General Fitzhugh Lee (Robert E. Lee's nephew) discovered that Hooker had left his right flank, west of Chancellorsville, hanging in the air (that is, neither protected by a river, ridge or other natural feature nor bent back, entrenched, and supported). That exposed flank proved irresistible to Lee and Jackson. Jackson proposed and Lee agreed that a surprise flanking march to the west and north should be made by Jackson to attack that inviting Union right flank the next day. Stonewall proposed that he be given two-thirds of the 45,000 men Lee had brought out of Fredericksburg, and Lee consented.[20] With a mere 15,000 facing the bulk of Hooker's army, Lee distracted Union attention away from Jackson's march and camouflaged his own weakness by brazenly initiating minor assaults along the lines throughout the day.

This daring gamble, which avoided a frontal attack on the numerically superior Army of the Potomac, proved successful. The now insecure Hooker ignored repeated reports that Rebel forces were marching around his army toward that hanging right flank he also had ignored. Shortly before dark, Jackson ascertained that Brigadier General Robert E. Rodes was "ready" and gave him the bland order, "You can go forward then." Major portions of Jackson's 30,000-man corps came crashing

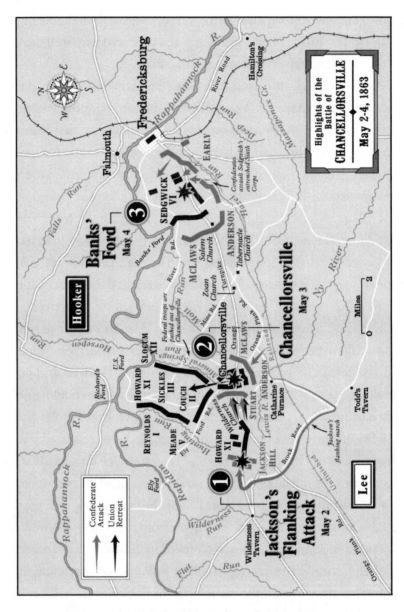

Highlights of the Battle of Chancellorsville (May 2–4, 1863)
Map by David Deis, Dreamline Cartography, Northridge, CA

down the Orange Turnpike, caused panicked wildlife to flee toward the Union lines, caught unwary Union troops cooking their evening meals, and decimated the right wing of the Union Army.

There were several flaws in Jackson's march and attack, however, that rendered it less effective than it otherwise might have been. The 7:30 a.m. starting hour for the march was about three hours later than usual for Jackson. Also, the generally westward march was not conducted quickly enough to ensure its full success. Because of narrow roads and paths, it took twelve hours for the ten-mile march and setup of the attack. Early reports that the exposed flank was on the Orange Plank Road proved false, and additional time and daylight were consumed marching farther north to the Turnpike before turning east to prepare for the attack. The cumulative delays resulted in the attack starting between 5:15 and 6:00 p.m.—so close to sunset that it could not be fully developed and the initial Union surprise and panic could not be totally exploited. Furthermore, federal reserves quickly began building fortifications of logs and abatis (an obstacle of cut trees with sharp points aimed at attackers) that provided protection and enabled them to stop the onslaught.[21]

The attack itself was hampered by the fact that many of Jackson's men did not get involved. Brigadier General Alfred H. Colquitt, an incompetent Georgia political general, severely reduced the impact of the lead division's five-brigade attack by stopping his own brigade, on Jackson's right flank, and blocking Brigadier General Stephen D. Ramseur's North Carolina Brigade behind him. Colquitt thus took at least 20 percent of the leading edge of the attacking force out of the attack by ignoring Jackson's orders to stop for nothing and instead heeding a false warning from a staff member that Union troops were on their right flank.

The rout on the Union right nevertheless was a major success, and Major General Oliver O. Howard's 11th Corps fled eastward for more than two miles into a gap left by Major General Daniel E. Sickles' 3rd Corps, most of which had moved south without authority to attack Jackson's rear guard in the area of Catherine Furnace.[22] But there would be hell to pay by the Confederates for the time-consuming manner in which the surprise attack had been arranged and then unfolded.

Darkness, confusion, and heroic stands by some Union forces brought the advance to a halt. In particular, Rodes' frontline division was devastated and stopped by artillery fire. The following division, that of the inexperienced Brigadier General Raleigh E. Colston, became badly intermingled with Rodes' division beginning shortly after the assault started. Colston himself described the chaotic situation: "Brigades, regiments, and companies had become so mixed that they could not be handled, besides which the darkness of evening was so intensified by the shade of the dense woods that nothing could be seen a few yards off. The halt at that time was not a mistake but a necessity." General Rodes later explained that the charge was halted at about 7:15 p.m. because of confusion and darkness.[23] Next, the accidental shooting of Jackson by his own men as he sought a route to the Union rear in the moonlit darkness took the heart out of the Confederate momentum. His successor, A. P. Hill, also was injured that evening, and cavalryman Jeb Stuart assumed command of Jackson's corps early the next morning.

Jackson and his moonlit party had been decimated by fire from the 18th North Carolina when they tried to return to the Rebel lines and were mistaken for Union cavalry. Jackson's left arm was shattered by two bullets, and his right palm was struck by a smoothbore musket bullet. He endured a painful litter ride to a field hospital, where his medical director amputated his left arm just below the shoulder. When informed of Jackson's condition, Lee said, " ... any victory is dearly bought which deprives us of the services of General Jackson, even for a short time." Lee later added, "He has lost his left arm, but I have lost my right."[24] Eight days later Jackson died of pneumonia at nearby Guinea Station, and Lee had lost the only corps commander who was compatible with his hands-off style of command.

Jackson's assault also took a heavy toll on his attacking troops. Although they routed the shocked infantry at the point of assault, the Rebels met more and more resistance as they advanced down the Turnpike past its intersection with the Orange Plank Road. Particularly devastating to them was the Union artillery (twenty or more guns at Hazel Grove and thirty-four more at Fairview Plateau) that blunted their progress. A federal artillery officer described the scene:

> It was dusk when [Jackson's] men swarmed out of the woods for a quarter of a mile in our front… They came on in line, five and six deep…. I gave the command to fire, and the whole line of artillery was discharged at once. It fairly swept them from the earth; before they could recover themselves the line of artillery had been loaded and was ready for the second attack… [against which] I poured in the canister for about twenty minutes, and the affair was over.[25]

Another problem resulting from Jackson's flanking march was that Lee's forces were separated and vulnerable to a counterattack—especially the two smaller contingents with Lee south and east of Chancellorsville and with Early back at Fredericksburg. Although the inept Hooker failed to take advantage of this situation, Stuart and Lee were left with no choice but desperately to launch offensives the next morning from the west and south respectively toward Chancellorsville so that they could join their forces.

Hooker made their task easier that night by ordering the evacuation of Hazel Grove, the commanding prominence in the middle of the Wilderness that was an ideal artillery position and the key to the battlefield. On the advice of then Colonel Porter Alexander, Stuart gave the orders that resulted in the dawn capture of Hazel Grove from its Union remnants. Alexander posted fifty guns on Hazel Grove and devastated Union forces to the north and east. Because of Hooker's failure to use more than half of his forces in the fighting (possibly due in part to his being knocked unconscious by a shell fragment from one of Alexander's guns), the Confederates' attack and effort to merge their divided forces were successful—although costly in terms of dead and wounded. That very day Jedediah Hotchkiss described the fighting from the Rebel perspective: "We united the two wings of our army and drove the enemy, by a vigorous and bloody onset, out of his strong works at Chancellorsville and took possession of that place, the loss being very heavy on both sides."[26] The merger of Confederate troops was followed by a wild celebration as General Lee rode in on Traveller and accepted the accolades of his gritty fighters. That emotional scene may have been the apex of the Confederacy.

The celebration did not last long, however. No sooner had Lee and Stuart joined their forces when serious problems developed with Early's small isolated force at Fredericksburg. Lee received word that John Sedgwick's 6th Corps had broken through Early's defenses at Fredericksburg, and Lee then moved east with McLaws' Division and some of Anderson's to block Sedgwick at Salem Church from getting through to Hooker. Although hemmed in by the passive McLaws on the west, the late-arriving Anderson on the south, and an aggressive Early on the east, Sedgwick defended his position skillfully, killed and wounded many overly aggressive Confederate attackers, and then escaped north across the Rappahannock via Scott's Ford on the night of May 4–5. In Porter

Alexander's opinion, Lee wasted a whole day trapping and attacking the outnumbered Sedgwick instead of going after him immediately.[27] This delay gave Sedgwick time to entrench, inflict severe casualties on the Rebels, and ultimately to escape.[28]

All the while Lee was trying to destroy Sedgwick, the hapless Hooker stood by and did nothing while his forces remaining in the Chancellorsville area outnumbered Lee's there by a four-to-one margin. Hooker missed a grand opportunity to trap Lee's army between his and Sedgwick's troops. Never one to pass up a chance to attack, Lee hurried back to Chancellorsville on May 5, after Sedgwick's nighttime retreat, in an effort to assault Hooker's forces before they could similarly retreat across the Rappahannock. Lee's forces arrived too late. General Winfield Scott Hancock was overseeing an orderly and well-defended retreat, and Lee was fortunate not to have had the opportunity to attack. In fact, according to Alexander, Lee was saved from disaster by Hooker's May 5–6 retreat back across the river:

> There was still another occasion when I recalled ruefully Ives's prophecy that I would see all the audacity [on Lee's part] I wanted to see, & felt that it was already over-fulfilled: but when, to my intense delight, the enemy crossed the river in retreat during the night, & thus saved us from what would have been probably the bloodiest defeat of the war. It was on the 6th of May 1863 at the end of Chancellorsville... Hooker's entire army, some 90,000 infantry, were in the Wilderness, backed against the Rapidan [actually the Rappahannock], & had had nearly three days to fortify a short front, from the river above to the river below. And, in that dense forest of small wood, a timber slashing in front of a line of breastworks could in a few hours make a position absolutely impregnable

to assault. But on the afternoon of the 5th Gen. Lee gave orders for a grand assault the next morning by his whole force of about 40,000 infantry, & I was all night getting my artillery in position for it. And how I did thank God when in the morning the enemy were gone![29]

Bitterly disappointed at the failure to launch the ill-conceived offensive[30] that he had hoped would bring a grand victory, Lee erupted when Brigadier General Dorsey Pender reported to him that the federal entrenchments had been abandoned overnight. He demeaned him by saying, "Why, General Pender! That is the way you young men always do. You allow those people to get away. I tell you what to do, but you don't do it! Go after them! Damage them all you can!"[31] The reality, according to David Lowe, was that "Hooker would have repulsed Lee's proposed frontal assault and inflicted dreadful casualties, but he lacked confidence to put his offensive/defensive inversion to the ultimate test."[32] Earl Hess added, "The fact that Lee was more than ready to strike at the bridgehead indicates that he had learned no lesson about the tactical strengths of well-made field fortifications."[33]

Chancellorsville, Jackson's last battle, also proved to be Lee's last major "victory." The classic flanking maneuver employed by Jackson was not to be repeated. After Jackson's death there was no one forceful enough (and only Longstreet apparently tried) to convince Lee of the necessity to preserve his most precious resource, his army, by remaining on the defensive whenever possible and by flanking, rather than frontally assaulting, superior enemy forces. There also was no one left capable of converting Lee's discretionary orders into daring success on the battle-field.[34]

Although often regarded as Lee's greatest victory, Chancellorsville was a tribute to the incompetence of Hooker under fire and, most importantly, was a disaster for the South.[35] It has been called a Pyrrhic victory that was "a mortal blow to the vitality" of Lee's army.[36] Another historian said, "It looked to be a great Confederate victory, but the appearance was deceiving."[37] Against the advice of his more competent subordinates, Hooker had sent his cavalry away from the battle, failed to use much of his infantry, meekly surrendered one strong position after another, and failed to take advantage of his artillery and infantry superiority.[38] Nevertheless, after the havoc wreaked by Jackson's flanking maneuver, the Confederates decimated themselves in a series of frontal attacks on Union defenders, who effectively relied on hastily constructed field fortifications. As a result, while killing and wounding 10,700 (11 percent) Yankees, the Rebels themselves suffered an intolerably high— and irreplaceable—11,100 (19 percent) killed and wounded of their own. Although the Union Army suffered more total casualties (17,287 to 12,764), the total numbers killed and wounded on the two sides were about equal.[39] Outnumbered four to one at the outset of the war and devastated by their 1862 losses, the Confederates could not afford many more battles in which they suffered 19 percent casualties to their foes' 11 percent.

His numerical losses were serious enough to cause Lee to change his army's manner of counting casualties by eliminating "slight injuries,"[40] to complain of his numerical inferiority, and to make one of his periodic appeals to President Davis for reinforcements from elsewhere. With both Vicksburg and Chattanooga threatened, Lee, on May 10, opposed sending one of Longstreet's divisions to the West and argued to Seddon that unless he was reinforced he would have "to withdraw into the defences around Richmond... The strength of this army has been reduced by the casualties in the late battles."[41] The next day Lee wrote Davis: "It would seem therefore that Virginia is to be the theater of action, and this army, if possible, ought to be strengthened... I think that you will agree with me that every effort should be made to reinforce this army in order to oppose the large force which the enemy seems to be concentrating against it."[42] Once again, Lee had squandered his army and then sought compensating reinforcements from elsewhere.

Chancellorsville demonstrated Lee's propensity for offensive strategy and tactics. In his September 1863 report on that battle, Lee admitted its costliness: "Attacking largely superior numbers in strongly entrenched positions[, our soldiers'] heroic courage overcame every obstacle of nature and art, and achieved a triumph most honorable to our arms.... The returns... will show the extent of our loss, which from the nature of the circumstances attending the engagements could not be otherwise than severe. Many valuable officers and men were killed or wounded in the faithful discharge of duty."[43] That battle also displayed his Virginia-only focus as he refused to part with Longstreet beforehand and sought reinforcements afterward. While his focus on Virginia had serious ramifications elsewhere, Lee's aggressive strategy and tactics again resulted in irreplaceable losses to his own army.

Perhaps as damaging as Lee's actual losses was the overconfidence that Chancellorsville inspired in Confederate minds—particularly in the mind of Robert E. Lee.[44] On May 21, Lee wrote to Hood about the men in the Army of Northern Virginia: "I agree with you in believing that our army would be invincible if it could be properly organized and officered. There never were such men in an army before. They will go anywhere and do anything if properly led."[45] Every tactical gamble Lee had taken appeared to have been successful, the enemy had been driven from the field and across the Rappahannock, and there seemed no task beyond the capability of his brave army. Lee's actions in the succeeding weeks reflected a fatal belief that the Army of Northern Virginia was invincible.[46] His belief, according to Porter Alexander, was shared at that time by his army:

But, like the rest of the army generally, nothing gave me much concern so long as I knew that Gen. Lee was in command. I am sure there can never have been an army with more supreme confidence in its commander than that army had in Gen. Lee. We looked forward to victory under him as confidently as to successive sunrises.[47]

Lee's overconfident army, however, had seen its last major "victory."

Lee, with Jackson no longer at his side, next made the fateful decision to invade the North—a decision that carried him to disastrous defeat at Gettysburg. He did so only after rejecting pleas that he send part of his army to rescue the 30,000 troops being bottled up near Vicksburg, Mississippi, by Ulysses S. Grant. Seddon and Longstreet initially recommended to President Davis either that course of action or a reinforcement of Bragg for an assault in Middle Tennessee. They could have argued that Chancellorsville demonstrated that Lee could survive and even win without Longstreet.[48]

On May 10, Lee bluntly rejected Seddon and Longstreet's proposal that one of Longstreet's divisions be sent to aid Vicksburg. Then, while Grant took Jackson, Mississippi; won the critical Battle of Champion's Hill; and moved toward Vicksburg; the Confederacy's leadership met in Richmond to debate the issue of whether to send some of Lee's troops to trap Grant between Jackson and John Pemberton's 30,000-man army in Vicksburg. Lee himself met with Davis and Seddon on May 15. Using all the political capital earned by his Chancellorsville "victory," Lee was able to convince Davis that Richmond would be threatened if Lee's army was reduced in strength and that the best defense of Richmond would be an offensive campaign into the North. Lee demonstrated his lack of a national strategic vision by arguing that this issue was a "question between Virginia and the Mississippi." He also argued that the oppressive

Mississippi climate would cause Grant to withdraw from the Vicksburg area in June.[49]

Lee prevailed, and on May 26 the Confederate Cabinet authorized him to launch a northern offensive in the East. As Lee moved north, he unrealistically wrote to Davis that his eastern offensive might even result in the Union recalling some of its troops from the West. Lee hedged his bet by coupling this statement with a request that troops be transferred to Virginia from the Carolinas to protect Richmond, threaten Washington, and aid his advance.[50] Although Longstreet acquiesced in Lee's strategic offensive, he spent a great deal of time trying to convince Lee to go on the tactical defensive once in the North in an effort to repeat the defensive victory at Fredericksburg. Confederate General Wade Hampton later complained that he thought the Pennsylvania campaign would enable the Confederates to choose a battlefield but that instead "we let Meade [appointed Union army commander just before Gettysburg] choose his position & we then attacked."[51]

Lee's correspondence indicates that he went north with mixed intentions. These are reflected in two June 25 letters Lee wrote to Davis. In the first, he said, "I think I can throw Genl Hooker's army across the Potomac and draw troops from the south, embarrassing their plan of campaign in a measure, if I can do nothing more and have to return."[52] Later that day, he seemed to reflect Longstreet's view: "It seems to me that we cannot afford to keep our troops awaiting possible movements of the enemy, but that our true policy is, as far as we can, so to employ our own forces as to give occupation to his at points of our own selection."[53] Historian Charles P. Roland concluded that Lee's "overriding strategic goal … was to convince a majority of the Northern people that they were incapable of winning the war, or that the price of such a victory was higher than it was worth."[54]

Alexander later stated that sending troops to the West would have been a better use of them, would have taken advantage of the South's interior lines, and was successful when used that autumn (at Chickamauga) under less favorable circumstances.[55] Lee's failure to send troops to either Vicksburg or middle Tennessee, in order to maintain his own army at full strength, was a significant factor in:

- the fall of Vicksburg,
- the loss of the Mississippi Valley to Union control,
- a retreat by Bragg's army out of Tennessee and northern Alabama after he had been forced to send troops to aid Vicksburg,
- the loss of Chattanooga, and
- the continuing Union success in the Mississippi Valley and middle theaters that ultimately would spread through Georgia to Lee's own back door.

As historian Archer Jones explained, "This opening of the Mississippi had a profound effect by spreading hope in the North for an early victory and in the South widespread pessimism."[56]

The Confederate Army of Tennessee had been considerably weakened that spring and summer because the Confederate commissary in Atlanta shipped massive foodstuffs to Lee and virtually nothing to Bragg.[57] Not only did Lee refuse to send troops to the West, but he unrealistically implored Bragg to invade Ohio to complement Lee's planned incursion into Pennsylvania.[58] He did this at a time when Bragg had only 50,000 troops in Tennessee to either hold Tennessee or send assistance to Vicksburg. At the time, Union strength in the Middle and Mississippi theaters was 214,000.[59]

DISASTER AT GETTYSBURG

Gettysburg—the finale to Confederate military prospects in the East—exposed Lee at his worst. As was the case when he went north in 1862, the numbers dictated that an embarrassing retreat and perceived defeat would be the ultimate result.[60] Alexander later expressed his concern that Lee's nearest ammunition supply railhead was at Staunton, Virginia, 150 wagon-miles from Gettysburg.[61] Just as in 1862, Lee was moving north with a badly weakened army but was blinded by its recent tactical success.[62] In addition, Lee spread his forces all around south-central Pennsylvania without knowing the location of the Army of the Potomac.

In going north again, Lee was demonstrating his flawed philosophy that the best defense was a good offense.[63] He hoped to draw Hooker's army out of Virginia and have the two armies live off the Pennsylvania countryside during the summer and early fall. He succeeded in taking everyone north, but his stay was shorter than he had hoped, and his ultimate retreat to the Rappahannock line confirmed his defeat. Gettysburg was Lee's final major strategic offensive campaign.[64]

Following Chancellorsville and Jackson's death, Lee reorganized his 75,000-man army. From two infantry corps of four divisions each, he created three corps, each having three divisions. The 1st Corps was commanded by Longstreet, the 2nd by Ewell, and the 3rd by A. P. Hill. Neither Ewell nor Hill had worked directly under Lee's command, and neither of them was Stonewall Jackson. Thus, Lee's offensive strategy and tactics had adversely affected the entire command structure of his army.[65] Lee's failure to adjust his style, expectations, and orders to the poorer and less experienced generals in his army after Chancellorsville would prove to be troublesome and even disastrous.

Jeb Stuart commanded the cavalry division, and his swashbuckling style led to serious problems soon after Lee's army started north on June 3. On the eve of this departure on a major invasion of the North, Stuart's cavalrymen seemed less interested than usual. One Confederate captain later explained that the troops were "worried out by the military foppery and display (which was Stuart's greatest weakness)."[66]

Lee's lax oversight of Stuart and the cavalry arm of his army led to one near-disaster and to one real disaster. Stuart's cavalry was supposed to be protecting Lee's right flank and hiding his northward movement from Yankee eyes. On June 5, Stuart's approximately 9,500 officers and men held a grand parade at Brandy Station near the Orange and Alexandria Railroad—to the joy of the local ladies and to the disgust of the Confederate infantry.[67] Their only disappointment was that the commanding general could not be there. But Stuart received another opportunity to strut his forces when Lee arrived on the 7th and requested another review the next day. Thus the cavalry's spectacle was repeated on June 8, one day before the date Lee had ordered them to move across the Rappahannock to cover the continuing northward march of Ewell and Longstreet. A pleased Lee wrote his wife, " ... I reviewed the cavalry in this section yesterday. It was a splendid sight. The men & horses looked well. They had recuperated since last fall. Stuart was in all his glory."[68]

Early the next morning (June 9), the Confederates, instead of moving out themselves, were caught off guard by a dawn attack launched by Brigadier General Alfred Pleasonton's Union calvary. 11,000 Union troopers crossed the Rappahannock at Beverly and Kelly's fords and launched attacks on Stuart's scattered forces. They got all the way to Brandy Station and Stuart's headquarters at nearby Fleetwood House before being repulsed by Confederate cavalry under Brigadier Generals Rooney Lee (Robert E. Lee's son) and William E. "Grumble" Jones, their horse artillery, and ultimately Rebel infantry.[69] Stuart almost lost his artillery, and an all-day battle swirled around Fleetwood Hill, which changed hands four times. Union losses were about nine hundred to the

Rebels' five hundred,[70] but the Northern horsemen achieved their goal
of pinpointing the location of the bulk of the Army of Northern Virginia
while demonstrating, for the first time, their ability to initiate and sustain
a credible offensive.[71] The Battle of Brandy Station was a tactical draw
but a Union strategic victory, and it marked the end of the dominance
of the Confederate cavalry over their Union counterparts.

Embarrassed by his lack of preparedness and near-defeat at Brandy
Station, Stuart sought to redeem himself later in June by setting off on
another grand swing around a Union army. Lee, instead of reining in
the flamboyant Jeb, provided Stuart with such ambiguous orders that
Lee's invasion of Pennsylvania and most of the battle at Gettysburg were
carried out without Lee knowing the location of his enemy. Amazingly,
Lee repeated the same error Hooker had just committed when he
stripped himself of cavalry for the entire battle at Chancellorsville. Lee
allowed Stuart to depart with half his cavalry and to take along his best
subordinate commanders while leaving others to screen and scout for
the army commander.

How could this have happened? Simply, Stuart had a series of orders
to choose from and decided upon the most exciting and glorious opportunity offered to him. Utilizing the confusing discretion Lee had provided to him, Stuart engaged in a meaningless frolic-and-detour and
did not rejoin Lee until late the second day at Gettysburg. Stuart decided
to pass behind the Union Army and cross the Potomac east of the Blue
Ridge Mountains after effectively screening Lee's northward movement
in successful cavalry actions at Aldie, Middleburg, and Upperville.
Beginning on June 24, he swung to the east of the northward-moving
Union Army and thus separated his troopers from the rest of Lee's army.
Although he entered Pennsylvania only a few miles east of Gettysburg,
Stuart had no idea where Lee was and therefore headed farther north to
Carlisle instead of west to Gettysburg. All the while Stuart was slowed
down by a captured wagon train that he regarded as precious booty.

As a result of this eight-day ego trip, Stuart did not join Lee at Gettysburg until the evening of July 2—too late to be of any real assistance. Lee had to learn, on June 28, from a spy of Longstreet's, about Meade's appointment to succeed Hooker and Meade's army's northward movement across the Potomac. Lee had no idea which Union corps were going to arrive when at Gettysburg, was frustrated by his lack of knowledge of enemy movements as the fighting started on July 1,[72] and on the critical next day had to base his plan of battle on skimpy and incorrect information concerning Union strength in the area of the Round Tops south of Gettysburg. Although Lee rebuked Stuart upon his tardy arrival at Gettysburg by saying, "Well, General Stuart, you are here at last,"[73] Lee had only himself to blame for letting his strong-willed cavalry commander get away from his army.[74]

Lee's vague orders to Stuart presaged a series of such orders that plagued the Confederates throughout the entire Gettysburg campaign. Some defenders of Lee have attempted to justify Lee's ambiguous orders as an essential part of his aggressive tactics and strategy. If so, dangerously vague orders may also be seen as another disadvantage of the offensive style of warfare that lost the war.

While Stuart campaigned east of the Blue Ridge, Lee was having success to the west. Ewell's 2nd Corps led the northward sweep and routed 9,000 Yankee defenders of Winchester, Virginia, on June 14 and 15. Word of the rout reached Richmond the next day, when Confederate Chief of Ordnance Josiah Gorgas ominously noted Lee's movement in his journal: "What the movement means it is difficult to divine. I trust we are not to have the Maryland campaign over again."[75]

After Winchester, Ewell, Hill, and Longstreet moved their respective corps, in that order, through Sharpsburg and Hagerstown, Maryland, and across the Mason-Dixon Line into the Cumberland Valley of Pennsylvania, Ewell moved his leading corps through Chambersburg and then eastward through the mountains to York and Carlisle.

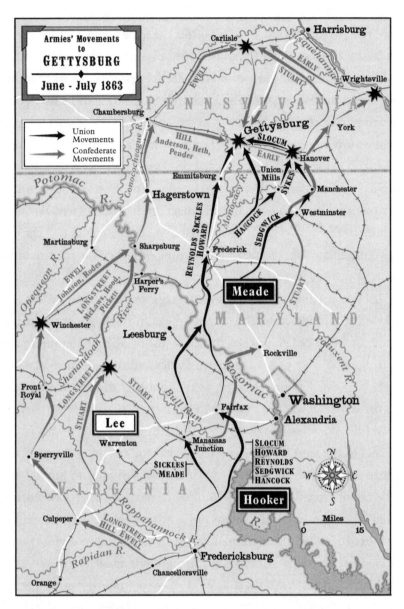

Armies' Movements to Gettysburg (June–July 1863)
Map by David Deis, Dreamline Cartography, Northridge, CA

In the midst of this movement, Lee finally revealed to Davis the scope of his planned offensive by belatedly requesting backup diversionary reinforcements. Lee wanted his offensive campaign to be aided by a diversionary action that would require Rebel troops from other areas not under his command. He requested Davis to move troops from Richmond and the Carolinas, under Beauregard's command, to create a diversion near Culpeper Court House in central Virginia while his own army moved into Pennsylvania. On June 23 and twice on June 25, he wrote to Davis that an army should be raised in the southeast under General Beauregard and moved to Culpeper Court House to threaten Washington.[76] In one of the June 25 letters, he explained that his own northward movement "has aroused the Federal Government and people to great exertions, and it is incumbent upon us to call forth all our energies."[77] Davis declined to do so because Confederate soldiers were needed to guard Richmond against 16,000 Union troops on the Virginia Peninsula and to guard Charleston, South Carolina, against a major Union offensive.[78] Lee's unrealistic, but typical, suggestion to reinforce Virginia overlooked the facts that Grant by then had Pemberton trapped in Vicksburg and that Beauregard already had sent reinforcements to Tennessee.

By June 28, Ewell was in position to move on the Pennsylvania capital of Harrisburg. Meanwhile Lee, unaware of the whereabouts of the Union Army, was with Hill and Longstreet back at Chambersburg. That night Lee learned from Thomas Harrison, one of Longstreet's spies, that Meade had replaced the hapless Hooker as commander of the 95,000-man Army of the Potomac and that his army had moved north to Frederick, Maryland. Lee decided to meet them east of the mountains. Realizing the necessity to concentrate his numerically inferior force but not sure where the enemy was, Lee sent orders to Ewell to head back toward either Cashtown or Gettysburg.[79]

Day 1 of Gettysburg (July 1, 1863) brought Lee's army a stiff rebuff, a fortuitous success, and finally a missed opportunity for victory. The prior day the Confederates had discovered a division of federal cavalry under Brigadier General John Buford at Gettysburg when they headed there in hopes of obtaining shoes from local factories. Thus, the next morning a stronger Confederate force, the divisions of Major Generals Henry Heth and Dorsey Pender of Hill's corps, headed east from Cashtown toward Gettysburg to deal with Buford.

Because of Stuart's absence and Lee's consequent ignorance concerning the whereabouts of General Meade's forces, Heth's and Pender's infantry divisions found more than they had bargained for. Initially they were handicapped by the fact that two-thirds of Lee's army was going to have to use a single route, the Chambersburg Pike or Cashtown Road, to get to Gettysburg. Heth, under somewhat puzzling orders from Lee not to bring on a general engagement,[80] pushed ahead with two brigades. Why was Heth sent against a position known to be held by Union forces if he was not to bring on a general engagement? Was he to stand in place when he encountered resistance and back up two-thirds of Lee's army on a single road?

On June 30, Buford had astutely recognized the tactical value of the high ground south of Gettysburg and decided to save it for the main Union Army once it arrived. Instead of putting his own cavalrymen on those hills, therefore, he deployed them during the night west and north of the town so they could delay the Confederates until Union infantry arrived. He sent word to his superior, Pleasonton, the Army of the Potomac's cavalry commander, that Hill's corps was massed back of Cashtown nine miles west and that Hill's pickets were in sight. He also passed along rumors that Ewell was coming south over the mountains from Carlisle.[81]

In a fierce struggle that began at 5:30 a.m. on July 1, Buford's cavalry stubbornly resisted the 7,500-man advance of two brigades of Heth's Division. With the firing of the first shot, Buford had sent word of the fighting to Major General John F. Reynolds, commander of the 1st Corps. Reynolds, then eight miles away at Emmitsburg, Maryland, ordered his 9,500 infantrymen to shed their baggage and speedily march to Gettysburg.

Buford sent skirmishers west on the Chambersburg Pike to Herr's and Belmont School House ridges west of his McPherson's Ridge campsite. Their determined resistance, aided by Spencers and other repeating rifles, forced the Confederates to spend more than a precious hour deploying into a battle line. Meanwhile, Reynolds arrived and conferred with Buford about the critical situation. Reynolds then went back to hasten his infantry to the front, sent word to Howard to speed his 11th Corps to Gettysburg, and sent a message to Meade advising him that Gettysburg was to be the collision point of the East's two armies.

Heth, enjoying momentary superiority, ordered his two brigades forward. Buford's skirmishers grudgingly gave up the forward ridges and a small stream called Willoughby Run. They gradually fell back to McPherson's Farm on McPherson's Ridge only a mile west of Gettysburg. Buford sent a message to Meade describing the battle, stating that Hill's entire corps was moving on Gettysburg, and advising that Confederate troops had been discovered approaching Gettysburg from the north.[82] The nature of the battle changed when Reynolds' men, led by the Iron Brigade, began arriving at the scene shortly after 10:00 a.m. That proud brigade was the 1st Brigade of the 1st Division of the 1st Corps of the Army of the Potomac and was composed of stalwart black-hatted troops from the Upper Midwest. Although Reynolds was instantly killed by a Rebel sharpshooter while directing his troops in an assault on

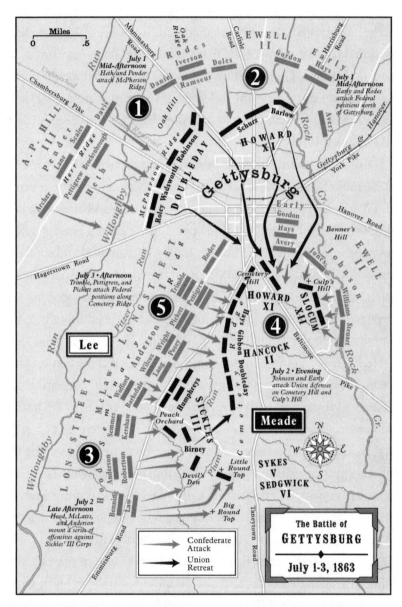

The Battle of Gettysburg (July 1–3, 1863)
Map by David Deis, Dreamline Cartography, Northridge, CA

Archer's brigade, this Union counterattack was devastating and drove the Confederates back toward Herr's Ridge. Buford's brilliant delaying tactics had saved the day and perhaps the entire battle, and Reynolds had arrived in the nick of time to repel the first serious Confederate assault at Gettysburg.[83]

Back at Cashtown, Lee had heard the sounds of battle and started toward Gettysburg. The impact of Stuart's absence was reflected in Lee's comments as he headed toward the fateful battlefield: "I cannot think what has become of Stuart; I ought to have heard from him long before now.... In the absence of reports from him, I am in ignorance of what we have in front of us here. It may be the whole Federal army, or it may be only a detachment. If it is the whole Federal force, we must fight a battle here...."[84]

As the Union forces gained strength, so did Lee's. Down Mummasberg Road from the northwest came Rodes' 8,000-man division of Ewell's 2nd Corps, which had been as far north as Carlisle. They arrived about 11:00 a.m., the same time as advance elements of Howard's 11th Corps arrived to impede their advance. Because of Reynolds' death, Howard assumed overall command of the Union forces and Major General Carl Schurz took command of the 11th Corps. About noon Rodes' artillery began shelling the Union lines, and by 2:00 p.m. his infantry launched an assault on Schurz's troops north of town. At about the same time, Meade learned of Reynolds' death and dispatched Hancock from Taneytown to go to Gettysburg to take command (even though the unreliable Howard was senior to him).

Rodes' five-brigade attack from the northwest was uncoordinated and ineffective. Brigadier General Alfred Iverson Jr.'s Brigade was slaughtered and then pinned down by Union troops who may have fired 100,000 shots at them from behind a stone wall. Iverson lost more than 900 of his 1,400 men, that 66 percent casualty rate being the highest for any Rebel brigade at Gettysburg.[85] Rodes failed to break through the 11th Corps' lines, and the Confederate situation looked bleak. Good fortune, however, arrived around 3:00 p.m. in the person of Jubal Early and his 5,500-man division (also of Ewell's Corps). Moving from Carlisle toward Cashtown, Early had heard the battle and headed south on roads approaching Gettysburg from the north and north-northeast. These approaches brought Early's division in on Schurz's exposed right flank.

Although the arrival of Rodes' and Early's divisions of Ewell's 2nd Corps prevented a disastrous defeat of A. P. Hill's men coming down the bottlenecked Chambersburg Pike, their earlier arrival would have been even better. Because of Stuart's absence and Lee's consequent ignorance of the Union Army's precise whereabouts, Lee had ordered Ewell to march from Carlisle to either Cashtown or Gettysburg. Ewell's choice of Cashtown resulted in a several-hour delay in his corps' arrival at Gettysburg. Had Ewell been ordered to march directly to Gettysburg, his men should have been able to drive out Buford's and Reynolds' troops, reduce Hill's and their own casualties, and occupy the high ground above the town before the arrival of Union reinforcements.

But this was not the end of the problems that resulted from Lee's ignorance of the Union Army's whereabouts. Lee, still at Cashtown as the morning fighting erupted in Gettysburg, was advised by a messenger from Ewell, Major G. Campbell Brown, that Ewell was heading south toward the sounds of battle. Lee asked about Stuart, ordered Ewell to send scouting parties to look for Stuart, and then incredibly told Major Brown that he (Lee) did not want a major engagement brought on.[86]

Even worse, Lee then used the critical Chambersburg Pike to send Ewell's other division (under Major General Edward "Old Allegheny" Johnson) and Ewell's entire ten-mile-plus train of wagons eastward toward Gettysburg. That division and Ewell's train were on the same road as Hill's and Longstreet's corps because of Lee's Cashtown-or-

Gettysburg orders to Ewell. Lee's use of the Chambersburg Pike for a crucial ten-hour period to move Ewell's wagon-train, estimated at fourteen miles long by McLaws,[87] compounded the bottleneck on that road. Meade, on the other hand, had his army marching full-bore for Gettysburg on several roads with their trains behind. Lee's action delayed the arrival near Gettysburg of Longstreet's leading divisions, those of McLaws and Hood, until midnight and later.[88] Incredibly, Lee had bottlenecked seven of his nine divisions on a single road[89] and thereby retarded their arrival for both the first and second days of battle at Gettysburg.

Nevertheless, as a result of Early's fortuitous afternoon arrival on the field, when Lee arrived on Herr's Ridge from Cashtown, he observed the pleasing panorama of the 11th Corps' line crumbling and its troops starting to retreat. Lee hastily sent Heth's badly beaten-up division and Dorsey Pender's fresh brigade into the fray west of town around 3:30 p.m. Initially Lee did not hesitate to take advantage of his momentary numerical and positional superiority and the opportunity to destroy two Union corps before Meade had his whole army up.

Between three and five o'clock in the afternoon on Day 1, it looked as though Gettysburg was going to be a great victory for Lee. Ewell's two-division attack from the north forced the outflanked 11th Corps to flee south in disarray into Gettysburg and through the town to Cemetery and Culp's hills. Uncovered by that retreat, the exhausted Union 1st Corps troops, who had been defending the Chambersburg Pike approach west of town for several hours, had no choice but to retreat to Seminary Ridge and ultimately to Cemetery Hill.

Hancock arrived at Cemetery Hill before 4:00 p.m. in time to see the massive retreat of two Union corps, sent some troops to unoccupied Culp's Hill, and started the men entrenching. Around 5:00 p.m., Slocum began arriving with his 8,500-man 12th Corps, but it deployed along Cemetery Ridge south of the high ground of Cemetery and Culp's hills.

Therefore, an immediate attack by all of Lee's forces had an excellent chance of dislodging the minimal Union forces from their position on the heights. The likelihood of their success was demonstrated by Ewell's near-success on those same hills 24 hours later.

Although Stonewall Jackson was dead, Lee persisted in issuing ambiguous orders that only Jackson could have turned into victories. Lee, with at least a 35,000-21,000 manpower superiority through the late afternoon and evening, did not aggressively take charge of the field nor order any of Hill's troops to their front and left to join or support an attack by Ewell on the two hills. Ewell and Early were on their own. At this point, Ewell should have had over 10,000 men still able to attack—especially 5,000 relatively fresh men in four brigades of Early's division. Early's men were actively pursuing the Union troops through the town and could have continued up the hills while panic reigned. Instead, Early halted the pursuit and sent two brigades off to the east because of a report of Union troops coming in from that direction.[90] Receiving Early's report and conflicting information concerning Union strength on Culp's Hill, Ewell decided not to assault.

With Union troops in chaotic retreat through the town, Lee committed two egregious errors. First, he failed to take firm control of all troops he had on hand and deploy them for a maximum-strength attack on the 80-foot-high Cemetery Hill and the 100-foot-high Culp's Hill, the dominant heights in the immediate vicinity of the town. He ignored and failed to utilize all troops other than Ewell's, particularly A. P. Hill's, and thus failed to take advantage of his numerical superiority.

Second, at 4:30 p.m. he issued a merely discretionary order, via Major Walter Taylor, to the stalled Ewell to take the high ground. Given the critical nature of the situation, Lee's orders to Ewell were appalling: Ewell was to take the heights "if he found it practicable, but to avoid a general engagement until the arrival of the other divisions of the army,"[91] which were being hurried to Gettysburg. This order seems inexplicable because there had been a general engagement since early that day, the remaining Confederate forces were caught in a Chambersburg Pike traffic jam, and the Union presence would inevitably increase much more than the Confederates'. In the absence of a mandatory order to immediately take those critical positions, the hesitant Ewell not surprisingly failed to move on Culp's and Cemetery hills before the outnumbered and disorganized Union forces there had dug in and been reinforced.[92]

Even the arrival at dusk of Ewell's third division, that of "Old Allegheny" Johnson, was not sufficient to encourage the reticent Ewell, unmoved by Lee's weak order, to take the high ground—at the very least the dominant heights of Culp's Hill. Virtually all of Ewell's generals urged an assault on the high ground; they included Early, who had passed up the earlier opportunity to do so when he alone would have been responsible.[93] Major General Isaac R. Trimble asked for a single regiment to take the two hills and stalked away in disgust when Ewell declined to attack.[94] At this same time, Lee deliberately and inexplicably held the unbloodied troops of Major General Richard H. Anderson's division in Hill's corps nearby in reserve apparently because Lee's whole army was not yet concentrated and he lacked information on the enemy's strength.[95] For these reasons, leading Gettysburg historian Edwin B. Coddington concluded, "Responsibility for the failure of the Confederates to make an all-out assault on Cemetery Hill on July 1 must rest with Lee."[96] Similarly, Gettysburg guide and historian Gary Kross pointed to Lee's failure to order support from Hill's corps as one reason why Ewell was justified in not attacking.[97] This late-day episode was the only time on July 1 that either side did not immediately use all the forces it had gotten to Gettysburg.

Lee, Ewell, and Early's hesitation proved disastrous. Lee's failure to take full advantage of his temporary superiority and to issue a definitive attack order to Ewell left his enemy in control of the high ground for the final two days of the battle. As a result, Union forces retained the commanding heights which Buford, Reynolds, and Hancock had successively determined to protect and hold because they were the key to battlefield control at Gettysburg.

Based on Lee's no-general-engagement warnings on July 1 and a postwar explanation by him, Lee's reticence to command an all-out assault on the first day at Gettysburg appears to have been due to his desire to have his entire army on the field before undertaking a "general engagement." This wishful approach seems strange in light of the facts that even a greater proportion of the Union Army was absent, Lee outnumbered his adversary, and every passing hour allowed the Yankees to move toward numerical and positional superiority. Later that evening, and again the next morning, Lee compounded the error by allowing Ewell, Early, and Rodes to decline to attack the high ground or to move around to Lee's right flank. This indecisiveness resulted in Ewell's corps being of little value for the duration of the battle.[98] Meanwhile, on the afternoon of July 1, Meade was moving all his corps toward Gettysburg in hopes of attacking Lee before his army reunited. Although those hopes were foiled, his prompt actions put strong forces in place on high ground to repel any head-on Confederate offensive.[99]

On the morning of July 2, Lee expressed his disappointment concerning the events of the prior late afternoon: "We did not or could not pursue our advantage of yesterday and now the enemy are in a good position."[100] This statement amounted to a rebuke of Ewell, but Lee must have known that he bore at least as much responsibility as Ewell for the army's failure to seize the commanding heights on that vital first day at Gettysburg. With Confederate casualties at 6,500 and the Union's at 9,000, Lee had won an engagement but missed an opportunity to win the Battle of Gettysburg.

By that next morning, the situation had radically changed. Hancock's 13,000-man 2nd Corps and Sickles' 12,000-man 3rd Corps arrived early. Thus, instead of three corps with 21,000 men on the battlefield, the Union now had five corps and 35,000 men, and two more corps (the 5th and 6th) with 28,000 more men were forced-marching about thirty and thirty-six miles, respectively, to get there that day. Instead of scrambling to find any kind of position as they had done on the prior day, the Northerners had established a strong line running from near Little Round Top (two miles south of town) north along Taneytown Road and Cemetery Ridge to Cemetery Hill and then curving east to Culp's Hill and southeast parallel to the Baltimore Pike. The Yankees had equal and then superior numbers, an imposing defensive position, and the advantage of interior lines (which permitted them to quickly move soldiers to threatened points in their lines). Meade's army ultimately had 27,000 men per mile along a three-mile inverted-fishhook line while Lee's army had 10,000 men per mile along a five-mile semicircle.[101] That disparity augured ill for Lee's army.

On July 2, Lee erred again—in several ways. Because of the absence of much of Stuart's cavalry, Lee ordered skimpy and consequently inadequate reconnaissance of the Union left. Somehow these small scouting parties failed to detect federal forces on the south end of Cemetery Ridge and on and near Little Round Top. As a result, he erroneously believed that the round tops and the areas around them were not occupied by Union troops.[102] Also, the reconnaissance was early, and the attack was late.

Lee ordered Longstreet with his two delayed and exhausted divisions to undertake a several-mile march and then to attack the left flank of the Union forces. In doing so, Lee ignored Longstreet's cautious advice to move south of Gettysburg, seek a strong defensive position and await a Union attack. Late the prior afternoon Longstreet and Lee had watched the retreat of the Yankee forces to the high ground immediately south of Gettysburg and discussed what to do the following day. Longstreet wanted to turn the Union left flank, establish a strong position and await an attack.[103] Ironically, at about that same hour, Union General Hancock was sending a message to Meade that the Union's strong position would be difficult to take but could be turned.[104] Longstreet argued that the Union forces would be compelled to attack any Confederate force placed between them and Washington and that bringing on this Fredericks-burg-type situation was consistent with a strategically offensive and tactically defensive campaign, which is what Longstreet thought had been agreed upon. Perhaps desperate for a convincing victory to justify his gambling invasion of the North and concerned about his medium-term supply situation, Lee insisted upon an attack. To Lee's assertion, "If the enemy is there tomorrow, we must attack him," Longstreet apparently replied, "If he is there tomorrow, it will be because he wants you to attack—a good reason, in my judgment, for not doing so."[105]

In his Gettysburg Battle Report, Lee later justified his deliberate offensives of July 2nd and 3rd on the grounds that retreat would have been difficult and awaiting attack was impractical because of foraging difficulties.[106] General E. Porter Alexander had the following thoughts about Lee's rationale:

> Now when it is remembered that we stayed for three days longer on that very ground, two of them days of desperate battle, ending in the discouragement of a bloody repulse, & then successfully withdrew all our trains & most of the wounded through the mountains; and, finding the Potomac too high to ford, protected them all & foraged successfully for over a week in a very restricted territory along the river, until we could build a bridge, it does not seem improbable

that we could have faced Meade safely on the 2nd at Gettysburg without assaulting him in his wonderfully strong position. We had the prestige of victory with us, having chased him off the field & through the town. We had a fine defensive position on Seminary Ridge ready at our hand to occupy. It was not such a really wonderful position as the enemy happened to fall into, but it was no bad one, & it could never have been successfully assaulted.... We could even have fallen back to Cashtown & held the mountain passes with all the prestige of victory, & popular sentiment would have forced Meade to take the aggressive.[107]

Historian Daniel Bauer studied the food supplies that would have been available to Lee had he gone on the defensive in Pennsylvania and concluded that Lee had the resources to go on the defensive and erred greatly when he allowed resource concerns to negate that alternative.[108]

Not only were there problems with Lee's offensive strategy on July 2, his execution of it proved disastrous. Lee again failed to give clear and forceful orders to Ewell's corps, and the result was an abysmal lack of coordination between the Confederates' left and right flanks. Lee's plan called for Ewell to demonstrate against the Union right and to attack if an opportunity developed and for Longstreet to attack the Union left. Even though Ewell's timidity had clearly been demonstrated the prior day, Lee failed to adequately oversee his efforts on the 2nd. As a result, the day passed with no assault by the Confederate left wing to divert attention from Longstreet's attack on the Union left flank.[109]

Likewise, Lee failed to oversee, personally or through staff, the execution of his orders on the right flank. No one ascertained the precise secure route that Hood and McLaws' divisions of Longstreet's corps needed to take to reach their attack positions. This lack of oversight

compounded Longstreet's difficulties in proceeding to the southern
Union flank without being observed by the Yankees. Alexander commented on this particular situation:

> That is just one illustration of how time may be lost in han-
> dling troops, and of the need of an abundance of competent
> staff officers by the generals in command. Scarcely any of our
> generals had half of what they needed to keep a constant &
> close supervision on the execution of important orders. An
> army is like a great machine, and in putting it into battle it is
> not enough for its commander to merely issue the necessary
> orders. He should have a staff ample to supervise the execu-
> tion of each step, & to promptly report any difficulty or mis-
> understanding. There is no telling the value of the hours
> which were lost by that division that morning.[110]

Some of the postwar defenders of Lee and critics of Longstreet, such as
Jubal Early[111] and Pendleton,[112] contended that Lee had ordered Longstreet to attack at dawn. There is no credible evidence to support this
contention. Alexander commented that this position was not believable,
that Lee would have ordered Longstreet's troops into position during
the night if he desired a dawn attack, and that the enemy's position was
never thoroughly determined until morning.[113] Lee, having personally
delayed Longstreet's divisions for ten hours the prior afternoon and
having caused them to arrive near Gettysburg in the wee hours of July
2, was well aware of their inability to initiate an early morning assault
in a position miles away from their bivouac. Because of the Chambersburg Pike congestion, Longstreet's two primary divisions to be used in
the attack had arrived near Gettysburg at midnight (McLaws' Division)
and dawn (Hood's Division).

In fact, Lee ordered a scouting expedition around dawn[114] and was not in a position to order an attack until he had specific information, based on daylight observations, on who should be attacked where. At about 11:00 a.m., Lee finally issued his only specific attack order of the day, directing Longstreet to proceed south to get into position to attack.[115] In addition, Lee at that time specifically consented to Longstreet's request that his attack be delayed until Brigadier General Evander Law's Brigade of Hood's Division could be brought up.[116] Law, another victim of the Chambersburg Pike bottleneck, had set out at about 3:00 a.m. and arrived on the scene around noon. In light of his actions and knowledge, Lee could not have expected an attack before mid-afternoon. Even Douglas Southall Freeman, who severely criticized Longstreet for delaying the attack, contended that Lee virtually surrendered control to Longstreet and concluded, "It is scarcely too much to say that on July 2 the Army of Northern Virginia was without a commander."[117] As commanding general of that army and on-scene commander of the battle, Lee was responsible for where and when Longstreet attacked.

As Longstreet proceeded on his southward march toward the Union left, he received reliable scouting reports that the Union left flank was "hanging in the air" and could be rolled up. Twice he passed this information on to Lee and requested permission to launch a flanking attack. Lee declined, however, and repeated his order to attack—probably under the erroneous impression that he still was ordering a flanking attack of some sort. McLaws and Hood's divisions had difficulty finding their way on unfamiliar roads to their designated attack positions and even had to turn back and retrace their steps when they discovered that a point on the line of march was visible from a Union signal station on Little Round Top. They were being guided by Captain Samuel L. Johnston of Lee's staff, and Lee himself rode part of the way south with Longstreet.[118] Lee oversaw and approved Longstreet's troop dispositions.[119]

Beginning their attack after 4:00 p.m., Longstreet's forces fought bravely in the Wheatfield, Peach Orchard, and Devil's Den, and almost succeeded in capturing both Big Round Top and Little Round Top. The near success indicates what a victory might have been achieved if Lee had turned Longstreet's men loose for a flanking attack instead of squandering them in frontal assaults along the Union lines on Cemetery Ridge. Stonewall Jackson was dead, and the Lee-Jackson charismatic relationship which had been present at Second Manassas and Chancellorsville had no worthy successor. Nevertheless, the attack had prospects for success had it been properly planned, executed, and supervised. Union General Sickles had advanced his 3rd Corps, contrary to orders, into a vulnerable position in the Peach Orchard along Emmitsburg Road well in front of the original Union line along Cemetery Ridge. Instead of simultaneously attacking the north-to-south Union line along their entire front, however, the Confederates attacked piecemeal. Hood's Division first attacked the Union left flank for an extended period of time before McLaws' Division was ordered to attack Sickles' center and right. This staggered, or in echelon, attack enabled the Union defenders to respond to each successively threatened position.

When Hood, McLaws, and their brigadiers first got into position, they had been surprised to find large Union troop concentrations in areas they had been informed were devoid of enemy forces. Both Hood and McLaws sought Longstreet's permission to avoid the desperate frontal assault they envisioned, but Longstreet, having failed numerous times to change Lee's mind over the prior twenty-four hours, directed that Lee's attack order be carried out.[120] In addition, Lee personally refused Hood's final request to send a brigade around the Union flank on the Round Tops.[121]

Each of the individual Confederate attacks was successful in driving back the enemy and capturing territory, but their overall impact was greatly reduced by uncoordinated timing. The attacks did not begin until 4:30 p.m. First, Hood's men attacked on the far south of the battlefield, crossed and followed Plum Run, captured Devil's Den below the Round Tops, and would have captured Little Round Top but for the courage of Colonel Joshua Chamberlain and his 20th Maine Regiment. Hood's attack was underway before two of McLaws' brigades moved against Sickles' overextended position to Hood's north. Later McLaws' other two brigades belatedly entered the fray. In fierce fighting, the Confederates drove Sickles' corps from the Peach Orchard, engaged in bitter combat for control of the adjoining Wheatfield, and finally drove the defenders back to the northern base of Little Round Top.

To their north, Dick Anderson's Division of Hill's 3rd Corps participated very ineffectively in the late stages of the attack. One brigade advanced haphazardly, and another never moved off Seminary Ridge. Throughout the day, Hill's corps and much of Anderson's Division acted as though they were unaware of Lee's plans or any role for them in the struggle. Lee may have intended them to join in the sequential attacks beginning at the southern end of his line but took no actions to get them properly aligned or to bring all of them into the fray as the afternoon turned to evening.[122]

On the Union side, Hancock took advantage of the disjointed Confederate attack and sent reinforcements to each successively attacked position. The 2nd Corps went to the Round Tops and to Sickles' left, and the 5th Corps reinforced Sickles. The 6th Corps, which arrived at 2:00 p.m. after marching thirty-four miles in seventeen hours, and the 12th Corps backed up the others and stopped the Confederates before they could get to Cemetery Ridge. As a result, by the time Sickles' line finally was broken and the Wheatfield secured, darkness was beginning to fall and additional Union troops had moved into position to back up Sickles and hold the Cemetery Ridge line. At one critical juncture, the

Rebels broke the Union's Wheatfield lines and were about to advance onto Cemetery Ridge. Hancock sent in the 262-man 1st Minnesota Regiment to push them back at all costs—which they did. The failed Confederate frontal attack in echelon cost them 6,500 casualties (to the Union's 6,000) and was reminiscent of similar failures by Lee's army during the Seven Days' Campaign.

Where was Lee while this major, uncoordinated, and costly attack was falling apart? He was overlooking the battle from the cupola and elsewhere at the Lutheran Seminary on Seminary Ridge, part of the time with Generals Hill and Heth. He neither sent nor received more than a message or two and apparently sent only one order during the battle.[123] He had given his orders many hours before when conditions were radically different, but he merely stood by and watched the bloody assault falter and fail. In a prelude to the more famous events of the next day, Lee allowed one third of his force to attack while the others remained in place.[124] In sharp contrast, George Meade actively moved his forces all over the battlefield to meet each new attack, took corrective actions when he discovered Sickles' disastrous abandonment of his assigned position, and used this "hands-on" approach throughout the entire battle to prevent a Rebel breakthrough along his critical Cemetery Ridge line.

In fact, Longstreet's assault of July 2 was only the first of three unco-ordinated attacks by Lee's army in a thirty-six-hour period. Bruce pointed to Lee's failure, on both July 2 and 3, to launch properly coor-dinated attacks: "For two days, Gettysburg presents the spectacle of two desperately fought and bloody battles by less than one third of [Lee's] army on each occasion, the other two thirds looking on, for the conflict was visible from nearly every point on the Confederate lines. Does not all this present another question to solve [than] whether a corps commander was quick or slow? Was the commander-in-chief justified in assigning such a task to such a force?"[125]

Lee's uncoordinated assaults continued that night when Ewell's forces finally attacked Cemetery Hill. They were twenty-four hours too late for a likely success and several hours too late to coordinate with Longstreet. Nevertheless, the brave men of two brigades fought their way to the top of Cemetery Hill. Failures of high command to provide support, however, compelled them to retreat. Ewell failed to commit his artillery to support the assault, while Early never committed a reserve brigade to the battle. Once again, the attack on Cemetery Hill was planned in echelon—Johnson to attack first, followed by Early and then Rodes. The reality was an ineffective assault by one brigade after another and the failure of many brigades to engage at all. In fact, two brigades had completed their successful attacks and been compelled to withdraw before Rodes launched his forces from the town itself. In summary, the tactics were poorly planned and executed. The result was a failure to secure and hold Cemetery Hill, which dominated the north end of the battlefield. Early on the morning of July 2, Confederate Major General Edward Johnson assaulted Culp's Hill with even less success.[126]

In fact, as Alexander points out, Lee wasted Ewell's 2nd Corps by leaving it in an isolated and harmless position northeast of the primary struggles on the second and third days of Gettysburg:

> Ewell's troops were all placed beyond, or N.E. of Gettysburg, bent around toward the point of the fish hook of the enemy's position. It was an awkward place, far from our line of retreat in case of disaster, & not convenient either for reinforcing others or being reinforced. And... this part of the enemy's position was in itself the strongest & it was practically almost

unassailable. On the night of the 1st Gen. Lee ordered him
withdrawn & brought around to our right of the town. Gen.
Ewell had seen some ground he thought he could take &
asked permission to stay & to take it. Gen. Lee consented, but
it turned out early next morning that the position could not
be taken. Yet the orders to come out from the awkward place
he was in—where there was no reasonable probability of his
accomplishing any good on the enemy's line in his front &
where his artillery was of no service—were never renewed &
he stayed there till the last. The ground is there still for any
military engineer to pronounce whether or not Ewell's corps
& all its artillery was not practically paralysed & useless by its
position during the last two days of the battle.[127]

In conclusion, the second day of Gettysburg was a disaster for which the
Commanding General of the Army of Northern Virginia must be held
accountable. Over the objection of the corps and division commanders
involved, Lee ordered Longstreet's 1st Corps to launch a frontal, in-
echelon assault on strong Union positions. Lee stood idly by while Hill's
3rd Corps in the center of the Confederate lines and directly in front of
Lee did little to assist Longstreet.[128] Finally, Lee neither moved Ewell's
2nd Corps to an effective supporting attack position nor ensured that
it attacked the Union right flank at the same time Longstreet was attacking the Union left. Instead, the Rebels attacked the high ground on the
Union left hours after the end of Longstreet's assault. Lee failed to coordinate Ewell's attack with Longstreet's, and Ewell failed to coordinate his
own attacking forces with each other.[129]

Lee's performance the next day was even worse. Frustrated by his
two successive days of failure, he compounded his errors on the third
and final day of Gettysburg.[130] His original plan for that day again

involved simultaneous attacks by Ewell on the Rebels' left and Longstreet on their right. This plan was thwarted when Meade ordered a Union attack on Ewell's forces, which had occupied Union trenches the prior evening. During the five-hour early morning battle at the north end of the battlefield, Ewell's Rebels unsuccessfully tried again and again to capture Culp's Hill. Federal forces still held that critical position at mid-morning on the fateful third of July.[131]

With Ewell engaged, Lee changed his mind and decided to attack the center of the Union line. The prior evening Union Major General John Newton, Reynolds' replacement as commander of the 1st Corps, had told Meade that he should be concerned about a flanking movement by Lee and that Lee would not be "fool enough" to frontally attack the Union Army in the strong position into which the first two days' fighting had consolidated it.[132] Around midnight, however, Meade told Gibbon that his troops in the center of the Union line would be attacked if Lee went on the offensive the next day. Gibbon told Meade that if that occurred Lee would be defeated.[133]

Lee, however, saw things differently. Again ignoring the advice and pleas of Longstreet, Lee canceled early morning orders by Longstreet for a flank attack and instead ordered the suicidal assault that was to be known forever as Pickett's Charge.[134] After studying the ground over which the attack would occur, Longstreet said to Lee, "The 15,000 men who could make a successful assault over that field had never been arrayed for battle."[135] Longstreet was not alone in his bleak assessment of the chances for success. Brigadier General Ambrose "Rans" Wright said there would be no difficulty reaching Cemetery Ridge but that staying there was another matter because the "whole Yankee army is there in a bunch."[136] On the morning of the third, Brigadier General Cadmus Wilcox told his fellow brigadier, Richard Garnett, that the Union position was twice as strong as Gaines' Mill at the Seven Days' Battle.[137]

Unlike Lee, these generals realized that the combination of artillery, rifled infantry, and entrenchments would prove fatal to a Rebel assault.[138]

Demonstrating the extreme, almost blind, faith the Confederate troops had in Lee, Alexander commented that, "…like all the rest of the army I believed that it would come out right, because Gen. Lee had planned it."[139] But historian Bevin Alexander severely criticized Lee's ordering of Pickett's Charge: "When his direct efforts to knock aside the Union forces failed, Lee compounded his error by destroying the last offensive power of the Army of Northern Virginia in Pickett's charge across nearly a mile of open, bullet-and-shell-torn ground. This frontal assault was doomed before it started."[140] A few months later, Lee himself may have admitted that Longstreet's flanking plan was a better idea. [141] Historian Stephen Sears concluded that Lee's battle plan for July 3 was "barren and uninformed," based on ignorance of the condition of his army and the battlefield, and intended to win a battle of wills with Longstreet.[142]

The famous attack was preceded by a massive artillery exchange—so violent and loud that it was heard one hundred forty miles away. Just after 1:00 p.m., Alexander unleashed his 170 Rebel cannons against the Union forces on Cemetery Ridge. 200 Federal cannons responded. Across a mile of slightly rolling fields, the opposing cannons blasted away for ninety minutes. The Confederate goal was to soften up the Union line, particularly to weaken its defensive artillery capacity, prior to a massive assault on the center of that line. Instead of falling on the federal batteries, many of the Rebel shells sailed beyond their targets and fell on the Union rear, including General Meade's headquarters.

Alexander's cannonade continued until his supply of ammunition was dangerously low. A slowdown in the Union artillery response gave the false impression that the Confederate cannonade had inflicted serious damage. Although Alexander received some artillery assistance from

Hill's guns to Alexander's north, there were almost no rounds fired from Ewell's five artillery battalions northeast of the main Confederate line. Artillery fire was the one thing that Ewell certainly could have provided, but the Commanding General and his chief of artillery also failed to coordinate this facet of the offensive.[143] A simultaneous cavalry attack by Jeb Stuart's 6,000 troopers on the Union rear east of town was thwarted by the cavalry of Union Brigadier Generals David M. Gregg and George A. Custer.[144]

The time of decision and death was at hand for many of the 55,000 Confederates and 75,000 Yankees. The Rebels were about to assault a position that Alexander described as "almost as badly chosen as it was possible to be." His rationale:

> Briefly described, the point we attacked is upon the long shank of the fishhook of the enemy's position, & our advance was exposed to the fire of the whole length of that shank some two miles. Not only that, that shank is not perfectly straight, but it bends forward at the Round Top end, so that rifled guns there, in secure position, could & did enfilade the assaulting lines. Now add that the advance must be over 1,400 yards of open ground, none of it sheltered from fire, & very little from view, & without a single position for artillery where a battery could get its horses & caissons under cover.
>
> I think any military engineer would, instead, select for attack the bend of the fishhook just west of Gettysburg [Cemetery Hill]. There, at least, the assaulting lines cannot be enfiladed, and, on the other hand the places selected for assault may be enfiladed, & upon shorter ranges than any other parts of the Federal lines. Again there the assaulting column will only be exposed to the fire of the front less than

half, even if over one fourth, of the firing front upon the shank.[145]

Around 2:30 p.m., Alexander ordered a ceasefire and hurried a note off to General Longstreet. It said, "If you are coming at all, you must come at once or I cannot give you proper support, but the enemy's fire has not slackened at all. At least 18 guns are still firing from the cemetery itself." Longstreet, convinced of the impending disaster, could not bring himself to give a verbal attack order to Major General George E. Pickett. Instead he merely nodded his indication to proceed after Pickett asked him, "General, shall I advance?"[146] On the hidden western slopes of Seminary Ridge, nine brigades of 13,000 men began forming two mile-and-a-half-long lines for the assault on Cemetery Ridge. Pickett gave the order, "Up men, and to your posts! Don't forget today that you are from old Virginia!"[147] With that, they moved out.

After sending his "come at once" message, Alexander noticed a distinct pause in the firing from the cemetery and then clearly observed the withdrawal of artillery from that planned point of attack. Ten minutes after his earlier message and while Longstreet was silently assenting to the attack, Alexander sent a frantic note: "For God's sake come quick. The 18 guns are gone. Come quick or I can't support you."[148] To Alexander's chagrin, however, the Union Chief of Artillery Henry J. Hunt moved five replacement batteries into the crucial center of the line. What Alexander did not yet know was that the Union firing had virtually ceased in order to save ammunition to repel the coming attack. Hunt had seventy-seven short-range guns in the position the Rebels intended to attack, as well as numerous other guns, including long-range rifled artillery, along the line capable of raking an attacking army.

The Rebel lines opened ranks to pass their now-quiet batteries and swept on into the shallow valley between the two famous ridges. A gasp arose from Cemetery Ridge as the two long Gray lines, a hundred fifty yards apart, came into sight. It was three o'clock, the hottest time of a scorching day, and 40,000 Union soldiers were in position to directly contest the hopeless Confederate assault. Many defenders were sheltered by stone walls or wooden fences. Their awe at the impressive parade coming their way must have been mixed with an understandable fear of battle and a confidence in the strength of their numbers and position.

Their brave Rebel counterparts must have had increasing fear and decreasing confidence with every step they took toward the stronghold on Cemetery Ridge.[149] Their forty-seven regiments (including nineteen from Virginia and fourteen from North Carolina) initially traversed the valley in absolute silence except for the clunking of their wooden canteens. Although a couple of swales provided temporary shelter from most Union view and rifle fire, the Confederates were under constant observation from Little Round Top to the southeast. Long-range artillery fire began tearing holes in the Confederates' bodies and lines. Then they approached and turned slightly left to cross the Emmitsburg Pike. At that point, they had marched into the middle of a Union semicircle of rifles and cannon. They attempted to maintain their perfect parade order, but all hell broke loose as federal cannons exploded along the entire ridge line—from Cemetery Hill on the north to Little Round Top on the south.

The cannons' double loads of canister (pieces of iron) and Minié balls from 40,000 Union rifles cut down the Confederate front ranks. The slaughter was indescribably horrible, but the courageous Rebels closed ranks and marched on. Taking tremendous losses, they started up the final rise toward the copse of trees that was their goal. They had come so far that they were viciously assaulted from the front, both their flanks and even their rear. Especially devastating was the rifle fire from a Vermont brigade point-blank into the Rebel right flank. Gaping holes opened in Confederates' bodies and their now-merged lines, and their numbers dwindled to insignificance. The survivors let loose their Rebel yell and charged the trees near the center of Cemetery Ridge. With cries of "Fredericksburg," the men in blue decimated the remaining attackers with canister and Minié balls. General Armistead led the final surge. He and one hundred fifty others crossed the low stone wall, but all of them were killed, wounded or captured within minutes. Armistead was mortally wounded.

Just as the Union soldiers recognized a Fredericksburg-like scenario, General Lee at long last did so as well. From 1,700 yards away, he watched the smoke-shrouded death throes of his grand assault. He saw his Gray and Butternut troops disappear into the all-engulfing smoke on the ridge and then saw some of them emerge in retreat. Fewer than 7,000 of the original 13,000 were able to make their way through the carnage and return to Seminary Ridge. There was no covering fire from Alexander's cannon because he was saving his precious ammunition to repel the expected counterattack. As the survivors returned to the Confederate lines, Lee met them and sobbed, "It's all my fault this time."[150] It was.[151]

Lee and Longstreet tried to console Pickett, who was distraught about the slaughter of his men.[152] Lee told him that their gallantry had earned them a place in history, but Pickett responded: "All the glory in the world could never atone for the widows and orphans this day has made."[153] To his death, Pickett blamed Lee for the "massacre" of his division.[154]

The result of Lee's Day 3 strategy was one of the worst single-charge slaughters of the whole bloody war.[155] The Confederates suffered at least 7,500 casualties (5,600 killed and wounded) to the Union's 1,500. More than 1,000 Rebels were killed in a 30-minute bloodbath. Brigadier General Richard Garnett, whose five Virginia regiments led the assault, was killed, and 950 of his 1,450 men were killed or wounded. Virtually wiped out were three regiments, the 13th and 47th North Carolina and 18th Virginia.[156]

That night Lee rode alone among his troops. At one point he met Brigadier General John D. Imboden, who said, "General, this has been a hard day on you." Lee responded, "Yes, it has been a sad, sad day to us." He went on to praise Pettigrew and Pickett's men and then made the puzzling statement, "If they had been supported as they were to have been—but for some reason not fully explained to me were not—we would have held the position and the day would have been ours. Too bad. Too bad. Oh, too bad."[157] General Alexander found Lee's comment inexplicable since Lee personally had overseen the entire preparation and execution of the disastrous charge.[158] According to Gettysburg historian Gary Kross, Lee's biggest mistake probably was failing to use enough men for the attack.[159] In other words, Lee failed to send enough troops to have any chance of breaking the Union lines and sustaining the attack afterward. For the third time in twenty-four hours, Lee had overseen an ineffective, inadequately supported attack by about a third of his army.

Even if Lee was nonplussed, his officers had little difficulty seeing the folly of Pickett's Charge and its parallel to the senseless Union charges at Fredericksburg the previous December. Having lost over half his 10,500 men in the July 3 charge, Pickett submitted a battle report highly critical of that assault—and probably of Lee. Lee declined to accept the report and ordered it rewritten.[160] Pickett never did. Historian Russell Weigley saw Pickett's Charge as a mini-version of the history of Lee's army: "Those 15,000 Confederates who followed their red battleflags through solid shot, canister, grape shot, and minnie [sic] balls from Seminary to Cemetery Ridge on the humid afternoon of July 3, 1863, deserve all the romantic rhapsodizing they have received, for soldiers never fought more bravely to rescue so mistaken a strategic design. Much the same might be said for the whole tragic career of the Army of Northern Virginia."[161]

The only saving grace for Lee's battered army was that General Meade, believing his mission was not to lose rather than to win, failed to immediately follow up his victory with an infantry counterattack on the stunned and disorganized Confederates. To Lincoln's chagrin, Meade developed a case of the "slows" reminiscent of McClellan after Antietam and took nine days to pursue and catch Lee, who was burdened by a seventeen-mile ambulance train carrying 12,700 of his wounded.[162] After missing his chance for a quick and decisive strike, Meade wisely did not attack Lee's strongly entrenched position at Williamsport, Maryland, on the Potomac River. As the Confederates waited to cross, their officers hoped for a Union assault: "Now we have Meade where we want him. If he attacks us here, we will pay him back for Gettysburg. But the Old Fox is too cunning."[163] Similarly, Alexander recalled: " … oh! how we all did wish that the enemy would come out in the open & attack us, as we had done them at Gettysburg. But they had had their lesson, in that sort of game, at Fredbg. [Fredericksburg] & did not care for another."[164] Lee's army crossed the receding river and returned ignominiously to Virginia.[165] Even the retreat from Gettysburg had been costly for Lee's army; they suffered more than 5,000 casualties to their opponents' more than 1,000.[166]

General Alexander concluded, "Then perhaps in taking the aggressive at all at Gettysburg in 1863 & certainly in the place & dispositions for the assault on the 3rd day, I think, it will undoubtedly be held that [Lee] unnecessarily took the most desperate chances & the bloodiest road."[167] Similarly, Wade Hampton wrote:

> To fight an enemy superior in numbers at such a terrible
> disadvantage of position in the heart of his own territory,

when freedom of movement gave him the advantage of accepting his own time and place for accepting battle, seems to have been a great military blunder… the position of the Yankees there was the strongest I ever saw… we let Meade choose the position and then we attacked.[168]

After the war, Lee provided his rationale for having attacked on the second and third days at Gettysburg:

> It had not been intended to deliver a general battle so far from our base unless attacked, but coming unexpectedly upon the whole Federal Army, to withdraw through the mountains with our extensive trains would have been difficult and dangerous. At the same time we were unable to await an attack, as the country was unfavorable for collecting supplies in the presence of the enemy who could restrain our foraging parties by holding the mountain passes with local and other troops. A battle had therefore become, in a measure, unavoidable, and the success already gained gave hope of a favorable issue.[169]

Lee, in fact, had not come upon "the whole Federal army." That whole army was not on the battlefield until late on the second day of the Gettysburg struggle. Later, even after suffering three days of terrible losses, Lee in fact was able to retreat safely through the mountains after the three-day battle. In addition, Lee's army managed to live off the country north of the Potomac for nine more days. Thus, Lee's rationale justifies neither his series of frontal attacks on the second day nor the suicidal charge on the third day.[170] Historian Troy D. Harmon recently contended that Lee consistently strove at Gettysburg to sever the Union salient on Cemetery Hill.[171] If that was his plan, his disjointed attacks failed to achieve that objective. It is easier to sympathize with Porter Alexander's assessment that "Never, never, never did Gen. Lee himself bollox a fight as he did this."[172]

A recent analysis of Gettysburg's results by James McPherson questions the high cost to the Confederates:

> But we might ask whether [Confederates' Gettysburg] spoils were worth the 28,000 or more casualties suffered by Confederates in the campaign as a whole, including the nightmare retreat. Of this number at least 18,000 men were gone for good from the Army of Northern Virginia—dead, imprisoned, or so badly wounded that they could never fight again. And we might also ask whether, even though Gettysburg was not a decisive turning point toward imminent Union victory, it might have been a decisive turning point away from a Confederate victory that could have demoralized the Army of the Potomac and the Northern people and might also have neutralized the loss of Vicksburg.[173]

Lee's strategic campaign into the North had reaped its inevitable result, the appearance of defeat, and an unforeseen actual military defeat. Rhode Islander Elisha Hunt Rhodes' July 9 diary entry typified Northern elation over Gettysburg: "I wonder what the South thinks of us Yankees now. I think Gettysburg will cure the Rebels of any desire to invade the North again."[174] Historian Archer Jones provided this analysis: "Lee... suffered a costly defeat in a three-day battle at Gettysburg. In losing perhaps as many as 28,000 men to the North's 23,000, the battle became a disaster of depletion for the Confederate Army, and his inevitable retreat to Virginia, seemingly the result of the battle rather than his inability to forage, made it a serious political defeat also."[175]

Considering the nearly equal number of combatants at Gettysburg, Lee's losses were staggering in both absolute and relative terms. Of the 75,000 Confederates, 22,600 (30 percent) were killed or wounded. The toll of general officers was appalling: six dead, eight wounded, and three captured. Just as significantly, the Southern field grade officers suffered very high casualties, and their absence would be felt for the duration of the war.[176] Of the 83,300 Union troops at Gettysburg, 17,700 (21 percent) were killed or wounded.[177] Total Rebel casualties were about 28,000, while Union casualties were about 23,000.[178] Despite the fact that his losses were higher in absolute and proportional terms, Lee told Davis, "Our loss has been very heavy, that of the enemy's is proportionally so."[179]

The Richmond papers, and thus many others in the South, initially reported Gettysburg as a Confederate victory.[180] Thus the South did not at first realize the extent of its losses in Pennsylvania. By July 31 Lee had deluded himself into calling the campaign a "general success."[181] A Virginia private who had fought at Gettysburg wrote his sister with a different view: "We got a bad whiping… they are awhiping us… at every point… I hope they would make peace so that we that is alive yet would get home agane… but I supose Jef Davis and Lee don't care if all is killed."[182]

Regardless of what was known when, Lee's strategy and tactics at Gettysburg were the same he had employed for the entire thirteen months he had commanded the Army of Northern Virginia. He attacked too often, and too often he initiated frontal attacks. Lee's approach had resulted in a terrible toll of death and injury. When he assumed command in June 1862, his army numbered about 80,000. In the next fourteen months, he had that many troops killed and wounded. From the Seven Days' through Cedar Mountain, Second Manassas, Chantilly, South Mountain, Antietam, Fredericksburg, Chancellorsville, and finally

Gettysburg, Lee's little army had suffered about 80,000 killed and wounded (an average of 19.2 percent per battle) while inflicting about 73,000 deaths and injuries (13.2 percent per battle) on the enemy.[183] Having lost the equivalent of the army he had inherited (a total casualty rate of over 100 percent), Lee was dependent on reinforcements from elsewhere for his army's survival.

Not only had the outnumbered army of Lee suffered more casualties in absolute terms, its percentages of losses relative to those of the Federals were staggering. During the Seven Days' Battle, Lee's army had 21 percent killed or wounded (to the enemy's 11 percent), at Second Manassas it lost 19 percent (to the Federals' 13 percent), at Antietam Lee lost an appalling 23 percent (to the "attacking" McClellan's 16 percent), at Fredericksburg Lee's generally entrenched forces lost only 6 percent (to Burnside's 11 percent), in his Chancellorsville "victory" Lee lost 19 percent (to Joe Hooker's 11 percent), and then at Gettysburg came the crushing three-day loss of 30 percent of Lee's remaining troops (to Meade's loss of 21 percent).[184] Lee's offensive strategy and tactics were causing his seriously undermanned army to lose irreplaceable troops at an unsustainable rate—a casualty rate far greater than that of his stronger opponent. Lee was fighting as though he had unlimited resources; he was fighting as though he were a Union general with the burden of winning, not stalemating, the war.

British Colonel Fremantle discussed the flaw of Lee's aggressiveness: "Don't you see your system feeds upon itself? You cannot fill the places of these men. Your troops do wonders, but every time at a cost you cannot afford."[185] Lee's own General Harvey Hill similarly described the folly of the Army of Northern Virginia's penchant for the tactical offensive: "We were very lavish of blood in those days, and it was thought to be a very great thing to charge a battery of artillery or an earth-work lined with infantry... The attacks on the Beaver Dam intrenchments, on the heights of Malvern Hill, at Gettysburg, etc., were all grand, but of exactly the kind of grandeur which the South could not afford."[186] All of the attacks mentioned by Hill had been personally ordered by Lee.

In a little over a year, therefore, Lee's army had lost as many men as it had on its rolls when he took command and was losing its strength at a far faster rate than its manpower-rich foe. While the North, with its four-to-one manpower advantage, could afford its casualties and replace the men it lost, Lee's aggression had seriously depleted the supply of Confederate men of fighting age in the East, drained men from the rest of the Confederacy, and made his ultimate military defeat inevitable— unless Lincoln lost the war at the ballot box in 1864.

In summary, Gettysburg demonstrated all of Lee's weaknesses. He initiated an unnecessary strategic offensive that, because of his army's inevitable return to Virginia, would be perceived as a retreat and thus a defeat. He rejected alternative uses for Longstreet's corps that could have avoided or mitigated critical losses of the Mississippi River (including Vicksburg and then Port Hudson, Louisiana) and middle and south- eastern Tennessee (including Chattanooga). His tactics were inexcusably and fatally aggressive on days two and three, he failed to take charge of the battlefield on any of the three days, his battle plans were ineffective, and his orders (especially to Stuart and Ewell) were vague and too dis- cretionary. Particularly concerning the Stuart fiasco, historian Patrick Brennan concluded, "Ill-defined objectives, contradictory orders, over- confidence, and poor use of resources all conspired to embarrass Lee's operation, much of it traceable to the army commander himself and his staff."[187] Gettysburg thus was Lee at his worst.

Not only would Lee's entire Army of Northern Virginia never again invade the North; it had been so damaged that it had become vulnerable to a war of attrition. All hope of foreign intervention ended as England and France even halted deliveries on ships to the Confederates.[188] That

European action was influenced not only by Lee's Gettysburg Campaign itself but by the cumulative impact of the western and middle theater losses that were facilitated by Lee's refusal to provide troops elsewhere. Confederate Ordnance Chief Josiah Gorgas, on July 28, bemoaned the rapid change of Rebel fortunes resulting from its defeats at Vicksburg, Port Hudson, and Gettysburg:

> Lee failed at Gettysburg, and has recrossed the Potomac & resumed the position of two months ago, covering Richmond. Alas! he has lost fifteen thousand men and twenty-five thousand stands of arms. Vicksburgh and Port Hudson capitulated, surrendering thirty five thousand men and forty-five thousand arms. It seems incredible that human power could effect such a change in so brief a space. Yesterday we rode on the pinnacle of success—to-day absolute ruin seems to be our portion. The Confederacy totters to its destruction.[189]

GRANT CAPTURES VICKSBURG AND ANOTHER REBEL ARMY

For a full appreciation of the mid-1863 damage done by Lee and the contrasting successes of Grant, it is necessary to examine Grant's brilliant Vicksburg Campaign. During the spring and early summer of 1863, Grant carried out the finest campaign of the Civil War and one of the greatest campaigns in military history. Two of the Civil War's best historians shared that view. James M. McPherson called the Vicksburg Campaign "the most brilliant and innovative campaign of the Civil War," and T. Harry Williams called it "one of the classic campaigns of the Civil War and, indeed, of military history." In fact, the *U.S. Army Field Manual*

100–5 (May 1986) described it as "the most brilliant campaign ever fought on American soil" and said "It exemplifies the qualities of a well-conceived, violently executed offensive plan."[190]

Vicksburg, the Gibraltar of the West, was the key to Union control of the Mississippi. It and Port Hudson to its south were the only remaining Confederate strongholds on the river. Early in the war, Lincoln himself had pinpointed Vicksburg's importance when he pointed to a national map and said, "See what a lot of land these fellows hold, of which Vicksburg is the key. The war can never be brought to a close until that key is in our pocket."[191]

Having been stymied in his earlier efforts to reach and capture Vicksburg, Grant decided to march his army southward down the west bank of the Mississippi to get well below Vicksburg. He planned to load his men on transports that would first have to be floated past the guns of Vicksburg, transport his army to the Mississippi shore south of Vicksburg, strike inland against any Confederate forces brought to bear, and eventually strike and capture Vicksburg. He had spent months poring over maps and charts to singlehandedly devise this approach. This daring plan was opposed as too risky by Grant's strong subordinate commanders, including Sherman, McPherson, and Logan. Yet, Grant would carry out his campaign plan and thereby accomplish phenomenal achievements with a surprisingly small loss of Union personnel.[192]

Grant was hindered during his Vicksburg planning by McClernand, a disloyal corps commander who had lobbied and continued to lobby for Grant's job. McClernand's efforts included the by-then familiar efforts to accuse Grant of being intoxicated on the job. When those rumors again reached Washington, Assistant Secretary of War Charles A. Dana was sent to observe Grant. Ironically, Dana soon became an admirer of Grant and one of his most effective supporters during the Vicksburg Campaign and the rest of the war.[193]

Vicksburg was a fortified bastion. Surrounded by fortifications (including nine major forts or citadels), the city had one hundred seventy-two guns that commanded all approaches by water and land. It was protected by a 30,000-troop garrison. Grant had three options for attacking it: (1) return to Memphis for an overland approach from the north and east, (2) cross the river and directly assault the city, or (3) march his troops down the west bank of the Mississippi, cross the Mississippi, and approach the city from the south and east. Grant rejected the first option because going back would be morale-deflating (Grant hated to retrace his steps) and the second because it involved, Grant said, "immense sacrifice of life, if not defeat." Historian Edwin C. Bearss said, "The third alternative was full of dangers and risks. Failure in this venture would entail little less than total destruction. If it succeeded, however, the gains would be complete and decisive."[194]

Early April brought receding waters and the emergence of roads from Milliken's Bend northwest of Vicksburg to other west bank points on the Mississippi downstream from that city. Grant planned to march his troops over those roads to a location where he could ferry them to the east bank of the river. To do that, he had to enlist the support of Admiral Porter to get steamships and transport vessels from north of Vicksburg past that city to the location where Grant's troops would be awaiting ferry transportation.[195]

The cooperative Porter agreed to Grant's plan and eagerly set about organizing the vessels for a maritime parade past Vicksburg. He warned Grant that the ironclad vessels could not return upstream against the strong currents past Vicksburg's guns—that this transit would be the point of no return. In preparation for the transit, Porter directed that boilers on the steamships be hidden and protected by barriers of cotton and hay bales, as well as bags of grain. Beginning at 10:00 p.m. on April

16, Porter led the fleet of seven ironclad gunboats, four steamers, and an assortment of towed coal barges downstream. Coal barges and excess vessels were lashed to the sides of critical vessels to provide additional protection.[196] Confederate bonfires illuminated the Union vessels, which were under fire for two hours as they ran the gauntlet past the Vicksburg guns. Those guns fired five hundred twenty-five rounds and scored sixty-eight hits. Miraculously, only one vessel was lost, and no one on the vessels was killed.[197] Grant now had his basic marine transportation in place.[198]

Fortunately, Rebel General Pemberton at Vicksburg did not connect the passage of Porter's vessels with the possibility of a Union march down the west bank and an amphibious crossing. Back in Richmond, Lee told Davis that Grant "can derive no material benefit" from Porter's movement and predicted that the addition of more artillery at Vicksburg would prevent Porter from repeating his performance. In contrast, a nineteen-year-old Vicksburg gunner perceptively wrote in his diary, "Their object, I think, in going below is to cross troops and try and get in the rear of Vicksburg."[199]

Beginning on March 31, Grant had started McClernand's four-division corps on the land route from Milliken's Bend to New Carthage below Vicksburg. Construction of the narrow line of advance and supply down the west bank required backbreaking canal digging, road building and repairing, and bridge building. After the transports had slipped by Vicksburg, Grant visited New Carthage on April 17 and approved an alternate but longer 40-mile west bank route to Perkins' Plantation, twelve miles south of New Carthage. Preparing the way for this march required building four bridges totaling 2,000 feet across bayous.[200]

Grant returned to Milliken's Bend and, on April 20, issued Special Orders No. 110 for the march by his entire army. McClernand's 13th

Corps was to be followed by McPherson's 17th, and then Sherman's 15th.[201] On the critical issue of gathering supplies, Grant's order stated:

> Commanders are authorized and enjoined to collect all the beef cattle, corn and other necessary supplies on the line of march; but wanton destruction of property, taking of articles useless for military purposes, insulting citizens, going into and searching houses without proper orders from division commanders, are positively prohibited. All such irregularities must be summarily punished.

Realizing that the area of their intended operations and the single line of march were inadequate to fully supply his troops, Grant ordered a second collection of vessels to bring some additional supplies south past Vicksburg. Thus, on the night of April 22, six more protected steamers towing twelve barges loaded with rations steamed past Vicksburg under the command of Colonel Clark Lagow of Grant's staff. Despite Lee's prediction, five of the steamers and half of the barges made it through the gauntlet of artillery batteries, which fired three hundred ninety-one rounds. Most of the vessels were commanded and manned by army volunteers from "Black Jack" Logan's division because the civilian vessel crews did not want to run the Vicksburg gauntlet.[202]

Grant now had all his vessels (seven transports and fifteen or sixteen barges), a modicum of supplies, and a gathering invasion force. Sherman and Porter had serious doubts about the viability of eventually supplying Grant's army via a poor, swampy road on the west bank of the Mississippi River and then across the river and into Mississippi. Nevertheless, Grant pressed forward with his plan and started McPherson's corps south from New Carthage on April 25.[203]

Meanwhile Grant had created four diversions to the north and east of Vicksburg to deflect Confederate attention from his campaign plans.

First, he had sent Major General Frederick Steele's troops in transports one hundred miles northward up the Mississippi River toward Greenville, Mississippi. This movement led General Pemberton in Vicksburg to conclude that Grant was retreating (to reinforce Rosecrans in eastern Tennessee) and to allow about 8,000 Rebel troops to be transferred from Mississippi back to Bragg in Tennessee.[204]

Second, Grant had initiated a cavalry raid from Tennessee to Louisiana through the length of central and eastern Mississippi. Incurring a mere handful of casualties, Colonel Benjamin H. Grierson conducted the most effective strategic cavalry raid of the entire war. Grant had devised this diversionary mission back on February 13, when he sent the following simple, flexible, and brilliant suggestion in a dispatch to Hurlbut in Tennessee:

> It seems to me that Grierson with about 500 picked men might succeed in making his way South and cut the rail-road East of Jackson Miss. The undertaking would be a hazardous [*sic*] one but it would pay well if carried out. I do not direct that this shall be done but leave it for a volunteer enterprise.

On April 17, Grierson rode out of LaGrange, Tennessee, in command of 1,700 cavalrymen and a six-gun battery.[205]

In the early days of the raid, Grierson deftly split off part of his force, primarily to confuse the Confederates as to his location and intentions. First, on April 20, he sent one hundred seventy-five men determined to be incapable of completing the mission (the "Quinine Brigade") and a gun back to LaGrange with prisoners and captured property. Then the next day he sent a regiment and another gun east to break up the north/south Mobile & Ohio Railroad and to create even more confusion. To ensure that significant enemy forces were not present in towns that he raided, Grierson assembled a group of nine handpicked men, the

"Butternut Guerillas," who scouted ahead dressed in Confederate uniforms and clothes.[206]

With another detached force drawing substantial Confederate infantry and cavalry away from his main force, Grierson continued south to the east/west railroad in the heart of Mississippi. There he destroyed two trains (both filled with ammunition and commissary stores), tore up the railroad, and tore down the telegraph line—both linking Meridian to the east with Jackson and Vicksburg to the west. With the disruption of the key railroad to Vicksburg and the destruction of millions of dollars worth of Confederate assets (including thirty-eight railcars), Grierson's mission was complete—except for his final escape.[207]

Pemberton, who had sent troops to head off Grierson before he reached the railroad, sent additional soldiers to try to cut off the escape of the raiders.[208] The raid's effect on Pemberton is reflected in the fact that on April 27 he sent seventeen messages to Mississippi commands about Grierson's raiders and not a single one about Grant's buildup on the west bank of the Mississippi River. By April 29, Pemberton had further played into Grant's hands by sending all his cavalry in pursuit of Grierson; he advised his superiors: "The telegraph wires are down. The enemy has, therefore, either landed on this side of the Mississippi River, or they have been cut by Grierson's cavalry… All the cavalry I can raise is close on their rear."[209]

Sixteen days and six hundred miles after starting their dangerous venture, Grierson's men rode south out of Mississippi and reached the safety of Union lines at Baton Rouge, Louisiana, on May 2—two days after Grant's amphibious landing at Bruinsburg on the Mississippi. They had survived several close calls, created havoc in their wake, and performed their primary mission of diverting attention from Grant's movements west and south of Vicksburg. They had inflicted one hundred casualties and captured over five hundred prisoners. Miraculously, all this had been accomplished with fewer than twenty-five casualties. There was good reason for Sherman to call it the "most brilliant expedition of the Civil War."[210]

Grant's third diversion involved another cavalry foray. At the same time as Grierson traveled the length of Mississippi, other Union forces went on the offensive far to the east. Colonel Abel D. Streight led a "poorly mounted horse and mule brigade" from Middle Tennessee into Alabama and drew the ever-dangerous cavalry of Nathan Bedford Forrest away from Grierson and his various detachments.[211]

To completely confuse Pemberton, Grant used a fourth diversion. While he was moving south with McClernand and McPherson on the west bank (Louisiana shore), Grant had Sherman's 15th Corps threaten Vicksburg from the north. On April 27, Grant directed Sherman to proceed up the Yazoo River and threaten the bluffs northeast of Vicksburg. On April 29, Sherman debarked ten regiments of troops and appeared to be preparing an assault while eight naval gunboats bombarded the Confederate forts at Haines' Bluff. Having suffered no casualties, Sherman withdrew on May 1 to hastily follow McPherson down the west bank of the Mississippi. His troops were ferried across the river on May 6 and 7.[212]

Grant, meanwhile, had joined McClernand at New Carthage on the west bank on April 23. Grant next ordered the troops to proceed south another twenty-two miles to Hard Times, a west bank area directly across the river from Grand Gulf, Mississippi. Ten thousand soldiers were moved farther south by vessel, and the rest of the men bridged three bayous and completed their trek to Hard Times by April 27. Although on April 28 Confederate Brigadier General John S. Bowen at Grand Gulf could see the Union armada gathering across the river and urgently requested reinforcements from Pemberton in Vicksburg, Pemberton was focused on Grierson and Sherman. Thus he refused to send

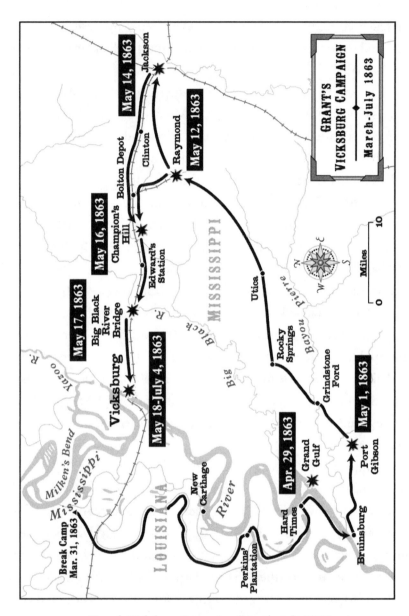

Grant's Vicksburg Campaign (March–July 1863)
Map by David Deis, Dreamline Cartography, Northridge, CA

reinforcements south toward Grand Gulf until late on April 29—when they were too late to halt the amphibious crossing.[213]

On April 29, with 10,000 of McClernand's troops embarked on vessels for a possible east bank landing, Porter's eight gunboats attacked the Confederate batteries on the high bluffs at Grand Gulf. After five and a half hours and the loss of eighteen killed and about fifty-seven wounded, the Union fleet had eliminated the guns of Fort Wade but not those of Fort Coburn, which stood forty feet above the river and had a forty-foot-thick parapet. A disappointed Grant watched from a small tugboat, and Porter eventually halted the attack.[214]

The persistent Grant, however, did not give up; he simply moved south. That night, the 10,000 troops left the vessels and marched across a peninsula while Porter slipped all of his vessels past the Confederate guns. Grant sent orders that night to Sherman to immediately head south with two of his three divisions. On the morning of April 30, Grant moved across and down the Mississippi to Bruinsburg, Mississippi, and landed troops without opposition.[215] In his memoirs, Grant explained the great relief he felt after the successful landing:

> When this was effected I felt a degree of relief scarcely ever equalled since. Vicksburg was not yet taken it is true, nor were its defenders demoralized by any of our previous moves. I was now in the enemy's country, with a vast river and the stronghold of Vicksburg between me and my base of supplies. But I was on dry ground on the same side of the river with the enemy. All the campaigns, labors, hardships and exposures from the month of December previous to this time that had been made and endured, were for the accomplishment of this one object.[216]

Under the cover of several diversions, Grant had daringly marched his army through Louisiana bayous down the west bank of the Mississippi and launched one of the largest amphibious operations (involving 24,000 troops) ever conducted prior to D-Day on June 6, 1944. Historian Terrence J. Winschel concluded:

> The movement [down the west bank] was boldly conceived and executed by a daring commander willing to take risks. The sheer audacity of the movement demonstrated Grant's firmness of purpose and revealed his many strengths as a commander. The bold and decisive manner in which he directed the movement set the tone for the campaign and inspired confidence in the army's ranks.[217]

The first day ashore, Grant pushed McClernand two miles inland to high, dry ground and then onward toward the town of Port Gibson, which had a bridge across Big Bayou Pierre that led to Grand Gulf (which Grant coveted as a supply base on the Mississippi). Meanwhile, Grant oversaw the continuous transport of more of his troops across the Mississippi well into the night. Aided by the light of huge bonfires, McPherson's soldiers were transported until a 3:00 a.m. collision between two transports stopped the operation until daylight.[218]

Back upriver Sherman was beginning to move south but remained skeptical of the feasibility of the long, vulnerable supply line. There was reason to be skeptical. As historian James R. Arnold observed, "Grant was at the end of an exceedingly precarious supply line, isolated in hostile territory, positioned between Port Hudson and Vicksburg—two well-fortified, enemy-held citadels—outnumbered by his enemy, and with an un-fordable river to his rear. Few generals would have considered this anything but a trap. Grant judged it an opportunity."[219]

The next day, May 1, brought conflict and the first of Grant's five victories in battles leading to the siege of Vicksburg: the Battle of Port Gibson.[220] Two Confederate brigades, which had belatedly marched as many as forty-four miles from near Vicksburg, and the garrison from Grand Gulf had crossed the bridge over the North Fork of Bayou Pierre at Port Gibson. They confronted McClernand's troops about three miles west of Port Gibson. The Confederate left fell back under intense attack from three of McClernand's divisions as Union sharpshooters picked off the brave and effective Rebel gunners manning the defenders' artillery. Following the initial Rebel retreat, McClernand and visiting Illinois Governor Yates delivered victory remarks and did some politicking with the troops. Grant put an end to those proceedings and ordered the advance to resume. Meanwhile, Grant had reinforced McClernand's left wing with two of McPherson's brigades, and that wing similarly drove the Confederates back toward Port Gibson in the face of Confederate artillery. Victory was confirmed the next morning (May 2), when Grant's soldiers found Port Gibson abandoned by the Confederates, who had crossed and burned the bridges across Big Bayou Pierre (to Grand Gulf) and Little Bayou Pierre.[221] Although Grant's troops were on the offensive all day at Port Gibson, the two sides' casualties were surprisingly comparable—almost nine hundred each.[222]

Despite narrow roads, hilly terrain, and dense vegetation that aided the defenders, Grant's superior force had gained the inland foothold it needed and access to the interior. The battle set the tone for those that followed in the campaign and affected the morale of the winners and losers. Through deception and celerity, Grant would consistently outnumber his foes on five battlefields in eighteen days although his troops were outnumbered by the Confederates scattered around western Mississippi. That concentration of force proved decisive. From Vicksburg, Pemberton accurately and somewhat desperately telegraphed

Richmond: "A furious battle has been going on since daylight just below Port Gibson…. Enemy's movement threatens Jackson, and, if successful, cuts off Vicksburg and Port Hudson from the east…" With minimal losses, Grant was moving inland. Meanwhile, a rattled Pemberton sent an urgent message to his field commanders directing them to proceed at once—but neglecting to say to where.[223]

After his troops had quickly built a bridge across Little Bayou Pierre, Grant accompanied McPherson northeast to Grindstone Ford, the site of the next bridge across Big Bayou Pierre. Fortunately, they found the bridge still burning and only partially destroyed. They made rapid repairs and crossed Big Bayou Pierre. Because Grant was now in a position to cut off Grand Gulf, the Confederates abandoned that river town and retreated north toward Vicksburg. At Hankinson's Ferry, north of Grand Gulf, the Confederates retreated across a raft bridge over the Big Black River, the only remaining geographical barrier between Grant and Vicksburg.[224]

On May 3, as Lee was finishing the Battle of Chancellorsville, Grant rode into the abandoned and ruined town of Grand Gulf, boarded the *Louisville*, took his first bath in a week, caught up on his correspondence, and rethought his mission. He had learned of the successful completion of Grierson's diversionary mission[225] and also of the time-consuming campaign of General Nathaniel P. Banks up the Red River. He decided to deviate radically from his orders, which called for him to send McPherson's corps south to Port Hudson to await the return of Banks and cooperate with Banks in the capture of Port Hudson—all of this before a decisive move on Vicksburg. Grant realized that he would lose about a month waiting to cooperate with Banks in taking Port Hudson, he would gain only about 12,000 troops from Banks, and the intervening time would give Confederates the opportunity to gather reinforcements from all over the South to save Vicksburg. Instead, Grant decided to move inland with McPherson's and McClernand's corps, and he ordered Sherman to continue moving south to join him with two of his three divisions.[226]

Therefore, before leaving Grand Gulf at midnight on May 3, Grant wrote to Halleck:

> The country will supply all the forage required for anything like an active campaign and the necessary fresh beef. Other supplies will have to be drawn from [the west bank]. This is a long and precarious route but I have every confidance [*sic*] in succeeding in doing it.
>
> I shall not bring my troops into this place but immediately follow the enemy, and if all promises as favorably hereafter as it does now, not stop until Vicksburg is in our possession.[227]

Grant was going for Vicksburg—now! Until Sherman's troops arrived, Grant had only 25,000 troops across the river to face 50,000 Confederates in Mississippi with as many as another 20,000 on the way.[228]

When he moved inland to Hankinson's Ferry at daybreak on May 4, Grant learned that McPherson's men had captured intact the bridge across the Big Black River and established a bridgehead on the opposite shore. While awaiting the arrival of Sherman's corps, Grant ordered McPherson and McClernand to probe the countryside, and the former's patrols discovered that the Confederates were fortifying a defensive line south of Vicksburg. Their patrols also were designed to create the impression that Grant would directly attack Vicksburg from the south. With the arrival of Sherman and the bulk of his corps on May 6 and 7, Grant was ready to move in force.[229]

Realizing that Vicksburg by now was well defended on the south and that its defenders could flee to the northeast if he attacked from the south, Grant decided on a more promising—but riskier—course of action. In the words of historian T. Harry Williams, "Then the general called dull and unimaginative and a mere hammerer executed one of the fastest and boldest moves in the records of war."[230] He cut loose from his base at Grand Gulf, withdrew McPherson from north of the Big Black River, and ordered all three of his corps to head northeast between the Big Black on the left and Big Bayou Pierre on the right. His goal was to follow the Big Black, cut the east/west railroad between Vicksburg and the state capital of Jackson, and then move west along the railroad to Vicksburg. In what historian Thomas Buell called "the most brilliant decision of his career," Grant "would attack first Johnston and then Pemberton before they could unite and thereby outnumber him, the classic example of defeating an enemy army in detail."[231]

Given the poor condition of the dirt roads, the tenuous supply situation, and the threat of Confederate interference from many directions, according to Vicksburg Campaign expert Ed Bearss, Grant's "decision to move northeast along the Big Black-Big Bayou Pierre watershed was boldness personified, and Napoleonic in its concept."[232] Historian William B. Feis concluded: "From the outset, Grant designed his movements to sow uncertainty in Pemberton's mind as to the true federal objective. The key to success, especially deep in Confederate territory, was to maintain the initiative and make the enemy guess at his objectives."[233] Noteworthy is Grant's determination to not only occupy Vicksburg but to trap Pemberton's army rather than allow it to escape to fight again. Historian Gary Ecelberger observed, "If successful Grant's strategy would not only control the city and free the Mississippi River, it was destined to force the annihilation or surrender of the Confederate troops defending it."[234]

As he would do later in Virginia, Grant stayed focused on defeating, capturing, or destroying the opposing army—not simply occupying geographic positions. Military historian Fuller pointed out that Grant's plan not only was daring and contrary to his instructions from Halleck, but that, just as importantly, he insisted that his commanders move with haste to execute it. His orders to them in those early days of May were filled with words urging them to implement his orders expeditiously. He clearly wanted to move quickly inland to negate any forces other than Pemberton's, destroy Vicksburg's supply line, and then quickly turn on Vicksburg with his own rear protected.[235]

As Grant moved inland, he planned to live off the previously unsacked countryside. His troops slaughtered livestock and harvested crops and gardens to obtain food and fodder. They also gathered an eclectic collection of buggies and carriages to assemble a crude and heavily guarded wagon train that would carry salt, sugar, hard bread, ammunition, and other crucial supplies from Grand Gulf to Grant's army. Grant would depend on those intermittent and vulnerable wagon trains to meet some of his needs for two weeks until a regular supply line was opened on the Yazoo River north of Vicksburg on May 21.[236]

From May 8 to 12, Grant's army moved out of its Grand Gulf beachhead and up this corridor with McClernand hugging the Big Black on the left and guarding all the ferries, Sherman in the center, and McPherson on the right. They gradually swung in a more northerly direction and moved within a few miles of the critical railroad without serious opposition. Then, on May 12, McPherson ran into stiff opposition south of the town of Raymond.[237] Aggressive assaults ordered by Confederate Brigadier General John Gregg, who believed he was facing a single brigade, threw McPherson's soldiers into disarray. Strong counterattacks led by Logan drove the outnumbered Confederates back into and through Raymond. Gregg's aggressiveness cost him eight hundred twenty casualties. McPherson reported four hundred forty-two casualties. Grant's campaign of maneuver and his concentration of force were resulting in progress at the cost of moderate casualties.[238]

Even more significantly, Grant's daring crossing of the Mississippi and inland thrust were wreaking havoc at the highest levels of the Confederacy. Pemberton, in command at Vicksburg, was caught between conflicting orders from President Jefferson Davis and Johnston. Davis told Pemberton that holding Vicksburg and Port Hudson was critical to connecting the eastern Confederacy to the Trans-Mississippi. The Northern-born Pemberton, who had been eased out of his Charleston, South Carolina, command for suggesting evacuation of that city, decided to obey the president and defend Vicksburg at all costs. He did this despite May 1 and 2 orders from Johnston that, if Grant crossed the Mississippi, Pemberton should unite all his troops to defeat him. Grant was the beneficiary of Pemberton's decision because Pemberton kept his fifteen brigades in scattered defensive positions behind the Big Black River while Grant moved away from them toward Jackson. Johnston belatedly moved from Tennessee to Pemberton's aid.[239]

The battle at Raymond caused Grant to realize the seriousness of the Confederate threat to his right flank—and then to his rear—if he simply continued north to the railroad and then turned west toward Vicksburg. He had received reports that Johnston had arrived in Jackson and reinforcements from the east and south were headed for that town. Jackson was the obvious rail junction for Confederate troops and supplies headed for Vicksburg. Thus, Grant decided to attack Jackson and eliminate it and the troops there as a threat to his Vicksburg campaign. On the evening of May 12, therefore, he issued orders for McPherson and Sherman to move on Jackson. They threatened Jackson by nightfall on May 13.[240]

That very evening Johnston arrived at Jackson. Advised by Gregg that Union troops were astride the railroad to Vicksburg, that only 6,000 Confederate troops were in the Jackson vicinity, and that Confederate reinforcements were on the way, Johnston hoped to assemble 12,000 troops at Jackson within a day and trap Grant between Pemberton's force and his. To accomplish this, he sent three couriers with messages directing Pemberton to organize a converging attack and, if practicable, attack the federal troops at Clinton. He stressed that "Time is all important." In a concurrent telegram to Seddon, Johnston concluded by saying, "I am too late."[241] In light of Grant's initiative and Pemberton's hesitance to carry out Johnston's order or abandon Vicksburg, Johnston was indeed too late.[242] Partly because Grant's spy network had advised him of Johnston's arrival and plans for reinforcement, Grant did not hesitate to continue his expedited offensive.[243]

Because of Grant's concentration of force at Jackson and despite torrential downpours, his troops were able to drive the Confederates from Jackson in less than a day of battle on May 14.[244] McPherson fought his way in from the west and Sherman from the southwest; they occupied the city by mid-afternoon. Jackson cost the Union about three hundred casualties while the Confederates suffered an estimated five hundred casualties and the loss of seventeen cannon. Confederate industrial losses in Jackson were significant. Johnston himself burned all the city's cotton and five million dollars in railroad rolling stock; Sherman followed that up by burning an arsenal, foundries, machine shops, and cotton factories and warehouses. During the assault, Pemberton spent the day probing southeast of Vicksburg for Grant's virtually nonexistent line of communication with Grand Gulf, and Johnston retreated from Jackson to the north away from Pemberton's movement. Even worse for the Rebels, Johnston turned back reinforcements that were moving toward Jackson by rail.[245]

Grant then learned from McPherson that one of Johnston's three couriers carrying his May 12 "attack" message to Pemberton was a Union spy. Thus, Grant learned of Johnston's order and immediately turned his army westward to deal with Pemberton. He ordered McClernand to

Bolton Station (Bolton Depot), about twenty miles west of Jackson and the nearest point to Jackson on the railroad where Johnston might merge his and Pemberton's forces. He also ordered McPherson to swiftly move west along the railroad and Sherman to destroy the railroads[246] and enemy property in and around Jackson. These actions were all accomplished without delay on May 15, and Grant at last was prepared to march directly toward Vicksburg.

At five in the morning on May 16, Grant learned from two railroad workers that Pemberton was supposedly moving toward him with about 25,000 troops. Grant immediately sent Sherman orders to cease his destructive work at Jackson and move hastily west to join Grant, McClernand, and McPherson. Meanwhile, Pemberton, having wasted his time on the southward movement to cut off Grant from his nonexistent base, had finally decided to obey his orders from Johnston and move east toward Jackson to confront Grant. Pemberton occupied a strong defensive position at Champion's Hill, astride the Vicksburg and Jackson Railroad and two parallel roads. Pemberton's men, however, were exhausted from their confused handling on May 15, while Grant's troops had been efficiently moved into a threatening position. [247]

At the May 16 Battle of Champion's Hill, Grant's 32,000 troops in McPherson's and McClernand's corps moved against 23,000 Confederate defenders. An aura of uncertainty hung over the Confederate troops as word spread of General Pemberton's belated decision, made that morning, to disengage from the enemy and move northeast to join Johnston. His decision (his third different strategic decision in three days as he tried to figure out what Grant was doing) came too late because the armies were soon locked in battle.[248] After an initial blocking action, Pemberton gave orders for some infantry to disengage by moving west and then northeast. His efforts were foiled by Grant's rapid movement, and the Rebels could not escape battle.[249]

Under Grant's oversight and McPherson's control, Union soldiers launched a late morning assault on the north side of the battlefield. By early afternoon, they not only had carried Champion's Hill, but they also had gained control of Jackson Road west of the crossroads, thereby cutting off one of Pemberton's only two escape routes back toward Vicksburg. In the process, they had shattered one Confederate division and captured sixteen precious guns.[250] Seeing the north end of his line collapsing, Pemberton ordered reinforcements from his right. At 2:30 that afternoon, veteran Arkansas and Missouri brigades launched a furious assault on the Union soldiers who only recently had taken control at the crossroads. The two Rebel brigades not only drove the Yankees out of the key crossroads but all the way back beyond the crest of Champion's Hill.[251]

Grant and McPherson organized yet another attack to regain the lost ground. As at Belmont, Donelson, and Shiloh, Grant took personal charge at a critical moment to turn adversity into victory. He said, "[Brigadier General Alvin P.] Hovey's division and [Colonel George] Boomer's brigade are good troops. If the enemy has driven them he is not in good plight himself. If we can go in here and make a little showing, I think he will give way." Led by a newly arrived division of McPherson's corps, the Federals made that "little showing" and drove the stubborn Rebels off Champion's Hill and out of the crossroads.[252] With Union forces pressing them all along the front and only one retreat route open, most of the Confederates fled across the Big Black River toward Vicksburg. One Rebel 7,000-man division was cut off, abandoned its twelve guns, and headed toward Jackson. By the time it reached Jackson, it had melted away to 4,000.[253]

The Battle of Champion's Hill involved about three hours of skirmishing and four hours of fierce fighting on Grant's center and right. Although Grant was on the offensive throughout the battle and attained

his goal of pushing the enemy toward Vicksburg, the numbers of his
dead and wounded were remarkably similar to his enemy's. Both sides
had about four hundred killed and 1,800 wounded, but Grant's two
hundred missing paled alongside the Confederates' 1,700 missing. In
addition, Grant captured thirty pieces of artillery and cut Loring's 7,000-
man division off from the rest of Pemberton's army.[254]

This battle closed the door on possible escape by Pemberton's army
and cleared the way for the siege of Vicksburg. It has been described by
James R. Arnold as "arguably the decisive encounter of the war." While
Pemberton had kept 40 percent of his troops behind the Big Black River,
Grant had pressed forward with all available troops and thereby gained
a crucial and decisive 3:2 manpower advantage. Grant later described
the military significance of the victory: "We were now assured of our
position between Johnston and Pemberton, without a possibility of a
junction of their forces."[255]

With the demoralized Confederates having moved back to the Big
Black River, Grant sent word to the trailing Sherman to head northwest
to cross that river at Bridgeport with his 15th Corps and thereby flank
Pemberton's troops. Yet, before Sherman arrived on their flank, the
Confederates had been beaten. At the Big Black River, the Confederates
again had a respectable defensive position from which to confront
Grant's assault. Inexplicably, however, they built a parapet of cotton bales
and dirt on the east side of the river instead of on the higher ground
west of the river. Thus they failed to fully utilize the river's defensive
potential during the brief battle that ensued. Pemberton's over-commit-
ment to the east bank included his withdrawal of all the artillery horses
to the west bank, thus making withdrawal of those guns east of the river
difficult or impossible.[256]

On the morning of May 17, Grant's troops arrived near the river and
came under fire as the Battle of the Big Black River began.[257] A brigade

of Iowa and Wisconsin troops scurried under fire to an old river mean-
der scar (an oxbow) near the center of the battlefield. From there they
launched a dramatic three-minute charge through a swamp and abatis
and entered the Confederate lines—to the shock of everyone on the
field. They captured many startled defenders while the rest of the Rebels
east of the deep river started a major "skedaddle." A few of them tried to
swim across the river while most scrambled back across two "bridges"
(one being a converted steamboat), which the Confederates then burned
behind them as they fled to Vicksburg. Although the bridge-burning
prevented Grant's immediate pursuit across the high river, the fast-
moving Union troops trapped at least a thousand Confederates on the
east side of the river. Thus, Grant captured those soldiers, eighteen guns,
and the last obstacle between his army and Vicksburg—at the small cost
of two hundred eighty casualties.[258]

As the Battle of the Big Black River was about to begin, an officer
from General Banks' staff arrived with a May 11 letter to Grant from
Halleck ordering Grant to return to Grand Gulf and cooperate with
General Banks in capturing Port Hudson. Grant told the startled officer
he was too late and that Halleck would not have given the order if he
had known of Grant's position. The next day, May 18, Grant crossed the
Big Black and met Sherman, who had crossed miles above as planned.
They rode together hastily toward their long-sought position on the
Yazoo River northeast of Vicksburg, where they could establish a base
for supplies from the Mississippi.[259] In his memoirs, Grant remembered
the moment of elation he shared with Sherman:

> In a few minutes Sherman had the pleasure of looking down
> from the spot coveted so much by him the December before
> on the ground where his command had lain so helpless for
> offensive action. He turned to me, saying that up to this

minute he had felt no positive assurance of success. This, however, he said was the end of one of the greatest campaigns in history and I ought to make a report of it at once. Vicksburg was not yet captured, and there was no telling what might happen before it was taken; but whether captured or not, this was a complete and successful campaign.[260]

As Grant approached Vicksburg, he could look back on the past eighteen successful days with satisfaction. He had entered enemy territory against a superior force and with no secure supply-line, fought and won five battles, severely damaged the Mississippi capital, driven away Johnston's relief force, driven Pemberton's army back into Vicksburg, inflicted over 7,000 losses on the enemy, separated Loring's 7,000 troops from the main enemy army, and thus had reduced Pemberton's army by 14,000 troops. Grant's own casualties were between 3,500 and 4,500. Bearss succinctly summarized the greatness of Grant's campaign to that point: "Students of history up to that time had to go back to the campaigns of Napoleon to find equally brilliant results accomplished in the same space of time with such corresponding small losses."[261]

Back in Richmond, Lee had convinced Davis not to expend resources opposing Grant's supposedly doomed campaign. Therefore, Grant could focus on Vicksburg without having his rear threatened by significant Rebel reinforcements. In any event, Grant wasted no time and immediately moved on Vicksburg with all three of his corps and ordered the first assault at 2:00 p.m. on May 19. Riding the momentum of his string of successes, Grant wanted to catch the defenders before they had an opportunity to fully organize. Although that assault tightened the noose around the town and resulted in Grant's troops achieving covered and advanced positions, it also demonstrated that capture of the town by assault would be difficult. It cost Grant nine hundred casualties to the

Rebels' two hundred. Nevertheless, Grant decided on a second assault. Therefore, on May 22, all three corps launched simultaneous attacks, bravely approached the enemy fortifications, and were repulsed. In response to dubious claims of success by McClernand, Grant sent him reinforcements and continued attacks elsewhere—causing additional casualties. Grant had 3,200 casualties while the defenders incurred about five hundred. With that final assault having failed, Grant settled in for a siege.[262]

In his memoirs, Grant expressed his regrets for the May 22 assault but explained his reasons for doing so:

> We were in a Southern climate, at the beginning of the hot season. The Army of the Tennessee had won five successive victories over the garrison of Vicksburg in the three preceding weeks... The Army of the Tennessee had come to believe that they could beat their antagonist under any circumstances. There was no telling how long a regular siege might last. As I have stated, it was the beginning of the hot season in a Southern climate. There was no telling what the casualties might be among Northern troops working and living in trenches, drinking surface water filtered through rich vegetation, under a tropical sun. If Vicksburg would have been carried in May, it would not only have saved the army the risk it ran of a greater danger than from the bullets of the enemy, but it would have given us a splendid army, well equipped and officered, to operate elsewhere with.[263]

General Fuller pointed out that Grant had seven reasons to attack rather than simply besiege Vicksburg: (1) Johnston was gathering an army in his rear, (2) a quick victory would allow Grant to attack Johnston, (3)

Union reinforcements [264] would be required to perfect the siege, (4) the troops were impatient to take Vicksburg, (5) the weather was getting hotter, (6) water was scarce, and (7) the men were not anxious to dig entrenchments. Although he has been criticized in hindsight for initiating the May 22 assault, Grant had sufficient reasons to justify his attempt to take the town by assault. Even though his casualties that day were five hundred killed and 2,550 wounded, Grant's casualties in the three prior weeks of fighting had been a mere seven hundred killed and 3,400 wounded. Cumulatively, these casualties were a fair price to pay for having struck at the heart of the western Confederacy and trapping a 30,000-man army in the citadel on the Mississippi whose capture would culminate in an extraordinarily significant Union victory.[265]

Shortly after the second assault, Grant finally relieved McClernand of his corps command after McClernand foolishly issued and sent to newspapers, without Grant's required approval, an order praising his own corps' performance and reflecting negatively on Sherman's and McPherson's corps. When Colonel James H. Wilson happily delivered the relief order to McClernand, the latter astutely commented, "Well, sir! I am relieved! By God, sir, we are both relieved."

From afar, Lee gave President Davis some belated advice on the Vicksburg situation and paid tribute to Grant's speedy execution of his campaign. On May 28, barely more than a week after downplaying Grant's chances for success in Mississippi, Lee revealed a fresh-found concern. He wrote, "I am glad to hear that the accounts from Vicksburg continue encouraging—I pray & trust that Genl Johnston may be able to destroy Grant's army—I fear if he cannot attack soon, he will become too strong in his position—No time should ever be given them to fortify. They work so fast."[266]

Separated from Julia since April, Grant may have resumed his drinking. On May 12, 1863, *Chicago Times* reporter Sylvanus Cadwallader allegedly observed Grant drinking three cups of whiskey from a barrel maintained for him by his chief of artillery, Colonel William L. Duff. And in early June during the siege of Vicksburg, Cadwallader allegedly saw Grant go on a two-day "bender" on board the steamboat *Diligence* while Grant was on an inspection tour on the Yazoo River. Cadwallader claimed that he had tried unsuccessfully to keep Grant from drinking during the trip, but Grant had sobered up when he returned to his headquarters. Cadwallader's account was far from contemporaneous, and he is not regarded as a reliable witness. There is evidence, however, that Grant did do some drinking during the boring period of the Vicksburg siege.[267]

There are many reports of Lincoln humorously rebuffing complaints about Grant's alleged drinking problem. In the midst of the Vicksburg campaign, Colonel T. Lyle Dickey of Grant's cavalry was sent to Washington with dispatches for the president and Secretary of War. When meeting with the president, Colonel Dickey assured the president that rumors about Grant's drinking were false. The president allegedly responded, " ….if those accusing General Grant of getting drunk will tell me where he gets his whiskey, I will get a lot of it and send it around to some of the other generals…"[268]

Grant's possible drinking episode, however, did not interfere with the business at hand. After the May 22 attack on Vicksburg, Grant had his troops dig in for a sustained siege. They dug trenches and protected them with sandbags and logs while Union sharpshooters kept the besieged defenders from interfering with the construction. With only four engineering officers in his army, Grant directed every West Point graduate to actively supervise the siege line construction. With Johnston assembling an "Army of Relief" consisting of 31,000 troops from all over the South to trap him, Grant received reinforcements of his own from Missouri, Tennessee, and Kentucky. His army grew from 51,000 to

77,000. As reinforcements arrived, Grant used them to cut off all communication out of Vicksburg south along the Mississippi, secure the
countryside back to the Big Black River, destroy bridges across that river,
and thus protect his army from being attacked by Johnston's force from
the east.[269]

Grant's risky campaign left him somewhat vulnerable to a Confederate counterattack between May 22 and June 8, when the first division of
Union reinforcements arrived. During that time, Grant had about 51,000
troops between Pemberton, with 29,500 men, and Johnston, with 22,000
that increased to 30,000 by June 3. But Lee's prevention of more reinforcements, together with Johnston's temerity and the lack of Confederate coordination, kept Grant from being attacked.

In Virginia, Lee learned that Grant had reached the Yazoo and optimistically speculated, "The enemy may be drawing to the Yazoo for the
purpose of reaching their transports and retiring from the contest, which
I hope is the case." As he would demonstrate again in 1864, Lee knew
nothing of Grant's tenaciousness or of his refusal to even consider
retreating. As historian Kenneth P. Williams concluded, "Grant's persistence during the winter and his brilliant campaign behind Vicksburg
had taught Lee nothing about the character of the soldier he would a
year later have to face."[270] More importantly to Grant, his president
recognized the greatness of what he had accomplished to this point.
Lincoln, on May 26, wrote, "Whether Gen. Grant shall or shall not con-
summate the capture of Vicksburg, his campaign from the beginning of
this month up to the twenty second day of it, is one of the most brilliant
in the world."[271]

On June 22, Grant learned that some of Johnston's cavalry had
crossed the Big Black River to threaten his rear. Immediately Grant put
Sherman in charge of the half of his army protecting against such an
attack and readied other forces to reinforce Sherman if needed. With

30,000 men and seventy-two guns, Sherman's "Army of Observation" guarded all of the Big Black River crossings. Johnston backed off.[272]

On June 25 and July 1, Union troops exploded mines in tunnels they had dug under the Confederate lines. Although these explosions did not afford the besiegers an opportunity to enter the city, they did force the defenders to further constrict their lines. For forty-seven days, the Confederate forces and Vicksburg residents were subjected to continuous Union fire from ships and shore that may have totaled 88,000 shells and killed perhaps twenty civilians. With deserters reporting that morale and food supplies were running low in Vicksburg and with his trenches having been advanced as far as possible, Grant planned an all-out assault for July 6. Ironically, Johnston had chosen that same date for his own long-delayed assault on Grant.[273]

For six weeks, Grant's soldiers dug day and night in order to advance their lines, set off explosions beneath the Rebel defenses, and improve their prospects for a final assault. Grant rejected some officers' views that another assault should have been launched before the one planned for July 6. After May 22, the siege of Vicksburg was a relatively bloodless one for Grant's army despite the fact that a siege usually is costlier for the besiegers than the defenders. Between May 23 and July 3, Grant's forces suffered 1,000 casualties to his enemies' 2,900.[274]

With the noose tightening and food running low, Pemberton finally relented. On the morning of July 3, he raised white flags and sent out a pair of officers to arrange an armistice during which capitulation terms could be negotiated. Pemberton's signalmen had decoded Porter's signals to Grant that he lacked adequate vessels to transport almost 30,000 prisoners to the North, and thus Pemberton held out for parole rather than imprisonment. To save Union transportation resources and encourage desertions by the freed and demoralized Rebel troops, Grant agreed to parole, not imprison, the Rebel troops. Pemberton's July 4 surrender of his 29,500-man army (along with 172 guns and 60,000 rifles) made the national holiday a memorable one for the North—especially in conjunction with Lee's July 1–3 defeat at Gettysburg. As a result of Vicksburg's fall, the Confederate commander at Port Hudson surrendered to Banks his 6,000 soldiers on July 9—thereby relinquishing the last Confederate position on the Mississippi.[275]

After the fall of Vicksburg, Grant sent Sherman back to Jackson in order to drive out Johnston and his troops and complete its destruction. As early as July 3, Grant had wired Sherman of the anticipated surrender, told him to "make your calculations to attack Johnston—destroy the [rail]Road North of Jackson," and promised him all of his army but one corps.[276] Sherman was aided by specific and accurate information on Johnston's forces provided by scout Charles Bell. The first of Sherman's 50,000-man force left their lines east of Vicksburg on July 5. The three-pronged army approached Jackson by July 9 and then besieged and bombarded the town. They forced Johnston to evacuate Jackson on July 16 and retreat to middle Alabama. Sherman's first successful independent command completed its mission by destroying all railroads within fifty miles of Jackson as well as what little of value remained in that unfortunate town.[277]

From May 1 at Port Gibson through the mid-July return to Jackson, Grant's Vicksburg and Banks' Port Hudson joint offensive resulted in the fall of Vicksburg, Port Hudson, and Jackson, as well as the capture of 241 guns in Grant's battles and another 51 at Port Hudson—all at a cost of one-third the losses suffered by the Confederates. Grant's and Banks' battlefield casualties totaled 14,846 while the Confederate casualties were 47,625. Of the 2,153 captured Confederate officers, fifteen were generals.[278] Grant's isolated Vicksburg Campaign ratio is even more impressive. His troops suffered about 9,400 casualties while inflicting about 41,000 on the enemy.[279] Considering that Grant was on the offensive, that he achieved his strategic goals, and that the defenders should have had a tactical advantage, his 1:4 casualty ratio is an amazing tribute to his great generalship.

Thus ended the greatest campaign of the war. Grant's aggressive campaign of maneuver that achieved great success with moderate casualties was described by Weigley as "one of the masterpieces of military history."[280] Although that campaign "was built on speed and deception and military brilliance," ironically, Bruce Catton explained, "[Grant] ... would be written off as a man with a bludgeon, a dull plodder who could win only when he had every advantage and need count no cost."[281]

Vicksburg was the culmination of Grant's offensive western campaigns. Catton summarized those campaigns: "The thrust which began at Cairo and was ending at Vicksburg had never been a matter of piling up overwhelming resources and trusting that something would break under the sheer weight of men and muscle.... This had been a business of finesse, of daring decisions and fast movement, of mental alertness and the ability to see and use an opening before it closed."[282] With a minimum of casualties, Grant deprived the Confederacy of much of Kentucky and Tennessee, made the Mississippi a Union highway, and cut off the western third of the Confederacy.

As Hattaway and Jones stated, "Grant succeeded because his superb campaign had embodied all of the elements that had made for Napoleon's victories—distraction, a penetration to threaten communications and turn the enemy, and the use of interior lines."[283] One-third of the Confederacy had been severed; horses and food from Texas, Mexico, and elsewhere beyond the river were denied to the Confederacy's main armies and population centers; sugar, salt, and cotton were denied to the Confederacy; huge amounts of weapons (60,000 rifles) and ammunition were captured; smuggling of weapons and other goods through Mexico was greatly hindered; and the river could resume its role as a highway for transporting Union commerce of the Midwest. Not only did the Union control the Mississippi Valley and isolate Texas, Arkansas, and western Louisiana, but the states of Mississippi and Alabama were no longer major arenas in the war.[284]

In his inimitable fashion, Lincoln eloquently summarized the impact of the Vicksburg Campaign: "The Father of Waters again goes unvexed to the sea."[285] James M. McPherson described this campaign's importance: "The capture of Vicksburg was the most important Northern strategic victory of the war, perhaps meriting Grant's later assertion that 'the fate of the Confederacy was sealed when Vicksburg fell.'"[286] Russell Weigley discussed Grant's low casualty rate during the Vicksburg Campaign: "[Grant] waged successfully the kind of campaign of maneuver, and eventually of siege, at a low cost in lives, that McClellan had only hoped to wage."[287]

As James Arnold concluded, the campaign was Napoleonic in Grant's logistical preparation, use of all available manpower, intelligent risk-taking, flexible adjustments to changing circumstances, and focus on the ultimate goal.[288] To carry out his plan, Grant had to proceed rapidly, avoid being crushed between two Confederate forces, effectively abandon his supply line, and live off the land until he obtained a secure position on the Mississippi in the Vicksburg area. With Grant directly involved all the way, his army crossed the river, fought and won five battles in eighteen days, twice drove the Rebels from the Mississippi capital of Jackson, trapped a 29,500-man army in Vicksburg, besieged that city, and accepted the surrender of both the city and the army on July 4, 1863. That same evening Lee's army began its retreat from the Gettysburg battlefield in Pennsylvania. Historian Alan Nevins observed, "The country had at last the military hero for which it had longed, and Grant's name was on every lip."[289] He was promoted to major general in the regular army, the nation's highest military rank at that time.[290] (Previously he had been a major general of volunteers, a wartime-only position.) Grant also received a letter of thanks and apology from the president, who obviously had been following his activities closely:

Major General Grant   Executive Mansion,
My Dear General: Washington, July 13, 1863.

    I do not remember that you and I ever met personally. I write this now as a grateful acknowledgment for the almost inestimable service you have done the country. I wish to say a word further. When you first reached the vicinity of Vicksburg, I thought you should do, what you finally did— march the troops across the neck, run the batteries with the transports, and thus go below; and I never had any faith, except in a general hope that you knew better than I, that the Yazoo Pass expedition, and the like, could succeed. When you got below and took Port Gibson, Grand Gulf and vicinity, I thought you should go down the river and join Ge. Banks; and when you turned Northward East of the Big Black, I feared it was a mistake. I now wish to make the personal acknowledgment that you were right, and I was wrong.

Yours very truly
A. Lincoln[291]

Perhaps the keys to the campaign's success, in Noah Andre Trudeau's words, were Grant's "bold leadership and shrewd risk-taking," and the facts that he "knew his objective and never lost sight of it." [292] For example, he had good intelligence but kept moving even when he did not and "refused to let inevitable uncertainty lead to paralysis."[293] Grant's campaign was noteworthy for its focus, deception, celerity, flexibility, maneuver, and cunning.[294] As Bearss concluded, "The oft told story that Grant was a heedless, conscienceless butcherer, devoid of the skills associated with history's great captains is shown by the Vicksburg Campaign to be a shallow canard."[295]

It was Lee, not Grant, who was campaigning in an exceedingly costly manner. While Lee's army of 75,000 was suffering 28,000 (37 percent) casualties in his simultaneous but disastrous Gettysburg Campaign, Grant carried out his brilliant Vicksburg Campaign with the loss of a mere 2,254 of his 29,373 troops (8 percent casualties) killed or wounded at Champion's Hill and 3,052 of his 45,556 troops (7 percent casualties) killed or wounded at Vicksburg itself.[296] For the entire campaign, Grant lost a total of 9,362 (1,514 killed, 7,393 wounded, and 453 missing or captured). The Confederates opposing Grant lost almost 41,000 men (2,000 killed, 5,000 wounded, and 33,718 captured.)[297]

The impact of the two campaigns on Confederate morale was crushing. In Richmond, War Department Clerk Jones wrote on July 8, "But, alas! we have sad tidings from the West. Gen. Johnston telegraphs from Jackson, Miss., that Vicksburg capitulated on the 4th inst. This is a terrible blow, and has produced much despondency." Twenty days later, Confederate Ordnance Chief Gorgas completed his diary entry on Vicksburg, Port Hudson, and Gettysburg with the realistic and prophetic words, "Yesterday we rode on the pinnacle of success—to-day absolute ruin seems to be our portion. The Confederacy totters to its destruction."[298]

In summary, the combined efforts of Grant and Lee in the spring and summer of 1863 probably determined the outcome of the Civil War. Grant appropriately went on the offensive, gained control of the Mississippi Valley, won an entire theater of the war, captured a huge enemy army, and boosted Union morale—all the while absorbing one-fourth the casualties he imposed on his foes. He was aided by Lee's refusal to make any troops available to oppose Grant's risky campaign deep into enemy territory. Meanwhile, Lee inappropriately went on the offensive, failed to gain territory or capture an army, doomed his prospects in the eastern theater, adversely affected the western and middle theaters, and deflated Confederate morale—all the while incurring intolerably higher losses than those he inflicted on his foes.

After that crucial summer, Grant's and Lee's later actions were somewhat anti-climactic but continued along the same lines as before. Grant continued the strategic and tactical offensives so necessary to Union victory, and Lee continued his myopic, one-theater efforts by hindering or stopping aid to other theaters and acting offensively whenever he had an opportunity to do so.

CHAPTER SEVEN

AUTUMN 1863:

LEE LENDS AN ASSIST
AS GRANT SAVES
CHATTANOOGA AND
A UNION ARMY

*Lee delays reinforcements and reduces Confederate troop strength
at Chattanooga, thereby assisting Grant in rescuing
and breaking out a Union army trapped there*

As if Lee had not done enough damage to the Confederate cause by the end of July 1863, he would compound the South's problems in the middle theater over the next few months. His primary means of doing so was to delay the Rebels' most significant inter-theater transfer of troops during the entire war and then interfere with their use in the middle theater to stimulate their return to his own precious Virginia theater. Lee's actions lost the opportunity for Rebel destruction or capture of the Union Army of the Cumberland at Chickamauga and Chattanooga, and instead prepared the way for Sherman's Atlanta Campaign of 1864.

During the late summer, fall, and winter of 1863, Lee's morale and health deteriorated. Gettysburg was the primary cause of Lee's depression. A month afterward, Lee submitted his resignation to Davis. In his resignation letter, Lee took full responsibility for Gettysburg and urged the appointment of someone in whom the army would have greater confidence.[1] Lee may have come to realize many of the mistakes he had made at Gettysburg, and perhaps he understood what effects his overall strategy and tactics had wrought on the Army of Northern Virginia. Davis, however, responded to Lee that there was no person in whom the army would have greater confidence and refused to accept Lee's resignation.[2]

The Tullahoma Campaign in eastern Tennessee was another result of Lee's having retained Longstreet to go to Gettysburg. A series of brilliant flanking movements across three mountain ranges by Rosecrans' Army of the Cumberland from late June to early September forced Bragg's Army of Tennessee into a succession of retreats from mid-Tennessee, through Chattanooga and into northwestern Georgia. Lee's continuing refusal to reinforce Bragg played a significant role in Bragg's outnumbered army losing southeastern Tennessee and then its direct rail connection with Richmond.

Gettysburg, however, did at least temporarily reduce Lee's pro-Virginia influence on Davis, and thereby help bring about the ultimate transfer of some of Lee's troops. Despite Lee's hopes and plans for another offensive against Meade, Davis at long last yielded to Longstreet and others' pleas and authorized Longstreet to move west. Longstreet had pressed Seddon and Lee in mid-August for some of his troops to be sent west.[3] Simultaneously, from the middle theater, since August 21, Bragg had been warning Richmond of a massive Tennessee offensive by Rosecrans and Burnside, who were then respectively threatening Chattanooga and Knoxville. Davis first summoned Lee to Richmond on August 24 to discuss the Tennessee/Georgia crisis, and, during the last week of August, Davis began pressing Lee on the possibility of sending reinforcements from Lee to the middle theater.

Those talks dragged on into early September. Lee, who usually argued that Union reinforcements on his front precluded transfers from his army, now argued that transfers away from Meade in the East (such as Burnside's 9th Corps) made Meade vulnerable to an offensive by Lee's full army. In fact, on August 31, Lee even ordered Longstreet to prepare for such an offensive.[4] At the same time, Lee declined Davis' request that he take command in the West. Lee declined on the grounds of poor health, ignorance of the West, and expected opposition from generals Lee had shipped to the western front (including William W. Loring, Earl Van Dorn, John B. Magruder, Theophilus H. Holmes, and Thomas F. Drayton).[5]

The Confederates' situation in Tennessee worsened with their September 3 abandonment of Knoxville in northeastern Tennessee. Burnside captured that city in an action that severed the direct rail route from Richmond to Chattanooga. While Lee argued with Davis about whether to send troops westward, Burnside had blocked the direct route for any such troops to reach Bragg at Chattanooga. After agreeing on September 5 to the movement of Longstreet's troops, Lee and Davis took two more days to agree on the details. Finally, on September 7, Davis ordered reinforcements from Lee to Bragg.[6]

As a result of the cumulative Lee-generated delays, Longstreet's troops did not begin to leave Orange Court House until September 9. McLaws' and Hood's divisions and Alexander's reserve artillery, all without supply wagons and horses, at long last began their time-consuming, circuitous route through the Carolinas and Georgia (1,000 miles on ten railroads) instead of being able to travel 500 rail-miles directly to the Chattanooga area via Knoxville.[7] Lee had turned a routine two- or three-day railroad trek into a ten-day nightmare. Rather than using direct tracks on the Eastern Tennessee & Virginia Railroad and the East Tennessee & Georgia Railroad, Longstreet's troops had to use a patchwork jumble of disconnected small railroads to reach Bragg at Chickamauga. The result of Lee's myopia was that only a third to half of Longstreet's infantry and none of his artillery arrived in time for the Battle of Chickamauga.[8]

After chasing Bragg into Georgia, Rosecrans had become careless, scattered his four corps (one cavalry) in pursuit of the Rebels, and reassembled them barely in time to repel a major offensive by Bragg on September 19 along Chickamauga Creek. Longstreet arrived by rail that night with about 5,000 reinforcements from Virginia to give Bragg a slight numerical edge, took command of the Rebel Army's left wing the next morning, and broke through and collapsed the right side of the Union line. While Rosecrans fled back to Chattanooga with the bulk of his army, George Thomas earned the name "The Rock of Chickamauga" by organizing and leading the remaining Union forces in a desperate army-saving defense at Snodgrass Hill (Horseshoe Ridge) all afternoon and early evening. Although Bragg had inflicted 16,000 casualties on the forces of Rosecrans, the constantly attacking Confederates lost 18,000 men in the two-day battle.[9]

Had more of Longstreet's 15,000 troops, as well as his artillery, arrived in time to fight and contest the Yankee retreat, Rosecrans' army might have been slaughtered or captured. Lee's reticence to leave Virginia himself or to part with any of his troops had cost the Confederates the opportunity for a significant success in the crucial middle theater.[10] For the next month, however, the military situation looked promising for the Confederates as they besieged and brought to near-starvation Rosecrans' army in Chattanooga.[11]

Meanwhile Bragg rekindled a preexisting and debilitating dispute between himself and all his corps commanders when he accused one of them, General Polk, of failing to attack on time at dawn on September 20 at Chickamauga. Longstreet fueled the insurrection that followed by participating in anti-Bragg meetings and co-signing a petition to President Davis urging Bragg's removal. Even Davis' trip to Tennessee and personal intervention failed to heal the rift. After hearing most of Bragg's subordinates call for his removal (in Bragg's presence), Davis made the egregious error of retaining his good friend Bragg and allowing him to sack all his corps commanders.

After Chickamauga, Lee would further undercut Southern prospects in the middle theater by machinations involving the departed Longstreet that greatly influenced the two sides facing off at Chattanooga. Once again, however, it was not merely Lee's negative actions that hurt the Confederacy. As at Vicksburg, it was brilliant, aggressive, and persistent actions by Grant that saved the trapped Union Army at Chattanooga and resulted in pushing the Confederates out of Tennessee.

Following his Vicksburg victory, Grant proposed that his army attack Mobile, Alabama, the last open Confederate port on the Gulf of Mexico. Halleck rejected Grant's proposal. The president himself explained to Grant that he agreed with the concept but that the recent French establishment of an emperor in Mexico made a Texas movement more urgent. Reflecting Grant's growing reputation in Washington, Lincoln and the promoted Assistant Secretary of War Charles Dana discussed the possibility of bringing Grant east to command the Army of the Potomac. Grant demurred on the grounds that he knew the players and terrain in the West and that such an appointment would upset the eastern generals.[12]

From July to September, Grant was in New Orleans. His visit, however, was rudely interrupted by the crisis in Tennessee. All that had gone before—Belmont, Donelson, Shiloh, Vicksburg—had prepared him for that crisis. Bruce Catton put it well: "Grant was ready, at last. The time of testing was over, and he had reached his full stature. He had developed—through mistakes, through trial and error, through steady endurance, through difficult lessons painfully learned, through the unbroken development of his own capacities—into the man who could finally lead the way through that open door [to victory]."[13]

The post-Chickamauga crisis centered on Chattanooga. That critical railroad and river crossroads town was a key transportation hub between the Deep South and Virginia, between the Mississippi River and the Carolinas, and between Nashville and the critical industrial city of Atlanta. Chattanooga, however, had become a trap for the Union forces there as Bragg's army occupied the high ground east, south, and south-west of the town. The Rebels limited the Union forces to a single, mountainous, and inadequate supply line over a sixty-mile wagon road from the Union railhead at Bridgeport, Alabama. Union rations were cut, animals were dying, and starvation threatened the troops.[14]

Realizing the critical nature of the situation, Lincoln, Stanton, and Halleck looked to Grant to resolve the crisis. In an October 3 dispatch, Halleck told Grant, "It is the wish of the Secretary of War that as soon as General Grant is able he will come to Cairo and report by telegraph." Grant arrived at Cairo on October 16, immediately telegraphed Halleck, and was advised the next day to proceed to the Galt House in Louisville to meet "an officer of the War Department." On his way to Louisville, Grant was met in Indianapolis by none other than Secretary of War Stanton, who had Grant's train flagged down so that he could join him.[15] Stanton accompanied Grant the rest of the way to Louisville and explained the desperate situation in Chattanooga. The Secretary then gave Grant the choice of two orders—both of which would name him commander of a new Military Division of the Mississippi, which included the Departments (Armies) of the Ohio (Burnside), the Cumberland (Rosecrans), and the Tennessee (Grant), and all territory between the Mississippi and the Alleghenies north of Banks in Louisiana.[16]

Following this October 16 appointment, Grant's top priority became saving Chattanooga. His first action was to replace Rosecrans with Thomas. He did this by accepting one of the alternative orders offered to him by Stanton—the one that relieved Rosecrans of command.[17] Grant wired Thomas, "I will be there as soon as possible. Please inform me how long your present supplies will last, and the prospect for keeping them up." Thomas replied that he and his troops would hold "until we starve."[18]

Meanwhile, on September 24, Stanton had ordered the 11th and 12th corps of the Army of the Potomac, under Hooker, to proceed by rail from Virginia to the Chattanooga area. The next day those troops began boarding trains for the 1,200-mile journey over seven railroads through Maryland, West Virginia, Ohio, Indiana, Kentucky, and Tennessee all the way to Bridgeport, Alabama. The movement of 20,000 troops, their baggage, and ten artillery batteries was completed in fifteen days, and their 3,000 horses and transport vehicles followed within about a week. This, the most efficient long-distance movement of troops in the Civil War, resulted in Grant ultimately receiving the fully equipped soldiers of those two corps for his Chattanooga operations.[19]

Grant began the arduous 60-mile trek by horse over the mountains from Bridgeport to Chattanooga as soon as he arrived by train at Bridgeport. Along the way, the animal-loving Grant must have been dismayed by the sight of thousands of horse and mule carcasses and the wreckage of numerous wagons—all evidence of the need to open a better supply route into Chattanooga. Upon his October 23 arrival in Chattanooga, Grant asked Halleck to promote Sherman to command the Army of the Tennessee in place of Grant; Halleck did so.[20]

Grant immediately conferred with Thomas and Thomas' staff, including Major General William F. "Baldy" Smith, Chief Engineer of the Army of the Cumberland. After scouting the area with Thomas and

Smith the next day, Grant approved Smith's creative plan to open an adequate supply-line to the town. Three nights later that plan was executed. Under the cover of darkness and fog between three and five o'clock on the morning of October 27, eighteen hundred Union troops in sixty pontoon boats floated downriver from Chattanooga around Moccasin Bend to Brown's Ferry. There they quickly overcame the surprised Confederate guards, ferried across another brigade of awaiting troops, and coordinated with the first of Hooker's soldiers coming up Lookout Valley. They repelled a Rebel counterattack and had a bridge built across the river by 4:30 p.m. This comparatively bloodless operation (with a mere twenty-one casualties) resulted in Grant's forces taking control of Lookout Valley and the Tennessee River below Chattanooga, thus opening the "Cracker Line" by which massive rations and supplies could be brought directly and efficiently from Bridgeport to Chattanooga. Grant's troops in Chattanooga celebrated the opening of the Cracker Line as the first barges carrying 400,000 rations and 39,000 pounds of forage arrived behind the steamer *Chattanooga*.[21]

Within four days of arriving, Grant had solved Chattanooga's supply crisis. Although Grant received the troops' praise for their sudden change of fortune, he gave credit for the breakthrough to Thomas and Smith in a dispatch to Halleck.[22] But Grant did deserve and receive credit for a new atmosphere he brought to the Union troops at Chattanooga. The just-arrived General Howard wrote later that fall, "This department was completely 'out of joint' when we first arrived ... I cannot be too thankful for the policy that placed these three Depts. under Grant." Years later a veteran said, "You have no conception of the change in the army when Grant came. He opened up the cracker line and got a steamer through. We began to see things move. We felt that everything came from a plan. He came into the army quietly, no splendor, no airs, no staff. He used to go about alone. He began the campaign the moment he reached the field."[23]

Bragg's Confederates must have been shocked by the suddenness and ease with which Grant had altered the Chattanooga situation. Instead of being bottled up in a valley and subsisting on short rations, the Union forces had a wide-open supply line that promised food, rations, forage, clothing, and other provisions—as well as a route for reinforcements from both the East and West. Grant himself later summarized the about-face that had occurred:

> In five days from my arrival in Chattanooga the way was open to Bridgeport and, with the aid of steamers and Hooker's teams, in a week the troops were receiving full rations. It is hard for any one not an eyewitness to realize the relief this brought. The men were soon re-clothed and also well fed; an abundance of ammunition was brought up, and a cheerfulness prevailed not before enjoyed in many weeks... I do not know what the effect was on the other side, but assume it must have been correspondingly depressing. [Jefferson] Davis had visited Bragg but a short time before, and must have perceived our condition to be about as Bragg described it in his subsequent report. "These dispositions," he said "faithfully sustained, insured the enemy's speedy evacuation of Chattanooga for want of food and forage. Possessed of the shortest route to his depot, and the one by which reinforcements must reach him, we held him at our mercy, and his destruction was only a question of time."[24]

In desperation, the shocked Confederates counterattacked the second night following the surprise Union assault. Longstreet's men came down from Lookout Mountain to attack Hooker's troops in Lookout Valley. Union Brigadier General John W. Geary at the Battle of Wauhatchie was badly outnumbered but held his position. Howard moved to the rescue

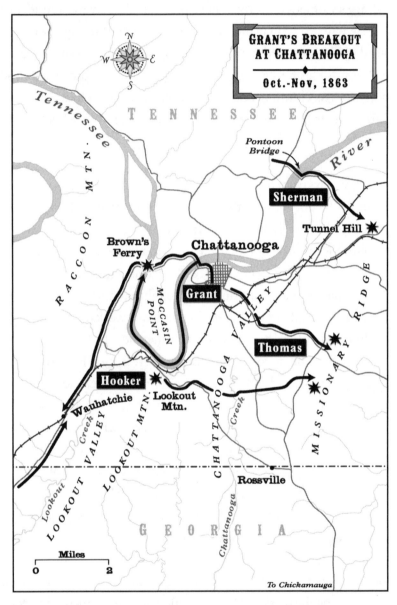

Grant's Breakout at Chattanooga (October–November, 1863)
Map by David Deis, Dreamline Cartography, Northridge, CA

from Brown's Ferry, engaged Confederates attacking from a foothill of Lookout Mountain on his left, drove them back, and captured the hill. The attack on Geary, meanwhile, was broken up by a stampede of his horses and mules toward the attackers, who mistook the stampede for a cavalry charge on the pitch-black night. The Union victory at Wauhatchie kept Lookout Valley open, guaranteed the security of the Cracker Line, and came at a minimal cost (216 casualties to the Rebels' 355). At a minuscule cost, therefore, Grant had saved a trapped army, opened and defended a useful supply and reinforcement route to Chattanooga, and shortly posed a serious threat to Bragg's encircling army.[25]

Having solved the supply problem, Grant spent the next month gathering his reinforcements, assembling an army of 80,000, and planning an assault on the six-mile Confederate line semi-encircling Chattanooga. With the eastern theater quiescent and the Mississippi theater essentially gone, the nation's attention focused on Chattanooga. Only the Union fully responded to the critical situation there. The presence of Hooker's 25,000 troops and Sherman's two corps from Mississippi swelled Grant's army and demonstrated Grant's grasp of the national situation and the vital importance of Chattanooga. On the other hand, Lee continued to have a devastating impact on Confederate fortunes in Grant's new theater. Lee stymied a Rebel plan to reinforce Chattanooga with 25,000 troops from Lee in Virginia and 10,000 from Johnston in Mississippi. President Davis rejected the plan at an October 11 council of war because Lee refused to provide more troops.[26]

Unbelievably, Lee and Davis not only prevented an increase of Bragg's force; they actually reduced it. Anxious to get back the bulk of Longstreet's corps, which Davis had belatedly pried loose from Lee and sent to Chickamauga, Lee had campaigned for Longstreet's return to Virginia. Within days of his temporary loss of Longstreet's 15,000 troops to the West, Lee began his efforts to get them back and thereby helped bring about a major military disaster for the Confederacy. Even before all those troops reached Bragg, Lee twice (on September 11 and 14) wrote to Davis about getting them back. On both September 23 and 25, he suggested to Davis that Longstreet and his two divisions be moved northeasterly from Chattanooga to take on Burnside in Knoxville. This conveniently would move Longstreet's forces toward Virginia and back to Lee, who stressed to Davis his urgent need for them.[27] At the same time, Lee wrote to Longstreet, "Finish the work before you, my dear general, and return to me. I want you badly and you cannot get back too soon."[28] On October 26, Lee wrote to Longstreet, "I missed you dreadfully and your brave corps... I hope you will soon return to me... I trust that we may soon be together again."[29]

On October 29, Davis passed Lee's idea for a Knoxville move on to Bragg, who knew that Longstreet had aggravated the discontent among Bragg's generals and correctly suspected that Longstreet wanted his command. Longstreet had seen his opportunity for that command destroyed by Davis. Therefore, for their separate reasons, Bragg and Longstreet agreed on November 3 that Longstreet should take his 15,000 troops to Knoxville and away from Bragg. This gambit reduced Bragg's strength to 36,000 against Grant's ultimate 80,000 and deprived Bragg of a reserve in the event of a Union breakthrough. Lee, Davis, Longstreet, and Bragg seemed determined to make Grant's breakout feasible.[30]

Pressured by Washington to relieve Burnside in Knoxville, Grant devised a plan to drive Bragg away from Chattanooga and put pressure on Longstreet to return to Chattanooga (and away from Knoxville). He wanted to cause Longstreet to return toward Chattanooga—but not quickly enough to help oppose Grant's own offensive. To do so, Grant had to move fast. Therefore, he immediately issued a battle plan sending Sherman against the Confederate right (north) wing all the way to the railroad in Bragg's rear (the pathway to Knoxville), sending Hooker against the Confederate left at Lookout Mountain, and having Thomas pressure the Confederate center to keep reinforcements from going to either flank. Ironically, the arrival of Sherman's troops on Grant's north flank caused Bragg to think they were headed toward Knoxville and to order 11,000 more of his troops to head there. They were in the process of doing so and were recalled when Grant attacked at Chattanooga.[31]

The first Union step was a November 23 one-mile forward movement by Thomas' troops against the center of the Confederate line when he turned what looked like a drill into a takeover of the advance Confederate lines and a prominent hill called Orchard Knob. That night, to the north, thousands of Sherman's men crossed the river in pontoon boats, established a beachhead, and then built a pontoon bridge for the men behind them. The next day Grant ordered Hooker to take Lookout Mountain, the 1,200-foot-high dominant landmark in the area that towered over the Tennessee River southwest of Chattanooga. His three divisions crossed Lookout Creek and proceeded to take control of the weakly-manned mountain in a daylong "Battle above the Clouds." The fighting on the upper half of the mountain was visible to cheering Union troops in the Tennessee River valley and to Grant and other generals on Orchard Knob in the center of the Union lines. Bragg ordered the mountain abandoned that night and thus ended the Confederates' sixty-three-day occupation of that dominant position. The Rebels suffered 1,250 casualties in its defense. Hooker's success cleared the way for his troops to advance through Chattanooga Valley on the Rebel left flank as part of an all-out assault on the remaining Confederates threatening Chattanooga.[32]

Grant ordered Sherman and his troops, who had marched over six hundred miles from Vicksburg and then crossed the Tennessee north of town, to attack Tunnel Mountain on the north end of Missionary Ridge, the dominant Confederate heights overlooking Chattanooga from the east.[33] Grant simultaneously ordered Hooker to drive from Lookout Mountain through Lookout Valley to threaten the south end of Missionary Ridge. Meanwhile, Grant held Thomas' troops in reserve between Sherman and Hooker, prepared to reinforce any breakthrough made by either of them. Sherman's offensive made little progress on November 24, but a full eclipse of the moon that evening seemed to auger significant developments the next day.

On November 25, however, Sherman continued to encounter serious problems because Tunnel Hill turned out to be a couple of ridges beyond its expected location—and behind a ravine. A frustrated Sherman sent small portions of his troops into deadly frontal assaults on well-planned defensive positions conceived by Confederate Major General Patrick R. Cleburne. Sherman's lack of progress was matched on the other end of the line by Hooker, who was having difficulty crossing the now bridgeless Chattanooga Creek in Lookout Valley. From his outpost on Orchard Knob between Chattanooga and Missionary Ridge, Grant observed Confederate reinforcements being shifted to deal with Sherman's attack on the north and became concerned about Sherman's welfare.[34]

To relieve the pressure on Sherman, Grant ordered Thomas' 23,000 infantrymen to assault the Rebel rifle pits at the base of Missionary Ridge. The attackers moved out in good order and, despite some defensive fire, quickly made their way to the base of Missionary Ridge, where the defending Rebels fled uphill. Thomas' men, however, soon realized they were in a no-man's-land where they were under fire from numerous Confederate riflemen and some artillery on the side and top of the ridge. A Union infantryman, Fred Knefler of the 79th Indiana, described the situation: "Nothing could live in or about the captured line of field works; a few minutes of such terrific, telling fire would quickly convert them into untenable hideous slaughter pens. There was no time or opportunity for deliberations. Something must be done and it must be done quickly." Given the option of retreating, dying, or continuing the assault, Union soldiers scrambled up the ridge to eliminate the source of the killing rifle-fire.[35]

Back at Orchard Knob, Grant and numerous generals watched in astonishment as Thomas' men scrambled up the ridge. Grant accusingly asked Thomas, "Who ordered those men up the ridge?" After Thomas denied knowledge, Grant turned to Thomas' deputy, Major General Gordon Granger, and asked, "Did you order them up, Granger?" Granger said he had not and explained, "When those fellows get started, all hell can't stop them." Grant mumbled that someone would "catch it" if the attack failed.[36]

Because of Confederate incompetence, Thomas' men had three things going for them. With Longstreet's 15,000 men having been sent away at Lee's suggestion and with most Confederates defending their flanks, Bragg did not have the numbers to withstand such a massive assault at the center of his line. Furthermore, the Confederates had placed their artillery at the geologic, instead of the military, crest of the ridge, and most of their guns therefore were too far back from the slope to be lowered and fired at the thousands of men desperately heading their way. Finally, these blunders had been compounded by Bragg's wasteful and foolish placement of a significant number of his troops in indefensible positions at the base of the ridge from which they were compelled to retreat—if they survived the initial assault.[37]

Virtually as one, hundreds and then thousands of Thomas' troops reached the summit and began wreaking havoc among fleeing Confederates. They shouted, "Chickamauga! Chickamauga!" as they avenged the embarrassing September defeat and retreat. A Union general humorously addressed his troops: "Soldiers, you ought to be court-martialed, every man of you. I ordered you to take the rifle pits and you scaled the mountain."[38]

The Lee-generated absence of Rebel reserves collapsed Bragg's army.[39] As the center of the Confederate line dissolved, troops from all sectors of that line abandoned their positions and fled toward Georgia. Bragg rode among his troops in a vain attempt to stop the retreating flood. To his cries of "Here is your commander!", they responded, "Here's your mule." Bragg had completely lost control of his army, many of his soldiers were captured, and thousands threw away their weapons. They abandoned forty-one guns (one-third of their total) and 7,000 firearms. By 7:00 p.m. Bragg had reached Chickamauga Station and telegraphed news of the debacle to Richmond. Despite determined pursuit by Sheridan, Cleburne saved the army with an effective rearguard defense at a strong defensive position. Sheridan's aggressive pursuit caught Grant's eye and played a role in a major promotion for him the following year.[40]

As Private Sam Watkins of Tennessee watched Bragg's demoralized soldiers retreat from Chattanooga, he observed:

> It was the first defeat our army had ever suffered, but the prevailing sentiment was anathemas and denunciations hurled against Jeff Davis for ordering Longstreet's corps to Knoxville, and sending off [Major] General [Joseph] Wheeler's and [Brigadier General Nathan Bedford] Forrest's cavalry, while every private soldier in the whole army knew that the enemy was concentrating at Chattanooga.[41]

Little did Watkins know that Lee's recommendation was behind Davis' actions in Tennessee. Lee's concern for his own theater of the war had hobbled the Confederate Army of Tennessee in the West, resulted in its retreat from Tennessee to Georgia, and cleared the way for Sherman's decisive 1864 Atlanta Campaign.

The Battle of Chattanooga certainly was not fought and won as Grant had planned. An excellent summary of the planning and execution was provided by "Baldy" Smith:

> The original plan contemplated the turning of Bragg's right flank, which *was not done*. The secondary plan of Thomas looked toward following up the success of Hooker at Lookout Mountain by turning the left flank of Bragg [through Rossville Gap], and then an attack by Thomas along his entire front. The Rossville Gap was not carried in time to be of more than secondary importance in the battle. The assault on the center before either flank was turned was never seriously contemplated, and was made without plan, without orders....[42]

The bottom line is that the victory did not occur where and how Grant planned but instead was the result of his aggressive use of all his forces to keep the pressure on the enemy at all points.

One Confederate soldier, captured and being taken to the rear, described Grant's compassion for the defeated and demoralized enemy prisoners. After telling how many other Union officers rode by without paying the prisoners any attention, the soldier wrote, "When General Grant reached the line of ragged, filthy, bloody, starveling, despairing prisoners strung out on each side of the bridge, he lifted his hat and held it over his head until he passed the last man of that living funeral cortege. He was the only officer in that whole train who recognized us as being on the face of the earth."[43]

Consistent with Lincoln's direction to "Remember Burnside," Grant immediately sent a relief expedition and supplies toward Knoxville.

Before that expedition began, six thousand of Burnside's troops had avoided being trapped, beaten Longstreet's 12,000 troops to Campbell's Station on the road to Knoxville, held them back in a daylong battle there on November 16, and retreated to Knoxville.[44] Later Burnside had thwarted Longstreet's assault on Knoxville, and the threat of the relief column drove Longstreet into the Tennessee mountains twenty miles east of Knoxville, where his troops spent a hard winter. Eastern Tennessee was now in Union hands.[45] With both Chattanooga and Knoxville secure, Lincoln finally tendered Grant, "and all under your command, my more than thanks—my profoundest gratitude—for the skill, courage, and perseverance with which you and they, over so great difficulties, have effected that important object."[46]

In Georgia, a retreating Rebel officer observed, "Captain, this is the death knell of the Confederacy. If we cannot cope with those fellows with the advantages we had on this line, there is not a line between here and the Atlantic Ocean where we can stop them." His captain responded, "Hush, Lieutenant. That is treason you are talking."[47] That Confederate despair reached all the way to Richmond, where President Davis reluctantly accepted the resignation of his friend Bragg as Commander of the Army of Tennessee and even more reluctantly replaced him with their mutual enemy, Joseph Johnston, after Lee declined the position.[48]

In the amazingly short period of time of about five weeks, Grant had converted a potential Union disaster at Chattanooga into a smashing success by assembling a potent force and keeping incessant pressure on the enemy. As he had done in his earlier western campaigns, Grant accomplished his success at Chattanooga with minimal casualties. Of his 56,400 troops engaged between November 23 and 25, Grant had 752 killed, 4,713 wounded and 349 missing—a total of 5,814 (10.3 percent). On the other side, Bragg's 46,165 troops had 361 killed; 2,160 wounded; and 4,146 missing (most captured)—a total of 6,667 (14.4 percent).[49]

Considering that Grant's troops were attacking an enemy entrenched on high ground above them, these statistics are an amazing tribute to Grant's intelligent but persistent aggression.

As 1863 was drawing to a close, Grant could look back at an unbroken series of successes, including Forts Henry and Donelson, Shiloh, Iuka, Corinth, Vicksburg, and Chattanooga. He had lopped off more than a third of the Confederacy and put Union armies in a position to split the remainder in half. At Vicksburg alone he had captured almost 30,000 of the enemy. According to McWhiney and Jamieson, Grant had done all of this fighting over a two-year period of time at a minimal cost of 23,500 killed and wounded (15 percent of the total 221,000 men who fought under his command in those battles and campaigns). A battle-by-battle breakdown of total Union and Confederate casualties (killed, wounded, and captured/missing) reveals that Grant imposed 82,847 casualties on the western Confederates while his armies suffered 36,688 casualties—a positive difference of 46,159. Grant had demonstrated that a Union general could aggressively maneuver and attack with great success at a relatively minimal cost.[50]

On the other hand, Lee's singular, grudging instance of supporting the western Confederate forces came about because of his reduced standing after Gettysburg. The reinforcements were delayed and weakened by Lee's reluctance; these flaws resulted in a less-than-complete victory at Chickamauga. The inter-theater troop transfer was further undermined by Lee's impatient efforts to retrieve Longstreet's two divisions. Although Bragg and Longstreet, for their own reasons, agreed with Davis' suggestion that Longstreet go off to Knoxville and thus weaken the Chattanooga lines, it was in fact Lee's idea that they had implemented.

Back in Virginia, Lee was having problems in his own theater even though Lincoln and Halleck were having trouble getting Meade to organize an aggressive offensive campaign.[51] Lee's depressed mental state appears to have aggravated the heart condition that had caused him great pain and disabled him the prior spring. Between September 20 and October 10 and again from October 31 to November 5, Lee was confined to an ambulance because of severe chest and back pains brought about by his deteriorating heart.[52]

On October 9, Lee launched his brief Bristoe Campaign after he learned that the 11th and 12th corps had been moved to Tennessee from Meade's army. Instead of sending troops to the colossal showdown at Chattanooga, Lee moved his army across the Rapidan and Rappahannock rivers in an effort to get around Meade's right flank. The campaign quickly ended in disaster. On October 14, at Bristoe Station, Virginia, three brigades under A. P. Hill were lured into a clever Yankee trap and decimated. From high ground, Hill had seen Meade's army marching north along the Orange and Alexandria Railroad toward Manassas Junction. Believing that they would catch the Union troops in a vulnerable condition while on the move, the Confederate brigades incautiously attacked the Union rear. Hidden Union forces along the railroad caught the attackers in a bloody ambush and killed, wounded, or captured almost 1,400 of them (including two brigadier generals who were killed). This disaster, caused by inadequate reconnaissance and rash offensive tactics, was one Lee could ill afford.[53]

Although Lee was not personally responsible for Bristoe Station, the same cannot be said for another disaster that occurred the following month. Lee himself, aggressive as ever, helped bring about the loss of 2,000 men along the Rappahannock. Lee hoped to lure Meade's forces across the river at Kelly's Ford and then to hit them with overwhelming force. To do this, he had Jubal Early establish and hold a bridgehead a few miles away at Rappahannock Station. Lee, however, played right into the hands of Meade, who ordered a demonstration at Kelly's Ford while planning an attack on the Confederates' vulnerable Rappahannock Station bridgehead.[54]

Lee, conferring late on November 7 with Early about the two Rebel brigades which had been advanced across the single pontoon bridge at Rappahannock Station, approved their being kept north of the bridge even in the face of hostile fire. This specific direction led to those 1,700 men being cut off and then killed, wounded or captured by Meade's attacking force. The combined fighting at the two crossings cost Lee 2,000 troops and four guns while his foes suffered only 400 casualties. Lee's adjutant, Major Walter Taylor, wrote to his fiancé that this debacle was "the saddest chapter in the history of this army."[55]

The Mine Run Campaign followed. To Lee's delight, Meade advanced across the Rapidan on November 26. Lee, of course, went on the offensive. His 2nd and 3rd Corps attacked the next day at Locust Church. The battle resulted in 550 Confederate deaths. Then both armies entrenched along Mine Run just west of Virginia's Wilderness—the old Chancellorsville battlefield. Lee, anticipating his 1864 modus operandi, entrenched his troops. Lee unsuccessfully tried to entice Meade into attacking his well-entrenched Confederates. When Meade refused to go for the bait, Lee characteristically decided to attack. In hopes of repeating Chancellorsville, Lee sent two divisions on a freezing nighttime march around the Union left. When they reached the Union trenches at dawn on December 2, the frozen Confederates found that Meade had retreated to the north.[56]

In December 1863, when he had no option but to remove Bragg, Davis again offered Lee command of the Army of Tennessee. Unsurprisingly, Lee, concerned exclusively about preserving the Old Dominion, declined the appointment. Once again Lee's stated reason for doing so was that he would not be likely to receive support from the subordinate generals in an area Lee had used as a dumping ground for failed eastern generals.[57]

While Lee had negatively affected Confederate fortunes in other theaters (especially at Vicksburg, Tullahoma, Chickamauga, and Chattanooga), he was more responsible for the fact that 1863 also had been a Confederate disaster in the East: the extremely costly "victory" at Chancellorsville, the death of Jackson, the lost opportunities and disastrous decimation at Gettysburg, the retreat to Virginia, and finally the disasters at Bristoe Station and Rappahannock Bridge. The reality was that the South was running out of men. The Confederacy had started with a real manpower shortage, but, under Lee's leadership, it had squandered that precious resource. As a result, the Confederacy would reap the whirlwind in 1864.

CHAPTER EIGHT

EARLY 1864:

BOTH GENERALS PREPARE
FOR CONFRONTATION

*Promoted to General-in-Chief, Grant goes East to retrain
the Army of the Potomac and plan a comprehensive national
campaign while Lee prepares for the inevitable assault*

I mmediately after his Chattanooga victory, Grant again proposed a winter offensive against Mobile, Alabama. He had proposed a simi- lar effort after capturing Vicksburg. Grant was not satisfied to sit idly by while more Confederate targets beckoned. Thus, on November 29, he proposed the Mobile campaign to Charles Dana, and he repeated the proposal in a December 7 letter to Halleck. In the words of Bruce Cat- ton, "[Grant] had at last reached the point where he could see that final triumph for the Union depended on crowding a beaten foe without respite, permitting no breathing spell in which the weaker antagonist could regain his balance and repair damages—using the superior power of the North, in short, to apply unrelenting pressure of a sort the

Confederacy had not the resources to resist."[1] He soon would have an opportunity to implement his national strategy.

Four Union generals emerged as leaders from the Chattanooga crisis and victory: Grant, Sherman, Thomas, and Sheridan. Their leadership would bring victories to the Union cause all over the nation in 1864 and 1865. Among that illustrious group, there was one clear leader of leaders: Grant.

Saving the army trapped in Chattanooga, breaking out of the Confederate trap, and driving Bragg's army back into Georgia guaranteed Grant greater fame and a historic promotion. From Palo Alto in Mexico through Missionary Ridge, he had fought twenty-seven battles—without defeat. He had captured two Confederate armies and soundly defeated a third.[2] On December 17, Congress recognized his accomplishments by passing a joint resolution thanking him and his officers and soldiers and directing that a gold medal be struck and presented to him.[3]

More significantly, Grant's aggressively achieved successes virtually compelled Congress and President Lincoln to offer him a promotion to lieutenant general—the first three-star American general since George Washington[4]—and Commander-in-Chief of the Union Armies. The bill reviving that rank was introduced by Elihu Washburne in the House and James Doolittle of Wisconsin in the Senate. The Senator calculated that Grant had won seventeen Civil War battles, captured 100,000 prisoners, and seized five hundred artillery pieces.[5]

Grant and Sherman did not remain inactive. Beginning on February 3, 1864, Sherman left Vicksburg and penetrated deeply into Mississippi east of Jackson. In this Meridian Campaign, a prelude to Sherman's more famous later marches, Sherman's 23,500 troops traveled light and basically lived off the countryside in the fertile, previously untouched "breadbasket" area of northern Mississippi. Casualties to Sherman's men were minimal. Despite the failure of Brigadier General William Sooy

Smith to join them with his cavalry, Sherman's men entered Meridian on February 14. In that vicinity, over a five-day period, Sherman's men destroyed sixty-one bridges, twenty locomotives, and one hundred fifteen miles of railroad track. He reported that "Meridian, with its depots, storehouses, arsenals, hospitals, offices, hotels, and cantonments no longer exists." Sherman then withdrew back to Vicksburg with the knowledge that an army could live off the countryside while destroying its resources—a lesson he would apply later in Georgia and the Carolinas. The damage to the Meridian area railroads was so extensive that it cost John Bell Hood's late 1864 campaign into Tennessee a month's delay and contributed to his defeats at Franklin and Nashville.[6]

Meanwhile, leaders of both national political parties expressed an interest in Grant's becoming president. A concerned Lincoln put out feelers on Grant's intentions and was relieved to see a letter Grant had written to an old Galena friend. In that letter, Grant had said, "I already have a pretty big job on my hands, and ... nothing could induce me to think of being a presidential candidate, particularly so long as there is a possibility of having Mr. Lincoln re-elected." Lincoln was so relieved that he immediately endorsed the bill creating the position of Lieutenant General of the Army. After congressional passage, the president signed the bill into law on February 26. Lincoln nominated Grant for the position on March 1, and the Senate confirmed him the next day. On March 3, Grant was ordered to Washington.[7]

Grant had commanded one army at Vicksburg and three armies at Chattanooga. Now he would command all the armies of the United States. He was in charge of nineteen departments and seventeen commanders.[8] His major job became coordinating their actions so that they were synchronized and mutually supporting.

Grant and his eldest son, Fred, arrived in Washington unheralded on March 8. They went to the Willard Hotel, where the desk clerk reluctantly offered them an inconvenient and ordinary room on the top floor. After Grant signed the register, the clerk quickly changed his attitude and offered Grant the best room in the house. Later Grant and his son became the center of attention in the hotel dining room as one enthusiastic patron stood on his chair and led the gawking crowd in three cheers for the general.[9]

That night Grant went to the White House to meet President Lincoln for the first time. The crowd parted for Grant to meet the president, who shook his hand, smiled, and said, "Why, here is General Grant! Well, this is a great pleasure, I assure you." Secretary of State William H. Seward introduced Grant to Mary Todd Lincoln and, when the crowd started chanting for Grant, had the short general stand on a couch to be seen by all. The pandemonium only increased.

The next day, March 9, Grant returned to the White House to receive his commission from the president. "The turning point of the entire Civil War would be when Grant took command. He had a completely different way of doing things," according to historian Gordon Rhea.[10] The Union now would have a general who had a broad national view of the war (something the Confederacy lacked), coordinated the activities of all theaters, and realized that destruction of Lee's army was the primary mission in the Virginia theater. Although Grant kept Meade as commander of the Army of the Potomac, he usually was its *de facto* commander. Never again would that army's soldiers be the victims of the incompetence or timidity so often demonstrated by their earlier commanders, Irvin McDowell, McClellan (twice), Pope, Burnside, Hooker, and Meade, who had suffered 144,000 casualties without moving the war to conclusion. They would be part of a coordinated nationwide assault on Confederate armies rather than on mere places. As Rhea said, "Their objective under Grant was the destruction of Confederate armies, and the days of short battles followed by months of inactivity were over. Henceforth, Union armies were to engage the armed forces of the rebellion and batter them into submission, giving no respite."[11] Historian Michael C. C. Adams has astutely observed that one of the turning points of the war probably was "the decision of Grant to march with the Army of the Potomac, for this ensured that Lee would be hit hard at last."[12]

On the Confederate side, Grant's old friend Longstreet knew what was coming. As renowned historian Bruce Catton told it,

> Over in the Army of Northern Virginia, James Longstreet was quietly warning people not to underestimate this new Yankee commander: "That man will fight us every day and every hour till the end of the war." Nobody in the North heard the remark, but the quality which had called it forth had not gone unnoticed. Here was the man who looked as if he would ram his way through a brick wall, and since other tactics had not worked perhaps that was the thing to try. At Fort Donelson and at Vicksburg he had swallowed two Confederate armies whole, and at Chattanooga he had driven a third army in head-long retreat from what had been thought to be an impregnable stronghold, and all anyone could think of was the hard blow that ended matters. Men seemed ready to call Grant the hammerer before he even began to hammer.[13]

Lincoln wanted an aggressive, proven winner to challenge and defeat Lee. Grant was his man. Troops in the Army of the Potomac agreed. Among them was soldier-artist Charles Ellington Reed, who welcomed Grant's appointment even though he foresaw tough fighting ahead: "placeing [*sic*] Grant in command is the grandest coup yet. It has inspired all with that confidence that insures success. I have not the slightest doubt but that we shall be gloriously successful this comeing [*sic*] campaign. There will be hard fighting without doubt. Many assert that our next battle will eclipse all others in magnitude and slaughter, but that remains to be seen."[14] Needing Grant to make substantial early progress to ensure his own reelection, Lincoln demonstrated his complete confidence in the general by telling Stanton to "leave him alone to do as he pleases."[15]

On March 10, the day after receiving his three-star commission, Grant visited Meade at the Army of the Potomac's Brandy Station, Virginia, headquarters. Meade graciously offered to step aside as army commander so that Grant could name someone of his own choosing. If Grant had any plans of making such a change (he may at one time have planned to appoint "Baldy" Smith[16]), Meade's gesture ended them. Grant assured him that he would retain the command. Although Grant avoided the politics of Washington by keeping his command in the field with Meade's army, Grant generally issued orders to the Army of the Potomac through Meade.[17] Keeping Meade, instead of commanding the army himself, may have been a mistake because of the ambiguity Grant created about who really was in charge. Bruce Catton observed, "At the very least it must be said that the dual command arrangement was a handicap,"[18] and Robert N. Thompson concluded that, as a result of Grant's intention to issue instructions through Meade, "the Army of the Potomac appeared to have two heads."[19]

Having decided to retain Meade in place and to accompany him in the field, Grant quickly made other important decisions. Sherman would command the three-army march on Atlanta, McPherson would replace him as commander of the Army of the Tennessee, and "Black Jack" Logan would replace McPherson.[20] In an early interview with Lincoln, Grant expressed his dissatisfaction with the eastern Union cavalry and secured the president's consent to bring Phil Sheridan east to command the Army of the Potomac's cavalry corps.[21] Grant's senior team was in place. By April 6, Grant also had assembled an experienced and professional personal staff. Unlike Lee, Grant had a large, competent staff and used it.[22]

Grant also took care of another important piece of business in Washington. His former superior, Halleck, requested to be relieved as general-in-chief in light of Grant's promotion. Grant cleverly arranged for Halleck to be chief-of-staff. Through this deft separation of administration from strategic command, "a crucial innovation in modern warfare," Grant had Halleck handle the political and handholding chores in Washington while Grant was free to command in the field.[23]

Although Meade was left in command of the Army of the Potomac, it quickly became known as "Grant's army." One reason for that may be that changes immediately began to take place. Inspectors general suddenly took an interest in what units were and were not doing; unit commanders had to reduce the discrepancy between "numbers present for duty" and "numbers present for duty, equipped;" discipline became tighter; infantrymen were drilled on how to fire a rifle (since so many abandoned weapons on battlefields had contained multiple Minié balls indicating they had never been fired); artillerymen were drilled on assembling and disassembling their guns; cavalrymen received new Spencer seven-shot repeater rifles; and the entire army benefitted from trainloads of supplies and equipment that arrived at Brandy Station.[24]

In March and April 1864, Grant devised a grand strategy that would put all Union troops on the offensive against their Confederate counterparts and thereby keep the latter from using their interior lines to transfer troops among theaters. This plan envisioned Sherman's three armies (the Cumberland, the Tennessee, and the Ohio) pushing Joseph Johnston's Army of Tennessee southeastward back toward Atlanta, Nathaniel Banks joining Sherman after capturing Mobile, General Franz

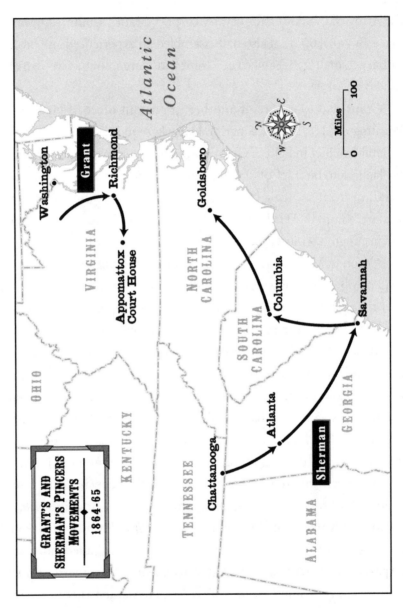

Grant's and Sherman's Pincers Movements (1864–65)
Map by David Deis, Dreamline Cartography, Northridge, CA

Sigel clearing Confederates out of the Shenandoah Valley, Major General Benjamin F. Butler directly attacking Petersburg-Richmond via the James River, and the Army of the Potomac going after Lee's Army of Northern Virginia until it was defeated or destroyed.[25] Every Union soldier and army had a role. As Lincoln told Grant and Grant told Sherman (without attribution), "Those not skinning can hold a leg."[26] Grant told Meade: "Lee's army will be your objective point. Wherever Lee's army goes, you will go also."[27]

This strategy would not only advance the offensive goals of the Union, but it also would preclude the Confederates from having the flexibility to converge their forces in a meaningful counterattack. Remembering earlier Confederate convergences at Shiloh and Chickamauga, Grant and Sherman were determined to prevent a repetition of them.[28] Grant declined a White House banquet in his honor so that he instead could quickly head west to meet with Sherman.[29] Coordination with Sherman was so important to Grant that he spent March 11–23 on a trip to visit him in Nashville, including extended consultations on Grant's return train ride from Nashville to Cincinnati. Grant made it clear that Sherman's primary objective was Johnston's Army of Tennessee and that his secondary objective was Atlanta. Grant's hope was that a successful campaign there would divide the remaining Confederacy in half.[30]

On his return trip, Grant was accompanied to Cincinnati by his friends and confidants, Sherman and Grenville Dodge. There they laid out maps and planned their end-the-war campaigns. Sherman later said that Grant's plan was simple: Grant would go for Lee, and Sherman would go for Joe Johnston.[31] Grant's primary concern then and later was to ensure that Sherman's thrust in Georgia and Meade's in Virginia would keep the Confederates so occupied that they could not reinforce each other. To protect against the possibility of Confederate inter-theater transfers, he wrote to Sherman:

> What I now want more particularly to say is, that if the two main attacks, yours and the one from here, should promise great success, the enemy may, in a fit of desperation, abandon one part of their line of defense, and throw their whole strength upon the other, believing a single defeat without any victory to sustain them better than a defeat all along their line, and hoping too, at the same time, that the army meeting with no resistance, will rest perfectly satisfied with their laurels, having penetrated to a given point south, thereby enabling them to throw their force first upon one and then on the other.
>
> With the majority of military commanders they might do this. But you have had too much experience in traveling light, and subsisting upon the country, to be caught by any such ruse. I hope my experience has not been thrown away. My directions, then, would be, if the enemy in your front shows signs of joining Lee, follow him up to the full extent of your ability. I will prevent the concentration of Lee upon your front, if it is in the power of this army to do it.[32]

Sherman promised Grant that he would "ever bear in mind that Johnston is at all times to be kept so busy that he cannot, in any event, send no [sic] part of his command against you or Banks."[33]

As Grant planned his campaign against Lee, at least he was moderately free of presidential interference. In Grant's first interview with Lincoln, the president told him he was not a military man and would not interfere but that he was opposed to procrastination.[34] That was a problem he would not have with Grant. Lincoln wrote him, "The particulars of your plans I neither know, or seek to know. You are vigilant and self-reliant; and, pleased with this, I wish not to obtrude any constraints or restraints upon you."[35] Lincoln was confident that he finally had a forceful and effective general in the East, where Union commanders had little to show for all their losses—except the casualties Lee's ever-attacking army had suffered.[36] Grant, however, was to be handicapped in 1864 by incompetent political generals (Sigel, Banks, Butler) commanding many of his ancillary campaigns and by the waste of resources on the Red River Campaign, which he opposed.[37]

Union intelligence confirmed the springtime arrival of Longstreet's 1st Corps back in the main Virginia theater and pinpointed its location at Gordonsville, about a day's march from Lee's other two corps near the Rapidan River.[38] As late as March 25, Lee remained doubtful that Grant, the westerner, would direct the primary Union assault against his army in Virginia rather than against Johnston's army in Georgia. Lee reminded Davis of the ruses Grant had used at Vicksburg, told him he doubted the first Union effort would be against Richmond, and concluded that Grant's first efforts would be against Johnston in Georgia or Longstreet in Tennessee. Lee seems not to have contemplated Grant directing the simultaneous assaults by two Union armies of 100,000 or more apiece.[39]

Grant's primary decision concerning his advance in Virginia was whether to move to the east or west of Lee. An advance to the west was more likely to force Lee to fight in the open and thereby enhance the value of Grant's supremacy in overall numbers and especially in artillery. That course of action, however, would compel Grant to rely on tenuous overland lines of supply via questionable roads and a single rail line. Grant decided to move east of Lee so that he could utilize Union waterborne transportation to supply his troops via all the rivers and streams that fed into the Potomac River and Chesapeake Bay. That route also would facilitate coordination with the movements on the James River of Butler, in whom Grant had little or no confidence. In addition, the fords across the Rapidan were more accessible by the eastern route, Longstreet's corps was farther away, and the previous November Lee had taken thirty hours to defend his right flank in the same area.[40]

William Feis captured the gist of Grant's strategy as he began the Overland Campaign:

> In any event, the endgame for Grant was not the capture of strategic points but the destruction of Lee's army, and he could achieve this in one of two ways. He could fight him on open ground or in the Wilderness, or perhaps force him to retreat. Even if Lee withdrew, Grant understood that it would only delay the inevitable. To prevail in this war, the military might of the Confederacy had to be destroyed. At some point, therefore, Grant would have to stand toe to toe with Lee and beat him, regardless of the circumstances. Nothing short of this would guarantee the death of the rebellion.[41]

In the same letter in which Grant told Meade that his objective was Lee's army, Grant also advised that Burnside's independent 9th Corps would be brought east to add another 25,000 men to the Union forces in Virginia.[42] With the addition of Burnside's 9th Corps, the Army of the Potomac had 120,000 soldiers against Lee's 66,000.[43] Although Grant would move toward Richmond, he would do so because Lee had to defend the Confederate capital and major rail hub and manufacturing center. In the words of Jean Edward Smith, "Richmond was to be attacked because it was defended by Lee, not Lee because he defended Richmond."[44] Grant also realized that an army's communications and supply were vital to its survival and went after Lee's communications and supply routes whenever possible.[45]

Taking the initiative and clinging to Lee's army, however, would be costly. According to Rhea, "The very nature of Grant's assignment guaranteed hard fighting and severe casualties. Mistakes there were. The facts, however, do not support the caricature of Grant as a general who eschewed maneuver in favor of headlong assaults and needlessly sacrificed his men. Quite the opposite is true."[46] Grant was prepared to pay the price to end the war and get Lincoln reelected. This time, unlike earlier eastern efforts, the price would buy results.

In just two months, Grant took control of all Union armies and worked out his grand strategy to end the war. Grant realized that Lee had seriously weakened his and other Confederate armies through the massive casualties of 1862 and 1863. Therefore, Union armies would continuously pressure the Confederates everywhere and continue to do so until the war was won.[47] Grant decided to use all of the Union's military forces to keep the Confederates on the defensive everywhere and thereby preclude their sending reinforcements to each other.[48] This strategy generally deprived the Rebels of the advantage they possessed by virtue of their inner, shorter lines of communication and reflected Grant's determination to take advantage of the Union's manpower superiority. Grant's strategy resulted in Union victory in less than a year.

As Grant planned his nationwide offensives, Lee spent the winter and spring of 1864 simplistically urging an offensive by Johnston through barren mountains (with few foraging opportunities) into middle Tennessee—even though Johnston had virtually no mobile supply capability and had half the strength of Sherman, who was opposing him.[49] Relying on false rumors that five western Union corps were being moved to Virginia, Lee insisted that a Johnston offensive was necessary to relieve pressure on Virginia.[50]

Sherman later contrasted Lee's myopia unfavorably to Grant's sweeping national strategy:

> [Lee] never rose to the grand problem which involved a con-
> tinent and future generations. His Virginia was to him the
> world.... He stood at the front porch battling with the flames
> whilst the kitchen and house were burning, sure in the end
> to consume the whole.... Grant's "strategy" embraced a con-
> tinent, Lee's a small State; Grant's "logistics" were to supply
> and transport armies thousands of miles, where Lee was
> limited to hundreds.[51]

Given Grant's desire to seek out and destroy Lee's army, Lee played right
into his hands. During 1862 and 1863, Lee's hyper-aggression had
reduced the Army of Northern Virginia to a mere shadow of what it had
been or what it still could have been.[52] Because of the North's virtually
unlimited manpower resources (especially since it would employ as
many as 180,000 African-Americans in its army by war's end),[53] Lee
probably had militarily lost the war by the beginning of 1864. That is, if
the war continued to its military conclusion, the Confederacy would
lose.

If Lee could, however, find some way to preserve the forces he had
left and perhaps even provide some support to the defense of Atlanta,[54]
the Confederacy might be able to maintain a stalemate sufficient to win
the war at the Northern ballot boxes in November 1864. In March 1864,
Longstreet described this connection between the military events of
1864 and that year's presidential election: "Lincoln's re-election seems
to depend upon the result of our efforts during the present year. If he is
re-elected, the war must continue, and I see no way of defeating his reelection except by military success."[55]

But it was a long time from April to November, and Lee was not a patient man. Lee aggressively sought out the Army of the Potomac, underestimated Grant's tenacity and cunning, launched attacks as though he had a surplus of manpower, and periodically committed costly blunders. As a result, the leadership and manpower of Lee's army were further decimated—despite his efforts to strip the Carolinas to reinforce his own army—and the war went so badly for the South that Lincoln was reelected over the accommodating McClellan and the Confederacy thereby was doomed.

In early 1864, as he had done on many prior occasions, Lee sought to strengthen his own army at the expense of forces elsewhere. That April, while the Army of Tennessee faced a massive offensive by Sherman, Lee made his familiar argument that "the great effort of the enemy in this campaign will be made in Virginia."[56] On April 7, Lee wrote to Bragg: "I think every preparation should be made to meet the approaching storm, which will apparently burst on Virginia, & unless its force can be diverted by an attack in the West, that troops should be collected to oppose it."[57] Based on that hypothesis and rumors Lee passed on to Richmond about western Federals coming east, Lee astoundingly requested part of Johnston's cavalry and recommended that Johnston's army take the offensive against Sherman. At that time, the Union numerical advantage was 198,000 to 74,000 in the middle theater and 148,000 to 82,000 in the East.[58] Contrary to Lee's advice, Johnston went on the defensive and preserved his forces much more effectively than did Lee. Persistent to a fault, Lee in May requested Davis to send him more troops from Florida, Georgia, and the Carolinas.[59]

Thus, as the crucial campaigns of 1864 approached, Grant and Lee continued demonstrating the traits that had characterized their efforts in the first three years of the war. Grant took a national perspective and planned to aggressively attack all Confederate forces. Meanwhile, Lee stressed the overwhelming importance of the Virginia theater; sought reinforcements for his army from elsewhere; and provided pathetic advice concerning, and no reinforcements for, the middle theater. The ultimate results were the fall of Atlanta, the reelection of Lincoln, and the loss of the war.

CHAPTER NINE

SPRING 1864:
GRANT ATTACKS AND
BESIEGES LEE

With Lincoln's reelection in the balance, Grant moves the Army of the Potomac against Lee's Army of Northern Virginia at the Wilderness, Spotsylvania Court House, North Anna River, and Cold Harbor before crossing the James River and threatening Petersburg.

rant's 46-day Overland Campaign at long last put him head-to-head against Lee, whose army Grant was determined to defeat—if not destroy. It took Grant less than two months to get his army to the Richmond-Petersburg area with an opportunity for immediate success and less than a year to defeat Lee and end the Civil War. In his memoirs, Grant looked back at the start of that campaign:

Soon after midnight, May 3rd–4th, the Army of the Potomac moved out… to start upon that memorable campaign, destined to result in the capture of the Confederate capital and the army defending it. This was not to be accomplished, however, without as desperate fighting as the world has ever witnessed; not to be consummated in a day, a week, a month, or a single season. The losses inflicted, and endured, were destined to be severe; but the armies now confronting each other had already been in conflict for a period of three years, with immense losses in killed, by death from sickness, captured and wounded; and neither had made any real progress toward accomplishing the final end.... So here was a standoff. The campaign now begun was destined to result in heavier losses, to both armies, in a given time, than any previously suffered; but the carnage was to be limited to a single year, and to accomplish all that had been anticipated or desired at the beginning of that time. We had to have hard fighting to achieve this.[1]

On April 18, Grant reviewed the 6th Corps and received a mixed review from an observer, Elisha Hunt Rhodes, a Rhode Islander who rose from private to lieutenant colonel during the war: "General Grant is a short thick set man and rode his horse like a bag of meal. I was a little disappointed in the appearance, but I like the look of his eye."[2]

Grant's plans for several simultaneous assaults were undermined by three incompetent political generals who still commanded Union troops because Lincoln needed their election-year support. First, Massachusetts Democrat Butler failed in the direct assault on the Richmond-Petersburg area. After landing his 40,000-man Army of the James at Bermuda Hundred, a peninsula between the Appomattox and James Rivers, Butler foolishly spent a week building fortifications instead of immediately attacking. This delay enabled Beauregard to gather reinforcements from North Carolina, march north from Petersburg, and engage Butler at Drewry's Bluff, about six miles south of Richmond. Beauregard's surprise attack drove Butler away from the Richmond-Petersburg rail-road and back into Bermuda Hundred. Butler had failed to occupy the Confederate works at Drewry's Bluff or to take any other action to permanently cut the supply-line from Petersburg to Richmond. As a result of his reticence and incompetence, Butler remained so bottled up in Bermuda Hundred that Grant thereafter withdrew troops from But-ler for use under productive generals elsewhere.[3]

Failure also marked the Shenandoah Valley campaign of the Ger-man-American Major General Franz Sigel. He had attracted into the Union Army many German-Americans who proudly proclaimed, "I fights mit Sigel."[4] His May 1864 campaign, however, was a disaster. With 9,000 troops, he headed south up the Shenandoah Valley but was routed by Major General John C. Breckinridge's 5,300 troops (including 247 Virginia Military Institute cadets) at the Battle of New Market on May 15. Grant replaced him with Major General David Hunter on May 26; military necessity overrode political considerations.[5]

Far to the southwest, on the Red River, another Massachusetts Dem-ocratic general, Nathaniel Banks, was matching the ineptitude of Butler and Sigel. His second and strategically pointless campaign up the Red River in Louisiana had been stopped cold by a crushing defeat at Sabine Crossroads (or Mansfield), which was followed by a downriver retreat in which Banks nearly lost his army. Banks' demoralized forces were then unable to carry out Grant's plans for an assault on the port city of Mobile, Alabama.[6]

Fortunately for Grant, the other major Union campaign of that spring and summer was in the capable hands of Grant's good friend Sherman. He commanded the armies of the Cumberland, the Tennessee, and the Ohio. During the month of May, Sherman made steady progress, moving from the Tennessee border toward Atlanta in northwestern Georgia. He engaged in fights at Dalton, Resaca, and Dallas but focused

primarily on moving around the flanks of Joseph Johnston's Army of
Tennessee and moving closer to Atlanta. Through June and into early
July, Sherman avoided frontal assaults (except his costly effort at Kennesaw Mountain) and continued to move around Johnston's flanks.
Sherman's maneuvers enabled him to avoid fighting Johnston at rivers
or at strong defensive fortifications prepared by Johnston. The decisive
moment came on July 8, when Sherman's left flank crossed the Chattahoochee and threatened Atlanta.[7]

Back at Culpeper, Virginia, Grant planned and then initiated his
campaign against Lee. On the night of May 3, he met with his personal
staff and discussed the coming campaign. He wanted to destroy or seriously damage the Army of Northern Virginia before it reached the
existing fortifications at Richmond. Grant explained that he wanted all
his commanders to focus on enemy armies rather than enemy cities.[8]
Finally, he previewed and invited full staff participation:

> I want you to discuss with me freely from time to time the
> details of the orders given for the conduct of a battle, and
> learn my views as fully as possible as to what course should
> be pursued in all the contingencies which may arise. I expect
> to send you to the critical points of the lines to keep me
> promptly advised of what is taking place, and in cases of great
> emergency, when new dispositions have to be made on the
> instant, or it becomes suddenly necessary to reinforce one
> command by sending to its aid troops from another, and
> there is not time to communicate with headquarters, I want
> you to explain my views to commanders, and urge immedi-
> ate action, looking to cooperation, without waiting for spe-
> cific orders from me.[9]

Grant, unlike Lee, clearly empowered his personal staff.

Just after midnight on May 4, Grant launched his famous Overland Campaign[10] as Meade's Army of the Potomac and then Burnside's independent (of Meade) 9th Corps crossed the Rapidan at Germanna and Ely's fords. Grant had a total of about 120,000 men under his command. As the Union troops crossed the fords and headed toward the Wilderness, Grant received a Union signal-corps intercept indicating that Lee was rushing troops to intercept the advance. A satisfied Grant commented, "That gives me the information I wanted. It shows that Lee is drawing out from his position and is pushing across to meet us."[11] Grant wanted a battle, and Lee obliged by moving toward Grant's forces in the Wilderness.

Historian James F. Epperson provided an insightful analysis of the manner in which the armies of Grant and Lee came into contact in the Wilderness:

> Actually, Grant's plan called for the Army of the Potomac to wheel southwest toward Lee's army, and Grant was quite willing to engage Lee within the confines of the Wilderness. Lee did not figure out Grant's plan. Quite to the contrary, Lee precipitated the battle by essentially ordering his advanced infantry corps to find out Grant's intentions. And there is no reliable evidence from the period to support the notion that Lee actually wanted a battle within the Wilderness, while there is substantial evidence that Lee wanted to fight behind the entrenchments at Mine Run.[12]

Grant was aware that Longstreet's corps was some distance beyond the corps of Ewell and Hill, and he hoped to bring on a battle before Longstreet arrived. Although Lee had a total of 66,000 troops at his disposal,[13]

he had put himself at a distinct disadvantage because of Longstreet's
location back at Orange Court House. Because of the prepositioning of
Longstreet, Lee only had two-thirds of his troops for the Wilderness
conflict on May 5, and Longstreet did not arrive on the battlefield until
midmorning on May 6. Longstreet's men did not start marching toward
the Wilderness until 11:00 a.m. on May 4, many hours after Grant's
troops started crossing the Rapidan River.

Given Lee's desire to intercept Grant's forces in the Wilderness, it is
surprising how slowly he brought his three corps to bear. If Lee's intent
was to use Longstreet to protect the important railroad junction at
Gordonsville, he took a tremendous gamble by using all of one of his
three corps for that purpose when a lesser force could have provided
sufficient security or at least an adequate warning capability. General
Alexander was especially critical of Lee's poor positioning of Longstreet's
corps at Mechanicsville, some forty-three miles from the battlefield
behind the Confederates' left flank. He found it particularly puzzling in
light of Lee's statement on May 2 that he expected Grant to turn the
Confederates' right flank. Alexander described what he saw as a grand
missed opportunity:

> The first day, naturally, offered us far the greatest chances.
> Grant's army was not all in hand, & had had no time to make
> breastworks. It was at a great disadvantage in the Wilderness
> & could not use its superiority in artillery. We had here the
> one rare chance of the whole campaign to involve it in a panic
> such as ruined Hooker on the same ground.... What proved
> a drawn battle when begun by three divisions reinforced by
> two more after six hours & by three more 18 hours later
> might have proved a decisive victory if fought by all eight
> from the beginning.[14]

Because of Lee's failure to have his forces at full strength and in place to meet Grant's army as it entered the Wilderness, May 4 was a successful day for the Blue Army. Although still strung out at the end of the day, they had moved all their forces across the Rapidan with no opposition.

While Longstreet was coming up, Lee sent his other two corps on a reconnaissance-in-force eastward on the parallel Orange Turnpike and Orange Plank Road.[15] Epperson commented that "[a]pparently, Lee did not think Grant was turning toward him, for he sent two thirds of his army forward on separated roads with no good line of communication between them and with the remaining one-third of his army a full day's march to the rear."[16]

After the entire Union Army crossed the Rapidan without interference, fierce fighting erupted in the Wilderness on May 5, and the vicious Battle of the Wilderness continued for two whole days.[17] Grant's operations in that battle were adversely affected by the failure of the federal cavalry, under the ineffective command of Brigadier General James H. Wilson (Grant's former aide), to provide adequate and accurate information on the approaching Confederates. Despite having orders to send out reconnaissance patrols on each of the major roads in the area, Wilson failed to maintain adequate pickets at key locations and to detect the proximity of Confederate troops on the evening of May 4 and the morning of May 5. Nevertheless, Grant was determined to attack Lee as soon as the enemy was located and, because of Lee's poor positioning of Longstreet, he wanted to do so before Longstreet's 1st Corps arrived. Close to 8:30 a.m., Grant urged Meade to attack: "If any opportunity presents [it]self for pitching into a part of Lee's Army do so without giving time for [di]sposition."[18] Against their wishes, the strung-out, frontline Union troops therefore were ordered to attack and did engage the Confederates before Lee was at full strength.[19]

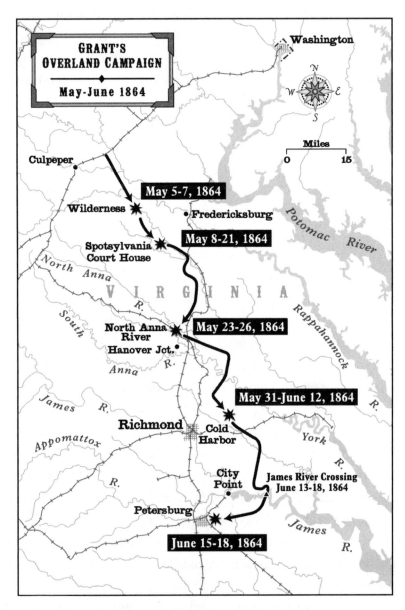

The Overland Campaign (May–June 1864)
Map by David Deis, Dreamline Cartography, Northridge, CA

Early on the afternoon of May 5, accordingly, Major General Gouverneur K. Warren's Union 5th Corps attacked Lieutenant General Richard Ewell's 2nd Corps at Saunders' Field on the Orange Turnpike, the northern east/west approach to Fredericksburg. Ewell's men held their ground and counterattacked. That fighting spread south to Higgerson's Field and north along Culpeper Mine Road, continued all afternoon and evening, and resulted in tremendous casualties to both sides.[20]

To the south, Major General Winfield Scott Hancock and his Union 2nd Corps had proceeded south on the Brock Road with plans to turn west toward Lee on a road south of the Orange Plank Road. His plans were disrupted by the fighting well to his rear and the threat posed by Hill's 3rd Corps, which was marching east on the Orange Plank Road. Hill was headed for the intersection of the Plank Road and Brock Road, where he would split the Union forces. While a division from Major General John Sedgwick's 6th Corps initially delayed Hill's approach, Hancock hastened to carry out orders from Grant and Meade to reverse his course on the Brock Road and get back to the Plank Road to stop Hill.[21]

Of course, Grant did not just want Hill stopped; he wanted an attack on Hill. Hancock's corps began arriving at the crucial intersection at 3:00 p.m., and his troops launched their major assault down the Orange Plank Road around 4:30 p.m. Bloody fighting continued all afternoon and into the darkness. Hill had been firmly stopped and potential disaster averted.[22]

As to the first day's fighting at the Wilderness, Overland Campaign historian Rhea concluded that Grant had been impatient and his coordination sloppy. However, he said, "there was still something about the quiet man's style that promised a new era of warfare in Virginia.... Grant would keep trying until he got it right."[23] More positively, historian Don

Lowry explained how Grant took the initiative: "It was Grant, matching tactics to strategy, who ordered an attack on Lee as soon as his forces were encountered, in order to put him on the defensive and keep him too busy to launch one of his famous flank attacks."[24]

That evening Grant chatted with Henry Wing, a young reporter who was returning to Washington to file his story. Grant gave him a verbal message to deliver to President Lincoln. At two o'clock in the morning of June 7, Wing saw Lincoln and delivered the message: "[Grant] told me I was to tell you, Mr. President, that there would be no turning back." Lincoln happily embraced the reporter.

On the night of June 5, Lee left Hill's battered and disorganized forces in an advanced and exposed position on the Orange Plank Road. He failed to withdraw them, as Hill himself requested, under cover of darkness despite the fact that Hill's flanks were exposed to attack from a massive accumulation of federal forces and the non-arrival of Longstreet. According to one Confederate sharpshooter, they "lay in the shape of a semicircle, exhausted and bleeding, with but little order or distinctive organization." Lee inexplicably was relying upon Longstreet's early arrival although he knew that Longstreet had said he would march at 1:00 a.m. from a point from which it had taken a messenger ninety minutes to ride to Lee. That same night Grant decided to have Hancock attack along the Plank Road and Burnside's 9th Corps pierce the unguarded center between the Confederate forces on the Turnpike and the Plank Road and then swing left (south) to hit Hill's left flank and rear. The attack was set for 5:00 a.m.[25]

Thus, Grant took advantage of the opportunity Lee had offered and Hancock attacked Hill at dawn. Despite Burnside being a "no-show," Hancock routed Hill's forces. Imminent disaster loomed for the Rebels until the long-awaited arrival of Longstreet's 1st Corps saved the day. Lee was so excited by its arrival that he announced, "I want to lead the

Texas Brigade in this charge!" He was dissuaded by Brigadier General John Gregg's Texans, who yelled, "Go back, General Lee, go back! We won't go on unless you go back!" The Confederates then completed and stabilized their line.[26]

Hill's retreating forces were reinforced by Longstreet, who stabilized the Confederate line and then counterattacked. When Confederate artillery shells began landing near Grant's headquarters, an officer there suggested to Grant that the headquarters be moved. Grant responded, "It strikes me it would be better to order up some artillery and defend the present position." Lee later authorized Longstreet to counterattack around the exposed southern flank of the Union forces via an abandoned railroad bed. Longstreet initially surprised the Union defenders and, in Hancock's postwar words, "rolled me [Hancock] up like a wet blanket." Longstreet was driving back the 2nd Corps troops when he was hit by friendly fire from Confederates on the Plank Road as he dangerously swept across their front. His serious throat and shoulder wounds brought the attack to an immediate halt.[27]

That afternoon, however, Lee once again played into Grant's hands. The Union line at the Brock Road/Plank Road intersection was not as vulnerable as it may have appeared in the initial moments of Longstreet's surprise flank assault. Just after 4:00 p.m., Lee personally launched a thirteen-brigade frontal assault against Union fortifications along Brock Road that were perpendicular to the Orange Plank Road. "At nearly every point of attack, Lee's troops were stopped by a deadly curtain of musketry and cannon fire."[28] The Rebels were repulsed with heavy losses.[29]

That same morning and afternoon, inconclusive fighting continued to the north on and near the Orange Turnpike. The increasingly incompetent Ewell, relying on the unreliable Jubal Early, ignored Brigadier General John B. Gordon's accurate, eyewitness information that the Union right flank was open to attack. When Lee finally learned about

Gordon's observations and advice, he ordered a late-afternoon attack around the Union right flank. Although the attack was initially successful, all of Gordon's troops eventually were either swallowed up or repulsed by Union troops and darkness.[30]

After two days of vicious, confused, and bloody fighting in the Wilderness, both armies were further shocked as wounded soldiers were burned alive in the fires spreading through the woods between the lines. Grant's forces had taken almost 18,000 casualties in two days, while Lee had lost over 11,000 troops. Grant, however, had achieved his strategic goal of attaching himself to Lee's army—within forty-eight hours of starting his campaign. Lee had cooperated perfectly with Grant's plans to go after Lee's army and had again suffered large losses that he could not make up. While Grant lost 15 percent of his soldiers, Lee lost a critical 20 percent of his strength—identical to their war-long percentages lost in battle. Lee's offensive had destroyed any reserve he might assemble, and he was compelled to remain on the defensive and rarely counterattack for the rest of the war.[31]

Unlike his eastern predecessors after Seven Days', Fredericksburg, and Chancellorsville, Grant was not persuaded to retreat as a result of the bloody fighting and great loss of life at the Wilderness. He was determined to carry on—even if some of his officers needed some bucking up. Shortly after Gordon's attack late on the second day of battle, one of Grant's generals told him that a crisis existed and that Lee would throw his whole army on the Union rear and cut off its communications. Grant sent a message to the entire Army of the Potomac when he responded:

> Oh, I am heartily tired of hearing about what Lee is going to
> do. Some of you always seem to think he is suddenly going
> to turn a double-somersault and land in our rear and on both

of our flanks at the same time. Go back to your command, and try to think what we are going to do ourselves instead of what Lee is going to do.[32]

On May 7, the day after the Battle of the Wilderness, Elisha Hunt Rhodes no longer had any qualms about Grant: "If we were under any other General except Grant I should expect a retreat, but Grant is not that kind of a soldier, and we feel that we can trust him."[33] Another more skeptical soldier said that Grant "has come up from the Western army, where they have been fighting skirmish-lines, and has found that we have lines of battle to fight here, and he is now studying how to get back across the Rapidan."[34] In fact, that very morning Grant had issued orders to Meade to spend the day preparing for a flank movement southeast toward Spotsylvania Court House.[35]

The defining moment of the Overland Campaign was Grant's decision, after engaging in the fierce fight in the Wilderness, to not retreat across the Rappahannock as his eastern predecessors would have done but instead to move southeast and on toward Richmond.[36] Jean Edward Smith called it "the final turning point of the war."[37] Rhea explained the impact of Grant's determination and forward movement after the Wilderness:

> Hooker had treated his loss in the Wilderness as a defeat. Grant lost more troops in the Wilderness, but rather than retreat he pushed on. Defensively-minded commanders such as McClellan, Burnside, Hooker, and Meade considered as defeats setbacks that Grant shrugged off as mere tactical reverses. It was this new way of thinking that got the Army of the Potomac through stalemates at the Wilderness, Spotsylvania, North Anna, and Cold Harbor, and on to victory.[38]

And Sherman put it in the context of the men Grant had lost and would lose: "Undismayed, with a full comprehension of the importance of the work in which he was engaged, feeling as keen a sympathy for his dead and wounded as anyone, and without stopping to count his numbers, he gave his orders calmly, specifically, and absolutely—'Forward to Spotsylvania.'"[39]

When his troops realized that Grant was ordering an advance, they went wild. Grant had to order them not to cheer for fear of revealing their movement. As he often did, historian Shelby Foote caught the spirit of that moment:

> But now a murmur, swelling rapidly to a chatter, began to move back down the column from its head, and presently each man could see for himself that the turn, beyond the ruins of the Chancellor mansion, had been to the right. They were headed south, not north; they were advancing, not retreating; Grant was giving them another go at Lee.... There were cheers and even a few tossed caps, and long afterwards men were to say that, for them, this had been the high point of the war.[40]

Thus, on the night of May 7–8, the Army of the Potomac marched off to try to outflank the Army of Northern Virginia. Lee himself expected a retreat and advised Seddon that the "enemy has abandoned his position and is moving towards Fredericksburg."[41] Grant's decision to continue the campaign, however, sent a message not only to his own Union troops but also to Lee and his army. In the words of Michael C. C. Adams,

> This forward move must also have demonstrated to the rebel generals that they were playing a different kind of game from

the one with McClellan, Hooker, and Meade. A shrewd observer might have sensed that here was the beginning of the end for an army that could no longer rely on the mental intimidation of its opponent to compensate for its own weakness in numerical strength.[42]

While riding toward Spotsylvania Court House along the Brock Road, Grant, Meade, and members of their staffs accidentally left the main road and drifted toward the Confederate lines. So determined was Grant not to turn back that he at first objected to doing so. Colonel Horace Porter described the incident: "General Grant at first demurred when it was proposed to turn back, and urged the guide to try and find some crossroad leading to the Brock Road, to avoid retracing our steps. This was an instance of his marked aversion to turning back, which amounted almost to a superstition."[43]

Lee gave orders to move at 4:00 a.m. on May 8 toward the east in pursuit of what he believed were the fleeing Federals. Fortunately for Lee, a new corps commander, Major General Richard H. Anderson, replacing the injured Longstreet, could find no place to bivouac in the smoke-filled Wilderness, decided to begin the eastward trek three hours early at 1:00 a.m., and kept going once he saw the slow progress being made. Anderson's men had to follow a newly cut, stump-filled trail as they paralleled the Union Army's southeasterly march. Ahead of and parallel to Anderson, on the Brock Road northwest of Spotsylvania Court House, Confederate cavalry delayed the Union infantry for critical hours before giving way to superior numbers and firepower. As a result of the cavalry's delaying tactics and Anderson's early start and all-night forced march, his infantrymen were able to intercept and block—by a matter of seconds or minutes—the southward advance of the Union forces near Spotsylvania Court House. Lee's army entrenched

in the vicinity of the Brock Road northwest of the courthouse, and
Grant's army sought a way to get around or through Lee's position.

Unfortunately for Grant and the Army of the Potomac, confusion
reigned on the southeasterly march toward Spotsylvania Court House.[44]
Sheridan's cavalry and Warren's infantry got in each other's way, Confederate cavalry delayed the Union movement, and Meade reversed a
Sheridan order that would have blocked a Confederate advance.[45]

One ramification of the confused Union movement toward Spotsylvania Court House was a finger-pointing confrontation between
Meade and Sheridan. They each blamed the other for the fiasco. Sheridan, frustrated by Meade's desire to keep the cavalry close to his infantry,
told Meade that he could defeat Confederate Cavalry commander "Jeb"
Stuart if given the chance. When Meade repeated what he thought was
a ridiculous boast to Grant, the commanding general shocked Meade
by ordering him to take Sheridan up on his offer. As a result, Sheridan
was sent off on a mission that resulted in Stuart's death at Yellow Tavern
but left Grant without the eyes of his cavalry during the ensuing days at
Spotsylvania.[46]

Spotsylvania deteriorated into another bloodbath, primarily because
of a defective alignment and tactics condoned and authorized by Lee
himself. The initial battlefield array at Spotsylvania was the haphazard
result of the Confederates rushing southeast and frantically blocking the
Union advance around the Rebel right flank. As the armies settled in, it
became obvious that a half-mile-wide central portion of the Confederate
line jutted northward one mile from a generally straight alignment and
that this projection was vulnerable to an attack on both flanks. Because
of its shape, this salient became known as the "Mule Shoe." Lee strengthened the position with artillery but did not straighten his line.[47] After two
unsuccessful attacks, Grant ordered an attack on the Mule Shoe.
Union Colonel Emory Upton led a well-conceived, twelve-regiment

surprise attack on the left flank of the Mule Shoe. He carried the Confederate trenches and failed to succeed in a major rout only because his attack was unsupported on his flanks. Although forced to retreat, Upton had taken a thousand prisoners, killed and wounded many rebels, and confirmed the already-apparent vulnerability of the Mule Shoe—a confirmation noted by Grant but apparently not Lee.[48]

Grant and Meade made plans for a full-scale, concentrated attack similar to Upton's against the Mule Shoe early on May 12. On May 11, as he planned for the assault, Grant apprised Halleck of the situation and expressed his determination to keep fighting. That letter began with this famous paragraph:

> We have now ended the sixth day of very heavy fighting. The result to this time is much in our favor. But our losses have been heavy as well as those of the enemy. We have lost to this time eleven General officers killed, wounded or missing, and probably twenty thousand men. I think the loss of the enemy must be greater we having taken over four thousand prisoners, in battle, whilst he has taken from us but few except stragglers. I am now sending back to Belle Plaines [*sic*] all my wagons for a fresh supply of provisions, and Ammunition, and propose to fight it out on this line if it takes all Summer.[49]

Although the Mule Shoe was slightly elevated, that vulnerable projection could not be properly defended unless covered by substantial artillery. Despite that weakness, Lee played into Grant's hands by personally approving removal of the Mule Shoe's protective artillery during the night of May 11. He apparently mistook the noise of Grant's preparation for an assault as a retreat toward Fredericksburg and interpreted Rebel scouts' reports of a massive movement of Union wagons toward Fredericksburg as separate evidence of a retreat by Grant. As Grant advised Halleck, the wagons were going back for rations and ammunition. Lee told Brigadier General Henry Heth, "My opinion is the enemy are preparing to retreat tonight to Fredericksburg.... We must attack those people if they retreat." Thus, Lee, as usual, was anxious to attack and once again erroneously believed Grant was retreating. If so, he had not studied Grant's western campaigns or his advance immediately after their Wilderness encounter; the word "retreat" was not in Grant's vocabulary.[50]

No sooner had the big guns been moved when Rebel pickets in front of the Mule Shoe began hearing sounds indicating the possibility of a massive Union assault. Desperate attempts to recall the guns were too late; they merely resulted in the guns being brought back just in time to be captured. Before dawn, 20,000 Union troops under Hancock attacked in a massive column formation and overran virtually the entire Mule Shoe area. The absence of Confederate artillery greatly assisted the attack. Burnside's corps kept pressure on the Rebel right, and Wright's 6th Corps promptly responded to orders to support Hancock; however, Warren's 5th Corps apparently was slow to do so.[51] The Union attackers nevertheless captured two generals; 4,000 other prisoners; twenty artillery pieces; and thirty Rebel colors. Lee personally ordered a frantic and violent counterattack. Although the Confederates were able to recapture the area after many hours of fierce, often hand-to-hand, combat, they lost thousands of irreplaceable men in the struggle to defend, recapture and then hold the Mule Shoe—especially at its most fiercely contested point, known ever after as the "Bloody Angle." At long last, on May 13, Lee moved the survivors out of the Mule Shoe and back to the security of a new, straightened line.[52]

Off and on through May 18, Grant ordered continued assaults on sectors of Lee's line that Grant believed had been weakened by troop movements. None of them was successful. Grant's infectious aggression and determination, however, kept Union spirits up. For example, on May 17, Elisha Hunt Rhodes reported the loss of half his division but wrote, "I am well and happy and feel that at last the Army of the Potomac is doing good work. Grant is a fighter and bound to win."[53]

On May 18, Grant learned of the Union disasters at Bermuda Hundred and in the Shenandoah Valley that would enable Lee to be reinforced. On that day, Grant ordered the final assault at Spotsylvania Court House. About 12,000 troops attacked over the ground where the Mule Shoe had been, but they were repelled firmly by small-arms and artillery fire. Their casualties were over 1,500 while the Confederate defenders' casualties were negligible. Seeing nothing to be gained by more assaults at Spotsylvania after almost twelve days of them, Grant decided to move southeast once again.[54]

The final battle at Spotsylvania was the Battle of Harris Farm on May 19.[55] Fortunately for Grant, Lee had decided to send Ewell's 2nd Corps (minus most of its artillery) against and around the supposedly weakened Union right in what was intended as a reconnaissance-in-force or a disruptive raid. For once, Union soldiers could fire on exposed attackers. Newly arrived and inexperienced New York, Massachusetts, and Maine heavy artillery regiments (now fighting as infantrymen) acquitted themselves well, stopped the progress of Ewell's attack, and imposed heavy casualties on the 2nd Corps. When Ewell realized that he had overreached, was two miles from the rest of Lee's army, and was in danger of losing his isolated corps, he settled into defensive positions. His corps fought off Union attackers and retreated during the night. Ewell lost at least nine hundred men, while the "green" Union heavy artillery units suffered about 1,500 casualties and earned the respect of the army's veterans. Before the end of May, Lee relieved Ewell of command. On the Union side, Grant noted that Warren again was slow and had missed an opportunity to cut off the isolated 2nd Corps.[56]

As Spotsylvania drew to a close, it was clear that this campaign was going to be costly to both sides. Grant and Lee suffered casualties at Spotsylvania amazingly similar to those they had incurred at the Wilderness—just over a much longer period of time. Grant had lost a militarily tolerable 18,400 men (killed, wounded, missing/captured) while Lee had incurred 13,400 casualties. Because Grant outnumbered Lee by 2:1 and had more reinforcements available, he could tolerate that 3:2 ratio of casualties as he moved toward his goal of defeating or destroying Lee's army. Lee, on the other hand, was seeing his army disappear through 24,500 two-battle casualties that he could not tolerate, and the South was beginning to use up its last reinforcements. Virtually all Confederate soldiers in South Carolina, coastal Georgia, and eastern Florida were ordered to Virginia at Lee's request, and he also received reinforcements from the Shenandoah Valley. Lee's army was back up to between 50,000 and 55,000 troops, but that number would decline for the rest of the war because the supply of reinforcements had virtually been exhausted. Lee's heavy losses were draining troops from the region Joseph Johnston was defending.[57]

Grant's persistence in pursuing his campaign came as a surprise to many Confederates. Evander M. Law, one of Lee's generals, later said that he knew that Grant had been aggressive in the West, " but we were not prepared for the unparalleled stubbornness and tenacity with which he persisted in his attacks under the fearful losses which his army sustained at the Wilderness and at Spotsylvania."[58]

Grant's attacks had just about wrecked Ewell's 2nd Corps. Ewell had started the campaign with 17,000 troops and had only 6,000 left after the first two battles. Lee's corps commanders also were in bad shape. Longstreet was wounded and out of action for many months, Ewell had become increasingly erratic and undependable before he was replaced, and Hill was sick during Spotsylvania and not in command until May 21.

In fact, after these first two battles of the campaign, Lee had lost twenty of his fifty-seven corps, division, and brigade commanders (35 percent) while Grant had lost only ten of sixty-nine (14 percent).[59]

A Union officer's letter from Spotsylvania described the Confederate defenses that the Union forces faced: "It is a rule that, when the rebels halt, the first day gives them a good rifle-pit; the second, a regular infantry parapet with artillery in position; and the third a parapet with an abattis in front and entrenched batteries behind. Sometimes they put this three days' work into the first twenty-four hours." He explained, "our men can, and do, do the same," but he cautioned, "but remember, our object is offense—to advance."[60] He, like Grant, understood the Union's mission.

On May 20, Grant sent Hancock's corps ahead alone in hopes of drawing Lee out in an attack on an isolated corps. Grant sent Warren's corps after Hancock's and invited Lee to attack someone somewhere. When the invitation was not accepted, Burnside and Wright's corps followed the other two. The movement of all Grant's corps compelled Lee to respond in order to protect Richmond.[61] The Union forces came upon Lee at the North Anna River. On May 23, Hancock successfully attacked Lee's rearguard posted north of the river at the Chesterfield Bridge on Telegraph Road, drove them into and across the river, and captured hundreds of prisoners.[62] Upstream from the bridge, near Jericho Mill, other Union troops crossed the river and repulsed an attack by A. P. Hill's corps. The next day, an ill Lee rebuked Hill with the stinging words: "Why did you let these people cross the river? Why did you not drive them back as General Jackson would have done?"[63]

On May 24, some of Burnside's troops (under drunken Brigadier General James H. Ledlie) recklessly attacked the point of an inverted "V" Confederate line that Lee had brilliantly established south of the river. The "V" not only was inherently strong but also, by resting its point on the North Anna, split the Union attackers so that either wing would have to cross the river twice to reinforce the other. The Rebels, therefore, easily repelled the attack. The next day Lee could have attacked the spread-out and divided Union troops, but his ill and bedridden condition, combined with his failure to delegate, prevented a Confederate counterattack, and a disappointed Lee kept muttering, "We must strike them a blow. We must not let them pass us again. We must strike them a blow."[64]

By May 26, Grant had the divided wings of his army protected with newly dug earthworks and better connected by a series of pontoon bridges. In addition, Grant's flanks were patrolled by Sheridan's cavalry, which had returned to him on May 24. Thus, Grant and Lee were stalemated. Neither could easily attack the other without heavy losses.[65] Given his inability to effectively attack Lee's inverted "V" at the North Anna River and the fact that Lee again had been reinforced, Grant decided it was time to move on. He did so on May 27. His optimism was reflected in a dispatch he sent the prior day: "Lee's army is really whipped....Our men feel that they have gained morale over the enemy and attack with confidence. I may be mistaken but I feel that our success over Lees [sic] army is already insured."[66] Grant's hopes were premature.

Under cover of darkness on the night of May 26–27, Grant had Meade delicately withdraw his troops from their positions opposite Lee's army and move southeast. After considering the possibility of moving around Lee's left flank and crossing several small rivers, Grant decided in favor of crossing a single river, the Pamunkey, which had the additional advantage of providing White House Landing as a base of supply off the Chesapeake Bay.[67] According to Rhea, "Grant's virtually bloodless withdrawal from the North Anna and his shift to Hanovertown ranks among the war's most successful maneuvers."[68]

Most of the Union troops crossed the Pamunkey River at Hanover-town and Nelson's Crossing just above the Totopotomoy Creek on May 28. Southwest of the crossing, screening Union cavalry engaged in a fierce battle at Haw's Shop. They fought Rebel cavalry that Lee had moved to block Grant from coming west to attack the Virginia Central Railroad. The Confederates slowed the Union march for five hours and confirmed for Lee that Grant was across the Pamunkey. Both sides missed opportunities to seriously damage their opponents, and the result was a draw with each side suffering several hundred casualties.[69]

On May 29, the still-ailing Lee replaced the ill and ineffective Ewell with Jubal Early as commander of his 2nd Corps. When Warren's corps crossed the Totopotomoy that same day, Lee saw an opportunity to counterattack that isolated corps. He ordered Early to do so ("Send out a brigade and see if those people are in force."[70]) and told him, "We must destroy this Army of Grant's before he gets to [the] James River. If he gets there it will become a siege, and then it will be a mere question of time."[71] On May 30, therefore, Early sent a brigade into a deadly trap set by the Union 5th Corps. Colonel Edward Willis (who had been approved for promotion to brigadier) was killed, and his brigade, "perhaps the cream of the Confederate [2nd] Corps," according to Rhea, was decimated. Union casualties were about four hundred twenty and Confederate about four hundred fifty. This Union victory at Bethesda Church may have encouraged Grant to think that Lee's army was demoralized and ready to be broken.[72]

Meanwhile Grant had ordered General "Baldy" Smith's 18th Corps to sail from Bermuda Hundred to Grant's new supply base at White House Landing on the Pamunkey River and then to join Grant and Meade. With 10,000 troops, Smith arrived at White House Landing on May 30. Looking ahead, Grant on that same day requested Halleck to send all the pontoons in Washington to City Point near Bermuda

Hundred on the James River. For his part, Lee told Davis he needed reinforcements to prevent "disaster" and was successful in getting Major General Robert F. Hoke's 7,000-man division sent to him from Beauregard in Richmond/Petersburg.[73]

By the end of May, Grant's casualties were pouring back into Washington by the boatload. The wounded men filled twenty-one Washington-area hospitals. There was "dark talk that Grant, although dogged, was also a butcher who harbored too little regard for human life."[74] The Northern press was calling Grant a "butcher."[75] The fighting and bloodshed did not cease. In the running battles and skirmishes from the North Anna to the Totopotomoy and then Cold Harbor between May 26 and June 2, Grant and Lee each incurred almost 4,000 casualties.[76]

That "dark talk" certainly increased after the next development: Cold Harbor. Sheridan's cavalrymen arrived at the Cold Harbor crossroad on May 31, forcefully repelled the advance of a Confederate brigade on the morning of June 1, and were then relieved by Wright's 6th Corps, which had orders from Grant to attack immediately. Wright's corps began arriving at 10:00 a.m. that morning. Believing his men too tired and deciding to wait for Smith's reinforcements from Bermuda Hundred, Wright did not attack until later.[77]

Belatedly reinforced by "Baldy" Smith (who had marched on the wrong road from White House Landing under outdated or erroneous orders), Wright finally attacked the partially-organized Confederate Cold Harbor line at 5:00 p.m. on June 1. The 30,000 troops of Wright's and Smith's corps were repelled in most places, broke through a gap in the Rebel lines, captured hundreds of prisoners, and then were sealed off by a counterattack. The Union attackers' casualties may have been in the thousands, while the Rebel defenders lost between five and six hundred.[78]

Despite Grant's desire to attack again quickly as both armies converged on Cold Harbor, the Confederates ended up with a day and a half to construct seven miles of strong fortifications to protect against the expected Union attack. Grant's plans to attack at 5:00 a.m. on June 2 were delayed by the 6:30 a.m. arrival of Hancock's corps, and his plans to attack at 5:00 p.m. that day were delayed until 4:30 the following morning by the exhausted condition of Hancock's men. Therefore, the Confederates were well prepared for the expected attack. Fearing the worst, many Union troops wrote farewell letters to their loved ones and pinned their names on their uniforms to ensure that their bodies were well-marked for identification in the event they did not survive the attack.[79]

Grant was seven miles from Richmond, had just been reinforced, and believed he had no choice but to attempt to break Lee's army and perhaps win the war. He gave Meade another chance to demonstrate his command skills by placing him in operational charge for the day; Meade failed to reconnoiter, coordinate, or command. Some of the Union forces launched a frontal assault on the southern end of Lee's line at 4:30 a.m. on June 3. The well-entrenched defenders shot down any exposed Union soldier. Large numbers died in a short period, and the attack lasted no more than an hour. Hours later Burnside attacked on the north end of the line. Grant lost about 3,500 to 4,000 men in the early-morning assault and about another 2,500 during the rest of the day.[80] After several hours of waffling by Meade about whether to call off the assaults, Grant interviewed the corps commanders and then ordered an end to the attacks. Rhea observed, "Far from behaving like an uncaring 'butcher,' Grant intervened to save lives when Meade, seemingly paralyzed by indecision, appeared incapable of acting."[81]

In his immediate June 3 post-action report to the War Department, Grant falsely stated, "Our loss was not severe nor do I suppose the Enemy to have lost heavily."[82] It is likely that he was trying damage control in light of Northern press criticism of his casualties.[83] Grant's more honest, later brief summary of the attack was: "The assault cost us heavily and probably without benefit to compensate; but the enemy was not cheered by the occurrence sufficiently to induce him to take the offensive."[84]

Cold Harbor has been the major black mark on Grant's record.[85] For example, Harold Simpson wrote, "In a little over *eight minutes,* Grant lost almost 7,000 men and earned for himself the sobriquet, 'The Butcher.'"[86] Grant himself later said in his memoirs,

> I have always regretted that the last assault at Cold Harbor was ever made…. At Cold Harbor no advantage whatever was gained to compensate for the heavy loss we sustained. Indeed, the advantages other than those of relative losses, were on the Confederate side. Before that, the Army of Northern Virginia seemed to have acquired a wholesome regard for the courage, endurance, and soldierly qualities generally of the Army of the Potomac…. This charge seemed to revive their hopes temporarily; but it was of short duration. The effect upon the Army of the Potomac was the reverse. When we reached the James River, however, all effects of the battle of Cold Harbor seemed to have disappeared.[87]

Rhea, who has exhaustively studied the Overland Campaign, explained that Grant was only seven miles from Richmond, Lee's weakened army had a river at its back, and Bethesda Church and the June 1 breakthrough seemed to indicate Lee's army was on the verge of collapse. Meade ineffectively oversaw the uncoordinated attack by only half the Union troops against un-reconnoitered Confederate lines. Rather than the 7,000 to 15,000 men Grant is supposed to have lost in that early-morning assault,[88] Rhea stated that battlefield records show that Grant lost no more than 3,500 to 4,000 troops—many less than Lee in similar assaults at Seven Days', Gettysburg, and Chancellorsville.[89] "The traditional figure of 7,000 Union casualties in the first thirty minutes certainly is too high. While Grant's army definitely absorbed tremendous casualties in that time, the grand total probably fell several thousand short of 7,000."[90] For the entire day, Rhea calculated that Grant suffered slightly more than 6,000 casualties, while Lee took about 1,000 to 1,500.[91]

Assistant Secretary of War Charles Dana, who was with Grant at Cold Harbor, later analyzed that battle:

> This was the battle of Cold Harbor, which has been exaggerated into one of the bloodiest disasters of history, a reckless, useless waste of human life. It was nothing of the kind. The outlook warranted the effort. The breaking of Lee's lines meant his destruction and the collapse of the rebellion. Sheridan took the same chances at Five Forks ten months later, and won; so did Wright, Humphreys, Gibbon and others at Petersburg [on April 2, 1865].[92]

Even after Cold Harbor, morale remained high among many officers and soldiers in Grant's force. On June 3, Elisha Hunt Rhodes wrote: "Nothing seems to have been gained by the attack today, except that it may be that it settles the question of whether the enemy's line can be carried by direct assault or not. At any rate General Grant means to hold on, and I know that he will win in the end."[93] Captain Charles Francis Adams Jr. wrote that "so far Grant has out-generalled Lee and he has, in spite of his inability to start Lee one inch out of his fortifications, maneuvered himself close to the gates of Richmond."[94] Even a soldier in one of the hard-hit corps wrote, "We have the gray backs in a pretty close corner at present and intend to keep them so. There is no fall back in Grant." [95] He certainly had that right.

Union Major General Jacob D. Cox noted that, "Grant was slower than Sherman in learning the unprofitableness of attacking fieldworks, and his campaign was by far the most costly one.... There were special reasons which led Grant to adhere so long to the more aggressive tactics, which need to be weighed in any full treatment of the subject...."[96] On May 22, Sherman explained, "Grant's battles in Virginia are fearful but necessary. Immense slaughter is necessary to prove that our Northern armies can and will fight."[97]

After the abortive attack of June 3 and following an unseemly dispute between Grant and Lee about conditions for retrieving wounded from between the lines, the troops on both sides settled into a deadly standoff in which sharpshooters picked off anything that moved in the enemy lines. The broiling sun, the danger of being shot, and the smells of the battlefield made the conditions unbearable. Within ten days Grant would move on once again.[98]

As the confrontation at Cold Harbor came to a close, both sides could look back at almost six weeks of virtually incessant fighting. During the final two weeks, along the Totopotomoy and at Cold Harbor, Lee at long last achieved something close to the 3:1 casualty ratio he needed for victory. During that time, Grant's forces had suffered over 17,000 casualties to Lee's more than 8,000. Those results, however, were too little and too late to affect the ultimate outcome of the war. Between the Wilderness and Cold Harbor, Grant had lost 53,000 of his 122,000 troops to death or wounds, while Lee's 70,000 troops (including reinforcements) had incurred 33,000 such casualties. Thus, Lee had lost an irreplaceable 47 percent while Grant had lost a replaceable and militarily tolerable 43 percent. In addition, the Army of Northern Virginia had lost twenty-two of its fifty-eight generals (eight killed, twelve wounded, and two captured).[99]

Grant quickly determined to restore the morale of his soldiers and to threaten Richmond by making a surprise crossing of the James River. According to Jean Edward Smith, "For Grant, Cold Harbor had been a setback, not a defeat."[100] On June 5, Grant revealed his movement plans to Halleck and said, "My idea from the start has been to beat Lee's Army, if possible, north of Richmond, then after destroying his lines of communication North of the James river to transfer the Army to the South side and besiege Lee in Richmond, or follow him South if he should retreat."[101] Given the Rebels' continuous use of defensive fortifications since their abortive attacks at the Wilderness, Grant stated that such a movement was necessary to avoid "a greater sacrifice of human life" than he was willing to make.[102]

As a prelude to his secret move, Grant on June 6 sent Sheridan on his "Second Raid" to destroy much of the Virginia Central Railroad, a key supply route from the Shenandoah Valley to Richmond, and to connect with General Hunter, whose troops were to destroy the James River Canal at Lynchburg. Both Sheridan and Hunter failed. Confederate cavalry commanded by Wade Hampton kept Sheridan from reaching his critical goal of Gordonsville and drove him into retreat at the Battle of Trevilian's Station on June 11 and 12. Jubal Early and the 2nd Corps arrived from Richmond in time to save Lynchburg from the dawdling Hunter and to drive him back into West Virginia. The one positive result for Grant of Sheridan's expedition was that Hampton's response deprived Lee of the eyes of his own cavalry for a critical period when Grant moved his army again.[103]

Back at Cold Harbor, Grant planned for and then began his secret backdoor assault on Petersburg via a crossing of the James River. On

June 5, he requested more vessels from Washington and ordered Horace
Porter and Cyrus Comstock of his staff to locate a suitable crossing of
the James River. They reported their findings to Grant on June 12.
Behind a massive screen of cavalry and one corps (Warren's 5th), Grant
evacuated his line one corps at a time. First, W. F. Smith's 18th Corps
marched east back to White House Landing and traveled by vessel via
the Pamunkey and York rivers, Chesapeake Bay, Hampton Roads, and
the James River to Bermuda Hundred, where they arrived on June 14.[104]

Meanwhile, all the other corps moved out from Cold Harbor without being discovered and, behind a screen established at Malvern Hill
by Warren's corps, crossed the Chickahominy River via three separate
crossings—two fixed bridges and a pontoon bridge. Confederate General E. Porter Alexander described how the Rebels could have pounced
on and crushed the isolated 5th Corps on the afternoon of June 13—but
for one problem: "The only trouble about that was that we were entirely
ignorant of the fact that it was isolated. On the contrary,… Warren's
corps had taken up its line so near to Riddell's Shop as to give us the idea
that it was the advance corps of Grant's whole army pushing toward
Richmond on the road from Long Bridge."[105] As Jean Edward Smith
observed, "[t]he Army of the Potomac—115,000 men—had marched
away so quietly that Confederate pickets had not observed its departure."[106]

On June 14, Hancock's corps crossed the James by boat from Wilcox's
Landing and established a bridgehead around Windmill Point on the
south shore. Those actions cleared the way for construction of—to that
time—the world's longest pontoon bridge, over which the rest of Grant's
army crossed on June 15 and 16. Grant took a tremendous gamble that
he would be able to detach his large army from Lee's, construct and use
a 2,100-foot bridge across a river with a four-foot tidal range, and cross
that river without being attacked with his army split on two sides of the

river. As the crossing succeeded, Dana wired Stanton, "All goes on like a miracle."

As early as 7:00 p.m. on June 15, Grant's advance troops were attacking Petersburg, with Lee twenty-five miles away. Grant had stolen a march on Lee, and a prompt, competent attack on Petersburg by the relocated army would have cost Lee both Petersburg and Richmond, which was dependent on supply by rail through Petersburg. But incompetence on the part of Grant's corps commanders prevented the seizure of that key railroad junction so critical to Richmond's survival.[107]

How badly had Grant fooled Lee with his unprecedented massive crossing of the mile-wide James? Beauregard at Petersburg had predicted Grant's movement in June 7 and 9 dispatches, sent telegraphic warnings and a personal emissary to Lee on the 14th, and continued to send dire reports and reinforcement requests on the 15th and 16th. General Alexander later concluded that Grant's initial attack at Petersburg late on the 15th could have been another Cold Harbor, but "General Lee did not have a soldier there to meet him! Grant had gotten way from US completely & was fighting *Beauregard*. The Army of Northern Virginia had lost him, & was sucking its thumbs by the roadside 25 miles away, & wondering where he could be!"[108] In General Fuller's words, "*Lee* had been completely out-generalled."[109]

Even after the assaults on Petersburg began, Lee continued to doubt Beauregard's claims. Even after Grant's troops began attacking Petersburg, Lee sent five telegrams to Beauregard questioning his assertions that Grant's army had crossed the James.[110] At 6:40 p.m. on June 17, more than two days after Grant's first attack on Petersburg, Beauregard sent an attention-grabbing dispatch to Lee indicating that he would attempt that night to fall back from outer to inner lines and might have to abandon the city. That night, while he indeed was falling back, Beauregard sent, one after the other, two colonels and a major as personal emissaries to convince Lee of the desperateness of the situation. The two colonels initially were rebuffed by Lee, but the major convinced Lee that the broad representation of three Union corps among captured prisoners demonstrated that Grant indeed was across the James in strength.[111]

Finally, about three days late, Lee got his army underway to Petersburg. At long last, Lee realized that he had been duped and was in danger of losing Petersburg, Richmond, and the war. Thus, on June 18, he sent an urgent 3:30 a.m. message to the Superintendent of the Richmond and Petersburg Railroad asking whether trains could run to Petersburg, directing that cars be sent for troops wherever they could be picked up, and stating finally, "It is important to get troops to Petersburg without delay."[112] He also telegraphed Early, who had been sent to defend Lynchburg, that Grant was in front of Petersburg and that Early should attack quickly and then either carry out the original plan to move down the Valley or move to Petersburg "without delay."[113]

Meanwhile, a number of Grant's corps commanders displayed incredible incompetence and timidity that cost them the opportunity to capture a severely undermanned Petersburg. The first attack, on June 15, was made by W. F. Smith's corps with Hancock's corps in support. After Smith wasted most of the day, he finally attacked with 16,000 troops against a mere 2,200 defenders. His overwhelming superiority forced Beauregard to fall back to new positions, but Smith failed to take the entire garrison, allowed his "weary" men to be replaced by Hancock's soldiers, and rested them before their goal had been achieved. Hancock's arrival to support Smith apparently had been delayed by a missing order and delayed rations. The next day saw halfhearted attacks by the 2nd, 18th, and newly-arrived 9th Corps. Even the arrival of the 5th Corps on June 17 was followed by uncoordinated and unsuccessful attacks. Union troops and commanders may have been suffering from "Cold Harbor fever."[114]

On June 18 at dawn, with the newly arrived 6th Corps further bolstering their strength, the Federals launched a 70,000-man, five-corps assault on Petersburg. They overran the recently abandoned Confederate outer lines and seriously threatened to finally take the town. As at Spotsylvania, Lee's troops appeared on scene just in time to stop a federal advance and save the day. Four hours after Lee began arranging for their transportation from north of Richmond, Confederates began pouring into their comrades' defensive lines at 7:30 that morning. They continued to do so until 11:00 a.m. About an hour later, the attackers tried again. After another unsuccessful assault at 4:00 p.m., a frustrated and perhaps angry Grant called off the attacks.[115] His attacking army had incurred over 11,000 casualties while the defenders suffered only 4,000.[116] Not until April 2 of the next year would Grant order another frontal assault; in fact, he expressly prohibited such assaults.[117] Siege warfare would commence.

Some analysts have dramatically—and somewhat inaccurately—criticized Grant's Overland Campaign. John Waugh, for example, said, "Grant had covered some sixty miles and lost nearly 60,000 men—a thousand per mile, 2,000 a day, three [actually two] for every one of Lee's men—a number equal in size to the entire Confederate army he faced. Now, after all of that, the war in the South had come down to a siege."[118] Although Grant's forces had incurred about 64,000 casualties between May 5 and June 18, Lee's army had suffered about 37,000 casualties during the same period.[119] While both armies lost about half their troops during that time,[120] Grant could count on more reinforcements. Lee's army, however, had begun a downward spiral in strength that would continue until the war's end. The war had evolved to a condition that Lee wanted to avoid.

Lee's casualties were so significant that units from elsewhere totaling 24,495 men had come to reinforce him.[121] These reinforcements to Lee weakened critical areas to which Sherman would be heading, and the South was now essentially out of reinforcements. Besides his hard-to-replace manpower losses, Lee had another serious problem. Between June 1, 1862, when he assumed command, and December 31, 1863, Lee's army had 19 of its generals killed, including four in the Antietam Campaign and five more at Gettysburg. These losses were followed by the deaths of eight more generals in May 1864, including three during Lee's last major tactical offensive at the Wilderness, two at Spotsylvania, and two at Yellow Tavern.[122] Leadership in his army had become a serious problem.

Rhea analyzed Grant's losses in the campaign:

> Did Grant pay too great a human cost in waging his Overland Campaign? Critics emphasized that he lost approximately 55,000 soldiers in forty days, nearly as many men as Lee had in his army at the beginning of the campaign. Lee, however, lost about 33,000 troops in that same period. While Grant's subtractions were numerically greater than Lee's, his percentage of loss was smaller. Grant's losses amounted to about 45 percent of the force he took across the Rapidan; Lee's reached slightly over 50 percent. And while Grant could draw upon a deep manpower pool for reinforcements, Lee's potential was limited. In the game of numbers, Grant was coming out ahead. He was losing soldiers at a lower percentage than was his adversary, and he possessed greater capacity to replace his losses.[123]

Catton reinforced the view that the Union could endure Grant's attrition but the Confederacy could not absorb Lee's. He wrote:

> Yet it was not actually just a campaign of attrition. The significant thing is that Lee was deprived of the opportunity to

maneuver, to seize the openings created by his opponent's mistakes, to make full use of the dazzling ability to combine swift movements and hard blows which had served him so well in former campaigns. Against Grant, Lee was not able to do the things he had done before. He had to fight the sort of fight he could not win.[124]

Although the Overland Campaign had not yet resulted in the surrender of Richmond or Lee's army, Grant had succeeded in bottling up the bulk of Lee's troops in Richmond and Petersburg—a situation that Lee himself had said would be fatal[125]—and in seriously damaging Lee's army. James M. McPherson provided a perceptive analysis of that campaign:

> Grant did not admit culpability for the heavy Union casualties in the whole campaign of May and June 1864. Nor should he have done so, despite the label of "butcher" and the later analyses of his "campaign of attrition." It did turn out to be a campaign of attrition, but that was more by Lee's choice than by Grant's. The Union commander's purpose was to maneuver Lee into a position for open-field combat; Lee's purpose was to prevent this by entrenching an impenetrable line to protect Richmond and his communications. Lee was hoping to hold out long enough and inflict sufficient casualties on Union forces to discourage the people of the North and prevent Lincoln's reelection. Lee's strategy of attrition almost worked. That it failed in the end was owing mainly to Grant, who stayed the course and turned the attrition factor in his favor. Although the Confederates had the advantage of fighting on the defensive most of the time, Grant inflicted almost as high a percentage of casualties on Lee's army as vice versa.[126]

Rhea concluded: "Contrary to the image urged by Grant's detractors, the general's campaign against Lee reveals a warrior every bit as talented as his famous Confederate counterpart. Grant understood the importance of seizing the initiative and holding tight to his offensive edge to keep Lee off balance and prevent him from going on the offensive."[127] Lee now paid the price for emasculating his army in 1862 and 1863; his army was so weakened that it could not effectively counterattack and could not tolerate an exchange of casualties with Grant's forces.

Throughout the Overland Campaign, both commanding generals demonstrated again and again the traits that had characterized their battles and campaigns in the first three years of the war. Staying on the strategic and tactical offensive, Grant seriously weakened Lee's army, compelled Lee to retreat to a siege situation at Richmond and Petersburg, and kept Lee from reinforcing the Confederates facing Sherman in Georgia. His game plan for Lee's defeat and Lincoln's reelection was working.

Lee, on the other hand, paid the price for his costly aggressiveness of 1862 and 1863 through an inability to counterpunch with power. He suffered irreplaceable losses (37,000 casualties) through unwise attacks and defensive mistakes; constantly underestimated the determined aggressiveness of Grant; received 24,500 reinforcements during the campaign; and maintained his Virginia-only myopic view of the war.[128] By the end of the short campaign, he faced a siege situation that he had said would doom his army. He was correct.

CHAPTER TEN

LATE 1864:

GRANT AND SHERMAN MOVE
TOWARD VICTORY

*While Grant pins Lee down in Petersburg and Richmond,
Union forces capture Atlanta, the Shenandoah Valley, and
Mobile Harbor; Lincoln wins reelection; Sherman marches
through Georgia; and George Thomas virtually destroys
John Bell Hood's Army of Tennessee.*

During the second half of 1864, Grant kept Lee pinned down in
Petersburg and Richmond, encouraged Sherman's success in
Georgia, and finally drove the Confederates out of the Shenandoah Valley. As part of Grant's grand strategy, he pressured Lee in Virginia while Sherman advanced through Georgia. Taking minimal
casualties, Grant tightened the noose around Lee's army and readied the
way for victory in 1865.[1] One of Grant's constant efforts was to threaten
Lee's supply lines by extending his own left flank and making cavalry
raids beyond the lines.

The two armies then settled into siege warfare, a situation Lee had
previously said would spell defeat for his army.[2] With the partial siege of

Petersburg and Richmond, the first moment had arrived when Lee should have considered ending the slaughter. He must have known that military victory in the long run was impossible. General Alexander later explained that Lee had the ability, but not the will, to halt the proceedings:

> It is, indeed, a fact that both the army and the people at that time would have been very loth to recognize that the cause was hopeless. In the army, I am sure, such an idea was undreamed of. Gen. Lee's influence could doubtless have secured acquiescence in it, for his influence had no bounds; but nothing short of that would. He would not have opposed any policy adopted by President Davis; so the matter was really entirely within the president's power.[3]

Although Alexander believed peace then would have saved thousands of lives and up to a billion dollars of property for the South, he agreed with the decision to fight to the bitter end in order to save the honor of the Army of Northern Virginia.[4]

Grant's first problem after the siege began was that Early and his 2nd Corps were on the loose northward down the Shenandoah Valley—and Grant did not know it. His intelligence system broke down, and Grant was not aware of Early's position until Early neared Frederick, Maryland, on an ill-conceived approach to Washington. After Early had driven Hunter away from Lynchburg, Lee could have ordered Early to return to Richmond, reinforce Johnston at Atlanta, or do something else. The brilliant strategic move would have been to reinforce Johnston, who was being overwhelmed by Sherman's numerical superiority and needed to hold Atlanta if Lincoln was to be defeated in the November presidential election. As reflected in their correspondence all that year, that was the move most feared by Grant and Sherman. Instead, on June 27, Lee authorized Early to proceed north down the Shenandoah Valley to threaten Washington. Early's orders contained a quixotic authorization for him to go around Washington and free Confederate prisoners at the isolated Point Lookout prison camp far southeast of Washington.[5]

Although the fortifications and forts surrounding Washington made it unlikely that Early would accomplish much, he created a stir. Early's 18,000 troops made their way north down the Shenandoah and entered Maryland. Early demanded and received ransoms of $20,000, $1,500, and $200,000, respectively, from the citizens of Hagerstown, Middletown, and Frederick. At first Grant refused to believe reports that Early was in Maryland. On July 3, Grant reported that "Early's corps is now here." Two days later, Grant, apparently concerned about continuing reports of Early's possible movement, told Stanton and Halleck that he would send a full corps to Washington if the city was threatened; they declined. After Meade reported to Grant that deserters claimed Early was heading for Maryland and Washington, Grant sent a division of the 6th Corps north by vessel to Baltimore as an insurance policy.[6]

Finally realizing where Early was, Grant ordered the rest of the 6th and all of the 19th Corps north to defend Washington. The initial 5,000-man division greatly strengthened the force that was cobbled together by General Lew Wallace at Monocacy Creek, south of Frederick, to oppose Early's advance. They supplemented the 2,800 untested soldiers Wallace had under his own command. Wallace carefully picked the battlefield site, where the Baltimore & Ohio Railroad, the Georgetown Pike to Washington, and the Baltimore Pike (National Road) all crossed the river.[7]

During the July 9 Battle of Monocacy,[8] Wallace's makeshift force fiercely held the three bridges at those crossings. After hours of fighting at the bridges, Early, however, had his cavalry cross the river at a ford a mile downstream from the fighting and then attack the Union left flank.

After the cavalry were driven back, a three-brigade infantry attack finally drove Wallace's men back toward Baltimore after seven hours of fighting.[9]

The Battle of Monocacy delayed Early a day, and two divisions of seasoned 6th Corps troops had arrived from Grant and were waiting for him in Washington by the time he arrived at midday on July 11. After being driven away from Washington, Early undertook a long retreat—plus a detour to burn Chambersburg, Pennsylvania, on July 30 when the residents were unable to raise sufficient tribute money.[10] The net result of Early's quixotic, five-week raid was that Lee had used one of his three corps to cause Grant to send two of his seven corps away from Richmond.

With Atlanta critically threatened by Sherman, there was a much better use for any surplus troops that Lee could spare. Instead of sending Early on a futile thrust toward Washington and then into Pennsylvania, Lee would have produced more effective results by sending a comparable number of troops south to oppose Sherman in Georgia. By sending those 18,000 surplus troops to Georgia, Lee could have increased Johnston's 57,000-man army defending Atlanta by almost 30 percent. That increase would have had a substantial impact whether Johnston attacked or stayed on the defensive against Sherman. Such a movement was the very thing Grant was concerned about preventing during all of his 1864 campaign.[11] Grant had erred in allowing Early's corps to escape his grasp, but Lee saved Grant's dual campaigns by wasting Early's corps. As Stephen Ambrose concluded, if Lee had sent Early to Johnston, "Grant's entire campaign, with its tremendous losses, would have been a failure."[12]

Unlike Grant, however, Lee again was proving himself to be a theater, not a national, general. Even General Alexander criticized Lee's futile attempt to bluff Grant, whom he said could not be bluffed, and Lee's failure to use the Rebels' internal lines to reinforce Johnston, "the very strongest play on the military board. Then every man sent might have counted for his full weight in a decisive struggle with Sherman &, if it proved successful, then Early might return bringing a large part of Johnston's army with him to reinforce Lee."[13] In early July, Grant sent Sherman a message expressing his concern that Early's men were going to reinforce Johnston against Sherman, and on July 15 Grant wrote Halleck that his greatest fear was that the Confederates would do just that.[14] Another Confederate leader saw those same possibilities: Brigadier General Josiah Gorgas, chief of confederate ordnance, wrote: "I still think that my notions were correct at the outset of Sherman's movement when I advocated the detachment of 10,000 men to Georgia, even at the risk of losing Petersburgh [sic] & the Southern R.R. It would have ruined Sherman, & with his ruin, gone far to make the north tired of the war."[15] But, fortunately for Sherman, Lee had a different idea.

By the time Lee sent Early north from Lynchburg on June 27, it should have been clear to Lee that Sherman's three armies in Georgia, originally totaling 110,000 men, presented a serious threat to the Confederacy, to the chance to beat Lincoln in November's election, and even to Lee's own army. Beginning on May 3, Sherman had pushed toward Atlanta with Major General James B. McPherson's Army of the Tennessee, Major General John M. Schofield's Army of the Ohio, and George Thomas' Army of the Cumberland. Through a series of flanking moves, interspersed with a couple of foolish direct assaults, Sherman had relentlessly moved seventy miles from the Tennessee-Georgia border southeasterly to the environs of Atlanta, the railroad and manufacturing center of the Confederate heartland. The absence of major battles had resulted in Sherman's forces suffering 11,000 casualties and Johnston's original 66,000 troops incurring 9,000 casualties—low casualties for two months of constant contact.

By June 19, Sherman had reached Kennesaw Mountain, a mere twelve miles from Atlanta. Lee had notice by telegram that Atlanta was in real trouble—and with it the South. There was plenty of time—a few weeks—to get troops to Atlanta while the city could still be saved. But instead of sending Early's corps, or a comparable number of troops, to assist in the defense of Atlanta, Lee sent no one and then proceeded to make the situation in Georgia even worse.

On July 17, with the concurrence of Lee, Davis replaced Johnston with Hood. Davis was dissatisfied with what he perceived to be Johnston's lack of aggressiveness. Johnston and Jefferson Davis had a long history of acrimony that had developed into deep mutual hatred by July 1864. Johnston believed that Davis had not given him appropriate seniority among Confederate generals at the outset of the war, that Davis had placed him in a powerless position as Commander of the Department of the West while Pemberton and Bragg were losing Vicksburg and Chattanooga respectively, and that Davis was constantly second-guessing his strategy and tactics. Sherman's persistent and successful campaign not only brought his armies across the Chattahoochee River and within five miles of Atlanta on July 8 and 9, but also brought the Davis-Johnston feud to a head.

By this time, Davis was disconcerted by the series of retreats to Atlanta by Johnston, was totally frustrated by Johnston's refusal to explain his future plans, and thus resolved to replace him immediately in a last desperate effort to save Atlanta. This move was encouraged by Bragg, who had caused much discord among western Confederate generals, had been relieved for cause after losing Chattanooga, and now implausibly was serving as chief military advisor to Davis, his longtime friend. Davis and Bragg both disliked Johnston, and Hood, a new major general and new corps commander under Johnston, had been sending both of them secret, self-serving, and false reports critical of Johnston's campaign. Hood lied to them about his own battlefield failures during the campaign and about the alleged willingness to retreat of Johnston and Hardee (Hood's major competitor to replace Johnston)—when, in fact, Hood had opposed attacks and urged retreats over Johnston and Hardee's opposition. Hood's calculated campaign for Johnston's command won the crucial support of Bragg, who also remembered Hardee's earlier opposition to Bragg when Bragg commanded the Army of Tennessee.[16]

Replacing Johnston with Hood was inexcusable. Hood, who had lost the use of an arm at Gettysburg and had lost a leg at Chickamauga, was an overly aggressive general whom even Lee had described as "all lion, none of the fox."[17] His record of costly frontal assaults included not only the Seven Days' and Gettysburg. His men also had been slaughtered at Antietam the previous September; when afterwards asked the whereabouts of his division, Hood had responded, "dead on the field."[18] Again, as recently as June 22 at Kolb's Farm near Atlanta, Hood's troops had been decimated in battle. Hood, who had commanded a corps for only a few months, was a protégé of Lee's. Lee had fostered Hood's overzealousness.[19]

Before replacing Johnston with the conniving and hotheaded Hood, Davis consulted with his trusted military advisor, Lee. At this point, Lee had the opportunity to prevent what Bruce Catton has called the most grievous error of the war. Lee knew Davis' decision was unwise but did not use his great influence to veto it. On July 12, Davis sent Lee a telegram stating that he was relieving Johnston and asking for Lee's evaluation of Hood as Johnston's successor. Lee responded as follows: "Telegram of today received. I regret the fact stated. It is a bad time to release the commander of an army situated as that of Tennessee. We may lose Atlanta and the army too. Hood is a bold fighter. I am doubtful as to other qualities necessary."[20]

Obviously concerned about this matter, Lee wrote to Davis later that same day:

> I am distressed at the intelligence conveyed in your telegram of today. It is a grievous thing to change commander of an army situated as is that of the Tennessee. Still if necessary it ought to be done. I know nothing of the necessity. I had hoped that Johnston was strong enough to deliver battle.... Hood is a good fighter, very industrious on the battle field, careless off, & I have had no opportunity of judging of his action, when the whole responsibility rested upon him. I have a high opinion of his gallantry, earnestness & zeal. [Lieutenant] Genl [William J.] Hardee has more experience in managing an army....[21]

A couple of days later Secretary of War Seddon visited Lee and discussed the matter further. As had Davis, Seddon told Lee Johnston was being relieved and sought Lee's advice on a successor. Lee expressed his regret about the apparent need for a change but did not provide definitive counsel concerning a replacement.

Although Douglas Southall Freeman claimed that Lee opposed Johnston's removal and Hood's appointment, the record supports a contrary conclusion. Lee failed to affirmatively oppose Hood, which was necessary in light of Davis' known hatred of Johnson and his stated intention to select him. Lee also made several positive statements concerning Hood (calling him a bold fighter with gallantry and zeal) that would have pushed Davis toward naming Hood. These statements were particularly helpful to Hood because Davis was disgusted with Johnston's constant retreats and was looking for someone who would fight. The worst part of Lee's advice was his statements that Hood was good on the battlefield and questionable otherwise; the truth was that Hood's greatest flaw was that he was dangerously reckless on the battlefield itself. Hood's recklessness on the field was capable of destroying his own army, and it did.

In summary, Lee, when consulted by Davis, made no effort to forcefully dissuade the president from making this disastrous appointment. Perhaps Lee saw and admired something of himself in Hood and therefore did not criticize Hood's battlefield performance. In that regard, it is interesting to consider Johnston's comparison of himself to Lee in Johnston's response to Davis' July 17 order relieving him of command:

> … Sherman's army is much stronger compared with that of Tennessee than Grant's compared with that of Northern Virginia. Yet the enemy has been compelled to advance much more slowly to the vicinity of Atlanta than to that of Richmond and Petersburg, and has penetrated much deeper into Virginia than into Georgia.[22]

Davis' appointment of Hood drew a mixed reaction; Confederates had their doubts, and the Yankees were elated. Confederate General Arthur M. Manigault later remembered that "the army received the announcement with very bad grace, and with no little murmuring."[23] Confederate Private Sam Watkins called Hood's appointment "the most terrible and disastrous blow that the South ever received," and described how fellow Army of Tennessee soldiers cried or deserted after the elevation of the "over-rated" Hood.[24] The only place where Hood's appointment brought joy was in the Union command. John Schofield, Hood's West Point roommate, told Sherman that Hood was bold, rash, and courageous and would quickly hit Sherman "like hell."[25] Sherman alerted his commanders to the risk of attack, advised them that "Each army commander will accept battle on anything like fair terms," and wrote to his wife that he was pleased by the change. He had good reason to be happy.[26]

After replacing Johnston as commander of the Army of the Tennessee, Hood, promoted to full general, predictably and immediately went on the offensive. Beginning on July 20, Hood launched frontal assaults on strong Union positions at Peach Tree Creek, then Decatur (Atlanta) (July 22), and finally Ezra Church (July 28). The results were so disastrous that on August 5 Davis, who must have been having second thoughts, provided his newly appointed army commander with some ironic tactical advice: "The loss consequent upon attacking the enemy in his entrenchments requires you to avoid that if practicable."[27]

During the preceding two months of the Atlanta campaign, Johnston had lost 9,000 men to Sherman's 11,000. In a little more than a week, Hood lost an appalling 14,000 more to Sherman's mere 4,000.[28] Parenthetically, Early's 18,000 troops would have made up all, and prevented some, of Hood's losses if Lee had sent them to Georgia, instead of Maryland, in late June or early July. Significantly, Hood's losses made Atlanta vulnerable.

A month later, on August 31, Hood lost more than 4,000 men (15 percent casualties) at Jonesboro, where he criticized his subordinate Hardee's assault as feeble because of the low percentage of casualties.[29] With their win at Jonesboro, the Union forces controlled all the railroads into Atlanta, which Hood therefore was compelled to evacuate on September 1. Once Hood took command, the struggle for Atlanta became a bloodbath. The 100-day campaign had cost the Union 32,000 casualties and the Confederates 35,000—almost three-fourths of these Rebel casualties occurring after Hood succeeded Johnston.[30] Because Sherman had a 2-to-1 manpower advantage, the Southerners could not afford to trade casualties of this scope.

Bruce Catton explained how Lee's failure to stop Hood's ascension to command cost the Democrats an opportunity to push Lincoln out of the White House:

> Worse yet, William Tecumseh Sherman captured Atlanta. Sherman had moved against Joe Johnston's Confederate army the same day Grant crossed the Rapidan. From the distant North his campaign had looked no more like a success than the one in Virginia. If it had not brought so many casualties, it had seemed no more effective at ending Rebel resistance. Wise old Joe Johnston, sparring and side-stepping and shifting back, had a very clear understanding of the home-front politics behind the armies. His whole plan had been to keep Sherman from forcing a showdown until after the election, on the theory that victory postponed so long would look to the people up North like victory lost forever, and his strategy had been much more effective than his own government could realize. To President Davis, Johnston's course had seemed like sheer faintheartedness, and he had at last dismissed Johnston and put slugging John B. Hood in his place. Hood had gone in and slugged, and Sherman's army had more slugging power—so now, with the Democrats betting the election on the thesis that the war effort was a flat failure, decisive success had at last been won [by Sherman].[31]

The Confederates' weakened condition compelled Hood to flee westward and make a feeble attempt to destroy Sherman's railroad supply line. Sherman at first followed Hood but finally convinced Grant that Sherman's superiority was so great that he could split his army and break loose on his famous March to the Sea.

Only three months later, on November 29, Hood allowed Schofield's 20,000-man augmented Army of the Ohio to escape a trap Hood had carefully set at Spring Hill, Tennessee. The next day, in disgust and fury, Hood deliberately ordered the slaughter of his own Army of Tennessee (21 percent casualties) in a suicidal attack at Franklin, Tennessee. Captain Sam Foster of Texas said that Franklin, where six Confederate generals were killed, five wounded and one captured, was not war: "It can't be called anything else than cold-blooded murder."[32] Two weeks later, the remnants of Hood's army were routed (with 26 percent casualties) in the Battle of Nashville, where Hood foolishly used his 25,000 remaining soldiers to challenge 77,000 of the enemy.[33] In a mere six months, Hood had reduced a proud army of 57,000 to a battered collection of 18,000 survivors, who retreated across the Tennessee River into Alabama in the middle of winter.[34]

The documentary evidence shows that Lee did not recommend to Davis that he reject Hood and instead select Hardee. It shows that perhaps Lee thought that would be the proper action. But, given Davis' stated predisposition to name Hood and Bragg's well-known dislike for Johnston and Hardee, Lee's dancing around the issue and failure to make a straightforward recommendation could only have one result: Davis' proceeding to make the disastrous appointment of Hood.

Lee's error in acquiescing in Hood's appointment eventually eliminated the Army of Tennessee as a southern buffer for Lee's own army.[35] It allowed Sherman to move his unchallenged force on a destructive march through Georgia and the Carolinas (causing thousands of desertions from Lee's army) and was about to result in Sherman and Grant's encirclement of the Army of Northern Virginia when Petersburg and Richmond fell in April 1865.

Toward the end of June, meanwhile, Grant authorized Pennsylvania Volunteer miners under Burnside's command to dig a five-hundred-foot tunnel under the Confederate fortifications at Petersburg. By July 23, they had finished their digging and were ready to detonate eight tons of explosives under the Confederate lines. In the latter days of July, Grant transferred troops north toward Richmond. By doing so, he duped Lee into moving four of seven infantry divisions from Petersburg to Richmond and thereby weakened that sector of Lee's line. Then, on the night of July 29–30, Grant surreptitiously brought most of his troops back to the Petersburg front in an effort to exploit the expected breakthrough from the planned explosion. Early on the morning of July 30, Union troops set off a massive explosion under the Confederate lines, thereby creating a huge opening and an opportunity for a breakthrough.[36]

With Grant's approval, Meade, however, had ordered a last-minute replacement for the African-American troops who had been trained to lead the assault. General Ledlie, the division commander of the replacement troops, cowered in a bunker behind the lines—drunk again (as he had been at the North Anna River). Therefore, contrary to Grant's orders stressing "the absolute necessity of pushing entirely beyond the enemy's present line," Ledlie's men entered the Crater but then hesitated to move farther. The belated and ineffective Union advance provided the shocked Confederates with time to reorganize and counterattack. The Rebel response resulted in a slaughter of Union troops in the Crater. What Grant later called "this stupendous failure" resulted in 4,000 Union casualties while the Confederates suffered only 1,500. Ledlie at last was removed from command.[37]

Grant was more successful in establishing and maintaining control of the James River north of his City Point base at the intersection of the James and Appomattox Rivers. From June 20 onward, his forces held a fortified bridgehead on the northwest bank of the James at the narrow horseshoe curve called Deep Bottom (because the James River was very deep at that point). For the next two months, they cleared Confederate mines from the river and blocked the creeks flowing into it. Lee declined Early's request for artillery and infantry that were necessary to dislodge Grant's forces, and the Union troops thus prevented a Rebel blockade of the river, safeguarded their City Point base of operations, and kept viable their ability to transfer troops between the Petersburg and Richmond fronts.[38]

In late July, Grant sent Hancock and Sheridan on a mission to challenge the northern end of Lee's lines, divert Lee's attention from the planned mine explosion in Petersburg, widen the Union bridgehead on the north side of the James River, and thus more effectively threaten Lee's Richmond lines. At what became known as the First Battle of Deep Bottom, aggressive Rebel defenders caused Hancock to hesitate and not use his overwhelming numerical advantage. Although Hancock failed to achieve his mission (except to divert Lee's attention), he imposed more casualties than he incurred.[39]

Feeling more confident after the Crater debacle, Lee, in early August, sent Major General Joseph B. Kershaw's division to reinforce Early in the Valley. By doing so, he missed another opportunity to reinforce the Confederate forces (then under Hood) in their continuing struggle against Sherman outside Atlanta.

The advantages of being on the defensive were again demonstrated in late August when, in additional attacks on the Weldon Railroad, the Union lost 4,500 men (to 1,600 Confederates) in securing a hold on the tracks at Globe Tavern, on August 18–21, and then lost 2,700 more (to 700 Rebels) in a trap sprung on Hancock at Reams Station several miles to the south on August 25. However, in between these defensive victories for Lee was a foolish August 21 attack in the same Weldon Railroad area. Lee directed an assault on Union breastworks that resulted in 1,500 casualties to the enemy's 300. On both sides of the action, Lee continued to demonstrate the tremendous advantage of being on the defensive.

In the summer of 1864, however, the North was growing impatient. During July and August 1864, Grant and his army were tied down in a siege of Petersburg and Richmond while Sherman and his armies were locked in a siege at Atlanta. These stalemates were particularly frustrating and depressing when considered in light of the high casualties the Union armies, particularly Grant's, had suffered since the beginning of May. Peace Democrats were successfully causing many Northerners to question whether the war was worth fighting. Many appeals were blatantly racist; they asked whether it was worth shedding white blood to free Negro slaves. When the Democrats adopted a Peace Platform and nominated popular ex-Union General George McClellan as their presidential candidate in late August, things looked very bleak for Lincoln and the Union.

Lincoln was re-nominated for president on the Union ticket, but he seriously doubted that he would win another term because of the bleak battlefield situation. In August, he told a friend, "You think I don't know I am going to be beaten, but I do and unless some great change takes place, badly beaten."[40] On August 23, Lincoln despairingly wrote the following note at a Cabinet meeting:

> This morning, as for some days past, it seems exceedingly
> probable that this administration will not be re-elected. Then
> it will be my duty to so cooperate with the President-elect as
> to save the Union between the election and the inauguration,
> as he will have secured his election on such ground that he
> cannot possibly save it afterward.[41]

He had all the Cabinet members sign the statement.[42] Three days later, Confederate cartographer Jedediah Hotchkiss came to a similar conclusion in a letter to his wife: "The signs are brightening, and I still confidently look for a conclusion of hostilities with the ending of

'Old Abe's' reign."[43] In the words of Beringer and others, "[M]ost Confederates agreed that they needed to mobilize Union discontent and undermine Union will sufficiently so that voters would select a peace candidate to replace Lincoln."[44]

During August, Grant dealt with manpower issues. In mid-August, he wrote to his friend and political advocate, Congressman Elihu Washburne:

> The rebels have now in their ranks their last man. The little boys and old men are guarding prisoners, guarding rail-road bridges and forming a good part of their garrisons for intrenched positions. A man lost by them can not be replaced. They have robbed the cradle and the grave equally to get their present force. Besides what they lose in frequent skirmishes and battles they are now loosing [sic] from desertions and other causes at least one regiment per day.[45]

Grant foresaw a Union victory if the North was true to itself and rejected Southern hopes for the election of a peace candidate.[46]

Grant recognized that prisoner exchanges benefitted the Confederates, who had limited manpower. On August 18, he wrote, "If we commence a system of exchanges which liberates all prisoners taken we will have to fight on until the whole South is exterminated. If we hold those caught they amount to no more than dead men. At this particular time to release all rebel prisoners [in the] North would insure Sherman's defeat and would compromise our safety here."[47] The next day he wrote, "We ought not to make a single exchange nor release a prisoner on any pretext whatever until the war closes. We have got to fight until the military power of the South is exhausted and if we release or exchange prisoners captured it simply becomes a War of extermination."[48]

At the same time, Lee's concerns expressed in an August 24 letter to the Secretary of War confirmed Grant's view: "Unless some measures can be devised to replace our losses, the consequences may be disastrous.... Without some increase of our strength, I cannot see how we are to escape the natural military consequences of the enemy's numerical superiority."[49]

By mid-August, Grant was aware from the Bureau of Military Intelligence (BMI) that Lee had sent reinforcements to the Shenandoah and believed he could take advantage of their absence. By threatening Richmond on the north end of the battle-lines, Grant thought Lee would have to weaken Petersburg so much in response that Petersburg could be taken. Thus, he had Hancock, with 29,000 troops, move on Richmond, which was defended by a well-entrenched force of 7,700. Due to serious bungling and lack of coordination, this Second Battle of Deep Bottom, from August 14 to 20, resulted in little progress (other than overrunning and capturing eight large guns that threatened Union control of the James) being made by the Union forces, which incurred 2,900 casualties while imposing about 1,500 on the defenders.[50] But Grant was keeping the pressure on Lee.

That approach was consistent with a Grant-Lincoln exchange of views that occurred that same month. Halleck initiated the communications by writing that possible Northern draft riots would necessitate the withdrawal of troops from the Army of the Potomac to deal with the insurrections. Grant strongly disagreed, contended that state militias would have to deal with any riots, and said, "If we are to draw troops from the field to keep the loyal states in the harness it will prove difficult to suppress the rebellion in the disloyal states. My withdrawel [*sic*] now from the James River would insure the defeat of Sherman." Lincoln then chimed in and wired Grant, "I have seen your despatch expressing your unwillingness to break your hold where you are. Neither am I willing. Hold on with a bull-dog gripe [*sic*], and chew & choke, as much as possible."[51]

The "great change" that Lincoln needed for reelection occurred in Georgia the day after the Democrats' August 31 nomination of McClellan as their presidential candidate. Hood was compelled to abandon Atlanta on September 1. Sherman occupied it the next day, the North went wild in celebration, and Lincoln's reelection was virtually assured.[52] On September 12, Grant sent a personal letter to Sherman that was delivered by Colonel McPherson of Grant's staff. He closed by congratulating Sherman on his Atlanta campaign: "In conclution [*sic*] it is hardly necessary for me to say that I feel you have accomplished the most gigantic undertak[ing] given to any General in this War and with a skill and ability that will be acknowledged in history as unsurpassed if not unequalled." Grant told Sherman that he was sending McPherson to get Sherman's views on future actions, but Grant did suggest the possibility of moves on Mobile and Savannah.[53] Grant was thinking ahead on a national scale.

After Early's July 30 burning of Chambersburg, Pennsylvania, Grant took action to end the Confederate use of the Shenandoah Valley as an avenue for raiding the North and supplying Lee. Secretary of War Stanton had previously rejected Sheridan as commander of all the forces there because of Sheridan's young age (33). Grant, nevertheless, was determined to get his aggressive cavalryman directly involved. Thus, he sent Sheridan and another division of cavalry to the Shenandoah and wired Halleck, "Unless Gen. Hunter is in the field in person I want Sheridan put in command of all the troops in the field with instructions to put himself south of the enemy and follow him to the death. Wherever the enemy goes let our troops go also."[54]

After reading this dispatch, Lincoln sent Grant an August 3 wire quoting the above words and then prodding Grant to do more:

> This, I think, is exactly right, as to how our forces should move. But please look over the despatches [*sic*] you may have receved [*sic*] from here, even since you made that order, and discover, if you can, that there is any idea in the head of any one here, of "putting our army *South* of the enemy" or of ["] following him to the *death*" in any direction. I repeat to you it will neither be done nor attempted unless you watch it every day, and hour, and force it.[55]

Taking the president's not-so-subtle hint, Grant immediately left his City Point headquarters and headed north to resolve this situation. He went directly to Monocacy, Maryland, where he met General Hunter. Since Hunter was unable to tell Grant where the enemy was, Grant decided to smoke out the enemy troops by sending a trainload of soldiers four miles west of Harper's Ferry to draw them out. Because Grant also ordered Hunter's cavalry and wagons to move west in search of Confederates and explained that Sheridan would command in the field, Hunter requested that he be relieved of command. Grant gladly complied and thus had Sheridan where he wanted him—in charge of 30,000 troops charged with clearing the Valley of Confederates. Grant would not be disappointed.[56] Between August 13 and 20, Grant moved troops north of the James to keep Lee from reinforcing the Shenandoah.[57]

From June 22 to August 21, Grant had intermittently focused on extending his south-of-Petersburg lines westward to block the north/south Weldon Railroad, over which Lee's army was receiving many of its supplies from Weldon, North Carolina. After unsuccessfully moving on that railroad in late June with a loss of 3,000 troops, Grant's forces tried again in August. Warren's 5th Corps extended its line three miles to the west, took and fortified a position on the railroad, and then held on against a Confederate counterattack at the Battle of Globe Tavern (Weldon Railroad) on August 18–21. Thereafter, the Confederates had to bypass the section of that railroad held by Grant's troops via a thirty-mile detour by wagon, and thus Richmond/Petersburg was more difficult to supply. The battle had cost Lee 1,200 killed or wounded out of his almost 15,000 soldiers, while Grant had used over 20,000 troops and had 1,303 killed or wounded. Grant's missing and captured exceeded Lee's four hundred by about 2,600.[58]

On September 15, Grant left City Point for another visit with Sheridan. In his memoirs, Grant said he went to Harper's Ferry to discuss an offensive greater than Stanton or Halleck would have authorized if he had tried to communicate by telegraph. Grant brought a campaign plan with him but kept it in his pocket when Sheridan produced a plan of his own—another indicator of Grant's willingness to delegate authority. Grant wanted an end to years of pussyfooting by Union generals in the Valley, and he was now certain that Sheridan was the man to do it. Thus began Sheridan's successful 1864 Shenandoah Valley campaign.[59]

On September 19, at Opequon Creek (Winchester), Sheridan took 5,000 casualties to impose 4,000 casualties on Early and drive him south. Three days later, at Fisher's Hill, Sheridan repeated his assault and, at a cost of only 500 casualties, imposed 1,200 casualties on Early and drove him farther south.[60] Sheridan chased Early so far up the Valley that Sheridan lost contact with Washington. To allay Lincoln's fears that Lee would successfully reinforce Early against Sheridan, Grant told him he would attack Lee to keep him from doing so. To do that, Grant issued September 28 orders to Ord's 18th and Major General David B. Birney's 10th Corps, as well as Brigadier General August V. Kautz's cavalry, to threaten the Richmond end of Lee's lines.[61]

Between September 29 and October 2, Grant launched simultaneous offensives on both ends of the Petersburg/Richmond siege lines; captured important Fort Harrison outside Richmond, thus inducing Lee to launch a costly and unsuccessful counterattack against that fort; and compelled Lee to extend his lines three miles farther west of Petersburg, thereby thinning and weakening Lee's defensive perimeter. Utilizing excellent Bureau of Military Intelligence information, Grant and Sheridan caught Kershaw's division in transition between Richmond and the Shenandoah Valley while Grant was conducting his successful dual assaults against Lee's weakened army. A few days later, Grant's troops used Spencer repeating rifles to repulse a Lee-directed assault along Darbytown Road.[62]

A month later, on October 19, Early surprised Sheridan's troops at Cedar Creek and drove them in retreat toward Winchester. The absent Sheridan arrived just in time to stop the panicked retreat, organize a counterattack, and rout and drive Early's soldiers from the Lower Valley for the final time. Both sides withdrew most of their remaining troops to the Richmond/Petersburg front, and significant fighting in the Shenandoah was over. Although Sheridan had suffered 5,900 casualties to Early's 2,900, his third and final major victory in the Valley in about 35 days provided more grist for the Lincoln reelection mill.[63]

After all the September fighting, Lee the next month again proposed to Grant that prisoner exchanges be resumed. Grant responded that exchanges could be resumed if Lee agreed that African-American prisoners would be exchanged "the same as white soldiers." Lee, in turn, replied that "…Negroes belonging to our citizens are not considered subjects of exchange and were not included in my proposition." Grant, therefore, declined resumption of exchanges, in accordance with Lincoln's policy on the matter—a policy that cost Lincoln votes in the November election.[64]

In the Deep South, meanwhile, Admiral David Dixon Farragut had taken major actions against Mobile, Alabama, a key port and rail center that had long been on Grant's list of primary targets. Not only was it the last major open port on the Gulf, but Mobile was the only extant rail connection point between Mississippi and Alabama and the rest of the Confederacy. Lincoln's reelection prospects were enhanced by Farragut's "Damn the torpedoes—Full speed ahead" charge into Mobile Bay on August 5 and the August 23 capture of Fort Morgan, which controlled that bay. Although the city itself was not occupied until April 1865, its use as a Confederate port was ended by Farragut's actions.[65] The morale-boosting impact of the Mobile Bay victory was captured by Secretary of State William H. Seward, who said, "Sherman and Farragut have knocked the bottom out of the [Democrats'] Chicago platform."[66]

In late October, Grant made his final pre-winter effort to cut Lee's supply lines. On October 24, he ordered Meade on an October 27 movement west from the Weldon Railroad toward the South Side Railroad. Meade was rebuffed with over 1,700 casualties to the enemy's less than 1,000.[67] Grant protected Meade's movement with a simultaneous effort by Butler on the far north end of the lines. Butler made some progress but was similarly rebuffed when he tried to drive headlong down the Darbytown Road instead of first turning the Confederate flank.[68]

Riding the wave of Atlanta, Mobile Bay, and Shenandoah military victories, Lincoln convincingly won reelection. Lincoln won 2,200,000 votes (55 percent) to McClellan's 1,800,000 (45 percent). The 78 percent of the military vote received by Lincoln reflected soldiers' satisfaction with how the war was going. Lincoln's electoral college advantage was 212 to 21. Although these statistics seem to reflect a landslide, the election was much closer than it appeared. The switch of a mere 1 percent of the votes (29,935 out of 4,031,195) in Connecticut, Illinois, Indiana, New York, Oregon, and Pennsylvania would have given McClellan the ninety-seven additional electoral votes he needed to barely win with one hundred eighteen electoral votes.[69] The relative closeness of the vote provided an inkling of what might have been if Lee had conserved his manpower, reinforced the opposition to Sherman, and kept Atlanta from falling before the election.

Jefferson Davis refused to accept the fact that the game was up and insisted that Lincoln's reelection had changed nothing. But Southern citizens' demoralization and Southern soldiers' desertions said the contrary.[70] Based on his own earlier statements, Lee should have known that further resistance was futile and would only bring more death and destruction to the South and its armies. Nevertheless, on November 12, he wrote to his wife that she should "make up your mind that Mr. Lincoln is reelected President" and "we must therefore make up our minds for another four years of war."[71]

After occupying Atlanta, Sherman deliberated on what to do next. As early as September 10, Grant talked about sending Union troops to Savannah. Sherman's response mentioned several possible Georgia targets and the possibility that he could "sweep the whole State of Georgia." On September 12, Grant sent Lieutenant Colonel Porter to visit Sherman and get his views on future operations.[72]

Sherman watched and then followed as Hood moved north and then west toward and eventually into Alabama. Initially Hood went after Sherman's supply line, the Western and Atlantic Railroad, from Chattanooga to Atlanta. Finally, Sherman decided that pursuing Hood and protecting his own extended supply line was getting him nowhere. Instead, on October 9, Sherman made a radical proposal to Grant: Sherman should break loose from his supply line, destroy the railroad between Chattanooga and Atlanta (his supposed lifeline), and "move through Georgia smashing things to the sea." Sherman told Grant, "I can make Savannah, Charleston or the mouth of the Chattahoochee" and asked for quick approval.[73] That same evening, Grant succinctly gave his approval: "Your dispatch of to-day received. If you are satisfied the trip to the sea coast can be made holding the line of the Tennessee River firmly you may make it destroying all the rail-road South of Dalton or Chattanooga, as you think best."[74] Grant gave final approval to Sherman's proposal after Sherman sent George Thomas and John Schofield (with the 12,000-man Army of the Ohio) to defend Tennessee against a likely incursion by Hood.[75]

On November 16, Sherman left Atlanta with about 60,000 troops, deftly feinted moves toward different destinations, and wreaked a path of destruction sixty miles wide from Atlanta to Savannah. Slocum commanded the two-corps Left Wing, Howard commanded the two-corps Right Wing, and Brigadier General Judson Kilpatrick commanded the cavalry. They destroyed railroads, factories, and Confederate arsenals. They seized anything that could be eaten by men, horses, or mules. Despite orders to the contrary, they burned and pillaged at will.[76] When Lincoln grew concerned about Southern press reports that Sherman's men were demoralized and starving, Grant told Lincoln not to worry.[77]

Confederate General Hardee, a Georgia native, came back to his home state, raised some troops, and harassed Sherman's unstoppable force as it continued toward Savannah. After a 280-mile trek, Sherman arrived at Savannah's outskirts and began his siege of that city on December 10. In order to establish contact with the federal fleet that had arrived off Savannah, a Union division had to assault and capture Fort McAllister—Sherman's first hard fighting since Atlanta. Once he had access to the shipboard mails, Sherman was able to read a December 3 letter from Grant. In that letter, Grant expressed his confidence in Sherman and his awareness of the relationship of their mutual activities:

> Not liking to rejoice before the victory is assured I abstain from congratulating you and those under your command until bottom has been struck. I have never had a fear however for the result.

Since you left Atlanta no very great progress has been made here. The enemy has been closely watched though and prevented from detaching against you.[78]

Although Hardee's force of about 10,000 defenders inexplicably and inexcusably were allowed to escape the city into South Carolina, Sherman occupied Savannah in time to make it a Christmas present to the president. He wired the president: "I beg to present to you as a Christmas-gift the city of Savannah, with one-hundred and fifty heavy guns and plenty of ammunition, also about twenty-five thousand bales of cotton."[79] The greatest significance of the capture of Savannah was that it gave Sherman an ocean base for supplies. For the balance of the war, his army could be supplied with ammunition and other essentials by sea and rail through Atlantic Ocean ports.[80]

Sherman's march from Atlanta to Savannah had a devastating effect on the Georgia countryside and towns and had a demoralizing effect on the inhabitants, their soldier relatives serving with Lee and elsewhere, and the entire South. In his memoirs, Grant gave full credit to Sherman for the conception and execution of this critical march:

> ... the question of who devised the plan of march from Atlanta to Savannah is easily answered: it was clearly Sherman, and to him also belongs the credit of its brilliant execution. It was hardly possible that any one else than those on the spot could have devised a new plan of campaign to supersede one that did not promise success.[81]

Meanwhile in Tennessee, Grant's national campaign achieved more success with Thomas' devastating defensive victory at Franklin and his smashing offensive victory at Nashville. After his suicidal attack at Franklin, Hood ordered his battered army to proceed toward Nashville.

With his inadequate force, Hood fortified in front of Nashville while Thomas consolidated his forces and received reinforcements. For the next two weeks, Grant urged Thomas to attack; Grant's attempted micromanagement of Thomas demonstrates that Grant had less confidence in Thomas than he did in Sherman.[82] On December 15 and 16, Thomas launched a massive assault on Hood's forces and inflicted another 6,600 casualties—26 percent of the remaining Army of Tennessee. The broken remnants of Hood's army headed back to Alabama in frigid winter conditions. Aided by two rivers and the horrid weather that slowed his pursuers, Hood escaped—much to Grant's chagrin. In five months, however, Hood had reduced the Army of Tennessee from 57,000 to 18,000.[83]

Loss of Atlanta, destruction of the Army of Tennessee, and the capture of Savannah after Sherman's destructive march through Georgia contributed to despair in the South. That despair had reached some true believers in the Confederate cause. As early as October 8, 1864, Varina Davis, the president's wife, was writing to Charleston, South Carolina, diarist Mary Chesnut, "Strictly between us, *Things look* very anxious here...."[84] On November 20, Mrs. Davis wrote to Mrs. Chesnut, "Only I mean that I am so forlorn that they do not tell me how forlorn they think I am...."[85] In late December, Mrs. Chesnut reflected her own concerns: "Savannah—a second Vicksburg business.... Neither the governor of Georgia nor the governor of South Carolina moving hand or foot. *They have given up*."[86]

During the second half of 1864, therefore, Grant tightened the noose around Richmond and Petersburg and oversaw successful operations in other theaters. Nowhere did Union forces suffer significant casualties compared with those they imposed on the enemy—especially when considered in light of their offensive missions and significant accomplishments. By the end of 1864, Grant's nationwide campaign had succeeded in capturing Atlanta, Savannah, Mobile harbor, and the Shenandoah Valley; reelecting Lincoln; virtually destroying the Army of Tennessee; and laying the groundwork for the final defeat of Lee and the Confederacy.

From November 1864 until the following April, Lee, with his unparalleled standing among Confederate leaders, appears to have had the power to bring the war to a halt by simply resigning. Lee must have realized he was in a hopeless near-siege situation, Lincoln's reelection ended hope for a political settlement, and Sherman was running roughshod through the Deep South. There is no indication, however, that he attempted to tell Davis that further resistance was hopeless, and it is likely that Davis would have rejected any advice to stop the war—particularly given his later hopes that the struggle could be continued even after Lee surrendered at Appomattox the following April. Nevertheless, Lee's stature and standing were so great that his resignation would have caused massive desertions and brought virtually all the fighting to an end. Lee could have presented Davis with a *fait accompli*, but he chose to carry on the war in the glorious cavalier tradition and thereby caused the loss of thousands of lives and the destruction of hundreds of millions of dollars worth of southern property.

In summary, while Grant was pressing on to ultimate victory, Lee was pressing on to ultimate defeat.

CHAPTER ELEVEN

EARLY 1865:
LEE SURRENDERS
TO GRANT

Sherman marches through the Carolinas, Wilmington falls,
Grant's troops extend the Confederates and break through
at Petersburg, Lee's Army abandons Richmond, and
Lee surrenders to Grant at Appomattox Court House.

I n the first months of 1865, Grant would concentrate virtually all his forces in the Carolina/Virginia theater to bring the war to a decisive end. As the year opened, Grant had Lee pinned down in Richmond and Petersburg, Sherman was poised to march virtually unmolested through the Carolinas from Savannah, and George Thomas was prepared to send tens of thousands of troops eastward from Tennessee to Virginia after his rout of Hood at Franklin and Nashville. The Union was threatening to close Wilmington, the Confederacy's last major port.

The end was clearly inevitable. About 40 percent of Confederate soldiers east of the Mississippi had deserted during the fall and early winter.[1] On December 31, 1864, less than half of the Confederacy's soldiers were present with their units.[2] In desperation, Lee requested that General E. Kirby Smith's Trans-Mississippi Army be transferred to Virginia.[3] Therefore, 1865 should have witnessed no fighting. But Lee had yet to call a halt to the bloody proceedings. The thousands of deaths that year were a macabre tribute to his chivalry and sense of honor and duty.

As the result of a January 19, 1865, act of the Confederate Congress and Davis' grudging appointment, Lee became Commander-in-Chief of all Confederate forces and in that capacity continued the hopeless struggle. Lee's appointment demonstrated the unused power he held because it resulted from pressure by the Confederate Congress and the Virginia Legislature on Davis, who was reluctant to yield any power.[4]

As the Confederacy's condition deteriorated in early 1865, a half-hearted effort to achieve peace resulted in a February 3 conference on the steamer *River Queen* in Hampton Roads, Virginia. When Lincoln made it clear to the Confederate representatives that the Southern states' return to the Union and an end to slavery were required, the talks went nowhere. Lee had clearly not made Davis understand that the military situation was hopeless. Before leaving for those talks, Lincoln had wired Grant, "Let nothing which is transpiring change, hinder, or delay your Military movements or plans." Grant responded that he would keep his soldiers "in readiness to move at the shortest notice if occasion should justify it."[5]

Word of the peace negotiations and anti-Davis developments in Richmond further increased Southern despondency. In late January, Mrs. Chesnut wrote: "Here is startling news. Politely but firmly the Virginia legislature requests Jeff Davis and all of his cabinet to resign.... And we have sent [Alexander] Stephens, [John Archibald] Campbell— all who never believed in this thing—to negotiate for peace. No hope— no good. Who dares hope?"[6] In Richmond, Gorgas reflected a mixture of melancholy and dependence on Lee:

Jan 15 [1865] In this dark hour of our struggle there is of course strong feeling against the administration for having mismanaged our affairs. This must be expected in adversity.

Jan 25 [1865] I have outlived my momentary depression, & feel my courage revive when I think of the brave army in front of us, sixty thousand strong. As long as Lee's army remains intact there is no cause for despondency. As long as it holds true we need not fear. The attacks of the enemy will now all be directed against that Army. Sherman from the South, Thomas from the West and Grant in front.[7]

With despondency turning to despair throughout the South, Lee nevertheless carried on the hopeless struggle to preserve the honor of his army—and perhaps to preserve his own honor.

Grant's army and the threat it posed to Richmond seemed to be the sole concern of Lee and the paralyzed Confederate Government. They were slow to respond to the danger represented by Sherman and his resupplied 60,000-man army. Optimistically, Lee had sent one dispatch in which he spoke of achieving two incompatible goals: stopping Sherman and holding Charleston.[8] Doing both was unrealistic with the few Confederate troops available in the Carolinas. Besides Hardee's small force that had escaped Savannah, there were only local militia and the reassembled remnants of the Army of Tennessee, which had come northeast from Alabama to oppose Sherman.

Initially Grant had intended to move Sherman's troops by vessel from Savannah to either Richmond or North Carolina. When Sherman realized how long it would take to gather the necessary transports, however, he instead proposed a march through the Carolinas. Grant promptly approved. As early as January 21, Grant was making arrangements for up to 30,000 western troops to be brought east to the ports of

Wilmington and New Bern, North Carolina, from which they could move inland to reinforce Sherman.[9]

Sherman later explained the importance of his intended march through the Carolinas: "Were I to express my measure of the relative importance of the march to the sea and of that from Savannah northward, I would place the former at one, and the latter at ten, or the maximum."[10] The plan was brilliant; it allowed Sherman to destroy the railroads supplying Lee from the Carolinas as he moved to close Lee's back door.[11]

Late in December, with Sherman outside Savannah, Grant had analyzed Lee's vulnerability to Sherman's actions. On December 18, Grant wrote to Sherman about Lee's focus on Richmond: "If you capture the garrison of Savannah it certainly will compel Lee to detach from Richmond or give us nearly the whole South. My own opinion is that Lee is averse to going out of Virginia, and if the cause of the South is lost he wants Richmond to be the last place surrendered. If he has such views it may be well to indulge him until everything else is in our hands."[12]

It would be two more months before Lee turned his attention to Sherman, and he did so with no help from his own army. On February 22, he recalled Davis' old enemy, Joseph Johnston, to active duty as commander of the Western Army remnants charged with stopping Sherman. Lee's recall order to Johnston reflected unrealistic expectations about what Johnston could accomplish with the limited troops at hand: "Assume command of the Army of Tennessee and all troops in Department of South Carolina, Georgia, and Florida. Assign General Beauregard to duty under you, as you may select. Concentrate all available forces and drive back Sherman."[13] The reality was that Lee's attention to Sherman came far too late to do any good.[14]

Lee meanwhile was seeing his army melt away. On February 25, he wrote, "Hundreds of men are deserting nightly...."[15] Union Colonel

Elisha Hunt Rhodes provided confirmation of that; he reported continuing Confederate desertions, including the arrival of ten deserters on February 21 and one hundred sixty of them on February 25.[16] Between February 15 and March 18, there were 3,000 deserters from Lee's army.[17] The situation became so bad that, in March, Lee reported 1,094 desertions in a ten-day period, and one entire division left *en masse*.[18] During March, numerous regimental and brigade commanders requested the Confederate Adjutant's Office in Richmond to drop from the rolls captains and lieutenants who had deserted.[19] Appomattox Campaign historian William Marvel calculated that, between March 10 and April 9, from 14,400 to 20,400 of Lee's soldiers deserted.[20]

These desertions were due not only to the strains of trench warfare and life. A major factor was the impact of Sherman's campaign: it caused a reduction of food and supplies coming to Lee's army, and, as Bevin Alexander observed, it resulted in "letters from home, which reflected the despair and helplessness of families and friends who had watched Sherman's unchecked progress and witnessed the destruction of their property."[21] Lee's manpower situation became so desperate that, in January, he and Davis agreed to exchange their African-American prisoners and in March the Confederate Congress belatedly passed a bill to recruit African-American soldiers.[22] These actions came too late as the Confederacy completed its war-long failure to utilize its slaves as soldiers.[23]

Because of the continued incompetence of Butler, Wilmington, North Carolina, remained open to blockade-runners as 1865 began. Both sides recognized its importance and acted accordingly. After Sherman captured Atlanta and Mobile was blocked, Grant gave his approval for troops to be used in an amphibious assault designed to close Wilmington. Similarly, Lee sent a division of troops to defend the city; President Davis, however, overruled Lee's choice of a commander and put his (Davis') friend, Braxton Bragg, in command there instead of his enemy, P. G. T. Beauregard.[24]

On Christmas Eve, Butler exploded a naval vessel near Fort Fisher, guarding the approach to Wilmington, in an effort to destroy that fort. As early as December 3, Grant had expressed his skepticism about the exploding-ship tactic: "Owing to some preparations Admiral Porter and Gen. Butler are making to blow up Fort Fisher, and which, whilst I hope for the best, do not believe a particle in…."[25] The ship explosion, which failed to damage the fort, was a fiasco—as was Butler's Christmas Day amphibious assault on Fort Fisher. Infuriated that Butler had ignored his orders to at least besiege the fort, Grant urged Lincoln to relieve Butler of his command. On January 4, 1865, Lincoln at long last removed the political general, who had, in the words of Chris Fonvielle, a "singular blend of arrogance and military ineptitude." Having approved Sherman's plans for a march up through the Carolinas, Grant was determined to not only close Wilmington to Confederate commerce but to capture and open it as a means of resupplying Sherman via the Cape Fear River and Wilmington's three railroads. Grant then designated Brigadier (Brevet Major) General Alfred H. Terry as Butler's replacement to cooperate with Porter in taking Fort Fisher and Wilmington.[26]

On January 13, Terry landed his 9,000 troops four miles north of the fort. The next day Porter softened the Confederate land defenses by shelling the fort's guns protecting that side. On January 15, Terry and Porter continued their coordination and successfully stormed the weakened fort with a combined force of soldiers, sailors, and marines. Bragg, who had ignored numerous pleas from Fort Fisher for reinforcements, simply returned to Richmond.[27]

For the additional manpower needed to complete the capture of Wilmington, Grant assigned Schofield and his 23rd Corps, which only recently had come east from Tennessee. Schofield, who superseded Terry as the Union commander by virtue of his seniority, arrived with one division on February 7 and began his advance on February 11. A combined naval and ground assault resulted in the February 19 capture of Fort Anderson, closer to the city. The Union forces continued their assaults and approached the city. Bragg returned from Richmond just in time to evacuate the Confederacy's last port city on the night of February 21–22. The fall of Wilmington opened three rail routes for possible resupply of Sherman's ongoing advance into the Carolinas. Grant sent railroad rolling stock by water from Virginia to reinforce and supply Sherman. The city's fall also opened the Cape Fear River, which immediately was used to supply Sherman at Fayetteville. Conversely, no more foreign supplies would come to Lee or Johnston through the Union blockade.[28] Grant's investment of troops in the Wilmington campaign, therefore, paid real dividends. As Fionvielle concluded, "The fall of Wilmington did not end the Confederacy, but it hastened its downfall by guaranteeing the success of Sherman's Carolinas Campaign."[29]

On February 1, Sherman had left Savannah for the major offensive thrust of 1865. His men were eager to wreak havoc in South Carolina. One Union soldier exclaimed, "Here is where treason began, and by God, here is where it will end!"[30] Sherman wrote to Halleck that he almost trembled at the fate of South Carolina.[31] With that fervor, Sherman's soldiers advanced through the wintry swamps of southern South Carolina at a pace that amazed their opponents. In a manner similar to the March to the Sea, Slocum's Army of Georgia was the Left Wing of the advance, Howard's Army of the Tennessee was the Right Wing, and Brevet Major General Kilpatrick led the 3rd Cavalry Division. They headed for the South Carolina capital of Columbia while cavalry bluffed movements toward Augusta, Georgia, on the left and Charleston, South Carolina, on the right.[32]

Virtually unopposed, Sherman raced over the rivers and through the swamps of South Carolina to the capital at Columbia. The only delays were to rebuild burned bridges, corduroy roads, and fend off cavalry skirmishers. Columbia was burned on February 17; controversy still exists as to whether the wind-driven fire's primary cause was Confederates' torching of their cotton stockpiles or arson by drunken Union soldiers and other looters. Sherman's juggernaut moved on.[33]

Sherman's march on Columbia cut many of the railroad connections to Charleston and compelled the military evacuation of that "Cradle of the Confederacy" on February 15. Beauregard positioned his forces forty-five miles north of Columbia to protect Charlotte, North Carolina. Sherman, however, moved northeast toward Goldsboro and unification with Schofield and at least 21,000 soldiers who previously had entered North Carolina to capture Wilmington and were now moving inland.[34]

As he had in 1864, Sherman still had concerns about the possibility of Lee shifting troops to oppose his advance:

> ... the only serious question that occurred to me was, would General Lee sit down in Richmond (besieged by General Grant), and permit us, almost unopposed, to pass through the States of South and North Carolina, cutting off and consuming the very supplies on which he depended to feed his army in Virginia, or would he make an effort to escape from General Grant, and endeavor to catch us inland somewhere between Columbia and Raleigh?[35]

Grant and Sherman had been concerned about such a merger since the beginning of their simultaneous campaigns in May 1864. Sherman said that, "if Lee is a soldier of genius, he will seek to transfer his army from Richmond to Raleigh or Columbia; if he is a man simply of detail, he will remain where he is, and his speedy defeat is sure." On March 1, 1865, Johnston proposed such a merger to Lee, who declined to turn on Sherman until the Federals had crossed the Roanoke River, a mere fifty-five miles south of Petersburg. At the time, Johnston had about 21,000 troops to take on Sherman's forces: 60,000 soldiers of his own and perhaps another 30,000 with Schofield coming inland from the North Carolina coast. Each Confederate army would lose separately.[36] Lee did allow the 14,000 troops who had been defending Fort Fisher, Wilmington, and its environs to remain in North Carolina.[37]

As to Lee's capability of affecting events, Grant commented of him at the time, "All the people except a few political leaders in the South will accept whatever he does as right and will be guided to a great extent by his example."[38] This view was shared by Gorgas, who on March 2 wrote:

> People are almost in a state of desperation, and but too ready to give up the cause.... It must be confessed that we are badly off for leaders both on the council & on the field. Lee is about all we have & what public confidence is left rallies around him, and he it seems to me fights without much heart in the cause. I do him wrong perhaps, but I don't think he believes we will or can succeed in this struggle. The President has alas! lost almost every vestige of the public confidence. Had we been successful his errors and faults would have been overlooked, but adversity magnifies them.[39]

On March 8 to 10, Bragg's 8,500 troops halted Schofield's westward movement at Kinston, North Carolina. The delay was temporary only because Sherman's overwhelming force was moving farther northeast with little hindrance. He took Fayetteville on March 11, crossed the Cape Fear and Black rivers, and continued northeast toward a rendezvous with Schofield at Goldsboro. Grant earlier had selected Goldsboro as Sherman's goal because it was the junction of two railroads, the Wilmington and Weldon and the Atlantic and North Carolina, that would facilitate troop and supply movements from Wilmington, New Bern, and Morehead City on the coast.[40]

Slocum's left wing of Sherman's army was delayed by Hardee's troops at Averasboro between the Black and Cape Fear rivers on March 15 and 16.[41] Then on March 19–21, two isolated divisions of that wing were attacked by Johnston's combined forces at Bentonville. Sherman's forces incurred 1,500 casualties while inflicting 2,600 on the Confederates. Seeking to avoid a costly end-of-the-war frontal assault on Johnston's lines, Sherman passed up an opportunity to reinforce a breakthrough by one of his divisions.[42]

To avoid the merging federal forces, Johnston retreated north to Smithfield. As a result, on March 23 Sherman and Schofield merged their forces at Goldsboro into a 90,000-man threat to Johnston's less than 20,000 troops. Sherman's army thus completed its 425-mile march, which historian Bevin Alexander described as "the greatest march in history through enemy territory."[43]

Things were going no better for the Confederates in the Shenandoah. The forces of both Early and Sheridan had been reduced by winter transfers to the Richmond area. Sheridan decided to end Confederate occupation of any part of the Valley and promptly did so. He moved south on February 25 and pushed aside Early's cavalry at Mount Crawford on March 2. The next day Sheridan decimated Early's infantry at Waynesboro. Early retreated through the Blue Ridge Mountains toward Charlottesville, thereby ending any Confederate Army presence in the valley that had once been its primary breadbasket in the East.

On the Petersburg front, meanwhile, Grant was making survival more difficult for the Army of Northern Virginia. In February, his army of 118,000 faced Lee's army of 68,000 (56,000 fit for fighting) along a front of over thirty miles.[44] On February 5 to 7, Grant pushed back the Confederates at Hatcher's Run on the far western end of the lines below and west of Petersburg and then extended his (and, in response, the Confederate) lines an additional two miles. Grant's army had moved closer to the South Side Railroad and the Boydton Plank Road, key supply routes for Lee's army.[45]

In addition, Grant's continual extension of his line was weakening Lee's defensive strength by stretching out his defenders. In August 1864, Lee had about 65,000 soldiers defending a twenty-seven-mile front—about 2,500 men per mile. By March 1865, however, Lee was defending a thirty-five-mile front with 53,000 troops—a greatly reduced 1,500 men per mile.[46]

Not only was Grant lengthening and weakening Lee's line, he also was fortifying his own so efficiently that he freed up men to launch the final campaign of the war. David W. Lowe explained this development:

> In the war's last months, Federal engineers strengthened every fort on the Petersburg front into a self-sufficient fortress capable of meeting an assault from any direction. Artillery fields of fire were carefully refined, using diverse facings and restricting embrasures to generate the maximum degree of mutual support among the forts. The engineers proposed to denude the connecting parapets of troops and place the brunt of defense on the artillery and garrisons of 150–300 men—about 900 men per mile of front—certainly the most efficient use of entrenchments of the war.[47]

In a desperate attempt to force Grant to shorten his lines and perhaps aid an escape of Lee's army to North Carolina, Lee launched a March 25 pre-dawn assault from his Petersburg lines on Fort Stedman. Although initially successful in capturing that fort (perhaps because the defenders thought the attackers were deserters coming over to their lines), the Confederate attackers were driven back or surrounded by an immediate counterattack and deadly crossfire from every direction—particularly from the well-positioned nearby forts. The untrapped survivors retreated without 4,000 of their comrades, who were killed, wounded, or captured. Grant's army had lost a few more than a thousand men. Fort Stedman was to be Lee's last offensive.[48]

On March 26, Lieutenant Colonel Elisha Hunt Rhodes reported on the previous day's happenings:

> We had a very exciting day yesterday. At daylight the Rebels charged upon Fort Stedman on the 9th Corps front and got possession. Our division was ordered to march to the relief of the 9th Corps. The distance was about five miles, and we made it at a double quick most of the time and arrived in season to see a Division commanded by [Brigadier] Gen. John [F.] Hartranft of Penn. recapture the fort with many prisoners. We got a good shelling as we passed the Rebel forts and lost two horses from our division.[49]

The failure of Lee's desperate assault on Fort Stedman affected both Lee and Grant. Lee finally argued to Davis that his army should attempt to join with Johnston to defeat Sherman and then turn on Grant. On the other side of the lines, Grant sensed an enhanced opportunity to end the stalemate. On March 24, he had issued orders to Meade for a movement by Ord and Sheridan that was to begin on March 29 with Ord bringing three divisions from the far right to the far left of Grant's lines. Grant said that the movement was "for the double purpose of turning the enemy out of his present position around Petersburg, and to insure the success of the Cavalry under general Sheridan… in its efforts to reach and destroy the South Side and Danville rail-road[s]."[50] Lee's losses at Fort Stedman improved the prospects for success on the far left.[51]

Using Ord's men to fill the lines vacated by the 2nd Corps, Grant completed the shift of manpower to create a mobile force of Major General Andrew A. Humphreys' 2nd and Warren's infantry 6th Corps plus Sheridan's 9,000-man cavalry corps. With that force, Grant intended to finally get around the Confederate right flank and cut off the South-side and Danville railroads—the last ones supplying, respectively, Petersburg and Richmond. The Union troops started moving west on March 27, and Lee sent the cavalry of his nephew Fitzhugh Lee and five brigades of Pickett's infantry to oppose them. By moving at least 5,500 cavalry and 5,000 infantry southwest out of the Petersburg fortifications, Lee was fulfilling one of Grant's goals: drawing the Confederates into a fight with few, if any, fortifications.[52]

On March 29, Elisha Hunt Rhodes expressed anticipation of a movement and confidence in his commanders: "Still on picket and very quiet, although every man is on the alert. Something is about to happen. We are all ready to move, and if I did not know our leaders I should feel that we were in trouble and about to retreat. But I feel sure that the enemy are about to leave Petersburg, and we are held in readiness to pursue them."[53]

That same day saw a successful advance by two of Warren's 6th Corps divisions onto the key Boydton Plank Road as a result of their success at the Battle of Lewis' Farm. Encouraged by this development, Grant told Sheridan to forget a railroad raid and instead work with the 5th Corps to turn the Confederate flank. When Sheridan asked instead for the 6th Corps, with which he had worked in the Shenandoah Valley, Grant declined his request because the 5th Corps was closer to Sheridan.[54]

The 5th Corps stayed in place on March 30 because of heavy rain, the issuance of three days' rations, and a confusion about orders. On March 31, however, at White Oak Road (Gravelly Run or Hatcher's Run), Warren allowed two of his four divisions to be separately attacked and routed before he finally drove back Confederate Major General Bushrod R. Johnson's infantry division across White Oak Road. Union casualties totaled almost 1,900, while Johnson reported that he lost 800. The action, however, did prevent Johnson from reinforcing Pickett, who faced Sheridan farther west. Grant and Meade took critical note of Warren's performance and wondered why he had allowed the enemy troops to entrench after their retreat.[55]

To the west of the 5th Corps on that same day, Pickett and Fitzhugh Lee's 10,600 soldiers hit Sheridan's strung-out 9,500 troopers hard in the Battle of Dinwiddie Court House[56] and forced them back until Sheridan actively oversaw a last-ditch stand to avoid collapse. With the Confederates on the offensive throughout that day, Sheridan imposed 750–1,000 casualties on them while suffering no more than 400 himself. Although he had been stymied by Pickett from reaching Five Forks, Sheridan saw an opportunity and that evening told one of Grant's aides, "[Pickett's] force is in more danger than I am in—if I am cut off from the Army of the Potomac, it is cut off from Lee's army, and not a man in it should ever be allowed to get back to Lee."[57] Nearby, Colonel Elisha Hunt Rhodes heard the fighting and wrote, "The fight has raged all day on the 2nd Corps front to our left, and we have been under arms waiting for something to turn up. It means fight within a few hours, and may God give us a victory. Grant knows what he is doing and I am willing to trust him to manage Army affairs."[58] Colonel Rhodes would not be disappointed.

On the evening of March 31, Grant agreed with Sheridan's assessment of Pickett's isolation and vulnerability. Therefore, Grant ordered

Warren, through Meade, to withdraw a division and send it to reinforce Sheridan. Within hours Grant accepted a Meade recommendation and ordered Warren to move his entire corps west to strike Pickett. Due to Meade's delayed and confused orders and the prior destruction of a key bridge, Warren's corps arrived on the morning of April 1 well after Sheridan expected them. As soon as he was ordered to reinforce Sheridan, Warren had told Meade that he would have to build a replacement bridge over the swollen Gravelly Run; that forty-foot bridge was completed at 2:00 a.m. Sheridan, unaware of Warren's difficulties, wanted to attack immediately but had to delay until the arrival of all Warren's troops. Warren inexplicably and foolishly waited three hours before personally reporting to Sheridan at 11:00 a.m., and Sheridan's anger at Warren increased as the day progressed.[59]

During the night, Pickett had learned of the approach of Warren's infantry, which threatened to isolate him, and withdrew from Dinwiddie Court House back to a more secure line at Five Forks. During that movement, Pickett received a forceful and unfriendly message from Lee: "Hold Five Forks at all hazards. Protect road to Ford's Depot and prevent Union forces from striking the Southside Railroad. Regret exceedingly your forced withdrawal, and your inability to hold the advantage you gained."[60]

Lee correctly appreciated the value of Five Forks in protecting the South Side Railroad, but he probably failed to appreciate the difficult situation faced by Pickett with only about 10,000 soldiers defending a mile and three-quarter line and opposed by an increasingly superior adversary. Although Pickett advised Lee of his situation and requested a diversionary action, he and his cavalry commander, Fitzhugh Lee, negligently left the front lines and joined Major General Thomas L. Rosser at his shad bake behind Hatcher's Run, perhaps a mile from the front. Fitzhugh Lee went even after being advised that Union cavalry had driven away the Confederate cavalry between the Confederates at

Five Forks and the rest of the Army of Northern Virginia. It was to be a costly fish fry.[61]

At 4:00 p.m., the Battle of Five Forks finally got under way. Sheridan's 10,000 cavalry, generally dismounted, manned the bulk of the attacking Union line and took the brunt of the Rebel defenders' fire. To Sheridan's right, Warren's 12,000 troops were to come in on the left flank of Pickett's infantry. Because of an erroneous map and faulty reconnaissance, Warren's troops were misaligned and got into the fight only after changing the direction of their march. Warren desperately directed his divisions toward the fighting and even chased down one that had marched well past the battle. Brigadier General Joshua Chamberlain worked with Sheridan on the front lines to throw all available troops into the struggle as Pickett's leaderless troops bravely held on but finally broke and ran. One reason they broke is that the bulk of Warren's troops finally appeared on their left flank and rear. Back at the shad bake, Pickett and Fitzhugh Lee learned of the battle from couriers. Pickett got through to Five Forks to participate in the rout while Fitzhugh Lee was trapped behind Hatcher's Run with Rosser's cavalry.[62]

After the prior night's delayed march by Warren's 5th Corps, although primarily the fault of Meade and a missing bridge, Grant had authorized Sheridan to relieve Warren of command. After Warren's "tardy" arrival, his misdirected attack, and his absence from the front lines while he retrieved his errant divisions, Sheridan used that authority. When Warren's chief of staff reported to Sheridan late in the battle, Sheridan told him, "By God, sir, tell General Warren he wasn't in the fight." When a subordinate suggested that he rethink his decision, Sheridan roared, "Reconsider, hell! I don't reconsider my decisions. Obey the order!" At 7:00 p.m. a messenger brought Warren written orders replacing him as corps commander with Brigadier General Charles Griffin, who was promptly promoted to major general.[63]

With the sacking of Warren, Grant had completed a clean sweep of all his senior commanders except Meade as he entered the final phase of the war. A. A. Humphreys had succeeded the ailing Hancock as 2nd Corps commander; Wright had replaced the dead Sedgwick at the 6th Corps; John G. Parke had replaced Burnside, who had long commanded the 9th Corps; John Gibbon had replaced "Baldy" Smith at the 24th Corps, and Ord had replaced the incompetent Butler as Commander of the Army of the James.[64] All involved were major generals. The new leadership guaranteed there would be no hesitation in the war's last days.

Sheridan's cavalry and Warren's infantry had achieved a great victory at Five Forks, devastated Pickett's command, killed or wounded more than five hundred, taken between 2,000 and 2,500 prisoners, turned Lee's right flank, and opened the way to the South Side Railroad. Remnants of Pickett's five brigades were in full retreat, and Grant ordered artillery fire all along the line in anticipation of a full-scale attack the next day. After receiving the news of the Sheridan/Warren victory from Colonel Porter, Grant quietly retired to his tent, drafted orders, and then announced to the celebrating officers, "I have ordered a general assault along the lines."[65]

April 2 was a critical day in the history and ultimate demise of the Army of Northern Virginia. Following up on the victory at Five Forks the preceding day, Union troops captured Sutherland Station on the South Side Railroad, four miles east of Five Forks, and thereby severed Lee's lifeline. More significantly, Union forces executed Grant's order for an all-out assault on the Confederate lines at Petersburg, which he assumed would be weakened by Lee's manpower shifts to the west. Grant also attacked to preclude any possible counterattack on Five Forks by the ever-aggressive Lee.[66]

At Petersburg, Wright's 6th Corps exploited a weakness where a creek breached the Confederate line, used a 14,000-man wedge to attack at first light (about 4:40 a.m.) along a one-mile front, and by 5:15 a.m. had achieved a complete breakthrough. Alongside Wright's, Ord's and Humphrey's corps were likewise successful in overrunning the Confederate lines in their fronts. At midday, Grant's forces assaulted two Confederate forts at Petersburg; they captured one, and the defenders of the other then fled. Lee sent President Davis a message, saying "I think it is absolutely necessary that we should abandon our position to-night...." It was delivered to Davis as he attended Sunday services in Richmond. Davis immediately began preparations for the Confederate Government and treasury to leave Richmond by rail.[67] Lee sacrificed more men to hold the Union forces at bay for the additional hours required for Davis, Lee, and the dwindling Army of Northern Virginia to flee. Although there was no hope that his army would survive more than weeks, Lee did not advise surrender or threaten to resign. Thus, the killing continued for one more week.

Grant's well-conceived assault broke Lee's line in less than thirty minutes, killed Lieutenant General A. P. Hill, compelled the evacuation of Petersburg and Richmond, and sent Lee's army in a westward retreat. He accomplished these tasks with fewer casualties than he imposed on the Rebels. While Grant may have suffered casualties of about 4,000, Lee's army lost between 5,000 and 5,500—about 10 percent of Lee's remaining force. As A. Wilson Greene concluded, "[t]he engagements of April 2 doomed the Confederate war effort in Virginia."[68]

Before abandoning Richmond, Lee ordered the senseless burning of large quantities of Confederate supplies in the city. The resulting fires burned much of Richmond. As Grant's troops occupied the city on April 3, Lee's army fled westward. The Appomattox Campaign had begun.[69] The Rebel troops generally followed the Appomattox River on their ninety-mile retreat but were slowed by having to cross and re-cross the river and its tributary creeks. Their flight was accompanied by Union cavalry and infantry moving on their left flank in order to keep them from moving toward North Carolina and Johnston—as well as by Union forces following directly behind them.

Lee's plan was to have his forces head for Amelia Court House on the Richmond and Danville (R&D) Railroad, where Lee later claimed rations and supplies were supposed to be waiting. None were there, however, when the Confederates arrived on April 5. It is quite possible that Lee's staff, specifically Colonel Walter Taylor, failed to issue an order for those materials in the haste of evacuating Richmond (and Taylor's haste to get to his evening wedding on April 2). More significantly, Lee had to wait an extra day at Amelia Court House for Ewell's column, which was delayed by a missing pontoon bridge in crossing the Appomattox River.[70] Lee's predicament was worsened by the fact that some of Grant's cavalry had already gotten ahead of his troops and were eight miles southwest at Jetersville astride the R&D. Even farther southwest, by the morning of April 6, Ord's Army of the James was at Burke (Burkeville Junction), where the R&D joined the Southside Railroad.[71]

With the R&D forcefully blocked, Lee had no choice but to leave the R&D and head west. Hoping to find supplies from Lynchburg on the Southside Railroad northwest of Burke, Lee ordered a forced march westward toward Farmville. But disaster befell his army on April 6 when Anderson and Early's divisions fell behind and were trapped at Sayler's (or Sailor's) Creek by Sheridan's cavalry and the 2nd and 6th Union Corps. Overlooking the battlefield, Lee exclaimed, "My God, has the army been dissolved?" He did lose about a third of it that day. The Confederates lost most of their wagon train, had about 2,000 killed or wounded, and had another 7,000 (including at least nine generals) taken prisoner—at a cost to Grant of only 1,200 casualties.[72] Did Lee then give up the hopeless mismatch to halt further bloodshed? No, he continued west.

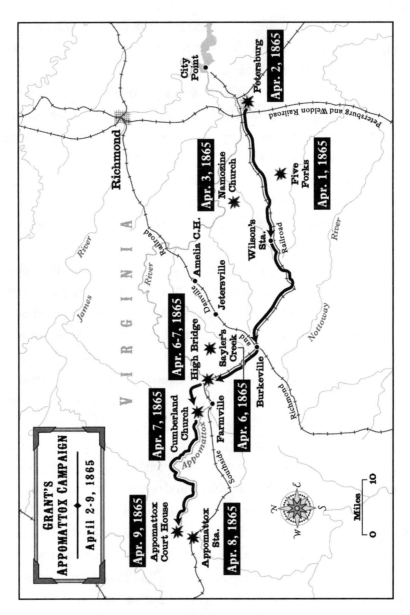

The Appomattox Campaign (April 2–9, 1865)
Map by David Deis, Dreamline Cartography, Northridge, CA

On April 6, Lee's survivors at last found rations in railcars on the Southside Railroad at Farmville. They had only partially removed the rations when the arrival of federal soldiers ended that operation. The railcars were moved west toward Appomattox Station, and Lee's remaining forces crossed the Appomattox River for the last time.[73] Lee, however, now found his army trapped between the Appomattox and James rivers. His soldiers headed west once again—this time toward a place called Appomattox Court House. But Phil Sheridan's cavalry was well ahead of them. He had captured the trainloads of Rebel rations at Appomattox Station on the Southside Railroad, and blocked any farther advance by the Army of Northern Virginia. Lincoln, who had been at City Point since March 24, saw a positive report from Sheridan and on the morning of April 7 wired Grant, "Gen. Sheridan says 'If the thing is pressed I think that Lee will surrender.' Let the *thing* be pressed."[74] That apparently was Lincoln's last written communication to Grant, who did indeed "press the thing."

Grant recognized that the human chess-match was nearly over and on the afternoon of April 7 made his first overture to Lee:

> General, The result of the last week must convince you of the hopelessness of further resistance on the part of the Army of Northern Va. in this struggle. I feel that it is so and regard it as my duty to shift from myself, the responsibility of any further effusion of blood by asking of you the surrender of that portion of the C. S. Army known as the Army of Northern Va.[75]

That night, his army's third consecutive night of marching, Lee responded with an inquiry about the terms Grant would allow:

General, I have recd your note of this date. Though not enter-
taining the opinion you express of the hopelessness of further
resistance on the part of the Army of N. Va. I reciprocate your
desire to avoid useless effusion of blood & therefore before
Considering your proposition ask the terms you will offer on
condition of its surrender.[76]

Lee's response was delayed by delivery difficulties and did not arrive until
the morning of April 8. Grant promptly responded with a minimal
requirement:

Your note of last evening, in reply to mine of same date, asking the conditions on which I will accept the surrender of the
Army of N. Va. is just received. In reply I would say that *peace*
being my great desire there is but one condition I insist upon,
namely: that the men and officers surrendered shall be dis-
qualified for taking up arms again, against the Government
of the United States, until properly exchanged.

I will meet you or will designate Officers to meet any
officers you may name for the same purpose, at any point
agreeable to you, for the purpose of arranging definitely the
terms upon which the surrender of the Army of N. Va. will
be received.[77]

In a response to Grant that night, Lee expressed an unrealistic view that
the end was not necessarily imminent but then reluctantly agreed to a
meeting with Grant:

General, I recd at a late hour your note of today—In mine of
yesterday I did not intend to propose the Surrender of the

Army of N. Va—but to ask the terms of your proposition. To be frank, I do not think the emergency has arisen to call for the Surrender of this Army; but as the restoration of peace should be the Sole object of all, I desired to know whether your proposals would lead to that end. I cannot therefore meet you with a view to Surrender the Army of N—Va—but as far as your proposal may affect the C. S. forces under my Command & tend to the restoration of peace, I should be pleased to meet you at 10 A m tomorrow on the old stage road to Richmond between the picket lines of the two armies—[78]

Although Lee may not yet have been willing to accept the inevitable, several of his officers were. They held an informal council, and Pendleton approached Longstreet about advising Lee to surrender. Fully understanding the depth of Lee's continuing reluctance to surrender, Longstreet refused to do so and responded, "If General Lee doesn't know when to surrender until I tell him, he will never know."[79] Although Longstreet did not intend this meaning, Lee had clearly demonstrated during the preceding several months that he did not know when to surrender.

After receiving Grant's response and observing and receiving reports of his army's surrounded condition, Lee finally decided to surrender. At long last and when there was no alternative but ungentlemanly guerrilla warfare, Lee had accepted the inevitable. Lee's reluctance, however, was demonstrated by his statement that, "There is nothing left for me to do but to go and see General Grant, and I would rather die a thousand deaths."[80] He went into the Union lines looking for Grant. As Lee went through the Union lines under a flag of truce, he belatedly remembered that the outgunned Confederates facing Ord and others ought to send out a flag of truce of their own. As Lee directed, Longstreet sent an officer with the white flag as a federal offensive was about to start. That officer was accompanied back to the Rebel lines by a brash Union cavalry commander, young General Custer, who made a pompous demand for the Confederate Army's unconditional surrender. When Custer repeated his demand to Longstreet, the 1st Corps commander dressed down Custer and told him he could either wait for Lee or attack. A humbled Custer returned to his lines, and all awaited developments at the highest level.[81]

When he was unable to find Grant, Lee wrote to him: "General: I received your note of this morning on the picket line, whither I had come to meet you and ascertain definitely what terms were embraced in your proposal of yesterday with reference to the surrender of this army. I now request an interview in accordance with the offer contained in your letter of yesterday, for that pu[r]pose."[82]

Their subordinate officers quickly arranged for the historic meeting of Grant and Lee in Appomattox Court House at the home of Wilmer McLean. The unfortunate McLean had moved to that peaceful town after his home had been hit by artillery during the First Battle of Bull Run (Manassas) in 1861. During the rather awkward meeting, Grant extended generous terms to Lee. He paroled Lee's 28,000 remaining men and allowed his officers to keep their horses. The only condition was that the Confederates not again take up arms against the United States. After confirming Lee's acceptance of his terms, Grant asked for writing materials and reduced the terms to writing on the spot. He agreed to Lee's additional request that any artilleryman or cavalryman who had brought his own horse to war could take one horse back home; Grant said that would help in the planting of crops. At Lee's request, Grant ordered Sheridan to provide rations for Lee's men. They then signed the surrender agreement, and Lee departed.[83]

The next day Lee issued his final order to what was left of his once grand army. With language that could have been accurately and timely used six months earlier, his General Order No. 9 said:

> After four years of arduous service marked by unsurpassed courage and fortitude, the Army of Northern Virginia has been compelled to yield to overwhelming numbers and resources.
>
> I need not tell the brave survivors of so many hard fought battles, who have remained steadfast to the last, that I have consented to this result from no distrust of them; but feeling that valor and devotion could accomplish nothing that could compensate for the loss that must have attended the continuance of the contest, I determined to avoid the useless sacrifice of those whose past services have endeared them to their countrymen....[84]

At long last, the bloody struggle was almost over. Over the next month, another hundred minor engagements closed out the fighting. A mind-boggling 620,000 Americans—260,000 Confederates and 360,000 Yankees—had died of wounds and disease. About 214,00 died on the battlefield. Robert E. Lee's offensives of 1862, 1863, and even 1864 had accounted for many of those deaths—on both sides—and guaranteed the ultimate defeat of the outmanned Confederacy.

Lee's final wartime mistake had been his failure to halt the fighting when it no longer served any sane purpose. Lee should have resigned his commission and position; the demoralized South was ready for an end to the war.[85] As Jeffry Wert stated, "Confederate resistance during the final weeks, if not months, of the war had been valiant, hopeless, and ultimately tragic. Tens of thousands of men on both sides were killed or maimed on battlefields or died wretchedly in prisons and hospitals. During Lee's retreat from Petersburg, more than 6,000 of his troops were killed or wounded."[86] Lee's final failure accounted for thousands of meaningless deaths. After the fall of Atlanta or certainly after Lincoln's reelection, Lee should have, in his own words, realized that "... valor and devotion could accomplish nothing that could compensate for the loss that must have attended continuance of the contest [and] determined to avoid the useless sacrifice of those whose past services have endeared them to their countrymen."[87]

Lee's surrender to Grant on April 9, 1865, effectively ended the Civil War. Once again Grant had achieved his goal with a militarily reasonable loss of men. During the entire expanded Appomattox Campaign, about 9,000 of Grant's 80,000 actively involved soldiers (11 percent) were killed or wounded as they broke through the Petersburg lines and pursued Lee to Appomattox. They killed or wounded almost 7,000 of Lee's 50,000 troops (13.5 percent) and took thousands of prisoners along the way.[88]

In the chase from Petersburg to Appomattox Court House, Grant used about 80,000 troops to pursue 50,000 Confederates. Appomattox Campaign historian William Marvel described how, on April 9, Confederate General Gordon claimed in an address to his troops that Lee surrendered only 8,000 troops to Grant's 60,000 and thus started the myth of Appomattox Campaign numbers relied upon by defenders of The Lost Cause. Rejecting claims by Lee's adjutant, Colonel Walter Taylor, that Lee faced 6:1 odds and had only 25,000 troops as the Appomattox pursuit began, Marvel carefully reviewed the official records and other sources and concluded that Lee started the chase with between 51,000 and 57,000 men. Marvel pointed out that the numbers of Gordon and Taylor are difficult to reconcile with the published list of 28,231 Confederates who surrendered and were paroled at Appomattox. Similarly, Marvel demolished Taylor's claim that Grant had 162,000 troops and instead concluded that Grant started the chase with about 80,000 men—less than a two-to-one edge.[89] Thus, Lee still had a large force at his disposal as he abandoned Petersburg and Richmond, but Grant's aggressive pursuit with a somewhat larger force quickly brought Lee's army to bay.

Grant's war-ending successes of 1864–65 were due to his aggressiveness, perseverance, and implementation of a multi-theater strategy. Meade's Army of the Potomac, under the personal supervision of Grant, did suffer high casualties during its drive to Petersburg and Richmond. However, it imposed an even higher percentage of casualties on Lee's army. Grant's determination to destroy Lee's army was demonstrated by three actions he took during and immediately after the Battle of the Wilderness, the first conflict of that campaign. Within a two-day period, he advised Lincoln that there would be "no turning back," told his officers to focus on what they could do and not what Lee might do, and made the crucial decision to continue south after the bloody two-day battle. As historian Michael C. C. Adams explained, Grant, a Westerner, was the first federal general in the East not intimidated by Lee and the myth of Southern fighting superiority.[90]

Within less than seven weeks, Grant's army compelled Lee to retreat to a nearly besieged position at Richmond and Petersburg, which Lee had previously said would be the death-knell of his own army. Gregory A. Mertz concluded: "The campaign reached Richmond only because Lee retreated to the defenses of the capital city. When U.S. Grant became commander of all Union armies and chose to make his headquarters in the eastern theater, he intended to take the war to the Army of Northern Virginia and pound Lee into submission. He battled the legendary Confederate leader and his army in the Wilderness and never looked back."[91]

At the same time, Grant was overseeing and facilitating a coordinated attack against Confederate forces all over the nation, particularly

Sherman's campaign from the Tennessee border to Atlanta. As he had hoped, Grant succeeded in keeping Lee from sending reinforcements to Georgia. Sherman took Atlanta and thus guaranteed the crucial reelection of Lincoln. Sherman ultimately broke loose on a virtually unimpeded sweep through Georgia and the Carolinas that doomed the Confederacy. Thus, in the words of Herman Hattaway, the war "was decided by Grant's superior strategy: the use of simultaneous advances in widely separated scenes of action."[92] Grant's 1864–65 nationwide coordinated offensive against the Rebel armies not only won the war but demonstrated that he was a national general with a broad vision while Lee was a theater general suffering from Virginia myopia.

Furthermore, an analysis of the losses suffered by the four commanders' armies involved in the two major 1864 campaigns (Overland and Atlanta) reveals that Grant's percentage of casualties, although higher than Sherman's, was better than those of the Confederate commanders:

Armies and Generals	Total Troops	Total Casualties
Army of Tennessee (Johnston/Hood)	66,000	35,000 (53 percent)[93]
Army of Northern Virginia (Lee)	70,000	42,000 (46 percent)[94]
Army of the Potomac, etc. (Grant)	122,000	50,000 (41 percent)[95]
Armies of the Tennessee, the Ohio, and the Cumberland (Sherman)	110,000	32,000 (29 percent)[96]

These numbers indicate that, even when he pressed for pre-election victory, Grant incurred a lower percentage of casualties than Lee or Lee's protégé Hood. The bottom line is that vicious, aggressive fighting involving the significant movement of two large Union forces resulted in significant casualties on both sides in both theaters. By 1864, most combatants were using accurate rifled muskets (often breech-loading rifles), rifled artillery, and sometimes repeating weapons that required less reloading—which cumulatively resulted in more rapid and accurate firing. Also, soldiers had become expert at quickly creating field fortifications and making almost any assault extremely costly.

As Assistant Secretary of War Dana concluded, "Grant in eleven months secured the prize with less loss than his predecessors suffered in failing to win it during a struggle of three years."[97] To the end, therefore, Grant was persistent, aggressive, dogged, and determined, but he rarely incurred unnecessary casualties. During the Appomattox Campaign, as was his usual practice, he maneuvered his army and avoided frontal assaults as best he could and attacked when he believed he had to. With Lee's surrender, Grant had demonstrated that he knew what had to be done to achieve victory, and he had done it.

Lee, on the other hand, had constantly incurred intolerable and unnecessary casualties while continuing a war that had been rendered hopeless by the fall of Atlanta, the reelection of Lincoln, and the surge of Sherman through the Carolinas.

CHAPTER TWELVE

A COMPARISON OF GRANT AND LEE

From the earliest postwar days, Lee was praised as a military genius. Typical is this statement by Lee's Adjutant-General Walter H. Taylor: "It is well to bear in mind the great inequality between the two contending armies, in order that one may have a proper appreciation of the difficulties which beset General Lee in the task of thwarting the designs of so formidable an adversary, and realize the extent to which his brilliant genius made amends for paucity of numbers, and proved more than a match for brute force, as illustrated in the hammering policy of General Grant."[1] Taylor typified the denigration of Grant that accompanied the deification of Lee. The cult of Lee worshipers began with former Civil War generals who had fought ineffectively under him. They sought to polish their own tarnished reputations and restore Southern pride by deliberately distorting the historical record and creating the myth of the flawless Robert E. Lee.[2] More recently, Richard McMurry wrote, "[Lee] stands as the colossus of Confederate military history—the only Southern army commander to enjoy any degree of success."[3]

Although Lee was generally worshipped for the first hundred years after the Civil War, there were exceptions. In 1929 and 1933, British Major General J. F. C. Fuller criticized Lee while praising Grant.[4] He described Lee as "in several respects... one of the most incapable Generals-in-Chief in history," and criticized him for his narrow Eastern perspective and his over-aggressiveness in several campaigns.[5] The works of T. Harry Williams and Thomas L. Connelly (especially his *The Marble Man: Robert E. Lee and His Image in American Society* [1977]) tied Lee to the Myth of the Lost Cause, explained deliberate pro-Lee distortions of the historical record, and further questioned Lee's strategy and tactics. A classic reevaluation of Lee was Alan T. Nolan's *Lee Considered: General Robert E. Lee and Civil War History* (1991).[6] Currently, the reappraisal of Lee continues, and, as J. F. C. Fuller said, "The truth is, the more we inquire into the generalship of Lee, the more we discover that Lee, or rather the popular conception of him, is a myth...."[7]

On the other hand, Grant's often-tarred reputation has ascended while Lee's has declined. In his memoirs, Grant noted the impact of those Southern historians who were creating the Myth of "The Lost Cause":

> With us, now twenty years after the close of the most stupendous war ever known, we have writers—who profess devotion to the nation—engaged in trying to prove that the Union forces were not victorious; practically, they say, we were slashed around from Donelson to Vicksburg and to Chattanooga; and in the East from Gettysburg to Appomattox, when the physical rebellion gave out from sheer exhaustion.[8]

In fact, several pro-Confederate writers attacked Grant as soon as the shooting stopped. One of those was Richmond newspaperman Edward

Pollard, who, in *The Lost Cause: A New Southern History of the War of the Confederates* (1866), said that Grant "contained no spark of military genius; his idea of war was to the last degree rude—no strategy, the mere application of the *vis inertia*; he had none of that quick perception on the field of action which decides it by sudden strokes; he had no conception of battle beyond the momentum of numbers."[9]

Even Northern historians criticized Grant. In 1866, *New York Times* war correspondent William Swinton wrote in his *Campaigns of the Army of the Potomac* that Grant relied "exclusively on the application of brute masses, in rapid and remorseless blows."[10] John C. Ropes told the Military Historical Society of Massachusetts that Grant suffered from a "burning, persistent desire to fight, to attack, in season and out of season, against intrenchments, natural obstacles, what not."[11]

Mediocre Confederate General Jubal Early led the way, along with incompetent Confederate General William Nelson Pendleton, in creating the Myth of the Lost Cause. In doing so, they felt compelled to belittle the accomplishments of Grant. In 1872, in a speech on Lee's birthday, Early said, "Shall I compare General Lee to his successful antagonist? As well compare the great pyramid which rears it majestic proportions in the Valley of the Nile, to a pygmy perched on Mount Atlas."[12] At least, he admitted that Grant was successful.

Historian Gary Gallagher fairly recently criticized the selectiveness and merits of Early's (and others') criticisms of Grant:

> Absent from Early's work, as well as that of other writers who portrayed Grant as a butcher, was any detailed treatment of Grant's brilliant campaign against Vicksburg, his decisive success at Chattanooga, or his other western operations. Moreover, critics failed to grasp that Grant's tactics in 1864 went against his preferred style of campaigning. He fought

Lee at every turn primarily because he wished to deny Jefferson Davis the option of shifting Confederate troops from Virginia to Georgia where they might slow Sherman's progress.[13]

In 1881, Jefferson Davis joined the parade of Grant critics when he launched this criticism of Grierson's effective 1863 raid (which barely affected civilians in Davis's native Mississippi): "Among the expeditions for pillage and arson [, Grierson's raid] stands prominent for savage outrages against defenseless women and children, constituting a record alike unworthy a soldier and a gentleman."[14] The 1880s publication of *Battles and Leaders of the Civil War*, containing the recollections of the war's participants, provided former Confederates with an opportunity to impugn Grant. For example, Lieutenant General Evander M. Law wrote, "What a part at least of his own men thought about General Grant's methods was shown by the fact that many of the prisoners taken during the [Overland] campaign complained bitterly of the 'useless butchery' to which they were subjected."[15]

Easterners, who controlled most of the newspapers and publishing houses, did not like Grant, "whom they saw as an uncouth westerner." In the wake of the numerous scandals in which his presidential appointees were involved, Grant's continuing support for the rights of African-Americans and Native Americans during his years as president, and intellectuals' revulsion at the materialism of the Industrial Age, many Northerners joined Southerners in glorifying Lee and his army and in attacking Grant as a butcher.[16] It is difficult to overestimate the damage to Grant that these writings caused and the virtual indelibility of the image they created of Grant the Butcher.

In fact, it was another Richmond newspaper reporter-turned-historian, Douglas Southall Freeman, who placed Lee on a pedestal at Grant's expense. In his four-volume treatise, *R. E. Lee*, Freeman idolized Lee in describing all the details of his generalship. Freeman criticized Grant for hammering Lee's forces instead of maneuvering more, but even Freeman did concede that Grant's efforts had not been in vain: "Lee did not lose the battles but he did not win the campaign. He delayed the fulfillment of Grant's mission, but he could not discharge his own. Lee found few opportunities of attacking the enemy in detail or on the march.... And in some subtle fashion General Grant infused into his well-seasoned troops a confidence they had never previously possessed."[17]

A pro-Lee disciple of Freeman's, Clifford Dowdey, was harder on Grant than Freeman was. In his 1960 *Lee's Last Campaign: The Story of Lee and His Men Against Grant*, Dowdey described Grant as a "boring-in type of attacker, who usually scorned finesse."[18] The anti-Grant tradition is not dead. It has been recently continued in Paul D. Casdorph's 1992 *Lee and Jackson: Confederate Chieftains* and Ernest B. Furgurson's 2000 *Not War But Murder: Cold Harbor 1864*. Casdorph grossly overestimated Grant's Cold Harbor casualties as including 13,000 killed ("dead or dying") and referred to "union hordes" and the "Yankee Goliath."[19]

Significant praise for Grant, other than from his subordinates and fellow officers, first came from overseas. British military historian and Major-General J. F. C. Fuller strongly endorsed the greatness of Grant in *The Generalship of Ulysses S. Grant* in 1929 and then in *Grant and Lee: A Study in Personality and Generalship* in 1932. Fuller concluded that Grant was a superior strategist, possessed common sense, recognized what needed to be done to win the war, and deserved the major credit for doing so. He compared Grant quite favorably to Lee, found that Lee consistently throughout the war lost a higher percentage of his troops than Grant or other adversaries he faced, and that Lee much more than Grant—and for no good reason—sacrificed his troops in frontal assaults and continued to do so until he had no more to sacrifice.

Another British military historian, John Keegan, also found cause to praise Grant. He did so in *The Mask of Command* (1987). There he discussed Grant in a chapter entitled "Grant and Unheroic Leadership." He praised Grant's fighting skills and concluded, "But in retrospect, great though Grant's generalship is seen to be, it is his comprehension of the nature of the war, and of what could and could not be done by a general within its defining conditions, that seems the more remarkable."[20]

The most comprehensive sympathetic treatment of Grant came with the works of Bruce Catton. He first wrote of Grant in the second and third volumes of the famous Civil War trilogy, *Mr. Lincoln's Army* (1951), *Glory Road* (1952), and the Pulitzer Prize-winning *A Stillness at Appomattox* (1953). Having come to admire Grant above other Civil War generals, Catton then proceeded to write *U.S. Grant and the American Military Tradition* (1954) (the bulk of which is entitled "The Great Commander"), *This Hallowed Ground: The Story of the Union Side in the Civil War* (1956), *Grant Moves South* (1960) (describing Grant's Civil War career through Vicksburg in glowing terms), and *Grant Takes Command* (1968) (taking him through the end of the war). The prolific Catton also produced *The Coming Fury: The Centennial History of the Civil War* (1961), *Terrible Swift Sword* (1963), and *Never Call Retreat* (1965). Like Grant himself, said Stephen W. Sears, Catton was "quiet and unassuming and unpretentious and business-like."[21]

A contemporary of Catton's, T. Harry Williams, was a renowned Civil War scholar and a strong proponent of Grant. Williams found him superior to Lee and others in *Lincoln and His Generals* (1952) and to his fellow Union generals in *McClellan, Sherman and Grant* (1962). In the former book, Williams succinctly stated, "Grant was, by modern standards, the greatest general of the Civil War."[22]

In their exhaustive 1983 study of the war, *How the North Won: A Military History of the Civil War*, Herman Hattaway and Archer Jones concluded that Grant was responsible for recognizing the North's need to effectively use its superiority. Although they disclaimed the significance of turning points, they concluded that Grant's seizure of Forts Henry and Donelson and his approval of Sherman's March to the Sea were decisive events.

Although he relied on Bruce Catton's work, William S. McFeely treated Grant with much less sympathy in his 1981 *Grant: A Biography*. McFeely's Grant seemed uncaring about the death around him. This first "modern" biography of Grant reinforced earlier negative impressions with such characterizations of Grant as "a man of limited though by no means inconsequential talents to apply to whatever truly engaged his attention." McFeely made it appear that Grant's second-day offensive at Shiloh was a spur-of-the-moment idea conceived only that morning, and he then criticized Grant for failing to pursue the Rebels with his exhausted army. He claimed it was Grant's rivalry with McClernand that got him focused on Vicksburg. McFeely asserted that "Grant's strategy was to make sure more Southerners than Northerners were killed. It was a matter of simple arithmetic...." Of the Overland Campaign, he said, "In May 1864 Ulysses Grant began a vast campaign that was a hideous disaster in every respect save one—it worked. He led his troops into the Wilderness and there produced a nightmare of inhumanity and inept military strategy that ranks with the worst such episodes in the history of warfare." Jean Edward Smith later cited McFeely's work as a biography written by an academic historian who was influenced by the Vietnam War and denigrated Grant's critical role in Union victory.[23]

A return to the Catton sympathetic approach marked the 1997 *Ulysses S. Grant: Soldier & President* written by Geoffrey Perret and the 2000 *Ulysses S. Grant: Triumph over Adversity, 1822–1865* by Brooks D. Simpson. Perret praised Grant's "military genius" and credited him with creating two concepts that the U.S. Army has been using ever since:

the use of converging columns (Grant's 1864–5 national strategy) and the wide envelopment (Grant's sweeping around Lee's flank throughout 1864 and 1865).[24] Simpson described a non-idealized Grant and praised his common sense, imagination, and perseverance. On the issue of Grant's tactics, Simpson concluded:

> He was less successful at shaking the perception that he was a ham-handed tactician who freely wasted the lives of his own men. This reputation was largely based on the pervasive impression of his generalship left by the 1864 campaign in Virginia. That during the Vicksburg and Chattanooga campaigns combined, Grant's forces suffered fewer losses than did Lee's troops at Gettysburg escaped most people's notice; that he was far more frugal with human life than his leading Confederate counterpart… is recognized by only a few. He preferred to take prisoners than to slay foes; he emphasized movement and logistics over slugging it out. Even his campaigns in Virginia show a general who… shifted units and probed for weaknesses, mixing assaults with marches, constantly seeking new approaches.[25]

Jean Edward Smith's 2001 book entitled simply *Grant* is an excellent, sympathetic biography of Grant. He pointed to Grant's decisiveness at Fort Donelson, his Vicksburg campaign's amphibious crossing, his moving forward after the Wilderness, and his surreptitious crossing of the James River as examples of Grant's greatness. He contended that Grant was the strategic master of his Confederate counterparts, had a lower casualty rate than Lee, and demonstrated his strategic skills by focusing on enemy armies rather than on mere geographic goals. Smith not only described the greatness of Grant as a Civil War general but also the many overlooked positive aspects of his eight-year presidency. Smith detailed President Grant's efforts to protect Negroes' rights in the postwar South and Indians' rights in the West and said that "mainstream historians, unsympathetic to black equality, brutalized Grant's presidency."[26]

In the past several years, Grant's conduct of the Overland Campaign has received exhaustive and generally positive treatment at the hands of Gordon C. Rhea. His four books were *The Battle of the Wilderness* (1994), *The Battles for Spotsylvania Court House and the Road to Yellow Tavern* (1997), *To the North Anna River* (2000), and *Cold Harbor* (2002). In those volumes and a series of contemporaneous articles, Rhea contended that Grant had been unfairly labeled a "butcher," that his casualties were proportionately less than Lee's, and that Grant was an innovative and effective general who focused on and achieved his strategic objectives.

In summary, Ulysses Grant got off to a bad start among postwar historians, but his military accomplishments have received increasing, if erratic, recognition since about 1930. Serious historical reestablishment of his multi-theater, war-winning record continues.[27] With this historical perspective as background, we can now undertake a comparative analysis of Grant and Lee.

Those two generals shared many characteristics, but in many ways they were quite different. An examination of Grant and Lee's general military skills, military management skills, and personal attributes reveals why Grant won and Lee lost the war.[28]

GENERAL MILITARY SKILLS

Aggressiveness

Both generals were quite aggressive. Grant's aggressiveness was consistent with the North's superior manpower and its need to proactively win the war, while Lee's was inconsistent with the South's inferior manpower and its need only for a deadlock. In short, Grant's aggressiveness won the war while Lee's lost it. General Fuller encapsulated the contrary effects of the two generals' aggressiveness: " ... the fact remains that Grant's pugnacity fitted the general strategical situation—the conquest of the South, whilst Lee's audacity more than once accelerated rather than retarded this object."[29] Ironically, the Overland Campaign of 1864, for which Grant is criticized as taking too many casualties, demonstrates what Lee could have done had he stayed on the strategic and tactical defensive throughout the war. As historian Alan Nolan concluded, "The truth is that in 1864, Lee himself demonstrated the alternative to his earlier offensive strategy and tactics."[30]

Lee was too aggressive. With one-quarter the manpower resources of his adversary, Lee exposed his forces to unnecessary risks and ultimately lost the gamble.[31] The gamble was unwarranted because Lee only needed to play for a tie; instead he made the fatal mistake of going for the win. Lee failed to accept the reality that the North had to conquer the South; instead he tried to conquer the North—or at least destroy its eastern army.[32] Military historian Russell Weigley blamed Lee's stubbornness for Gaines' Mill, Malvern Hill, the mistaken Maryland Campaign, and his risking his entire army by fighting at Antietam.[33] Bevin Alexander compared Lee unfavorably to Jackson on the issue of over-aggressiveness: "Jackson was a military genius. He had found a way to avoid making frontal assaults against the massed power of the Union Army. This was the essence of his intellectual breakthrough. But Lee had not absorbed the lesson. And this sealed the fate of the Confederacy."[34]

Many have argued that Lee had no choice but to be recklessly aggressive because the South had no other way to win the war. Among them was Joseph L. Harsh, who contended that Lee hoped to destroy the Northern will to fight by going on the offensive and thus causing high

Northern casualties and destroying its will to continue a long, costly war. Others have argued that Lee's aggressiveness was compelled by Southerners' expectations that he take the offensive.[35] Ironically, Lee's aggressiveness caused high, intolerable Southern casualties and played a major role in the decline of Southern morale and willingness to continue the war.[36] As Alan Nolan argued, because the South was so badly outnumbered and the burden was on the North to win the war, Lee's grand strategy should have been a defensive one that did not squander the scarce manpower of the Confederacy.[37]

Those supporting Lee's aggressiveness sometimes fail to acknowledge that the Confederacy had advantages of its own. It consisted of a huge, 750,000-square mile territory which the Federals would have to invade and conquer.[38] It also had the interior lines and was able to move its troops from place to place over shorter distances via a complex of well-placed railroads. The burden was on the North to win the war;[39] a deadlock would confirm secession and the Confederacy.[40] Historian James M. McPherson put it succinctly: "The South could 'win' the war by not losing; the North could win only by winning."[41] Concurring with that analysis was Southern historian Bell I. Wiley, who said: "… the North also faced a greater task. In order to win the war, the … North had to conquer the South while the South could win by outlasting its adversary.… The South had reason to believe that it could achieve independence. That it did not was due as much, if not more, to its own failings as to the superior strength of the foe."[42]

The Confederates' huge strategic advantage and their missed opportunities were confirmed by an early war analysis of the struggle by a military analyst writing in the *Times* of London. The analyst said, "… It is one thing to drive the rebels from the south bank of the Potomac, or even to occupy Richmond, but another to reduce and hold in permanent subjection a tract of country nearly as large as Russia in Europe.… No war of independence ever terminated unsuccessfully except where the disparity of force was far greater than it is in this case. Just as England during the [American] revolution had to give up conquering the colonies, so the North will have to give up conquering the South."[43] The Confederate Secretary of War agreed with this view at the start of the war: "there is no instance in history of a people as numerous as we are inhabiting a country so extensive as ours being subjected if true to themselves."[44] Yet another Southern historian commented:

> In the beginning the Confederate leaders and most of the southern population believed the Confederacy had a strong prospect of success; many scholars today endorse this view.... The Confederate war aim, which was to establish southern independence, was less difficult in the purely military sense than the Union war aim, which was to prevent the establishment of southern independence. The Confederacy could achieve its aim simply by protecting itself sufficiently to remain in existence. The Union could achieve its aim only by destroying the will of the southern population through invasion and conquest.[45]

The South's primary opportunity for success was to outlast Lincoln, and the deep schisms among Northerners throughout the War made this a distinct possibility. Northerners violently disagreed on slavery, the draft, and the war itself.[46] As early as May 1863, Josiah Gorgas noted in his journal the North's susceptibility to a political defeat: "No doubt that the war will go on until at least the close of [Lincoln's] administration. How many more lives must be sacrificed to the vindictiveness of a few unprincipled men! for there is no doubt that with the division of sentiment existing at the North the administration could shape its policy either for peace or for war."[47]

Confederate General Alexander confirmed the Confederacy's need to wear down, not conquer, the North:

> When the South entered upon war with a power so immensely her superior in men & money, & all the wealth of modern resources in machinery and transportation appliances by land & sea, she could entertain but one single hope of final success. That was, that the desperation of her resistance would finally exact from her adversary such a price in blood & treasure as to exhaust the enthusiasm of its population for the objects of the war. We could not hope to conquer her. Our one chance was to wear her out.[48]

A Southern victory was not out of the question.[49] After all, it had been only eighty years since the supposedly inferior American revolutionaries had vanquished the mighty Redcoats of King George III[50] and it was less than fifty years since the outgunned Russians had repelled and destroyed the powerful invading army of Napoleon. The feasibility of such an outcome is demonstrated by the fact that, despite numerous crucial mistakes by Lee and others, the Confederates still appeared to have political victory in their grasp in the late summer of 1864, when Lincoln himself despaired of winning reelection that coming November.

Twice during the war Lee went into the North on strategic offensives with scant chance of success, lost tens of thousands of irreplaceable officers and men in the disasters of Antietam and Gettysburg, and inevitably was compelled to retreat.[51] These retreats enabled Lincoln to issue his crucial Emancipation Proclamation, created an aura of defeat that doomed any possibility of European intervention, and played a major role in destroying the South's morale and will to fight. Finally, Lee's offensive strategy and tactics so seriously weakened the Confederacy's fighting capability that its defeat was perceived as inevitable by the time of the crucial 1864 presidential election.

It was Lee's strategy and tactics that dissipated irreplaceable manpower—even in his "victories." His tactical losses at Seven Days' (especially Malvern Hill), his strategic defeats at Antietam and Gettysburg, and his costly "wins" at Second Bull Run and Chancellorsville—all in 1862 and 1863—made possible Grant's and Sherman's successful 1864 campaigns against the armies defending Richmond and Atlanta and created the aura of Confederate defeat that Lincoln exploited to win reelection. If Lee had performed differently, the North could have been fatally split on the war issue, Democratic nominee George B. McClellan might have defeated Lincoln, and the South could have negotiated an acceptable settlement with the compromising McClellan. Although some have contended that McClellan would not have allowed the South to remain outside the Union,[52] he often had demonstrated both his reticence to engage in the offensive warfare necessary for the Union to prevail and his great concern about Southerners' property rights in slaves. It would not have been out of character for McClellan to have sought a ceasefire immediately after the election and thereby have stopped Northern momentum and created a situation in which Southern independence was possible.[53]

Northern victory affirmed the correctness of Grant's aggressiveness. Unlike most Union generals, who were reticent about taking advantage of the North's numerical superiority and unwilling to invade the Confederacy that had to be conquered, Grant knew what had to be done and did it. Grant's war-ending 1864 Overland Campaign against Lee's army reflected Grant's war-long philosophy that "The art of war is simple enough. Find out where your enemy is. Get at him as soon as you can. Strike him as hard as you can and as often as you can, and keep moving on."[54] Bruce Catton said it prosaically: "Better than any other Northern soldier, better than any other man save Lincoln himself, [Grant] understood the necessity for bringing the infinite power of the growing nation to bear on the desperate weakness of the brave, romantic, and tragically archaic little nation that opposed it...."[55]

General Cox said, "[Grant] reminds one of Wellington in the combination of lucid and practical common-sense with aggressive bull-dog courage."[56] In the words of T. Harry Williams, Grant "made his best preparations and then went in without reserve or hesitation and with a simple faith in success."[57] He advanced aggressively and creatively, and he attacked with vigor, but he usually avoided suicidal frontal attacks.[58] In light of the large number of battles fought by his armies, the total of 154,000 killed and wounded suffered by his commands was surprisingly small—especially when considered in light of the 209,000 killed and wounded among the soldiers commanded by Lee.[59]

Examples of Grant's successful aggressiveness are numerous. He carried out his Belmont diversion in the vicinity of enemy forces several times his own. At the beginning of the Henry/Donelson campaign, in the words of Kendall Gott, "He landed a petty force of about 15,000 in the midst of nearly 45,000 enemy soldiers who could have massed against him."[60] His second-day counterattack at Shiloh turned stalemate or defeat into victory. His unexcelled Vicksburg Campaign into enemy territory where he was outnumbered marked the war's turning point. His aggressiveness at Chattanooga saved an army and set the stage for permanent victory in the middle theater. Finally, his aggressive Overland Campaign won the war in less than a year.

On the down side, Grant's aggressiveness caused him to focus so much on what he intended to do to the enemy that he at times became vulnerable to enemy surprises. Examples of these unexpected events were the initial Rebel breakout from Fort Donelson, the surprise Confederate attack on the first day at Shiloh, and Jubal Early's 2nd Corps breaking free from the Grant-Lee deadlock in June 1864. His battlefield control and perseverance turned the first two events into major Union victories, and he was able to nullify Early's foray because Lee kept Early in the eastern theater.[61]

Not only did Grant recognize the need for the Union armies to be on the offensive, but he also was cognizant of the need for them to damage, destroy, or capture Confederate armies—instead of merely gaining control of geographic positions. He had, in Jean Edward Smith's words, an "instinctive recognition that victory lay in relentlessly hounding a defeated army into surrender."[62] Only three armies surrendered while the Civil War raged: Buckner's at Fort Donelson, Pemberton's at Vicksburg, and Lee's at Appomattox. They all surrendered to Grant in an affirmation that, as Albert Castel said, "… he always sought, not merely to defeat, but to destroy the enemy."[63]

Casualties

Wartime casualties need to be placed in the context of the populations of the North and South. At the outset of the war, the North had tremendous population and resource advantages over the South. The North had 22 million people, while the South had only nine million, of whom 3.5 million were slaves.[64] Unless therefore the South found a way to fully involve those slaves in the war effort (and on the Confederate side), it faced a 4-to-1 general population disadvantage. More relevantly, the North had 4,070,000 men of fighting age (15 to 40), and the South had only 1,140,000 white men of fighting age. Considering that immigration and defecting slaves further augmented the North's forces, the crucial bottom line is that the Union had an effective combat manpower advantage of 4:1 over the Confederacy. The South could not afford to squander its limited manpower.

Of the nearly three million men (two million Union and 750,000 Confederate)[65] who served in the military during the war, 620,000 died (360,000 Union and 260,000 Confederate), 214,938 in battle and the rest from disease and other causes.[66] While many Northerners were in the military for brief periods of time (many of them serving twice or more), most Southern military personnel were compelled to stay for the duration. Amazingly, almost one-fourth of Southern white males of military age died during the war—virtually all of them from wounds or war-related diseases. The primary point of all these statistics is that the South was greatly outnumbered and could not afford to squander its resources by engaging in a war of attrition. Robert E. Lee's deliberate disregard of this reality may have been his greatest failure. As James M. McPherson wrote, "For the war as a whole, Lee's army had a higher casualty rate than the armies commanded by Grant. The romantic glorification of the Army of Northern Virginia by generations of Lost Cause writers has obscured this truth."[67]

The results of Lee's faulty strategies and tactics were catastrophic. His army suffered almost 209,000 casualties—55,000 more than Grant and more than any other Union or Confederate Civil War general. Although Lee's army inflicted a war-high 240,000 casualties on its opponents, about 117,000 of those occurred in 1864 and 1865[68] when Lee was on the defensive and Grant engaged in a deliberate war of adhesion (achieving attrition and exhaustion) against the army Lee had fatally depleted in 1862 and 1863.[69] Astoundingly (in light of his reputation), Lee's percentages of killed and wounded suffered by his troops were worse than those of his fellow Confederate commanders. During the first fourteen months that Lee commanded the Army of Northern Virginia (through the retreat from Gettysburg), he took the strategic and tactical offensive so often with his undermanned army that he lost 98,000 men while inflicting 120,000 casualties on his Union opponents.[70] The manpower-short Confederacy could not afford to trade numerous casualties with the enemy. During each major battle in the critical and decisive phase of the war from June 1862 through July 1863, Lee was losing an average 19 percent of his men while his manpower-rich enemies were suffering casualties at a tolerable 13 percent.[71]

By 1864, therefore, Grant had a 120,000-man army and additional reserves to bring against Lee's 65,000 and, by the sheer weight of his numbers, imposed a fatal 47 percent casualty rate on Lee's army while losing a militarily tolerable 43 percent of his own replaceable men, as he drove from the Rappahannock to the James River and created a terminal threat to Lee's army and Richmond.[72] The high casualties sustained by Grant's army in 1864 were substantially because "he was then under considerable political pressure to end the war quickly before the autumn presidential election."[73]

Had Lee not squandered Rebel resources during the three preceding years, the Confederacy's 1864 opportunity for victory might have been realized. It was Lee's strategy and tactics that dissipated irreplaceable manpower—even in his "victories." His army lost at Malvern Hill, Antietam, Gettysburg, the Shenandoah Valley, Petersburg, and Appomattox. His army took unnecessarily high casualties in those defeats, as well as throughout the entire Seven Days' Battle and at Chancellorsville. Lee's army's 1862–3 casualties made possible Grant's successful 1864 campaign of adhesion to Lee's army. Finally, the losses Lee's army suffered at the Wilderness and Spotsylvania were higher than he could afford and helped to create the aura of Confederate defeat that Lincoln exploited to win reelection.[74]

Fuller concluded, "If anything, Lee rather than Grant deserves to be accused of sacrificing his men."[75] Gordon Rhea similarly concluded that

"Judging from Lee's record, the rebel commander should have shared in Grant's 'butcher' reputation."[76] James McPherson compared the casualties of Lee and Grant: "Indeed, for the war as a whole, Lee's armies suffered a higher casualty rate than Grant's (and higher than any other army). Neither general was a 'butcher,' but measured by that statistic, Lee deserved the label more than Grant."[77]

Far from being the uncaring slaughterer of men, Grant again and again displayed his feelings about the contributions of the ordinary soldier. After Chattanooga, for example, he alone raised his hat in salute to a ragged band of Confederate prisoners through which Union generals and their staffs were passing, and at Hampton Roads late in the war he spoke to a group of Rebel amputees about better artificial limbs that were being manufactured.[78]

A fresh and comprehensive analysis of all the casualties (killed, wounded, and missing/captured) in all of Grant and Lee's campaigns and battles reinforces the brilliance of Grant's accomplishments. Appendix II, "Casualties in Grant's Battles and Campaigns," contains a fairly exhaustive list of various historians' and other authorities' estimates of those casualties. This author has made a best estimate of the casualties and, at the end of that appendix, created a table of best estimates of those casualties for the entire war. While Grant's armies were incurring a total of 153,642 casualties in those battles for which he was responsible and on which he had some effect, they were imposing a total of 190,760 casualties on the enemy. That positive total casualty differential of 37,118 should put to rest any negative analyses of Grant's performance.

In their thought-provoking book, *Attack and Die: Civil War Military Tactics and the Southern Heritage*, Gordon McWhiney and Perry D. Jamieson provided some astounding numbers related to Grant's major battles and campaigns. First, they determined that, in his five major campaigns and battles of 1862–3, he commanded a cumulative total of 220,970 soldiers and that 23,551 of them (11 percent) were either killed or wounded. Second, they determined that, in his eight major campaigns and battles of 1864–5 (when he was determined to defeat or destroy Lee's army as quickly as possible), he commanded a cumulative total of 400,942 soldiers and that 70,620 of them (18 percent) were either killed or wounded. Third, they determined that during the course of the war, therefore, he commanded a cumulative total of 621,912 soldiers in his major campaigns and battles and that a total of 94,171 of them (a militarily tolerable[79] 15 percent) were either killed or wounded.[80] These loss percentages are remarkably low—especially considering the fact that Grant was on the strategic and tactical offensive in most of these battles and campaigns.

It may be helpful to put these numbers in perspective by comparing them to the casualty figures for the Army of Northern Virginia under Lee's command and to those for other Confederate commanders. Incomplete figures show that Lee, in his major campaigns and battles, commanded a cumulative total of 598,178 soldiers, of whom 121,042 were either killed or wounded—a total loss of 20.2 percent, about one-third higher than Grant. Other major Confederate commanders with higher percentages killed or wounded than Grant were Generals Braxton Bragg (19.5 percent), John Bell Hood (19.2 percent), and Pierre Gustave Toutant Beauregard (16.1 percent).[81]

Similarly, Lee's generals were mortally wounded in battle at a much higher rate than those under other Confederate commanders. After Lee took command of the Army of Northern Virginia, he lost two of the three mortally wounded Confederate lieutenant generals (corps commanders), four of the seven mortally wounded Confederate major generals (division commanders), and 33 of 53 mortally wounded Confederate brigadier generals (brigade commanders).[82]

McWhiney and Jamieson also tallied those Civil War battles in which either side incurred the heaviest percentage of losses suffered by one side during the entire war. Of the nineteen battles in which one side lost nineteen percent or more of its troops (killed or wounded), only "one" involved such a loss by Grant's troops (and that was actually two battles—29.6 percent at Wilderness and Spotsylvania combined). Given the number of battles Grant's armies fought, this is a surprising, but informative, result. Contrarily, Lee's army suffered the highest percentage of such losses in a single battle at Gettysburg (30.2 percent) and the fifth and seventh highest such losses at Antietam (22.6 percent) and Seven Days' (20.7 percent).[83]

Writing in 1898, Charles Dana, Assistant Secretary of War during the Civil War, analyzed this facet of Grant's Overland Campaign: "There are still many persons who bitterly accuse Grant of butchery in this campaign. As a matter of fact, Grant lost fewer men in his successful effort to take Richmond and end the war than his predecessors lost in making the same attempt and failing." Dana examined the specific casualties suffered by Union troops in the East under Grant's predecessors and then under Grant. Under Generals McDowell, McClellan, Pope, Burnside, Hooker, and Meade, the Union's eastern armies, according to Dana's table of statistics, had 15,745 killed, 76,079 wounded, and 52,101 missing or captured for a total of 143,925 casualties between May 24, 1861, and May 4, 1864. He then calculated Grant's losses between May 5, 1864 and April 9, 1865 as 15,139 killed, 77,748 wounded, and 31,503 missing or captured for a total of 124,390. Dana concluded that these numbers showed that "Grant in eleven months secured the prize with less loss than his predecessors suffered in failing to win it during a struggle of three years."[84]

"Lee lost more troops than any other general in the war and 'if a general could be called a butcher, Lee is probably more of a butcher than

Grant,' said [historian Gordon] Rhea."[85] Geoffrey Perret commented on this paradox: "After Cold Harbor, [Grant] was an easy target for those who called him 'Butcher Grant.' Lee was more reckless with men's lives, yet got away with it. The list of costly, doomed frontal assaults in Lee's career is remarkably long, but he was not known as 'Butcher Lee.'"[86] Appendices I and II show that Lee's army incurred about 55,000 more casualties that Grant's armies (209,000 versus 154,000)—an amazing comparison since Grant had the burden of taking the attack to his enemies while Lee should have been on the strategic and tactical defensive.

Tactics

Although Lee's purported "tactical genius" was trumped by Grant's "superior talent in grand strategy,"[87] Lee is famed for his tactical management of battles. He was the tactical victor in several 1862–63 battles and generally performed well on the tactical defensive against Grant in 1864.[88] However, Lee's tactics proved fatally defective. His tactical defects were that he was too aggressive on the field,[89] he frequently failed to take charge of the battlefield, his battle plans were too complex[90] or simply ineffective, and his orders were too vague or discretionary.

Lee's first problem was that his tactics, like his strategy, were too aggressive.[91] Bevin Alexander pointed out that in 1862 alone Lee had "an obsession with seeking battle to retrieve a strategic advantage when it had gone awry or he thought it had." Thus, at Beaver Dam Creek (Gaines' Mill), Frayser's Farm (Glendale), Malvern Hill, and Antietam, he resorted to "desperate, stand-up, head-on battle" that resulted in great losses. "This fixation was Lee's fatal flaw. It and Lee's limited strategic vision cost the Confederacy the war."[92] Elsewhere Alexander concluded, "Lee never understood the revolution that the Minié ball had brought to battle tactics.... This tendency to move to direct confrontation, regardless of the prospects of the losses that would be sustained, guaranteed Lee's failure as an offensive commander."[93]

Although sometimes creative (particularly when Stonewall Jackson was involved), too often those tactics failed to adequately consider the advantages new weaponry gave to defensive forces. Rifled muskets (ones with grooves rifled in their bores to spin bullets for accuracy) and bullets which expanded in the bores to follow the grooves (Minié balls) greatly increased the accuracy and range of infantry firepower (from 100 yards to between 400 and 1,000 yards), thereby providing the defense with an unprecedented advantage.[94] Fuller called the Civil War "the war of the rifle bullet," and rifle bullets (primarily Minié balls) accounted for 90 percent of the about 214,000 battlefield deaths and 469,000 wounded during the war.[95] This advanced weaponry made assaults increasingly difficult.

Despite the fact that seven of eight Civil War frontal assaults failed,[96] Lee just kept attacking. Battles in which Lee damaged his army with overly aggressive tactics include the Seven Days' (particularly Mechanicsville, Gaines' Mill, and Malvern Hill), Second Manassas, Chantilly, Antietam, Chancellorsville, Gettysburg, Rappahannock Station, the Wilderness, and Fort Stedman. Archer Jones pointed to Lee's periodic misplaced elation, when he refused to "quit while he was ahead," and cited Malvern Hill, Chantilly, the end of Chancellorsville, and Pickett's Charge as examples.[97]

The North had more advanced weaponry and had it earlier in the war. Its Model 1861 Springfield rifle, with an effective range of 200–400 yards, could kill at a distance of 1,000 yards or more. Most infantrymen (especially Federals) had rifles by some time in 1862, Union cavalry had breech-loading (instead of muzzle-loading guns) repeating rifles by 1863, and even some Union infantry had these "repeaters" (primarily Spencer rifles) in 1864 and 1865.

Demonstrating this trend, Rhode Islander Elisha Hunt Rhodes experienced an improvement in weaponry during the war. In June 1861 he was first issued one of many muskets that he described as "old fashioned smooth bore flint lock guns altered over to percussion locks."[98] Late the following month, when other Rhode Islanders' enlistments expired after First Bull Run, Rhodes' unit members traded their smoothbore weapons for Springfield rifles.[99] Three years later, in July 1864 in the Shenandoah Valley, Captain Rhodes wrote: "I have forty of my men armed with Spencer Repeating rifles that will hold seven cartridges at one loading. I have borrowed these guns from the 37th Mass. who are armed with them and have used them for some time."[100]

Appreciation of the great reliance upon rifles by both sides in the conflict can be gleaned from the following estimates provided by Paddy Griffith in his thought-provoking *Battle Tactics of the Civil War*. He estimated that the Confederate Government procured 183,000 smoothbore muskets and 439,000 rifles and that the Union obtained 510,000 smoothbores and an astounding 3,253,000 rifles, including 303,000 breechloaders and 100,000 repeaters.[101] The increased effectiveness of breechloaders, rather than muzzleloaders, was demonstrated by Union cavalry on the first day at Gettysburg (July 1, 1863) and by Union defenders on the second day at Chickamauga just two months later.[102]

Musketry and the new lethal force of rifle power accounted for as many as 80 percent of the Civil War's battlefield casualties. The improved arms gave the defense a tremendous advantage against exposed attacking infantry or cavalry. Use of trenches from 1863 on further increased the relative effectiveness of infantry defenders' firepower. Similar improvements in artillery ranges and accuracy also aided the defense. Rhodes, for instance, wrote on February 14, 1862: "The 4th Battery 'C' 1st Rhode Island Light Artillery came over [to Washington, D.C.] from Virginia this morning and exchanged their brass guns for steel rifle cannon."[103] The old smooth-bore cannons had ranges of 1,000 to 1,600 yards while the new rifled artillery had ranges of 4,000 to 6,000 yards.

Despite these significant new advantages held by the defense, during battle after battle, Lee frontally attacked and counterattacked with his splendid and irreplaceable troops. Military historian Bevin Alexander asserted that Lee's obsession with seeking battle and his limited strategic vision lost the war.[104] The short-term results of Lee's overly aggressive tactics were his troops' injury, death, and capture; the long-term results were dissipation of the South's finite resources and loss of the war.[105]

Lee was not alone in failing to adequately compensate for the new effectiveness of defensive firepower, but, as the leading general of a numerically inferior army for almost three years, he could not afford to make that mistake. In fact, Lee lost 20.2 percent of his soldiers in battle while imposing only 15.4 percent losses on his opponents. This negative difference in percentage of casualties (4.8 percent) was exceeded among Confederate generals only by Lee's protégé Hood (19.2 percent casualties; minus 13.7 percent difference) and by Pemberton, who surrendered his army at Vicksburg. For example, neither Joseph Johnston (10.5 percent casualties; minus 1.7 percent difference), Bragg (19.5 percent casualties; minus 4.1 percent difference) nor Beauregard (16.1 percent casualties; minus 3.3 percent difference) sacrificed such percentages of their men in unjustified frontal assaults as did Lee.[106] Lee's statistics substantially improved when he generally went on the defensive—finally and much too late—after the Battle of the Wilderness in early May 1864.

In addition to his aggressiveness, Lee had other tactical problems. His second problem was his failure to take charge on the battlefield. Lee explained his approach to a Prussian military observer at Gettysburg: "I think and work with all my powers to bring my troops to the right place at the right time; then I have done my duty. As soon as I order them into battle, I leave my army in the hands of God." To interfere later, he said, "does more harm than good."[107] "What Lee achieved in boldness of plan and combat aggressiveness he diminished through ineffective command and control."[108]

The third problem with Lee's tactics was his propensity to devise battle plans which either required impossible coordination and timing or which dissipated his limited strength through consecutive, instead of concurrent, attacks. For example, the Seven Days' Battle was a series of disasters in which Lee relied upon unrealistic coordination and timing that resulted in Confederate failures and extreme losses. Again, the second and third days at Gettysburg featured three uncoordinated attacks on the Union line by separate portions of Lee's forces when a simultaneous assault might have resulted in an important Confederate breakthrough or seizure of high ground.

Lee's fourth tactical problem was that his orders often were too vague or discretionary, an issue discussed more fully below. The pre-Gettysburg orders to Stuart and the Gettysburg Day One orders to Ewell are examples of this problem. In Philip Katcher's words, "Lee's failure adequately to order his generals to perform specific actions or discipline them if they failed was probably his greatest character defect.... One of his staunchest defenders [Fitzhugh Lee] agreed: 'He had a reluctance to oppose the wishes of others, or to order them to do anything that would be disagreeable and to which they would not consent.[']" [109] Almost a century ago, George Bruce concluded, "Every order and act of Lee has been defended by his staff officers and eulogists with a fervency that excites suspicion that, even in their own minds, there was need of defence to make good the position they claim for him among the world's great commanders."[110]

Grant's tactics proved superior to Lee's. While Grant was aggressive, he was compelled to be so by the North's burden to win (not stalemate) the war. Of all his assaults, only Cold Harbor, the second assault at

Vicksburg, and the post-Bloody Angle assault at Spotsylvania were, in hindsight, unjustified. Grant was well-known for his control of the battlefield (e.g., Fort Donelson, Shiloh, and Champion's Hill). His battle plans were rarely too complex. Finally, his orders were neither vague nor too discretionary; those to Sherman and Sheridan were masterpieces.

Lucid and Effective Orders

Unlike those of Lee and many other generals on both sides, Grant's orders were lucid and unambiguous—even when issued in the heat of battle.[111] General Meade's chief of staff commented that "there is one striking feature of Grant's orders; no matter how hurriedly he may write them on the field, no one ever has the slightest doubt as to their meaning, or even has to read them over a second time to understand them."[112] Horace Porter described Grant's drafting of a flurry of orders after his arrival at Chattanooga: "His work was performed swiftly and uninterruptedly, but without any marked display of nervous energy. His thoughts flowed as freely from his mind as the ink from his pen; he was never at a loss for an expression, and seldom interlined a word or made a material correction."[113] R. Steven Jones said, "Historians have always regarded Grant's orders as some of the clearest in the war, rarely leaving room for misunderstanding or misinterpretation."[114] Finally, Williamson Murray concluded, "[Grant] could express his thoughts verbally and on paper with a succinctness and eloquence that is remarkable."[115]

One reason that Grant's orders were lucid is that they were simple. His oral and written orders tended to be simple and goal-oriented with the means of execution left to the discretion of his subordinates. Jean Edward Smith concluded, "The genius of Grant's command style lay in its simplicity. Better than any Civil War general, Grant recognized the battlefield was in flux. By not specifying movements in detail, he left his subordinate commanders free to exploit whatever opportunities developed."[116] That approach reflected Grant's willingness to delegate discretionary authority to Sherman, Sheridan, Meade, and other subordinates.

Lee's ambiguous, and often verbal, orders created real problems. On numerous occasions his orders were too vague[117] or discretionary, characteristics that were enhanced by the verbal nature of many of them. Examples of flawed orders are Lee's Malvern Hill attack order ("ludicrous on its face," according to Brian Burton[118]), confusing or discretionary orders to Stuart as Lee's army moved north prior to Gettysburg, and his orders to Ewell to take the high ground "if practicable" at the end of Gettysburg's first day. There are times for discretionary orders, but Lee overused them—especially with generals who needed firmer direction. In his study of Lee's 1861 western Virginia campaign, Martin Fleming explained the basis for Lee's overuse of discretionary orders: "Lee was not a stern commander. He tended to avoid personal controversy and worked best with commanders with whom he was familiar, giving them broad discretion in carrying out their orders."[119] Reinforcing that theme, Gettysburg historian Kross said, "Lee wanted his corps, division, brigade and even regimental commanders to think and act for themselves. Therefore, it was easy to mistake his orders for suggestions, or at best discretionary instructions."[120]

Both the small size of Lee's staff and his under-use of them resulted in the issuance of verbal orders when written ones would have been more effective. Jones cited an instance where Lee's chief of staff ineffectively relayed Lee's wishes to General Early at Fredericksburg during the Battle of Chancellorsville; the misunderstanding resulted in Early's unintended and premature, but temporary, evacuation of Fredericksburg.[121]

Maneuverability

Although he was consistently on the strategic offensive, Grant used the art of maneuver as much as possible. His Vicksburg Campaign, described by Thomas Buell as "the equivalent of a Second World War blitzkreig,"[122] was a classic surprise maneuver that caught his adversaries completely off-guard. It demonstrated that he was, according to Edwin Bearss, "daring and innovative."[123] At Chattanooga, he maneuvered on both of Bragg's flanks before the central attack on Missionary Ridge broke through. During his Overland Campaign, he kept maneuvering around Lee's right flank until he had forced Lee back to the lethal siege situation at Richmond/Petersburg. As Jean Edward Smith concluded, Grant's detaching a 115,000-man army from his foe and secretly crossing the James River "was a perilous maneuver and an incredible tactical accomplishment, and it in no way diminishes Patton's accomplishment [in changing fronts during the Battle of the Bulge in 1944] to say that it pales alongside Grant's withdrawal from Cold Harbor and his crossing of the James in June 1864."[124] General Fuller concluded:

> Grant has gone down to history as a bludgeon general, a general who eschewed manoeuvre and who with head down, seeing red, charged his enemy again and again like a bull: indeed an extraordinary conclusion, for no general, not excepting Lee, and few generals in any other war, made greater use of manoeuvre in the winning of his campaigns, if not of his battles. Without fear of contradiction, it may be said that Grant's object was consistent; strategically it was to threaten his enemy's base of operations, and tactically to strike at the rear, or, failing the rear, at a flank of his enemy's army.[125]

Lee's record on maneuverability is more mixed. His movement away from McClellan on the Peninsula and into central Virginia to oppose Pope and win at Second Manassas was brilliant. His turning Jackson loose for the famous flanking movement at Chancellorsville worked well with qualifications. Less auspicious were Lee's loss of control during the Seven Days' Battle, his maneuvering his army into a desperate and dangerous position at Antietam (where he lacked space for any counterattack), and his scrambling and desperate attempts to maneuver at Gettysburg.

Handling Their Opponents

Both generals were fortunate to face opponents of questionable talents. Among Grant's victims were Floyd, Pillow, Pemberton, Beauregard, and Bragg. Likewise, Lee faced weak Union generals in the East: McClellan, Pope, Burnside, and Hooker. Bevin Alexander pointed to the "missteps and blunders" of eastern Union commanders as a major reason for Lee's success.[126] As Richard McMurry concluded, "It was thus not until mid-1863 that the Federals on the eastern front had a reasonably stable and competent leader [Meade] to pit against Lee."[127] Both Grant and Lee probably made some of their opponents look worse than others would have. When they finally faced each other, Grant almost won the war in two months and did win it in less than a year.[128]

One reason for Grant's success against Lee and others probably was his lack of concern about who his opponent was. As Steven Woodworth commented, "Grant made the Army of the Tennessee in his own image— aggressive, businesslike, eager to get the job done, and unconcerned about what the enemy might be doing."[129] He clearly expressed his attitude when, on the second day of the Wilderness battle, he exclaimed, "Oh, I am heartily tired of hearing about what Lee is going to do.... Go back to your command, and try to think what we are going to do ourselves instead of what Lee is going to do."[130]

In a study of Grant's use of military intelligence, William Feis provided a slightly different perspective. He disagreed with Sherman's conclusion that his friend Grant "don't care a damn for what the enemy does out of his sight." After analyzing Grant's increasing use of intelligence throughout the war, Feis concluded, "In reality, he cared a great deal about what the enemy did on the 'other side of the hill,' but unlike Henry Halleck, George McClellan, or William Rosecrans, he refused to allow that concern to become an obsession in which the search for 'perfect' information became an end in itself, effectively stifling intuitive risk taking."[131]

After his early, but costly, successes against less-than-impressive Union generals, Lee may have been victimized by his own success. Historian Brian Murphy concluded, "To his detriment,... [Lee] seemed to believe his army was invincible and treated the enemy and his plans with contempt. Eighty years later the Japanese would call this 'victory disease.' For Lee it culminated in the defeat at Gettysburg."[132] That belief also cost him in 1864 and 1865. For example, early in the Overland Campaign, Lee acted on the basis of faulty assumptions that Grant would retreat—both after the Wilderness and during Spotsylvania Court House fighting.

MILITARY MANAGEMENT SKILLS

Taking Charge on the Battlefield

While Grant excelled at personally taking charge on the battlefield, Lee too often failed to do so. Grant's taking charge was part of what Bruce Catton described as Grant's military realism. Grant learned as early as Belmont and Fort Donelson that in every hotly-contested battle there is a critical time when both armies are exhausted and the battle is in the balance and that "the one which can nerve itself for one more attack at such a time is very likely to win." Grant applied that lesson again at Shiloh, Champion's Hill, and Chattanooga.[133] He erred, however, in ceding too much battlefield control to Meade during the Overland Campaign.

Lee's failure to take charge of the battlefield was a glaring problem throughout the entire Seven Days' Battle and the three days at Gettysburg. Specifically, he would take a "hands-off" attitude even though he was on the scene and disaster was developing or opportunities beckoned. Lee himself may have provided a partial explanation for some of his army's failures in these situations. In a variation of his earlier quote, Lee is reputed to have said, "I strive to make my plans as good as my human skill allows, but on the day of battle I lay the fate of my army in the hands of God; it is my generals' turn to perform their duty."[134]

In fact, Lee too often left battle tactics to others who were obviously failing even when Lee was personally present on the battlefield—effectively leaving those decisions to no one except perhaps his God. Lee's hands-off approach is demonstrated by the dearth of written orders issued by him once a battle had started—something that distinguished him from many other generals in the war. Part of Lee's problem in this area may have been his failure to provide himself with an adequate staff, a failure described below.

Use of Available Resources

Grant's effective recognition and utilization of the North's superior resources distinguished him from most other Union generals. Gary Gallagher said, "The North always enjoyed a substantial edge in manpower and almost every manufacturing category, but none of Grant's predecessors proved equal to the task of harnessing and directing that latent strength. Grant's ability to do so stands as one of his greatest achievements."[135] James Arnold added, "When he massed for battle he brought every available soldier to the field, sublimating those secondary considerations that so often consumed the attention and resources of weaker generals."[136] For example, he concentrated his forces brilliantly in each Vicksburg Campaign battle and thereby negated the Confederates' overall numerical superiority in that theater.

In sharp contrast to Lee and McClellan, Grant rarely pleaded for reinforcements.[137] In fact, Grant was rather unique in fighting uncomplainingly with the soldiers he had on hand. "He rarely complained, never asked for reinforcements, and went ahead and did the job with whatever resources were available."[138] Grant did the best he could with the resources he had—a trait he identified with, and probably acquired from, his Mexican War idol, Zachary Taylor.[139] Even when he could have used more troops, he made do with what he had. Lincoln confirmed this when he said, "General Grant is a copious worker and fighter, but a very meager writer or telegrapher. [Grant] doesn't worry and bother me. He isn't shrieking for reinforcements all the time. He takes what troops we can safely give him … and does the best he can with what he has got."[140]

Unlike McClellan, Grant did not grossly exaggerate the strength of his opponents in an effort to secure reinforcements, excuse inaction, or justify a potential defeat. Lincoln told his Third Secretary, "[Grant] doesn't ask me to do impossibilities for him, and he's the first general I've had that didn't."[141] When Grant did ask for more troops, he did so in a subtle manner, such as, "The greater number of men we have, the shorter and less sanguinary will be the war. I give this entirely as my views and not in any spirit of dictation—always holding myself in readiness to use the material given me to the best advantage I know how."[142]

Ironically, the more successful Grant was in advancing into Confederate territory, consistent with the Union's strategic goals, the more manpower he needed to establish garrisons and to provide logistical support for his frontline troops.[143] By late 1863 and in 1864, Grant decided to deal with this problem by conducting army-size raids with little or no logistical support, destroying the Confederate infrastructure, and reducing the need for garrisons and supply lines in his rear.[144] His efficiently moving on Vicksburg, sending Sherman on his Meridian Campaign, approving Sherman's March to the Sea, and reducing the Washington, D.C., garrisons in 1864 all were consistent with this approach.

Lee, to the contrary, consistently requested reinforcements from other theaters—a practice partially caused by the large number of casualties his aggressiveness imposed on his own army. Buell faulted Lee for not effectively developing his resources: "Artillery would undergo incremental improvements but would remain inferior to its Federal counterpart. Engineering, cartography, communications, intelligence, and logistical support would persist in being consistently mediocre."[145]

Use of Assigned Generals

Grant's mentoring led to the growth and effectiveness of Sherman, Sheridan, McPherson, and numerous other Union generals. Although Grant became frustrated with generals he perceived as lacking timely aggressiveness and with incompetent political generals, he rehabilitated several eastern generals who had been shipped west after less than glowing careers in the East. Among these generals who served at least somewhat successfully under Grant were Hooker, Howard, and Burnside. After becoming general-in-chief, Grant was a team player who used four generals who were retained for political reasons: Banks, Burnside, Butler, and Sigel. After they ultimately failed him, he relieved them from command.[146]

Grant's liberal use of generals assigned and ultimate shunting of incompetents out of the war contrasted with the practices of Lee, who "dumped" his less successful generals, such as Magruder and Huger, on other theaters. Another distinction was that Lee's *laissez-faire* style of management led to situations in which his army's setbacks were blamed on his lieutenants' failure to comply with his wishes or orders. As Buell explained, Lee's leadership style may have been a cause of that problem:

> Lee's lieutenants were typically proud, independent, fractious, egotistical, confrontational, and thin-skinned—attributes of fighters, sure enough, but pure hell to deal with when Lee needed conformity and cooperation. All his life, Lee had avoided confrontation. He was a mediator, a conciliator, instinctively deferential. It was Lee's way to speak in quiet, civil tones, to use the self-deprecating understatement, to employ circumlocution to avoid unpleasantness.[147]

Thus, Grant spoke clearly and usually punished failure. Lee spoke indirectly and transferred failures without adequately addressing the underlying issues.

Use of Staff

Grant made excellent use of his staff, but Lee did not. While Lee's staff "consisted mainly of lieutenant colonels who were primarily clerks,"[148] Grant's staff ultimately included some generals and, in T. Harry Williams' words, "was an organization of experts in the various phases of strategic planning." In fact, the 1864–65 Army of the Potomac's large staff was headed by a major general and included several brigadier generals.[149] A prime example of an excellent staff officer was Horace Porter, who served as Grant's aide-de-camp beginning in the spring of 1864. Grant used him as his personal emissary to Sherman in Georgia in late 1864 and relied upon him for advice in selecting the commander for the successful assault on Fort Fisher. According to Richard Owens, Porter described Grant as "direct, open, intelligent, offensive-minded, dedicated, and having 'singular mental powers which are rare military qualities.'"[150] Porter also pointed out that Grant "studiously avoided performing any duty which some one else could do as well or better than he, and in this respect demonstrated his rare powers of administration and executive methods."[151]

R. Stephen Jones' exhaustive analysis of Civil War generals' use of personal staffs revealed that Porter was just one of several military professionals Grant used effectively as members of his personal staff—particularly in the second half of the war. By the time of the Overland Campaign, Grant had progressed, in the phrases of Jones, from a "civilian staff" to an "accidental staff" to a "professional staff." As early as Shiloh, one of Grant's aides was positioning artillery, another herding troops to the right area, and two others trying to get Lew Wallace's Division into the fight. Throughout the Overland Campaign, Grant frequently sent members of his personal staff as his emissaries and even as his alter egos to far sectors of the battlefield and to other theaters, such as Georgia. Jones' study concluded that only Grant, among Civil War generals, took the lead in expanding the duties of personal staff and that he developed something close to the Prussian system of delegation of responsibility.[152] He summarized Grant's role as a commonsense innovator in the use of staff:

> In Grant, all of the factors compatible with staff advancement came together: large armies, cooperative operations, and a willingness to experiment with staff improvements. Grant was not a staff reformer; he was a competent, intelligent general looking for more efficient ways to fight a complicated war. As such, he spent no time talking or writing about staff work. He did not promote his innovations as a model for the whole United States Army. He simply found a creative way

to use an organizational element available to all Civil War generals—the personal staff—and made it his right hand of command.[153]

Lee's staff, on the contrary, was small and usually headed by a colonel or lieutenant colonel. His maintenance of a small staff is somewhat surprising in light of the obvious damage caused by this practice in the Seven Days' Campaign, his first major one. During Seven Days', said Bevin Alexander, "Lee's staff organization was defective. He had made no arrangements for continuing communication with the separate columns.... The result was that Lee lost all grip of the battle and each commander operated too independently and without coordination."[154] In his study of the Seven Days' Campaign, Brian Burton concluded that Lee's staff work problems showed up in "the lack of good guides, the lack of cooperation among units, and the lack of well-written orders."[155]

When Lee surrendered at Appomattox, his personal staff members signing the parole agreement along with Lee consisted of a mere four lieutenant colonels and two majors.[156] In between Seven Days' and Appomattox, short staffing probably helped cause the damaging Missing Order in the Maryland Campaign, aided the lack of coordination at Gettysburg, deprived Lee's army of a substitute when Lee fell ill at the North Anna River, and did other damage to Lee's cause.[157] Freeman commented on Lee's small staff: "No general ever had more devoted service than he received from his personal assistants, but surely no officer of like rank ever fought a campaign comparable to that of 1864 with only three men on his staff, and not one of the three a professional soldier."[158] Historian Buell concluded that Lee did more and more staff work himself because he chose not to commit the time and resources to improving his staff.[159]

T. Harry Williams described the adverse personal impact on Lee of his having a small staff: "It would not be accurate to say that Lee's general staff were glorified clerks, but the statement would not be too wide of the mark. Certainly his staff was not, in the modern sense, a planning staff, which was why Lee was often a tired general."[160] Staffing problems, with resultant poor coordination, had a greater effect on offensive than defensive tactics,[161] and thus would have been a particularly troublesome problem for Lee.

Use of Cavalry

According to Eric J. Wittenberg, "Ulysses S. Grant was the master of the strategic raid."[162] The most strategically effective cavalry raid of the entire war was Grierson's length-of-Mississippi incursion that disrupted transportation to Vicksburg and distracted Vicksburg's commander while Grant moved into position and began his amphibious crossing of the Mississippi leading to the fall of Vicksburg and the opening of the Mississippi. In May of 1864, Grant unleashed Sheridan on his raid toward Richmond that resulted in Jeb Stuart's death and distracted Lee from Grant's movement around Lee's right flank at Spotsylvania Court House.[163] Although Sheridan was unsuccessful in cutting off Lee's army during his June 1864 "Second Raid" and was defeated at Trevilian Station, it was Sheridan's later raid-in-force that led to the crucial Union Victory at Five Forks and the breakdown of Lee's defenses, and ultimately his army, in April 1865.

Lee's use of cavalry was often flawed. After Jeb Stuart first rode around McClellan's army outside Richmond in 1862 and determined that McClellan's right flank was hanging, Lee failed to fully utilize that information to send Stuart and Jackson on sweeping end runs to get on McClellan's flank and rear. According to Bevin Alexander, during the latter Seven Days' battles, Lee wasted his cavalry by having Stuart's entire force idling along the Chickahominy instead of seeking up-to-date information on McClellan's location and vulnerabilities.[164] Even when Stuart finally discovered the vulnerability of Harrison's Landing to attack from Evelington Heights, Stuart demonstrated the lack of control by Lee and forfeited the advantage by prematurely disclosing his position on the heights.

Lee's loss of control over Stuart's whereabouts for many days prior to and during the Battle of Gettysburg, combined with Lee's failure to order scouting missions by other cavalry during that time, left Lee largely ignorant of the movements and position of the Army of the Potomac. That ignorance may have caused his over-cautiousness on the afternoon of July 1, 1863, when a major victory was within his grasp. In addition, that ignorance caused the costly frontal, rather than flanking, assault by Longstreet's corps the next day.

PERSONAL ATTRIBUTES

Perseverance

Both generals possessed great perseverance. Grant's resulted in Union victory, but Lee's proved to be foolhardy and extremely costly. Grant's dogged determination was demonstrated on numerous occasions, including his counterattack on the second day of Shiloh, his numerous efforts to capture Vicksburg, his continuing south against Lee and Richmond after the Battle of the Wilderness, and his crossing of the James River shortly after the disaster at Cold Harbor.

Dogged perseverance, including a disinclination to retrace his steps, was an important aspect of Grant's character. He displayed this trait when he persisted in his efforts to capture Vicksburg and launched his daring campaign across the Mississippi south of Vicksburg instead of returning to Memphis to restart another overland campaign from the north. During that campaign, James R. Arnold stated, Grant "accepted war's uncertainty by flexibly adjusting to new circumstances while maintaining a determined focus on the main chance."[165]

Again, in 1864–5, Grant demonstrated his perseverance (Gordon Rhea called it "persistence") as he carried out his campaign of adhesion against Lee's Army of Northern Virginia and achieved all his goals within a year.[166] As he explained in his official reports, "The battles of the Wilderness, Spotsylvania, North Anna, and Cold Harbor, bloody and terrible as they were on our side, were even more damaging to the enemy, and so crippled him as to make him wary ever after of taking the offensive."[167] That comment was typical of Grant's "refusal to treat reverses as defeats."[168] Even a critic of Grant's tactics noted his perseverance on significant matters: "Tactically rigid, strategically flexible, grand-strategically unrelenting—such was the generalship of U.S. Grant."[169]

James R. Arnold summed up Grant's determination and focus throughout the war: "Grant was a simple man who dealt with the facts as he found them. While his contemporaries saw war in all its complexities and too often took counsel of their fears, from Belmont to Appomattox Grant saw the main chance, stuck to it, and thus led his armies to victory."[170]

By contrast, Lee's perseverance after Lincoln's reelection, after the fall of Wilmington, and again during Sherman's drive through the Carolinas, merely resulted in countless additional deaths. The time had come to end the war, but Lee did nothing. Revered and loved by his troops and the entire South, Lee certainly had the power to bring down the curtain on the great American bloodbath. His resignation would have brought about a massive return of Southern soldiers to their homes and would have destroyed the Army of Northern Virginia's, and ultimately the Confederacy's, will to fight. But he did nothing. For five more months after Lincoln's reelection, up until the last hours at Appomattox, Lee continued the futile struggle. The result of Lee's failure to resign was continued death and destruction throughout the South. This senseless continuation of the slaughter was Lee's final failure.

Moral Courage

Another distinguishing feature of Ulysses Grant was what he himself called "moral courage." His friend William T. Sherman observed this trait in Grant:

> But I tell you where he beats me, and where he beats the world. He don't care a damn for what the enemy does out of his sight.... He uses such information as he has, according to his best judgment. He issues his orders and does his level best to carry them out without much reference to what is going on about him.[171]

As James McPherson pointed out, moral courage went beyond the physical courage that Grant and others had demonstrated while carrying out Mexican War attacks under the command of others:

> This was a quality different from and rarer than physical courage.... Moral courage involved a willingness to make decisions and give the orders. Some officers who were physically brave shrank from this responsibility because decision risked error and initiative risked failure. This was George B. McClellan's defect as a commander; he was afraid to risk his army in an offensive because he might be defeated. He lacked

the moral courage to act, to confront that terrible moment of truth, to decide and to risk.[172]

General Fuller said, "In the Vicksburg campaign Grant's moral courage has seldom been equalled, certainly seldom surpassed."[173] A one-time subordinate, General Cox, said, "[Grant's] quality of greatness was that he handled great affairs as he would little ones, without betraying any consciousness that this was a great thing to do."[174] Even a former foe, Porter Alexander, observed, "Grant was undoubtedly a great commander. He was the first which the Army of the Potomac ever had who had the moral courage to fight his army for what it was worth. He was no intellectual genius, but he understood arithmetic."[175] T. Harry Williams noted that Grant's approach was to "seek out the enemy and strike him until he is destroyed"—an approach that required "a tremendous will and a dominant personality."[176] Grant had both; he had character.

Decisiveness was a strong aspect of Grant's moral courage. Grant was decisive. Colonel James F. Rusling of the Quartermaster General's staff recalled an incident demonstrating Grant's deliberate decisiveness. In the winter of 1863–4, a quartermaster officer approached Grant for approval of millions of dollars of expenditures for the coming Atlanta campaign, and Grant approved the expenditure after briefly examining the papers involved. Questioning Grant's swift decision, the officer asked him if he was sure he was right. Grant replied, "No, I am not, but in war anything is better than indecision. *We must decide.* If I am wrong we shall soon find it out and can do the other thing. But *not to decide* wastes both time and money and may ruin everything."[177] In discussing Grant's positive effect on the mindset of the usually victorious Army of the Tennessee, Steven E. Woodworth pointed to his prompt and decisive counterattack at Shiloh: "Perhaps in part at least it was not so much that Grant infused confidence into his army as that he refrained from destroying—by timid campaigning—the confidence of men who knew they had survived the worst the enemy had to throw at them."[178]

Moral courage is a trait that Lee shared with Grant. No one can say that Lee was afraid to fight his army or to implement his gambling strategy to win the war with offensives against his enemy. His personal bravery and moral courage inspired his outnumbered army to strategic and tactical successes that won the hearts of Confederates. He truly was audacity personified. Had he been a Union general, his moral courage and audacity would have won the war.

Religion

Grant was not a churchgoer, and there is little evidence that any religious beliefs or practices shaped his Civil War activities. Lee, on the other hand, was openly religious and constantly referred to God in his official and personal correspondence. His oft-quoted comments about leaving his army in the hands of God seem to indicate, not only a reason for his frequent inactivity on the battlefield, but an acceptance of its predestined fate. Freeman described Lee's acceptance: "Whatever befell the faithful was the will of God, and whatever God willed was best. In every disaster, he was to stand firm in the faith that it was sent by God for reasons that man could not see."[179] Lee praised God for his armies' victories and after the war conceded, "We have appealed to the God of battles, and He has decided against us."[180] On the contrary, Grant seems not to have seen the hand of God in military outcomes and instead always to have pressed for results that he believed could be achieved only by his and his armies' actions.

Temperance

Persistent rumors of Grant's alleged drunkenness plagued him throughout the war. Although he may have inherited alcoholic tendencies from his grandfather, been greatly affected by a little alcohol, and had a drinking problem when separated from his family (as demonstrated in the early 1850s), Grant is never known to have been drinking—let alone drunk—during battle or at other than quiescent times during the war.[181] The stories about his drinking or being drunk during the war were "usually circulated by dishonest war contractors, corrupt subordinates, or jealous rivals whom Grant had reprimanded, dismissed, or supplanted."[182]

Recollections about Grant's drinking during the war may have been exaggerated by reporter Sylvanus Cadwallader, who was noted for inaccuracies and self-promoting exaggerations, and by John Rawlins, who wanted credit for being the watchdog over Grant's drinking.[183] There is, however, evidence that Grant did "go on a bender" while things were quiet during the Vicksburg siege.[184]

Nevertheless, Grant's struggle to restrain his drinking may have been an asset. Historian James M. McPherson, for example, concluded that:

> [Grant's] predisposition to alcoholism may have made him a better general. His struggle for self-discipline enabled him to understand and discipline others; the humiliation of pre-war failures gave him a quiet humility that was conspicuously absent from so many generals with a reputation to protect; because Grant had nowhere to go but up, he could act with more boldness and decision than commanders who dared not risk failure.[185]

To the contrary, Lee had no drinking problem and was not noted for his alcohol consumption. His premier biographer, Douglas Southall Freeman, described Lee's abstemiousness, his declining liquor, his preferring ice water to mint juleps and soda-water and ice cream to "strong potations," his hatred of whiskey, his avoidance of strong drink as a hindrance to self-mastery, and his consumption of wine "rarely and in small quantities."[186] Lee's temperance probably increased the respect in which he was held.

VISION

National Perspective/Grand Strategy

While Lee was strictly a Virginia-focused, one-theater commander who constantly sought reinforcements for his theater and resisted transfers to other theaters, Grant had a broad, national perspective, rarely requested additional troops from elsewhere, and uncomplainingly provided reinforcements to locations not under his command. Contrasting examples of their approaches are Lee's retention of Longstreet for his Gettysburg campaign, Lee's delay of Longstreet's transfer to Chickamauga, Lee's maneuvering to get Longstreet back to Virginia from Chattanooga, Grant's cooperation in sending reinforcements to Buell in Kentucky to oppose Bragg in late 1862, Grant's numerous proposals for campaigns against Mobile, and his war-winning, multi-theater strategic plan for operations beginning in May 1864. J. F. C. Fuller concluded, "Unlike Grant, [Lee] did not create a strategy in spite of his Government; instead, by his restless audacity, he ruined such strategy as his Government created."[187]

Critical to Grant's success and Union victory in the war was that Grant early in the war recognized the need to focus, and thereafter stayed focused, on defeating, capturing, or destroying opposing armies. He did not simply occupy Fort Donelson, Vicksburg, and Richmond. Instead, he maneuvered his troops in such a way that he captured enemy armies in addition to occupying important locations. Unlike McClellan, Hooker, and Meade, who ignored Lincoln's admonitions to pursue and destroy enemy armies, and Halleck, who was satisfied with his hollow capture of Corinth, Grant believed in and practiced that approach, which was so critical to Union victory.[188]

Grant's armies incurred the bulk of their casualties in the Overland Campaign of 1864. In Gordon C. Rhea's words, "[t]he very nature of Grant's [offensive] assignment guaranteed severe casualties."[189] Although Meade's Army of the Potomac, under the personal direction of Grant, did suffer high casualties that year during its drive to Petersburg and Richmond, it imposed an even higher percentage of casualties on Lee's army. In addition, that federal army compelled Lee to retreat to a nearly besieged position at Richmond and Petersburg, which Lee had previously said would be the death knell of his own army. Rhea concluded, "A review of Grant's Overland Campaign reveals not the butcher of lore, but a thoughtful warrior every bit as talented as his Confederate opponent."[190] At the same time as he advanced on Lee's army and Richmond, Grant was overseeing and facilitating a coordinated attack against Confederate forces all over the nation, particularly Sherman's campaign from the Tennessee border to Atlanta.

As he had hoped, Grant succeeded in keeping Lee from sending reinforcements to Georgia, Sherman's capture of Atlanta virtually ensured the crucial reelection of Lincoln, and Sherman ultimately broke loose on a barely contested sweep through Georgia and the Carolinas that doomed the Confederacy. Grant's 1864–65 nationwide coordinated offensive against the Rebel armies, as stated before, not only won the war but demonstrated that he was a national general with a broad vision.

Nevertheless, all too often Grant has been regarded as a "hammerer and a butcher who was often drunk, an unimaginative and ungifted clod who eventually triumphed because he had such overwhelming superiority in numbers that he could hardly avoid winning."[191] Although the Overland Campaign proved costly to the Army of the Potomac, it was fatal for Lee's Army of Northern Virginia. Grant took advantage of the fact that Lee had gravely weakened his outnumbered army in 1862 and 1863 and successfully conducted a campaign of adhesion against Lee's Army of Northern Virginia. As Rhea concluded, Grant provided the backbone and leadership that the Army of the Potomac had been lacking:

> … it was a very good thing for the country that Grant came east. Had Meade exercised unfettered command over the Army of the Potomac, I doubt that he would have passed beyond the Wilderness. Lee would likely have stymied, or even defeated the Potomac army, and Lincoln would have faced a severe political crisis. It took someone like Grant to force the Army of the Potomac out of its defensive mode, and aggressively focus it on the task of destroying Lee's army.[192]

Historian Jeffry Wert described how Grant's strategic vision and perseverance (see above) combined to reinforce each other: "On May 4, 1864, more than a quarter of a million Union troops marched forth on three fronts. There would be no turning back this time. This time, a strategic vision guided the movements, girded by an iron determination—the measure of Ulysses S. Grant's greatness as a general."[193] Williamson Murray saw the same traits: "Ulysses Simpson Grant was successful where other union generals failed because he took the greatest risks and followed his own vision of how the war needed to be won, despite numerous setbacks."[194]

According to historian T. Harry Williams, Lee, unlike Grant, had little interest in a global strategy for winning the war, and:

What few suggestions [Lee] did make to his government
about operations in other theaters than his own indicate that
he had little aptitude for grand planning.... Fundamentally
Grant was superior to Lee because in a modern total war he
had a modern mind, and Lee did not.... The modernity of
Grant's mind was most apparent in his grasp of the concept
that war was becoming total and that the destruction of the
enemy's economic resources was as effective and legitimate
a form of warfare as the destruction of his armies.[195]

Lee's strategy concentrated all the resources he could obtain and retain
almost exclusively in the eastern theater of operations, while fatal events
were occurring in the Mississippi Valley and middle theaters (primarily
in Tennessee, Mississippi, Georgia, and the Carolinas).[196] His approach
overlooked the strength of the Confederacy in its size and lack of communications, which required the Union to conquer and occupy it.[197]
Historian Archer Jones provided an analysis tying together Lee's two
strategic weaknesses (aggressiveness and Virginia myopia): "More convincing is the contention that if the Virginia armies were strong enough
for an offensive they were too strong for the good of the Confederacy.
They would have done better to spare some of their strength to bolster
the sagging West where the war was being lost."[198]

Lee's solitary focus on Virginia should not have been surprising. After
declining command of the Union's armies at the start of the war, Lee
immediately resigned his U.S. military commission and assumed command of the Virginia militia. When he did so, he stated, "I devote myself
to the service of my native State, in whose behalf alone will I ever again
draw my sword."[199] His "Virginia parochialism"[200] hampered the South
during the entire war. To the detriment of the Confederacy, Lee was a
Virginian first and a Confederate second. This trait was harmful, even

though he was not the commander-in-chief, due to his crucial role as Davis' primary military advisor throughout the war.[201]

Even more significantly, Lee's actions played a role in major Confederate western defeats at Vicksburg, Tullahoma, Chattanooga, and Atlanta. He refused to send reinforcements before or during Grant's campaign against Vicksburg; contributed to the gross undermanning of the Confederate forces during the Tullahoma Campaign and at Chattanooga; and played a critical role in the disastrous ascension of Hood to command in the West that led to the fall of Atlanta and the destruction of the Army of Tennessee.

Throughout the war, Lee was obsessed with operations in Virginia and urged that additional reinforcements be brought to the Old Dominion from the West, where Confederates defended ten times the area in which Lee operated. Thomas L. Connelly and Archer Jones concluded that, "Lee actually supplied little general strategic guidance for the South. He either had no unified view of grand strategy or else chose to remain silent on the subject."[202] Often Lee prevailed upon President Jefferson Davis to refuse or only partially comply with requests to send critical reinforcements to the West.[203]

In April 1863, for example, Lee opposed sending any of his troops to Tennessee even though the Union had sent Burnside's 9th Corps there. Using arguments that one of his supporters called bizarre, Lee opposed concentration against the enemy and favored concurrent offensives by all Confederate commands against their superior foes. Lee used similar arguments the next month when he declined to involve his soldiers in an effort to save Vicksburg (and a Confederate army of 30,000) and thereby prevent Union control of the Mississippi River. In addition, the lack of eastern reinforcements caused Braxton Bragg's Army of Tennessee to retreat in the mid-1863 Tullahoma Campaign from middle Tennessee through Chattanooga into Georgia, thereby losing Tennessee and the vital rail connection between northern Alabama and southern Tennessee in the "West" and Richmond and other eastern points.

Only once, in late 1863, did Lee consent to a portion of his army being sent west. On that occasion, Lee delayed those troops' departure from Virginia for over two weeks and caused many of them to arrive only after the Battle of Chickamauga—and without their artillery. Despite Lee's non-support, the barely reinforced Rebels won at Chickamauga and drove the Yankees back into Chattanooga. Lee's delays, however, had deprived the Rebels of perhaps an additional 10,000 troops and the artillery that might have destroyed, rather than merely repelled, Rosecrans' Army of the Cumberland. Nevertheless, that army was besieged and threatened by starvation in Chattanooga. Almost immediately, however, Lee undercut his grudging assistance by promoting the prompt return to him of his Virginia troops. His promotion of Longstreet's return led to movement of Longstreet's 15,000 troops away from Chattanooga just before the Union forces broke out of Chattanooga against Bragg's vastly outnumbered army.

Lee compounded his erroneous strategic approach to the West by acquiescing in the disastrous elevation of his protégé, the obsessively aggressive John Bell Hood, to full general and command of the Army of Tennessee at the very moment Sherman reached Atlanta in July 1864. Within seven weeks Hood lost Atlanta, and within six months he destroyed that army. During that significant summer, Lee squandered Jubal Early's 18,000-man corps on a demonstration against Washington instead of sending those troops to Atlanta, where they could have played a vital role defending that city under the command of either Johnston or Hood. These events enabled Sherman to march unmolested through Georgia and the Carolinas and ultimately to pose a fatal backdoor threat to Lee's own Army of Northern Virginia.[204]

Some may question whether Lee should have sent troops to the "West," where allegedly incompetent generals would have simply squandered them. There are several problems with that position. First, many of those western generals were so outnumbered (more than Lee was) that they were simply outflanked by their Union opponents (e.g., Bragg in mid-1863 and Johnston in mid-1864) in vast areas that afforded greater maneuverability than did Virginia. Second, Lee declined several opportunities to take command in the West, where he could have commanded troops moved from the East but where he had little interest and probably had an inkling things were more difficult than he knew or wanted to know. Third, the success of the few troops that Lee finally provided for Chickamauga demonstrated what might have been if Lee had sent more of Longstreet's troops and done so in a timely manner. Fourth, Jubal Early's corps could have provided invaluable assistance in preventing the fall of Atlanta prior to the crucial 1864 presidential election. Finally, Lee himself squandered troops in the East (particularly at Seven Days', Chancellorsville, Antietam, and Gettysburg), lost the war doing what he did, and could hardly have done worse sending some troops to the undermanned "West."

In summary, Grant won the Mississippi theater, saved the Union Army in the middle theater, and then won the eastern theater and the war. Lee lost the eastern theater and adversely affected Confederate prospects in the other theaters. How important were those other theaters (often referred to collectively as "the West")? Richard McMurry, after arguing that Lee was justified in his actions, conceded: "Finally, it seems that, as the Civil War evolved, the really decisive area—the theater where the outcome of the war was decided—was the West. The great Virginia battles and campaigns on which historians have lavished so much time and attention had, in fact, almost no influence on the outcome of the war. They led, at most, to a stalemate while the western armies fought the war of secession to an issue."[205] Weigley criticized Lee's failure to appreciate the significance of Tennessee as the South's primary granary and meat source, as well as the importance of the mines, munitions plants, manufacturing, and transportation facilities in Georgia and Alabama.[206] Grant's national perspective prevailed while Lee's myopic views badly hurt the Confederacy.

Political Common Sense

Unlike McClellan, Beauregard, Joseph Johnston, and many other Civil War generals, Grant made it his business to get along with his president. In the words of Thomas Goss, "Unlike many of his fellow commanders, Grant was willing to support the political goals of the administration as they were presented to him."[207] That cooperation included tolerating political generals, such as McClernand, Sigel, Banks, and Butler, until Grant had given them enough rope to hang themselves. Michael C. C. Adams explained Grant's willingness to work with Lincoln: "Grant's freedom from acute awareness of class may also partially explain his excellent working relationship with Lincoln. Grant was one of the few top generals who managed to avoid looking down on the common-man president. He took his suggestions seriously and benefited accordingly."[208] Grant's loyalty was rewarded when Lincoln allowed him to designate colonels and generals for promotion and to remove the remaining unsuccessful political generals—especially after Lincoln's 1864 reelection.[209]

Grant extended his cooperative attitude to Stanton, who reciprocated by directing his staff officers to comply with Grant's wishes. Grant's political antennae also kept him from "retreating" back up the Mississippi River to begin a fresh campaign against Vicksburg in the spring of 1863 or moving back toward Washington after 1864 Overland Campaign "setbacks" because of the negative public reaction and morale impact such regressive movements would provoke among his soldiers and the public.[210]

Lee was similar to Grant in his cultivating an excellent working relationship with his president. Lee's war-long correspondence with Davis virtually drips with deference—a deference that the ultra-sensitive Davis appreciated and reciprocated. It was partially Lee's circumspect politeness to Davis that resulted in the sharp contrast between the Davis-Lee relationship and those between Davis and Joseph Johnston and P. G. T. Beauregard. Lee had great influence on Davis; they had none.

CONCLUSIONS

Far from being a butcher of the battlefield, Grant determined what the North needed to do to win the war and did it. Grant's record of unparalleled success—including Belmont, Forts Henry and Donelson, Shiloh, Iuka, Corinth, Raymond, Jackson, Champion's Hill, Vicksburg, Chattanooga, the Wilderness, Spotsylvania Court House, Petersburg, and Appomattox—establishes him as the greatest general of the Civil War.

As renowned Civil War scholar T. Harry Williams concluded, Grant was an enigma to many: "He hated war, and yet found his place there above all his fellows. No wonder he is difficult to understand, and no wonder he has not been more fully appreciated." While the strategy fascinated him, he loathed the actual slaughter.[211]

Grant won the war by excelling in three theaters. He fought six Confederate armies, defeated all of them, and captured three of them[212]—the only three captures of armies during the war until after Appomattox. He succeeded for two years in the West with amazingly minimal casualties—particularly when compared with those of his foes. He conquered the Mississippi Valley and chased the Confederates out of Chattanooga and Tennessee. His later casualties in the East were militarily acceptable considering that the presidential election demanded swift and aggressive action and that he defeated Lee, captured his army, and took Petersburg and Richmond—in less than one year after initiating the Overland Campaign.

Ulysses Grant has acquired the unfortunate and unfair label of "butcher" because of the 1864 campaign of adhesion he conducted against Robert E. Lee to secure final victory for the Union. Grant's dogged persistence as he moved beyond the Wilderness and Spotsylvania caused one Southerner to say, "We have met a man this time, who either does not know when he is whipped, or who cares not if he loses his *whole* army."[213] During that campaign, some described him as a "butcher" or "murderer."[214] As Russell F. Weigley concluded, however, "there is no good reason to believe that the Army of Northern Virginia could have been destroyed within an acceptable time by any other means than the hammer blows of Grant's army."[215]

That campaign represented a deliberate effort by Grant and President Abraham Lincoln to take advantage of the fact that Lee had chewed up his Army of Northern Virginia during the prior two years and rendered it, and the Confederacy, vulnerable to a nationwide offensive campaign that would bring the hostilities to a final halt. Such an aggressive campaign inevitably would result in heavy Union losses, and, again in Weigley's words, "[i]t was the grim campaign to destroy the Confederacy by destroying Lee's army that was to give Grant his reputation as a butcher."[216] Despite that undeserved reputation, Grant was the most successful general of the Civil War and one of the greatest in military history.

Lee, on the other hand, has been overrated by romantic proponents of the Myth of the Lost Cause, historians who could not conceive of the possibility of a Confederate victory, and others overwhelmed by the

North's preponderance of resources or the first hundred years of pro-Lee Civil War historiography. Instead of staying on the tactical and strategic defensive and preserving the limited manpower of the South, Lee squandered his manpower through over-aggressive strategy and tactics. In addition, he undermined the Confederacy by claiming and expending a massive percentage of the South's troops in his beloved Virginia theater while depriving other vital theaters of the soldiers necessary for their defense.

To Grant, along with Lincoln, must go the credit for Union victory, and to Lee, along with Jefferson Davis, must go the blame for Confederate defeat.

APPENDIX I

CASUALTIES IN GRANT'S BATTLES AND CAMPAIGNS

Determining the number of casualties is one of the most difficult issues in writing about the Civil War. Not only did the Union and the Confederacy calculate their casualties differently, but individual armies on both sides took different approaches to doing so. The deterioration of the Army of Tennessee in late 1864 and of the Army of Northern Virginia in 1864 and 1865 resulted in a dearth of complete and reliable Confederate records of their casualties for the last two calendar years of the war.

Defining casualties is another aspect of the problem. A full casualty count includes killed, wounded, missing, and captured, but many records and writers include only killed and wounded. Distinctions between killed and wounded became difficult because of battle-related deaths that occurred during the days, weeks, and months after a battle. The missing category was particularly amorphous because it might or might not include soldiers who had wandered away or deserted under cover of battle—as well as those captured by the enemy.

Another problem has been determining the number of combatants on either side in order to calculate percentages of casualties. The complexity of this chore can be demonstrated by the following description of three different ways that Union troops were counted:

- **Present:** Including all personnel for whom rations had to be issued;
- **Present for Duty:** Excluding personnel on sick call or recuperating from wounds and those under arrest, but including musicians, teamsters, hospital personnel, and other uniformed noncombatants; and
- **Present for duty equipped:** Including only combat-ready enlisted men and their officers; the number of men armed and ready to fight, excluding field musicians, teamsters, hospital personnel, and other uniformed noncombatants.[1]

The Confederates used the first two categories but, instead of the third one, used "Effectives," which included only enlisted men present and under arms.[2]

In 1883, Frederick Phisterer made the first significant attempt to summarize Civil War casualties (especially Union casualties) in his *Statistical Record of the Armies of the United States*.[3] He was followed in 1888 by William F. Fox, whose years of labor resulted in the comprehensive *Regimental Losses in the American Civil War* with its Union regiment-by-regiment breakdown of casualties.[4] The foremost authority on civil war casualties was Thomas L. Livermore, whose *Numbers & Losses in the Civil War in America, 1861–1865* (1901) has been the starting point, and often the finishing point, for many later writers and statisticians. Livermore's entire concise tome explains how he derived his numbers. Unfortunately, his work contains few late-war Confederate statistics.

In his 1933 classic, *Grant and Lee: A Study in Personality and Generalship*, Fuller included a valuable appendix listing the strength, killed,
wounded, and missing of both sides in fifty-eight Civil War battles.
About two-thirds of his numbers were taken from Livermore, but he
expanded the Confederate statistics. He also analyzed those figures and
came to some startling conclusions. First, in their respective (and separate) 1862–63 battles, Lee had 16.20 percent of his men killed or
wounded while Grant's losses were only 10.03 percent. Second, where
both sides' losses are known in the battles listed, the Federals lost 11.07
percent and the Confederates 12.25 percent—both higher than Grant's
overall total of 10.225 percent and lower than Lee's 1862–63 total of
16.20 percent even though the Confederate totals include Lee's own
numbers. In other words, Fuller found that Grant lost a smaller percentage of his troops than Lee, Grant lost a smaller percentage of his troops
than other Union generals, and Lee lost a greater percentage of his troops
than other Confederate generals.[5]

A more recent analysis of killed and wounded is found in Grady
McWhiney's and Perry D. Jamieson's *Attack and Die: Civil War Military
Tactics and the Southern Heritage* (1982).[6] In their opening chapter, "It
Was Not War—It Was Murder," they assembled an illuminating series
of statistical tables analyzing the number of killed and wounded (only)
incurred by Union and Confederate commanders. The following significant statistical nuggets come from the tables in *Attack and Die*: Grant
lost an average of 18.1 percent of his troops per battle while imposing a
20.7 percent loss on his opponents. Before 1864, Grant lost 23,551 of his
220,970 men (11 percent) in his major battles and campaigns. In
1864–65, he lost 70,620 of his 400,942 men (18 percent). For the whole
war, he lost 94,171 of 621,912 (15 percent).[7] Their detailed analyses result
in a range between 15 and 18 percent for Grant's losses.

Any analysis that only includes the killed and wounded understates
the impact of a general, such as Grant, who successfully trapped and

captured three enemy armies. Also, the "missing/captured" numbers often included men who actually died in battle but whose deaths were not confirmed by their commands. Therefore, the following tables are an attempt to reconstruct the *total* casualties on both sides in battles and campaigns involving Grant.

The following tables contain comprehensive lists of various historians' and other authorities' estimates of either or both sides' casualties in most of Grant's campaigns and battles. Several observations are in order:

- There is considerable dependence on the numbers developed by Livermore.
- The numbers provided by directly interested parties, such as Grant and Jefferson Davis, are biased and inaccurate.
- The numbers are fairly consistent with each other (perhaps due to the use of Livermore and similar early sources).
- There are overlaps, gaps, and inconsistencies because different sources calculate the dates of certain battles and campaigns differently.
- The exact numbers of casualties cannot be known; some respectable authors and sources provide different statistics for the same battle.
- For the last year of the war, Confederate statistics are incomplete or missing because there are inadequate Confederate records for that period.
- Some recent exhaustive studies (such as Young, "Numbers and Losses") provide the best available information on certain battles or campaigns.

At the end of each significant and relevant campaign and battle is my estimate of the total casualties on both sides. I have based my estimates on what I deemed to be the most reliable sources cited—both long-respected sources that have not been disproved and more recent sources that reflect detailed and conscientious research. Often, I have made campaign estimates rather than estimates for each individual battle in those campaigns. The summary table contains my estimates of the war-long total casualties incurred and imposed by Grant's armies when they were under his command and control. (The Shenandoah Valley and Arkansas Post, for example, did not meet that "command and control" standard.) That summary table reveals that Grant's armies in the West, including the Middle Theater at Chattanooga, imposed 84,187 casualties while incurring only 36,688. It also shows that his aggressive eastern campaign to end the war resulted in his armies inflicting 106,573 casualties on the Confederates while themselves suffering 116,954. For the entire war, therefore, his armies imposed 190,760 casualties on the enemy while incurring 153,642. Thus, Grant's armies imposed 37,118 more casualties on their opponents than they incurred themselves.

CASUALTIES RESULTING FROM CAMPAIGNS AND BATTLES OF ULYSSES S. GRANT

[Unless otherwise noted, the numbers are the total of killed and wounded on each side. An asterisk (*) indicates the number includes missing and captured, as well as killed and wounded. "Missing" includes captured unless indicated otherwise. The term "k&w" means killed and wounded.]

BELMONT (November 7, 1861)

Source	Confederate	Union
Arnold, *Armies of Grant*[8]	105 killed	90 killed
	419 wounded	400 wounded
	117 missing	100 captured

Buell, *Warrior Generals*[9]		600+*
Current, *Encyclopedia*[10]	105 killed	80 killed
	409 wounded	322 wounded
	117 missing	99 missing
Foote, *Civil War*[11]	600+*	600+*
Fox, *Regimental Losses*[12]	105 killed	80 killed
	419 wounded	322 wounded
	117 missing	99 missing
Fuller, *Grant and Lee*[13]	105 killed	79 killed
	419 wounded	289 wounded
	117 missing	117 missing
Grant, *Memoirs*[14]	642*	425*
Hattaway and Jones, *How the North*[15]	641*	607*
Heidler & Heidler, *Encyclopedia*[16]	641* (105 killed)	607* (120 killed)
Marshall-Cornwall, *Grant*[17]	641*	485*
Phisterer, *Statistics*[18]	966*	90 killed
		173 wounded
		235 missing
Polk, "Polk and Belmont"[19]	642*	c. 600*
Roberts, "Belmont"[20]	641*	610*
Smith, *Grant*[21]	642*	607* (19%)
Author's Best Estimate:	**641***	**501***

FORT HENRY (February 6, 1862)

Source	Confederate	Union
Marshall-Cornwall, *Grant*[22]	90*	0

FORT DONELSON (February 13–16, 1862)

Source	Confederate	Union
Arnold, *Armies of Grant*[23]	16,500 captured	
Badeau, *Grant*[24]	2,500+ k&w	425 killed
		1,616 wounded/
	14,623 captured	missing
Beringer et al., *Why the South Lost*[25]	16,623* (79%)	2,832* (10.5%)
Buell, *Warrior Generals*[26]	2,832* (10%)	

Cobb, *American Battlefields*[27]	2,000 killed	500 killed
		2,108 wounded
	17,000 captured	
Cooling, "Forts"[28]	15,000 captured	
Foote, *Civil War*[29]	c. 2,000 plus	c. 3,000*
	12,000+ captured	
Fox, *Regimental Losses*[30]	466 killed	500 killed
	1,534 wounded	2,108 wounded
	13,829 captured	224 missing
Fuller, *Grant and Lee*[31]	11,500 surrendered	3,000*
		and
	2,000 k&w	500 killed
		2,108 wounded
	14,623 captured/	224 missing
	missing	
Gott, *Where the South*[32]	327 killed	480 killed
	1,127 wounded	1,926 wounded
	12,392 captured	208 missing
Heidler & Heidler, *Encyclopedia*[33]	1,500–3,500 k&w	500 killed
		2,108 wounded
	15,000 captured	221 missing
Johnson & Buel, *Battles and Leaders*[34]	2,000 k&w	510 killed
		2,152 wounded
	9,000–15,000	224 missing
	captured	
Jones, "Military Means"[35]	16,600*	3,800*
Livermore, *Numbers*[36]	2,000 k&w	500 killed
		2,108 wounded
	14,623 captured/	224 missing
	missing	
Marshall-Cornwall, *Grant*[37]	2,000 "casualties"	2,886*
	& 14,623 captured	
McPherson, *Battle Cry*[38]	500 killed	
	1,000+ wounded	
	12,000–13,000	
	captured	

McWhiney & Jamieson, *Attack*[39]		2,608
Phisterer, *Statistics*[40]	15,067*	446 killed
		1,735 wounded
		150 missing
Papers of Grant[41]	12,000–17,750 captured	
Smith, *Grant*[42]	14,000 captured	3,000 (11%)
Walsh, "*Whip*"[43]	c. 2,000 k&w	2,608 k&w
Williams, *Lincoln Finds*[44]	12,000–15,000 captured	
Author's Best Estimate:	**16,000***	**2,832***

SHILOH (PITTSBURG LANDING) (April 6–7, 1862)

Source	Confederate	Union
Allen, "Shiloh!"[45]	1,728 killed	1,754 killed
	8,012 wounded	8,408 wounded
	959 missing	2,885 missing
Arnold, *Armies of Grant*[46]	10,700*	13,700*
Badeau, *Grant*[47]	1,728 killed	1,700 killed
	8,012 wounded	7,495 wounded
	957 missing	3,022 missing
Beauregard, "Shiloh"[48]	10,699*	
Beringer et al., *Why the South Lost*[49]	10,600* (26.5%)	13,000* (20.7%)
Boritt, *Why the Confederacy Lost*[50]	10,600*	13,000*
Buell, *Warrior Generals*[51]	10,694* (27%)	13,047* (21%)
Catton, *Grant Moves South*[52]	10,000+*	13,000+*
Cobb, *American Battlefields*[53]	10,703*	13,017*
Current, *Encyclopedia*[54]	10,694*	13,047*
Daniel, *Shiloh*[55]	1,728 killed	1,754 killed
(incomplete Confederate reports)	8,012 wounded	8,408 wounded
	959 missing	2,885 missing
Davis, *Rise and Fall*[56]	1,728 killed	1,500 killed
(Union figures are for first day only)	8,012 wounded	6,634 wounded
	959 missing	3,086 missing
Donald et al., *Civil War*[57]	10,699*	13,047*
Esposito, *West Point Atlas*[58]	10,700*	13,700*

Feis, *Grant's Secret Service*[59]		13,047*
Foote, *Civil War*[60]	1,723 killed	1,754 killed
	8,012 wounded	8,408 wounded
	959 missing	2,885 captured
Fox, *Regimental Losses*[61]	1,723 killed	1,754 killed
	8,012 wounded	8,408 wounded
	959 missing	2,885 missing
Fuller, *Generalship of Grant*[62]	10,699*	13,573*
Fuller, *Grant and Lee*[63]	1,723 killed	1,754 killed
	8,012 wounded	8,408 wounded
	959 missing	2,885 missing
Grant, "Shiloh"[64]	1,728–4,000 killed	1,754 killed
	8,012 wounded	8,408 wounded
	959 missing	2,885 missing
Hattaway and Jones, *How the North*[65]	10,699*	13,047*
Heidler & Heidler, *Encyclopedia*[66]	1,700+ killed	1,700+ killed
	8,000+ wounded	8,000+ wounded
Johnson & Buel, *Battles and Leaders*[67]	1,728 killed	1,754 killed
	8,012 wounded	8,408 wounded
	959 missing	2,885 missing
Jones, "Military Means"[68]	10,600*	13,000*
Livermore, *Numbers*[69]	1,723 killed	1,754 killed
	8,012 wounded	8,408 wounded
	959 missing	2,885 missing
Lowe, "Field Fortifications"[70]	9,740	10,160
Marshall-Cornwall, *Grant*[71]	10,694–10,699*	13,000+*
Martin, *Shiloh*[72]	10,699*	13,047*
McFeely, *Grant*[73]	1,723 killed	1,754 killed
McWhiney & Jamieson, *Attack*[74]	9,735 (24%)	10,162 (16%)
Nevins, *Ordeal of the Union*[75]	10,699*	13,047*
Phisterer, *Statistics*[76]	10,699*	1,735 killed
		7,882 wounded
		3,956 missing
Roland, *American Iliad*[77]	1,723 killed	1,754 killed
	8,012 wounded	8,508 wounded
	959 missing	2,885 missing

Sherman, *Memoirs*[78]	1,700 killed	
		7,495 wounded
		3,022 captured
Smith, *Grant*[79]	1,728 killed	1,754 killed
	8,012 wounded	8,408 wounded
	959 missing	2,885 missing
Walsh, *"Whip"*[80]	12,000*	13,000*
Williams, *Lincoln Finds*[81]	1,723 killed	1,754 killed
	8,012 wounded	8,508 wounded
	959 missing	2,885 missing
Woodworth, *Nothing But Victory*[82]	9,740 k&w	10,162 k&w
	957 missing	2,103 missing
Author's Best Estimate:	**10,694***	**13,147***

IUKA (September 19, 1862)

Source	Confederate	Union
Allen, "Crossroads"[83]	86 killed	144 killed
	496 wounded	598 wounded
		40 missing
Badeau, *Grant*[84]	1,438*	
Cozzens, *Darkest Days*[85]	85 killed	141 killed
(Confederate and Union	410 wounded	613 wounded
estimates of Confederate	157 missing	36 missing
casualties differed	and	
considerably)	385–520 killed	
	692–1,300 wounded	
	181–361 captured	
Foote, *Civil War*[86]	535*	790*
Fox, *Regimental Losses*[87]	86 killed	141 killed
	408 wounded	613 wounded
	199 missing	36 missing
Fuller, *Grant and Lee*[88]	782*	144 killed
		598 wounded
		40 missing
Hattaway and Jones, *How the North*[89]	1,500*	800*

Heidler & Heidler, *Encyclopedia*[90]	1,516*	782*
Lamers, *Edge of Glory*[91]	385 killed	141 killed
	692 wounded	613 wounded
	361 captured	36 missing
Marshall-Cornwall, *Grant*[92]	700*	790*
Phisterer, *Statistics*[93]	1,516*	144 killed
		598 wounded
		40 missing
Smith, *Grant*[94]	535*	790*
Snead, "With Price"[95]	86 killed	141 killed
	408 wounded	613 wounded
	200 abandoned	36 missing
Suhr, "Iuka"[96]	1,500*	800*
Author's Best Estimate:	**1,600***	**790***

CORINTH (October 3–4, 1862) (Grant not present[97])

Source	Confederate	Union
Allen, "Crossroads"[98]	505 killed	355 killed
	2,150 wounded	1,841 wounded
	2,183 missing	324 missing
Badeau, *Grant*[99]	1,423 killed	315 killed
(Union reports)	2,225 captured	1,812 wounded
		232 missing
Catton, *Grant Moves South*[100]	Almost 5,000*	2,500*
Cobb, *American Battlefields*[101]	c. 4,800 k&w	2,520*
	1,700 missing	
Cozzens, *Darkest Days*[102]	505 killed	355 killed
(Confederate numbers	2,150 wounded	1,841 wounded
include Hatchie River, Oct. 5)	1,657 missing	324 missing
Current, *Encyclopedia*[103]	594 killed	315 killed
	2,162 wounded	1,812 wounded
	2,102 missing	232 missing
Foote, *Civil War*[104]	4,233*	2,520*
Fox, *Regimental Losses*[105]	505 killed	401 killed
(Includes Hatchie River, Oct. 5)	2,150 wounded	2,334 wounded

	2,183 missing	355 missing
Fuller, *Grant and Lee*[106]	473 killed	355 killed
	1,197 wounded	1,841 wounded
	1,763 missing	324 missing
Grant, *Memoirs*[107]	1,423 killed	315 killed
	? wounded	1,812 wounded
	2,225 captured	232 missing
Hattaway and Jones, *How the North*[108]	473 killed	355 killed
	1,197 wounded	1,841 wounded
	1,763 missing	324 missing
Heidler & Heidler, *Encyclopedia*[109]	1,423 killed	315 killed
	5,692 wounded	1,812 wounded
	2,268 captured	232 missing
Johnson & Buel, *Battles and Leaders*[110]	505 killed	355 killed
(Confederate numbers	2,150 wounded	1,841 wounded
include Hatchie River, Oct. 5)	2,183 missing	324 missing
Lamers, *Edge of Glory*[111]	1,423 killed	355 killed
	5,000 wounded	1,841 wounded
	2,268 missing	324 missing
Marshall-Cornwall, *Grant*[112]	4,838* (24%)	3,000–3,090*
		(17%)
Livermore, *Numbers*[113]	473 killed	355 killed
	1,997 wounded	1,841 wounded
	1,763 missing	324 missing
Phisterer, *Statistics*[114]	14,221*	315 killed
		1,812 wounded
		232 missing
Rosecrans, "Corinth"[115]	1,423 killed	355 killed
	c. 5,000 wounded	1,841 wounded
	2,268 captured	324 captured
Smith, *Grant*[116]	5,000*	2,000*
Williams, *Lincoln Finds*[117]	2,470 k&w	2,196 k&w
	1,763 missing	324 missing
Woodworth, *Nothing But Victory*[118]	almost 4,000	2,500+
Author's Best Estimate:	**6,188***	**2,520***

HATCHIE RIVER (October 5, 1862) (Grant not present)

Source	Confederate	Union
Cozzens, *Darkest Days*[119]	9 killed	570*
	30 wounded	
	300 captured	
Foote, *Civil War*[120]	c. 600*	c. 600*
Phisterer, *Statistics*[121]	500*	400*
Williams, *Lincoln Finds*[122]	605*	570*
Author's Best Estimate:	**339***	**600***

CHICKASAW BAYOU AND BLUFFS (December 26–29, 1862) (Grant not present)

Source	Confederate	Union
Badeau, *Grant*[123]	63 killed	175 killed
	134 wounded	930 wounded
	10 missing	43 missing
Bearss, *Vicksburg*[124]	58 killed	213 killed
	119 wounded	1,016 wounded
	10 missing	561 missing
Beringer et al., *Why the South Lost*[125]	207*	1,776*
Fox, *Regimental Losses*[126]	57 killed	208 killed
	120 wounded	1,005 wounded
	10 missing	563 missing
Fuller, *Grant and Lee*[127]	63 killed	208 killed
	134 wounded	1,005 wounded
	10 missing	563 missing
Hattaway and Jones, *How the North*[128]	207*	1,776*
Livermore, *Numbers*[129]	63 killed	208 killed
	134 wounded	1,005 wounded
	10 missing	563 missing
Marshall-Cornwall, *Grant*[130]	207*	1,776*
Morgan, "Chickasaw Bluffs"[131]	63 killed	208 killed
	134 wounded	1,005 wounded
	10 missing	563 missing

Phisterer, *Statistics*[132]	207*	191 killed
		982 wounded
		756 missing
Woodworth, *Nothing But Victory*[133]	"light"	1,776*

ARKANSAS POST (POST OF ARKANSAS, FORT HINDMAN) (January 11, 1863) (Grant not present)

Source	Confederate	Union
Arnold, *Grant Wins*[134]	150 killed	4,791 captured
Bearss, *Vicksburg*[135]	60 killed	134 killed
	73 wounded	898 wounded
	80 missing	29 missing
	4,791 captured	
Fox, *Regimental Losses*[136]		134 killed
		898 wounded
		29 missing
Livermore, *Numbers*[137]	28 killed	134 killed
	81 wounded	898 wounded
	4,791 captured	29 missing
Marshall-Cornwall, *Grant*[138]	140 k&w	1,061*
	4,791 captured	
Phisterer, *Statistics*[139]	5,500*	129 killed
		831 wounded
		17 missing
Sherman, *Memoirs*[140]	c. 150 killed	79+ killed
	4,791 captured	440+ wounded

PORT GIBSON (May 1, 1863)

Source	Confederate	Union
Arnold, *Grant Wins*[141]	400+ k&w	850 k&w
(incomplete Confederate reports)	387–580+ missing	25 missing
Badeau, *Grant*[142]	448 k&w	130 killed
	650 captured	718 wounded
Bearss, *Vicksburg*[143]	60 killed	131 killed
	340 wounded	719 wounded
	387 missing	25 missing

Current, *Encyclopedia*[144]	60 killed	131 killed
	340 wounded	719 wounded
	387 missing	25 missing
Fuller, *Grant and Lee*[145]	1,650*	130 killed
		718 wounded
		5 missing
Grant, *Memoirs*[146]		131 killed
		719 wounded
		25 missing
Heidler & Heidler, *Encyclopedia*[147]	About 800	About 800
Marshall-Cornwall, *Grant*[148]	1,650*	850*
Martin, *Vicksburg*[149]	787*	849*
"Opposing Forces," *Battles and Leaders*[150]		131 killed
		719 wounded
		25 missing
Phisterer, *Statistics*[151]	1,650*	130 killed
		718 wounded
		5 missing
Smith, *Grant*[152]	832*	875*
Winschel, "Grant's Beachhead"[153]	68+ killed	131 killed
(incomplete Confederate reports)	380+ wounded	719 wounded
	384+ missing	25 missing

RAYMOND (May 12, 1863)

Source	Confederate	Union
Arnold, *Grant Wins*[154]	515+*	442*
(incomplete Confederate reports)		
Badeau, *Grant*[155]	100 killed	69 killed
	305 wounded	341 wounded
	15+ missing	30 missing
Bearss, *Vicksburg*[156]	73 killed	68 killed
	252 wounded	341 wounded
	190 missing	37 missing
Foote, *Civil War*[157]	514*	442*
Fox, *Regimental Losses*[158]	73 killed	66 killed
	252 wounded	339 wounded
	190 missing	37 missing

Grant, *Memoirs*[159]	100 killed	66 killed
	305 wounded	39 wounded
	415 captured	37 missing
Hattaway and Jones, *How the North*[160]	c. 500*	c. 500*
Heidler & Heidler, *Encyclopedia*[161]	72 killed	66 killed
	252 wounded	339 wounded
	190 missing	37 missing
	and	
	100 killed	66 killed
	305 wounded	339 wounded
	415 captured	37 missing
Martin, *Vicksburg*[162]	505*	432*
"Opposing Forces"[163]		66 killed
		339 wounded
		37 missing

JACKSON (May 14, 1863)

Source	Confederate	Union
Arnold, *Grant Wins*[164]	c. 845*	300*
Badeau, *Grant*[165]	845*	41 killed
		249 wounded
Bearss, *Vicksburg*[166]	17+ killed	42 killed
(incomplete Confederate reports)	64+ wounded	251 wounded
	7+ missing	118 missing
Current, *Encyclopedia*[167]	Under 400*	300*
Foote, *Civil War*[168]	200+*	48 killed
		273 wounded
		11 missing
Fox, *Regimental Losses*[169]		42 killed
		251 wounded
		7 missing
Grant, *Memoirs*[170]	845*	42 killed
		251 wounded
		7 missing
Martin, *Vicksburg*[171]	800+ captured	

"Opposing Forces"[172]		42 killed
		251 wounded
		7 missing

CHAMPION'S HILL (CHAMPION HILL) (May 16, 1863)

Source	Confederate	Union
Arnold, *Armies of Grant*[173]	3,800+*	410 killed
(incomplete Confederate reports)		1,844 wounded
		187 missing
		(7% total
		casualties)
Arnold, *Grant Wins*[174]	381+ killed	410 killed
(incomplete Confederate reports)	1,018+ wounded	1,844 wounded
	2,411+ missing	187 missing
Badeau, *Grant*[175]	3,000–4,000 k&w	26 killed
		1,842 wounded
	Almost 3,000	189 missing
	captured	
Bearss, "Grant Marches West"[176]	381+ killed	410 killed
	1,018+ wounded	1,944 wounded
	2,441+ missing	187 missing
Bearss, *Vicksburg*[177]	381+ killed	396 killed
(incomplete Confederate reports)	1,081+ wounded	1,838 wounded
	2,441+ missing	187 missing
Buell, *Warrior Generals*[178]	3,851* (19%)	2,441* (8%)
Catton, *Grant Moves South*[179]	3,800*	2,400+*
Cobb, *American Battlefields*[180]	3,800*	2,400*
Ecelbarger, *Black Jack Logan*[181]	3,800*	2,400*
Editors, *Great Battles*[182]	4,300*	2,400*
Esposito, *West Point Atlas*[183]	3,851*	2,441*
Foote, *Civil War*[184]	3,624*	2,441*
Fox, *Regimental Losses*[185]	380 killed	410 killed
	1,018 wounded	1,844 wounded
	2,441 missing	187 missing
Fuller, *Generalship of Grant*[186]	4,082*	2,438*

Fuller, *Grant and Lee*[187]	381 killed	410 killed
	1,800 wounded	1,844 wounded
	1,670 missing	187 missing
Grant, *Memoirs*[188]		410 killed
		1,844 wounded
	2,500+ captured	187 missing
Hattaway and Jones, *How the North*[189]	381 killed	410 killed
	1,800 wounded	1,844 wounded
	1,670 missing	187 missing
Heidler & Heidler, *Encyclopedia*[190]	About 3,800*	About 2,400*
		and
	3,624*	2,441*
Livermore, *Numbers*[191]	381 killed	410 killed
	c.1,800 wounded	1,844 wounded
	c.1,670 missing	187 missing
Marshall-Cornwall, *Grant*[192]	1,400 k&w	2,441*
	2,500 captured	
Martin, *Vicksburg*[193]	400 killed	400 killed
	1,000 wounded	1,800 wounded
	200 missing	2,400 missing
McPherson, *Battle Cry*[194]	3,800*	2,400*
McWhiney & Jamieson, *Attack*[195]		2,254*
Miers, *Web of Victory*[196]	3,624*	2,500*
"Opposing Forces"[197]		410 killed
		1,844 wounded
		187 missing
Phisterer, *Statistics*[198]	4,300*	426 killed
		1,842 wounded
		189 missing
Smith, *Grant*[199]	3,840*	2,441*
Williams, *Lincoln Finds*[200]	3,851*	2,441*

BIG BLACK RIVER (BIG BLACK RIVER BRIDGE) (May 17, 1863)

Source	Confederate	Union
Arnold, *Grant Wins*[201]	3 killed	39 killed
(one Confederate division only)	9 wounded	237 wounded
	473 missing	3 missing

Source	Confederate	Union
Badeau, *Grant*[202]	1,751 captured	29 killed
		242 wounded
Barton, "Charge"[203]		279*
Bearss, *Vicksburg*[204]	4+ killed	39 killed
(incomplete Confederate reports)	16+ wounded	237 wounded
	1,019+ missing	3 missing
Civil War Times, *Great Battles*[205]	1,752 captured	39 killed
		237 wounded
Foote, *Civil War*[206]	1,751*	276 k&w
		3 missing
Fox, *Regimental Losses*[207]		39 killed
		237 wounded
		3 missing
Freeman, "Big Black River"[208]	1,751*	279*
Goodman, "Decision"[209]	? killed	39 killed
	? wounded	237 wounded
	1,151 captured	3 missing
Grant, *Memoirs*[210]	1,751 captured	39 killed
		237 wounded
		3 missing
Heidler & Heidler, *Encyclopedia*[211]	1,024*	under 300*
		and
	1,751*	279*
Martin, *Vicksburg*[212]	1,800 captured	Under 300*
"Opposing Forces"[213]		39 killed
		237 wounded
		3 missing
Smith, *Grant*[214]	1,751*	200*

VICKSBURG ASSAULT (May 19, 1863)

Source	Confederate	Union
Arnold, *Grant Wins*[215]	c. 200*	157 killed
		777 wounded
		8 missing
Bearss, *Vicksburg*[216]	8+ killed	157 killed
(incomplete Confederate reports)	62+ wounded	777 wounded
	2+ missing	8 missing

Civil War Times, *Great Battles*[217]	c. 250*	157 killed 777 wounded 8 missing
Cobb, *American Battlefields*[218]	900*	
Fox, *Regimental Losses*[219]		157 killed 777 wounded 8 missing
Marshall-Cornwall, *Grant*[220]		942*
Martin, *Vicksburg*[221]	Under 100*	Under 1,000*
"Opposing Forces"[222]		157 killed 777 wounded 8 missing
Trudeau, "Climax at Vicksburg"[223]	About 200*	157 killed 777 wounded 8 missing
Winschel, "Siege"[224]		942*

VICKSBURG ASSAULT (May 22, 1863)

Source	Confederate	Union
Arnold, *Grant Wins*[225]		3,199*
Badeau, *Grant*[226]		3,000 k&w
Bearss, *Vicksburg*[227] (incomplete Confederate reports)	82+ killed 242+ wounded 0+ missing	502 killed 2,550 wounded 147 missing
Buell, *Warrior Generals*[228]	3,199* (7%)	
Cobb, *American Battlefields*[229]	3,200*	
Ecelbarger, *Black Jack Logan*[230]	3,000+*	
Esposito, *West Point Atlas*[231]	3,200*	
Fox, *Regimental Losses*[232]		502 killed 2,550 wounded 147 missing
Fuller, *Grant and Lee*[233]		502 killed 2,550 wounded 147 missing
Hattaway and Jones, *How the North*[234]	Under 500*	502 killed 2,550 wounded 147 missing

Heidler & Heidler, *Encyclopedia*[235]	Over 3,000*	
Livermore, *Numbers*[236]		502 killed
		2,550 wounded
		147 missing
Lowe, "Field Fortifications"[237]	500	3,200
Marshall-Cornwall, *Grant*[238]		3,199*
Martin, *Vicksburg*[239]	500*	3,200*
McFeely, *Grant*[240]		3,200*
"Opposing Forces"[241]		502 killed
		2,550 wounded
		147 missing
Smith, *Grant*[242]		3,000+*
Trudeau, "Climax at Vicksburg"[243]	500*	502 killed
		2,550 wounded
		147 missing
Winschel, "Siege"[244]	Under 500*	3,199*

VICKSBURG TRENCHES AFTER TWO ASSAULTS
(May 23–July 4, 1863)

Source	Confederate	Union
Arnold, *Grant Wins*[245]	805 killed	104 killed
(incomplete Confederate reports)	1,938 wounded	419 wounded
	129 missing	7 missing
Bearss, *Vicksburg*[246]	817+ killed	91 killed
(Confederates May 18–July 4, incomplete)	1,952+ wounded	391 wounded
(Union June 23–July 4)	164+ missing	118 missing
Fox, *Regimental Losses*[247]		147 killed
		613 wounded
		9 missing
Hattaway and Jones, *How the North*[248]	2,872*	4,910*
(includes the two assaults)		104 killed
"Opposing Forces"[249]		419 wounded
		7 missing
Phisterer, *Statistics*[250]	31,277*	545 killed
(May 18–July 4, 1863)		3,688 wounded
		303 missing

Trudeau, "Climax at Vicksburg"[251]	875 killed	104 killed
	2,169 wounded	419 wounded
	158 missing	119 missing

VICKSBURG CAMPAIGN (May 1–July 4, 1863)

Source	Confederate	Union
Arnold, *Armies of Grant*[252]	8,000+ k&w	1,514 killed
	29,491 captured	7,395 wounded
		453 missing
Arnold, *Grant Wins*[253] (including Port Hudson)	47,625*	14,846*
Badeau, *Grant*[254]	12,000 k&w	1,243 killed
		7,095 wounded
	42,000 captured	535 missing
Chambers, *Oxford Companion*[255]	10,000 k&w	9,000 k&w
	29,396 surrendered	
Cobb, *American Battlefields*[256]	10,000 k&w	10,000*
	20,000 surrendered	
Davis, *Rise and Fall*[257]	5,632*	8,875*
	28,000 surrendered	
Ecelbarger, *Black Jack Logan*[258]	29,500 surrendered	
Esposito, *West Point Atlas*[259]		9,362*
Fox, *Regimental Losses*[260]		1,514 killed
		7,395 wounded
		453 missing
Fuller, *Generalship of Grant*[261]	10,000 k&w	1,243 killed
		7,095 wounded
	37,000 captured	535 missing
Fuller, *Grant and Lee*[262]	10,000 k&w	1,243 killed
		7,095 wounded
	37,000 captured	535 missing
Grant, *Memoirs*[263]	31,600 surrendered	
Hattaway and Jones, *How the North*[264]	29,396 captured	
Heidler & Heidler, *Encyclopedia*[265]	29,396 captured	
Livermore, *Numbers*[266]	29,396 surrendered	

Marshall-Cornwall, *Grant*[267]	10,000* plus	4,500* prior to siege 31,600 captured and
	39,490*	9,362*
McPherson, *Battle Cry*[268] (May 1–18 only)	7,200*	4,300*
McWhiney & Jamieson, *Attack*[269]	29,396* (100%)	3,052 (7%)
"Opposing Forces"[270] (incomplete Confederate reports)	1,260 killed 3,572 wounded 33,718 missing	1,514 killed 7,395 wounded 453 missing
Poulter, Keith, "Stop Insulting"[271]	38,000+*	10,142*
Sherman, *Memoirs*[272]	10,000 k&w 3,000 missing 43,000 captured	1,243 killed 7,095 wounded 535 missing
Trudeau, "Climax at Vicksburg"[273]	29,491 captured	
Walsh, *"Whip"*[274]	48,000*	10,500*
Weigley, *American Way of War*[275]	About 39,000*	About 9,400*
Williams, *Lincoln Finds*[276]	29,396 captured	1,514 killed 7,395 wounded 453 missing
Author's Best Estimate:	**40,718***	**9,362***

RETURN TO JACKSON, MISSISSIPPI (July 9–16, 1863) (Grant not present)

Source	Confederate	Union
Badeau, *Grant*[277]	71 killed 504 wounded 1,000+ captured	Under 1,000*
Current, *Encyclopedia*[278]	600*	1,132*
Fox, *Regimental Losses*[279]	71 killed 504 wounded 765 missing	129 killed 762 wounded 231 missing
Martin, *Vicksburg*[280]	c. 1,300*	c. 1,100*
Author's Best Estimate:	**1,340***	**1,122***

BROWN'S FERRY (October 27, 1863)

Source	Confederate	Union
Sword, "Battle above Clouds"[281]		21

WAUHATCHIE (October 29, 1863) (Grant not present)

Source	Confederate	Union
Grant, *Memoirs*[282]	150+ killed 100+ captured	416 k&w
Cozzens, *Shipwreck*[283]	356*	216*
Sword, "Battle above Clouds"[284]	356*	216*

LOOKOUT MOUNTAIN (November 24, 1863)

Source	Confederate	Union
Sword, "Battle above Clouds"[285]	1,251	

CHATTANOOGA (November 23–25, 1863)

Source	Confederate	Union
Arnold, *Armies of Grant*[286]	6,667*	5,824*
Badeau, *Grant*[287]	361 killed 2,180 wounded 6,146 missing	757 killed 4,529 wounded 330 missing
Buell, *Warrior Generals*[288]		5,824* (10%)
Catton, *Grant Takes Command*[289]		5,824* (under 10%)
Cobb, *American Battlefields*[290]	6,667*	5,824*
Cozzens, *Shipwreck*[291]	361 killed 2,180 wounded 6,142 captured	684 killed 4,329 wounded 322 missing
David et al., *Civil War*[292]	6,667*	5,824*
Davis, *Rise and Fall*[293]	"Our loss in killed and wounded was much less."	757 killed 4,529 wounded 337 missing
Donald et al., *Civil War*[294]	6,667*	5,824*
Esposito, *West Point Atlas*[295]	6,667*	5,824*
Foote, *Civil War*[296]	361 killed 2,160 wounded 4,146 missing	753 killed 4,722 wounded 349 missing

Fox, *Regimental Losses*[297]	361 killed	687 killed
	2,160 wounded	4,346 wounded
	4,146 missing	349 missing
		and
		752 killed
		4,713 wounded
		349 missing
Fuller, *Grant and Lee*[298]	361 killed	753 killed
	2,160 wounded	4,722 wounded
	4,146 missing	349 missing
Grant, "Chattanooga"[299]	361 killed	752 killed
	6,100+ captured	4,713 wounded
		350 missing
Grant, *Memoirs*[300]	6,142 captured	757 killed
		4,529 wounded
		330 missing
Hattaway and Jones, *How the North*[301]	6,667*	5,824*
Heidler & Heidler, *Encyclopedia*[302]	About 6,900*	About 5,400*
Johnson & Buel, *Battles and Leaders*[303]	361 killed	752 killed
	2,180 wounded	4,713 wounded
	4,146 missing	350 missing
Livermore, *Numbers*[304]	361 killed	753 killed
	2,160 wounded	4,722 wounded
	4,146 missing	349 missing
Marshall-Cornwall, *Grant*[305]	2,541 k&w	5,815*
	4,146 captured	
		and
	8,683*	5,815*
McWhiney & Jamieson, *Attack*[306]	2,521 (6%)	5,475 (10%)
Phisterer, *Statistics*[307]	8,684*	757 killed
		4,529 wounded
		330 missing
Smith, *Grant*[308]	Under 2,700	5,475
	4,146 missing	349 missing
Walsh, *"Whip"*[309]	Almost 6,700*	5,800*
Author's Best Estimate:	**6,667***	**5,814***

KNOXVILLE ASSAULT (November 29, 1863) (Grant not present)

Source	Confederate	Union
Foote, *Civil War*[310]	129 killed	8 killed
	458 wounded	5 wounded
	226 captured	
Heidler & Heidler, *Encyclopedia*[311]	800+*	

KNOXVILLE CAMPAIGN (November–December 1863) (Grant not present)

Source	Confederate	Union
Foote, *Civil War*[312]	1,142*	693*
Heidler & Heidler, *Encyclopedia*[313]	1,296*	681*

MERIDIAN CAMPAIGN (February 1864) (Grant not present)

SHERMAN'S MARCH

Source	Confederate	Union
Hattaway, "Hard War"[314]		21 killed
		61 wounded
	400 captured	81 missing

WILLIAM SOOY SMITH'S ANCILLARY CAVALRY MOVEMENT

Source	Confederate	Union
Hattaway, "Hard War"[315]	25 killed	54 killed
	75 wounded	179 wounded
		155 missing
Castel, "History in Hindsight"[316]	144 total	2 killed
		386 wounded/missing

WILDERNESS (May 5–7, 1864)

Source	Confederate	Union
Alexander, *Fighting for the Confederacy*[317]	2,000 killed	2,246 killed
	6,000 wounded	12,037 wounded
	3,400 missing	3,383 missing
Buell, *Warrior Generals*[318]		17,666* (17%)
Catton, *Grant Takes Command*[319]	2,265 killed	10,220 wounded
		2,902 missing

Catton, *Stillness*[320]		c. 15,000*
Civil War Times, *Great Battles*[321]	c. 11,400*	15,000+*
Cobb, *American Battlefields*[322]	7,750–10,800*	18,000*
Current, *Encyclopedia*[323]	c. 7,500*	17,666*
Esposito, *West Point Atlas*[324]	7,750–11,400*	15,000–18,000*
Foote, *Civil War*[325]	7,800*	17,666*
Fox, *Regimental Losses*[326]		2,246 killed
		12,037 wounded
		3,383 missing
Freeman, *Lee*[327]	Less than 7,666*	17,666*
Fuller, *Generalship of Grant*[328]	11,400*+	17,666*
Fuller, *Grant and Lee*[329]	7,750+*	17,666*
		and
		2,246 killed
		12,037 wounded
		3,383 missing
Hassler, *Commanders*[330]	8,000+*	17,666*
Hattaway, "Changing Face"[331]	7,500+*	2,246 killed
		2,037 wounded
		3,383 missing
Hattaway and Jones, *How the North*[332]	c. 7,500*	17,666*
Heidler, *Encyclopedia*[333]	10,000*	18,000*
Livermore, *Numbers*[334]	c. 7,750*	2,246 killed
		12,037 wounded
		3,383 missing
Marshall-Cornwall, *Grant*[335]	11,400*	17,666*
McPherson, *Battle Cry*[336]	Under 10,500*	17,500*
Mertz, "Wilderness II"[337]	11,000*	17,666*
Phisterer, *Statistics*[338]	11,400*	5,597 killed
		21,463 wounded
		10,677 missing
Rhea, "'Butcher' Grant"[339]	11,000*	18,000*
Smith, *Grant*[340]	11,000* (18%)	17,666* (18%)
		2,246 killed
		12,037 wounded
		3,383 missing

Source	Confederate	Union
Steere, *Wilderness*[341]	8,700*	2,246 killed
		12,037 wounded
		3,383 missing
Taylor, *Lee*[342]	17,666*	
U.S. War Department[343]		2,261 killed
		8,785 wounded
		2,902 missing
Young, "Numbers and Losses"[344]	1,495 killed	
	7,690 wounded	
	238 wounded/ captured	
	1,702 missing	
Author's Best Estimate:	**11,125***	**17,666***

SPOTSYLVANIA COURT HOUSE (May 8–21, 1864)

Source	Confederate	Union
Alexander, *Fighting for the Confederacy*[345]		2,725 killed
		13,413 wounded
		2,258 missing
Civil War Times, *Great Battles*[346]		17,000+*
Cobb, *American Battlefields*[347]	c. 9,500*	18,000*
Current, *Encyclopedia*[348]	c. 10,000*	17,500*
Esposito, *West Point Atlas*[349]	9,000–10,000*	17,000–18,000*
Fox, *Regimental Losses*[350]		2,725 killed
		13,416 wounded
		2,258 missing
Fuller, *Generalship of Grant*[351] (May 8–12 only)	c. 12,000*	14,322*
Fuller, *Grant and Lee*[352]		
May 10 assault		753 killed
		3,347 wounded
May 12 assault	5,500? k&w	6,020 k&w
	4,000 missing	800 missing
Hassler, *Commanders*[353]		18,399*
Heidler & Heidler, *Encyclopedia*[354]	About 12,000*	About 18,000*
Livermore, *Numbers*[355]		10,120 k&w

(May 10 & 12)		800 missing
Lowe, "Field Fortifications"[356]	8,000	16,100
Marshall-Cornwall, *Grant*[357]	10,000*	18,399*
Phisterer, *Statistics*[358]	9,000*	4,177 killed
		19,687 wounded
		2,577 missing
Rhea, "'Butcher' Grant"[359]	12,500*	18,000*
Taylor, *Lee*[360]		18,399*
U.S. War Department[361]		2,271 killed
		9,360 wounded
		1,970 missing
Young, "Numbers and Losses"[362]	1,467 killed	
	4,783 wounded	
	452 wounded/	
	captured	
	5,719 missing	
Author's Best Estimate:	**13,421***	**18,399***

DREWRY'S (DRURY'S) BLUFF (May 16, 1865) (Grant not present)

Source	Confederate	Union
Alexander, *Fighting for the Confederacy*[363]	354 killed	390 killed
	1,610 wounded	1,721 wounded
	220 missing	1,390 missing
Heidler and Heidler, *Encyclopedia*[364]	c. 2,000*	c. 4,000*
Marshall-Cornwall, *Grant*[365]	3,499*	6,245*

NORTH ANNA, TOTOPOTOMOY, BETHESDA CHURCH AND SHERIDAN'S CAVALRY RAID (May 23–June 1, 1864) (Grant present at North Anna only)

Source	Confederate	Union
Alexander, *Fighting for the Confederacy*[366]	304 killed	223 killed
(North Anna only)	1,513 wounded	1,460 wounded
	200 missing	290 missing
Cobb, *American Battlefields*[367]	2,517*	2,623*
(North Anna only)		

Source	Confederate	Union
Fox, *Regimental Losses*[368]		591 killed 2,734 wounded 661 missing
Fuller, *Grant and Lee*[369]	2,000? k&w	223 killed 1,460 wounded 290 missing
Marshall-Cornwall, *Grant*[370] (North Anna & Totopotomoy only)	2,000?*	3,986*
Phisterer, *Statistics*[371]	2,000*	223 killed 1,460 wounded 290 missing
Rhea, "'Butcher' Grant"[372] (North Anna only)	1,600*	2,600*
Taylor, *Lee*[373]		3,986*
U.S. War Department[374] (North Anna & Totopotomoy only)		285 killed 1,150 wounded 217 missing
Young, "Numbers and Losses"[375]	460 killed 1,918 wounded 109 wounded/ captured 1,279 missing	
Author's Best Estimate:	**3,766***	**3,986**

COLD HARBOR (May 31–June 12, 1864)

(# Indicates these numbers are for June 3 only)

Source	Confederate	Union
Arnold, *Armies of Grant*[376]		13,153* and almost 6,000#[377]
Beringer et al., *Why the South Lost*[378]	1,500*#	7,000*#
Buell, *Warrior Generals*[379]		12,000* (11%)
Casdorph, *Lee and Jackson*[380]	13,000*#	
Catton, *Grant Takes Command*[381]	Under 1,500*#	7,000+*#
Catton, *Stillness*[382]		7,000*#
Current, *Encyclopedia*[383]	1,500*#	7,000*#

Esposito, *West Point Atlas*[384]	1,500*#	7,000*#
Fox, *Regimental Losses*[385]		1,844 killed
		9,077 wounded
		1,816 missing
Freeman, *Lee*[386]	1,200–1,500*#	7,000*#
Fuller, *Generalship of Grant*[387]	1,300*#	1,100 killed#
		4,517 wounded#
		and
(June 1–12)		12,737*
Fuller, *Grant and Lee*[388]		1,100 killed#
		4,517 wounded#
		1,400? missing#
		and
	1,700?* k&w	1,905 killed
		10,570 wounded
		2,546 missing
Hassler, *Commanders*[389]	1,700*#	12,737*
Heidler & Heidler, *Encyclopedia*[390]	1,500*#	7,000*#
Jones, *Right Hand*[391]	1,500*#	7,000*#
"Lee and Grant, 1864"[392]	1,500*#	about 7–8,000*#
Livermore, *Numbers*[393] (June 1–3)		c. 12,000 k&w
Lowe, "Field Fortifications"[394]	1,500#	3,000–3,500#
Lowry, *No Turning Back*[395]		7,000*#
Marshall-Cornwall, *Grant*[396]	1,500?*	12,737*
O'Beirne, "Valley"[397]		5,500*#
Phisterer, *Statistics*[398]	1,700*	1,905 killed
		10,570 wounded
		2,456 missing
Rhea, "'Butcher' Grant"[399]	5,000*	13,000*
Rhea, "Cold Harbor"[400]	1,500*#	6,000*#
Rhea, *Cold Harbor*[401]	1,000–1,500*#	6,000+*#
Taylor, *Lee*[402]		12,738*
U.S. War Department[403]		1,769 killed
(May 31–June 12)		6,752 wounded
		1,537 missing

Young, "Numbers and Losses"[404]	83 killed	
	3,313 wounded	
	67 wounded/ captured	
	1,132 missing	
Author's Best Estimate:	**4,595***	**12,737***

TREVILIAN RAID (June 7–24, 1864) (Grant not present)

Source	Confederate	Union
Fox, *Regimental Losses*[405]		141 killed
		709 wounded
		579 missing
Phisterer, *Statistics*[406]	370*	85 killed
(June 11–12 at Trevilian Station only)		490 wounded
		160 missing
Taylor, *Lee*[407]		1,512*
Young, "Numbers and Losses"[408]	83 killed	
	380 wounded	
	1 wounded/ captured	
	318 missing	

OVERLAND (RICHMOND) CAMPAIGN (WILDERNESS TO PETERSBURG)(May–June, 1864)

Source	Confederate	Union
Boritt, *Why the Confederacy Lost*[409]	32,000*	55,000*
Casdorph, *Lee and Jackson*[410]	32,000*	50,000*
Dana, *Recollections*[411]		7,621 killed
		38,339 wounded
		8,966 missing
Davis, *Rise and Fall*[412]		Almost 100,000*
Donald et al., *Civil War*[413]	24,000*	55,000*
Esposito, *West Point Atlas*[414]	20,000–40,000*	55,000*
Fuller, *Generalship of Grant*[415]	c. 33,000* (43%)	c. 55,000* (34%)
Freeman, *Lee*[416]	c. 30,000*	c. 64,000*
Grant, *Memoirs*[417]		32,633*

Groom, *Shrouds of Glory*[418]		54,000*
Hassler, *Commanders*[419]	20,000*	60,000*
Heidler & Heidler, *Encyclopedia*[420]		c. 50,000*
		and
	c. 33,500*	Almost 55,000*
McPherson, *Battle Cry*[421]	35,000+*	c. 65,000*
McWhiney & Jamieson, *Attack*[422]	c. 32,000 (46%)	c. 50,000 (41%)
Miers, *Last Campaign*[423]	32,000*	50,000*
Nolan, "Demolishing the Myth"	32,000 (45.7%)	50,000 (41%)
Rhea, *Spotsylvania*[424]	23,000* (33%)	33,000+* (28%)
(Through May 12 only)		
Smith, *Grant*[425]	35,000*	Almost 65,000*
Taylor, *Lee*[426]		54,926*
U.S. War Department[427]		6,586 killed
		26,047 wounded
		6,626 missing
Walsh, "*Whip*"[428]	32,000*	50,000*
Weigley, *American Way of War*[429]	32,000*	55,000*
Young, "Numbers and Losses"[430]	32,631*	
	4,206 killed	
	17,705 wounded	
	859 wounded/	
	captured	
	9,861 missing	

PETERSBURG ASSAULTS (June 15–18, 1864) (Grant not present)

Source	Confederate	Union
Buell, *Warrior Generals*[431]	8,150* (13%)	
Current, *Encyclopedia*[432]	c. 4,000*	10,586*
Fox, *Regimental Losses*[433]		1,688 killed
		8,513 wounded
		1,185 missing
Fuller, *Grant and Lee*[434]	8,150*	
Livermore, *Numbers*[435]	8,150*	
Lowe, "Field Fortifications"[436]	4,000	10,000
Marshall-Cornwall, *Grant*[437]	3,000?*	9,964*

Phisterer, *Statistics*[438]		1,298 killed
		7,474 wounded
		1,814 missing
Trudeau, *The Last Citadel*[439]	4,000*	8,150 k&w
		1,814 missing
Author's Best Estimate:	**4,000***	**11,386***

WILSON-KAUTZ RAID (June 22–30, 1864) (Grant not present)

Source	Confederate	Union
Fox, *Regimental Losses*[440]		71 killed
		262 wounded
		1,119 missing
Phisterer, *Statistics*[441]	300*	76 killed
		265 wounded
		700 missing
Trudeau, *Last Citadel*[442]		81 killed
		261 wounded
		1,113 missing

FIRST DEEP BOTTOM RUN/STRAWBERRY PLAINS (July 26–29, 1864)

Source	Confederate	Union
Suderow, "Glory Denied"[443]	471 k&w	62 killed
		340 wounded
		208 captured
		86 missing
Fox, *Regimental Losses*[444]		62 killed
		340 wounded
		86 missing

THE CRATER (THE MINE), PETERSBURG (July 30, 1864)

Source	Confederate	Union
Catton, *Grant Takes Command*[445]	c. 4,000*	
Catton, *Stillness*[446]		3,798*
Civil War Times, *Great Battles*[447]	c. 1,500	c. 4,400*
Current, *Encyclopedia*[448]	1,500*	4,000*

Esposito, *West Point Atlas*[449]	4,400*	
Fox, *Regimental Losses*[450]		504 killed
		1,881 wounded
		1,413 missing
Freeman, *Lee*[451]	c. 1,500*	
Fuller, *Grant and Lee*[452]		2,864 k&w
		929 missing
Hassler, *Commanders*[453]	1,200*	4,000+*
Livermore, *Numbers*[454]	619+ k&w	2,864 k&w
(incomplete Confederate reports)	563+ missing	929 missing
Marshall-Cornwall, *Grant*[455]	3,000?*	4,400*
McPherson, *Battle Cry*[456]	Under 2,000*	4,000*
McWhiney & Jamieson, *Attack*[457]		2,865
Phisterer, *Statistics*[458]	1,200*	419 killed
		1,679 wounded
		1,910 missing
Trudeau, *Last Citadel*[459]	361+ killed	504 killed
	727+ wounded	1,881 wounded
	403+ missing	1,413 missing

SECOND DEEP BOTTOM RUN/STRAWBERRY PLAINS
(August 14–19, 1864)

Source	Confederate	Union
Buell, *Warrior Generals*[460]	2,901* (10%)	
Fox, *Regimental Losses*[461]		327 killed
		1,851 wounded
		721 missing
Livermore, *Numbers*[462]		328 killed
		1,852 wounded
		721 missing
McWhiney & Jamieson, *Attack*[463]	2,180	
Phisterer, *Statistics*[464]	1,100*	400 killed
		1,755 wounded
		1,400 missing
Suderow, "Nothing But a Miracle"[465]	1,100 k&w	2,180 k&w
	400 captured	721 captured

Trudeau, *Last Citadel*[466]	1,000*	328 killed 1,852 wounded 721 missing

WELDON RAILROAD (SIX MILE HOUSE) (August 18–21, 1864) (Grant not present)

Source	Confederate	Union
Arnold, *Armies of Grant*[467]	720*	592 k&w 2,150 captured
Current, *Encyclopedia*[468]	c. 1,600*	4,455*
Fox, *Regimental Losses*[469]		251 killed 1,148 wounded 2,897 missing
Fuller, *Grant and Lee*[470]	1,200? k&w 419 missing	198 killed 1,105 wounded 3,152 missing
Hassler, *Commanders*[471]	4,455*	
Livermore, *Numbers*[472]	211 killed 990 wounded 419 missing	198 killed 1,105 wounded 3,152 missing
Marshall-Cornwall, *Grant*[473] (August 18–24)	7,020*	3,720?*
McWhiney & Jamieson, *Attack*[474]		1,303
Phisterer, *Statistics*[475]	4,000*	212 killed 1,155 wounded 3,176 missing
Trudeau, *Last Citadel*[476]	c. 1,600*	251 killed 1,149 wounded 2,879 missing

REAM'S STATION (REAMS STATION) (August 25, 1864) (Grant not present)

Source	Confederate	Union
Fox, *Regimental Losses*[477]		140 killed 529 wounded 2,073 missing

Phisterer, *Statistics*[478]	1,500*	127 killed
		546 wounded
		1,769 missing
Trudeau, *Last Citadel*[479]	814*	117+ killed
		439+ wounded
		2,046+ missing

NEW MARKET HEIGHTS/CHAFFIN'S FARM AND FORTS HARRISON AND GILMER (September 28–30, 1864)

Source	Confederate	Union
Fox, *Regimental Losses*[480]		383 killed
		2,299 wounded
		645 missing
Fuller, *Grant and Lee*[481]		783 killed
		4,328 wounded
		645 missing
Hassler, *Commanders*[482]	2,000*	3,327*
Livermore, *Numbers*[483]		383 killed
		2,299 wounded
		645 missing
McWhiney and Jamieson, *Attack*[484]		2,682
Phisterer, *Statistics*[485]	2,000*	400 killed
		2,029 wounded
Trudeau, *Last Citadel*[486] (includes Peebles Farm)	c. 3,000*	6,322*

FIFTH UNION OFFENSIVE AT PETERSBURG (September 29–October 2, 1864)

Source	Confederate	Union
Sommers, *Richmond Redeemed*[487]	3,041*	6,322*

DARBYTOWN ROAD (October 7, 1864)

Source	Confederate	Union
Fox, *Regimental Losses*[488]		49 killed
		253 wounded
		156 missing
Trudeau, "Unerring Firearm"[489]	600–1,000*	458*

HATCHER'S RUN/BURGESS MILL/BOYDTON PLANK ROAD (October 27–28, 1864)

Source	Confederate	Union
Current, *Encyclopedia*[490]		1,758*
Fox, *Regimental Losses*[491]		166 killed
		1,028 wounded
		564 missing
Fuller, *Grant and Lee*[492]		166 killed
		1,028 wounded
		564 missing
Hassler, *Commanders*[493]		1,758*
Heidler & Heidler, *Encyclopedia*[494]	Under 1,000*	Over 1,700*
Livermore, *Numbers*[495]		166 killed
		1,028 wounded
		564 missing
McWhiney and Jamieson, *Attack*[496]		1,194
Phisterer, *Statistics*[497]	1,000*	156 killed
		1,047 wounded
		699 missing
Trudeau, *Last Citadel*[498]	1,416*	3,428*

DABNEY'S MILLS/HATCHER'S RUN (February 5–7, 1865)

Source	Confederate	Union
Bergeron, "Hatcher's Run"[499]	1,000*	171 killed
		1,181 wounded
		187 missing
Current, *Encyclopedia*[500]		1,300+*
Fox, *Regimental Losses*[501]		171 killed
		1,181 wounded
		187 missing
Livermore, *Numbers*[502]		170 killed
		1,160 wounded
		182 missing
McWhiney and Jamieson, *Attack*[503]		1,330

Phisterer, *Statistics*[504]	1,200*	232 killed
		1,062 wounded
		186 missing
Trudeau, *Last Citadel*[505]	c. 1,000*	171 killed
		1,181 wounded
		187 missing

FORT STEDMAN (STEADMAN) (March 25, 1865)

Source	Confederate	Union
Current, *Encyclopedia*[506]	4,400–5,000*	
Esposito, *West Point Atlas*[507]	5,000*	
Fox, *Regimental Losses*[508]		72 killed
		450 wounded
		522 missing
Freeman, *Lee*[509]	Almost 4,800–5,000*	
Fuller, *Generalship of Grant*[510]	4,000*	2,080*
Fuller, *Grant and Lee*[511]	4,000?*	2,080*
Hassler, *Commanders*[512]	4,000*	2,000*
Heidler & Heidler, *Encyclopedia*[513]	2,500–3,500	72 killed
		450 wounded
		522 missing
Marvel, "Retreat"[514]	3,000*	1,000*
McPherson, *Battle Cry*[515]	Almost 5,000*	2,000
Phisterer, *Statistics*[516]	2,681*	68 killed
		337 wounded
		506 missing
		and
(Federal counterattack)	834*	103 killed
		864 wounded
		209 missing
Smith, *Grant*[517]	5,000*	under 1,500*
Trudeau, *Last Citadel*[518]	2,681–4,000*	2,134*
(includes later Federal counterattack)		

WHITE OAK ROAD (March 31, 1865) (Grant not present)

Source	Confederate	Union
Fox, *Regimental Losses*[519]		177 killed
		1,134 wounded
		556 missing
Phisterer, *Statistics*[520]	1,235*	177 killed
		1,134 wounded
		556 missing

DINWIDDIE COURT HOUSE (March 31, 1865) (Grant not present)

Source	Confederate	Union
Fox, *Regimental Losses*[521]		67 killed
		354 wounded
Crawford, "Dinwiddie Court House"[522]	800–1,000*	400*
Fuller, *Grant and Lee*[523]	1,050*?	2,198 k&w
(including White Oak Road)		583 missing
Livermore, *Numbers*[524] (March 29–31,		2,198 k&w
including White Oak Road)		583 missing

FIVE FORKS (April 1, 1865) (Grant not present)

Source	Confederate	Union
Calkins, "Five Forks"[525]	545 k&w	104 killed
		670 wounded
	2,000–2,400 captured	57 missing
Catton, *Grant Takes Command*[526]	4,500 captured	
Current, *Encyclopedia*[527]	4,500+*	Under 1,000*
Esposito, *West Point Atlas*[528]	4,500 captured	
Fox, *Regimental Losses*[529]		124 killed
		706 wounded
		54 missing
Freeman, *Lee*[530]	3,244 captured	
Marvel, "Retreat"[531]	5,000 captured	
Phisterer, *Statistics*[532]	8,500*	124 killed
		706 wounded
		54 missing

		Trudeau, *Storm*[533]	605 k&w	103 killed
				670 wounded
			2,400 captured	57 missing

PETERSBURG BREAKTHROUGH (April 2, 1865)

Source	Confederate	Union
Current, *Encyclopedia*[534]		3,300–4,100*
Fox, *Regimental Losses*[535]		296 killed
		2,565 wounded
		500 missing
Fuller, *Grant and Lee*[536]		625 killed
		3,189 wounded
		326 missing
Livermore, *Numbers*[537]		625 killed
		3,189 wounded
		326 missing
Phisterer, *Statistics*[538]	3,000*	296 killed
		2,565 wounded
		500 missing

PETERSBURG CAMPAIGN (June 15, 1864–April 3, 1865)

Source	Confederate	Union
Cobb, *American Battlefields*[539]	28,000*	42,000* or 59,000* [apparently a mistaken use of the 59,000 total troops Lee had at the start of the Petersburg siege]
Current, *Encyclopedia*[540]	At least 28,000*	42,000*
Trudeau, *Last Citadel*[541]	c. 28,000	c. 42,000
Author's Best Estimate:	**28,000***	**42,000***

SAILOR'S (SAYLER'S) CREEK (April 6, 1865) (Grant not present)

Source	Confederate	Union
Calkins, "Final Bloodshed"[542]		7,700 captured
Fox, *Regimental Losses*[543]		166 killed
		1,014 wounded
Freeman, *Lee*[544]	7,000–8,000*	
Glynn, "Black Thursday"[545]	c. 8,000 captured	
Heidler & Heidler, *Encyclopedia*[546]	c. 7,700 captured	
McPherson, *Battle Cry*[547]	6,000 captured	
Phisterer, *Statistics*[548]	7,000*	166 killed
		1,014 wounded
Smith, *Grant*[549]	2,000 k&w	
	6,000 captured	
Trudeau, *Last Citadel*[550]	6,000–7,000 captured	
Trudeau, *Storm*[551]	8,000*	1,180 k&w

APPOMATTOX CAMPAIGN (April 2–9, 1865)

Source	Confederate	Union
Buell, *Warrior Generals*[552] (March 29–April 9)	10,780* (10%)	
Civil War Times, *Great Battles*[553]	28,231 surrendered	
Current, *Encyclopedia*[554]	28,000* and Almost 30,000 surrendered	9,000*
Fuller, *Grant and Lee*[555]	22,349 surrendered	1,316 killed
		7,750 wounded
		1,714 missing
Hassler, *Commanders*[556]	28,000 surrendered	10,780*
Heidler & Heidler, *Encyclopedia*[557]	c. 28,000 surrendered	
Livermore, *Numbers*[558]	6,266	1,316 killed
		7,750 wounded
		1,714 missing
Marshall-Cornwall, *Grant*[559]	54,000*	10,515*
Marvel, *Lee's Last Retreat*[560]	26,000*	

(March 25–April 9)	28,000 surrendered	
	14,400–20,400 deserted	
McWhiney and Jamieson, *Attack*[561]	6,666 (14%)	9,066 (8%)
Phisterer, *Statistics*[562]	26,000 surrendered	
Porter, *Campaigning*[563]	1,200 killed	1,316 killed
(March 29–April 9)	6,000 wounded	7,750 wounded
	75,000 captured	1,714 missing
Simpson, *Hood's Texas Brigade*[564]	28,231 surrendered	
Author's Best Estimate:	**41,666***	**10,780***

SUMMARY TABLE OF AUTHOR'S BEST ESTIMATES OF CASUALTIES INCURRED BY BOTH SIDES IN MAJOR CAMPAIGNS AND BATTLES OF ULYSSES S. GRANT

Campaign/Battle	Total Confederate Casualties	Total Union Casualties
Belmont	641*	501*
Fort Donelson	16,000*	2,832*
Shiloh	10,694*	13,147*
Iuka	1,600*	790*
Corinth/Hatchie River	6,527*	3,120*
Vicksburg Campaign	40,718*	9,362*
Return to Jackson	1,340*	1,122*
Chattanooga	6,667*	5,814*
WESTERN TOTALS	84,187*	36,688*
Wilderness	11,125*	17,666*
Spotsylvania Court House	13,421*	18,399*
North Anna River, etc.	3,766*	3,986*
Cold Harbor	4,595*	12,737*
Petersburg Assaults	4,000*	11,386*
Petersburg Siege/Campaign	28,000*	42,000*
Appomattox Campaign	41,666*	10,780*

EASTERN TOTALS	106,573*	116,954*
TOTALS (killed, wounded, missing/captured)	190,760*	153,642*
NET DIFFERENCE	+37,118*	

APPENDIX II

CASUALTIES IN LEE'S BATTLES AND CAMPAIGNS

See the introduction to Appendix I. The same principles apply here.

In their *Attack and Die*, McWhiney and Jamieson provided incomplete statistics on soldiers killed and wounded (not missing or captured) in Lee's army and its opponents. In the battles and campaigns they included, Lee's army killed and wounded 134,602 (15.4%) of the enemy while having 121,042 (20.2%) of their own killed or wounded. Lee's 20.2 percent killed and wounded rate was the highest among the major Confederate generals—exceeding Braxton Bragg's 19.5 percent and John Bell Hood's 10.2 percent (McWhiney and Jamieson, *Attack and Die*, pp. 19–22).

The final table in this appendix contains my estimates of the war-long total casualties incurred and imposed by Lee's armies when they were under his command and control. This summary table reveals that Lee's army imposed 240,322 casualties on the enemy while incurring

208,922. Thus, Lee's soldiers imposed 31,400 more casualties on their opponents than they suffered themselves.

Appendices I and II facilitate a comparison of the casualty records of Grant and Lee. Lee's army incurred 55,280 more casualties than Grant's armies (208,922 versus 153,642). Lee's army imposed 49,562 more casualties on the enemy than Grant's armies imposed on their enemies (240,322 versus 190,760). Grant's armies had a positive casualty balance versus their opponents of 37,118 (190,760 minus 153,642), while Lee's army had a positive balance of 31,400 (240,322 minus 208,922).

Thus, their records are somewhat similar except that Lee, supposedly on the strategic defensive and fighting for a manpower-short Confederacy, exceeded Grant's casualties by more than 55,000.

CASUALTIES RESULTING FROM CAMPAIGNS AND BATTLES OF ROBERT E. LEE

[Unless otherwise noted, the numbers are the total of killed and wounded on each side. An asterisk (*) indicates the number includes missing and captured, as well as killed and wounded. "Missing" includes captured unless indicated otherwise. The term "k&w" means killed and wounded.]

MECHANICSVILLE/BEAVER DAM CREEK (June 26, 1862)

Source	Confederate	Union
Burton, *Extraordinary Circumstances*[1]	c. 1,400*	361*
Current, *Encyclopedia*[2]	1,484*	361*
Eicher, *Longest Night*[3]	1,484*	49 killed
		207 wounded
		105 missing
Fox, *Regimental Losses*[4]		49 killed
		207 wounded
		105 missing
Freeman, *R. E. Lee*[5]	1,350*	361*
Fuller, *Grant and Lee*[6]	1,484*	49 killed
	(9.1% k&w)	207 wounded
		105 missing
		(1.6% k&w)

Freeman, *Lieutenants*[7]	c. 1,400	
Heidler & Heidler, *Encyclopedia*[8]	c. 1,475*	361*
Konstam, *Seven Days*[9]	Nearly 1,500	360
Livermore, *Numbers*[10]	1,484*	49 killed
		207 wounded
		105 missing
Lowe, "Field Fortifications"[11]	1,400	360
McPherson, *Atlas*[12]	1,484*	361*
Robertson, *Jackson*[13]	Almost 1,500*	c. 375*

GAINES' [GAINES'S] MILL (June 27, 1862)

Source	Confederate	Union
Alexander, *Lost Victories*[14]	8,000+ k&w	4,000 k&w
		2,380 missing
Burton, *Extraordinary Circumstances*[15]	c. 8,700 k&w	6,837*
Current, *Encyclopedia*[16]	8,751*	6,837*
Eicher, *Longest Night*[17]	8,751*	894 killed
		3,107 wounded
		2,836 missing
Fox, *Regimental Losses*[18]		894 killed
		3,107 wounded
		2,836 missing
Freeman, *Lieutenants*[19]	8,000*	6,837*
Freeman, *R. E. Lee*[20]	8,000+*	894 killed
		3,107 wounded
		2,836 missing
Fuller, *Grant and Lee*[21]	8,751*	894 killed
	(15.3% k&w)	3,107 wounded
		2,836 missing
		(11.7% k&w)
Heidler & Heidler, *Encyclopedia*[22]	c. 8,750*	6,837*
Johnson & Buel, *Battles and Leaders*[23]	589+ killed	894 killed
(incomplete Confederate reports)	2,671+ wounded	3,107 wounded
	24+ missing	2,836 missing
Konstam, *Seven Days*[24]	1,483 killed	894 killed
	6,402 wounded	3,114 wounded
	108 missing	2,829 missing

Livermore, *Numbers*[25]	8,751*	894 killed
		3,107 wounded
		2,836 missing
Lowe, "Field Fortifications"[26]	8,700	4,100
McPherson, *Atlas*[27]	8,750*	6,837*
Thomas, *Lee*[28]	7,993*	6,837*

GARNETT'S FARM (June 27, 1862)

Source	Confederate	Union
Burton, *Extraordinary Circumstances*[29]	c. 200*	105 k&w
		13 missing

GOLDING'S [GARNETT'S] FARM (June 28, 1862)

Source	Confederate	Union
Burton, *Extraordinary Circumstances*[30]	182*	6–7*
Fox, *Regimental Losses*[31]		37 killed
		227 wounded
		104 missing

SAVAGE [SAVAGE'S] STATION (June 29, 1862)

Source	Confederate	Union
Fox, *Regimental Losses*[32]		80 killed
		412 wounded
		1,098 missing
Heidler & Heidler, *Encyclopedia*[33]	c. 500*	c. 1,000*
Konstam, *Seven Days*[34]	473*	1,038 k&w
		2,500 captured
Thomas, *Lee*[35]	444*	914*

GLENDALE/FRASER'S FARM/FRAYSER'S FARM /WHITE OAK SWAMP (June 30, 1862)

Source	Confederate	Union
Burton, *Extraordinary Circumstances*[36]	c. 3,500*	c. 2,800*
Current, *Encyclopedia*[37]	3,615*	2,853*
Eicher, *Longest Night*[38]	638 killed	297 killed
	2,814 wounded	1,696 wounded
	221 missing	1,804 missing

Fox, *Regimental Losses*[39]   210 killed
                                                                1,513 wounded
                                                                1,130 missing

Heidler & Heidler, *Encyclopedia*[40]   3,673*   3,797*
                                                                (1,800 missing)

Konstam, *Seven Days*[41]   638 killed   297 killed
                                                2,814 wounded   1,696 wounded
                                                221 missing   1,804 missing

Robertson, *Jackson*[42]   3,315*
Sears, "Glendale"[43]   638 killed   297 killed
                                                2,814 killed   1,696 wounded
                                                221 missing   1,804 missing

Thomas, *Lee*[44]   3,673*   3,797*

MALVERN HILL (July 1, 1862)

Source	Confederate	Union
Burton, *Extraordinary Circumstances*[45]	5,150 k&w 500 missing	2,100 k&w
Current, *Encyclopedia*[46]	5,355*	3,214*
Eicher, *Longest Night*[47]	5,355*	3,214*
Fox, *Regimental Losses*[48]		397 killed 2,092 wounded 725 missing
Fuller, *Grant and Lee*[49]	9.9% k&w	6.0% k&w
Heidler & Heidler, *Encyclopedia*[50]	869 killed 4,241 wounded 540 missing	314 killed 1,875 wounded 818 missing
Keegan, *Fields of Battle*[51]	1,000+ killed 4,000+ wounded	c. 400 killed <2,000 wounded
Kendall, "'Murder'"[52]	5,650*	3,000*
Konstam, *Seven Days*[53]	5,500*	3,200*
Lowe, "Field Fortifications"[54]	5,300*	3,000*
Robertson, *Jackson*[55]	5,650*	2,825+*
Weigley, *American Way of War*[56]	5,500*	

SAVAGE STATION, GLENDALE, MALVERN HILL
(June 29, June 30, and July 1, 1862)

Source	Confederate	Union
Livermore, *Numbers*[57]	8,602 k&w	724 killed
		4,245 wounded
	875 missing	3,067 missing

SEVEN DAYS' BATTLE (June 26–July 1, 1862)

Source	Confederate	Union
Alexander, *Lost Victories*[58]	20,168* (25%)	9,796 k&w
		6,000–10,000
		captured
Beringer, *Why the South*[59]	19,739	9,796
	(20.7% k&w)	(10.7% k&w)
Boritt, *Why the Confederacy Lost*[60]	20,000+*	<16,000*
Bradford, *Oxford Atlas*[61]	20,000*	16,000*
Burton, *Extraordinary Circumstances*[62]	3,478 killed	1,734 killed
	16,261 wounded	8,062 wounded
	875 missing	6,053 missing
Current, *Encyclopedia*[63]	19,739	9,796
		and
	3,286 killed	1,734 killed
	15,909 wounded	8,062 wounded
	946 missing	6,053 missing
Davis, *Stonewall*[64]	20,000+	
Donald et al., *Civil War*[65]	21,000*	16,000*
Eicher, *Longest Night*[66]	c. 20,000*	c. 16,000*
Esposito, *West Point Atlas*[67]	c. 20,000*	c. 16,000*
Foote, *Civil War*[68]	3,478 killed	1,734 killed
	16,261 wounded	8,062 wounded
	875 missing	6,053 missing
Fox, *Regimental Losses*[69]	3,478 killed	1,734 killed
	16,261 wounded	8,062 wounded
	875 missing	6,053 missing
Freeman, *Lieutenants*[70]	19,195 k&w	1,734 killed
	946 missing	8,062 wounded
		6,053 missing

Freeman, *R. E. Lee*[71]	3,286 killed	1,734 killed
	15,909 wounded	8,062 wounded
	946 missing	6,053 missing
Fuller, *Grant and Lee*[72]	3,478 killed	1,734 killed
	16,261 wounded	8,062 wounded
	875 missing	6,053 missing
	(20.7% k&w)	(10.7% k&w)
Gallagher, *Civil War*[73]	20,000+*	16,000+*
Hattaway & Jones, *How the North*[74]	20,000+*	<16,000
Heidler & Heidler, *Encyclopedia*[75]	20,500*	(3,500 killed)
Johnson & Buel, *Battles and Leaders*[76]	3,286 killed	1,734 killed
	15,909 wounded	8,062 wounded
	940 missing	6,053 missing
Konstam, *Seven Days*[77]	20,614*	16,849*
Livermore, *Numbers*[78]	3,478 killed	1,734 killed
	16,261 wounded	8,062 wounded
	875 missing	6,053 missing
McClellan, "Peninsular Campaign"[79]	2,823 killed	1,734 killed
	13,703 wounded	8,062 wounded
	3,223 missing	6,053 missing
McPherson, *Atlas*[80]	20,141*	15,849*
McWhiney & Jamieson, *Attack*[81]	19,739 (20.7%)	9,796 (10.7%)
Nolan, "Demolishing the Myth"[82]	19,739 (20.7%)	9,796 (10.7%)
Phisterer, *Statistics*[83]	17,583*	1,582 killed
		7,709 wounded
		5,958 missing
Weigley, *American Way of War*[84]	3,286 killed	
		15,909 wounded
		946 missing
Woodworth, *Civil War Generals*[85]	20,614*	15,849*
Author's Best Estimate	**20,000***	**16,000***

CEDAR MOUNTAIN (August 9, 1862)(Lee not present)[86]

Source	Confederate	Union
Alexander, *Lost Victories*[87]	229 killed	2,381*
		1,047 wounded

Civil War Times, *Great Battles*[88]	1,276*	2,377*
Current, *Encyclopedia*[89]	c. 1,400*	c. 2,600*
Esposito, *West Point Atlas*[90]	1,365*	2,381*
Fox, *Regimental Losses*[91]	223 killed	314 killed
	1,060 wounded	1,445 wounded
	31 missing	622 missing
Freeman, *Lieutenants*[92]	229 killed	2,381*
		1,047 wounded
Fuller, *Grant and Lee*[93]	231 killed	314 killed
	1,107 wounded	1,445 wounded
		594 missing
Heidler & Heidler, *Encyclopedia*[94]	1,341*	314 killed
		1,445 wounded
		622 missing
Johnson & Buel, *Battles and Leaders*[95]	241 killed	314 killed
	1,120 wounded	1,445 wounded
	4 missing	622 missing
Livermore, *Numbers*[96]	231 killed	314 killed
	1,107 wounded	1,445 wounded
		594 missing
McPherson, *Atlas*[97]	1,400*	2,500*
Phisterer, *Statistics*[98]	1,307*	450 killed
		660 wounded
		290 missing
Author's Best Estimate:	**1,300***	**2,400***

SECOND MANASSAS/SECOND BULL RUN (August 28–30, 1862)

Source	Confederate	Union
Alexander, *Lost Victories*[99]	<9,100 k&w	10,200 k&w
	81 missing	7,000 missing
Beringer et al., *Why the South*[100]	9,108	10,096
	(18.8% k&w)	(13.3% k&w)
Boritt, *Why the Confederacy Lost*[101]	9,000*	16,000*
Civil War Times, *Great Battles*[102]	1,550 killed	1,750 killed
	7,750 wounded	8,450 wounded
	100 missing	4,250 missing
	(17%)	(20%)

Cobb, *American Battlefields*[103]	1,481 killed	1,721 killed
	7,627 wounded	8,372 wounded
	89 missing	5,958 missing
Current, *Encyclopedia*[104]	9,108	10,096
	and	
	c. 9,000*	16,000+*
Esposito, *West Point Atlas*[105]	9,500*	14,500*
Foote, *Civil War*[106]	1,481 killed	1,724 killed
	7,627 wounded	8,372 wounded
	89 missing	5,958 missing
Fox, *Regimental Losses*[107]	1,481 killed	1,747 killed
	7,627 wounded	8,452 wounded
	89 missing	4,263 missing
Freeman, *R. E. Lee*[108]	9,112*	14,462*
Gallagher, *Civil War*[109]	9,200* (18.4%)	16,000* (21.3%)
Heidler & Heidler, *Encyclopedia*[110]	1,481 killed	1,724 killed
	7,627 wounded	8,372 wounded
	89 missing	5,958 missing
Hennessy, "Second Manassas"[111]	1,300 killed	1,700 killed
	7,000 wounded	8,200 wounded
Johnson & Buel, *Battles and Leaders*[112]	1,553 killed	1,747 killed
	7,812 wounded	8,452 wounded
	109 missing	4,263 missing
McWhiney & Jamieson, *Attack*[113]	9,108 (18.8%)	10,096 (13.3%)
Nolan, "Demolishing the Myth"[114]	9,108 (19%)	10,096 (13.3%)
Phisterer, *Statistics*[115]	10,700*	14,800*
Thomas, *Lee*[116]	9,500*	14,500*
Weigley, *American Way of War*[117]	9,197* (19%)	16,054* (13%)
Author's Best Estimate:	**9,500***	**14,400***

SECOND MANASSAS & CHANTILLY
(August 27–September 2, 1862)

Source	Confederate	Union
Eicher, *Longest Night*[118]	1,481 killed	1,724 killed
	7,627 wounded	8,372 wounded
	89 missing	5,958 missing

Fuller, *Grant and Lee*[119]	1,481 killed	1,724 killed
	7,627 wounded	8,372 wounded
	89 missing	5,958 missing
	(18.7% k&w)	(13.2% k&w)
Livermore, *Numbers*[120]	1,481 killed	1,724 killed
	7,627 wounded	8,372 wounded
	89 missing	5,958 missing
McPherson, *Atlas*[121]	9,197*	16,054*

CHANTILLY (September 1, 1862)

Source	Confederate	Union
Heidler & Heidler, *Encyclopedia*[122]	c. 500*	c. 700*
Phisterer, *Statistics*[123]	800*	1,300*
Author's Best Estimate:	**800***	**1,300***

HARPER'S FERRY (September 12–15, 1862)(Lee not present)

Source	Confederate	Union
Cobb, *American Battlefields*[124]	286*	219 k&w
		12,000+
		captured
Current, *Encyclopedia*[125]	39 killed	12,500 captured
		247 wounded
Fox, *Regimental Losses*[126]		44 killed
		173 wounded
		12,520 missing
Fuller, *Grant and Lee*[127]	500*	80 killed
		120 wounded
		11,583 captured
Heidler & Heidler, *Encyclopedia*[128]	12,419 captured	
Hotchkiss, *Make Me a Map*[129]	11,090 captured	
Johnson & Buel, *Battles and Leaders*[130]		44 killed
		173 wounded
		12,520 captured
McPherson, *Atlas*[131]	286*	12,500 captured
Phisterer, *Statistics*[132]	500*	80 killed
		120 wounded
		11,583 missing
Author's Best Estimate:	**286***	**11,783***

CRAMPTON'S GAP (September 14, 1862)(Lee not present)

Source	Confederate	Union
Heidler & Heidler, *Encyclopedia*[133]	c. 800*	533*

SOUTH MOUNTAIN (September 14, 1862)(Lee not present)

Source	Confederate	Union
Fuller, *Grant and Lee*[134]	325 killed	325 killed
	1,560 wounded	1,403 wounded
	800 missing	85 missing
	(10.5% k&w)	(6.8% k&w)

SOUTH MOUNTAIN & CRAMPTON'S GAP (September 14, 1862)(Lee not present)

Source	Confederate	Union
Current, *Encyclopedia*[135]	387 killed	438 killed
	1,768 wounded	1,821 wounded
	1,279 missing	87 missing
Eicher, *Longest Night*[136]	325 killed	443 killed
	1,560 wounded	1,807 wounded
	800 missing	75 missing
Fox, *Regimental Losses*[137]		438 killed
		1,821 wounded
		87 missing
Gallagher, *Civil War*[138] (South Mtn. Only)	2,700*	2,300*
Phisterer, *Statistics*[139]	4,343*	443 killed
		1,806 wounded
		76 missing
Author's Best Estimate:	**3,434***	**2,346***

ANTIETAM/SHARPSBURG (September 17, 1862)

Source	Confederate	Union
Alexander, *Lost Victories*[140]	c. 1,500 killed	2,108 killed
	7,800 wounded	9,450 wounded
	1,000 missing	753 missing
	(31% casualties)	

Bailey, *Bloodiest Day*[141]	1,546 killed	2,108 killed
	7,752 wounded	9,549 wounded
	1,018 missing	753 missing
Beringer et al., *Why the South*[142]	11,724	11,657
	(22.6% k&w)	(15.5% k&w)
Black, *Seventy Battles*[143]	2,700 killed	2,108 killed
	9,024 wounded	9,549 wounded
	2,000 missing	753 missing
Buell, *Warrior Generals*[144]	10,000+*	12,000+*
Cobb, *American Battlefields*[145]	10,318*	12,410*
Cox, *Reminiscences*[146]	11,172	12,410
Current, *Encyclopedia*[147]	11,724	11,657
	and	
	1,546 killed	2,108 killed
	7,754 wounded	9,549 wounded
	1,018 missing	753 missing
Donald et al., *Civil War*[148]	10,318*	(31%) 12,401*
Eicher, *Longest Night*[149]	2,700 killed	2,010 killed
	9,024 wounded	9,416 wounded
	1,043 missing	2,000 missing
Esposito, *West Point Atlas*[150]	c. 13,700*	c. 12,350*
Foote, *Civil War*[151]	<11,000*	>12,000*
Fox, *Regimental Losses*[152]		2,108 killed
		9,549 wounded
		753 missing
Freeman, *R. E. Lee*[153]	10,700*	12,410*
Fuller, *Grant and Lee*[154]	2,700 killed	2,108 killed
	11,724 wounded	9,549 wounded
	c. 2,000 missing	753 missing
	(22.6% k&w)	(15.5% k&w)
Gallagher, *Civil War*[155]	10,300+*	almost 12,500*
Hattaway & Jones, *How the North*[156]	13,725*	12,469*
Heidler & Heidler, *Encyclopedia*[157]	14,000*	12,000*
	(2,700 killed)	(2,100 killed)
	and	
	1,546 killed	2,108 killed

	7,752 wounded	9,540 wounded
	1,108 missing	753 missing
	(31%)	(25%)
Johnson & Buel, *Battles and Leaders*[158]	1,512 killed	2,108 killed
	7,816 wounded	9,549 wounded
	1,844 missing	753 missing
Livermore, *Numbers*[159]	2,700 killed	2,108 killed
	11,724 wounded	9,549 wounded
	c. 2,000 missing	753 missing
Lowe, "Field Fortifications"[160]	9,500	11,650
McPherson, *Atlas*[161]	10,318*	12,401*
McWhiney & Jamieson, *Attack*[162]	11,724 (22.6%)	11,657 (15.5%)
Nolan, "Demolishing the Myth"[163]	11,724 (22.6%)	11,657 (10.5%)
Phisterer, *Statistics*[164]	25,899*	2,010 killed
		9,416 wounded
		1,043 missing
Thomas, *Lee*[165]	1,546 killed	2,108 killed
	7,754 wounded	9,549 wounded
	1,018 missing	753 missing
Weigley, *American Way of War*[166]	13,724*	12,410*
Woodworth, *Davis & Lee*[167]	c. 11,000*	c. 12,000*
Author's Best Estimate:	**11,500***	**12,400***

SHEPHERDSTOWN (September 19–20, 1862)(Lee not present)

Source	Confederate	Union
Fox, *Regimental Losses*[168]		71 killed
		161 wounded
		131 missing

MARYLAND CAMPAIGN (September 12–20, 1862)

Source	Confederate	Union
Foote, *Civil War*[169]	13,609*	27,276*
Fox, *Regimental Losses*[170]		1,886 killed
		9,348 wounded
		1,367 missing

Freeman, *Lieutenants*[171]	13,609 or more*	27,767*
Freeman, *R. E. Lee*[172]	13,609*	
Weigley, *American Way of War*[173]	13,724*	23,410*

FREDERICKSBURG (December 13, 1862)

Source	Confederate	Union
Alexander, *Lost Victories*[174]	5,309*	12,647*
Beringer et al., *Why the South*[175]	4,656	10,884
	(6.4% k&w)	(10.9% k&w)
	and	
	5,300*	12,500*
Bradford, *Oxford Atlas*[176]	5,300*	12,600*
Cobb, *American Battlefields*[177]	5,300*	12,600*
Current, *Encyclopedia*[178]	<5,000*	<13,000*
Donald et al., *Civil War*[179]	600 killed	1,284 killed
	5,300*	9,600 wounded
		12,600*
Eicher, *Longest Night*[180]	595 killed	1,284 killed
	4,061 wounded	9,600 wounded
	653 missing	1,769 missing
Esposito, *West Point Atlas*[181]	5,000+*	10,000+*
Foote, *Civil War*[182]	4,201*	12,653*
Fox, *Regimental Losses*[183]	596 killed	1,284 killed
	4,068 wounded	9,600 wounded
	651 missing	1,769 missing
Freeman, *Lieutenants*[184]	4,201*	
Freeman, *R. E. Lee*[185]	5,309*	12,653*
Fuller, *Lee and Grant*[186]	595 killed	1,284 killed
	4,061 wounded	9,600 wounded
	653 missing	1,769 missing
	(6.4% k&w)	(10.3% k&w)
Gallagher, *Civil War*[187]	5,300*	12,650*
Hattaway & Jones, *How the North*[188]	5,309*	12,653*
Heidler & Heidler, *Encyclopedia*[189]	4,201*	12,653*
Johnson & Buel, *Battles and Leaders*[190]	608 killed	1,284 killed
	4,116 wounded	9,600 wounded
	653 missing	1,769 missing

Jones, *Right Hand*[191]	5,300*	12,600*
Livermore, *Numbers*[192]	595 killed	1,284 killed
	4,061 wounded	9,600 wounded
	653 missing	1,769 missing
Lowe, "Field Fortifications"[193]	1,750	7,700
McWhiney & Jamieson, *Attack*[194]	4,656 (6.4%)	10,884 (10.9%)
Nichols, *Reynolds*[195]	5,309*	12,653*
Phisterer, *Statistics*[196]	4,576*	1,180 killed
		9,028 wounded
		2,145 missing
Thomas, *Lee*[197]	5,377*	12,653*
	(4,700 k&w)	(11,000 k&w)
Weigley, *American Way of War*[198]	5,300*	12,700*
Author's Best Estimate:	**4,201***	**12,653***

KELLY'S FORD (March 17, 1863)(Lee not present)

Source	Confederate	Union
Fox, *Regimental Losses*[199]	11 killed	6 killed
	88 wounded	50 wounded
	34 missing	22 missing
Heidler & Heidler, *Encyclopedia*[200]	133*	78*
Author's Best Estimate:	**133***	**78***

CHANCELLORSVILLE (May 1–4, 1863)

Source	Confederate	Union
Alexander, *Fighting for the Confederacy*[201]	1,665 killed	1,575 killed
	9,081 wounded	9,594 wounded
	2,018 missing	5,676 missing
Alexander, *Lost Victories*[202]	13,156*	16,804*
Beringer et al., *Why the South*[203]	10,746	11,116
	(18.7% k&w)	(11.4% k&w)
	and	
	12,700* (21%)	16,800 (15%)
Bradford, *Oxford Atlas*[204]	12,800*	17,300*
Cobb, *American Battlefields*[205]	12,821*	17,278*

Current, *Encyclopedia*[206]	10,746* and c. 13,000*	11,116* c. 18,000*
Eicher, *Longest Night*[207]	1,665 killed 9,081 wounded 2,018 missing	1,606 killed 9,762 wounded 5,919 missing
Esposito, *West Point Atlas*[208]	13,000*	17,000*
Fox, *Regimental Losses*[209]	1,665 killed 9,081 wounded 2,018 missing	1,606 killed 9,762 wounded 5,919 missing
Freeman, *Lieutenants*[210]	1,683 killed	9,277 wounded 2,196 missing
Fuller, *Grant and Lee*[211]	18.7% k&w	11.4% k&w
Gallagher, *Civil War*[212]	12,674*	17,287*
Hattaway & Jones, *How the North*[213]	1,665 killed 9,081 wounded 2,018 missing (21%)	1,606 killed 9,762 wounded 5,919 missing (15%)
Heidler & Heidler, *Encyclopedia*[214]	13,000*	18,000*
Hess, "Spades"[215]	13,460*	17,304*
Johnson & Buel, *Battles and Leaders*[216]	1,649 killed 9,106 wounded 1,708 missing	1,606 killed 9,762 wounded 5,919 missing
Livermore, *Numbers*[217]	1,665 killed 9,081 wounded 2,018 missing	1,575 killed 9,594 wounded 5,676 missing
Lowe, "Field Fortifications"[218]	11,100	10,750
McPherson, *Atlas*[219]	14,000*	17,000*
McWhiney & Jamieson, *Attack*[220]	10,746 (18.7%)	11,116 (11.4%)
Nichols, *Reynolds*[221]	12,821*	17,278*
Nolan, "Demolishing the Myth"[222]	10,746 (18.7%)	11,116 (11.4%)
Phisterer, *Statistics*[223]	12,281*	1,512 killed 9,518 wounded 5,000 missing
Weigley, *American Way of War*[224]	<13,000*	>17,000*
Author's Best Estimate:	**12,764***	**17,287***

BRANDY STATION/BEVERLY FORD (June 9, 1863)(Lee not present)

Source	Confederate	Union
Carhart, *Lost Triumph*[225]	500*	900*
Current, *Encyclopedia*[226]	51 killed	1,651*
		250 wounded
		132 missing
Fox, *Regimental Losses*[227]	51 killed	81 killed
	250 wounded	403 wounded
	132 missing	382 missing
Heidler & Heidler, *Encyclopedia*[228]	525*	935*
Phisterer, *Statistics*[229]	700*	500*
Trudeau, *Gettysburg*[230]	c. 523*	866*
Author's Best Estimate:	**523***	**866***

WINCHESTER (June 13–15, 1863)(Lee not present)

Source	Confederate	Union
Fox, *Regimental Losses*[231]	47 killed	95 killed
	219 wounded	348 wounded
	3 missing	4,000 missing
Heidler & Heidler, *Encyclopedia*[232]	269*	4,000 captured
Phisterer, *Statistics*[233]	850*	3,000*
Author's Best Estimate:	**269***	**4,443***

ALDIE, MIDDLEBURG, UPPERVILLE (June 10–24, 1863) (Lee not present)

Source	Confederate	Union
Fox, *Regimental Losses*[234]	65 killed	78 killed
	279 wounded	307 wounded
	166 missing	228 missing
Author's Best Estimate:	**510***	**613***

HANOVER, PENNSYLVANIA (June 30, 1863)(Lee not present)

Source	Confederate	Union
Fox, *Regimental Losses*[235]	9 killed	19 killed
	50 wounded	73 wounded
	58 missing	123 missing

Heidler & Heidler, *Encyclopedia*[236]   c. 150* under 200
Author's Best Estimate: **150***   **200***

GETTYSBURG (July 1–3, 1863)

Source	Confederate	Union
Alexander, *Fighting for the Confederacy*[237]	3,072 killed	2,592 killed
	14,497 wounded	12,709 wounded
	5,434 missing	5,150 missing
Beringer et al., *Why the South*[238]	22,638 k&w	17,684 k&w
	(30.2% k&w)	(21.2% k&w)
	and	
	28,000* (33%)	23,000* (20%)
Black, *Seventy Battles*[239]	Up to 28,000*	23,000*
Boritt, *Why the Confederacy Lost*[240]	c. 28,000*	23,000*
Bradford, *Oxford Atlas*[241]	29,000+*	23,000+*
Civil War Times, *Great Battles*[242]	3,903 killed	3,564+ killed
	18,735 wounded	14,529 wounded
	5,425 missing	5,365 missing
Cobb, *American Battlefields*[243]	c. 28,063*	23,000+*
Current, *Encyclopedia*[244]	22,638*	17,684*
	and	
	(Incomplete totals: 3,155 killed	
	4,427 killed	14,529 wounded
	12,179 wounded	5,365 missing
	5,592 missing)	
	c. 28,000	
Donald et al., *Civil War*[245]	28,000*	23,000*
Eicher, *Longest Night*[246]	c. 28,000+*	3,149 killed
	although reported as: 14,503	
	wounded	
	4,637 killed	5,161 missing
	12,391 wounded	
	5,846 missing	
Esposito, *West Point Atlas*[247]	almost 28,000*	23,049*

Foote, *Civil War*[248]	25,000-28,000*	3,155 killed
	(Reported by Lee as:	14,529 wounded
	2,592 killed	5,365 missing
	12,709 wounded	
	5,150 missing)	
	12,227 recorded	
	as captured in	
	Union records	
	(see note)	
Fox, *Regimental Losses*[249]	2,592 killed	3,070 killed
	12,706 wounded	14,497 wounded
	5,150 missing	5,434 missing
Freeman, *Lieutenants*[250]	2,592 killed	3,155 killed
	12,709 wounded	14,529 killed
	5,150 missing	5,365 missing
	(Official reports	
	inconsistent with	
	12,227 reported as	
	captured by Union)	
Fuller, *Lee and Grant*[251]	3,903 killed	3,155 killed
	18,735 wounded	14,529 wounded
	5,425 missing	5,365 missing
	(30.1% k&w)	(20.0% k&w)
Hattaway & Jones, *How the North*[252]	28,063*	23,049*
Heidler & Heidler, *Encyclopedia*[253]	20,000*	23,000*
	(2,500 killed)	(3,000 killed)
	and	
	28,000*	3,149 killed
		14,501 wounded
		5,157 missing
Johnson & Buel, *Battles and Leaders*[254]	2,592 killed	3,072 killed
	12,709 wounded	14,497 wounded
	5,150–12,227	5,434 missing
	missing (see note)	

Livermore, *Numbers*[255]	3,903 killed	3,155 killed
	18,735 wounded	14,529 wounded
	5,425 missing	5,365 missing
	(see note)	
McPherson, *Atlas*[256]	20,000-28,000*	23,000*
McWhiney & Jamieson, *Attack*[257]	22,638 (30.2%)	17,684 (21.2%)
Nichols, *Reynolds*[258]	20,000+*	20,000+*
Nofi, *Gettysburg*[259]	28,500*	23,050*
Nolan, "Demolishing the Myth"[260]	22,638 (30.2%)	17,684 (21.2%)
Official Records[261]	2,592 killed	3,155 killed
	12,709 wounded	14,529 killed
	5,150 missing	5,365 missing
	(Official reports inconsistent with 12,227 reported as captured by Union)	
Phisterer, *Statistics*[262]	31,621*	2,834 killed
		13,709 wounded
		6,643 missing
Thomas, *Lee*[263]	Perhaps 28,000*	
Trudeau, *Gettysburg*[264]	22,874*	22,813*
Weigley, *American Way of War*[265]	c. 23,000*	
Author's Best Estimate:	**28,000***	**23,000***

PICKETT'S CHARGE AT GETTYSBURG (July 3, 1863)

Source	Confederate	Union
Lowe, "Field Fortifications"[266]	5,600	1,500
Nichols, *Reynolds*[267]	Almost 10,000	
Nofi, *Gettysburg*[268]	6,500*(60%)	1,500 (25%)

EAST CAVALRY FIELD BATTLE, GETTYSBURG (July 3, 1863)

Source	Confederate	Union
Carhart, *Lost Triumph*[269]	250*	30 killed
		149 wounded
		75 missing

LEE'S RETREAT FROM GETTYSBURG (MARYLAND)
(July 6–16, 1863)

Source	Confederate	Union
Alexander, "Ten Days"[270]	5,000+*	1,000+*
Fox, *Regimental Losses*[271]	34 killed	99 killed
	195 wounded	379 wounded
	241 missing	356 missing
Author's Best Estimate:	**5,000***	**1,000***

SCATTERED FIGHTING IN VIRGINIA (July 21–August 27, 1863)

Source	Confederate	Union
Fox, *Regimental Losses*[272]		76 killed
		224 wounded
		95 missing

BRISTOE STATION (October 14, 1863)(Lee not present)

Source	Confederate	Union
Berkoff, "Botched Battle"[273]	1,302*	331*
Current, *Encyclopedia*[274]	<1,400*	<600*
Fox, *Regimental Losses*[275]	136 killed	50 killed
	797 wounded	335 wounded
	445 missing	161 missing
Heidler & Heidler, *Encyclopedia*[276]	c. 1400*	546*
McPherson, *Atlas*[277]	1,360*	350*
Author's Best Estimate:	**1,378***	**546***

KELLY'S FORD (November 7, 1863)

Source	Confederate	Union
Fox, *Regimental Losses*[278]	359*	6 killed
		50 wounded
		22 missing

RAPPAHANNOCK STATION (November 7, 1863)

Source	Confederate	Union
Fox, *Regimental Losses*[279]	1,674*	83 killed
		328 wounded
		6 missing

KELLY'S FORD & RAPPAHANNOCK STATION
(November 7, 1863)

Source	Confederate	Union
Current, *Encyclopedia*[280]	2,023*	264*
Heidler & Heidler, *Encyclopedia*[281]	almost 2,000*	400*
McPherson, *Atlas*[282]	1,800 captured	
Weigley, *American Way of War*[283]	2,023*	419*
Welsh, *Dual Disasters*[284]	2,000+*	419*
Author's Best Estimate:	**2,000***	**400***

MINE RUN (Nov. 27–December 1, 1863)

Source	Confederate	Union
Current, *Encyclopedia*[285]	601*	1,653*
Foote, *Civil War*[286]	629*	1,653*
Fox, *Regimental Losses*[287]	110 killed	173 killed
	570 wounded	1,099 wounded
	65 missing	381 missing
Fuller, *Grant and Lee*[288]	110 killed	173 killed
	570 wounded	1,099 wounded
	65 missing	381 missing
Heidler & Heidler, *Encyclopedia*[289]	545*	950*
Livermore, *Numbers*[290]	110 killed	173 killed
	570 wounded	1,099 wounded
	65 missing	381 missing
Phisterer, *Statistics*[291]	500*	100 killed
		400 wounded
Author's Best Estimates:	**601***	**1,653***

POST-GETTYSBURG CASUALTIES IN 1863
(July 4–December 31, 1863)

Source	Confederate	Union
Foote, *Civil War*[292]	4,255*	4,406*

LEE'S ARMY'S BATTLES AND CAMPAIGNS IN 1864–1865

Since Lee and Grant fought head-to-head in 1864 and 1865, the statistics for those years apply equally to Lee and Grant. See the Grant numbers in Appendix I for detailed numbers that also apply to Lee. The following are the author's best estimates of the Lee- and Grant-related casualties for those years.

Campaign/Battle	Confederate	Union
WILDERNESS (May 5–7, 1864)	11,125*	17,666*
SPOTSYLVANIA COURT HOUSE		
(May 8–21, 1864)	13,421*	18,399*
NORTH ANNA, TOTOPOTOMOY,		
BETHESDA CHURCH AND		
SHERIDAN'S CAVALRY RAID		
(May 23–June 1, 1864)		
(Lee present at North Anna only)	3,766*	3,986*
COLD HARBOR		
(May 31–June 12, 1864)	4,595*	12,737*
PETERSBURG ASSAULTS		
(June 15–18,1864)		
(Lee not present)	4,000*	11,386*
PETERSBURG SIEGE/CAMPAIGN		
(June 15, 1864–April 3, 1865)	28,000*	42,000*
APPOMATTOX CAMPAIGN		
(April 2–9, 1865)	41,666	10,780

SUMMARY TABLE OF AUTHOR'S ESTIMATES OF CASUALTIES INCURRED BY BOTH SIDES IN MAJOR CAMPAIGNS AND BATTLES OF ROBERT E. LEE

Campaign/Battle	Total Confederate Casualties	Total Union Casualties
Seven Days'	20,000*	16,000*
Cedar Mountain	1,300*	2,400*
Second Manassas	9,500*	14,400*
Chantilly	800*	1,300*
Harper's Ferry	286*	11,783*
Crampton's Gap & South Mountain	3,434*	2,346*

Antietam/Sharpsburg	11,500*	12,400*
Fredericksburg	4,201*	12,653*
Kelly's Ford	133*	78*
Chancellorsville	12,764*	17,287*
Brandy Station	523*	866*
Winchester (June 1863)	269*	4,443*
Aldie, Middleburg, Upperville	510*	613*
Hanover	150*	200*
Gettysburg	28,000*	23,000*
Retreat from Gettysburg	5,000*	1,000*
Bristoe Station	1,378*	546*
Kelly's Ford & Rappahannock Stn.	2,000*	400*
Mine Run	601*	1,653*
Wilderness	11,125*	17,666*
Spotsylvania Court House	13,421*	18,399*
North Anna River, etc.	3,766*	3,986*
Cold Harbor	4,595*	12,737*
Petersburg Assaults	4,000*	11,386*
Petersburg Siege/Campaign	28,000*	42,000*
Appomattox Campaign	41,666*	10,780*
TOTALS (killed, wounded, missing/captured)	208,922*	240,322*
NET DIFFERENCE	+31,400*	

ACKNOWLEDGMENTS

Special credit for his lucid maps goes to my cartographer, David Deis of Dreamline Cartography of Northridge, California. His professionalism, promptness, and patience are remarkable.

The following readers of my manuscript provided me with many critical comments and invaluable advice. Due to their diligence and knowledge, the book's quality was vastly improved and many errors were avoided.

These reviewers were:

- Mary Crouter, long-time colleague and wordsmith par excellence;
- Ed Baldridge, mentor, teacher, and historian;
- Larry Clowers, the Ulysses Grant of the 2000s;
- Steve Farbman, an editor with an inquiring mind;
- Doré Hunter, my first government boss and lifelong friend;

- Brian Jones, remarkably creative writer;
- Elaine Economides Joost, my last government boss and a great editor;
- James MacDonald, a perfectionist at all he touches;
- Chic Pollock, intellectual professor;
- Kaye Pollock, lifelong educator;
- Ed Powell, military mastermind, and
- Gary Rosecrans, a polished professor.

Special thanks to Maria Ruhl, Regnery's Managing Editor, and especially to Tess Civantos, Assistant Managing Editor, for making this manuscript reader-friendly for non-academic readers. Finally, I appreciate the cooperation of Harry Crocker, Vice President and Executive Editor of Regnery, and Alex Novak, Associate Publisher of Regnery History, for making this softcover edition happen.

As to those errors that remain in this book, I take full responsibility.

NOTES

CHAPTER 1

1. Grant, Ulysses S., *Memoirs and Selected Letters: Personal Memoirs of U.S. Grant, Selected Letters 1839–1865* (New York: Literary Classics of the United States, Inc., 1990) (Reprint of 1885 edition) [hereafter Grant, *Memoirs*], p. 27.

2. Ibid., pp. 28–29, 1122; Warner, Ezra J., *Generals in Blue: Lives of the Union Commanders* (Baton Rouge and London: Louisiana State University Press, 1964) [hereafter Warner, *Generals in Blue*], pp. 183–84; Simon, John Y. (ed.), *The Papers of Ulysses Grant* (28 vols.)(Carbondale and Edwardsville: Southern Illinois University Press, 1967–2006)[hereafter *Papers of Grant*], I, pp. 3–4; Smith, Jean Edward, *Grant* (New York: Simon & Schuster, 2001)[hereafter Smith, *Grant*], p. 25; Catton, Bruce, *U.S. Grant and the American Military Tradition* (Boston: Little, Brown and Company, 1954)[hereafter Catton, *Grant*], pp. 15, 19. Congressman Thomas Hamer appointed Ulysses to the Military Academy, at the request of Jesse Grant despite the fact that an 1832 political dispute had led the elder Grant to attack Hamer in the appropriately named Georgetown, Ohio, *The Castigator* (Sept. 25, 1832) ("...he would at any time sacrifice a tried personal friend, to buy over two enemies, who will answer present purpose:—That he cares not who sinks as long as he swims—and that he is alike faithless in his political principles, and his personal attachments."). Smith, *Grant*, p. 25.

3. Grant, *Memoirs*, p. 129.

4. Ibid., pp. 31–35, 1122–23; Warner, *Generals in Blue*, p. 184.

5. Smith, *Grant*, p. 28.

6. Grant, *Memoirs*, pp. 34–35.

7. Ibid., pp. 36–39, 1123; Warner, *Generals in Blue*, p. 184; *Papers of Grant*, I, xxxvii.

8. Nagel, *Lees of Virginia*, pp. 164–82; Thomas, Emory M., *Robert E. Lee: A Biography* (New York and London: W.W. Norton & Company, 1995) [hereafter Thomas, *Lee*], pp. 23–29.

9. Nagel, *Lees of Virginia*, pp. 164–84; Thomas, *Lee*, pp. 24–36; Connelly, *Marble Man*, p. 177.

10. Thomas, *Lee*, p. 40; Nagel, *Lees of Virginia*, pp. 207–26; Connelly, *Marble Man*, p. 177.

11. Thomas, *Lee*, p. 44.

12. Ibid., pp. 36–55.

13. *Papers of Grant*, I, xxxvii.

14. Grant, *Memoirs*, pp. 41–42. It should be noted that Grant's statements of opposition to the Mexican War primarily occurred decades later when it was convenient to attack the war brought on by a Democratic president. Winders, Richard Bruce, *Polk's Army: The American Military Experience in the Mexican War* (College Station: Texas A&M University Press, 1997), pp. 204–6.

15. McWhiney, Grady and Jamieson, Perry D., *Attack and Die: Civil War Military Tactics and the Southern Heritage* (Tuscaloosa: The University of Alabama Press, 1982) [hereafter McWhiney and Jamieson, *Attack and Die*], p. 156.

16. Grant, *Memoirs*, p. 50.

17. Smith, *Grant*, pp. 42, 52–53.

18. Grant to Julia Dent, May 11, 1846, *Papers of Grant*, I, pp. 84–87 at 86.

19. Grant, *Memoirs*, p. 65, 81, 1124; Smith, *Grant*, p. 56.

20. McPherson, James N., "The Unheroic Hero," *The New York Review of Books*, LXVI, No. 2 (Feb. 4, 1999), pp. 16–19 [hereafter McPherson, "Unheroic Hero"], pp. 16–17.

21. Grant, *Memoirs*, pp. 69–70. "Back of the famous soldier who was to go slouching off to the supreme moment of his career at Appomattox Courthouse wearing a private's blouse, mud-stained pants and boots and no sword

at all, stood somewhere the remembered example of Old Rough-and-Ready, who would have done it just the same way." Catton, *Grant*, p. 28.

22. Murphy, Brian John, "Grant versus Lee," *Civil War Times*, XLIII, No. 1 (April 2004), pp. 42–49, 63–66 [hereafter Murphy, "Grant versus Lee"] at p. 45.

23. McPherson, "Unheroic Hero," p. 16; Grant, *Memoirs*, pp. 83–85; Catton, *Grant*, p. 37. Polk's treatment of Taylor backfired: "General Taylor's victory at Buena Vista, February 22d, 23d, and 24th, 1847, with an army composed almost entirely of volunteers who had not been in battle before, and over a vastly superior force numerically, made his nomination for the Presidency by the Whigs a foregone conclusion." Grant, *Memoirs*, p. 85. Ironically, Polk, in May 1846, had initially replaced Scott with Taylor when Scott complained that Polk's interference placed him in "the most perilous of all positions, a fire upon my rear from Washington and the fire in front from the Mexicans." Wheelan, Joseph, "Polk's Manifest Destiny," *The History Channel Magazine*, Vol. 4, No. 1 (Jan./Feb. 2006), pp. 41–45 at p. 43.

24. Smith, *Grant*, p. 67; Marshall-Cornwall, James, *Grant as Military Commander* (New York: Barnes & Noble Books, 1995) (Reprint of 1970 edition) [hereafter Marshall-Cornwall, *Grant*], p. 31.

25. Thomas, *Lee*, pp. 113–42.

26. Ibid., pp. 140–41; Murphy, "Grant versus Lee," p. 45.

27. Ibid., p. 152.

28. Ibid., p. 64.

29. Ibid., pp. 36, 64, 69.

30. Jamieson, Perry D., "Background to Bloodshed: The Tactics of the U.S.–Mexican War and the 1850s," *North & South*, Vol. 4, No. 6 (Aug. 2001), pp. 24–31 [hereafter Jamieson, "Background"] at p. 29.

31. McWhiney & Jamieson, *Attack and Die*, pp. 28–29.

32. Jamieson, "Background," p. 30.

33. Thomas, *Lee*, p. 173, citing Lee to Edward Childe, January 9, 1857.

34. Ibid., p. 186, citing Lee to Rooney Lee, December 3, 1860.

35. Ibid., citing Lee to Annette Carter, January 16, 1861, and Lee to Markie Williams, January 22, 1861.

36. Ibid., pp.130–31, 1125–26.

37. Grant to Julia Dent Grant, Aug. 9, 1852, *Papers of Grant*, I, pp. 251–53.

38. Anderson, "Grant's Struggle with Alcohol," p. 20; Grant, *Memoirs*, p. 1126.

39. *Papers of Grant*, I, pp. 311–15; Anderson, "Grant's Struggle with Alcohol," pp.19–20.

40. Grant to Julia Dent Grant, Feb. 2, 1854, *Papers of Grant*, I, pp. 316–18.

41. Grant to Julia Dent Grant, Feb. 6, 1854, Ibid., pp. 320–22.

42. Grant to Julia Dent Grant, Mar. 6 and 25, 1854, Ibid., pp. 322–24, 326–28.

43. Ibid., pp. 328–33. There is considerable dispute about whether Grant was drunk while serving as a paymaster at Humboldt, California. See Epperson, James F., Letter to Editor, *Columbiad*, Vol. 3, No. 2 (Summer 1999), pp. 8–9, citing the following from Charles Ellington's *The Trial of U.S. Grant*: "At this date, so far removed from the time in question, it is impossible to know whether the payroll episode did indeed take place." Jean Edward Smith concluded that circumstantial evidence indicates that the "story rings true." Smith, *Grant*, p. 87.

44. Ibid., pp. 1126–27; Warner, *Generals in Blue*, p. 184. Drinking problems may have been the immediate cause of Grant's resignation, and he may have had no more than a few off-duty drinking bouts during the Civil War. He had no drinking problem when he was with his wife, and when Grant was away from her his friend and chief-of-staff, John Rawlins, usually kept him from drinking. McPherson, "Unheroic Hero," p. 19.

45. Anderson, "Grant's Struggle with Alcohol," pp. 20–21. "Grant had served in the Army for fifteen years, performed well, and gained valuable experience. During those fifteen years, he had occasionally indulged in periods of drinking, but these generally had been confined to social occasions or when he had little to occupy his time and was separated from his family. There is no indication that prior to his resignation Grant drank more than was typical for a man of the time. Unfortunately, Grant incautiously allowed others to see him when inebriated, and he left the Army with a reputation as a heavy drinker." Ibid., p. 21.

46. Grant, *Memoirs*, pp. 141–42, 1127–28; *Papers of Grant*, I, pp. 336–55; Warner, *Generals in Blue*, p. 184.

47. Grant, *Memoirs*, p. 1128; Warner, *Generals in Blue*, p. 184; Anderson, "Grant's Struggle with Alcohol," p. 21.

CHAPTER 2

1. Grant, *Memoirs*, pp. 152–55, 1128–29; Smith, *Grant*, pp. 100–105.

2. Grant, *Memoirs*, pp. 157–59; Anderson, "Grant's Struggle with Alcohol," p. 21; Smith, *Grant*, pp. 105–7.

3. Fuller, J. F. C., *Grant and Lee: A Study in Personality and Generalship* (Bloomington: University of Indiana Press, 1957) (reprint of 1932 edition) [hereafter Fuller, *Grant and Lee*], p. 59.

4. Grant, *Memoirs*, pp. 160–62, 1129; Smith, *Grant*, pp. 107–111.

5. Orders No. 7, June 18, 1861, *Papers of Grant*, II, pp. 45–46.

6. Smith, *Grant*, pp. 108–9.

7. Ibid., p. 111.

8. Grant, *Memoirs*, pp. 163–65.

9. Ibid., pp. 168–71, 1129. Grant's appointment as brigadier general was backdated to May 17, 1861, making him thirty-fifth in seniority in the U.S. Army (headed by Winfield Scott). Smith, *Grant*, p. 113.

10. Grant to Captain Speed Butler, August 23, 1861, *Papers of Grant*, II, p. 131. The "Pillow" reference is to Confederate Brigadier General Gideon J. Pillow, who gained notoriety in the Mexican War for having a ditch dug on the wrong side of his fortifications.

11. Smith, *Grant*, p. 116.

12. Grant, *Memoirs*, pp. 171–73, 1129; Smith, *Grant*, pp. 117–18.

13. Roberts, Donald J., II, "Belmont: Grant's First Battle," *Military Heritage*, Vol. 2, No. 6 (June 2001) [hereafter Roberts, "Belmont"], pp. 40–49 at p. 43.

14. Grant, *Memoirs*, pp. 172–75, 1129; Smith, *Grant*, pp. 118–20. In addition to notifying Frémont of his intended move on Paducah, Grant also sent a telegram to the speaker of the Kentucky legislature advising him of the Confederate occupation of Columbus in violation of that Commonwealth's neutrality. Grant, *Memoirs*, p. 176; Smith, *Grant*, p.119.

15. Feis, William, *Grant's Secret Service: The Intelligence War from Belmont to Appomattox* (Lincoln, Nebraska, and London: The University of Nebraska Press, 2002) [hereafter Feis, *Grant's Secret Service*], pp. 21–25.

16. Nagel, *Lees of Virginia*, p. 267; Thomas, *Lee*, pp. 187–88. The offer to Lee reflected General Scott's admiration for Lee, who had performed heroically under Scott during the Mexican War.

17. Lee to Sydney Smith Lee, April 20, 1861, Dowdey, Clifford and Manarin, Louis H., *The Wartime Papers of R. E. Lee* (New York: Bramhall House, 1961) [hereafter *Papers of Lee*], p. 10 [emphasis added]. Because Dowdey and Manarin took the liberty of correcting Lee's spelling and grammatical errors,

more accurate versions of Lee's correspondence often can be found else-where.

18. Union General Winfield Scott, also a native Virginian, had received the first offer of this position but declined. Allan, William, "Memoranda of Conversations with General Robert E. Lee," pp. 7–24, [hereafter Allan, "Conversations"] in Gallagher, Gary W. (ed.), *Lee the Soldier* (Lincoln and London: University of Nebraska Press, 1996) [hereafter Gallagher, *Lee the Soldier*], p.10.

19. Crocker, H. W., III, *Robert E. Lee on Leadership: Executive Lessons in Character, Courage, and Vision* (Roseville, California: Prima Publishing, 1999, 2000) [hereafter Crocker, *Lee*], pp. 49–50.

20. Thomas, *Lee*, pp. 189–98; Nagel, *Lees of Virginia*, pp. 268–71.

21. Fleming, Martin K., "The Northwestern Virginia Campaign of 1861: McClellan's Rising Star—Lee's Dismal Debut," *Blue & Gray Magazine*, X, Issue 6 (Aug. 1993), pp. 10–17, 48–54, 59–65 [hereafter Fleming, "Northwestern Virginia Campaign"], p. 16.

22. Waugh, John C., *The Class of 1846: From West Point to Appomattox: Stonewall Jackson, George McClellan and Their Brothers* (New York: Warner Books, Inc., 1994) [hereafter Waugh, *Class of 1846*], p. 265.

23. Wiley, Bell Irvin, *The Road to Appomattox* (Baton Rouge and London: Louisiana State University Press, 1994; originally Memphis: Memphis State College Press, 1956) [hereafter Wiley, *Road to Appomattox*], p. 47.

CHAPTER 3

1. An excellent synopsis of the fighting in western Virginia is found in Fleming, "Northwestern Virginia Campaign," *supra*.

2. On Lee's western Virginia experiences, see Freeman, Douglas Southall, *R. E. Lee*, 4 vols. (New York and London: Charles Scribner's Sons, 1934–5) [hereafter Freeman, *R. E. Lee*], I, pp. 531–604; Newell, Clayton R., *Lee vs. McClellan: The First Campaign* (Washington, D.C.: Regnery Publishing, Inc., 1996) [hereafter Newell, *Lee vs. McClellan*].

3. Freeman, *R. E. Lee*, I, pp. 552–53; Newell, *Lee vs. McClellan*, 216, 232.

4. Fleming, "Northwestern Virginia Campaign," p. 62. Freeman and Newell share Fleming's judgment that Lee seriously erred in relying upon Colonel

Rust for this critical assignment. Freeman, *R. E. Lee*, I, p. 575 (referring to Rust as "an unskilled volunteer"); Newell, *Lee vs. McClellan*, pp. 232–33.

5.   Freeman, *R. E. Lee*, I, p. 594; Newell, *Lee vs. McClellan*, p. 238; Fuller, *Grant and Lee*, pp. 137–38.

6.   "[Lee's] habit of issuing broad orders and leaving details to his subordinates had led to a series of lost opportunities as the Confederate military leaders in western Virginia delayed and bickered." Newell, *Lee vs. McClellan*, p. 263.

7.   Lee, Captain Robert E., *Recollections and Letters of General Robert E. Lee* (New York: Konecky & Konecky, 1966) [hereafter Lee, *Recollections*], pp. 52–53.

8.   Feis, *Grant's Secret Service*, pp. 48–52; Foote, Shelby, *The Civil War: A Narrative* (New York: Random House, 1958–1974) (3 vols.) [hereafter Foote, *Civil War*], I, p. 149.

9.   Roberts, "Belmont," pp. 43–45. Polk's son described the effect of Grant's deceptions: "Polk had been deterred from sending in the first instance a larger force to meet Grant's attack by the reports which his scouts made of the movements of the transports upon the river, and of the position and numbers of the columns from Fort Holt and Paducah,—all tending to show that the landing upon the opposite shore of the river was a mere feint, while the real design was an attack on Columbus." Polk, William M., "General Polk and the Battle of Belmont," in Johnson, Robert Underwood and Buel, Clarence Clough (eds.), *Battles and Leaders of the Civil War*, 4 vols. (New York: Thomas Yoseloff, Inc., 1956; reprint of Secaucus, New Jersey: Castle, 1887–8) [hereafter Johnson and Buel, *Battles and Leaders*], I, pp. 348–57 at p. 349.

10.   Roberts, "Belmont," pp. 45–49; Grant, *Memoirs*, pp. 177–84; Smith, *Grant*, pp. 128–30; McFeely, William S., *Grant: A Biography* (New York and London: W.W. Norton & Company, 1981) [hereafter McFeely, *Grant*], p. 93.

11.   Wallace, Lew, "The Capture of Fort Donelson," in Johnson and Buel, *Battles and Leaders*, I, pp. 328–429 [hereafter Wallace, "Donelson"] at p. 404.

12.   Smith, *Grant*, pp. 133–34.

13.   Fox, William F., *Regimental Losses in the American Civil War, 1861–1865: A Treatise on the Extent and Nature of the Mortuary Losses in the Union Regiments, with Full and Exhaustive Statistics Compiled from the Official Records on File in the State Military Bureaus and at Washington* (Dayton: Morningside House, Inc., 1985) (Reprint of Albany: Brandow Printing Company, 1898) [hereafter Fox, *Regimental Losses*], pp. 543, 549. For details on casualties in

this and later battles and campaigns of Grant, see Appendix I, "Casualties in Grant's Battles and Campaigns." There I have listed others' estimates of casualties and then made my own best estimate of those casualties—by selecting or combining the estimates I found most reliable.

14. Grant, *Memoirs*, pp. 185–86; Roberts, "Belmont," p. 49; Smith, *Grant*, pp. 130–32; Hattaway, Herman, and Jones, Archer, *How the North Won: A Military History of the Civil War* (Urbana and Chicago: University of Illinois Press, 1983, 1991) [hereafter Hattaway and Jones, *How the North Won*], p. 53.

15. Grant, *Memoirs*, p. 188; Feis, *Grant's Secret Service*, p. 63.

16. Grant, *Memoirs*, p. 189; Smith, *Grant*, pp. 135–40; McFeely, *Grant*, pp. 96–97; Catton, Bruce, *Grant Moves South* (Boston: Little, Brown and Company, 1960)[hereafter Catton, *Grant Moves South*], pp. 123–25, 129–32; Grant to Halleck, January 28 and 29, 1862, *Papers of Grant*, IV, pp. 99–102. Grant's problems in dealing with Halleck have been ascribed by British Major-General and military historian J. F. C. Fuller to Halleck's being a "cautious, witless pedant who had studied war, and imagined that adherence to certain strategical and tactical maxims constituted the height of generalship." Fuller added, "It may be said, without fear of contradiction, that throughout the war Halleck was worth much more than the proverbial army corps to the Confederate forces." Fuller, J. F. C., *The Generalship of Ulysses S. Grant* (New York: Da Capo Press, Inc., 1991) (reprint of 1929 edition)[hereafter Fuller, *Generalship of Grant*], p. 79.

17. Smith, *Grant*, pp. 140–41.

18. Grant, *Memoirs*, pp. 189–90; Cooling, Benjamin Franklin, "Forts Henry and Donelson: Union Victory on the Twin Rivers," *Blue & Gray Magazine*, IX, Issue 3 (Feb. 1992), pp. 10–20, 45–53 [hereafter Cooling, "Forts"] at p. 13; Smith, *Grant*, p. 141.

19. Cooling, Benjamin Franklin, *Forts Henry and Donelson: The Key to the Confederate Heartland* (Knoxville: The University of Tennessee Press, 1987) [hereafter Cooling, *Forts*], pp. 101–11; Cooling, "Forts," pp. 13–17; Smith, *Grant*, p. 147; Taylor, Jesse, "The Defense of Fort Henry," in Johnson and Buel, *Battles and Leaders*, I, pp. 368–72 at pp. 370–71.

20. Cooling, "Forts," p. 20; Smith, *Grant*, p. 153.

21. Cooling, *Forts*, pp. 115–23.

22. Grant, *Memoirs*, pp. 190–95; Cooling, "Forts," p. 17; Smith, *Grant*, p. 148; Cooling, *Forts*, pp. 113–15.

23. Cooling, "Forts," p. 20.

24. Smith, *Grant*, p. 149.

25. Grant, *Memoirs*, pp. 196–97. The Fort Donelson operation marked the beginning of the great partnership between Grant and Sherman, which is discussed in Glatthaar, Joseph T., *Partners in Command: The Relationships Between Leaders in the Civil War* (New York: The Free Press, 1994)[hereafter Glatthaar, *Partners in Command*], pp. 135–61 and Flood, Charles Bracelon, *Grant and Sherman: The Friendship That Won the Civil War* (New York: Farrar, Straus and Giroux, 2005).

26. For details of the Battle of Fort Donelson. See Gott, Kendall D., *Where the South Lost the War: An Analysis of the Fort Henry–Fort Donelson Campaign, February 1862* (Mechanicsburg, Pennsylvania: Stackpole Books, 2003) [hereafter Gott, *Where the South Lost*]; Cooling, *Forts*, and Cooling, "Forts."

27. Cooling, *Forts*, pp. 140–46; Cooling, "Forts," pp. 45–46; Wallace, "Donelson," pp. 411–2.

28. Cooling, *Forts*, pp. 147–60; Cooling, "Forts," pp. 46–47; Wallace, "Donelson," pp. 413–14.

29. Cooling, *Forts*, pp. 166–83; Cooling, "Forts," pp. 47–48; Wallace, "Donelson," pp. 415–21. Major General Lew Wallace later rhetorically asked, "Why did [Floyd] not avail himself of the dearly bought opportunity, and march his army out?" Ibid., p. 418.

30. Wallace, "Donelson," pp. 421–22.

31. Grant, *Memoirs*, p. 205.

32. Cooling, *Forts*, pp. 183–99; Cooling, "Forts," pp. 48–49; Smith, *Grant*, pp. 157–60.

33. Smith, *Grant*, p. 160.

34. Grant, *Memoirs*, pp. 197–207; Cooling, *Forts*, pp. 200–23; Cooling, "Forts," pp. 51–52; Smith, *Grant*, pp. 160–61; Wallace, "Donelson." pp. 425–26.

35. Grant, *Memoirs*, pp. 207–11; Smith, *Grant*, pp. 165–66; Wallace, "Donelson," pp. 426–28; Grant to Buckner, Feb. 16, 1862, *Papers of Grant*, IV, p. 218; Buckner to Grant, Feb. 16, 1862, Ibid., note.

36. Selcer, Richard F., "A Legend Is Born," *Civil War Times*, XLV, No. 10 (Jan. 2007), pp. 22–31.

37. Williams, T. Harry, *McClellan, Sherman and Grant* (New Brunswick: Rutgers University Press, 1962)[hereafter Williams, *McClellan, Sherman and Grant*], p. 88.

38. Cooling, "Forts," p. 49.

39. Ibid., p. 52.

40. Grant to Brigadier General George W. Cullum, *Papers of Grant*, IV, p. 223.

41. Foote, *Civil War*, I, pp. 214–15.

42. Davis, William C., *Jefferson Davis: The Man and His Hour* (Baton Rouge: Louisiana State University Press, 1991)[hereafter Davis, *Jefferson Davis*], pp. 398–99.

43. Jones, J. B., *A Rebel War Clerk's Diary at the Confederate States Capital* (Philadelphia: J. B. Lippincott & Co., 1866) (1982 reprint) (2 vols.) [hereafter Jones, *Diary*], I, p. 111.

44. Grant, *Memoirs*, p. 214; Cooling, "Forts," p. 53; Smith, *Grant*, pp. 151–52, 164, 166.

45. Catton, Bruce, *Terrible Swift Sword* (Garden City, New York: Doubleday & Company, Inc., 1963), p. 163.

46. Hattaway and Jones, *How the North Won*, xv.

47. Fox, *Regimental Losses*, pp. 543, 549. See Appendix I.

48. Davis, Jefferson, *The Rise and Fall of the Confederate Government*, 2 vols. (New York: Da Capo Press, Inc., 1990; reprint of 1881 edition)[hereafter Davis, *Rise and Fall*], p. 376; Thomas, *Lee*, p. 212, citing Jefferson Davis to Joseph E. Brown, November 6, 1861. Freeman also concluded that Davis wrote to the two governors because of strong opposition to Lee. Freeman, *R. E. Lee*, I, p. 607.

49. Thomas, *Lee*, pp. 215–16; Weigley, Russell F., *The American Way of War: A History of United States Military Strategy and Policy* (New York: Macmillan Publishing Co., Inc., 1973) [hereafter Weigley, *American Way of War*], p. 101.

50. On Lee's service in the Southeast, see Freeman, *R. E. Lee*, I, pp. 605–31; Thomas, *Lee*, pp. 212–17 (Chapter 17, "Low–Country Gentlemen Curse Lee").

CHAPTER 4

1. Smith, *Grant*, pp. 168–71; Buell, Thomas B., *The Warrior Generals: Combat Leadership in the Civil War* (New York: Crown Publishers, Inc., 1997) [hereafter Buell, *Warrior Generals*], pp. 168–70.

2. McFeely, *Grant*, p. 104; Halleck to McClellan, March 3, 1862, *The War of Rebellion: A Compilation of the Official Records of the Union and Confederate*

Armies (Washington: Government Printing Office, 1880–1901) (128 vols.) [hereafter OR], Ser. I, VII, p. 680, *Papers of Grant*, Vol. 4, p. 320n; Halleck to Grant, March 4, 1862, OR, Ser. I, X, Part II, p. 3, *Papers of Grant*, Vol. 4, pp. 319–20n; Grant, *Memoirs*, pp. 219–20; Grant, Ulysses S., "The Battle of Shiloh," in Johnson and Buel, *Battles and Leaders*, I, pp. 464–86 [hereafter Grant, "Shiloh"] at pp. 465–66; Halleck to Grant, March 4, 1862, *Papers of Grant*, IV, p. 319–21n.

3.   Halleck to Grant, March 6, 1862, OR, Ser. I, X, Part II, p. 15 (misdated Feb. 6, 1862), *Papers of Grant*, Vol. 4, p. 331n; Grant to Halleck, March 7 and 9, 1862, OR, Ser. I, X, Part 2, pp. 15, 21, *Papers of Grant*, Vol. 4, pp. 331, 334; Grant, *Memoirs*, p. 220; Badeau, Adam, *Military History of Ulysses S. Grant, from April, 1861, to April, 1865* (New York: D. Appleton and Company, 1868) (3 vols.) [hereafter Badeau, *Grant*], I, p. 60.

4.   Halleck to McClellan, March 3, 1862, OR, Ser. I, VII, pp. 679–80, *Papers of Grant*, Vol. 4, p. 320n; McClellan to Halleck, March 3, 1862, OR, Ser. I, VII, p. 680, *Papers of Grant*, Vol. 4, p. 320n; Halleck to McClellan, March 4, 1862, OR, Ser. I, VII, p. 682, *Papers of Grant*, Vol. 4, p. 320n; Williams, *McClellan, Sherman and Grant*, pp. 90–91; Grant, *Memoirs*, pp. 220–21; Allen, Stacy D., "Shiloh! The Campaign and First Day's Battle," *Blue & Gray Magazine*, Vol. XIV, Issue 3 (Feb. 1997), pp. 6–27, 46–64 [hereafter Allen, "Shiloh! I"] at p. 13; Smith, *Grant*, pp. 172–77; *Papers of Grant*, IV, pp. 319–59; Badeau, *Grant*, pp. 60–8; Marszalek, John, "Henry Halleck Captures Corinth in 1862," *Civil War Times* (Feb. 2006), historynet.com/cuti/bl–henry–halleck/–64k; Murphy, Brian J., "The Secret War Between Grant & Halleck," *Civil War Times*, XLV, No. 6 (August 2006), pp. 44–49 at p. 49.2

5.   Grant, *Memoirs*, pp. 222–23.

6.   Catton, Bruce, "The Generalship of Ulysses S. Grant," [hereafter Catton, "Generalship of Grant"] in McWhiney, Grady (ed.), *Grant, Lee, Lincoln and the Radicals: Essays on Civil War Leadership* (New York: Harper & Row, 1966) (Reprint of Chicago: Northwestern University Press, 1964), pp. 3–30 [hereafter McWhiney, *Grant, Lee*] at p. 14.

7.   Williams, *McClellan, Sherman and Grant*, p. 92; Grant, *Memoirs*, p. 223.

8.   Grant, *Memoirs*, pp. 224–25.

9.   For details and comprehensive battle-maps of the Battle of Shiloh, see Daniel, Larry J., *Shiloh: The Battle That Changed the Civil War* (New York: Simon & Schuster, 1997) [hereafter Daniel, *Shiloh*], pp. 143–292; Allen,

"Shiloh! I"; Allen, Stacy D., "Shiloh! The Second Day's Battle and Aftermath," *Blue & Gray Magazine*, XIV, No. 4 (April 1997), pp. 6–27, 45–55 [hereafter Allen, "Shiloh! II"]. Also see Johnson and Buel, *Battles and Leaders*, I, pp. 464–610.

10. Allen, "Shiloh! I," p. 24; Grant to Halleck, April 5, 1862, *Papers of Grant*, V, p. 13; Grant to Halleck, Ibid., pp. 13–14 at p. 14.

11. Allen, "Shiloh! I," pp. 19–21.

12. Allen, "Shiloh! I," pp. 46–47.

13. Grant, *Memoirs*, pp. 225–26; Allen, "Shiloh! II," pp. 8–10.

14. Grant, *Memoirs*, pp. 226, 236; Swift, Gloria Baker and Stephens, Gail, "Honor Redeemed: Lew Wallace's Military Career and the Battle of Monocacy," *North & South*, Vol. 4, No. 2 (Jan. 2001), pp. 34–46 [hereafter Swift & Stephens, "Honor Redeemed"] at pp. 36–39; Johnson and Buel, *Battles and Leaders*, I, pp. 607–10. For more on the Grant/Wallace miscommunication and dispute, see "'If He Had Less Rank': Lewis Wallace," in Woodworth, Steven E. (ed.), *Grant's Lieutenants from Cairo to Vicksburg* (Lawrence: University Press of Kansas, 2001) [hereafter Woodworth, *Grant's Lieutenants*], pp. 63–89.

15. Swift & Stephens, "Honor Redeemed," pp. 38–39 [editorial note by Keith Poulter]; June 21, 1885 note of Ulysses S. Grant in Grant, "Shiloh," pp. 468–69; Allen, "Shiloh! II," p. 10.

16. Woodworth, Steven E., "Shiloh's Harsh Training Ground," *America's Civil War*, pp. 34–40 [hereafter Woodworth, "Shiloh's Training Ground"]. Those three generals' divisions lost almost 7,000 of the nearly 11,000 casualties Grant's forces incurred at Shiloh. Ibid., p. 39.

17. Allen, "Shiloh! I," p. 47.

18. Ibid., pp. 24–27.

19. Grant, *Memoirs*, p. 227.

20. Allen, "Shiloh! I," p. 47.

21. Ibid., pp. 48–53; Johnston, William Preston, "Albert Sydney Johnston at Shiloh," in Johnson and Buel, *Battles and Leaders*, I, pp. 540–68 at pp. 564–65.

22. Allen, "Shiloh I," pp. 50–51.

23. Hinze, David C., "'At All Hazards': Ulysses S. Grant's instructions to Benjamin M. Prentiss left little doubt as to the importance of the Hornets' Nest at Shiloh," *Columbiad*, Vol. 3, No. 3 (Fall 1999), pp. 19–38 (hereafter Hinze, "'At All Hazards'") at pp. 19–27.

24. Ibid., pp. 24–29.

25. Ibid., pp. 29–30, quoting R. W. Hurdle, *Reminiscences of the Boys in Gray* (Mamie Yarey, editor) (New Orleans: Dante Publishing, 1912), p. 368.
26. Ibid., pp. 30–32; Grant, *Memoirs*, p. 228; Smith, Timothy B., "Myths of Shiloh," *America's Civil War*, Vol. 19, No. 2 (May 2006), pp. 30–36, 71 at pp. 33–36. Smith produced a postwar picture showing that the Hornets' Nest was a flat area, not a sunken road. Ibid., p. 33.
27. Hinze, "'At All Hazards,'" pp. 32–33; Woodworth, "Shiloh's Harsh," pp. 38–39; Allen, "Shiloh! I," p. 54.
28. Hattaway, "Changing Face," pp. 37–38.
29. Hinze, "'At All Hazards,'" pp. 32–36; Woodworth, "Shiloh's Training Ground," p. 39; Allen, "Shiloh I," p. 60. Grant may have thought that Prentiss had unnecessarily sacrificed troops by literally following Grant's order to "maintain that position at all hazards." Woodworth, "Shiloh's Training Ground," p. 39.
30. Allen, "Shiloh! I," pp. 60–61.
31. Hinze, "'At All Hazards,'" p. 36; Woodworth, "Shiloh's Harsh," p. 39
32. Grant, *Memoirs*, pp. 230–31.
33. Grant, "Shiloh," I, p. 474; Grant, *Memoirs*, p. 231.
34. Grant, "Shiloh," pp. 474–75; Beauregard, P. G. T., "The Campaign of Shiloh," in Johnson and Buel, *Battles and Leaders*, I, pp. 569–93 at p. 590; McWhiney and Jamieson, *Attack and Die*, p. 112; Suhr, Robert Collins, "Saving the Day at Shiloh," *America's Civil War*, XII, No. 6 (January 2000), pp. 34–41.
35. Allen, "Shiloh! II," p. 14.
36. Grant, *Memoirs*, pp. 232–33, 243–44; Allen, "Shiloh! I," p. 62.
37. Grant, *Memoirs*, pp. 233–34. When Grant had ordered Nelson's division to proceed from Savannah to Pittsburg Landing on the morning of April 6, Grant was not aware that Buell had arrived at Savannah and failed to report to Grant. Buell proceeded to hold Nelson's division at Savannah until 1:00 p.m., when Buell was personally satisfied that its advance was appropriate. Allen, "Shiloh! I," p. 47; Allen, "Shiloh! II," p.12
38. Grant, *Memoirs*, p. 234.
39. Ibid., pp. 234–35.
40. Beauregard to General S. Cooper, Asst. Adjutant-General, April 6, 1862, OR, Ser. I, Vol. X, Part I, p. 384.
41. Allen, "Shiloh! I," pp. 62–64.
42. Allen, "Shiloh! II," p. 7.

43. Smith, *Grant*, p. 204.

44. Allen, "Shiloh! II," pp. 10–14.

45. Ibid., pp. 14–19.

46. Grant, *Memoirs*, pp. 235–36; Allen, "Shiloh! II," pp. 10–27, 45–46, 51–54 (battle maps); Feis, *Grant's Secret Service*, pp. 100–1; Grant, "Shiloh," p. 478.

47. Allen, "Shiloh! II," p. 47; Weigley, *American Way of War*, p. 139.

48. Hattaway and Jones, *How the North Won*, p. 93.

49. Lee to John C. Pemberton, April 10, 1862, *Papers of Lee*, p. 145.

50. Lee to John C. Pemberton, April 20, 1862, Ibid., p. 150.

51. Lee to Thomas J. Jackson, April 21, 1862, OR, Ser. I, XII, Part III, pp. 859–60.

52. Lee to Thomas J. Jackson, April 25, 1862, Ibid., pp. 865–66.

53. Ibid. at p. 866; Glatthaar, *Partners in Command*, p. 23.

54. The Seven Days' Battle was the major exception.

55. Detailed accounts of the Peninsular Campaign, including the Seven Days' Battle, are in Sears, *To the Gates of Richmond: The Peninsular Campaign* (New York: Ticknor & Fields, 1992)[hereafter Sears, *To the Gates*]; Freeman, *R. E. Lee*, II, pp. 8–250; Nevins, Alan, *Ordeal of the Union* (New York and London: Charles Scribner's Sons, 1947–50) (8 vols.) [hereafter Nevins, *Ordeal*], VI, 34–64, 119–38.

56. Delcour, Melissa, "Lightning Strike in the Valley," *Military History*, Vol. 22, No. 3 (June 2005), pp. 26–32, 78.

57. For details of Jackson's Shenandoah Valley Campaign, see Robertson, James I., Jr., *Stonewall Jackson: the Man, the Soldier, the Legend* (New York: Macmillan Publishing USA, 1997) [hereafter Robertson, *Jackson*], pp. 323–457.

58. Livermore, Thomas L., *Numbers & Losses in the Civil War in America: 1861–1865* (Millwood, New York: Kraus reprint Co., 1977) (reprint of Bloomington: Indiana University Press, 1957) [hereafter Livermore, *Numbers & Losses*], p. 81.

59. Alexander, Bevin, *Lost Victories: The Military Genius of Stonewall Jackson* (New York: Henry Holt and Company, 1992)[hereafter Alexander, *Lost Victories*], pp. 80–81.

60. Reardon, Carol, "From 'King of Spades' to 'First Captain of the Confederacy': R. E. Lee's First Six Weeks with the Army of Northern Virginia," pp. 309–30 in Gallagher, *Lee the Soldier*, p. 312.

61. McClellan, with resources to spare and the necessity to win, should have been aggressive but was not; Lee, with scarce resources and only needing a deadlock, should have been defensive but was not.

62. Connelly, *Marble Man*, p. 17.

63. Gallagher, Gary W. (ed.), *Fighting for the Confederacy: The Personal Recollections of General Edward Porter Alexander* (Chapel Hill: University of North Carolina Press, 1989) [hereafter Alexander, *Fighting for the Confederacy*], p. 91.

64. Mewborn, Horace, "Jeb Stuart's Ride Around the Army of the Potomac, June 12–15, 1862," *Blue & Gray Magazine*, XV, Issue 6 (Aug. 1998), pp. 6–21, 46–54.

65. McClellan to Stanton, June 25, 1862, 6:15 p.m., OR, Ser. I, XI, Part I, p. 51.

66. Konstam, Angus, *Seven Days Battles 1862: Lee's Defense of Richmond* (Westport, Connecticut and London: Praeger, 2004), p. 24.

67. "Timing was all important; and unless all parts of the Confederate host acted in complete liaison, critical problems would arise instantly. Robertson, *Jackson*, p. 464.

68. Ibid., pp. 466–70.

69. "Nowhere in Jackson's orders was he required to be at a particular place at a specific time. He was unaware of how critical Lee and others thought it was to turn Porter's flank that afternoon. Hearing nothing from Lee, Jackson naturally concluded that nothing was pressing. Fighting would not take place until he got there." Ibid., p. 472. Historian David J. Eicher, however, described Jackson as the "weak link . . . whose performance was derelict" and concluded that four "times during the Seven Days battles Stonewall Jackson would exhibit lethargic, incompetent command behavior." Eicher, David J. *The Longest Night: A Military History of the Civil War* (New York: Simon & Schuster, 2002) [hereafter Eicher, *Longest Night*], p. 285.

70. Livermore, *Numbers & Losses*, p. 82.

71. Robertson, *Jackson*, pp. 466–98. For details of Jackson's exhausted condition and lack of sleep, as well as an ambiguous conclusion about the cause of his failure on June 30 (one of many Jackson failures at Seven Days'), see Freeman, *R. E. Lee*, II, Appendix II–3, "The Reason for Jackson's Failure at White Oak Swamp, June 30, 1862," pp. 572–82.

72. Robertson, *Jackson*, pp. 466–98.

73. "Jackson of the Chickahominy," *Civil War Times Illustrated*, XXVII, No. 2 (April 1988), pp. 30–33 at p. 32.

74. Robertson, *Jackson*, pp. 476–83.

75. Livermore, *Numbers & Losses*, pp. 82–83.

76. Porter, Fitz John, "Hanover Court House and Gaines's Mill," in Johnson and Buel, *Battles and Leaders*, II, pp. 319–343 at p. 343.

77. Robertson, *Jackson*, p. 484.

78. Alexander, *Lost Victories*, pp. 114–16.

79. Hill, Daniel H., "Lee Attacks North of the Chickahominy," in Johnson and Buel, *Battles and Leaders*, II, pp. 347–62 at pp. 361–62.

80. Robertson, *Jackson*, pp. 485–90.

81. Alexander, *Lost Victories*, p. 131.

82. Freeman, *R. E. Lee*, II, p. 176.

83. Sears, Stephen W., "Glendale: Opportunity Squandered," *North & South*, Vol. 5, No. 1 (Dec. 2001), pp. 12–24 [hereafter Sears, "Glendale"]; Robertson, *Jackson*, pp. 490–98. On the evening of June 30, Jackson fell asleep with food in his mouth while eating supper. Ibid., p. 495.

84. Alexander, *Fighting for the Confederacy*, pp. 110–11. E. Porter Alexander spent most of the war as the very competent artillery commander for James Longstreet's 1st Corps in Lee's Army of Northern Virginia. Because that army's artillery commander, William Nelson Pendleton, was incompetent, Alexander often served as Lee's *de facto* army artillery commander. Therefore, Alexander was a well-placed and reliable source.

85. Freeman, *R. E. Lee*, II, p. 202.

86. Robertson, *Jackson*, pp. 495–98. Two weeks later, Jackson said of his June 30 inactivity: "If General Lee had wanted me, He could have sent for me." Ibid., pp. 495–96.

87. Buell, *Warrior Generals*, p. 95.

88. Alexander, *Fighting for the Confederacy*, p. 111 (emphasis added).

89. Alexander, *Lost Victories*, p. 124; Wert, Jeffrey D., *General James Longstreet: The Confederacy's Most Controversial Soldier—A Biography* (New York: Simon & Schuster, 1993)[hereafter Wert, *Longstreet*], p. 146.

90. Robertson, *Jackson*, p. 501.

91. Ibid.

92. Bruce, George A., "Lee and the Strategy of the Civil War," pp. 111–38 [hereafter, Bruce, "Lee and Strategy"] in Gallagher, *Lee the Soldier*, p. 114.

93.   McWhiney & Jamieson, *Attack and Die*, p. 3.

94.   Ibid.

95.   Freeman, *R. E. Lee*, II, p. 218.

96.   Konstam, *Seven Days*, p. 81.

97.   Griffith, Paddy, *Battle Tactics of the Civil War*, (New Haven and London: Yale University Press, 1996) [hereafter Griffith, *Battle Tactics*], p. 170.

98.   Freeman, *R. E. Lee*, II, p. 218; Sears, *To the Gates*, p. 335; McWhiney & Jamieson, *Attack and Die*, p. 4. Some historians have borrowed Hill's "not war—but murder" comment about Lee's Malvern Hill attacks and applied it to Grant's later Cold Harbor assault. See, e.g., Furgurson, Ernest B., *Not War But Murder: Cold Harbor 1864* (New York: Alfred A. Knopf, 2000).

99.   Weigley, *American Way of War*, p. 91.

100. Adams, Michael C. C., *Fighting for Defeat: Union Military Failure in the East, 1861–1865* (Lincoln and London: University of Nebraska Press, 1978, 1992) [hereafter Adams, *Fighting for Defeat*], p. 91.

101. Bruce, "Lee and Strategy," p. 114.

102. Alexander, *Fighting for the Confederacy*, p. 120.

103. Freeman, *R. E. Lee*, II, p. 232.

104. Ibid., p. 241. It is hoped that Freeman was praising the Union leadership at the corps, division, and brigade levels—and not McClellan's as army commander. However, many pro-Lee historians, like Lee himself, seem to have admired McClellan, who made life so uncomplicated for Lee.

105. Konstam, Angus, *Seven Days Battles 1862: Lee's Defense of Richmond* (Westport, Connecticut and London: Praeger, 2004), p. 19.

106. Jones, Archer, "Military Means, Political Ends: Strategy," [hereafter Jones, "Military Means"] in Boritt, Gabor S. (ed.), *Why the Confederacy Lost* (New York and Oxford: Oxford University Press, 1992) [hereafter Boritt, *Why the Confederacy Lost*], p. 55.

107. Alexander, *Lost Victories*, p. 129.

108. Freeman said that, at the Seven Days' Battle, "Lee trusted too much to his subordinates, some of whom failed him almost completely...." Freeman, *R. E. Lee*, II, p. 241.

109. Grant, "Shiloh," p. 479.

110. See Appendix I.

111. Catton, "Leadership of Grant," p. 14.

112. Smith, *Grant*, p. 204.

113. Allen, "Shiloh! II," p. 50.

114. Daniel, *Shiloh*, pp. 304–9; Allen, "Shiloh! II," p. 49; Buell, *Warrior Generals*, pp. 178–79; Foote, *Civil War*, I, p. 351; Anderson, "Grant's Struggle with Alcohol," p. 22. Under the watchful eye of Major John Rawlins, Grant drank but stayed sober until late 1862. Rawlins denied the false accusations that Grant had been drinking during the Battle of Shiloh. Anderson, "Grant's Struggle with Alcohol," p. 22.

115. McWhiney and Jamieson, *Attack and Die*, pp. 8, 19–20, 158; Allen, "Shiloh! II," p. 48.

116. See Appendix II.

117. Freeman, *R.E.Lee*, II, pp. 244–45.

CHAPTER 5

1. McClellan to Stanton, July 3, 1862 in Sears, Stephen W. (ed.), *The Civil War Papers of George B. McClellan: Selected Correspondence 1860–1865* (New York: Ticknor & Fields, 1989), p. 333.

2. Alexander, *Lost Victories*, p. 151n. 6.

3. Lee to Thomas J. Jackson, July 27, 1862, *Papers of Lee*, p. 239.

4. Halleck to McClellan, Aug. 3, 1862, OR, Ser. I, XI, Part I, pp. 80–81; McClellan to Halleck, Aug. 4, 1862, OR, Ser. I, XI, Part I, pp. 81–82.

5. For details of Lee's Second Manassas campaign, see Hennessy, John J., *Return to Bull Run: The Campaign and Battle of Second Manassas* (New York: Simon & Schuster, 1993) and Hennessy, John, "The Second Battle of Manassas: Lee Suppresses the 'Miscreant' Pope," *Blue & Gray Magazine*, IX, Issue 6 (Aug. 1992), pp. 10–34, 46–58 [hereafter Hennessy, "Second Manassas"].

6. Hattaway and Jones, *How the North Won*, p. 223.

7. Livermore, *Numbers & Losses*, pp. 87–88. See Appendix II.

8. For details of Second Manassas, see Freeman, *R. E. Lee*, II, pp. 317–49; Time-Life Books Editors, *Voices of the Civil War: Second Manassas* (Alexandria, Virginia: Time-Life Books, 1995).

9. Freeman, *R. E. Lee*, II, p. 235. Consistent with pro-Lee historians' disparagement of Longstreet, Freeman disagreed with Lee's decision to take Longstreet's advice. The delay gave McClellan an extra day to get reinforcements to Pope, but McClellan was just delaying the reinforcements anyway—in an effort to ensure Pope's defeat. Bonekemper, Edward H., III, *McClellan and*

Failure: A Civil War Study of Fear, Incompetence and Worse (Jefferson, North Carolina: McFarland & Company, 2007), pp. 95–122.

10. Hennessy, *Return to Bull Run*, p. 57.

11. Fuller, *Grant and Lee*, p. 165.

12. Hennessy, "Second Manassas," p. 57. See Appendix II.

13. Lee to Jefferson Davis, September 3, 1862, *Papers of Lee*, pp. 292–94 at p. 293, September 4, 1862, pp. 294–95.

14. Lee to Jefferson Davis, September 3, 1862, Ibid., pp. 292–94 at p. 293.

15. Connelly, "Lee and the Western Confederacy," p. 124.

16. Buell, *Warrior Generals*, p. 104.

17. For detailed accounts of the Antietam (Sharpsburg) campaign, see Sears, Stephen W., *Landscape Turned Red: The Battle of Antietam* (New York: Book-of-the-Month Club, Inc., 1994) [hereafter Sears, *Landscape*]; Luvaas, Jay and Nelson, Harold W., *The U.S. Army War College Guide to the Battle of Antietam: The Military Campaign of 1862* (Carlisle, Pennsylvania: South Mountain Press, Inc., 1987); Priest, John M., *Antietam: The Soldiers' Battle* (Shippensburg, Pennsylvania: White Mane Publishing Company, Inc., 1989); Freeman, *R. E. Lee*, II, pp. 350–414; Nolan, Alan T. and Storch, Marc, "The Iron Brigade Earns Its Name," *Blue & Gray Magazine*, XXI, Issue 6 (Holiday 2004), pp. 6–20, 47–50 (including South Mountain maps and accompanied by detailed cornfield maps at pp. 56–63).

18. Buell, *Warrior Generals*, p. 122.

19. Lee to Jefferson Davis, September 8, 1862, *Papers of Lee*, p. 301.

20. McPherson, James M., *Crossroads of Freedom: Antietam* (Oxford: Oxford University Press, 2002) [hereafter McPherson, *Crossroads*], pp. 36–40, 56–61, 93–94, 141–46.

21. Piston, *Lee's Tarnished Lieutenant*, pp. 27–28.

22. Freeman, Douglas Southall, *Lee's Lieutenants: A Study in Command*, 3 vols. (New York: Charles Scribner's Sons, 1942–4; 1972 reprint) [hereafter Freeman, *Lee's Lieutenants*], II, p. 149.

23. Ibid., pp. 150–51.

24. Lee to Jefferson Davis, September 3, 1862, *Papers of Lee*, pp. 292–94 at p. 293.

25. Alexander, *Fighting for the Confederacy*, p. 139.

26. Lee to Jefferson Davis, September 13, 1862, *Papers of Lee*, pp. 306–7 at p. 307.

27. Piston, *Lee's Tarnished Lieutenant*, pp. 24–25.

28. *Papers of Lee*, pp. 301–3.

29. Wert, *Longstreet*, p. 184.

30. Gordon, Edward Clifford, "Memorandum of a Conversation with General Robert E. Lee," February 15, 1868, pp. 25–27 in Gallagher, *Lee the Soldier*, pp. 25–26.

31. Lee later complained that the lost order's discovery had caused him to miss an opportunity to concentrate his troops and *attack* McClellan's army. Allan, "Conversations," pp. 7–8.

32. Alexander, *Lost Victories*, p. 217.

33. Freeman, *R. E. Lee*, II, p. 370; Holsworth, Jerry W., "Uncommon Valor: Hood's Texas Brigade in the Maryland Campaign," *Blue & Gray Magazine*, XIII, Issue 6 (Summer 1996), pp. 6–20, 50–55 [hereafter Holsworth, "Uncommon Valor"], p. 11.

34. Holsworth, "Uncommon Valor," p. 11.

35. Ibid.

36. See Appendix II.

37. McPherson, *Crossroads*, p. 114.

38. Ibid., p. 115. H. W. Crocker III succinctly summarized McClellan's debilitating delays: "The odds against Lee changed with the clock, each advancing hour bringing him a greater surety. As Lee arranged his men at Sharpsburg, he brought barely a quarter as many troops as McClellan to the field. By afternoon, with the arrival of Jackson, he had shaved the odds to three to one. And at full strength, which he did not have until the battle was nearly over, he was still outnumbered by two to one." Crocker, *Lee*, p. 82.

39. Buell, *Warrior Generals*, p. 115.

40. Freeman, *R. E. Lee*, II, pp. 389–96.

41. Lowe, "Field Fortifications," p. 63.

42. Holsworth, "Uncommon Valor," p. 54; Fox, *Regimental Losses*, pp. 36, 556, 565.

43. Lowe, "Field Fortifications," p. 63. A vivid description of the Miller's cornfield fighting is in Cheeks, Robert C., "Carnage in a Cornfield," *America's Civil War*, Vol. 5, No. 2 (July 1992), pp. 30–37.

44. Robertson, *Jackson*, p. 617.

45. Chiles, Paul, "Artillery Hell! The Guns of Antietam," *Blue & Gray Magazine*, XVI, Issue 2 (Dec. 1998), pp. 6–18, 24–25, 41–59 at p. 49; McPherson, *Crossroads*, pp. 123–24; Alexander, *Military Memoirs*, p. 262; Catton, *Mr. Lincoln's Army*, p. 304; Pois and Langer, *Command Failure*, p. 55.

46. Sears, *Landscape*, p. 260.
47. For information supporting the view that McClellan intended to use Burnside only as a diversion, belatedly ordered his involvement, and later tried to use Burnside as a scapegoat, see Sears, *Landscape Turned Red*, Appendix II ("Burnside and His Bridge"), pp. 353–57. Also see Smith, Robert Barr, "Killing Zone at Burnside's Bridge," *Military History*, Vol. 21, No. 2 (June 2004), pp. 34–40 [hereafter Smith, "Killing Zone"].
48. Freeman, *R. E. Lee*, II, pp. 398–402; Waugh, *Class of 1846*, pp. 387–90.
49. Waugh, *Class of 1846*, p. 391; Smith, "Killing Zone," p. 39.
50. Sears, Stephen W., "McClellan at Antietam," *Hallowed Ground*, Vol. 6, No. 1 (Spring 2005), pp. 30–33 at p. 33.
51. Cox, Jacob Dolson, *Military Reminiscences of the Civil War* (New York: Charles Scribner's Sons, 1900)(2 vols.)[hereafter Cox, *Reminiscences*], I, pp. 350–52.
52. Ibid.; Cox, Jacob D., "The Battle of Antietam," in Johnson and Buel, *Battles and Leaders*, II, pp. 630–60 at pp. 656–58.
53. Holworth, "Uncommon Valor," pp. 54–55.
54. Alexander, *Lost Victories*, p. 253; Fuller, *Grant and Lee*, p. 169.
55. Alexander, *Fighting for the Confederacy*, p. 92.
56. This sixth blunder is mentioned in Alexander, Bevin, *Robert E. Lee's Civil War* (Avon, Massachusetts: Adams media Corporation, 1998) [hereafter Alexander, *Lee*], pp. 93, 114.
57. Freeman, *R. E. Lee*, II, p. 412.
58. Alexander, *Lost Victories*, p. 253–54.
59. Even Freeman criticized Lee's division of his forces in the Antietam campaign. Freeman, *R. E. Lee*, II, p. 411.
60. Bevin Alexander criticized Lee's failure to promptly leave Maryland: "... when the 1862 invasion of Maryland proved to be abortive, Lee did not retreat quickly into Virginia but allowed himself to be drawn into a direct confrontation at Antietam, which he had no hope of winning.... Since the Confederacy was greatly inferior to the North in manpower, any such expenditure of blood should have been made only for great strategic gains. Standing and fighting at Antietam offered no benefits, whereas a withdrawal into Virginia would have retained the South's offensive power." Alexander, Bevin, *How Great Generals Win* (New York and London: W.W. Norton & Company, 1993) [hereafter Alexander, *Great Generals*], p. 26.

61.   Jones, Archer, "Military Means," pp. 43–77, in Boritt, *Why the Confederacy Lost*, pp. 60–61.

62.   Hartwig, D. Scott, "Robert E. Lee and the Maryland Campaign," pp. 331–55 in Gallagher, *Lee the Soldier*, p. 352.

63.   Alexander, *Lost Victories*, p. 220.

64.   Lee to Jefferson Davis, September 19, 1862, OR, Ser. I, XIX, Part I, p. 142.

65.   Hattaway and Jones, *How the North Won*, p. 243.

66.   See Appendix II.

67.   Weigley, *American Way of War*, p. 111.

68.   Buell, *Warrior Generals*, p. 122.

69.   Beringer, Richard E.; Hattaway, Herman; Jones, Archer; and Still, William N. Jr., *Why the South Lost the Civil War* (Athens: University of Georgia Press, 1986) [hereafter Beringer et al., *Why the South Lost*], pp. 169, 179.

70.   George Bruce provided a postwar northern perspective: "Confederate writers take especial delight in recording that General Grant lost 39,000 men in getting his army to the James River, when he might have reached the same point by the use of transports with his army intact, but they never mention the fact that Lee in five months in 1862 had lost nearly 60,000 men in four battles, and still found Jackson's part of the army one hundred miles south and the remainder only sixty miles north of their starting-points, Grant, in 1864, moving forward toward final victory; Lee, in 1862, by his general policy, toward a sure defeat." Bruce, "Lee and Strategy," pp. 116–17.

71.   Sears, *Landscape*, p. 307.

72.   Weigley, *American Way of War*, p. 110.

73.   Freeman, *R. E. Lee*, II, pp. 406–8; Sears, *Landscape*, pp. 307–8.

74.   Lee to Jefferson Davis, September 21, 1862, OR, Ser. I, XIX, Part I, pp. 142–43 at p. 143.

75.   Sears, *Landscape*, p. 325.

76.   *Works of Lincoln*, V, p. 474.

77.   Freeman, *R. E. Lee*, II, p. 428.

78.   "By arguing that he always faced huge odds McClellan retained his popularity with the troops; failures were not attributed directly to him.... But in understating the strength of his army, McClellan gave it an unworthy definition of success: avoiding outright defeat became an accomplishment." Adams, *Fighting for Defeat*, p. 103.

79. "The long-term damage caused by McClellan was observed by one of his subordinates, General Jacob Cox, who observed, "The general who indoctrinates his army with the belief that it is required by its government to do the impossible, may preserve his popularity with the troops and be received with cheers as he rides down the line, but he has put any great military success far beyond his reach." Cox, *Reminiscences*, I, pp. 370–71.

80. Piston, *Lee's Tarnished Lieutenant*, p. 28.

81. Hattaway and Jones, *How the North Won*, p. 116.

82. Freeman, *R. E. Lee*, II, pp. 417–18.

83. Lee to Jefferson Davis, December 6, 1862, *Papers of Lee*, pp. 352–53 at p. 353.

84. Cox, *Reminiscences*, I, p. 453.

85. Nevins, *Ordeal*, VI, p. 345; Lee to Jefferson Davis, Dec. 6, 1862, *Papers of Lee*, pp. 352–53 at p. 353.

86. Lowe, "Field Fortifications," p. 63.

87. Rhodes, Elisha Hunt, *All for the Union: The Civil War Diary and Letters of Elisha Hunt Rhodes*, edited by Robert Hunt Rhodes (New York: Orion Books, 1985) [hereafter Rhodes, *All for the Union*], p. 90.

88. Barry, John M., *Rising Tide: The Great Mississippi Flood of 1927 and How It Changed America* (New York: Simon & Schuster, 1997), p. 48.

89. Lowe, "Field Fortifications," p. 63. About Fredericksburg, Confederate General Joseph E. Johnston commented, "What luck some people have. Nobody will ever come to attack me in such a place." Johnston to Louis T. Wigfall, December 15, 1862, quoted in McWhiney & Jamieson, *Attack and Die*, p. 159.

90. Lee to Samuel Cooper, "Battle Report of Fredericksburg Campaign," April 10, 1863, *Papers of Lee*, pp. 366–74 at p. 373; Allan, "Conversations," p. 13; O'Reilly, Frank A., "Lee's Incomplete Victory: Battle of Fredericksburg," *America's Civil War*, Vol. 14, No. 5 (Nov. 2001), pp. 30–37. After the war, Longstreet supported Lee's decision not to counterattack because of the difficulties of switching from the defensive to offensive. Longstreet, James, "The Battle of Fredericksburg" in Johnson and Buel, *Battles and Leaders*, III, pp. 70–85 at pp. 82–84.

91. Fuller, *Grant and Lee*, pp. 172–74.

92. Major-General Fuller said, " [At Fredericksburg], on the morning of December 14, [Lee] erred from over-caution, and as [Captain C. C.] Chesney says: 'Missed an opportunity of further advantage, such as even a great victory

has rarely offered; it must be borne in mind that his troops were not on this occasion suffering from over-marching, want of food and ammunition.'" Ibid., pp. 127–28.

93. Nevins, *Ordeal*, VI, pp. 366–67.

94. Freeman, *R. E. Lee*, II, p. 462; Hattaway and Jones, *How the North Won*, p. 308; Wert, *Longstreet*, p. 223.

95. See Appendix II.

96. Lee to James A. Seddon, January 10, 1863, *Papers of Lee*, pp. 388–90 at p. 389.

97. General Orders No. 16, Department of the Mississippi; Captain Nathaniel H. McLean to Grant, April 14, 1862, *Papers of Grant*, V, pp. 48–49; Halleck to Grant, April 14, 1862, OR, Ser. I, X, Part II, p. 106; Grant, *Memoirs*, p. 247.

98. Weigley, *American Way of War*, p. 139; Special Orders No. 35, Department of the Mississippi, April 30, 1862, *Papers of Grant*, V, p. 105.

99. Allen, Stacy D., "Corinth, Mississippi: Crossroads of the Western Confederacy," *Blue & Gray Magazine*, XIX, Issue 6 (Summer 2002), pp. 6–25, 36–51 [hereafter "Allen, "Crossroads"].

100. Grant, *Memoirs*, pp. 250–52; Cozzens, Peter, *The Darkest Days of the War: The Battles of Iuka & Corinth* (Chapel Hill and London: University of North Carolina Press, 1997)[hereafter Cozzens, *Darkest Days*], p. 17. Grant was unaware that, in the aftermath of Shiloh, Lincoln was resisting suggestions that he remove Grant by saying, "I can't spare this man; he fights." Williams, *McClellan, Sherman and Grant*, p. 96.

101. Allen, "Crossroads," pp. 12–24, 36 [siege map on p. 13]; Watkins, Sam R., *"Co. Aytch": Maury Grays, First Tennessee Regiment or a Side Show of the Big Show* (Wilmington, N.C.: Broadfoot Publishing Company, 1987) (Reprint of 1882 and 1952 editions)[hereafter Watkins, *"Co. Aytch"*], p. 71.

102. Grant, *Memoirs*, pp. 252–55; Allen, "Crossroads," pp. 24, 36; Cozzens, *Darkest Days*, pp. 31–33.

103. Grant, *Memoirs*, pp. 250–55; Suhr, Robert Collins, "Old Brains' Barren Triumph," *America's Civil War*, Vol. 14, No. 2 (May 2001), pp. 42–49 at p. 49; Woodworth, Steven E., *Nothing But Victory: The Army of the Tennessee, 1861–1865* (New York: Alfred A. Knopf, 2005)[hereafter Woodworth, *Nothing but Victory*], 207–9.

104. Grant, *Memoirs*, pp. 255; 256–57.

105. Weigley, *American Way of War*, p. 136.
106. Williams, *McClellan, Sherman and Grant*, p. 94.
107. Feis, *Grant's Secret Service*, p. 109; Cozzens, *Darkest Days*, p. 35.
108. Feis, *Grant's Secret Service*, p. 114.
109. Allen, "Crossroads," p. 37. For details on the Battle of Iuka, see Suhr, Robert Collins, "Small but Savage Battle of Iuka" *America's Civil War*, Vol. 12, No. 2 (May 1999), pp. 42–49 [hereafter Suhr, "Iuka"]; Cozzens, *Darkest Days*, pp. 66–134.
110. Snead, Thomas L., "With Price East of the Mississippi," in Johnson and Buel, *Battles and Leaders*, II, pp. 717–36 [hereafter Snead, "With Price"] at pp. 731–32; Suhr, "Iuka," pp. 44–48; Allen, "Crossroads," pp. 37–38; Woodworth, *Nothing But Victory*, p. 223. Acoustic shadows had similar effects at other Civil War battles, including Fort Donelson, Tennessee (1862); Gaines' Mill, Virginia (1862); Perryville, Kentucky (1862); Rappahannock Station, Virginia (1863), and Drewry's Bluff, Virginia (1864). Suhr, "Iuka," p. 48; Schiller, Herbert M., "Beast in a Bottle: Bermuda Hundred Campaign, May 1864," *Blue & Gray Magazine*, VII, Issue 1 (Oct. 1989), pp. 8–26 [hereafter Schiller, "Beast in a Bottle"] at p. 22; Smith, *Grant*, pp. 157, 218. Rosecrans' sympathetic biographer William M. Lamers contended that the sounds of battle were heard in the vicinity of Grant and Ord, their failure to attack may have been due to Grant's drunkenness or mistake, and Rosecrans did not have sufficient troops to safely block the Rebels' escape route. Lamers, William M., *The Edge of Glory: A Biography of General William S. Rosecrans, U.S.A.* (Baton Rouge: Louisiana State University Press, 1999) (Reprint and update of New York: Harcourt, Brace & World, 1961) [hereafter Lamers, *Edge of Glory*], pp. 102–30. It is hard to believe that Grant would knowingly have passed up an opportunity to attack—especially in a planned pincers movement situation. Speculation about Grant's alleged drunkenness is just that— speculation.
111. Grant, *Memoirs*, pp. 263–77; Suhr, "Iuka," pp. 48–49; Allen, "Crossroads," p. 38.
112. Suhr, "Iuka," p. 49; Cozzens, *Darkest Days*, p. 133. See Appendix I.
113. Allen, "Crossroads," pp. 38, 41; Suhr, Robert Collins, "Attack Written Deep and Crimson," Vol. 4, No. 3 (Sept. 1991), pp. 46–52 [hereafter Suhr, "Attack"] at p. 48. As Price's aide-de-camp, John Tyler, heard Price and Van Dorn debate

the proposed attack on Rosecrans, "It was becoming clear to Tyler why Rosecrans had graduated fifth in the West Point class of 1842 and Van Dorn fifth from the bottom." Cozzens, *Darkest Days*, p. 139.

114. Cozzens, *Darkest Days*, pp. 159–270, 305–306; Allen, "Crossroads," pp. 41–44; Suhr, "Attack," pp. 49–52; Cozzens, Peter, "Moving into Dead Men's Shoes: The Fight for Battery Robinett at the Battle of Corinth, Mississippi," *Civil War Times Illustrated*, XXXVI, No. 2 (May 1997), pp. 24–33, 47–49; Smith, *Grant*, p. 219.

115. Allen, "Crossroads," pp. 44–45; Cozzens, *Darkest Days*, pp. 274–77; Foote, *Civil War*, I, p. 725.

116. Grant, *Memoirs*, pp. 278–80.

117. For details of the Battle of Davis' Bridge, see Smith, Timothy B., "The Forgotten Battle of Davis' Bridge," *North & South*, Vol. 2, No. 5 (June 1999), pp. 68–79 [hereafter Smith, "Davis' Bridge"].

118. Grant, *Memoirs*, pp. 280–82; Allen, "Crossroads," p. 45; Cozzens, *Darkest Days*, pp. 280–90.

119. Smith, "Davis' Bridge," p. 79. The deteriorating relationship between Grant and Rosecrans was described in Gordon, Lesley J., "'I Could Not Make Him Do As I Wished': The Failed Relationship of William S. Rosecrans and Grant" in Woodworth, *Grant's Lieutenants*, pp. 109–27.

120. Grant, *Memoirs*, pp. 280–81; Cozzens, *Darkest Days*, pp. 298–304. In his version of Corinth, Rosecrans described his telegrams to Grant seeking permission to continue the pursuit and Grant's denial, and said, "Confederate officers told me afterward that they never were so scared in their lives as they were after the defeat before Corinth." Rosecrans, William S., "The Battle of Corinth," in Johnson and Buel, *Battles and Leaders*, II, pp. 737–60 [hereafter Rosecrans, "Corinth"] at pp. 754–56.

121. Grant, *Memoirs*, p. 281; Allen, "Crossroads," p. 46. See Appendix I for total Corinth/Hatchie River casualties.

122. Grant, *Memoirs*, pp. 281–82; Feis, *Grant's Secret Service*, p. 123.

123. Allen, "Crossroads," p. 47.

124. Grant, *Memoirs*, p. 283.

125. Weigley, *American Way of War*, p. 139.

126. Grant, *Memoirs*, p. 283; Grant to Halleck, Nov. 2, 1862, *Papers of Grant*, VI, p. 243.

127. Grant, *Memoirs*, pp. 283–86; Meyers, Christopher C., "'Two Generals Cannot Command This Army': John A. McClernand and the Politics of Command in Grant's Army of the Tennessee," *Columbiad: A Quarterly Review of the War Between the States*, Vol. 2, No. 1 (Spring 1998), pp. 27–41 [hereafter Meyers, "Two Generals"] at pp. 31–35.

128. Grant, *Memoirs*, pp. 286–88.

129. Ibid., p. 287; Grant to Sherman, Dec. 8, 1862, *Papers of Grant*, VI, pp. 406–7.

130. Grant, *Memoirs*, p. 289.

131. Ibid., pp. 289–93.

132. Ibid., pp. 289–91.

133. Ibid., p. 291. The same point was made in Badeau, *Grant*, I, pp. 140–41.

134. Grant, *Memoirs*, pp. 289, 292; Morgan, George W., "The Assault on Chickasaw Bluffs," in Johnson and Buel, *Battles and Leaders*, III, pp. 462–71 [hereafter Morgan, "Chickasaw Bluffs"]; Fox, *Regimental Losses*, pp. 23, 544, 550; Bearss, Edwin Cole, *Unvexed to the Sea: The Campaign for Vicksburg* (Dayton, Ohio: Morningside House, Inc., 1985, 1991) (3 vols.) [hereafter Bearss, *Vicksburg*], I, pp. 192–229.

135. Grant, *Memoirs*, pp. 292–93; Meyers, "Two Generals," p. 36.

136. Grant, *Memoirs*, pp. 293–95.

137. Ibid., p. 296.

138. Ibid., pp. 296–97.

139. Bearss, *Vicksburg*, I, pp. 431–50; Grant, *Memoirs*, pp. 297–98; Groom, Winston, *Shrouds of Glory. From Atlanta to Nashville: The Last Great Campaign of the Civil War* (New York: The Atlantic Monthly Press, 1995) [hereafter Groom, *Shrouds of Glory*], p. 89.

140. Bearss, *Vicksburg*, I, pp. 467–78; Grant, *Memoirs*, pp. 298–99.

141. Bearss, *Vicksburg*, I, pp. 479–548; Grant, *Memoirs*, pp. 299–301.

142. Bearss, *Vicksburg*, I, pp. 549–95; Grant, *Memoirs*, pp. 301–2; Groom, *Shrouds of Glory*, pp. 89–90.

143. Grant, *Memoirs*, pp. 303–5.

144. Arnold, James R., *Grant Wins the War: Decision at Vicksburg* (New York: John Wiley & Sons, Inc., 1997)[hereafter Arnold, *Grant Wins*], p. 52

145. Meyers, "Two Generals," p. 37.

146. The general, unlike his brother, spelled his name without an "e" on the end.

147. Smith, *Grant*, pp. 230–31.

148. Fuller, *Generalship of Grant*, p. 134.

CHAPTER 6

1. Hooker acquired the nickname "Fighting Joe" from a newsman's battle report that contained the phrase, "Fighting-Joe Hooker," which was modified to "Fighting Joe Hooker" in Northern newspapers. Hooker regretted the mistake and hated the sobriquet. Heidler, David S. and Heidler, Jeanne T. (eds.), *Encyclopedia of the American Civil War: A Political, Social, and Military History* (New York and London: W.W. Norton & Company, 2002)[hereafter Heidler and Heidler, *Encyclopedia*], p. 999; Warner, *Generals in Blue*, p. 234.

2. Freeman, *R. E. Lee*, II, p. 483; Allan, "Conversations," p. 17.

3. Connolly, Thomas Lawrence, *Autumn of Glory: The Army of Tennessee, 1862–1865* (Baton Rouge and London: Louisiana State University Press, 1971, 1991) [hereafter Connolly, *Autumn of Glory*], p. 94.

4. Freeman, *R. E. Lee*, II, p. 501.

5. Ibid., pp. 503–4; Connolly, *Autumn of Glory*, p. 104; Woodworth, Steven E., *Davis and Lee at War* (Lawrence: University of Kansas Press, 1995) [hereafter Woodworth, *Davis and Lee*], pp. 219–21.

6. Hattaway and Jones, *How the North Won*, p. 362.

7. James A. Seddon to Lee, April 6, 1863.

8. Hattaway and Jones, *How the North Won*, p. 362.

9. Lee to James A. Seddon, April 9, 1863, *Papers of Lee*, pp. 429–30; Lee to Jefferson Davis, April 16, 1863, Ibid., pp. 434–35. "[Lee's] new theories were rationalizations. Like his emphatic reaction, these were subconsciously designed to forestall the diminution of his army and prevent the derangement of his own plans for the spring campaign." Hattaway and Jones, *How the North Won*, p. 363.

10. Lee to General Samuel Cooper, Adjutant and Inspector General, April 16, 1863, *Papers of Lee*, pp. 433–34 at p. 434. Charles Roland observed, "Lee's curious listing of Vicksburg came of an erroneous notion that Federal operations there would soon have to quit because of the pestilential Mississippi summer. Apparently Davis, whose home was but a few miles from Vicksburg, never disabused Lee of this idea." Roland, Charles P., "The Generalship of Robert E. Lee," in McWhiney, *Grant, Lee*, pp. 31–71 at p. 43.

11. Woodworth, *Davis and Lee*, pp. 220–21.

12. Ibid., pp. 433–34.

13. Lee to his wife, April 19, 1863, *Papers of Lee*, pp. 437–38.

14. Connolly, *Autumn of Glory*, p. 114.

15. For details concerning Chancellorsville, see Sears, Stephen W., *Chancellors-ville* (Boston and New York: Houghton Mifflin Company, 1996) [hereafter Sears, *Chancellorsville*]; Furgurson, Ernest B., *Chancellorsville 1863: The Souls of the Brave* (New York: Alfred A. Knopf, 1992) [hereafter Furgurson, *Chancellorsville*]; Freeman, *R. E. Lee*, II, pp. 507–63.

16. Sears, *Chancellorsville*, p. 192; Hattaway and Jones, *How the North Won*, p. 379.

17. Sears, *Chancellorsville*, p. 180.

18. In April 1863 Lee had been suffering from a throat and chest infection, probably aggravating his underlying arteriosclerotic health problems. Hattaway and Jones, *How the North Won*, p. 379.

19. There has been a continuing dispute whether Hooker, a heavy drinker, lost his self-confidence because he had temporarily stopped drinking or because he had lapsed into drinking again. Sears, *Chancellorsville*, pp. 504–6.

20. Freeman, *Lee's Lieutenants*, II, pp. 546–47; Alexander, *Lost Victories*, pp. 304–5.

21. Sears, *Chancellorsville*, p. 280; Lowe, "Field Fortifications," p. 64.

22. O'Beirne, Kevin M., "A 'Perfect' But Flawed Campaign," *Military Heritage*, Vol. 2, No. 5 (April 2001), p. 65.

23. Sears, *Chancellorsville*, p. 287.

24. Freeman, *R. E. Lee*, II, pp. 533, 560.

25. McWhiney and Jamieson, *Attack and Die*, p. 4.

26. Hotchkiss, Jedediah, *Make Me a Map of the Valley: The Civil War Journal of Stonewall Jackson's Topographer* (Edited by Archie P. McDonald) (Dallas: Southern Methodist University Press, 1973, 1989)[hereafter Hotchkiss, *Make Me a Map*], p. 140. Stuart lost thirty percent of Jackson's remaining troops in bloody attacks on entrenched Union troops. Alexander, *Lost Victories*, p. 318. The fighting that morning cost the Confederates almost 9,000 dead, wounded and missing. Sears, *Chancellorsville*, p. 365.

27. Alexander, *Fighting for the Confederacy*, p. 213.

28. Rogan, George, "Salem Church: Final Federal Assault at Chancellorsville," *America's Civil War*, Vol. 11, No. 6 (Jan. 1999), pp. 42–48.

29. Alexander, *Fighting for the Confederacy*, p. 92.

30. Hattaway and Jones, *How the North Won*, p. 385.

31. Furgurson, *Chancellorsville*, p. 318.

32. Lowe, "Field Fortifications," p. 64.

33. Hess, Earl J., "'Set Your Spades to Work': Field Fortifications in the Chancellorsville Campaign," *North & South*, Vol. 9, No. 1 (March 2006), pp. 12–23 [hereafter Hess, "Spades"] at p. 21.

34. On several occasions, Jackson had recommended flanking offensive campaigns into the North, but Lee and Davis rejected his recommendations. Alexander, *Great Generals*, pp. 123–42; Allan, "Conversations," p. 15; Alexander, *Lost Victories*.

35. "[Chancellorsville] looked to be a great Confederate victory, but the appearance was deceiving." Alexander, *Lost Victories*, p. 322.

36. Hamlin, Augustus Choate, *The Battle of Chancellorsville*, p. 50 quoted in Fuller, *Grant and Lee*, p. 128.

37. Alexander, *Lost Victories*, p. 322.

38. Smith, Gene, "The Destruction of Fighting Joe Hooker," in *Battles and Leaders* (Supplement to American Heritage) (Washington: Library of Congress, 1995), pp. 10–17. Hooker barely used two of his best corps commanded by his best generals, Reynolds and Meade, despite those generals' efforts and pleas to get their corps involved. Nichols, Edward J., *Toward Gettysburg: A Biography of General John F. Reynolds* (State College: Penn State University Press, 1958)[hereafter Nichols, *Reynolds*], pp. 173–79.

39. Livermore, *Numbers & Losses*, pp. 98–99; Hess, "Spades," p. 21. Stephen Sears stated that the Confederates had 30 more soldiers killed than the Union and only 439 fewer wounded. Sears, *Chancellorsville*, p. 442. Although most later authorities used larger numbers than Livermore for Hooker's forces and those numbers reflect a greater manpower disparity, those larger numbers also reduce the casualty percentage suffered by Hooker's army. See Appendix II.

40. General Order No. 63, May 14, 1863, Fox, *Regimental Losses*, p. 559.

41. Lee to James A. Seddon, May 10, 1863, *Papers of Lee*, p. 482.

42. Lee to Jefferson Davis, May 11, 1863, Ibid., pp. 483–84.

43. Lee to Samuel Cooper (Battle Report of Chancellorsville Campaign), Sept. 23, 1863, Ibid., pp. 458–72 at p. 469.

44. McPherson, James M., *Battle Cry of Freedom: The Civil War Era* (New York: Ballantine Books, 1988) [hereafter McPherson, *Battle Cry of Freedom*], p. 645; Woodworth, *Davis and Lee*, p. 230.

45. Lee to John B. Hood, May 21, 1863, *Papers of Lee*, p. 490.

46. Pfanz, Harry W., *Gettysburg: The Second Day* (Chapel Hill and London: The University of North Carolina Press, 1987) [hereafter Pfanz, *The Second Day*], p. 4.

47. Alexander, *Fighting for the Confederacy*, p. 222.

48. McPherson, *Battle Cry of Freedom*, pp. 646–47.

49. Lee's arguments are reflected in his letters of April and May 1863. Lee to James A. Seddon, April 9, 1863; Lee to Samuel Cooper, April 16, 1863; Lee to Jefferson Davis, April 16, 1863; Lee to James A. Seddon, May 10, 1863; Lee to Jefferson Davis, May 11, 1863, *Papers of Lee*, pp. 430–31, 433–34, 434–35, 482, 483–84. See Connelly, Thomas Lawrence and Archer Jones, *The Politics of Command: Factions and Ideas in Confederate Strategy* (Baton Rouge: Louisiana State University Press, 1973) [hereafter Connelly and Jones, *Politics of Command*], p. 126–28; Sears, Stephen W., "'We Should Assume the Aggressive': Origins of the Gettysburg Campaign," *North & South*, Vol. 5, No. 4 (May 2002), pp. 58–66.

50. Lee to Jefferson Davis, June 23, 1863, *Papers of Lee*, pp. 527–28; Hattaway and Jones, *How the North Won*, pp. 401–2, 404. Steven Woodworth noted that, "Calling for Beauregard a month earlier, when the northern invasion itself was still being debated by the cabinet, would have made fatally obvious to the cautious president that what Lee had in mind was an all-out end-the-war gamble." Woodworth, *Davis and Lee*, pp. 238–39.

51. Hattaway and Jones, *How the North Won*, p. 414.

52. Lee to Jefferson Davis, June 25, 1863, *Papers of Lee*, pp. 530–31 at p. 531.

53. Lee to Jefferson Davis, June 25, 1863, Ibid., pp. 532–33 at p. 532. Bruce criticized Lee's post-battle rationale that he wanted to draw Hooker away from the Rappahannock and maneuver to gain a battlefield victory: "This discloses a piece of strategy with no definite objective, but one resting on a contingency. There is certainly something quixotic in the idea of moving an army two hundred miles for the purpose of finding a battlefield, leaving his base of supplies one hundred miles or more at the end of the railroad at Winchester, when able to carry along only ammunition enough for a single battle, as was necessarily the case." Bruce, "Lee and Strategy," p. 117.

54. Roland, Charles P. "Lee's Invasion Strategy," *North & South*, Vol. 1, No. 6 (1998), pp. 34–38 at p. 38.

55. Alexander, *Fighting for the Confederacy*, pp. 219–20.

56. Jones , "Military Means," in Boritt, *Why the Confederacy Lost*, p. 67.

57. Connelly, *Autumn of Glory*, p. 114.

58. Connelly, "Lee and the Western Confederacy," p. 124.

59. Ibid. "Lee's Pennsylvania campaign demanded that the Confederacy not use eastern reserves to attempt to lift the Vicksburg siege; Bragg, weakened to aid Johnston [near Vicksburg], was driven from Middle Tennessee by Rosecrans' brilliant Tullahoma campaign; and Johnston's fragment was too small to operate effectively against the heavily reinforced Grant." Hattaway and Jones, *How the North Won*, p. 415.

60. Beringer et al., *Why the South Lost*, pp. 264, 300; Jones, Archer, *Civil War Command & Strategy* (New York: The Free Press, 1992) [hereafter Jones, *Command & Strategy*], p. 168; "If on the other hand [Lee] fought a battle in Pennsylvania, he could choose his position and compel the Union army to fight another battle of Fredericksburg [what Longstreet recommended and Lee did not do]. But again Lee overlooked the political effect of fighting. Even a victorious defensive battle would look like a defeat because of the inevitable retreat of a raiding army forced to concentrate and unable to forage." Jones, "Military Means," in Boritt, *Why The Confederacy Lost*, p. 68.

61. Alexander, *Fighting for the Confederacy*, pp. 110, 222.

62. "Rather than a menace, Lincoln perceived Lee's raid, like the previous advance to Antietam, as an opportunity to strike the enemy when vulnerable and far from his base, 'the best opportunity' he said, 'we have had since the war began.'" Hattaway and Jones, *How the North Won*, p. 400.

63. In 1868 Lee allegedly told William Allan that his intentions in moving north were defensive: "First [Lee] did not intend to give general battle in Pa. if he could avoid it—the South was too weak to carry on a *war of invasion*, and his offensive movements against the North were never intended except as parts of a defensive system." Allan, "Conversations," p. 13. Lee's actions in 1862 and 1863 seem inconsistent with that description.

64. The classic study of Lee's Gettysburg campaign is Coddington, Edwin B., *The Gettysburg Campaign: A Study in Command* (New York: Charles Scribner's Sons, 1984) [hereafter Coddington, *Gettysburg Campaign*].

65. Weigley, *American Way of War*, p. 116.

66. Gallagher, Gary W., "Brandy Station: The Civil War's Bloodiest Arena of Mounted Combat, *Blue & Gray Magazine*, VIII, Issue 1 (Oct. 1990), pp. 8–22, 44–53; p. 13.

67. Blackford, William Willis, *War Years with Jeb Stuart* (Baton Rouge and London: Louisiana State University Press, 1945, 1993), pp. 211–12.

68. Ibid., pp. 212–13; Lee to his wife, June 9, 1863, *Papers of Lee*, pp. 506–7 at p. 507.

69. The early fighting at Brandy Station was described in Brennan, Patrick, "Thunder on the Plains of Brandy," *North & South*, Vol. 5, No. 3 (April 2002), pp. 14–34.

70. See Appendix II.

71. Carhart, Tom, *Lost Triumph: Lee's Real Plan at Gettysburg and Why It Failed* (New York: G.P. Putnam's Sons, 2005) [hereafter Carhart, *Lost Triumph*], pp. 113–14.

72. Sears, Stephen W., "The Lee of Gettysburg," *North & South*, Vol. 6, No. 5 (July 2003), pp. 12–19 [hereafter Sears, "Lee of Gettysburg"] at pp. 15–16.

73. Freeman, *Lee's Lieutenants*, III, p. 139.

74. In addition, Lee had skilled cavalry with him, including the 6th, 7th, 11th, and 35th Virginia cavalry regiments (heroes of Fleetwood Hill at Brandy Station), that he could have used, but did not, for scouting purposes. Nevertheless, after the war, Lee blamed Stuart for disobeying orders, keeping Lee uninformed and thereby forcing the fighting at Gettysburg. Allan, "Conversations," pp. 13–14, 17.

75. Wiggins, Sarah Woolfolk (ed.), *The Journals of Josiah Gorgas 1857–1878* (Tuscaloosa and London: The University of Alabama Press, 1955) [hereafter Gorgas, *Journals*], June 16, 1863, p. 70.

76. Lee to Jefferson Davis, June 23 and 25, 1863, *Papers of Lee*, pp. 527–28, 530–31, 532–33.

77. Lee to Jefferson Davis, June 25, 1863, Ibid., pp. 530–31 at p. 531.

78. McPherson, James M., *This Mighty Scourge: Perspectives on the Civil War* (Oxford: Oxford University Press, 2007) [hereafter McPherson, *Mighty Scourge*], pp. 60–61.

79. Pfanz, *The Second Day*, p. 20.

80. As explained later, Lee justified his non-mandatory attack orders to Ewell late on July 1 because Lee's whole army was not yet on the field. Likewise, his no-general-engagement orders early that same day may have been intended to avoid widespread conflict until Lee's entire army was present. This approach, however, overlooked the overall numerical superiority of the Army of the Potomac and the desirability of bringing on a general conflict in which Lee temporarily outnumbered his enemy. Lee's cautious approach to Get-

tysburg contrasted sharply with Grant's approach to Vicksburg, during which Grant, outnumbered in the theater, consistently sought battle as soon as he contacted the enemy.

81.   Luvaas, Jay and Nelson, Harold W. (ed.), *The U.S. Army War College Guide to the Battle of Gettysburg* (Carlisle, Pennsylvania: South Mountain Press, Inc., 1986), p. 5; Krolick, Marshall D., "Gettysburg: The First Day, July 1, 1863," *Blue & Gray Magazine*, V, Issue 2 (Nov. 1987), pp. 8–20 [hereafter Krolick, "The First Day"], pp. 14–15. On Buford's critical role on June 30 and July 1 at Gettysburg, see Longacre, Edward, *General John Buford: A Military Biography* (Conshohocken, Pennsylvania: Combined Books, 1995), pp. 179–203; Krolick, "The First Day."

82.   Kross, Gary, "Fight Like the Devil to Hold Your Own: General John Buford's Cavalry at Gettysburg on July 1, 1863," *Blue & Gray Magazine*, XII, Issue 3 (Feb. 1995), pp. 9–22; Kross, Gary, "Attack from the West," *Blue & Gray Magazine*, XVII, Issue 5 (June 2000), pp. 6–22, 44–50 at pp. 11–17; Krolick, "The First Day," p. 15.

83.   Schiller, Laurence D., "The Taste of Northern Steel: The Evolution of Federal Cavalry Tactics 1861–1865," *North & South*, Vol. 2, No. 2 (Jan. 1999), pp. 30–45, 80–84 at pp. 39–44; Hintz, Kalina Ingham, "When the General Fell: The Monumental Death of John F. Reynolds," *Blue & Gray Magazine*, XXII, No. 2 (Spring 2005), pp. 24–28.

84.   Coddington, *Gettysburg Campaign*, p. 281.

85.   Kross, Gary, "That One Error Fills Him with Faults: Gen. Alfred Iverson and His Brigade at Gettysburg," *Blue & Gray Magazine*, XII, Issue 3 (February 1995), 22, 52–53.

86.   Pfanz, *The Second Day*, p. 22.

87.   Ibid., p. 23.

88.   Pfanz made this Lee-Meade comparison and also concluded, "Obviously [Lee] did not expect a battle that would limit his army's ability to maneuver as early as 1 July or he would not have given hundreds of wagons precedence over much needed infantry." Ibid., p. 22.

89.   Wert, *Longstreet*, p. 255.

90.   Pfanz, Harry W., *Gettysburg—Culp's Hill and Cemetery Hill* (Chapel Hill and London: The University of North Carolina Press, 1993) [hereafter Pfanz, *Culp's and Cemetery Hills*], pp. 67–69.

91.   Ibid., p. 72; Coddington, *Gettysburg Campaign*, p. 315.

92. Ewell, who had been frustrated by a series of discretionary Lee-issued orders (including the one directing him to Cashtown or Gettysburg), refused to assault the high ground without an assurance from Lee of support on his right flank. Possibly he was influenced by Lee's criticism and relief of Magruder, who had unsuccessfully attacked the enemy at Malvern Hill as ordered by Lee the prior year. Swain, Robert L., "Generals at Odds," *Military History*, Vol. 23, No. 5 (July/Aug. 2006), pp. 38–45.

93. Piston, *Lee's Tarnished Lieutenant*, p. 49.

94. Freeman, *Lee's Lieutenants*, III, pp. 94–95.

95. Coddington, *Gettysburg Campaign*, pp. 316–17; Gallagher, "'If the Enemy Is There, We Must Attack Him': R. E. Lee and the Second Day at Gettysburg," pp. 497–521, in Gallagher, *Lee the Soldier*, p. 508.

96. Coddington, *Gettysburg Campaign*, p. 320. William Garrett Piston concluded likewise. Piston, *Lee's Tarnished Lieutenant*, p. 49.

97. Kross, Gary, "At the Time Impracticable: Dick Ewell's Decision on the First Day at Gettysburg with Excerpts from Campbell Brown's Journal," *Blue & Gray Magazine*, Vol. XII, Issue 3 (Feb. 1995), pp. 53–58 at p. 58. Kross cites several other reasons justifying Ewell's failure to attack. Ibid.

98. Sears, "Lee of Gettysburg," pp. 16–18.

99. Himmer, Robert, "July 1, 1863: George Gordon Meade's Lost Afternoon Re-examined," *North & South*, Vol. 9, No. 1 (March 2006), pp. 52–64.

100. Freeman, *R. E. Lee*, III, p. 91; Pfanz, *The Second Day*, p. 111.

101. Hattaway and Jones, *How the North Won*, p. 406.

102. Coddington, *Gettysburg Campaign*, pp. 372–74.

103. Ibid., pp. 360–63.

104. Ibid., p. 324.

105. Ibid., p. 361; Pfanz, *The Second Day*, p. 26. Pfanz admits that the exact dialogue will never be known. Pfanz, *The Second Day*, pp. 26–27. For arguments supporting Lee's decision to attack on July 2, see Bowden, Scott and Ward, Bill, "Last Chance for Victory," *North & South*, Vol. 4, No. 3 (March 2001), pp. 76–85.

106. Lee to Samuel Cooper, Battle Report of Gettysburg Campaign, January 20, 1864, *Papers of Lee*, p. 376.

107. Alexander, *Fighting for the Confederacy*, pp. 233–34.

108. Bauer, Daniel, "Did a Food Shortage Force Lee to Fight?: An Investigation into Lee's Claim That He Had to Attack at Gettysburg Because His Army

Lacked Sufficient Rations to Do Anything Else," *Columbiad: A Quarterly Review of the War Between the States*, Vol. I, No. 4 (Winter 1998), pp. 57–74 [hereafter Bauer, "Food Shortage?"].

109. Lee to Samuel Cooper, Battle Report of Gettysburg Campaign, January 20, 1864, *Papers of Lee*, pp. 569–85 at p. 577.

110. Alexander, *Fighting for the Confederacy*, p. 236.

111. Piston, *Lee's Tarnished Lieutenant*, p. 118.

112. Coddington, *Gettysburg Campaign*, p. 270.

113. Alexander, *Fighting for the Confederacy*, p. 237.

114. Pfanz, *The Second Day*, p. 106. Pfanz also said there were other early morning probes of the Union left by Colonel Armistead H. Long and Pendleton, the latter a major pro-Lee, anti-Longstreet commentator in the postwar decades. Ibid., pp. 105–6.

115. Coddington, *Gettysburg Campaign*, p. 378; Freeman, *R. E. Lee*, III, p. 93; Freeman, *Lee's Lieutenants*, III, p. 115.

116. Alexander, *Fighting for the Confederacy*, p. 278; Coddington, *Gettysburg Campaign*, p. 378.

117. Freeman, *R. E. Lee*, III, p. 150.

118. Coddington, *Gettysburg Campaign*, pp. 378–81; Freeman, *R. E. Lee*, III, pp. 95–97.

119. Piston, *Lee's Tarnished Lieutenant*, pp. 55–58.

120. Coddington, *Gettysburg Campaign*, p. 382.

121. Ibid., pp. 55–58.

122. Freeman, *R. E. Lee*, III, pp. 100–1.

123. Lee's inaction prompted Arthur J. L. Fremantle, a British military observer at Gettysburg, to comment, "It is evidently his system to arrange the plan thoroughly with the three corps commanders, and then leave to them the duty of modifying and carrying it out to the best of their abilities." Piston, "Cross Purposes" in Gallagher, Gary W., *The Third Day at Gettysburg & Beyond* (Chapel Hill & London: The University of North Carolina Press, 1994) [hereafter Gallagher, *Third Day*], pp. 31, 43.

124. Piston, *Lee's Tarnished Lieutenant*, p. 58. Lee's uncoordinated attacks at Gettysburg were similar to those of McClellan at Antietam the prior summer.

125. Bruce, "Lee and Strategy," p. 122.

126. Freeman, *R. E. Lee*, III, pp. 101–2; Pfanz, *Culp's and Cemetery Hills*, pp. 235–327.

127. Alexander, *Fighting for the Confederacy*, pp. 234–35. Similarly, Gary Pfanz criticized Lee for leaving Ewell, with one-third of Lee's outnumbered infantry, in an isolated position unsuited to offensive operations. Pfanz, *Second Day*, p. 426.

128. Pfanz faulted Lee for his hands-off supervision of Longstreet, whom Lee "… seems not to have hurried … along," and Hill ("He did not rectify Hill's faulty deployment of Anderson's division or his inadequate measures to sustain Anderson's attack…."). Pfanz, *Second Day*, pp. 426–27. For details on Hill's inadequate performance, see Ibid., pp. 99, 114, 386–87.

129. Tomasak, Peter. ""Glory to God! We Are Saved… Night Assault at Gettysburg," *North & South*, Vol. 1, No. 5 (1998), pp. 32–44.

130. For details of the third day, see Gallagher, *Third Day*, pp. 1–160; Coddington, *Gettysburg Campaign*, pp. 442–534.

131. Coddington, *Gettysburg Campaign*, pp. 465–76; Pfanz, *Culp's Hill & Cemetery Hill*, pp. 284–309; Pfanz, *Second Day*, p. 438; Kross, Gary, "Picketts's Charge! Including Supporting Actions on Culp's Hill," *Blue & Gray Magazine*, XVI, Issue 5 (June 1999), pp. 6–21, 38–51 [hereafter Kross, "Pickett's Charge"] at pp. 7–13.

132. Coddington, *Gettysburg Campaign*, p. 450.

133. Foote, *Civil War*, II, p. 525.

134. On this Lee-Longstreet dispute, see Piston, "Cross Purposes" in Gallagher, *Third Day*, pp. 31–55.

135. Coddington, *Gettysburg Campaign*, p. 460.

136. Ibid., p. 488.

137. Wert, *Longstreet*, p. 287.

138. Lowe, "Field Fortifications," p. 65. Lowe explained Lee's problem: "In the two years leading up to Gettysburg, both armies had steadily replaced outdated smoothbore muskets with rifle-muskets, thus improving the effective range of the standard shoulder arm from less than 100 yards to more than 300 yards. Within the last 100 yards the rifle-musket was considerably more accurate. It is estimated that less than fifteen percent of the frontline units at Gettysburg retained smoothbore muskets." Ibid.

139. Alexander, *Fighting for the Confederacy*, p. 254.

140. Alexander, *Great Generals*, p. 26.

141. Longstreet later stated that Lee had written to him in the 1863–64 winter that, "If I only had taken your counsel even on the 3d [July 3], and had moved

around the Federal left, how different all might have been." Longstreet, James, "Lee's Right Wing at Gettysburg," in Johnson and Buel, *Battles and Leaders*, III, pp. 339–53 at p. 349.

142. Sears, "Lee of Gettysburg," p. 18. "Thus it may be said that Pickett's Charge was more a product of Lee's will than of his head. He seems to have felt obliged to demonstrate to his lieutenants that his way was the right way, and the only way." Ibid., p. 19.

143. Alexander, *Fighting for the Confederacy*, p. 251.

144. For details of the East Cavalry Field battle, see Carhart, *Lost Triumph*, pp. 213–69.

145. Ibid., p. 252.

146. Ibid., pp. 258, 260; Coddington, *Gettysburg Campaign*, p. 500.

147. Freeman, *Lee's Lieutenants*, III, p. 157.

148. Coddington, *Gettysburg Campaign*, p. 501.

149. Confederate Captain Joseph Graham, of the Charlotte Artillery, wrote in late July 1863 of Pettigrew's infantry "mov[ing] right through my Battery, and I feared then I could see a want of resolution in our men. And I heard many say, 'that is worse than Malvern Hill,' and 'I don't hardly think that position can be carried,' etc., etc., enough to make me apprehensive about the result….." Gallagher, "Lee's Army" in Gallagher, *Third Day*, p. 23.

150. Alexander, *Fighting for the Confederacy*, p. 266; Coddington, *Gettysburg Campaign*, p. 526; Wert, *Longstreet*, p. 292.

151. Bruce, "Lee and Strategy," pp. 123–24.

152. Waugh, *Class of 1846*, p. 487.

153. Piston, *Lee's Tarnished Lieutenant*, p. 62.

154. Wert, *Longstreet*, p. 292.

155. "Properly led on the decisive afternoon at Gettysburg, George Pickett's Virginians and Johnston Pettigrew's Carolinians would not have been sent across the killing fields from Seminary to Cemetery Ridge, against the massed Union army. But their bravery at Chancellorsville had persuaded their general that they were invincible, and so he sent them. And so Gettysburg was lost, and so the war." Furgurson, *Chancellorsville*, p. 350.

156. Coddington, *Gettysburg Campaign*, pp. 525–26.

157. Freeman, *R. E. Lee*, III, pp. 133–34.

158. Alexander, *Fighting for the Confederacy*, pp. 278–80.

159. Kross, "Pickett's Charge," p. 51.

160. Fuller, *Grant and Lee*, p. 118.

161. Weigley, *American Way of War*, p. 117.

162. Lee to Jefferson Davis, July 29, 1863, *Papers of Lee*, pp. 563–64 at p. 563; Civil War Times Illustrated Editors (eds.), *Great Battles of the Civil War* (New York: Gallery Books, 1984) [hereafter Civil War Times, *Great Battles*], p. 314. Meade's failure to pursue Lee after Gettysburg, his ineffective Mine Run Campaign late in 1863, and a losing political battle with Sickles were some of the reasons that the hero of Gettysburg faded to the back pages of Civil War history. Haggerty, Charles, "George Who?," *Civil War Times Illustrated*, XLI, No. 4 (Aug. 2002), pp. 20–28.

163. Welch, Richard F., "Gettysburg Finale," *America's Civil War* (July 1993), pp. 50–57.

164. Alexander, *Fighting for the Confederacy*, p. 271.

165. Coddington, *Gettysburg Campaign*, pp. 535–74; Brown, Kent Masterson, "A Golden Bridge: Lee's Williamsport Defense Lines and His Escape across the Potomac," *North & South*, Vol. 2, No. 6 (Aug. 1999), pp. 56–65.

166. Alexander, Ted, "Ten Days in July: The Pursuit to the Potomac," *North & South*, Vol. 2, No. 6 (Aug. 1999), pp. 10–34 [hereafter Alexander, "Ten Days"] at pp. 20–21. Alexander described the retreat, Union pursuit, and several skirmishes in detail.

167. Ibid., p. 92.

168. McKenzie, John D., *Uncertain Glory: Lee's Generalship Re-Examined* (New York: Hippocrene Books, 1997) [hereafter McKenzie, *Uncertain Glory*], pp. 170–71.

169. Lee to Samuel Cooper, Battle Report of Gettysburg Campaign, January 20, 1864, *Papers of Lee*, pp. 569–85 at p. 576.

170. Lee's attacks at Gettysburg "were an unhappy caricature of the most unfortunate aspects of his tactics." Woodworth, *Davis and Lee*, p. 245. On available food for Lee's army, see Bauer, "Food Supplies?"

171. Harman, Troy D., *Lee's Real Plan at Gettysburg* (Mechanicsburg, Pennsylvania: Stackpole Books, 2003); Harman, Troy D., "The Unchanging Plan," *Civil War Times*, XLII, No. 3 (Aug. 2003), pp. 42–47.

172. Alexander to Thomas L. Rosser, April 19, 1901, quoted in Sears, "Lee of Gettysburg," p. 19.

173. McPherson, James M., "To Conquer a Peace?: Lee's Goals in the Gettysburg Campaign," *Civil War Times*, XLVII, No. 2 (March/April 2007), pp. 26–33 at p. 28.

174. Rhodes, *All for the Union*, p. 117.

175. Jones, "Military Means," in Boritt, *Why the Confederacy Lost*, p. 68.

176. Freeman, *Lieutenants*, III, pp. 190–97.

177. Livermore, *Numbers & Losses*, pp. 102–3.

178. See Appendix II.

179. Lee to Jefferson Davis, July 31, 1863, *Papers of Lee*, pp. 564–65 at p. 565.

180. Because of the misleadingly positive newspaper reports, Lee had cautioned his wife that "You will have learned before this reaches you that our success at Gettysburg was not as great as reported." Lee to his wife, July 12, 1863, Ibid., pp. 547–48 at p. 547; Gallagher, Gary W., "Lee's Army Has Not Lost Any of Its Prestige: The Impact of Gettysburg on the Army of Northern Virginia and the Confederate Home Front," pp. 1–30, in Gallagher, *Third Day*, p. 18.

181. Lee to Jefferson Davis, July 31, 1863, *Papers of Lee*, pp. 564–65 at p. 565. Historian and Lee critic Thomas L. Connelly marveled at Lee's judgment "three weeks after the South had lost Middle Tennessee, 47,000 men in the campaign at Vicksburg, the last link in the control of the Mississippi, over 27,000 at Gettysburg, and great political prestige in the Northwest." Connelly, Thomas Lawrence, "Robert E. Lee and the Western Confederacy: A Criticism of Lee's Strategic Ability," *Civil War History*, Vol. 15 (June 1969), pp. 116–32 [hereafter Connelly, "Lee and the West"] at p. 130.

182. Wiley, *Road to Appomattox*, pp. 64–65.

183. McWhiney and Jamieson, *Attack and Die*, p. 19.

184. Ibid. These numbers are killed and wounded only. "Principally, [Gettysburg] cost the Confederacy an immense number of killed and wounded, far greater in proportion to Lee's resources than the battle losses suffered by the Union. As President Davis later wrote, stressing the casualties: 'Theirs could be repaired, ours could not.'" Hattaway and Jones, *How the North Won*, p. 415.

185. Groom, Winston, *Shrouds of Glory. From Atlanta to Nashville: The Last Great Campaign of the Civil War* (New York: The Atlantic Monthly Press, 1995) [hereafter Groom, *Shrouds of Glory*], p. 42.

186. Wert, *Longstreet*, p. 151.

187. Brennan, Patrick, "It Wasn't Stuart's Fault," *North & South*, Vol. 6, No. 5 (July 2003), pp. 22–37 at p. 37.

188. Glatthaar, Joseph T., "Black Glory: The African-American Role in Union Victory," pp. 133–62 [hereafter Glatthaar, "Black Glory"] in Boritt, *Why the Confederacy Lost*, pp. 149–50.

189. Gorgas, *Journals*, July 28, 1863, p. 75.

190. McPherson, "Unheroic Hero," p. 18; Williams, *McClellan, Sherman and Grant*, p. 95; Goodman, Al W., Jr., "Grant's Mississippi Gamble," *America's Civil War*, Vol. 7, No. 3 (July 1994), pp. 50–56 [hereafter Goodman, "Grant's Gamble"] at p. 54; Winschel, Terrence J., "Vicksburg: 'Thank God. The Father of Waters again goes unvexed to the sea,'" *America's Civil War*, Vol. 16, No. 3 (July 2003), pp. 18–9 at p. 19. Grant's version of the Vicksburg Campaign is in Grant, Ulysses S., "The Vicksburg Campaign" in Johnson and Buel, *Battles and Leaders*, III, pp. 493–539 and in Grant, *Memoirs*, pp. 303–83.

191. Winschel, Terrence J., "Grant's March Through Louisiana: 'The Highest Examples of Military Energy and Perseverance,'" *Blue & Gray Magazine*, XIII, Issue 5 (June 1996), pp. 8–22 [hereafter Winschel, "Grant's March"] at p. 9.

192. Fuller, *Generalship of Grant*, p. 137.

193. Woodworth, *Nothing But Victory*, p. 317.

194. Winschel, "Grant's March," pp. 13–15.

195. Grant, *Memoirs*, pp. 305–6.

196. Ibid., pp. 306–8; Catton, *Grant Moves South*, pp. 411–15; Winschel, "Grant's March," p. 17; Poulter, Keith. "Decision in the West: The Vicksburg Campaign, Part II: Running the Batteries," *North & South*, Vol. 1, No. 3 (Feb. 1998), pp. 68–75 [hereafter Poulter, "Decision Part II"] at p 69.

197. Bearss, *Vicksburg*, II, pp. 53–74; Arnold, *Grant Wins*, p. 78.

198. Grant, *Memoirs*, pp. 306–8; Catton, *Grant Moves South*, pp. 411–15; Winschel, "Grant's March," p. 17; Poulter, "Decision Part II," p 69.

199. Smith, *Grant*, pp. 236–37; Arnold, *Grant Wins*, pp. 78–79.

200. Grant, *Memoirs*, p. 309; pp. 16–19; Nevins, *Ordeal*, VI, p. 415. Ever innovative, Grant had tried building a canal (the Duckport Canal) to assist in the movement from Hard Times to New Carthage, but the effort was unsuccessful. Winschel, "Grant's March," pp. 14–15.

201. Although the Union corps officially were numbered with Roman numerals (e.g., XVIII), I have used more reader-friendly Arabic numerals (e.g., 2nd or 18th) to describe them.

202. Bearss, *Vicksburg*, II, pp. 74–82; Grant, *Memoirs*, pp. 310–14; Smith, *Grant*, p. 237; Arnold, *Grant Wins*, pp. 79–81.

203. Arnold, *Grant Wins*, pp. 81–82.

204. Feis, *Grant's Secret Service*, pp. 144–45.

205. Williams, Kenneth P., *Grant Rises in the West* (Lincoln: University of Nebraska Press, 1997) (2 vols.) (Originally vols. 3 and 4 of *Lincoln Finds a General: A Military Study of the Civil War*, New York: Macmillan, 1952) [hereafter Williams, *Grant Rises in the West*], II, p. 339; Roth, Dave, "Grierson's Raid: A Cavalry Raid at Its Best, April 17–May 2, 1863," *Blue & Gray Magazine*, X, Issue 5 (June 1993), pp. 12–24, 48–65 [hereafter Roth, "Grierson's Raid"] at p. 13; Grant to Hurlbut, Feb. 13, 1863, *Papers of Grant*, VII, pp. 316–17 at p. 317. For more details on Grierson's raid, see Bearss, *Vicksburg*, II, pp. 187–236.

206. Roth, "Grierson's Raid," pp. 21–24.

207. Ibid., pp. 48–51.

208. Ibid., pp. 58–61.

209. Arnold, *Grant Wins*, p. 87; Williams, *Grant Rises in the West*, II, p. 345.

210. Weigley, Russell F., *A Great Civil War: A Military and Political History, 1861–1865* (Bloomington and Indianapolis: Indiana University Press, 2000) [hereafter Weigley, *Great Civil War*], p. 265; Roth, "Grierson's Raid," pp. 13, 64–65; Foote, *Civil War*, II, p. 334; Smith, *Grant*, p. 239; Arnold, *Grant Wins*, p. 87.

211. Feis, *Grant's Secret Service*, p. 146; Roth, "Grierson's Raid," pp. 48–49.

212. Grant, *Memoirs*, p. 318; Weigley, *Great Civil War*, p. 265; Catton, *Grant Moves South*, pp. 422–24; Winschel, "Grant's March," p. 19; Woodworth, *Nothing But Victory*, p. 334.

213. Feis, *Grant's Secret Service*, p. 158; Winschel, "Grant's March," p. 19; Dana, Charles A., *Recollections of the Civil War* (New York: Collier Books, 1898, 1963) [hereafter, Dana, *Recollections*, pp. 56–58; Arnold, *Grant Wins*, pp. 87–89.; Woodworth, *Nothing But Victory*, p. 341.

214. Grant, *Memoirs*, pp. 315–17; Winschel, "Grant's March," pp. 19–20.

215. Grant, *Memoirs*, pp. 317–21; Poulter, "Decision Part II," p. 75.

216. Grant, *Memoirs*, p. 321.

217. Winschel, "Grant's March," p. 22.

218. Winschel, Terrence J., "Grant's Beachhead for the Vicksburg Campaign: The Battle of Port Gibson, May 1, 1863," *Blue & Gray Magazine*, XI, Issue 3 (Feb. 1994), pp. 8–22, 48–56 [hereafter Winschel, "Grant's Beachhead"] at pp. 15–19.

219. Arnold, *Grant Wins*, p. 98.

220. For details and battle maps of the Battle of Port Gibson, see Winschel, "Grant's Beachhead"; Arnold, *Grant Wins*, pp. 101–18; and Bearss, *Vicksburg*, II, pp. 353–407. For battle maps of the battles of Port Gibson, Raymond, and Jackson, see Poulter, Keith, "Decision in the West: The Vicksburg Campaign, Part III," *North & South*, Vol. 1, No. 4 (April 1998), pp. 77–83 [hereafter Poulter, "Decision Part III"].

221. Grant, *Memoirs*, pp. 321–24; Winschel, "Grant's Beachhead," pp. 20–22, 48–55. Bearss, Ed, "The Vicksburg Campaign: Grant Moves Inland," *Blue & Gray Magazine*, XVIII, Issue 1 (October 2000), pp. 6–22, 46–52, 65 [hereafter Bearss, "Grant Moves Inland"] at p. 6; Goodman, "Grant's Gamble," pp. 52–56; Woodworth, *Nothing but Victory*, pp. 341–47. Even after the fall of Port Gibson, General Pemberton in Vicksburg had no idea what Grant was doing. He telegraphed his local commander, "Is it not probable that the enemy will himself retire tonight?" Goodman, "Grant's Gamble," p. 56.

222. Winschel, "Grant's Beachhead," p. 56.

223. Ibid.; Arnold, *Grant Wins*, pp. 116–17; Ballard, Michael B., "Misused Merit: The Tragedy of John C. Pemberton," in Woodworth, Steven E. (ed.), *Civil War Generals in Defeat* (Lawrence: University of Kansas Press, 1999), pp. 141–60 at p. 157; Woodworth, *Nothing But Victory*, p. 396.

224. Grant, *Memoirs*, pp. 324–27; Bearss, "Grant Moves Inland," p. 6; Weigley, *Great Civil War*, p. 265.

225. On May 3, Grant wrote to Halleck of Grierson's raid and concluded: "He has spread excitement throughout the State, destroyed railroads, trestle works, bridges, burning locomotives & rolling stock taking prisoners destroying stores of all kinds [*sic*]. To use the expression of my informant 'Grierson has knocked the heart out of the State." Grant to Halleck, May 3, 1863, *Papers of Grant*, VIII, p. 144.

226. Grant, *Memoirs*, pp. 326–28; Bearss, "Grant Moves Inland," pp. 6–7; Weigley, *Great Civil War*, p. 266.

227. Grant to Halleck, May 3, 1863, *Papers of Grant*, VIII, pp. 145–48 at pp. 147–48.

228. Poulter, "Decision III," p. 78.

229. Grant, *Memoirs*, pp. 328–29; Bearss, "Grant Moves Inland," pp. 7–8.

230. Williams, *McClellan, Sherman and Grant*, p. 95.

231. Buell, *Warrior Generals*, p. 247.

232. Grant, *Memoirs*, pp. 328, 330; Bearss, "Grant Moves Inland," pp. 8, 11 (quote on p. 8). On May 9, Grant wrote to Sherman: "I do not calculate upon the possibility of supplying the Army with full rations from Grand Gulf. I know it will be impossible without constructing additional roads. What I do expect however is to get up what rations of hard bread, coffee & salt we can and make the country furnish the balance.... A delay would give the enemy time to reinforce and fortify." Grant to Sherman, May 9, 1863, *Papers of Grant*, VIII, pp. 183–84. On May 10, Grant rejected a complaint from McClernand about "a very small number of teams" and pointed out that each corps had been provided with equal transportation. Grant to McClernand, May 10, 1863, *Papers of Grant*, VIII, pp. 192–93 at p. 193.
233. Feis, *Grant's Secret Service*, p. 160.
234. Ecelbarger, Gary, *Black Jack Logan: An Extraordinary Life in Peace and War*. (Guilford, Connecticut: The Lyons Press, 2005)[hereafter Ecelbarger, *Black Jack Logan*], pp. 132–33.
235. Fuller, *Generalship of Grant*, pp. 140–46.
236. Trudeau, Noah Andre, "Climax at Vicksburg," *North & South*, Vol. 1, No. 5 (June 1998), pp. 80–89 [hereafter Trudeau, "Climax at Vicksburg"] at p. 83.
237. For details on the Battle of Raymond, see Bearss, *Vicksburg*, II, pp. 483–517.
238. Grant, *Memoirs*, pp. 330–1; Bearss, "Grant Moves Inland," pp. 8–21; Arnold, *Grant Wins*, pp. 129–36; Fox, *Regimental Losses*, pp. 544, 550.
239. Bearss, "Grant Moves Inland," p. 10; Smith, *Grant*, p. 245; Davis, *Jefferson Davis*, pp. 501–4. For General Johnston's critique of Davis' involvement in the defense of Vicksburg, and particularly his refusal to provide reinforcements from west of the Mississippi, see Johnston, Joseph E., "Jefferson Davis and the Mississippi," in Johnson and Buel, *Battles and Leaders*, III, pp. 472–82. Johnston was responding to Davis' criticism of Johnston's conduct of the campaign in Davis, *Rise and Fall*, II, pp. 333–55. There Davis found no fault with Pemberton's conduct but stated that Johnston failed to act at all, let alone promptly, to come to Pemberton and Vicksburg's relief.
240. Grant, *Memoirs*, p. 332; Bearss, "Grant Moves Inland," pp. 21–22; Feis, "Charles S. Bell," pp. 28–29; Grant to McClernand, McPherson, and Sherman (three dispatches), May 12, 1863, *Papers of Grant*, VIII, pp. 204–8; Grant to McClernand (two dispatches), May 13, 1863, Ibid., pp. 208–9.
241. For a compelling argument that the loss of Vicksburg resulted from President Davis' ostrich-like behavior, Pemberton's incompetence, and Johnston's

reluctance to fight, see Winschel, Terrence J., "A Tragedy of Errors: The Failure of the Confederate High Command in the Defense of Vicksburg," *North & South*, Vol. 8, No. 7 (Jan. 2006), pp. 40–49.

242. Grant, *Memoirs*, p. 333; Bearss, "Grant Moves Inland," pp. 46–47.

243. Feis, *Grant's Secret Service*, p. 161.

244. For details on the Battle of Jackson, see Bearss, *Vicksburg*, II, pp. 519–58.

245. Grant, *Memoirs*, pp. 334–38; Bearss, "Grant Moves Inland," pp. 47–51, 65; "The Opposing Forces in the Vicksburg Campaign," in Johnson and Buel, *Battles and Leaders*, III, pp. 546–50 [hereafter "Opposing Forces"] at p. 549; Weigley, *Great Civil War*, p. 267; Wilson, Harold S., *Confederate Industry: Manufacturers and Quartermasters in the Civil War* (Jackson: University of Mississippi Press, 2002), pp. 192–93.

246. Feis, "Charles S. Bell," p. 29. Sherman's men tore up railroad ties and rails, set the ties on fire, heated the rails on those fires, and then bent the rails around trees and telegraph poles in what became known as "Sherman necklaces." Bearss, "Grant Moves Inland," p. 52.

247. Grant, *Memoirs*, pp. 340–41; Feis, *Grant's Secret Service*, p. 163; Bearss, Ed, "The Vicksburg Campaign. Grant Marches West: The Battles of Champion Hill and Big Black Bridge," *Blue & Gray Magazine*, XVIII, Issue 5 (June 2001), pp. 6–24, 44–52 [hereafter Bearss, "Grant Marches West"] at pp. 8–9. The Bearss article contains excellent maps of both those battles. For more details and battle maps on the Battle of Champion Hill, see Arnold, *Grant Wins*, pp. 147–99 and Bearss, *Vicksburg*, II, pp. 559–651.

248. Bearss, "Grant Marches West," pp. 9–11.

249. Ibid., p. 16.

250. Ibid., pp.12, 16–19; Arnold, *Grant Wins*, pp. 158–69.

251. Bearss, "Grant Marches West," pp. 13, 20–21; Arnold, *Grant Wins*, pp. 170–78.

252. Bearss, "Grant Marches West," pp. 14, 21–24; Arnold, *Grant Wins*, pp. 178–92; Foote, *Civil War*, II, pp. 372–73.

253. Bearss, "Grant Marches West," pp. 15, 44–45.

254. Grant, *Memoirs*, pp. 342–48; Livermore, *Numbers & Losses*, pp. 99–100; Bearss, "Grant Marches West," p. 45.

255. Arnold, *Grant Wins*, pp. 197–99; Foote, *Civil War*, II, p. 375; Grant, *Memoirs*, p. 349.

256. Grant, *Memoirs*, pp. 349–50; Bearss, "Grant Marches West," p. 45; Freeman, Kirk, "Big Black River," *Military Heritage*, Vol. 2, No. 3 (Dec. 2000), pp. 76–85

[hereafter Freeman, "Big Black River,"] at pp. 78–80; Goodman, Al W., Jr., "Decision in the West (Part IV): Between Hell and the Deep Sea: Pemberton's Debacle at Big Black River Bridge," *North & South*, Vol. 1, No. 5 (June 1998), pp. 74–79 [hereafter Goodman, "Decision"] at pp. 74–77.

257. For details and battle maps of the Battle of the Big Black River, see Freeman, "Big Black River"; Goodman, "Decision"; Arnold, *Grant Wins*, pp. 225–32; and Bearss, *Vicksburg*, II, pp. 653–89.

258. Grant, *Memoirs*, pp. 350–53; Bearss, "Grant Marches West," pp. 45–46; Freeman, "Big Black River," pp. 81–85; Goodman, "Decision," pp. 77–79; Barton, Dick, "Charge at Big Black River," *America's Civil War*, Vol. 12, No. 4 (Sept. 1999), pp. 54–61 [hereafter Barton, "Charge"].

259. Grant, *Memoirs*, pp. 350–54; Bearss, "Grant Marches West," p. 49.

260. Grant, *Memoirs*, p. 354. In fact, Sherman had verbally and by letter urged Grant before the crossing of the Mississippi not to undertake the risky campaign with no base or line of supply. Grant was more concerned about the impact in the North if he appeared to be retreating by returning to Memphis to restart a presumably safer overland campaign against Vicksburg. As soon as Vicksburg was besieged, Sherman himself revealed his earlier opposition. But Grant was fully forgiving: "[Sherman's] untiring energy and great efficiency during the campaign entitle him to a full share of all the credit due for its success. He could not have done more if the plan had been his own." Grant, *Memoirs*, p. 364.

261. Weigley, *American Way of War*, pp. 139–40; Bearss, "Grant Marches West," p. 52.

262. Grant, *Memoirs*, pp. 354–56; Bearss, *Vicksburg*, III, pp. 753–873. *Chicago Times* reporter Sylvanus Cadwallader observed and said of McClernand's May 22 attack: "McClernand had commenced his attack. He expected to succeed. But that he ever carried any part of the fortifications on his front, as he signaled Grant he had already done, was absolutely false." Cadwallader, Sylvanus, *Three Years with Grant* (New York: Alfred A. Knopf, 1956) [hereafter Cadwallader, *Three Years*], p. 92. Sherman agreed that McClernand had lied and thereby caused many additional casualties. Sherman, William Tecumseh, *Memoirs of General W. T. Sherman* (New York: Literary Classics of the United States, Inc., 1990) (reprint of 1885 second edition) [hereafter Sherman, *Memoirs*], pp. 352–53.

263. Grant, *Memoirs*, pp. 588–89.

264. Woodworth, *Nothing But Victory*, pp. 433–34.

265. Fuller, *Generalship of Grant*, p. 154; Livermore, *Numbers & Losses*, p. 100; Grant, *Memoirs*, p. 358.

266. Lee to Davis, May 28, 1863, Freeman, Douglas Southall (ed.), *Lee's Dispatches: Unpublished Letters of General Robert E. Lee, C.S.A. to Jefferson Davis and the War Department of The Confederate States of America, 1862–65* (Baton Rouge and London: Louisiana State University Press, 1994) (reprint of 1914 edition) [hereafter Freeman, *Lee's Dispatches*], pp. 96–99 at p. 98 [emphasis added].

267. Cadwallader, *Three Years*, pp. 70–71, 103–5; Anderson, "Grant's Struggle with Alcohol," p. 23; McFeely, *Grant*, pp.133–35; Epperson, James F., Letter to Editor, *Columbiad*, Vol. 3, No. 2 (Summer 1999), p. 8; Jones, R. Steven, *Right Hand of Command: Use & Disuse of Personal Staffs in the Civil War* (Mechanicsburg, Pennsylvania: Stackpole Books, 2000)[hereafter Jones, *Right Hand*], pp. 113–16. On June 6, Chief of Staff John Rawlins wrote a letter to Grant asking to be relieved from duty if Grant did not stop drinking. Rawlins thoughtfully left a copy of the letter for posterity—along with a similar letter from another occasion when Rawlins incorrectly thought that Grant had been drinking. Apparently, Rawlins wanted the historical record to show that he had been Grant's "alcohol nanny." Ibid., p. 114–16. "With a defender like Rawlins, Grant had no need of any enemies." Ibid., p. 116, quoting Bruce Catton.

268. Botkin, B. A. (ed.), *A Civil War Treasury of Tales, Legends and Folklore* (New York: Promontory Press, 1960)[hereafter Botkin, *Treasury*], pp. 243–44.

269. Grant, *Memoirs*, pp. 359–60, 1134; Arnold, James R., *The Armies of U.S. Grant* (London: Arms and Armour Press, 1995) [hereafter, Arnold, *Armies of Grant*], p. 127; Evans, E. Chris, "Return to Jackson: Finishing Stroke to the Vicksburg Campaign, July 5–25, 1863" *Blue & Gray Magazine*, XII, Issue 6 (Aug. 1995), pp. 8–22, 50–63 [hereafter Evans, "Return to Jackson"] at p.12; Trudeau, "Climax at Vicksburg," p. 86.

270. Smith, David M. "Too Little Too Late at Vicksburg," *America's Civil War*, Vol. 13, No. 2 (May 2000), pp. 38–44 [hereafter Smith, "Too Little"]; Williams, *Grant Rises in the West*, II, pp. 452–53.

271. Lincoln to I. N. Arnold, May 26, 1863, *Works of Lincoln*, Vol. VI, pp. 230–31 at p. 230.

272. Grant, *Memoirs*, p.368; Evans, "Return to Jackson," p. 12.

273. Grant, *Memoirs*, pp. 369–70; Leonard, Phillip A. B., "Forty-seven Days. Constant bombardment, life in bomb shelters, scarce food and water, and rapidly accumulating filth were the price of resistance for the resolute Confederate citizens of besieged Vicksburg, Mississippi," *Civil War Times Illustrated*, XXXIX, No. 4 (August 2000), pp. 40–49, 68–69; Evans, "Return to Jackson," p. 14; Smith, "Too Little," p. 44; Hickenlooper, Andrew, "The Vicksburg Mine" in Johnson and Buel, *Battles and Leaders*, III, pp. 539–42. Vicksburg residents' primary meats were mules and rats. Anonymous, "Daily Life during the Siege of Vicksburg," in Gienapp, William E. (ed.), *The Civil War and Reconstruction: A Documentary Collection* (New York and London: W.W. Norton and Company, 2001), pp. 159–62.

274. Morgan, Michael, "Digging to Victory," *America's Civil War*, Vol. 16, No. 3 (July 2003, pp. 22–29; Arnold, *Grant Wins*, p. 298.

275. Grant, *Memoirs*, pp. 374–84; Lockett, S. H., "The Defense of Vicksburg," in Johnson and Buel, *Battles and Leaders*, III, pp. 482–92 at p. 492. Lockett was the Confederate Chief Engineer at Vicksburg. Grant's decision to parole Pemberton's demoralized men placed a burden on the South to support them—even though hundreds of Confederates declined to be paroled and elected Union prison camp rather than face the possibility of fighting again. Thousands were ill and hardly able to move. Thousands of others spoke with their feet and headed home never to fight again. Faced with a disaster and having no weapons to enforce his orders, Pemberton gave his entire army a thirty-day furlough, which President Davis countermanded. Pemberton switched to staggered furloughs—after which most of his soldiers did not reappear to be "swapped" for Union prisoners captured elsewhere. The deserting troops became a public safety hazard throughout Mississippi, and Pemberton ordered railroad depot guards to shoot them if they did not leave trains on which they had swarmed to return home. Bearss, *Vicksburg*, III, pp. 1301–1310; Catton, Bruce, *This Hallowed Ground: The Story of the Union Side of the Civil War* (Garden City, New York: Doubleday & Company, Inc., 1956, 1962), p. 122; Arnold, *Grant Wins*, pp. 298–99; Davis, *Jefferson Davis*, pp. 508–9. Apparently, many of his soldiers, exchanged or unexchanged, did fight somewhere later, but the Rebels' Mississippi Valley army was gone and the theater was lost for good.

276. Grant to Sherman, July 3, 1863, OR, Ser. I, XXIV, Part III, p. 461; Grant to Sherman, July 3, 1863, *Papers of Grant*, VIII, p. 460.

277. Evans, "Return to Jackson"; Feis, "Charles S. Bell," pp. 30–31. Feis' article contains the detailed and accurate order of battle that Bell had prepared on Johnston's force in Jackson and delivered to Sherman. Ibid., p. 33.

278. Arnold, *Grant Wins*, p. 301; Fuller, *Generalship of Grant*, p. 158.

279. See Appendix I.

280. Weigley, *Great Civil War*, p. 264.

281. Catton, *Grant*, p. 105.

282. Ibid., p. 104.

283. Hattaway and Jones, *How the North Won*, p. 415.

284. Winschel, Terrence J., "Vicksburg the Key," *North & South*, Vol. 7, No. 7 (Nov. 2004), pp. 58–67; Evans, "Return to Jackson," p. 63.

285. Lincoln to James C. Conkling, Aug. 26, 1863, *Works of Lincoln*, VI, pp. 406–10 at p. 409.

286. McPherson, *Battle Cry*, p. 637.

287. Weigley, *American Way of War*, p. 140.

288. Arnold, *Grant Wins*, p. 4.

289. Nevins, *Ordeal of the Union*, VI, p. 425.

290. Smith, *Grant*, p. 256.

291. Basler, Roy P. (ed.), *The Collected Works of Abraham Lincoln* (New Brunswick: Rutgers University Press, 1953) (8 vols.) [hereafter *Works of Lincoln*], VI, p. 326

292. Trudeau, "Climax at Vicksburg," p. 88.

293. Feis, William B., "The War of Spies and Supplies: Grant and Grenville M. Dodge in the West, 1862–1864" in Woodworth, *Grant's Lieutenants*, pp. 183–98 at pp. 195–97; Feis, *Grant's Secret Service*, pp. 173–74.

294. Steven Woodworth commented that "Twenty years later [President] Davis still did not understand that Grant had no supply lines for the Confederates to cut or that Pemberton, in allowing himself to be bottled up in Vicksburg, had made the worst possible move." Woodworth, Steven E., *Jefferson Davis and His Generals: The Failure of Confederate Command in the West* (Lawrence: University Press of Kansas, 1990), p. 310.

295. Bearss, *Vicksburg*, III, p. 1311.

296. McWhiney and Jamieson, *Attack and Die*, pp. 8, 19–21, 158. See Appendices I and II.

297. "Opposing Forces" at pp. 549–50; Weigley, *American Way of War*, p. 140.

298. Jones, *Diary*, I, p. 374; Gorgas, *Journals*, July 28, 1863, p. 75.

CHAPTER 7

1. Lee to Jefferson Davis, August 8, 1863, *Papers of Lee*, pp. 589–90.

2. Taylor, Walter H., *General Lee: His Campaigns in Virginia, 1861–1865 with Personal Reminiscences* (Lincoln and London: University of Nebraska Press, 1994; reprint of Norfolk, Virginia: Nusbaum Books, 1906) [hereafter Taylor, *General Lee*], p. 221; Woodworth, *Davis and Lee*, p. 251.

3. Ibid., p. 150; Freeman, *Lee's Lieutenants*, III, pp. 221–22.

4. Connelly and Jones, *Politics of Command*, pp. 134–35; Lee to James Longstreet, August 31, 1863, *Papers of Lee*, p. 594.

5. Thomas, *Lee*, p. 309. In early December, Lee again declined command of the Army of Tennessee and gave similar reasons; on the issue of generals sent west, he wrote, "I also fear that I would not receive cordial co-operation...." Lee to Jefferson Davis, December 7, 1863, Freeman, Douglas Southall and McWhiney, Grady (eds.), *Lee's Dispatches: Unpublished Letters of General Robert E. Lee, C.S.A., to Jefferson Davis and the War Department of the Confederate States of America 1862–65* (Baton Rouge and London: Louisiana State University Press, 1957, 1994) [Update of Freeman's original 1914 edition], pp. 130–31.

6. Hattaway and Jones compared Lee's ultimate acquiescence with his May 1863 position: "Lee ran less risk, had less emotional investment, and hence less dissonance in September than he had had in the spring. He felt less need to keep all of his forces in Virginia; the need in the West appeared more pressing after the defeats in Mississippi and Tennessee. [Thus] he could easily accede to Davis's desire to apply the conventional strategy and reinforce the west with troops sent by rail from Virginia." Hattaway and Jones, *How the North Won*, p. 374. In fact, Lee did not "easily" accede to Davis' request.

7. Connelly, *Autumn of Glory*, pp. 150–53; Hattaway and Jones, *How the North Won*, p. 444.

8. McMurry, *Two Armies*, p. 67.

9. Brennan, Patrick, "Hell on Horseshoe Ridge," *North & South*, Vol. 7, No. 2 (March 2004), pp. 22–44; Powell, Dave, "The 96th Illinois and the Battles for

Horseshoe Ridge, 1863 and 1895," *North & South*, Vol. 8, No. 2 (March 2005), pp. 48–59.

10. Connelly, *Autumn of Glory*, pp. 152, 191.

11. For details of the struggle for Chattanooga, see Cozzens, Peter, *The Shipwreck of Their Hopes: The Battles for Chattanooga* (Urbana and Chicago: University of Illinois Press, 1994) [hereafter Cozzens, *Shipwreck*].

12. Smith, *Grant*, pp. 261–62; Grant, *Memoirs*, p. 388. Grant later complained that, as had happened after Corinth the prior year, Halleck broke up Grant's army and sent his troops where they "would do the least good." Ibid., p. 389.

13. Catton, *Grant Moves South*, p. 489.

14. Wilson, John, "Miracle at Missionary Ridge," *America's Civil War*, XII, No. 7 (misprinted as 6) (March 2000), pp. 42–49 (hereafter Wilson, "Miracle") at pp. 42–44.

15. Stanton at first walked up to Grant's bearded surgeon, extended his hand, and said, "How do you do, General Grant. I recognized you from your pictures." Catton, Bruce, *U.S. Grant and the American Military Tradition* (Boston: Little, Brown and Company, 1954), p. 113.

16. Grant, *Memoirs*, pp. 389, 403; McDonough, James Lee, *Chattanooga—A Death Grip on the Confederacy* (Knoxville: The University of Tennessee Press, 1984) [hereafter McDonough, *Chattanooga*], p. 49.

17. The other order would have left Rosecrans in command of the Army of the Cumberland.

18. McDonough, *Chattanooga*, p. 45; Feis, *Grant's Secret Service*, p. 177. Grant's descriptions of the Chattanooga Campaign are in Grant, Ulysses S., "Chattanooga," in Johnson and Buel, *Battles and Leaders*, III, pp. 679–711 [hereafter Grant, "Chattanooga"] and Grant, *Memoirs*, pp. 403–62.

19. Clark, John E., Jr., "Reinforcing Rosecrans by Rail: The movement of the Federal Eleventh and Twelfth Corps from Virginia was a wonder of strategy, logistics, and engineering," *Columbiad: A Quarterly Review of the War Between the States*, Vol. 3, No. 3 (Fall 1999), pp. 74–95 at pp. 74–87; Skoch, George F., "Miracle of the Rails," *Civil War Times Illustrated*, XXXI, No. 4 (Oct. 1992), pp. 22–24, 56–59; Clark, John E., Jr., *Railroads in the Civil War: The Impact of Management on Victory and Defeat* (Baton Rouge: Louisiana State University, 2001), pp. 146–209; Weber, Thomas, *The Northern Railroads in the Civil War, 1861–1865* (Bloomington and Indianapolis: Indiana Uni-

versity Press, 1952, 1999), pp. 181–86. The move to the West opened career opportunities for Major General O. O. Howard, who proved his value during Chattanooga, Knoxville, and the march to Atlanta, and then was selected by Sherman (over the more senior Joseph Hooker) to replace Major General James McPherson as Commander of the Army of the Tennessee when he was killed outside Atlanta. Dolzall, Gary W., "O. O. Howard's Long Road to Redemption," *America's Civil War*, Vol. 14, No. 5 (Nov. 2001), pp. 38–44. The two transferred corps commanders, Howard and Slocum, later commanded the two wings of Sherman's army marching through Georgia and the Carolinas.

20. Grant, *Memoirs*, pp. 411–12; McDonough, *Chattanooga*, pp. 53–54.

21. Grant, *Memoirs*, pp. 413–18; McDonough, *Chattanooga*, pp. 54–58, 76–85; Cozzens, *Shipwreck*, pp. 48–65; Sword, Wiley, "The Battle above the Clouds," *Blue & Gray Magazine*, XVIII, Issue 2 (Dec. 2000), pp. 6–20, 43–56 [hereafter Sword, "Battle above Clouds"] at pp. 13–14.

22. Grant to Halleck, Oct. 28, 1863, *Papers of Grant*, IX, p. 335.

23. Catton, Bruce, *Grant Takes Command* (Boston: Little, Brown and Company, 1968, 1969) [hereafter, Catton, *Grant Takes Command*], pp. 55–56; Berg, Gordon, "Opening the Cracker Line," *America's Civil War*, Vol. 19, No. 2 (May 2006), pp. 46–52. Rosecrans and "Baldy" Smith carried on a bitter postwar dispute about who deserved credit for conceiving the brilliant amphibious movement that opened the "Cracker Line." Ibid. at pp. 51–52.

24. Grant, *Memoirs*, pp. 418–19.

25. Grant, *Memoirs*, pp. 419–20; McDonough, *Chattanooga*, pp. 88–94; Cozzens, *Shipwreck*, pp. 74–100; Sword, "Battle above Clouds," pp. 16–19. Grant apparently got a laugh when the quartermaster in charge of the stampeding mules requested that they receive promotion to the rank of horses. Botkin, *Treasury*, pp. 332–33.

26. Ibid.; Bonekemper, Edward H., III, *How Robert E. Lee Lost the Civil War* (Fredericksburg: Sergeant Kirkland's Press, 1998) [hereafter Bonekemper, *How Lee Lost*], p. 142.

27. Connelly, "Lee and the West," p. 129. After advising Davis that Longstreet should be moved to eastern Tennessee "& thence rejoin me," Lee stated, "No time ought now to be lost or wasted. Everything should be done that can be done at once, so that the troops may be speedily returned to this department.

As far as I can judge they will not get here too soon." Lee to Davis, Sept. 23, 1863, *Papers of Lee*, pp. 602–4 at pp. 602–3.

28. Wert, *Longstreet*, pp. 320–21.

29. Lee to Longstreet, October 26, 1863, OR, Ser. I, LII, Part II, pp. 549–50 at p. 550.

30. Cozzens, *Shipwreck*, pp. 103–5; Wilson, "Miracle," pp. 44–45; Bonekemper, *How Lee Lost*, pp. 142–43; Connelly, "Lee and the West," p. 129; Wert, *Longstreet*, pp. 320–21. "Davis's suggestion that Bragg detach Longstreet was quixotic, reflecting both his lack of appreciation of the Union buildup at Chattanooga and the degree to which he was swayed by Robert E. Lee." Cozzens, *Shipwreck*, p. 103. For an analysis of the Knoxville expedition from the perspective of Hood's Texas brigade, see Simpson, Harold B., *Hood's Texas Brigade: Lee's Grenadier Guard* (Fort Worth: Landmark Publishing, Inc., 1970, 1999) [hereafter Simpson, *Hood's Texas Brigade*], pp. 345–58.

31. Grant, *Memoirs*, pp. 427–30; Sword, "Battle above Clouds," p. 43; Cozzens, *Shipwreck*, p. 125.

32. Grant, *Memoirs*, pp. 439–41; McDonough, *Chattanooga*, pp. 106–20, 129–40; Cozzens, *Shipwreck*, pp. 159–78; Wilson, "Miracle," p. 45; Sword, "Battle above Clouds," pp. 44–56.

33. Marszalek, *Sherman: A Soldier's Passion for Order* (New York: The Free Press, 1993) [hereafter Marszalek, *Sherman*], pp. 241–43.

34. Grant, *Memoirs*, pp. 443–45; McDonough, *Chattanooga*, pp. 143–60; Cozzens, *Shipwreck*, pp. 199–244.

35. McDonough, *Chattanooga*, pp. 161–89; Wilson, "Miracle," pp. 46–48; Morris, Roy, Jr., *Sheridan: The Life and Wars of General Phil Sheridan* (New York: Crown Publishers, Inc., 1992) [hereafter Morris, *Sheridan*], pp. 144–45; Wilson, "Miracle," p. 48; Catton, *Grant Takes Command*, 81–82.

36. Wilson, "Miracle," p. 48; Morris, *Sheridan*, p. 145; McDonough, *Chattanooga*, p. 167.

37. McDonough, *Chattanooga*, pp. 182–85.

38. Wilson, "Miracle," p. 49; Morris, *Sheridan*, p. 146; Cozzens, *Shipwreck*, pp. 289–99. One of the first soldiers to reach the top of Missionary Ridge was First Lieutenant Arthur MacArthur; for his heroism, he was awarded the Congressional Medal of Honor—an honor that was bestowed almost eighty years later on his son, Douglas MacArthur.

39.   Richard McMurry argued that the transfer of Longstreet's troops to Chick-
       amauga may have been a mistake: "Yet a few weeks after Longstreet arrived
       in the West, Bragg—motivated by his antipathy for Longstreet—depleted
       the western army by detaching the two divisions under Longstreet's com-
       mand and sending them off into the East Tennessee mountains. Soon after-
       ward, Bragg's weakened army was routed at Missionary Ridge and fell back
       into Georgia. Longstreet's divisions, cut off from the Army of Tennessee,
       eventually returned to Virginia. Lee sent troops to the Army of Tennessee;
       Bragg sent them away. Perhaps there is something to be said for a general's
       holding on to his men." McMurry, *Two Armies*, p. 151. McMurry did not
       explain that Lee had suggested to Davis the early return of Longstreet to
       Virginia by way of Knoxville. Davis, not Lee, sent Longstreet's troops to
       Chickamauga—over Lee's time-consuming objections. Davis, Bragg, and
       Longstreet agreed with Lee's suggestion to quickly send Longstreet away from
       Chattanooga prior to the breakout at Missionary Ridge.

40.   Grant, *Memoirs*, pp. 445–46; Wilson, "Miracle," p. 49; Smith, *Grant*, p. 280;
       Morris, *Sheridan*, p. 148; Broome, Doyle D., Jr., "Daring Rear-guard Defense,"
       America's Civil War, Vol. 6, No. 5 (Nov. 1993), pp. 34–40; Watkins, *"Co. Aytch,"*
       p. 125.

41.   Watkins, *"Co. Aytch,"* p. 128.

42.   Smith, William Farrar, "Comments on General Grant's 'Chattanooga'" in
       Johnson and Buel, *Battles and Leaders*, III, pp. 714–17 at p. 717. Years later
       when Grant was asked if Bragg had thought his position was impregnable,
       Grant responded with a smile, "Well, it *was* impregnable." Foote, *Civil War*,
       II, p. 859.

43.   Williams, *McClellan, Sherman and Grant*, p. 100.

44.   Dolzall, Gary W., "Muddy, Soggy Race to Campbell's Station," *America's Civil
       War*, Vol. 15, No. 3 (July 2002), pp. 26–32, 80.

45.   Cox, *Reminiscences*, II, pp. 20–41; Johnston, Terry A., Jr., "Failure before
       Knoxville: Longstreet's Attack on Fort Sanders, November 29, 1863," *North
       & South*, Vol. 2, No. 7 (Sept. 1999), pp. 56–75.

46.   Lincoln to Grant, Nov. 25, 1863, *Works of Lincoln*, VII, p. 30; Grant, *Memoirs*,
       pp. 452–58; Lincoln to Grant, Dec. 8, 1863, *Works of Lincoln*, VII, p. 53;
       Simpson, *Hood's Texas Brigade*, pp. 359–81. On activity at Knoxville, see
       Johnson and Buel, *Battles and Leaders*, III, pp. 731–52.

47.   Foote, *Civil War*, II, p. 859.

48. Davis, *Jefferson Davis*, pp. 527–31.

49. Livermore, *Numbers & Losses*, pp. 106–8; Fox, *Regimental Losses*, pp. 23, 546, 551.

50. McWhiney and Jamieson, *Attack and Die*, pp. 157–58. See Appendix I herein, "Casualties in Grant's Battles and Campaigns," especially the summary table at the end.

51. Ambrose, Stephen E., *Halleck: Lincoln's Chief of Staff* (Baton Rouge and London: Louisiana State University Press, 1962, 1990)[hereafter Ambrose, *Halleck*], pp. 147–49. Halleck observed that the eastern generals were "unwilling to attack, even very inferior numbers. It certainly is a very strange phenomenon." OR, Ser. I, XXIX, Part II, p. 277. That was a problem Grant would solve in 1864.

52. Thomas, *Lee*, pp. 277–79, 310.

53. Freeman, *R. E. Lee*, III, pp. 169–87; Hattaway and Jones, *How the North Won*, p. 471; Thomas, *Lee*, pp. 210–11; Berkoff, Todd S., "Botched Battle at Bristoe," *America's Civil War*, Vol. 16, No. 4 (Sept. 2003), pp. 22–29, 70–71.

54. Welsh, William E., "Dual Disasters on the Rappahannock," *America's Civil War*, Vol. 16, No. 5 (Nov. 2003), pp. 42–49 [hereafter Welsh, "Dual Disasters"]; Hattaway and Jones, *How the North Won*, p. 477.

55. Popchock, Barry, "Daring Night Assault," *America's Civil War* IV, No. 6 (July 1993), pp. 50–57.

56. Freeman, *R. E. Lee*, III, pp. 188–205.

57. Lee to Davis, OR, Ser. I, XXIX, Part II, p. 861; Connelly, "Lee and the West," p. 119.

CHAPTER 8

1. Catton, *Grant Takes Command*, p. 93; Grant to Halleck, Dec. 7, 1863, *Papers of Grant*, IX, pp. 500–1.

2. Waugh, John C., *Reelecting Lincoln: The Battle for the 1864 Presidency* (New York: Crown Publishers, Inc., 1997) [hereafter Waugh, *Reelecting Lincoln*], p. 121.

3. *Works of Lincoln*, VIII, 339.

4. Smith, *Grant*, p. 284. Winfield Scott had received a brevet (temporary) promotion to lieutenant general.

5. Ibid.

6. Hattaway, Herman, "Dress Rehearsal for Hell: In early 1864, Mississippi was a proving ground for the 'total war' that would make Sherman infamous—and victorious," *Civil War Times Illustrated*, XXXVII, No. 5 (Oct. 1998), pp. 32–39, 74–75; Fuller, *Generalship of Grant*, p.181; Marszalek, *Sherman*, pp. 253–54.

7. Grant, *Memoirs*, p. 469; Smith, *Grant*, pp. 284–87.

8. Jones, *Right Hand*, p. 192.

9. Simon, John Y., "Grant, Lincoln, and Unconditional Surrender," in Boritt, Gabor S. (ed.), *Lincoln's Generals* (New York and Oxford: Oxford University Press, 1994), pp. 161–98 [hereafter "Grant, Lincoln"] at p. 164.

10. Rhea quoted in "Reconsidering Grant and Lee: Reputations of Civil War Generals Shifting," Associated Press, http://www.cnn.com/2003/SHOWBIZ/books/01/08/wkd.Grant.vs.Lee.ap/index.html [hereafter "Reconsidering Grant and Lee"].

11. Rhea, "'Butcher' Grant," p. 46.

12. Adams, *Fighting for Defeat*, p. 150.

13. Catton, *Stillness*, pp. 39–40.

14. Campbell, Eric A., "'Slept in the mud, stood in the mud, kneeled in the mud,'" *America's Civil War*, Vol. 15, No. 6 (January 2003), pp. 50–55 at 54–55.

15. Reid, Brian Holden, "Civil-Military Relations and the Legacy of the Civil War" in Grant, Susan-Mary and Parish, Peter J. (eds.), *Legacy of Disunion: The Enduring Significance of the American Civil War* (Baton Rouge: Louisiana State University Press, 2003), pp. 151–70 at p. 157.

16. Perret, Geoffrey, *Ulysses S. Grant: Soldier & President* (New York: Random House, 1997) [hereafter Perret, *Grant*], p. 304.

17. Grant, *Memoirs*, pp. 470–71.

18. Catton, "Generalship of Grant," p. 24. Richard J. Sommers said, "Prudent and competent, Meade would never have lost the war in Virginia, but, unaided, he would never have won it, either." Sommers, Richard J., *Richmond Redeemed: The Siege at Petersburg* (Garden City: Doubleday & Company, 1981)[hereafter Sommers, *Richmond Redeemed*], p. 437.

19. Thompson, Robert N. "The Folly and Horror of Cold Harbor," *Military History*, Vol. 23, No. 8 (Nov. 2006), pp. 38–45. Thompson demonstrated the problems caused by this bifurcated command structure—including, most notably, at Cold Harbor.

20. Smith, *Grant*, pp. 292–94.

21. Grant, *Memoirs*, pp. 480–81.

22. Jones, *Right Hand*, pp. 59–60, 191–92, 219.

23. "Grant, Lincoln," pp. 168–69.

24. Catton, *Stillness*, pp. 37, 44–49.

25. Grant, *Memoirs*, pp. 478–79; Wert, Jeffry D., "All-out War," *Civil War Times*, LXIII, No. 1 (April 2004), pp. 34–40 [hereafter Wert, "All-out War"].

26. "Grant, Lincoln," p. 168; Grant to Sherman, April 4, 1864, *Papers of Grant*, X, pp. 251–53 at p. 253.

27. Hattaway and Jones, *How the North Won*, pp. 516–33; Grant to Meade, April 9, 1864, *Papers of Grant*, X, pp. 273–75 at p. 274; Bonekemper, *How Lee Lost*, pp. 145–46.

28. Connelly, Thomas Lawrence and Jones, Archer, *Politics of Command*, pp. 179–81.

29. In declining the White House dinner, Grant told Lincoln, "I appreciate the honor, but time is very important now, and I have had enough of this show business." The declination caused the *New York Herald* to exclaim, "We have found our hero." Smith, *Grant*, p. 294.

30. Grant, *Memoirs*, pp. 471–73. Some historians plausibly contend that seizing Atlanta was a major or primary objective of Grant. Hattaway and Jones, *How the North Won*, p. 532.

31. Smith, *Grant*, p. 296.

32. Connelly and Jones, *Politics of Command*, pp. 180–81.

33. Marzalek, *Sherman*, p. 263.

34. Grant, *Memoirs*, p. 473.

35. Lincoln to Grant, April 30, 1864, *Works of Lincoln*, VII, p. 324; Johnson and Buel, *Battles and Leaders*, IV, p. 112.

36. Rhea, "'Butcher' Grant," p. 45

37. Catton, "Generalship of Grant," pp. 22–24.

38. Ibid., pp. 201–3.

39. Thomas, *Lee*, p. 322; Lee to Davis, March 25, 1863, Freeman, *Lee's Dispatches*, pp. 140–43.

40. Grant, *Memoirs*, pp. 481–82; Feis, *Grant's Secret Service*, pp. 203–5; Grant to Meade, April 9, 1864, *Papers of Grant*, X, pp. 273–75 at p. 274.

41. Feis, *Grant's Secret Service*, p. 207.

42. Grant to Meade, April 9, 1864, *Papers of Grant*, X, pp. 273–75 at p. 275.

43. Ibid., p. 538; Young, "Numbers and Losses," p. 19. During the course of the Overland Campaign, Lee received about 24,500 reinforcements from elsewhere. Ibid., p. 19.

44. Smith, *Grant*, pp. 303–4.

45. Beringer et al., *Why the South Lost*, p. 316.

46. Rhea, "'Butcher' Grant," p. 47.

47. Even General Alexander grudgingly conceded that Grant "was no intellectual genius, but he understood arithmetic." Alexander, *Fighting for the Confederacy*, p. 346.

48. The one glaring failure to tie down the Rebels was Jubal Early's breaking loose in July 1864; Lee, true to form, kept him in the Virginia theater instead of using him to reinforce Atlanta.

49. Connelly and Archer, *Politics of Command*, pp. 143–52.

50. Ibid., p. 192.

51. Coburn, Mark. *Terrible Innocence: General Sherman at War* (New York: Hippocrene Books, 1993) [hereafter Coburn, *Terrible Innocence*], p. 123.

52. On February 17, 1864, the Confederate Congress did attempt to address the manpower problem by extending conscription to 17-year-old boys and 45- to 50-year-old men. Wiley, *Road to Appomattox*, p. 68.

53. Hattaway and Jones, *How the North Won*, p. 272.

54. "Grant aimed to keep Lee so occupied that he could not emulate the Chickamauga campaign by sending men to help oppose Sherman. Although Grant had hopes of capturing Richmond…, the essence of his strategy lay in Sherman's taking Atlanta and beginning his raid." Jones, "Military Means," in Boritt, *Why the Confederacy Lost*, p. 71.

55. James Longstreet to Brigadier General Thomas Jordan, March 27, 1864, quoted in McPherson, *Battle Cry of Freedom*, p. 721 and Piston, *Lee's Tarnished Lieutenant*, pp. 85–86.

56. Connelly, "Lee and the Western Confederacy II," p. 198; Weigley, *American Way of War*, p. 125.

57. Lee to Braxton Bragg, April 7, 1864, *Papers of Lee*, pp. 692–93 at p. 692.

58. Connelly, *Autumn of Glory*, pp. 303–13.

59. Lee to Davis, May 12, 1864, *Papers of Lee*, p. 728.

CHAPTER 9

1. Grant, *Memoirs*, p. 512.
2. Rhodes, *All for the Union*, p. 142.
3. Grant, *Memoirs*, pp. 490–94; Schiller, "Beast in a Bottle," pp. 8–26. "[Butler] was perfectly safe against an attack; but, as [Chief Engineer General] Barnard expressed it, the enemy had corked the bottle and with a small force could hold the cork in place." Grant, *Memoirs*, pp. 493–94. Also, see "Controversy: Was Butler 'Bottled Up'?," *Blue & Gray Magazine*, VII, Issue 1 (Oct. 1989), pp. 27–29.
4. Warner, *Generals in Blue*, p. 448.
5. Holsworth, Jerry W., "VMI at the Battle of New Market and Sigel's Defeat in the Shenandoah Valley," *Blue & Gray Magazine*, XVI, Issue 4 (April 1999), pp. 6–24, 40–52.
6. Bounds, Steve and Milbourn, Curtis, "The Battle of Mansfield," *North & South*, Vol. 6, No. 2 (Feb. 2003), pp. 26–40.
7. McMurry, Richard M., "Georgia Campaign: Rocky Face to the Dallas Line, The Battles of May 1864," *Blue & Gray Magazine*, VI, Issue 4 (April 1989), pp. 10–23, 46–62; Kelly, Dennis, "Atlanta Campaign. Mountains to Pass, A River to Cross, The Battle of Kennesaw Mountain and Related Actions from June 10 to July 9, 1864," *Blue & Gray Magazine*, VI, Issue 5 (June 1989), pp. 8–30, 46–58.
8. Jones, *Right Hand*, p. 194.
9. Ibid. ; Porter, Horace, *Campaigning with Grant* (New York: SMITHMARK Publishers, Inc.) (Reprint of 1897 edition) [hereafter Porter, *Campaigning with Grant*], pp. 37–38
10. Grant's 1864 Overland Campaign is described in detail in Trudeau, Noah Andre, *Bloody Roads South: The Wilderness to Cold Harbor, May–June 1864* (Boston, Toronto, London: Little, Brown and Co., 1989)[hereafter Trudeau, *Bloody Roads*]; Lowry, *No Turning Back*; Lowry, Don, *Fate of the Country: The Civil War from June–September 1864* (New York: Hippocrene Books, 1992)[hereafter Lowry, *Fate of the Country*]; Rhea, Gordon C., *The Battle of the Wilderness, May 5–6, 1864* (Baton Rouge and London: Louisiana State University Press, 1994) [hereafter Rhea, *Wilderness*]; Rhea, Gordon C., *The Battles for Spotsylvania Court House and the Road to Yellow Tavern: May 7–12,*

1864 (Baton Rouge and London: Louisiana State University, 1997) [hereafter Rhea, *Spotsylvania*]; Rhea, Gordon C., *To the North Anna River: Grant and Lee, May 13–25, 1864* (Baton Rouge: Louisiana State University Press, 2000) [hereafter Rhea, *North Anna River*]; Rhea, *Cold Harbor*; Wheeler, Richard, *On Fields of Fury: From the Wilderness to the Crater: An Eyewitness History* (New York: HarperCollins Publishers, 1991)[hereafter Wheeler, *On Fields of Fury*]; and Law, Evander M., "From the Wilderness to Cold Harbor" in *Battles and Leaders*, IV, pp. 118–44 [hereafter Law, "From the Wilderness to Cold Harbor"] at p. 143.

11. Feis, *Grant's Secret Service*, p. 207.
12. Epperson, "Chance Battle," p. 78.
13. Lee's strength was definitively calculated at 65,995 in Young, Alfred C., "Numbers and Losses in the Army of Northern Virginia," *North & South*, Vol. 3, No. 3 (March 2000), pp. 14–29 [hereafter Young, "Numbers and Losses"] at pp. 15–20.
14. Alexander, *Fighting for the Confederacy*, p. 349.
15. Trudeau, Noah Andre, "'A Frightful and Frightening Place'," *Civil War Times Illustrated*, XXXVIII, No. 2 (May 1999), pp. 42–55 [hereafter Trudeau, "Frightful Place"]; Epperson, "Chance Battle," pp. 88–89.
16. Epperson, "Chance Battle," p. 94.
17. For more details on the Battle of the Wilderness, see Rhea, *Wilderness*; Scott, Robert Garth, *Into the Wilderness with the Army of the Potomac* (Bloomington: Indiana University Press, 1985) [hereafter Scott, *Into the Wilderness*]; Trudeau, "Frightful Place."
18. Grant to Meade, May 5, 1864, 8:24 a.m., *Papers of Grant*, X, p. 399.
19. Trudeau, "Frightful Place," pp. 45–46; Epperson, "Chance Battle," pp. 84–86; Mertz, Gregory A., "No Turning Back: The First Day of the Wilderness," *Blue & Gray Magazine*, XII, Issue 4 (April 1995) pp. 8–23, 47–53 [hereafter Mertz, "Wilderness I"] at pp. 14–15. On the morning of May 5, Grant was aware from his signal tower behind the Rapidan that Confederates were approaching but, because of Wilson's inadequate performance, was not aware of Ewell's substantial and close presence on the Orange Turnpike. Demonstrating his intent to engage Lee, Grant issued orders changing the direction of his troops from a westerly and southwesterly direction to a more westerly approach to where he expected Lee to be. "Grant's orders clearly envisioned a westward advance toward Lee. Contrary to many casual accounts of the

campaign, Grant was not trying to steal a march past Lee's flank, but was turning to meet Lee's army." Epperson, "Chance Battle," pp. 86–87.

20. Trudeau, "Frightful Place," pp. 46–48; Mertz, "Wilderness I," pp. 20–23, 47–48. For more details on the first day's fighting at the Wilderness, see Mertz, "Wilderness I"; Freeman, Douglas Southall, *R. E. Lee* (New York and London: Charles Scribner's Sons, 1934–35) (4 vols.) [hereafter Freeman, *R. E. Lee*], III, pp. 269–83. Epperson contends that competent reconnaissance by Wilson would have discovered Ewell's late May 4 position on the Orange Turnpike and enabled Grant to pounce on the flank and front of his 17,200 men with a combined force of 51,000 men (the 2nd and 6th corps and a division from Burnside's 9th Corps). Epperson, "Chance Battle," p. 95.

21. Trudeau, "Frightful Place," pp. 48–9; Mertz, "Wilderness I," pp. 48–51.

22. Trudeau, "Frightful Place," p. 49; Mertz, "Wilderness I," pp. 51–52.

23. Rhea, *Wilderness*, p. 271.

24. Lowry, *No Turning Back*, p. 518.

25. Trudeau, Noah Andre, "'A Mere Question of Time': Robert E. Lee from the Wilderness to Appomattox Court House," pp. 523–58 [hereafter Trudeau, "Question of Time"], in Gallagher, *Lee the Soldier*, pp. 527–28; Mertz, "No Turning Back: The Second Day of the Wilderness" *Blue & Gray Magazine*, Issue 5 (June 1995), pp. 8–20, 48–50 [hereafter Mertz, "Wilderness II"], p. 11. For more details on the second day's fighting at the Wilderness, see Mertz, "Wilderness II"; Freeman, *R. E. Lee*, III, pp. 283–303.

26. Freeman, *R. E. Lee*, III, pp. 287–88.

27. Freeman, *R. E. Lee*, III, pp. 287–88; Mertz, "Wilderness II," pp. 11–19; Trinque, Bruce A., "Battle Fought on Paper," *America's Civil War*, Vol. 6, No. 2 (May 1993), pp. 30–36; Trudeau, "Frightful Place," pp. 50–52; Fuller, *Grant and Lee*, p. 76; Longstreet, James, *From Manassas to Appomattox: Memoirs of the Civil War in America* (New York: Smithmark Publishers, Inc., 1994) [hereafter Longstreet, *From Manassas to Appomattox*], pp. 562–65.

28. Trudeau, "Frightful Place," p. 52.

29. Mertz, "Wilderness II," pp. 19–20.

30. Trudeau, "Frightful Place," pp. 52–54.

31. Arnold, James R., *The Armies of U.S. Grant* (London: Arms and Armour Press, 1995), p. 186. Livermore, *Numbers & Losses*, p. 110; Mertz, "Wilderness II," p. 49; Fuller, *Generalship of Grant*, p. 239; Young, "Numbers and Losses," p. 26; Smith, *Grant*, p. 333. "Robert E. Lee assumed the tactical defensive after

the Battle of the Wilderness until the end of the year, and did some of the best fighting of his career." McWhiney & Jamieson, *Attack & Die*, p. 108.

32. Gilbert, Thomas D., "Mr. Grant Goes to Washington," *Blue & Gray Magazine*, XII, Issue 4 (April 1995), pp. 33–37 at 37; Porter, *Campaigning with Grant*, pp. 69–70; Lowry, *No Turning Back*, p. 223.

33. Rhodes, *All for the Union*, p. 146.

34. Mertz, "Wilderness II," p. 49.

35. Grant, *Memoirs*, pp. 536–37.

36. "Grant kept fighting, even after some battles other generals would consider defeats." "Reconsidering Grant and Lee." Grant later said he was trying to get between Lee and Richmond and also to protect Butler against a possible counterattack by Lee. Grant, *Memoirs*, p. 540.

37. Smith, *Grant*, p. 338.

38. Rhea et al., "What Was Wrong?," p. 15.

39. Sherman, William T., "The Grand Strategy of the Last Year of the War," in Johnson and Buel, *Battles and Leaders*, IV, pp. 247–59 at p. 248.

40. Foote, *Civil War*, III, pp. 190–91.

41. Lee to James A. Seddon, May 8, 1864, *Papers of Lee*, pp. 724–25 at p. 724.

42. Adams, *Fighting for Defeat*, p. 156.

43. Mertz, "Wilderness II," p. 50.

44. For details on the Battle of Spotsylvania Court House, see Rhea, Gordon C., "Spotsylvania: The Battles at Spotsylvania Court House, Virginia, May 8–21, 1864," *Blue & Gray Magazine*, I, Issue 6 (June–July 1984), pp. 35–48.

45. Grant, *Memoirs*, pp. 540–41; Lowry, *No Turning Back*, p. 518. Perhaps influenced by Sheridan's later removal of Warren from command at the end of the Battle of Five Forks in April 1865, Grant criticized Warren in his *Memoirs* for being slow to get to and reinforce Spotsylvania Court House. Grant, *Memoirs*, pp. 541–43.

46. Mertz, Gregory A., "Upton's Attack and the Defense of Doles' Salient, Spotsylvania Court House, Va., May 10, 1864," *Blue & Gray Magazine*, May 10, 1864," XVIII, Issue 6 (Summer 2001), pp. 6–25, 46–52 [hereafter Mertz, "Upton's Attack."] at pp. 7–8; Guttman, Jon, "Jeb Stuart's Last Ride," *America's Civil War*, Vol. 7, No. 2 (May 1994), pp. 34–40, 79–80; Rhea, *North Anna River*, pp. 35–64. In his memoirs, Grant praised Sheridan's performance and seemed unfazed by his sixteen-day absence. Grant, *Memoirs*, pp. 494–97.

47. Mertz, "Upton's Attack," p. 10; McWhiney and Jamieson, *Attack and Die*, p. 91.

48. Grant, *Memoirs*, pp. 549–50; Mertz, "Upton's Attack," pp. 16–25, 46–51; McWhiney and Jamieson, *Attack and Die*, pp. 91–99; Ambrose, Stephen E., *Upton and the Army* (Baton Rouge: Louisiana State University Press, 1993), pp. 30–34. Grant rewarded Upton with a battlefield promotion to brigadier general. Grant, *Memoirs*, p. 550.

49. Grant to Halleck, May 11, 1864, *Papers of Grant*, X, pp. 422–23 at p. 422.

50. McWhiney & Jamieson, *Attack and Die*, p. 116; Freeman, *R. E. Lee*, III, pp. 315–16, 433; Smith, *Grant*, pp. 349–50; Freeman, *Lee's Lieutenants*, III, p. 398. "Never had Lee made a more egregious miscalculation." Rhea, Gordon C., "Robert E. Lee, Prescience, and the Overland Campaign," *North & South*, Vol. 3, No. 5 (June 2000), pp. 40–50 at p. 45. Rhea's article summarized the major decisions of Lee (and some by Grant) in the Overland Campaign.

51. Warren's refusal to promptly execute Meade's order for him to attack in support of Hancock's primary assault led Grant to tell Meade, "If Warren fails to attack promptly send Humphreys to command his corps, and relieve him." Grant to Meade, May 12, 1864, *Papers of Grant*, X, pp. 433; Grant, *Memoirs*, p. 554. This incident and a similar refusal to attack at Mine Run the prior November constituted the first two strikes against Warren—and he was "struck out" by Phil Sheridan (with Grant's blessing) after unfairly perceived hesitance at the Battle of Five Forks in April 1865. Sears, Stephen W., *Controversies and Commanders: Dispatches from the Army of the Potomac* (Boston and New York: Houghton Mifflin Company, 1999)[hereafter Sears, *Controversies*], pp. 253–87 [chapter entitled "Gouverneur Kemble Warren and Little Phil"]. The same material is in Sears, Stephen W., "Gouverneur Kemble Warren and Little Phil," *North & South*, Vol. 1, No. 5 (1998), pp. 56–72 [hereafter Sears, "Warren and Little Phil"].

52. Grant, *Memoirs*, p. 553; McWhiney and Jamieson, *Attack and Die*, pp. 92–93; Rhea, Gordon C., "Mule Shoe Redemption," *America's Civil War*, Vol. 17, No. 2 (May 2004), pp. 46–53, 72.

53. Grant, *Memoirs*, pp. 555–58; Rhodes, *All for the Union*, p. 153.

54. Grant, *Memoirs*, pp. 560–61; Rhea, Gordon C., "Last Union Attack at Spotsylvania: The belief that one more hard blow would shatter the Confederate line at Spotsylvania may have been one of Ulysses S. Grant's greatest

miscalculations.," *Columbiad: A Quarterly Review of the War Between the States*, Vol. 3, No. 4 (Winter 2000), pp. 111–39; Grant to Meade, May 18, 1864, *Papers of Grant*, X, p. 464.

55. Rhea, Gordon C., "'They Fought Confounded Plucky': The Battle of Harris Farm, May 19, 1864," *North & South*, Vol. 3, No. 1 (Nov. 1999), pp. 48–66 [hereafter Rhea, "Harris Farm"]; Rhea, *North Anna River*, pp. 164–89.

56. Rhea, "Harris Farm," pp. 52–66; Rhea, *North Anna River*, pp. 167–89.

57. Bonekemper, *How Lee Lost*, p. 156; Fuller, *Generalship of Grant*, p. 255.

58. Law, "From the Wilderness to Cold Harbor," p. 142. Law added that "... Grant's constant 'hammering' with his largely superior force had, to a certain extent, a depressing effect upon both officers and men." Ibid., p. 144.

59. Miller, "Strike Them," p.14; Foote, *Civil War*, III, p. 223; Smith, *Grant*, p. 355.

60. Colonel Theodore Lyman to Elizabeth Russell Lyman, May 18, 1864, quoted in McWhiney and Jamieson, *Attack and Die*, pp. 75–76, citing Agassiz, George R. (Ed.) , *Meade's Headquarters, 1863–1865* (Boston, 1922).

61. Grant, *Memoirs*, pp. 560–61.

62. Grant, *Memoirs*, pp. 562–64; Miller, "Strike Them," pp. 20–22, 44. This encounter also was known as the Battle of Henagan's Redoubt.

63. Robertson, James I., Jr. *General A. P. Hill: The Story of a Confederate Warrior* (New York: Random House, 1987), p. 276; Trudeau, "Question of Time," p. 533.

64. Dowdey, Clifford, *Lee* (Gettysburg: Stan Clark Military Books, 1991) [reprint of 1965 edition] [hereafter Dowdey, *Lee*], p. 464; Miller, "Strike Them," pp. 50–54. General Ledlie somehow managed to get promoted to division commander and performed miserably and drunkenly again at the Battle of the Crater on June 30. General Fuller hypothesized that it was Lee's prior heavy loss of manpower, not illness, that precluded him from attacking Grant's divided forces. Fuller, *Generalship of Grant*, p. 267.

65. Lowry, *No Turning Back*, pp. 424, 518; Miller, "Strike Them," p. 55.

66. "Grant and Lee, 1864: From the North Anna to the Crossing of the James," *Blue & Gray Magazine*, XI, Issue 4 (April 1994), pp. 11–22, 44–58 [hereafter "Grant and Lee, 1864"] at p. 11; Grant to Halleck, May 26, 1864, *Papers of Grant*, X, pp. 490–91 at p. 491.

67. "Grant and Lee, 1864," pp. 12–13; Grant to Halleck, May 26, 1864, *Papers of Grant*, X, pp. 490–91.

68. Rhea, *Cold Harbor*, p. 388.

69. "Grant and Lee, 1864," pp. 13–16; Malone, Jeff, "Melee in the Underbrush," *America's Civil War*, Vol. 5, No. 5 (Nov. 1992), pp. 26–32. For a detailed study of the Battle of Haw's Shop, see Rhea, "'The Hottest Place I Ever Was In,'" *North & South*, Vol. 4, No. 4 (April 2001), pp. 42–57 [hereafter Rhea, "Hottest Place"]; Rhea, *Cold Harbor*, pp. 61–91.

70. "Grant and Lee, 1864," pp. 11, 20.

71. "Grant and Lee, 1864," pp. 16–17.

72. "Grant and Lee, 1864," p. 20; Rhea, Gordon C., "Butchery at Bethesda Church," *America's Civil War*, Vol. 14, No. 6 (January 2002), pp. 48–54, 80. For details of the Battle of Bethesda Church, also see Rhea, *Cold Harbor*, pp. 139–51.

73. Grant, *Memoirs*, pp. 568–75; "Grant and Lee, 1864," p. 20; Rhea, *Cold Harbor*, pp. 159–60.

74. Welles, *Diary*, II, pp. 44–45.

75. Fellman, Michael, *Citizen Sherman: A Life of William Tecumseh Sherman* (New York: Random House, 1995) [hereafter Fellman, *Citizen Sherman*], p.177.

76. See Appendices I and II.

77. "Grant and Lee, 1864," pp. 21–22, 44.

78. Ibid., pp. 22, 44–46.

79. "Grant and Lee, 1864," pp. 50, 54. Union soldiers had similarly pinned their names on their uniforms before an apparent assault (which was cancelled) at Mine Run the prior November. Ibid., p. 54.

80. Ibid.; Rhea, Gordon C., "Cold Harbor: Anatomy of a Battle," *North & South*, Vol. 5, No. 2 (Feb. 2002), pp. 40–62 [hereafter Rhea, "Cold Harbor"] at pp. 40–41. For a detailed description of the Battle of Cold Harbor, see Rhea, *Cold Harbor*, pp. 318–64. For a description of one Irish brigade's decimation at Cold Harbor, see O'Beirne, Kevin M., "Into the Valley of the Shadow of Death: The Corcoran Legion at Cold Harbor," *North & South*, Vol. 3, No. 4 (April 2000), pp. 68–81 [hereafter O'Beirne, "Valley"].

81. Rhea, *Cold Harbor*, p. 390.

82. Grant to Halleck, June 3, 1864, 2:00 p.m., *Papers of Grant*, XI, p. 9.

83. Long, David E., "Cover-up at Cold Harbor," *Civil War Times Illustrated*, XXXVI, No. 3 (June 1997), pp. 50–95.

84. Grant, *Memoirs*, pp. 585.

85. Ernest B. Furgurson's book on Cold Harbor is *Not War But Murder: Cold Harbor 1864* (New York: Alfred A. Knopf, 2000) [hereafter Furgurson, *Not War but Murder*]. Ironically, Confederate Major General Daniel H. Hill earlier used the phrase, "It was not war—it was murder," to describe Lee's assault on Malvern Hill at the end of the Seven Days' Campaign in 1862. Hill, Daniel H., "McClellan's Change of Base and Malvern Hill," in Johnson and Buel, *Battles and Leaders*, p. 394; Kendall, Drew J., "'Murder' at Malvern Hill," *Military History*, Vol. 19, No. 3 (Aug. 2002), pp. 42–48.

86. Simpson, *Hood's Texas Brigade*, pp. 419–20.

87. Grant, *Memoirs*, p. 588.

88. A typical summary is "Cold Harbor, for example, cost Grant seven thousand men in a charge that lasted less than an hour." Groom, *Shrouds of Glory*, p. 9. Likewise, "Grant had lost... seven thousand in less than an hour of June 3 at Cold Harbor...." Fellman, *Citizen Sherman*, p.195. On the high side is the statement, "Grant's assault was finally canceled when thirteen thousand Union troopers lay dead or dying." Casdorph, Paul D., *Lee and Jackson: Confederate Chieftains* (New York: Paragon House, 1992) [hereafter Casdorph, *Lee and Jackson*], p. 401.

89. Rhea, *Cold Harbor*, p. 386; "Reconsidering Grant and Lee."

90. "Lee and Grant, 1864," p. 56.

91. Rhea, *Cold Harbor*, pp. 382, 386; Rhea, "Cold Harbor," pp. 60–61.

92. Dana, *Recollections*, p. 187.

93. Rhodes, *All for the Union*, p. 158.

94. Smith, *Grant*, pp. 365–66. Adams belonged to the famous presidential Adams family of Massachusetts.

95. Ibid.

96. Cox, *Reminiscences*, II, p. 224.

97. William T. Sherman to Ellen Boyle Ewing, May 20, 1864, cited in McWhiney and Jamieson, *Attack and Die*, pp. 106–7.

98. McFeely, *Grant*, pp. 171–73; Lowry, *No Turning Back*, pp. 518–19.

99. McWhiney and Jamieson, *Attack and Die*, p. 116; Freeman, *Lee's Lieutenants*, III, pp. 512–13; Bonekemper, *How Lee Lost*, p. 158.

100. Smith, *Grant*, p. 368.

101. Grant to Halleck, June 5, 1864, *Papers of Grant*, XI, pp. 19–20 at p. 19. As to the morale of his army, Grant told Halleck, "The feeling of the two Armies

now seems to be that the rebels can protect themselves only by strong intrenchments, whilst our Army is not only confidant [sic] of protecting itself, without intrenchments, but that it can beat and drive the enemy whenever and wherever he can be found without this protection." Ibid., p. 20.

102. Ibid.

103. "Lee and Grant, 1864," pp. 56–57; Wittenberg, Eric J., "Sheridan's Second Raid and the Battle of Trevilian Station," *Blue & Gray Magazine*, XIX, Issue 3 (Feb. 2002), pp. 8–24, 45–50 [hereafter Wittenberg, "Sheridan's Second Raid"].

104. "Lee and Grant, 1864," p. 57.

105. Alexander, *Fighting for the Confederacy*, p. 420.

106. Smith, *Grant*, p. 370.

107. Trudeau, Noah Andre, *The Last Citadel: Petersburg, Virginia June 1864–April 1865* (Baton Rouge: Louisiana State University Press, 1991) [hereafter Trudeau, *The Last Citadel*], pp. 22–25.

108. Alexander, *Fighting for the Confederacy*, p. 422.

109. Fuller, *Generalship of Grant*, p. 285.

110. Lee to Beauregard, June 16, 1864, 10:30 a.m., *Papers of Lee*, p. 784; Lee to Beauregard, June 16, 1864, 3:00 p.m., Ibid., p. 785; Thomas, *Lee*, p. 337; Alexander, *Fighting for the Confederacy*, pp. 429–30; Lee to Beauregard, June 16, 1864, 4:00 p.m., *Papers of Lee*, p. 785; Lowry, *Fate of the Country*, p. 53; Freeman, *R. E. Lee*, III, p. 417; Lee to Beauregard, June 17, 1864, 6:00 a.m., *Papers of Lee*, p. 787; Lee to Beauregard, June 17, 1864, noon, Ibid., p. 788; Lee to Beauregard, June 17, 1864, 4:30 p.m., Ibid., p. 789.

111. Foote, *Civil War*, III, p. 438; Lowry, *Fate of the Country*, p. 56; Freeman, *Lee's Lieutenants*, III, p. 534; Freeman, *R. E. Lee*, III, p. 421; Trudeau, *The Last Citadel*, p. 51; Alexander, *Fighting for the Confederacy*, p. 430–31; Lee to E. H. Gill [Superintendent, Richmond and Petersburg Railroad], June 18, 1864, 3:30 a.m., *Papers of Lee*, p. 791.

112. Lee to E. H. Gill, June 18, 1864, 3:30 a.m., *Papers of Lee*, p. 791; Alexander, *Fighting for the Confederacy*, p. 431.

113. Lee to Jubal A. Early, June 18, 1864, *Papers of Lee*, p. 791; Alexander, *Fighting for the Confederacy*, p. 431.

114. Grant, *Memoirs*, p. 599–602; Hattaway and Jones, *How the North Won*, pp. 589–90; Nolan, Alan T., *Lee Considered: General Robert E. Lee and Civil War*

History (Chapel Hill and London: University of North Carolina Press, 1991) [hereafter Nolan, *Lee Considered*], p. 85.

115. Bonekemper, *How Lee Lost*, p. 163.

116. See Appendix I.

117. Heidler and Heidler, *Encyclopedia*, p. 1497.

118. Waugh, *Reelecting Lincoln*, p. 202.

119. See Appendices I and II.

120. James M. McPherson wrote, "Although the Confederates had the advantage of fighting on the defensive most of the time, they suffered almost as high a percentage of casualties as the Union forces in this campaign." McPherson, *Mighty Scourge*, p. 113.

121. Young, Alfred C., "Numbers and Losses in the Army of Northern Virginia," *North & South*, Vol. 3, No. 3 (March 2000), pp. 14–29 [hereafter Young, "Numbers and Losses"] at pp. 19–21.

122. Fox, *Regimental Losses*, pp. 571–72; Warner, Ezra J., *Generals in Gray: Lives of the Confederate Commanders* (Baton Rouge and London: Louisiana State University Press, 1959, 1991) [hereafter Warner, *Generals in Gray*].

123. Rhea, "'Butcher' Grant," p. 55.

124. Catton, "Generalship of Grant," p. 28.

125. Nolan, *Lee Considered*, p. 85.

126. McPherson, "Unheroic Hero," p. 19.

127. Rhea, *Cold Harbor*, xii.

128. Young, "Numbers and Losses," pp. 19, 26–27.

CHAPTER 10

1. Catton, "Generalship of Grant," pp. 28–29.

2. Nolan, Alan T., *Lee Considered: General Robert E. Lee and Civil War History* (Chapel Hill and London: University of North Carolina Press, 1991) [hereafter Nolan, *Lee Considered*], p. 85.

3. Alexander, *Fighting for the Confederacy*, p. 433.

4. Ibid.

5. Case, David, "The Battle That Saved Washington," *Civil War Times Illustrated*, XXXVII, No. 7 (Feb. 1999), pp. 46–56 [hereafter Case, "Battle,"] at p. 47. For details of Early's campaign, see Judge, Joseph, *Season of Fire: The Confederate*

Strike on Washington (Berryville, Virginia: Rockbridge Publishing Co., 1994) [hereafter Judge, *Season of Fire*]; Ambrose, *Halleck* , p. 179; Vandiver, Frank E., *Jubal's Raid: General Early's Famous Attack on Washington in 1864* (New York: McGraw-Hill Book Company, Inc., 1960).

6.   Case, "Battle," pp. 47–48; Cooling, Benjamin Franklin, "Monocacy: The Battle That Saved Washington," *Blue & Gray Magazine*, X, Issue 2 (Dec. 1992), pp. 8–18, 48–60 [hereafter Cooling, "Monocacy."] at pp. 13, 16; Hotchkiss, *Make Me a Map*, p. 215.

7.   Case, "Battle," pp. 48–49.

8.   For details on the Battle of Monocacy, see Cooling, "Monocacy"; Judge, *Season of Fire*, pp. 171–201; and Wittenberg, Eric J., "Roadblock en Route to Washington," *America's Civil War*, Vol. 6, No. 5 (Nov. 1993), pp. 50–56, 80–82.

9.   Case, "Battle," pp. 50–54; Cooling, "Monocacy," pp. 48–55; Swift and Stephens, "Honor Redeemed," pp. 42–44.

10.   Grant, *Memoirs*, pp. 605–7, 614; Alexander, Ted, "McCausland's Raid and the Burning of Chambersburg," *Blue & Gray Magazine*, XI, Issue 6 (August 1994), pp. 10–18, 46–61; Case, "Battle," pp. 55–56.

11.   Gallagher, Gary W., "'Upon Their Success Hang Momentous Interests': Generals," pp. 79–108 [hereafter Gallagher, "Upon Their Success"] in Boritt, *Why the Confederacy Lost*, p. 91.

12.   Ambrose, *Halleck*, p. 179.

13.   Alexander, *Fighting for the Confederacy*, p. 440.

14.   Hattaway and Jones, *How the North Won*, p. 604.

15.   Gorgas, *Journals*, Dec. 15, 1864, pp. 143–44.

16.   Connelly, *Autumn of Glory*, pp. 321–25, 371, 391–421; Watkins, "*Co. Aytch*," pp. 166–67.

17.   Hattaway and Jones, *How the North Won*, p. 607.

18.   Groom, *Shrouds of Glory*, p. 34.

19.   In late 1862, Lee had transferred Brigadier General W.H.C. Whiting out of his theater to make room for promoting Hood. McMurry, *Two Armies*, p. 134.

20.   Lee to Jefferson Davis, July 12, 1864, *Papers of Lee*, p. 821.

21.   Lee to Jefferson Davis, July 12, 1864, 9:30 p.m., *Papers of Lee*, pp. 821–22.

22.   Castel, Albert, *Decision in the West: The Atlanta Campaign of 1864* (Lawrence: University Press of Kansas, 1992), p. 362.

23. Davis, Stephen, "Atlanta Campaign. Hood Fights Desperately. The Battles of Atlanta: Events from July 10 to September 2, 1864," *Blue & Gray Magazine*, VI, Issue 6 (August 1989), pp. 8, 11.

24. Watkins, "*Co. Aytch*," pp. 167–69, 174–75.

25. Groom, *Shrouds of Glory*, p. 25.

26. Marszalek, John F., *Sherman: A Soldier's Passion for Order* (New York: Macmillan, Inc., 1993), p. 277. In his memoirs, Grant said of the change of command: "I know that both Sherman and I were rejoiced when we heard of the change." Grant, *Memoirs*, p. 632.

27. Connelly, *Autumn of Glory*, p. 433; Castel, Albert, *Decision in the West: The Atlanta Campaign of 1864* (Lawrence: University Press of Kansas, 1992), p. 362; Davis, Stephen, "Atlanta Campaign. Hood Fights Desperately. The Battles of Atlanta: Events from July 10 to September 2, 1864," *Blue & Gray Magazine*, VI, Issue 6 (August 1989), pp. 8, 11; Watkins, "*Co. Aytch*," pp. 167–69, 174–75; Groom, *Shrouds of Glory*, p. 25; Marszalek, *Sherman*, p. 277; Connelly, *Autumn of Glory*, p. 433; Hattaway and Jones, *How the North Won*, p. 609; Bonekemper, *How Lee Lost*, pp. 166–70; Powles, James M., " New Jersey's Western Warriors," *America's Civil War*, Vol. 14, No. 4 (Sept. 2001), pp. 46–52.

28. Hattaway and Jones, *How the North Won*, p. 609.

29. Groom, *Shrouds of Glory*, p. 53.

30. Ibid., p. 54.

31. Catton, Bruce, *The Army of the Potomac: A Stillness at Appomattox* (Garden City, New York: Doubleday & Company, Inc., 1953), pp. 294–95.

32. Groom, *Shrouds of Glory*, p. 218.

33. Ibid., p. 224; Hattaway and Jones, *How the North Won*, pp. 650–53.

34. Groom, *Shrouds of Glory*, p. 273.

35. Connelly, *Autumn of Glory*, pp. 429–513.

36. Grant, *Memoirs*, pp. 607–12.

37. Grant to Meade, July 24, 1864, *Papers of Grant*, XI, pp. 305–7 at p. 306; Grant, *Memoirs*, pp. 612–13; Hattaway and Jones, *How the North Won*, pp. 614–15; Livermore, *Numbers & Losses*, p. 116; Miller, "Strike Them," p. 53.

38. Suderow, Bryce A. "War Along the James," *North & South*, Vol. 6, No. 3 (April 2003), pp. 12–23.

39. Suderow, Bryce A. "Glory Denied: The First Battle of Deep Bottom, July 27th–29th, 1864," *North & South*, Vol. 3, No. 7 (Sept. 2000), pp. 17–32 [hereafter Suderow, "Glory Denied"].

40. Donald, David Herbert, *Lincoln* (New York: Simon and Schuster, 1995), p. 529.

41. Nevins, *Ordeal*, VIII, pp. 92–93.

42. Ibid., p. 92.

43. Miller, William J., *Mapping for Stonewall: The Civil War Service of Jed Hotchkiss* (Washington: Elliott & Clark Publishing, 1993), p. 143.

44. Beringer et al., *Why the South Lost*, p. 347.

45. Grant to Washburne, August 16, 1864, *Papers of Grant*, XII, pp. 16–17 at p.16.

46. Ibid., pp. 16–17.

47. Grant to Benjamin F. Butler, August 18, 1864, Ibid., p. 27.

48. Grant to William H. Seward, August 19, 1864, Ibid., pp. 37–38 at p. 38.

49. Lee to James A. Seddon, August 23, 1864, *Papers of Lee*, pp. 843–44.

50. Suderow, Bryce A., "'Nothing But a Miracle Could Save Us': Second Battle of Deep Bottom, Virginia, August 14–20, 1864," *North & South*, Vol. 4, No. 2 (Jan. 2001), pp. 12–32 [hereafter Suderow, "Nothing But Miracle"].

51. Halleck to Grant, Aug. 11, 1864, *Papers of Grant*, XI, pp. 424–25n; Grant to Halleck, August 15, 1864, Ibid., p. 424; *Works of Lincoln*, VII, p. 499; Lincoln to Grant, Aug. 17, 1864, *Papers of Grant*, XI, p. 225n; *Works of Lincoln*, VII, p. 499.

52. Groom, *Shrouds of Glory*, p. 53.

53. Grant to Sherman, Sept. 12, 1864, *Papers of Grant*, XII, pp. 154–55.

54. Grant, *Memoirs*, pp. 614–15; Grant to Halleck, August 1, 1864, *Papers of Grant*, XI, pp. 358–59 at p. 358; Goodwin, Doris Kearns, *Team of Rivals: The Political Genius of Abraham Lincoln* (New York: Simon & Schuster, 2005), p. 646.

55. Lincoln to Grant, August 3, 1864, *Works of Lincoln*, VII, p. 476; Grant, *Memoirs*, pp. 615–16.

56. Grant, *Memoirs*, pp. 616–17; Williams, T. Harry, *Lincoln and His Generals* (New York: Alfred A. Knopf, Inc., 1952) [hereafter Williams, *Lincoln and His Generals*], pp. 331–33.

57. Grant, *Memoirs*, pp. 617–18.

58. Grant, *Memoirs*, p. 602, 619; Wagner, Margaret E., Gallagher, Gary W., and Finkelman, Paul (ed.), *The Library of Congress Civil War Desk Reference* (New York: Simon & Schuster, 2002), p. 311; McWhiney and Jamieson, *Attack and Die*, pp. 19, 158.

59. Grant, *Memoirs*, pp. 620–21. For details of the 1864 Shenandoah Valley Campaign, see Wert, Jeffry D., *From Winchester to Cedar Creek: The Shenandoah Campaign of 1864* (Carlisle, Pennsylvania: South Mountain Press, Inc., 1987). For a brief synopsis, see Wert, Jeffry D., "Closing the Back Door: The Shenandoah Valley Campaign of 1864," *Hallowed Ground*, Winter 2004, pp. 25–30.

60. Grant, *Memoirs*, p. 622.

61. Ibid., p. 625.

62. Feis, *Grant's Secret Service*, pp. 246–49; Trudeau, Noah Andre, "That 'Unerring Volcanic Firearm,'" *Military History Quarterly*, Vol. 7, No. 4 (Summer 1995) [hereafter Trudeau, "Unerring Firearm"], pp. 78–87.

63. Grant, *Memoirs*, pp. 628–30.

64. McPherson, *Battle Cry of Freedom*, p. 800. To accusations that Grant's no-exchange policy was the cause of many prison-camp deaths, Professor James Gillispie retorted that such a policy was the only security against a widespread Confederate policy of executing African-American prisoners and their white officers and that it also was intended to shorten the war by reducing the number of combatants—especially on the Rebel side. Gillispie, James, Letter to Editor, *North & South*, Vol. 5, No. 7 (Oct. 2002), pp. 5–6.

65. Bergeron, Arthur W., Jr., "The Battle of Mobile Bay and the Campaign for Mobile, Alabama," *Blue & Gray Magazine*, XIX, Issue 4 (April 2002), pp. 6–21, 46–54; Thomas, Emory, "'Damn the Torpedoes…': The Battle for Mobile Bay," *Civil War Times Illustrated*, XVI, No. 1 (April 1977), pp. 4–10, 43–45.

66. McPherson, *Battle Cry of Freedom*, p. 775.

67. Grant, *Memoirs*, p. 630; Heidler and Heidler, *Encyclopedia*, p. 496.

68. Grant, *Memoirs*, p. 630.

69. Congressional Quarterly, Inc., *Presidential Elections 1789–1996* (Washington: Congressional Quarterly, Inc., 1997), p. 94; Bonekemper, Edward H., III, "Lincoln's 1864 Victory Was Closer Than It Looked," *Washington Times*, July 15, 2000 [hereafter, Bonekemper, "Lincoln's 1864 Victory"]; Appendix III, "The Critical Election of 1864: How Close Was It?" in Bonekemper, Edward H., III, *A Victor, Not a Butcher: Ulysses S. Grant's Overlooked Military Genius*

(Washington: Regnery Publishing, 2004) [hereafter Bonekemper, *Victor*], pp. 323–32.

70. Jones, "Military Means," in Boritt, *Why the Confederacy Lost*, p. 73, citing Confederate Vice President Stephens' statement that southern aspirations of prevailing had been sustained only by hopes that the northern peace advocates would succeed.

71. Thomas, *Lee*, p. 346.

72. Grant, *Memoirs*, pp. 632–36; Grant to Sherman, Sept. 10, 1864, *Papers of Grant*, XII, p. 144; Sherman to Grant, Sept. 10, 1864, Ibid., p. 144n; Grant to Sherman, Sept. 12, 1864, Ibid., pp. 154–55. Porter described the visit in Porter, *Campaigning with Grant*, pp. 287–96.

73. Sherman to Grant, 11:00 a.m., October 11, 1864, *Papers of Grant*, XII, p. 290n; Grant, *Memoirs*, p. 816.

74. Grant to Sherman, 11:30 p.m., October 11, 1864, Ibid., p. 290n.

75. Grant, *Memoirs*, pp. 636–40, 652–53.

76. Sherman's soldiers killed virtually no civilians and probably did less physical damage in Georgia than commonly alleged. Their anti-property activities became more wantonly destructive during their 1865 march through South Carolina. Kennett, Lee B., "'Hell' or 'High Old Times,'" *America's Civil War*, Vol. 17, No. 6 (Jan. 2005), pp. 46–52. General Kilpatrick acquired his nickname, "Kill Cavalry," by virtue of his reputation for unnecessarily sacrificing his men in battle.

77. Grant, *Memoirs*, pp. 631–38; Garavaglia, Louis A., "Sherman's March and the Georgia Arsenals," *North & South*, Vol. 6, No. 1 (Dec. 2002), pp. 12–22. For details of Sherman's March to the Sea, see Scaife, William R., "Sherman's March to the Sea: Events from September 3 to December, 1864, Including the Occupation of Atlanta, More Battles with the Unpredictable John Bell Hood, the Burning of Atlanta, 'Marching Through Georgia,' and the Fall of Savannah," *Blue & Gray Magazine*, VII, Issue 2 (Dec. 1989), pp. 10–32, 38–42.

78. Grant, *Memoirs*, pp. 648–50; Grant to Sherman, Dec. 3, 1864, *Papers of Grant*, XIII, pp. 56–57 at p. 56.

79. Sherman to Lincoln, Dec. 22, 1864, *Works of Lincoln*, VIII, p. 182n.

80. Grant, *Memoirs*, pp. 651–25; Durham, Roger S., "Savannah: Mr. Lincoln's Christmas Present," *Blue & Gray Magazine*, VIII, Issue 3 (Feb. 1991), pp. 8–18, 42–53.

81. Grant, *Memoirs*, p. 652.

82.   Ibid., pp. 654–55; McWhiney and Jamieson, *Attack and Die*, p. 21; Groom,
       Shrouds of Glory, pp. 156–224; Heidler and Heidler, *Encyclopedia*, pp. 771–72.
       A frustrated Grant had issued orders to relieve Thomas of command, but
       Lincoln and Halleck provided Thomas with enough time to attack before
       those orders could be delivered. Williams, *Lincoln and His Generals*, pp.
       343–44.

83.   Grant, *Memoirs*, pp. 655–61; McWhiney and Jamieson, *Attack and Die*, p. 21;
       Groom, *Shrouds of Glory*, pp. 224–75; Dolzall, Gary W, "Enemies Front and
       Rear," *America's Civil War*, Vol. 16, No. 2 (May 2003), pp. 38–45; Cox, *Remi-
       niscences*, II, pp. 358–74.

84.   Woodward, C. Vann, *Mary Chesnut's Civil War* (New Haven and London:
       Yale University Press, 1981) [hereafter Woodward, *Chesnut*], p. 664.

85.   Ibid., p. 675.

86.   Ibid., p. 694 (December 19, 1864 diary entry).

CHAPTER 11

1.   Jones, "Military Means," in Boritt, *Why the Confederacy Lost*, p. 74.

2.   Beringer et al., *Why the South Lost*, p. 333.

3.   Wiley, *Road to Appomattox*, p. 85; Jones, Archer, "Military Means" in Boritt,
       Why the Confederacy Lost, pp. 43–77 [hereafter Jones, Archer, "Military
       Means"] at p. 74; Beringer et al., *Why the South Lost*, p. 333; Connelly, "Lee
       and the West," p. 123.

4.   Wiley, *Road to Appomattox*, p. 85.

5.   Lincoln to William H. Seward, Jan. 31, 1865, *Works of Lincoln*, VIII, pp.
       250–51; Lincoln to Grant, Feb. 1, 1865, Ibid., p. 252; Grant to Lincoln, Feb.
       1, 1865, Ibid., p. 280n and *Papers of Grant*, XIII, pp. 344–45; Bergeron, Arthur
       W., Jr., "Three-day Tussle at Hatcher's Run," *America's Civil War*, Vol. 16, No.
       1 (March 2003), pp. 30–37 [hereafter Bergeron, "Hatcher's Run"] at p. 30.
       For all the relevant communications on this abortive conference, see Lincoln
       to the House of Representatives, Feb. 10, 1865, *Works of Lincoln*, VIII, pp.
       274–85. A month later, Lee tried to initiate discussions with Grant, who
       sought instructions and was told by Lincoln not to confer with Lee "unless
       it be for the capitulation of Gen. Lee's army, or on some minor, and purely,
       military matter." Lincoln to Grant, March 3, 1865, Ibid., pp. 330–31n.

6.   Woodward, *Chesnut*, pp. 706–7 (late January 1865 diary entry).

7.   Gorgas, *Journals*, Jan. 15 and 25, 1865, pp. 148–49.

8.   Connelly, *Autumn of Glory*, p. 529.

9.   Grant, *Memoirs*, pp. 671–74. For example, the 10,000-man 23rd Corps was moved by river, rail, and sea from Clifton, Tennessee, to Wilmington in a rapid movement reminiscent of the late 1863 movement of the 11th and 12th Corps from Virginia to Chattanooga. Longstreet, *From Manassas to Appomattox*, pp. 386–87.

10. Bradley, Mark L., "Last Stand in the Carolinas: The Battle of Bentonville, March 19–21, 1865," *Blue & Gray Magazine*, XIII, Issue 2 (Dec. 1995), pp. 8–22, 56–69 [hereafter Bradley, "Last Stand"] at p. 9.

11. Williams, *Lincoln and His Generals*, p. 347.

12. Grant to Sherman, December 18, 1864, *Papers of Grant*, XIII, pp. 129–30 at p. 130; Coburn, Mark, *Terrible Innocence: General Sherman at War* (New York: Hippocrene Books, 1993), pp. 191–92.

13. Hattaway and Jones, *How the North Won*, p. 667.

14. "The delay in appointing Johnston proved disastrous for the West. Johnston was no genius at strategy. But if he had been appointed earlier, he might have wrought some order, and concentration might have been effected. Instead, for almost two critical months in 1865, the Confederacy confronted Sherman in the Carolinas with nothing but chaos." Connelly, *Autumn of Glory*, p. 520.

15. Thomas, *Lee*, p. 348.

16. Rhodes, *All for the Union*, pp. 214–16.

17. Ibid., p. 349.

18. Wiley, *Road to Appomattox*, p. 72.

19. Marvel, William, *Lee's Last Retreat: The Flight to Appomattox* (Chapel Hill and London: The University of North Carolina Press, 2002)[hereafter Marvel, *Lee's Last Retreat*], pp. 5–6.

20. Ibid., p. 205.

21. Alexander, *Great Generals*, p. 167.

22. Glatthaar, Joseph T., "Black Glory" in Boritt, *Why the Confederacy Lost*, p. 160; Thomas, *Lee*, p. 347; Beringer et al., *Why the South Lost*, p. 373; Hattaway and Jones, *How the North Won*, p. 272.

23. Levine, Bruce, *Confederate Emancipation: Southern Plans to Free and Arm Slaves During the Civil War* (Oxford: Oxford University Press, 2006).

24. When Davis designated Bragg to defend Wilmington, a Virginia newspaper opined, "Braxton Bragg has been ordered to Wilmington. Goodbye Wilmington."

25. Fonvielle, Chris, "The Last Rays of Departing Hope: The Fall of Wilmington Including the Campaigns against Fort Fisher," *Blue & Gray Magazine*, XII, Issue 2 (Dec. 1994), pp. 10–21, 48–62 [hereafter Fonvielle, "Last Rays"] at pp. 16–19; Zentner, Joe and Syrett, Mary, "Confederate Gibralter," *Military History*, Vol. 19, No. 6 (Feb. 2003), pp. 26–32, 73 [hereafter Zentner and Syrett, "Confederate Gibralter"]; Grant to Sherman, Dec. 3, 1964, *Papers of Grant*, XIII, pp. 56–57 at p. 56.

26. Fonvielle, "Last Rays," pp. 20–21, 48–52. "The Wilmington expedit[ion] has proven a gross and culpable failure." Grant to Lincoln, Dec. 28, 1864, *Papers of Grant*, XIII, pp. 177–78 at p. 177.

27. Fonvielle, "Last Rays," pp. 52–57.

28. Grant, *Memoirs*, pp. 662–70, 680; Fonvielle, "Last Rays," pp. 57–62; Zentner and Syrett, "Confederate Gibralter," pp. 26–32, 73.

29. Fonvielle, "Last Rays," p. 62.

30. McPherson, *Battle Cry of Freedom*, p. 826.

31. Marszalek, *Sherman*, pp. 320–21.

32. Grant, *Memoirs*, p. 675.

33. Grant, *Memoirs*, pp. 681–82. On the burning of Columbia, see Evans, E. Chris, "'I Almost Tremble at Her Fate': When Sherman came to Columbia, South Carolina, secession's hotbed became a bed of coals," *Civil War Times Illustrated*, XXXVII, No. 5 (Oct. 1998), pp. 46–51, 60–67. Sherman's comment on the burning of Columbia was, "Though I never ordered it and never wished it, I have never shed many tears over the event, because I believe it hastened what we all fought for, the end of the war." Ibid. at p. 67. Also see Elmore, Tom, "The Burning of Columbia, South Carolina, February 17, 1865, *Blue & Gray Magazine* XXI, Issue 2 (Winter 2004), pp. 6–27.

34. Alexander, *Great Generals*, p. 164.

35. Sherman, *Memoirs*, p. 752.

36. Alexander, *Great Generals*, pp. 164–65, quoting Hart, Liddell, *Sherman: Soldier, Realist, American*, p. 356 and Sherman, *Memoirs*, p. 271.

37. Grant, *Memoirs*, pp. 679–80.

38. Fuller, *Grant and Lee*, p. 123.

39. Gorgas, *Journals*, March 2, 1865, pp. 153–54.

40. Cox, *Reminiscences*, II, pp. 431–44; Bradley, "Last Stand," p. 10–12.

41. For details on the Battle of Averasboro, see Bradley, Mark L., "Old Reliable's Finest Hour: The Battle of Averasboro, North Carolina, March 15–16, 1865," *Blue & Gray Magazine*, XVI, Issue 1 (Oct. 1998), pp. 6–20, 52–57.

42. For full details and battle maps of the Battle of Bentonville, see Bradley, "Last Stand."

43. Alexander, *Great Generals*, pp. 166–67.

44. Marvel, *Lee's Last Retreat*, p. 7.

45. Bergeron, "Hatcher's Run," pp. 30–37.

46. Lowe, David W., "Field Fortifications in the Civil War," *North & South*, Vol. 4, No. 6 (Aug. 2001), pp. 58–73 [hereafter Lowe, "Field Fortifications"] at p. 72.

47. Ibid.

48. Grant, *Memoirs*, pp. 691–93; McWhiney and Jamieson, *Attack and Die*, p. 165; Marvel, *Lee's Last Retreat*, pp. 9–11; Lowe, "Field Fortifications," p. 72; Fox, *Regimental Losses*, p. 548.

49. Rhodes, *All for the Union*, pp. 221–22.

50. Grant to Meade, March 24, 1865, *Papers of Grant*, pp. 211–14 at p. 211.

51. Grant, *Memoirs*, p. 693; Grant to Meade, March 24, 1865, *Papers of Grant*, XIV, pp. 211–14.

52. Sears, *Controversies*, pp. 263–64; Calkins, Chris, "The Battle of Five Forks: Final Push for the South Side," *Blue & Gray Magazine*, IX, No. 4 (April 1992), pp. 8–22, 41–52 [hereafter Calkins, "Five Forks"] at pp. 8–9.

53. Rhodes, *All for the Union*, p. 223.

54. Calkins, "Five Forks," pp. 10–11.

55. King, Curtis S., "Reconsider, Hell!," *MHQ: The Quarterly Journal of Military History*, Vol. 13, No. 4 (Summer 2001), pp. 88–95 [hereafter King, "Reconsider, Hell!"] at pp. 88–92; Sears, *Controversies*, pp. 269–71; Calkins, "Five Forks," pp. 11–13.

56. For details of the Battle of Dinwiddie Court House, see Crawford, Mark J., "Dinwiddie Court House: Beginning of the End," *America's Civil War*, Vol. 12, No. 1 (March 1999), pp. 50–56 [hereafter Crawford, "Dinwiddie Court House"].

57. Crawford, "Dinwiddie Court House," pp. 53–55; Calkins, "Five Forks," pp. 16–17.

58. Rhodes, *All for the Union*, p. 224.

59. King, "Reconsider, Hell!," p. 92: Sears, *Controversies*, pp. 272–74; Calkins, "Five Forks," pp. 17–18.

60. Calkins, "Five Forks," p. 18.

61. Ibid., pp. 18–22.

62. King, "Reconsider, Hell!," pp. 92–93; Sears, *Controversies*, pp. 279–81; Crawford, "Dinwiddie Court House," p. 56; Calkins, "Five Forks," pp. 41–50; Sears, "Warren and Little Phil," pp. 66–69.

63. King, "Reconsider, Hell," pp. 88, 94–95; Sears, *Controversies*, p. 281; Marvel, William, "Retreat to Appomattox," *Blue & Gray Magazine*, XXXVIII, Issue 4 (Spring 2001), pp. 6–24, 46–54 [hereafter Marvel, "Retreat"] at p. 6; Marvel, William, "Thorn in the Flesh," *Civil War Times Illustrated*, XLI, No. 3 (June 2002), pp. 42–49, 60–62; Greene, A. Wilson, "April 2, 1865: Day of Decision at Petersburg," *Blue & Gray Magazine*, XVIII, Issue 3 (Feb. 2001), pp. 6–24, 42–53 [hereafter Greene, "April 2, 1865"] at p. 6; Sears, "Warren and Little Phil," pp. 69–70 . Many military and civilian observers believed that Sheridan had acted out of jealousy and fear that Warren would receive credit for the victory. For example, the well-known battlefield artist Alfred Waud wrote on the back of a sketch of Warren's attack at Five Forks, "Sheridan and the ring he belongs to intends to grab all laurels no matter at the cost of what injustice." Marvel, *Lee's Last Retreat*, p. 16. Another view is that the firing of Warren was the final step in ridding the Army of the Potomac of McClellan loyalists: "[McClellanism's] final victim was Gouverneur Warren, sacked at the moment of victory at Five Forks in 1865 by Sheridan (at Grant's nod) because as a McClellan loyalist Warren represented all that was wrong with the Army of the Potomac." Rhea et al., "What Was Wrong?," pp. 12–18. Warren spent the seventeen years after his relief trying to restore his reputation. His last words before his November 1881 death were, "I die a disgraced soldier." Sears, *Controversies*, pp. 282–84. Unfortunately, it was three months after his death when Warren was exonerated by a court of inquiry appointed by President Rutherford B. Hayes. King, "Reconsider, Hell," p. 95. Grant had prevented the inquiry (presumably to protect Sheridan) while he was general-in-chief and then president. Sears, *Controversies*, p. 282–84. In his memoirs, Grant naturally supported Sheridan's relief of Warren (which Grant had authorized): "[Warren] could see every danger at a glance before he had encountered it. He would not only make preparations to meet the danger which might occur, but he would inform his commanding officer what

others should do while he was executing his move." Grant, *Memoirs*, p. 702. Grant did not want hesitance; he wanted immediate action. As a result, Generals Warren and Thomas, among others, earned Grant's wrath and criticism for what he perceived as their hesitance.

64. Smith, *Grant*, p. 399n.

65. Calkins, "Five Forks," pp. 50–51; Marvel, "Retreat," p. 6.

66. Grant, *Memoirs*, pp. 702–3; Greene, "April 2, 1864," p. 12; Calkins, "Five Forks," pp. 50–51.

67. Grant, *Memoirs*, pp. 703–5; Greene, "April 2, 1864," pp. 12–24, 42–50; Davis, Burke, *The Long Surrender* (New York: Vintage Books, 1989), pp. 21–32.

68. Hardy, Michael C., "'A Day of Carnage & Blood'," *America's Civil War*, Vol. 18, No. 1 (March 2005), pp. 38–44; Greene, "April 2, 1865, " p. 53.

69. For details on the Appomattox Campaign, see Marvel, *Lee's Last Retreat*; Marvel, "Retreat" [includes battle maps].

70. William Marvel contended that the missing pontoon bridge delayed Lee more than any missing rations. He blamed both on poor headquarters communication. Marvel, *Lee's Last Retreat*, pp. 44–51, 207–8; Marvel, William, "Many have offered excuses for the Confederate retreat to Appomattox, perhaps beginning with Robert E. Lee," *America's Civil War*, Vol. 14, No. 3 (July 2001), pp. 62–70 [hereafter Marvel, "Many Have Offered"] at pp. 66–70. He also attacked the "myth" of the missing rations' significance and laid the probable blame for their absence at the doorstep of Walter Taylor. Marvel, *Lee's Last Retreat*, pp. 207–13; Marvel, "Many Have Offered," p. 70.

71. Marvel, "Retreat," pp. 8–11.

72. Marvel, *Lee's Last Retreat*, pp. 67–94; Glynn, Gary, "Black Thursday for Rebels," *America's Civil War*, Vol. 4, No. 5 (Jan. 1992), pp. 22–29 [hereafter Glynn, "Black Thursday"]; Marvel, "Retreat," pp. 13–20; Calkins, Chris M., "Hurtling Toward the End," *America's Civil War*, Vol. 17, No. 1 (March 2004), pp. 38–44; Calkins, Chris M., "Final Bloodshed at Appomattox," *America's Civil War*, Vol. 14, No. 2 (May 2001), pp. 34–40 [hereafter Calkins, "Final Bloodshed"] at p. 36; Fox, *Regimental Losses*, p. 549; Heidler and Heidler, *Encyclopedia*, p. 1710.

73. Marvel, "Retreat," pp. 21–22.

74. Marvel, "Retreat," pp. 50–51; Lincoln to Grant, April 7, 1865, *Works of Lincoln*, VIII, p. 392.

75. Grant to Lee, April 7, 1865, *Papers of Grant*, XIV, page 361.

76. Lee to Grant, April 7, 1865, *Papers of Lee*, pp. 931–32 and *Papers of Grant*, Vol. 14, page 361n. In *Papers of Lee*, Dowdey and Manarin made editorial corrections to Lee's papers to make them as perfect as possible, while Simon republished Grant's correspondence as it was written (including all the errors). Simon similarly maintained the original accuracy of Lee's correspondence that he quoted in notes to Grant's correspondence. The Lee texts quoted here and below are the unedited Simon versions.

77. Grant to Lee, April 8, 1865, *Papers of Grant*, XIV, p. 367.

78. Lee to Grant, April 8, 1865, *Papers of Lee*, p. 932 and *Papers of Grant*, XIV, p. 367n.

79. Freeman, *Lee's Lieutenants*, III, p. 721; Longstreet, *Memoirs*, p. 620.

80. Thomas, *Lee*, p. 362.

81. Marvel, "Retreat," pp. 54.

82. Lee to Grant, April 9, 1865, *Papers of Lee*, p. 932; *Papers of Grant*, XIV, p. 371n.

83. Marvel, *Lee's Last Retreat*, p. 180.

84. General Order No. 9, April 10, 1865 in Freeman, *R. E. Lee*, IV, pp. 154–55 and (slightly modified version) *Papers of Lee*, pp. 934–35.

85. "The will to win had become so feeble by the close of the war's last winter that any expectation of again reviving it to a point of effective resistance was wishful thinking of the extremist sort. Hence the final battles about Richmond and in the West were but tragic afterglows of a fire that had already died." Wiley, *Road to Appomattox*, p. 72.

86. Wert, Jeffry D., "'No Retreat Was Ever Possible,'" *Civil War Times Illustrated*, XXXIX, No. 2 (May 2000), pp. 32–37 at p. 37.

87. General Order No. 9, April 10, 1865 in Freeman, *R. E. Lee*, IV, pp. 154–55 and (slightly modified version) *Papers of Lee*, p. 934.

88. McWhiney and Jamieson, *Attack and Die*, pp. 19, 158.

89. Marvel, *Lee's Last Retreat*, pp. 184, 201–6; Marvel, "Many Have Offered," pp. 62–66.

90. McMurry, Richard M., *Two Great Rebel Armies: An Essay in Confederate Military History* (Chapel Hill and London: University of North Carolina Press, 1989) [hereafter McMurry, *Two Armies*], pp. 44–50, quoting Adams, Michael C. C., *Our Masters the Rebels: A Speculation on Union Military Failure in the East, 1861–1865* (Cambridge, Mass., 1978).

91. Mertz, "Wilderness II," p. 49.

92. Hattaway, "Changing Face," p. 43.

93. Groom, *Shrouds of Glory*, p. 54

94. McWhiney and Jamieson, *Attack and Die*, p. 19. These are the casualties from Wilderness through Cold Harbor.

95. Ibid., pp. 19, 158. Again, for consistency with Lee's numbers, these only include casualties from the Wilderness through Cold Harbor.

96. Groom, *Shrouds of Glory*, p. 54.

97. Dana, *Recollections*, pp. 210–11.

CHAPTER 12

1. Taylor, *General Lee*, p. 231.

2. See Appendix I, "Historians' Treatment of Lee," in Bonekemper, *How Lee Lost*, pp. 207–214. On the "transcendental" myth of Lee, see Fuller, *Grant and Lee*, pp. 103–8. Longstreet was the favorite scapegoat, but Freeman used his three-volume *Lee's Lieutenants* to cast blame for Lee's defeat on Jackson, Stuart, A. P. Hill, D. H. Hill, and others in addition to Longstreet.

3. McMurry, *Two Armies*, p. 139.

4. Fuller, *Generalship of Grant*; Fuller, *Grant and Lee*.

5. Fuller, *Grant and Lee*, pp. 8, 257, 265–67.

6. See Bonekemper, *How Lee Lost*, pp. 211–14.

7. Fuller, *Generalship of Grant*, p. 375.

8. Grant, *Memoirs*, p. 115.

9. Pollard, Edward A., *The Lost Cause. A New Southern History of the War of the Confederates* (New York: Gramercy Books, 1994) (Reprint of New York: E. B. Treat & Company, 1866), p. 510.

10. Swinton, William, *Campaigns of the Army of the Potomac* (New York: Richardson,1866), p. 440.

11. Ropes, John C., "Grant's Campaign in Virginia in 1864," *Papers of the Military Historical Society of Massachusetts*, Vol. 4, p. 495, quoted in Rhea, *Cold Harbor*, xii.

12. Gallagher, "Upon Their Success," pp. 90–91, quoting Early, Jubal A., *The Campaigns of Gen. Robert E. Lee. An Address by Lieut. General Jubal A. Early, before Washington and Lee University, January 19th, 1872* (Baltimore: Murphy, 1872), p. 44.

13. Gallagher, "Upon Their Success," p. 91.

14. Davis, *Rise and Fall*, II, p. 335.

15. Law, "From the Wilderness to Cold Harbor," p. 143.

16. McMurry, *Two Armies*, p. 50.

17. Freeman, *R. E. Lee*, III, pp. 433–34, 447.

18. Dowdey, Clifford, *Lee's Last Campaign: The Story of Lee and His Men Against Grant—1864* (Wilmington, North Carolina: Broadfoot Publishing Company, 1988) (Reprint of New York: Little, Brown and Company, 1960), p. 93.

19. Casdorph, *Lee and Jackson*, p. 401; Furgurson, *Not War But Murder*.

20. Keegan, John, *The Mask of Command* (New York: Viking, 1987).

21. Sears, Stephen W. "All the Trumpets Sounded. Bruce Catton: An Appreciation," *North & South*, Vol. 3, No. 1 (November 1999), pp. 24–32 at p. 30. Ironically, the dust jacket of Catton's *Stillness* contained an invidious, non-Catton comparison of Grant and Lee: "[The Army of the Potomac's] leader was General Ulysses S. Grant, a seedy little man who instilled no enthusiasm in his followers and little respect in his enemies. Opposing Grant... was Robert E. Lee, the last great knight of battle. He was a god to his men and scourge to his antagonists."

22. Williams, *Lincoln and His Generals*, p. 312.

23. McFeely, *Grant*, pp. xii, 114–15, 122, 157, 165; Smith, *Grant*, p. 15.

24. Perret, *Grant*, pp. 321–22.

25. Simpson, Brooks D. *Ulysses Grant: Triumph Over Adversity, 1822–1865* (New York: Houghton Mifflin, 2000) [hereafter Simpson, *Grant*], p. 463.

26. Smith, *Grant*, pp. 14–15.

27. For a more thorough discussion, see Appendix I, "Historians' Treatment of Ulysses S. Grant," in Bonekemper, *Victor*, pp. 271–82.

28. For a discussion of Grant's winning traits, see Bonekemper, *Victor*, pp. 245–70.

29. Fuller, *Grant and Lee*, p. 267.

30. Nolan, *Lee Considered*, p. 260.

31. "Like Napoleon himself, with his passion for the strategy of annihilation and the climactic, decisive battle as its expression, [Lee] destroyed in the end not the enemy armies, but his own." Weigley, *American Way of War*, p. 127. "Even some generals who enjoy high reputations or fame have actually been predominantly direct soldiers who brought disaster to their side. One such general was Robert E. Lee, the *beau ideal* of the Southern Confederacy, who possessed integrity, honor, and loyalty in the highest degree and who also possessed skills as a commander far in excess of those of the Union generals

arrayed against him. But Lee was not, himself, a great general. Lee generally and in decisively critical situations always chose the direct over the indirect approach." Alexander, *Great Generals*, pp. 25–26. "Of all the army commanders on both sides, Lee had the highest casualty rate." McPherson, *Battle Cry of Freedom*, p. 472.

32. On his way to Gettysburg, Lee wrote to Jefferson Davis, "It seems to me that we cannot afford to keep our troops awaiting possible movements of the enemy, but that our true policy is, as far as we can, so to employ our own forces as to give occupation to his at points of our selection." Lee to Jefferson Davis, June 25, 1863, *Papers of Lee*, pp. 532–33 at p. 532. As Nolan pointed out, these were not the words of a general whose grand strategy was defensive—as it should have been. Nolan, *Lee Considered*, p. 73. "For a belligerent with the limited manpower resources of the Confederacy, General Lee's dedication to an offensive strategy was at best questionable." Weigley, *American Way of War*, p. 118.

33. Weigley, *American Way of War*, p. 111.

34. Alexander. *Lee*, p. 167.

35. Gallagher, "'Upon Their Success,'" pp. 105–7.

36. Harsh, Joseph L., "'As stupid a fellow as I am...': On the Real Military Genius of Robert E. Lee," *North & South*, Vol. 3, No. 5 (June 2000), pp. 60–71 at pp. 66–68.

37. Nolan, Alan T., "Demolishing the Myth: Evaluating Lee's Generalship," *North & South*, Vol. 3, No. 5 (June 2000), pp. 29–36.

38. Ibid., pp. 18, 35. "Thus space was all in favour of the South; even should the enemy overrun her border, her principal cities, few in number, were far removed from the hostile bases, and the important railway junctions were perfectly secure from sudden attack. And space, especially when means of communication are scanty, and the country affords few supplies, is the greatest of all obstacles." Henderson, G. F. R., *Stonewall Jackson and the American Civil War* (New York: Da Capo Press, Inc., 1988; reprint of New York: Grossett & Dunlap, 1943), p. 82.

39. Beringer et al., *Why the South Lost*, p. 49.

40. Union Major General Henry W. Halleck wrote, "... the North must conquer the South." Henry W. Halleck to Francis Lieber, March 4, 1863, quoted in McWhiney & Jamieson, *Attack & Die*, p. 6.

41. McPherson, *Battle Cry of Freedom*, p. 336.

42. Wiley, *Road to Appomattox*, p. 77.

43. Ibid.; Nolan, *Lee Considered*, p. 65; McPherson, *Battle Cry of Freedom*, p. 336, all quoting London *Times*, July 18, 1861, Aug. 29, 1862.

44. Hattaway and Jones, *How the North Won*, p. 18.

45. Roland, Charles P., *An American Iliad: The Story of the Civil War* (Lexington: University Press of Kentucky, 1991) [hereafter Roland, *American Iliad*], p. 41.

46. McPherson, *Battle Cry of Freedom*, pp. 591–611.

47. Gorgas, *Journals*, May 10, 1863, p. 66.

48. Alexander, *Fighting for the Confederacy*, p. 415.

49. "The point is that the South could still have won, save only for the rapid diminution and ultimate death of morale, the will to win, during the last year or two of the war." Beringer et al., *Why the South Lost*, p. 31.

50. Russell Weigley compared the rebels' prospects for success in the Revolution and the Civil War: "In both instances the rebels began their war in substantial control of their territory and needed only to conduct a successful defense of what they already held in order to win.... The Union advantages of proximity [to the South] and sea power were partially offset by the fact that the military strength of the rebels on land much more closely approached that of the established government than did the Revolutionary strength against the British in the War of American Independence." Weigley, *American Way of War*, pp. 92–93.

51. Nolan noted that " ... there was a profound difference between Federal casualties and Lee's casualties.... Lee's were irreplaceable...." Nolan, *Lee Considered*, p. 85.

52. Davis, William C., *The Cause Lost: Myths and Realities of the Confederacy* (Lawrence: University Press of Kansas, 1996), pp. 142–47.

53. "If McClellan had won, the war might have been lost, for though he pledged himself to carry on the struggle, many votes for him represented a desire for peace that might have become too powerful to resist. Undoubtedly, too, McClellan would have interfered with military policy and might have spoiled the grand plan." Adams, *Fighting for Defeat*, p. 161. "Had McClellan ... been elected president in November 1864, any military victory would have been robbed of any meaning." Murray, "Praise," p. 14.

54. Simpson, *Grant*, p. 458.

55. Catton, *Grant Moves South*, p. 489.

56. Cox, *Reminiscences*, II, p. 41.

57.   Williams, *McClellan, Sherman and Grant*, p. 77.

58.   "No Civil War general—not even Lee—was more aggressive than Grant. He assumed the offensive in nearly every campaign or battle he directed." McWhiney and Jamieson, *Attack and Die*, p. 157.

59.   See appendices I and II for details of their casualties imposed and incurred.

60.   Gott, Kendall D., *Where the South Lost the War: An Analysis of the Fort Henry–Fort Donelson Campaign, February 1862* (Mechanicsburg, Pennsylvania: Stackpole Books, 2003)[hereafter Gott, *Where the South*], p. 278. "General Grant is perhaps an extreme example of knowing his men and taking calculated risks." Ibid., p. 279.

61.   Catton, "Leadership of Grant," pp. 14–15.

62.   Smith, *Grant*, p. 213.

63.   Castel, Albert, "Why the North Won and the South Lost," *Civil War Times Illustrated*, XXXIX, No. 2 (May 2000), pp. 56–60 at p. 59.

64.   Hattaway and Jones, *How the North Won*, p. 17.

65.   Ibid., p. 440.

66.   McWhiney and Jamieson, *Attack and Die*, pp. 19–24, 158; *Washington Post*, May 28, 2001, p. A21. The 214,938 American battle deaths ranked behind the 291,557 in World War II, but ahead of 53,402 in World War I, 47,410 in the Vietnam War, 33,686 in the Korean War, 4,435 in the American Revolution, almost 3,000 in the ongoing Iraq War, 2,260 in the War of 1812, 1,733 in the Mexican War, 1,000 in the Indian Wars, 385 in the Spanish-American War, and 148 in the Gulf War. Ibid.

67.   McPherson, *Mighty Scourge*, p. 113.

68.   See appendices I and II.

69.   "Though Lee was at his best on defense, he adopted defensive tactics only after attrition had deprived him of the power to attack. His brilliant defensive campaign against Grant in 1864 made the Union pay in manpower as it had never paid before, but the Confederates resorted to defensive warfare too late; Lee started the campaign with too few men, and he could not replace his losses as could Grant." McWhiney and Jamieson, *Attack and Die*, pp. 164–65.

70.   See Appendix II.

71.   Livermore, *Numbers & Losses*, pp. 86–103.

72.   McWhiney and Jamieson, *Attack and Die*, p. 19; Livermore, *Numbers & Losses*, pp. 110–16.

73. Marshall-Cornwall, *Grant*, p. 224.
74. Fuller concluded that Lee's audacity more than once accelerated the Union's achievement of its strategic goal of conquering the South. Fuller, *Grant and Lee*, p. 267.
75. Fuller, *Generalship of Grant*, p. 372.
76. Rhea, *Cold Harbor*, xii.
77. McPherson, "Unheroic Hero," p. 19. Later McPherson wrote, "And if any general deserved the label 'butcher,' it was Lee. McPherson, *Mighty Scourge*, p. 113.
78. Williams, *McClellan, Sherman and Grant*, pp. 100–1.
79. See the casualty rates that follow in the text for other Civil War generals.
80. McWhiney and Jamieson, *Attack and Die*, p. 158.
81. Ibid., pp. 19–21.
82. Fox, *Regimental Losses*, pp. 571–73; Warner, *Generals in Gray*.
83. McWhiney & Jamieson, *Attack and Die*, pp. 10–11.
84. Dana, *Recollections*, pp. 187–89.
85. "Reconsidering Grant and Lee."
86. Perret, *Grant*, p. 332.
87. Murphy, "Grant versus Lee," p. 66.
88. Ibid., p. 48.
89. General James Longstreet said, "In the field, [Lee's] characteristic fault was headlong combativeness.... He was too pugnacious." Wert, Jeffrey D., *General James Longstreet: The Confederacy's Most Controversial Soldier—A Biography* (New York: Simon & Schuster, 1993) [hereafter Wert, *Longstreet*], p. 296.
90. Glatthaar, *Partners in Command*, p. 35.
91. "Robert E. Lee suffered his most decisive defeats while on the tactical offensive, at Malvern Hill and Gettysburg. Even when he was successful on the offensive, Lee used up thousands of irreplaceable troops in battles such as Second Manassas and Chancellorsville." McWhiney & Jamieson, *Attack & Die*, p. 108.
92. Alexander, *Lost Victories*, p. 221.
93. Alexander, *Lee*, pp. xi–xii.
94. McWhiney & Jamieson, *Attack & Die*, pp. 28–49; Beringer et al., *Why the South Lost*, pp. 14–16.
95. Fuller, *Grant and Lee*, p. 49; Howey, Allan W., "The Widow-makers," *Civil War Times Illustrated*, XXXVIII, No. 5 (Oct. 1999), pp. 48–51, 60 at p. 51.

Union soldiers had a total of two million Springfield-type rifle muskets, and their Rebel counterparts had 400,000 Enfield rifles from England. Ibid., pp. 50–51.

96. Fuller, *Grant and Lee*, p. 261.

97. Jones, Archer, "What Should We Think about Lee's Thinking?," *Columbiad*, 1, No. 2 (Summer 1997), pp. 73, 84–85.

98. Rhodes, *All for the Union*, p. 20.

99. Ibid., pp. 39–40.

100. Ibid., p. 172.

101. Griffith, *Battle Tactics*, p. 80.

102. Nosworthy, Brent, "Breechloaders Level the Playing Field," *Military History Quarterly*, Vol. 18, No. 3 (Spring 2006), pp. 80–83 at p. 83.

103. Rhodes, *All for the Union*, p. 54.

104. Alexander, *Lost Victories*, p. 221.

105. "... casualties, like defeats in battles and campaigns, eventually had non-military consequences. Both casualties and consequences adversely affected the morale of the home front as well as of the soldiers, undermining Confederate will to achieve independence." Beringer et al., *Why the South Lost*, p. 22.

106. McWhiney and Jamieson, *Attack and Die*, pp. 19–20.

107. Connelly, *Marble Man*, p. 199; Piston, William Garrett, "Cross Purposes: Longstreet, Lee, and Confederate Attack Plans for July 3 at Gettysburg" [hereafter, Piston, "Cross Purposes"] in Gallagher, *Third Day*, pp. 31, 43.

108. Glatthaar, *Partners in Command*, p. 35. "Lee's battlefield control was minimal." Piston, William Garrett, *Lee's Tarnished Lieutenant: James Longstreet and His Place in Southern History* (Athens and London: The University of Georgia Press, 1987) [hereafter Piston, *Lee's Tarnished Lieutenant*], p. 36.

109. Katcher, *Army of Lee*, p. 26.

110. Bruce "Lee and Strategy," p. 117.

111. McPherson, "Unheroic Hero," p. 17.

112. Keegan, *Mask of Command*, p. 200. Grant probably modeled his orders on those of Zachary Taylor, of whom Grant wrote, "Taylor was not a conversationalist, but on paper he could put his meaning so plainly that there could be no mistaking it. He knew how to express what he wanted to say in the fewest well-chosen words." Grant, *Memoirs*, p. 95.

113. Porter, *Campaigning with Grant*, p. 7.

114. Jones, *Right Hand*, p. 111. Jones cited evidence that Grant wrote his own orders because he could write them more quickly than explain to a clerk or aide what he wanted written. Ibid., pp. 111–12.

115. Murray, "Praise," p. 15.

116. Smith, *Grant*, p. 202.

117. Wiley, *Road to Appomattox*, p. 115.

118. Burton, Brian K., *Extraordinary Circumstances: The Seven Days Battles* (Bloomington and Indianapolis: Indiana University Press, 2001)[hereafter Burton, *Extraordinary Circumstances*], p. 396.

119. Fleming, "Northwestern Virginia," p. 62.

120. Kross, "Pickett's Charge," p. 16.

121. Jones, *Right Hand*, pp. 52–53, 56, 59.

122. Ibid., p. 247.

123. Bearss, *Vicksburg*, III, p. 1311.

124. Smith, *Grant*, p. 369.

125. Fuller, *Generalship of Grant*, p. 195.

126. Alexander, *Lee*, p. ix.

127. McMurry, *Two Armies*, p. 43.

128. McMurry added: "By the time Grant arrived in the East, Lee had lost Jackson and his army had passed its peak. Until some historian puts the question to a computer, we shall not know what would have happened if a Rebel army commanded by Lee, Longstreet, Jackson, and Stuart had faced a Union force under Grant, Sherman, Thomas, and Sheridan." Ibid. From another perspective, McMurry wrote, "Some historian who really wants to melt the microchips might try asking one of the infernal machines what would have happened if a Union army led by McClellan, Pope, Burnside, and Hooker had tangled with a band of Rebels under Joseph E. Johnston, Bragg, Hood, and Pillow." Ibid., p. 132.

129. Woodworth, Steven E., "The Army of the Tennessee and the Elements of Military Success," *North & South*, Vol. 6, No. 4 (May 2003), pp. 44–55 at p. 48.

130. Gilbert, Thomas D., "Mr. Grant Goes to Washington," *Blue & Gray Magazine*, XII, Issue 4 (April 1995), pp. 33, 37; Porter, *Campaigning with Grant*, pp. 69–70; Lowry, *No Turning Back*, p. 223.

131. Feis, *Grant's Secret Service*, p. 267. Feis' conclusions appeared earlier in Feis, William B., "'He Don't Care a Damn for What the Enemy Does out of His Sight,'" *North & South*, Vol. 1, No. 2 (Jan. 1998), pp. 68–81.

132. Murphy, "Grant versus Lee," p. 49.

133. Catton, *Grant Moves South*, p. 217; Arnold, *Armies of Grant*, p. 108.

134. Freeman, *R. E. Lee*, II, p. 347n.

135. Gallagher, "'Upon Their Success,'" p. 91.

136. Arnold, *Grant Wins*, p. 4.

137. Williams, *Lincoln and His Generals*, p. 271.

138. Smith, *Grant*, p. 138; Fuller, *Grant and Lee*, p. 81.

139. Grant, *Memoirs*, pp. 69–70.

140. Williams, *McClellan, Sherman and Grant*, pp. 97–98.

141. Stoddard, William O., Jr., *William O. Stoddard: Lincoln's Third Secretary* (New York: Exposition Press, 1955), pp. 197–98.

142. Williams, *McClellan, Sherman and Grant*, p. 97.

143. Weigley, *American Way of War*, p. 130.

144. Hattaway and Jones, *How the North Won*, xvi.

145. Buell, *Warrior Generals*, p. 96.

146. Those were four of the ten worst generals of the war, along with Grant's early-war superior Halleck, according to a 2004 panel of historians. Symonds, Craig L.; Simon, John Y.; Poulter, Keith; Newton, Steven H.; Sears, Stephen W., and Woodworth, Steven E., "Who Were the Worst Ten Generals?," *North & South*, Vol. 7, No. 3 (May 2004), pp. 12–25.

147. Buell, *Warrior Generals*, p. 96.

148. Ibid., p. 59.

149. Williams, *Lincoln and His Generals*, p. 313.

150. Owens, Richard H., "An Astonishing Career," *Military Heritage*, Vol. 3, No. 2 (Oct. 2001), pp. 64–73.

151. Porter, *Campaigning with Grant*, p. 250.

152. Jones, *Right Hand*, pp. 86–122, 176–219.

153. Ibid., p. 219.

154. Alexander, *Lost Victories*, p. 131n.

155. Burton, *Extraordinary Circumstances*, p. 395.

156. Wiley, *Road to Appomattox*, pp. 115–16; *Papers of Lee*, p. 935; Taylor, *General Lee*, p. 295.

157. Jones, *Right Hand*, pp. 48–60.

158. Freeman, *R. E. Lee*, III, p. 230. For details on the various members of Lee's staff throughout the war, see Ibid., I, pp. 638–43.

159. Buell, *Warrior Generals*, p. 96.

160. Williams, *Lincoln and His Generals*, p. 313.

161. Griffith, *Battle Tactics*, p. 56.

162. Wittenberg, "Sheridan's Second Raid," p. 8.

163. Ibid.

164. Alexander, *Lost Victories*, p. 117.

165. Arnold, *Grant Wins*, p. 4.

166. McPherson, "Unheroic Hero," pp. 18–19; Rhea, *Cold Harbor*, p. 388.

167. OR, Ser. I, XLVI , Part I, p. 22.

168. Rhea, *Cold Harbor*, p. 388.

169. Sommers, *Richmond Redeemed*, p. 443.

170. Arnold, *Armies of Grant*, p. 275.

171. Williams, *McClellan, Sherman and Grant*, p. 59.

172. McPherson, "Unheroic Hero," p. 18.

173. Fuller, *Generalship of Grant*, p. 190.

174. Cox, *Reminiscences*, II, p. 41.

175. Alexander, *Fighting for the Confederacy*, p. 346.

176. Williams, *McClellan, Sherman and Grant*, pp. 105–6.

177. Catton, *Grant Takes Command*, p. 105.

178. Woodworth, Steven E., "The Army of Tennessee and the Element of Military Success," *North & South*, Vol. 6, No. 4 (May 2003), pp. 44–55 at p. 52.

179. Freeman, *R. E. Lee*, IV, p. 452.

180. Rollins, Richard. "Robert E. Lee and the Hand of God," *North & South*, Vol. 6, No. 2 (Feb. 2003), pp. 12–25 at p. 18.

181. Anderson, "Grant's Struggle with Alcohol," p. 24; Perret, *Grant*, p. 262. "There is no evidence that he was under the influence at any moment of decision or that the habit interfered with his generalship. But the suspicion was always there, and it cropped up at regular intervals." Williams, *McClellan, Sherman and Grant*, p. 89.

182. McPherson, *Mighty Scourge*, p. 114.

183. Jones, *Right Hand*, pp. 113–16.

184. Bauer, Dan, "Who Knows the Truth About the Big Bender: Did U. S. Grant Leave His Army at Vicksburg in 1863 To Go on a Drinking Binge?", *Civil War Times Illustrated*, XXVII, No. 8 (Dec. 1988), pp. 34–43.

185. McPherson, *Battle Cry of Freedom*, p. 588.

186. Freeman, *R. E. Lee*, I, pp. 86, 175, 452; IV, p. 60.

187. Fuller, *Generalship of Grant*, p. 375.

188. McPherson, James M., "Lincoln and the Strategy of Unconditional Surrender," in Boritt, Gabor S. (ed.), *Lincoln, the War President: The Gettysburg Lectures* (New York and Oxford: Oxford University Press, 1992), pp. 29–62 at p. 45.

189. Rhea, *Cold Harbor*, xii.

190. Rhea, Gordon C., "'Butcher' Grant and the Overland Campaign," *North & South*, Vol. 4, No. 1 (Nov. 2000), pp. 44–55 [hereafter Rhea, "'Butcher' Grant"] at p. 47.

191. Williams, T. Harry, *McClellan, Sherman and* Grant (New Brunswick: Rutgers University Press, 1962) [hereafter Williams, *McClellan, Sherman and Grant*], p. 81.

192. Rhea et al., "What Was Wrong?," p. 15.

193. Wert, "All-out War," p. 40.

194. Murray, Williamson, "In Praise of Sam Grant," *Military History Quarterly: The Quarterly Journal of Military History*, Vol. 18, No. 4 (Summer 2006), pp. 6–15 [hereafter Williamson, "Praise"] at p. 6.

195. Williams, *Lincoln and His Generals*, pp. 312–13.

196. Connelly and Jones, *Politics of Command*, pp. 31–48. "To all these events in the West, Lee remained remarkably indifferent, despite President Davis's continuing to call upon him as a military adviser. He persistently underrated the strength and importance of Federal offensives in the West." Weigley, *American Way of War*, p. 125. Lee operated in an area of 22,000 square miles, while the western theater consisted of 225,000 square miles in seven states. Connelly, "Lee and the West," p. 118. "... a very real criticism of Lee is that while he managed to defend Richmond for almost three years, he allowed the rest of the Confederacy to be slowly eaten away." Katcher, Philip, *The Army of Robert E. Lee* (London: Arms and Armour Press, 1994), [hereafter Katcher, *Army of Lee*], p. 27. "... [Lee's] thoughts were always concentrated on Virginia, consequently he never fully realized the importance of Tennessee, or the strategic power which resided in the size of the Confederacy." Fuller, *Grant and Lee*, p. 255. Although defenders of Lee contend that he was merely an eastern army commander for most of the war, he frequently advised President Davis on national issues, including military strategy. Connelly, *Marble Man*, pp. 202–3.

197. Fuller, *Grant and Lee*, p. 41.

198. Jones, Archer, *Confederate Strategy from Shiloh to Vicksburg* (Baton Rouge and London: Louisiana State University Press 1991), p. 29.

199. Murphy, "Grant versus Lee," pp. 48–49 [emphasis added].

200. Weigley, *American Way of War*, p. 115.

201. "One might argue that Lee was consulted, at least after early 1862, on all or almost all major policy decisions; that his advice was often heeded; and that many of the strategic matters on which he was consulted dealt with armies other than his own, such as the Army of Tennessee or coastal defenses." Connelly, Thomas Lawrence, "The Image: Robert E. Lee in American Historiography," *Civil War History*, Vol. 19 (March 1973), pp. 50–64 at p. 64.

202. Connelly and Jones, *Politics of Command*, p. 33. Earlier, T. Harry Williams had concluded that "Lee was interested hardly at all in 'global' strategy, and what few suggestions he did make to his government about operations in other theaters than his own indicate that he had little aptitude for grand planning." Williams, *Lincoln and His Generals*, p. 313.

203. Lee's son Robert later described how Lee had advised Davis and the Secretary of War throughout the war on movements and dispositions of armies other than his own. Lee, *Recollections*, p. 103; Fuller, *Grant and Lee*, p. 113.

204. Lee's myopic view of the war cannot be justified by either (1) his command of a single army or (2) his lack of power to suggest a national strategy. Numerous Confederate army commanders made national strategic recommendations to President Davis and his secretaries of war. Lee himself had great influence on Davis but chose to use it primarily to aid his own army rather than to recommend national strategy. Connelly and Jones, *Politics of Command*, pp. 33–38.

205. McMurry, *Two Armies*, p. 154.

206. Weigley, *American Way of War*, pp. 118, 125.

207. Goss, Thomas J., *The War Within the Union High Command: Politics and Generalship During the Civil War* (Lawrence: University Press of Kansas, 2003)[hereafter Goss, *War*], p. 170.

208. Adams, *Fighting for Defeat*, p. 158.

209. Goss, *War*, pp. 174–91.

210. Williams, T. Harry, "The Military Leadership of North and South" in Donald, David Herbert (ed.), *Why the North Won the Civil War* (New York: Collier

Books, 1960), pp. 33–54 at pp. 50–52; Rafuse, Ethan S., "Not Since George Washington," *Civil War Times*, XLIII, No. 1 (April 2004), pp. 28–33 at p. 33.

211. Williams, *McClellan, Sherman and Grant*, p. 105; Fuller, *Grant and Lee*, p. 63, 68.

212. Murphy, "Grant versus Lee," p. 49.

213. Hattaway, "Changing Face," p. 42.

214. Welles, *Diary*, II, pp. 44–45; Jones, *Right Hand*, p. 200; Groom, *Shrouds of Glory*, p. 9. A 1993 article in *Blue & Gray Magazine* refers to the "butcher's bill" of the first two weeks of the Overland Campaign. Miller, "Strike Them," p. 13. On June 4, 1864, Navy Secretary Gideon Welles also wrote in his diary, "Still there is heavy loss, but we are becoming accustomed to the sacrifice. Grant has not great regard for human life." Welles, *Diary*, II, p. 45.

215. Weigley, *American Way of War*, p. 152.

216. Ibid., p. 142.

APPENDIX I

1. Nofi, Albert A., "Calculating Combatants," *North & South*, Vol. 4, No. 2 (Jan. 2001), pp. 68–69 at p. 69.

2. *Ibid.*

3. Phisterer, Frederick, *Statistical Record of the Armies of the United States* (Carlisle, Pennsylvania: John Kallman Publishers, 1996) (reprint of Edison, New Jersey: Castle Books, 1883) [hereafter Phisterer, *Statistical Record*].

4. Fox, *Regimental Losses*.

5. Fuller, *Grant and Lee*, pp. 286–87.

6. Beringer et al., *Why the South Lost*, pp. 458–81, contained a statistical analysis that criticized the *Attack and Die* conclusion that Confederates self-destructed but conceded that the high Rebel casualties helped depress southern morale.

7. McWhiney and Jamieson, *Attack and Die*, pp. 23, 158.

8. Arnold, *Armies of Grant*, pp. 31–32.

9. Buell, *Warrior Generals*, p. 147.

10. Current, Richard N. (ed.), *Encyclopedia of the Confederacy* (New York: Simon & Schuster, 1993) (4 vols.) [hereafter Current, *Encyclopedia*], I, p. 156.

11. Foote, *Civil War*, I, p. 152.

12. Fox, *Regimental Losses*, pp. 543, 549.
13. Fuller, *Grant and Lee*, p. 286.
14. Grant, *Memoirs*, p. 185.
15. Hattaway and Jones, *How the North*, p. 53.
16. Heidler and Heidler, *Encyclopedia*, p. 208.
17. Marshall-Cornwall, *Grant*, pp. 41, 228.
18. Phisterer, *Statistical Record*, p. 213.
19. Polk, William M., "General Polk and the Battle of Belmont," in Johnson and Buel, *Battles and Leaders*, I, pp. 348–57 at pp. 352–53.
20. Roberts, "Belmont," p. 49.
21. Smith, *Grant*, p. 130.
22. Marshall-Cornwall, *Grant*, p. 228.
23. Arnold, *Armies of Grant*, p. 47.
24. Badeau, *Grant*, I, pp. 51–52.
25. Beringer et al., *Why the South Lost*, p. 124.
26. Buell, *Warrior Generals*, p. 440.
27. Cobb, Hubbard, *American Battlefields: A Complete Guide to the Historic Conflicts in Words, Maps, and Photos* (New York: Macmillan, 1995) [hereafter Cobb, *American Battlefields*], p. 158.
28. Cooling, "Forts," p. 52.
29. Foote, *Civil War*, I, p. 215.
30. Fox, *Regimental Losses*, pp. 543, 549.
31. Fuller, *Grant and Lee*, pp. 144, 286.
32. Gott, *Where the South*, pp. 281–88.
33. Heidler and Heidler, *Encyclopedia*, p. 730.
34. Johnson and Buel, *Battles and Leaders*, I, p. 429.
35. Jones, "Military Means," p. 57.
36. Livermore, *Numbers & Losses*, p. 78.
37. Marshall-Cornwall, *Grant*, pp. 61, 228.
38. McPherson, *Battle Cry*, p. 402.
39. McWhiney and Jamieson, *Attack and Die*, p. 158.
40. Phisterer, *Statistical Record*, p. 213.
41. Grant to Halleck, Feb. 16, 1862, *Papers of Grant*, pp. 223–25 at p. 223, and p. 226n.
42. Smith, *Grant*, p. 165.

43. Walsh, George, *"Whip the Rebellion": Ulysses S. Grant's Rise to Command* (New York: Tom Doherty Associates, LLC, 2005)[hereafter Walsh, *"Whip"*], p. 57.

44. Williams, *Grant Rises in the West*, I, pp. 257–58.

45. Allen, "Shiloh! II," p. 48.

46. Arnold, *Armies of Grant*, p. 70.

47. Badeau, *Grant*, I, pp. 91–92.

48. Beauregard, "Shiloh," p. 593.

49. Beringer et al., *Why the South Lost*, p. 131.

50. Boritt, *Why the Confederacy Lost*, p. 58.

51. Buell, *Warrior Generals*, pp. 440, 442.

52. Catton, *Grant Moves South*, p. 247.

53. Cobb, *American Battlefields*, p. 168.

54. Current, *Encyclopedia*, I, p. 338.

55. Daniel, *Shiloh*, p. 322.

56. Davis, *Rise and Fall*, II, p. 58.

57. Donald, David Herbert; Baker, Jean Harvey; and Holt, Michael F., *The Civil War and Reconstruction* (New York and London: W.W. Norton & Company, 2001) [hereafter Donald et al., *Civil War*], p. 201.

58. Esposito, Vincent J. (ed.), *The West Point Atlas of American Wars* (New York, Washington, London: Frederick A. Prager, Inc., 1959) (2 vols.) [hereafter Esposito, *West Point Atlas*], I, Map 38 text.

59. Feis, *Grant's Secret Service*, p. 101.

60. Foote, *Civil War*, I, p. 350.

61. Fox, *Regimental Losses*, pp. 23, 543, and 549.

62. Fuller, *Generalship of Grant*, p. 116.

63. Fuller, *Grant and Lee*, p. 286.

64. Grant, "Shiloh," in Johnson and Buel, *Battles and Leaders*, I, p. 485.

65. Hattaway and Jones, *How the North Won*, p. 169.

66. Heidler and Heidler, *Encyclopedia*, p. 1779.

67. Johnson and Buel, *Battles and Leaders*, I, pp. 538–39.

68. Jones, "Military Means," p. 58.

69. Livermore, *Numbers & Losses*, pp. 79–80.

70. Lowe, "Field Fortifications," p. 65.

71. Marshall-Cornwall, *Grant*, pp. 78, 228.

72. Martin, David G., *The Shiloh Campaign, March–April 1862* (Bryn Mawr, Pennsylvania: Combined Books, 1987), p. 155.

73. McFeely, *Grant*, p. 115.

74. McWhiney and Jamieson, *Attack and Die*, pp. 8, 158.

75. Nevins, *Ordeal of the Union*, VI, p. 85.

76. Phisterer, *Statistical Record*, p. 213.

77. Roland, *American Iliad*, p. 63.

78. Sherman, *Memoirs*, p. 268.

79. Smith, *Grant*, p. 204.

80. Walsh, "*Whip*", p. 81.

81. Williams, *Grant Rises in the West*, I, p. 394.

82. Woodworth, *Nothing But Victory*, p. 202.

83. Allen, "Crossroads," p. 38.

84. Badeau, *Grant*, I, p. 115.

85. Cozzens, *Darkest Days*, p. 133.

86. Foote, *Civil War*, I, p. 720.

87. Fox, *Regimental Losses*, pp. 23, 544, 550.

88. Fuller, *Grant and Lee*, p. 286.

89. Hattaway and Jones, *How the North Won*, p. 252.

90. Heidler and Heidler, *Encyclopedia*, p. 1052.

91. Lamers, *Edge of Glory*, p. 115.

92. Marshall-Cornwall, *Grant*, pp. 93, 228.

93. Phisterer, *Statistical Record*, p. 214.

94. Smith, *Grant*, p. 218.

95. Snead, "With Price," p. 734.

96. Suhr, "Iuka," p. 49.

97. The designation "Grant not present" represents my subjective judgment that, although Grant had command responsibility for the battle, he was not sufficiently involved to have had a direct impact on the outcome of the battle.

98. Allen, "Crossroads," p. 46.

99. Badeau, *Grant*, I, p. 117.

100. Catton, *Grant Moves South*, p. 315.

101. Cobb, *American Battlefields*, p. 195.

102. Cozzens, *Darkest Days*, pp. 305–6.

103. Current, *Encyclopedia*, I, p. 415.

104. Foote, *Civil War*, I, pp. 724–25.

105. Fox, *Regimental Losses*, pp. 23, 544, 550.

106. Fuller, *Grant and Lee*, p. 286.

107. Grant, *Memoirs*, p. 281.

108. Hattaway and Jones, *How the North Won*, p. 256.

109. Heidler and Heidler, *Encyclopedia*, p. 500.

110. Johnson and Buel, *Battles and Leaders*, II, pp. 759–60.

111. Lamers, *Edge of Glory*, pp. 154–55.

112. Marshall-Cornwall, *Grant*, pp. 95–96, 228.

113. Livermore, *Numbers & Losses*, p. 94.

114. Phisterer, *Statistical Record*, p. 214.

115. Rosecrans, "Corinth," p. 756.

116. Smith, *Grant*, p. 219.

117. Williams, *Grant Rises in the West*, I, p. 104.

118. Woodworth, *Nothing but Victory*, p. 235.

119. Cozzens, *Darkest Days*, p. 292.

120. Foote, *Civil War*, p. 725.

121. Phisterer, *Statistical Record*, p. 214.

122. Williams, *Grant Rises in the West*, I, p. 104.

123. Badeau, *Grant*, I, p. 145.

124. Bearss, *Vicksburg*, I, pp. 224–29.

125. Beringer et al., *Why the South Lost*, p. 243.

126. Fox, *Regimental Losses*, pp. 23, 544, 550.

127. Fuller, *Grant and Lee*, p. 286.

128. Hattaway and Jones, *How the North Won*, p. 314.

129. Livermore, *Numbers & Losses*, pp. 96–97.

130. Marshall-Cornwall, *Grant*, pp. 105, 228.

131. Morgan, "Chickasaw Bluffs," pp. 468–69.

132. Phisterer, *Statistical Record*, p. 215.

133. Woodworth, *Nothing But Victory*, p. 279.

134. Arnold, *Grant Wins*, p. 45.

135. Bearss, *Vicksburg*, I, pp. 405, 415–19.

136. Fox, *Regimental Losses*, p. 23.

137. Livermore, *Numbers & Losses*, p. 98.

138. Marshall-Cornwall, *Grant*, pp. 106, 228.

139. Phisterer, *Statistical Record*, p. 215.

140. Sherman, *Memoirs*, p. 325.

141. Arnold, *Grant Wins*, p. 116.
142. Badeau, *Grant*, I, p. 211.
143. Bearss, *Vicksburg*, II, pp. 402–7.
144. Current, *Encyclopedia*, III, p. 1238.
145. Fuller, *Grant and Lee*, p. 386.
146. Grant, *Memoirs*, p. 358.
147. Heidler and Heidler, *Encyclopedia*, p. 1545.
148. Marshall-Cornwall, *Grant*, p. 112.
149. Martin, David G., *The Vicksburg Campaign* (New York: Wieser and Wieser, Inc., 1990) [hereafter Martin, *Vicksburg*], p. 94.
150. "The Opposing Forces in the Vicksburg Campaign," in Johnson and Buel, *Battles and Leaders*, III, pp. 546–50 [hereafter "Opposing Forces"] at p. 549. These numbers represent "the gist of all the data obtainable in the Official Records." Ibid., p. 546.
151. Phisterer, *Statistical Record*, p. 215.
152. Smith, *Grant*, p. 240.
153. Winschel, "Grant's Beachhead," p. 56.
154. Arnold, *Grant Wins*, p. 135.
155. Badeau, *Grant*, I, pp. 236–37.
156. Bearss, *Vicksburg*, II, pp. 515–17.
157. Foote, *Civil War*, II, p. 360.
158. Fox, *Regimental Losses*, pp. 544, 550.
159. Grant, *Memoirs*, pp. 331, 358.
160. Hattaway and Jones, *How the North Won*, p. 392.
161. Heidler and Heidler, *Encyclopedia*, pp. 1611, 2022.
162. Martin, *Vicksburg*, p. 97.
163. "Opposing Forces," p. 549.
164. Arnold, *Grant Wins*, p. 140.
165. Badeau, *Grant*, I, p. 249.
166. Bearss, *Vicksburg*, II, pp. 555–58.
167. Current, *Encyclopedia*, II, p. 838.
168. Foote, *Civil War*, p. 363.
169. Fox, *Regimental Losses*, p. 544.
170. Grant, *Memoirs*, pp. 337, 358.
171. Martin, *Vicksburg*, p. 99.
172. "Opposing Forces," p. 549.

173. Arnold, *Armies of Grant*, p. 109.

174. Arnold, *Grant Wins*, p. 196.

175. Badeau, *Grant*, I, pp. 269–70.

176. Bearss, "Grant Marches West," p. 45.

177. Bearss, *Vicksburg*, II, pp. 642–51.

178. Buell, *Warrior Generals*, pp. 440, 442.

179. Catton, *Grant Moves South*, p. 445.

180. Cobb, *American Battlefields*, p. 220.

181. Ecelbarger, *Black Jack Logan*, p. 143.

182. Civil War Times, *Great Battles*, p. 342.

183. Esposito, *West Point Atlas*, I, Map 105 text.

184. Foote, *Civil War*, II, p. 374.

185. Fox, *Regimental Losses*, pp. 544, 550.

186. Fuller, *Generalship of Grant*, p. 152.

187. Fuller, *Grant and Lee*, p. 286.

188. Grant, *Memoirs*, pp. 347, 358.

189. Hattaway and Jones, *How the North Won*, p. 393.

190. Heidler and Heidler, *Encyclopedia*, pp. 392, 2023–24.

191. Livermore, *Numbers & Losses*, pp. 99–100.

192. Marshall-Cornwall, *Grant*, p. 113.

193. Martin, *Vicksburg*, p. 110.

194. McPherson, *Battle Cry*, p. 630.

195. McWhiney & Jamieson, *Attack and Die*, p. 158.

196. Miers, Earl S., *The Web of Victory: Grant at Vicksburg* (Baton Rouge: Louisiana State University Press, 1984) (Reprint of New York: Alfred Knopf, 1955), p. 195.

197. "Opposing Forces," p. 549.

198. Phisterer, *Statistical Record*, p. 215.

199. Smith, *Grant*, p. 250.

200. Williams, *Grant Rises in the West*, II, p. 379.

201. Arnold, *Grant Wins*, pp. 228–32.

202. Badeau, *Grant*, I, p. 278.

203. Barton, "Charge," p. 60.

204. Bearss, *Vicksburg*, II, pp. 686–89.

205. Civil War Times, *Great Battles*, p. 344.

206. Foote, *Civil War*, II, p. 377.

207. Fox, *Regimental Losses*, p. 545.
208. Freeman, "Big Black River," pp. 84–85.
209. Goodman, "Decision," p. 79.
210. Grant, *Memoirs*, pp. 353, 358.
211. Heidler and Heidler, *Encyclopedia*, pp. 2024, 228.
212. Martin, *Vicksburg*, p. 111.
213. "Opposing Forces," p. 549.
214. Smith, *Grant*, p. 251.
215. Arnold, *Grant Wins*, p. 245.
216. Bearss, *Vicksburg*, III, pp. 773–80.
217. Civil War Times, *Great Battles*, p. 348.
218. Cobb, *American Battlefields*, p. 221.
219. Fox, *Regimental Losses*, p. 545.
220. Marshall-Cornwall, *Grant*, p. 114.
221. Martin, *Vicksburg*, p. 118.
222. "Opposing Forces," p. 549.
223. Trudeau, "Climax at Vicksburg," p. 82.
224. Winschel, Terrence, "The Siege of Vicksburg," *Blue & Gray Magazine*, XX, Issue 4 (Spring 2003), pp. 6–24, 47–50 [hereafter Winschel, "Siege of Vicksburg"] at p. 12.
225. Arnold, *Grant Wins*, p. 256.
226. Badeau, *Grant*, I, pp. 326–27.
227. Bearss, *Vicksburg*, III, pp. 862–73.
228. Buell, *Warrior Generals*, p. 440.
229. Cobb, *American Battlefields*, p. 221.
230. Ecelbarger, *Black Jack Logan*, p. 144.
231. Esposito, *West Point Atlas*, I, Map 106 text.
232. Fox, *Regimental Losses*, p. 545.
233. Fuller, *Grant and Lee*, p. 286.
234. Hattaway and Jones, *How the North Won*, p. 395.
235. Heidler and Heidler, *Encyclopedia*, p. 2025.
236. Livermore, *Numbers & Losses*, p. 100.
237. Lowe, "Field Fortifications," p. 65.
238. Marshall-Cornwall, *Grant*, p. 114.
239. Martin, *Vicksburg*, p. 126.
240. McFeely, *Grant*, p. 132.

241. "Opposing Forces," p. 549.
242. Smith, *Grant*, p. 252.
243. Trudeau, "Climax at Vicksburg," p. 85.
244. Winschel, "Siege of Vicksburg," p. 14.
245. Arnold, *Grant Wins*, p. 298.
246. Bearss, *Vicksburg*, III, pp. 957–68.
247. Fox, *Regimental Losses*, p. 545.
248. Hattaway and Jones, *How the North Won*, p. 411.
249. "Opposing Forces," p. 549.
250. Phisterer, *Statistical Record*, p. 215.
251. Trudeau, "Climax at Vicksburg," p. 88.
252. Arnold, *Armies of Grant*, p. 125.
253. Arnold, *Grant Wins*, p. 301.
254. Badeau, *Grant*, I, pp. 386, 398–99.
255. Chambers, John Whiteclay, II, *The Oxford Companion to American Military History* (Oxford: Oxford University Press, 1999), p. 756.
256. Cobb, *American Battlefields*, p. 223.
257. Davis, *Rise and Fall*, II, p. 349.
258. Ecelbarger, *Black Jack Logan*, p. 149.
259. Esposito, *West Point Atlas*, I, Map 107 text.
260. Fox, *Regimental Losses*, p. 23.
261. Fuller, *Generalship of Grant*, p. 158.
262. Fuller, *Grant and Lee*, pp. 183, 286.
263. Grant, *Memoirs*, p. 384.
264. Hattaway and Jones, *How the North Won*, p. 411.
265. Heidler and Heidler, *Encyclopedia*, p. 2026.
266. Livermore, *Numbers & Losses*, pp. 100–1.
267. Marshall-Cornwall, *Grant*, pp. 114, 177, 228.
268. McPherson, *Battle Cry*, p. 631.
269. McWhiney and Jamieson, *Attack and Die*, pp. 8, 21, 158.
270. "Opposing Forces," pp. 549–50.
271. Poulter, Keith, "Stop Insulting Robert E. Lee!," *North & South*, Vol. 1, No. 5 (1998), p. 6.
272. Sherman, *Memoirs*, p. 358.
273. Trudeau, "Climax at Vicksburg," p. 88.
274. Walsh, *"Whip"*, p. 210.

275. Weigley, *American Way of War*, p. 140.

276. Williams, *Grant Rises in the West*, II, p. 420.

277. Badeau, *Grant*, I, p. 397.

278. Current, *Encyclopedia*, II, p. 838.

279. Fox, *Regimental Losses*, pp. 545, 550.

280. Martin, *Vicksburg*, p. 180.

281. Sword, "Battle above Clouds," p. 14.

282. Grant, *Memoirs*, p. 420.

283. Cozzens, *Shipwreck*, p. 100.

284. Sword, "Battle above Clouds," p. 19.

285. Ibid., p. 54.

286. Arnold, *Armies of Grant*, p. 143.

287. Badeau, *Grant*, I, p. 524.

288. Buell, *Warrior Generals*, p. 441.

289. Catton, *Grant Takes Command*, p. 91.

290. Cobb, *American Battlefields*, pp. 231–33.

291. Cozzens, *Shipwreck*, p. 389.

292. Donald et al., *Civil War*, p. 369.

293. Davis, *Rise and Fall*, II, p. 365.

294. Donald et al., *Civil War*, p. 369.

295. Esposito, *West Point Atlas*, I, Map 116 text.

296. Foote, *Civil War*, II, p. 858.

297. Fox, *Regimental Losses*, pp. 23, 546, 551.

298. Fuller, *Grant and Lee*, p. 287.

299. Grant, "Chattanooga," p. 711.

300. Grant, *Memoirs*, p. 455.

301. Hattaway and Jones, *How the North Won*, pp. 461–62.

302. Heidler and Heidler, *Encyclopedia*, p. 415.

303. Johnson & Buel, *Battles and Leaders*, III, pp. 729–30.

304. Livermore, *Numbers & Losses*, pp. 106–8.

305. Marshall-Cornwall, *Grant*, pp. 128, 228.

306. McWhiney and Jamieson, *Attack and Die*, pp. 20, 158.

307. Phisterer, *Statistical Record*, p. 215.

308. Smith, *Grant*, p. 281.

309. Walsh, "*Whip*", p. 238.

310. Foote, *Civil War*, II, p. 865.

311. Heidler and Heidler, *Encyclopedia*, p. 1133.

312. Foote, *Civil War*, II, p. 865.

313. Heidler and Heidler, *Encyclopedia*, p. 1133.

314. Hattaway, "Hard War," p. 75.

315. Ibid.

316. Castel, Albert, "History in Hindsight: Sherman and Sooy Smith. William Tecumseh Sherman's war of words with William Sooy Smith may have been merely a case of sour grapes," *Columbiad: A Quarterly Review of the War between the States*, Vol. 3, No. 3 (Fall 1999), pp. 56–75 at 71.

317. Alexander, *Fighting for the Confederacy*, p. 385.

318. Buell, *Warrior Generals*, p. 441.

319. Catton, *Grant Takes Command*, p. 204.

320. Catton, *Stillness*, p. 91.

321. Civil War Times, *Great Battles*, p. 438.

322. Cobb, *American Battlefields*, p. 237.

323. Current, *Encyclopedia*, I, p. 338.

324. Esposito, *West Point Atlas*, I, Map 125 text.

325. Foote, *Civil War*, III, p. 188.

326. Fox, *Regimental Losses*, pp. 23, 546.

327. Freeman, *R. E. Lee*, III, p. 428.

328. Fuller, *Generalship of Grant*, p. 238.

329. Fuller, *Grant and Lee*, p. 215.

330. Hassler, *Commanders*, p. 211.

331. Hattaway, "Changing Face," p. 41.

332. Hattaway and Jones, *How the North Won*, p. 545.

333. Heidler and Heidler, *Encyclopedia*, p. 2113.

334. Livermore, *Numbers & Losses*, pp. 110–11.

335. Marshall-Cornwall, *Grant*, p. 228.

336. McPherson, *Battle Cry*, p. 726.

337. Mertz, "Wilderness II," p. 49.

338. Phisterer, *Statistical Record*, p. 216.

339. Rhea, "'Butcher' Grant," p. 48.

340. Smith, *Grant*, p. 333.

341. Steere, Edward, *The Wilderness Campaign* (New York: Bonanza Books, 1960), pp. 463, 472.

342. Taylor, *Lee*, p. 249.

343. Smith, *Grant*, p. 365.
344. Young, "Numbers and Losses," p. 26. All of Young's "killed" numbers included those mortally wounded, for which he provided numbers. He also spelled out the numbers of wounded who subsequently died. His are the most accurate statistics for the Overland Campaign.
345. Alexander, *Fighting for the Confederacy*, p. 385.
346. Civil War Times, *Great Battles*, p. 447.
347. Cobb, *American Battlefields*, pp. 239–40.
348. Current, *Encyclopedia*, I, p. 338.
349. Esposito, *West Point Atlas*, I, Map 133 text.
350. Fox, *Regimental Losses*, pp. 23, 546.
351. Fuller, *Generalship of Grant*, p. 252.
352. Fuller, *Grant and Lee*, p. 287.
353. Hassler, *Commanders*, p. 216.
354. Heidler and Heidler, *Encyclopedia*, p. 1841.
355. Livermore, *Numbers & Losses*, p. 112.
356. Lowe, "Field Fortifications," p. 65.
357. Marshall-Cornwall, *Grant*, p. 228.
358. Phisterer, *Statistical Record*, p. 216.
359. Rhea, "'Butcher' Grant," p. 49.
360. Taylor, *Lee*, p. 249.
361. Smith, *Grant*, p. 365.
362. Young, "Numbers and Losses," p. 26. Although Young's table shows a total of 12,451 casualties, his broken-down numbers total 12,421.
363. Alexander, *Fighting for the Confederacy*, p. 394.
364. Heidler and Heidler, *Encyclopedia*, p. 621.
365. Marshall-Cornwall, *Grant*, p. 228
366. Alexander, *Fighting for the Confederacy*, p. 394.
367. Cobb, *American Battlefields*, p. 245.
368. Fox, *Regimental Losses*, pp. 23, 547.
369. Fuller, *Grant and Lee*, p. 287.
370. Marshall-Cornwall, *Grant*, p. 228.
371. Phisterer, *Statistical Record*, p. 216.
372. Rhea, "'Butcher' Grant," p. 48.
373. Taylor, *Lee*, p. 249.
374. Smith, *Grant*, p. 365.

375. Young, "Numbers and Losses," pp. 26–27. Although Young's tables for Sheridan's raid, North Anna, and Totopotomoy show a total of 3,757 casualties, his broken-down numbers total 3,766. The totals of his broken-down numbers for those three battles are 617, 1,558, and 1,591, respectively.

376. Arnold, *Armies of Grant*, p. 221.

377. # indicates casualties on June 3 only.

378. Beringer et al., *Why the South Lost*, p. 349.

379. Buell, *Warrior Generals*, p. 441.

380. Casdorph, *Lee and Jackson*, p. 401.

381. Catton, *Grant Takes Command*, p. 267.

382. Catton, *Stillness*, p. 163.

383. Current, *Encyclopedia*, I, p. 367.

384. Esposito, *West Point Atlas*, I, Map 136 text.

385. Fox, *Regimental Losses*, pp. 23, 547.

386. Freeman, *R. E. Lee*, III, p. 391.

387. Fuller, *Generalship of Grant*, p. 274.

388. Fuller, *Grant and Lee*, p. 221, 287.

389. Hassler, *Commanders*, p. 218.

390. Heidler and Heidler, *Encyclopedia*, p. 465.

391. Jones, *Right Hand*, p. 199.

392. "Lee and Grant, 1864," p. 56.

393. Livermore, *Numbers & Losses*, p. 114.

394. Lowe, "Field Fortifications," pp. 65, 70.

395. Lowry, *No Turning Back*, p. 453.

396. Marshall-Cornwall, *Grant*, p. 228.

397. O'Beirne, "Valley," p. 77.

398. Phisterer, *Statistical Record*, p. 216.

399. Rhea, "'Butcher' Grant," p. 49.

400. Rhea, "Cold Harbor," pp. 60–61.

401. Rhea, *Cold Harbor*, p. 382.

402. Taylor, *Lee*, p. 249.

403. Smith, *Grant*, p. 365.

404. Young, "Numbers and Losses," p. 27. Although Young's table shows a total of 5,294 casualties, his broken-down numbers total 5,295.

405. Fox, *Regimental Losses*, p. 547.

406. Phisterer, *Statistical Record*, p. 217.

407. Taylor, *Lee*, p. 249.
408. Young, "Numbers and Losses," p. 27.
409. Boritt, *Why the Confederacy Lost*, p. 120.
410. Casdorph, *Lee and Jackson*, p. 401.
411. Dana, *Recollections*, p. 188.
412. Davis, *Rise and Fall*, II, p. 442.
413. Donald et al., *Civil War*, p. 378.
414. Esposito, *West Point Atlas*, I, Map 137 text.
415. Fuller, *Generalship of Grant*, p. 371.
416. Freeman, *R. E. Lee*, III, p. 446.
417. Grant, *Memoirs*, p. 597, quoting data from "A Statement of Losses Compiled in the Adjutant-General's Office."
418. Groom, *Shrouds of Glory*, p. 8.
419. Hassler, *Commanders*, p. 219.
420. Heidler and Heidler, *Encyclopedia*, pp. 466, 1639.
421. McPherson, *Battle Cry*, p. 742.
422. McWhiney and Jamieson, *Attack and Die*, p. 19, 158.
423. Miers, Earl Schenck, *The Last Campaign: Grant Saves the Union* (Philadelphia and New York: J. B. Lippincott Company, 1972), p. 122.
424. Rhea, *Spotsylvania*, pp. 319, 324.
425. Smith, *Grant*, p. 376.
426. Taylor, *Lee*, p. 249.
427. Smith, *Grant*, p. 365.
428. Walsh, *"Whip"*, p. 284.
429. Weigley, *American Way of War*, p. 144.
430. Young, "Numbers and Losses," p. 27. If Kenon's Landing and Trevilian Station battles are included, Young's numbers increase to 33,508, 4,313, 18,153, 861, and 10,181, respectively.
431. Buell, *Warrior Generals*, p. 441.
432. Current, *Encyclopedia*, III, p. 1198.
433. Fox, *Regimental Losses*, pp. 23, 547.
434. Fuller, *Grant and Lee*, p. 287.
435. Livermore, *Numbers & Losses*, p. 115.
436. Lowe, "Field Fortifications," p. 65.
437. Marshall-Cornwall, *Grant*, p. 228.
438. Phisterer, *Statistical Record*, p. 217.

439. Trudeau, *The Last Citadel*, p. 55.
440. Fox, *Regimental Losses*, p. 547.
441. Phisterer, *Statistical Record*, p. 217.
442. Trudeau, *The Last Citadel*, p. 90.
443. Suderow, "Glory Denied," p. 31.
444. Fox, *Regimental Losses*, p. 547.
445. Catton, *Grant Takes Command*, p. 325.
446. Catton, *Stillness*, p. 253.
447. Editors, *Great Battles*, p. 469.
448. Current, *Encyclopedia*, III, p. 1200.
449. Esposito, *West Point Atlas*, I, Map 139 text.
450. Fox, *Regimental Losses*, p. 547.
451. Freeman, *R. E. Lee*, III, p. 477.
452. Fuller, *Grant and Lee*, p. 287.
453. Hassler, *Commanders*, p. 227.
454. Livermore, *Numbers & Losses*, pp. 116–17.
455. Marshall-Cornwall, *Grant*, p. 228.
456. McPherson, *Battle Cry*, p. 760.
457. McWhiney & Jamieson, *Attack and Die*, p. 158.
458. Phisterer, *Statistical Record*, p. 217.
459. Trudeau, *The Last Citadel*, p. 127.
460. Buell, *Warrior Generals*, p. 441.
461. Fox, *Regimental Losses*, pp. 23, 547.
462. Livermore, *Numbers & Losses*, p. 117.
463. McWhiney & Jamieson, *Attack and Die*, p. 158.
464. Phisterer, *Statistical Record*, p. 217.
465. Suderow, "Nothing But a Miracle," p. 31.
466. Trudeau, *The Last Citadel*, p. 170.
467. Arnold, *Armies of Grant*, p. 246.
468. Current, *Encyclopedia*, III, p. 1200.
469. Fox, *Regimental Losses*, p. 547.
470. Fuller, *Grant and Lee*, p. 287.
471. Hassler, *Commanders*, p. 229.
472. Livermore, *Numbers & Losses*, p. 118.
473. Marshall-Cornwall, *Grant*, p. 228.
474. McWhiney & Jamieson, *Attack and Die*, p. 158.

475. Phisterer, *Statistical Record*, p. 217.

476. Trudeau, *The Last Citadel*, p. 174.

477. Fox, *Regimental Losses*, p. 547.

478. Phisterer, *Statistical Record*, p. 217.

479. Trudeau, *The Last Citadel*, p. 189.

480. Fox, *Regimental Losses*, p. 548.

481. Fuller, *Grant and Lee*, p. 287.

482. Hassler, *Commanders*, p. 230.

483. Livermore, *Numbers & Losses*, p. 128.

484. McWhiney and Jamieson, *Attack and Die*, p. 158.

485. Phisterer, *Statistical Record*, p. 217.

486. Trudeau, *The Last Citadel*, p. 217.

487. Sommers, *Richmond Redeemed*, pp. 473–99.

488. Fox, *Regimental Losses*, p. 548.

489. Trudeau, "Unerring Firearm," p. 86.

490. Current, *Encyclopedia*, III, p. 1201.

491. Fox, *Regimental Losses*, p. 548.

492. Fuller, *Grant and Lee*, p. 287.

493. Hassler, *Commanders*, p. 231.

494. Heidler and Heidler, *Encyclopedia*, p. 946.

495. Ibid., pp. 130–31.

496. McWhiney and Jamieson, *Attack and Die*, p. 158.

497. Phisterer, *Statistical Record*, p. 218.

498. Trudeau, *The Last Citadel*, pp. 248, 250–51.

499. Bergeron, "Hatcher's Run," p. 37.

500. Current, *Encyclopedia*, III, p. 1201.

501. Fox, *Regimental Losses*, p. 548.

502. Livermore, *Numbers & Losses*, pp. 133–34.

503. McWhiney and Jamieson, *Attack and Die*, p. 158.

504. Phisterer, *Statistical Record*, p. 218.

505. Trudeau, *The Last Citadel*, p. 322.

506. Current, *Encyclopedia*, III, p. 1201.

507. Esposito, *West Point Atlas*, I, Map 142 text.

508. Fox, *Regimental Losses*, p. 548.

509. Freeman, *R. E. Lee*, IV, p. 19.

510. Fuller, *Generalship of Grant*, p. 341.

511. Fuller, *Grant and Lee*, p. 287.
512. Hassler, *Commanders*, p. 239.
513. Heidler and Heidler, *Encyclopedia*, p. 753.
514. Marvel, "Retreat," p. 6.
515. McPherson, *Battle Cry*, p. 726.
516. Phisterer, *Statistical Record*, p. 218.
517. Smith, *Grant*, p. 393.
518. Trudeau, *The Last Citadel*, pp. 353–54.
519. Fox, *Regimental Losses*, p. 549.
520. Phisterer, *Statistical Record*, p. 218.
521. Fox, *Regimental Losses*, p. 549.
522. Crawford, "Dinwiddie Court House," p. 55.
523. Fuller, *Grant and Lee*, p. 287.
524. Livermore, *Numbers & Losses*, p. 137.
525. Calkins, "Five Forks," p. 51.
526. Catton, *Grant Takes Command*, p. 445.
527. Current, *Encyclopedia*, III, p. 1201.
528. Esposito, *West Point Atlas*, I, Map 142 text.
529. Fox, *Regimental Losses*, p. 549.
530. Freeman, *R. E. Lee*, IV, p. 40.
531. Marvel, "Retreat," p. 6.
532. Phisterer, *Statistical Record*, p. 218.
533. Trudeau, Noah Andre, *Out of the Storm: The End of the Civil War, April–June 1865* (Boston, New York, Toronto, London: Little, Brown and Company, 1994) [hereafter Trudeau, *Out of the Storm*], p. 45.
534. Current, *Encyclopedia*, III, p. 1201.
535. Fox, *Regimental Losses*, p. 549.
536. Fuller, *Grant and Lee*, p. 287.
537. Livermore, *Numbers & Losses*, p. 138.
538. Phisterer, *Statistical Record*, p. 218.
539. Cobb, *American Battlefields*, pp. 256, 258.
540. Current, *Encyclopedia*, III, p. 1201.
541. Trudeau, *The Last Citadel*, p. 419.
542. Calkins, "Final Bloodshed," p. 36.
543. Fox, *Regimental Losses*, p. 549.
544. Freeman, *R. E. Lee*, IV, pp. 91, 93.

545. Glynn, "Black Thursday," p. 29.
546. Heidler and Heidler, *Encyclopedia*, p. 1710.
547. McPherson, *Battle Cry*, p. 848.
548. Phisterer, *Statistical Record*, p. 218.
549. Smith, *Grant*, p. 398.
550. Trudeau, *The Last Citadel*, p. 414.
551. Trudeau, *Out of the Storm*, pp. 115–16.
552. Buell, *Warrior Generals*, p. 441.
553. *Civil War Times, Great Battles*, p. 560.
554. Current, *Encyclopedia*, I, p. 48.
555. Fuller, *Grant and Lee*, p. 287.
556. Hassler, *Commanders*, p. 240.
557. Heidler and Heidler, *Encyclopedia*, p. 72.
558. Livermore, *Numbers & Losses*, pp. 135–37.
559. Marshall-Cornwall, *Grant*, p. 228.
560. Marvel, *Lee's Last Retreat*, p. 205.
561. McWhiney and Jamieson, *Attack and Die*, pp. 19, 158. If the Confederate loss figure is supposed to be 6,266 (Livermore's number [usually used by McWhiney and Jamieson]) instead of 6,666, the Confederate loss percentage would be 13%.
562. Phisterer, *Statistical Record*, p. 219.
563. Porter, *Campaigning with Grant*, p. 492.
564. Simpson, *Hood's Texas Brigade*, p. 466.

APPENDIX II
1. Burton, *Extraordinary Circumstances*, p. 74.
2. Current, *Encyclopedia*, Vol. 2, p.1021.
3. Eicher, *Longest Night*, pp. 284–85.
4. Fox, *Regimental Losses*, p. 543.
5. Freeman, *R. E. Lee*, II, p. 135.
6. Fuller, *Grant and Lee*, pp. 273, 286.
7. Freeman, *Lieutenants*, I, p. 515n.
8. Heidler & Heidler, *Encyclopedia*, p. 1301.
9. Konstam, *Seven Days*, p. 37.
10. Livermore, *Numbers & Losses*, p. 82.

11. Lowe, David W., "Field Fortifications in the Civil War," *North & South*, Vol. 4, No. 6 (Aug. 2001), pp. 58–73 [hereafter Lowe, "Field Fortifications"] at p. 65.

12. McPherson, *Atlas*, p. 70.

13. Robertson, *Jackson*, p. 473.

14. Alexander, *Lost Victories*, p. 109.

15. Burton, *Extraordinary Circumstances*, p. 136.

16. Current, *Encyclopedia*, Vol. 2, p. 653.

17. Eicher, *Longest Night*, p. 288.

18. Fox, *Regimental Losses*, p. 543.

19. Freeman, *Lieutenants*, I, pp. 536, 538.

20. Freeman, *R. E. Lee*, II, p. 157.

21. Fuller, *Grant and Lee*, pp. 273, 286.

22. Heidler & Heidler, *Encyclopedia*, p. 802.

23. Johnson and Buel, *Battles and Leaders*, II, p. 342n.

24. Konstam, *Seven Days*, p. 53.

25. Livermore, *Numbers & Losses*, pp. 82–83.

26. Lowe, "Field Fortifications," p. 65.

27. McPherson, *Atlas*, p. 70.

28. Thomas, *Lee*, p. 238.

29. Burton, *Extraordinary Circumstances*, p. 146.

30. Ibid., p. 173.

31. Fox, *Regimental Losses*, p. 543.

32. Ibid., p. 543.

33. Heidler & Heidler, *Encyclopedia*, p. 1706.

34. Konstam, *Seven Days*, p. 60.

35. Thomas, *Lee*, p. 240.

36. Burton, *Extraordinary Circumstances*, p. 298.

37. Current, *Encyclopedia*, Vol. 2, p. 637.

38. Eicher, *Longest Night*, p. 293.

39. Fox, *Regimental Losses*, p. 543.

40. Heidler & Heidler, *Encyclopedia*, p. 848.

41. Konstam, *Seven Days*, p. 68.

42. Robertson, *Jackson*, p. 497.

43. Sears, "Glendale," p. 24.

44. Thomas, *Lee*, p. 241.

45. Burton, *Extraordinary Circumstances*, p. 357.

46. Current, *Encyclopedia*, Vol. 3, p. 996.

47. Eicher, *Longest Night*, p. 296.

48. Fox, *Regimental Losses*, p. 543.

49. Fuller, *Grant and Lee*, p. 273.

50. Heidler & Heidler, *Encyclopedia*, p. 1246.

51. Keegan, John, *Fields of Battle: The Wars for North America* (New York: Alfred A. Knopf, 1996), p. 243.

52. Kendall, Drew J., "'Murder' at Malvern Hill," *Military History*, Vol. 19, No. 3 (Aug. 2002), pp. 42–48 at p. 48.

53. Konstam, *Seven Days*, p. 81.

54. Lowe, "Field Fortifications," p. 65.

55. Robertson, *Jackson*, pp. 502–3.

56. Weigley, *American Way of War*, p. 107.

57. Livermore, *Numbers & Losses*, pp. 84–85.

58. Alexander, *Lost Victories*, p. 129.

59. Beringer et al., *Why the South*, p. 460.

60. Boritt, *Why the Confederacy Lost*, p. 55.

61. Bradford, James C., *Oxford Atlas of American Military History* (Oxford: Oxford University Press, 2003) [hereafter Bradford, *Oxford Atlas*], p. 73.

62. Burton, *Extraordinary Circumstances*, p. 386.

63. Current, *Encyclopedia*, Vol. 1, p. 338; Vol. 3, pp. 1400–1.

64. Davis, Burke, *They Called Him Stonewall: A Life of Lt. General T. J. Jackson, C.S.A.* (New York: Wings Books, 1988) (Reprint of New York: Rinehart, 1954), p. 258.

65. Donald, David Herbert; Baker, Jean Harvey; and Holt, Michael F., The Civil War and Reconstruction (New York and London: W.W. Norton & Company, 2001)[hereafter Donald et al., *Civil War*], p. 213.

66. Eicher, *Longest Night*, p. 296.

67. Esposito, *West Point Atlas*, I, Map 47.

68. Foote, *Civil War*, I, p. 516. Foote calculated that, because more Federals (half their wounded) had been captured and approximately half the uncaptured wounded on both sides would return to action, "the actual loss in combat strength, after recuperation of the injured, would be 14,000 Federals and 12,500 Confederates." Ibid.

69. Fox, *Regimental Losses*, pp. 543, 550.

70. Freeman, *Lieutenants*, I, p. 605n.

71. Freeman, *R. E. Lee*, II, pp. 230–31.

72. Fuller, *Grant and Lee*, pp. 273, 286.

73. Gallagher, Gary W., *The American Civil War: The War in the East 1861–May 1863* (Oxford: Osprey Publishing, 2001) [hereafter Gallagher, *Civil War*], p. 44.

74. Hattaway & Jones, *How the North Won*, p. 199.

75. Heidler & Heidler, *Encyclopedia*, p. 374.

76. Johnson and Buel, *Battles and Leaders*, II, pp. 187, 315, 317.

77. Konstam, *Seven Days*, p. 86.

78. Livermore, *Numbers & Losses*, p. 86.

79. McClellan, George B., "The Peninsular Campaign," in Johnson and Buel, *Battles and Leaders*, II, pp. 160–87 at p. 187.

80. McPherson, *Atlas*, p. 72.

81. McWhiney & Jamieson, *Attack*, pp. 8, 19.

82. Nolan, "Demolishing the Myth," p. 33.

83. Phisterer, *Statistics*, p. 214.

84. Weigley, *American Way of War*, p. 107.

85. Woodworth, *Civil War Generals*, p. 91.

86. The designation "Lee not present" represents my subjective judgment that, although Lee had command responsibility for the battle, he was not sufficiently involved to have had a direct impact on the outcome of the battle.

87. Alexander, *Lost Victories*, p. 159.

88. Civil War Times, *Great Battles*, pp. 183–84.

89. Current, *Encyclopedia*, Vol. 1, pp. 272–73.

90. Esposito, *West Point Atlas*, I, Map 56.

91. Fox, *Regimental Losses*, pp. 544, 550.

92. Freeman, *Lieutenants*, II, p. 43.

93. Fuller, *Grant and Lee*, p. 286.

94. Heidler & Heidler, *Encyclopedia*, p. 387.

95. Johnson and Buel, *Battles and Leaders*, II, pp. 495–96.

96. Livermore, *Numbers & Losses*, pp. 87–88.

97. McPherson, *Atlas*, p. 74.

98. Phisterer, *Statistics*, p. 214.

99. Alexander, *Lost Victories*, p. 202.

100. Beringer et al., *Why the South*, p. 460.

101.   Boritt, *Why the Confederacy Lost*, p. 59.

102.   Civil War Times, *Great Battles*, p. 209.

103.   Cobb, *American Battlefields*, p. 184.

104.   Current, *Encyclopedia*, Vol. 1, p. 338; Vol. 3, p. 1003.

105.   Esposito, *West Point Atlas*, I, Map 64.

106.   Foote, *Civil War*, I, p. 640.

107.   Fox, *Regimental Losses*, pp. 544, 550. Confederate data are from August 21 through September 2, and Union data are from August 16 through 31.

108.   Freeman, *R. E. Lee*, II, p. 344.

109.   Gallagher, *Civil War*, p. 46.

110.   Heidler & Heidler, *Encyclopedia*, p. 321.

111.   Hennessy, "Second Manassas," p. 57.

112.   Johnson and Buel, *Battles and Leaders*, II, pp. 497–500.

113.   McWhiney & Jamieson, *Attack*, pp. 8, 19.

114.   Nolan, "Demolishing the Myth," p. 33.

115.   Phisterer, *Statistics*, p. 214.

116.   Thomas, *Lee*, p. 254.

117.   Weigley, *American Way of War*, p. 109.

118.   Eicher, *Longest Night*, p. 334.

119.   Fuller, *Grant and Lee*, p. 286.

120.   Livermore, *Numbers & Losses*, pp. 88–89.

121.   McPherson, *Atlas*, p. 77.

122.   Heidler & Heidler, *Encyclopedia*, p. 400.

123.   Phisterer, *Statistics*, p. 214.

124.   Cobb, *American Battlefields*, p. 185.

125.   Current, *Encyclopedia*, Vol. 2, p. 744.

126.   Fox, *Regimental Losses*, p. 544.

127.   Fuller, *Grant and Lee*, p. 286.

128.   Heidler & Heidler, *Encyclopedia*, p. 930.

129.   Hotchkiss, Jedediah, *Make Me a Map*, p. 81.

130.   Johnson and Buel, *Battles and Leaders*, II, p. 618.

131.   McPherson, *Atlas*, p. 78.

132.   Phisterer, *Statistics*, p. 214.

133.   Heidler & Heidler, *Encyclopedia*, p. 514.

134.   Fuller, *Grant and Lee*, pp. 273, 286.

135.   Current, *Encyclopedia*, Vol. 4, p. 1513.

136. Eicher, *Longest Night*, p. 344.
137. Fox, *Regimental Losses*, p. 544.
138. Gallagher, *Civil War*, p. 52.
139. Phisterer, *Statistics*, p. 214.
140. Alexander, *Lost Victories*, p. 253.
141. Bailey, Ronald H., *The Bloodiest Day: The Battle of Antietam* (Alexandria, Virginia: Time-Life Books, 1984, 1985) p. 150.
142. Beringer et al., Why the South, p. 460.
143. Black, Jeremy (ed.), *The Seventy Great Battles in History* (London: Thanes & Hutson Ltd., 2005) [hereafter Black, *Seventy Battles*], p. 208.
144. Buell, *Warrior Generals*, pp. 121–22.
145. Cobb, *American Battlefields*, p. 185.
146. Cox, *Reminiscences*, I, p. 353, citing *Century War Book*, II, p. 603.
147. Current, *Encyclopedia*, Vol. 1, p. 338; Vol. 3, p. 1408.
148. Donald et al., *Civil War*, p. 221.
149. Eicher, *Longest Night*, p. 363.
150. Esposito, *West Point Atlas*, I, Map 69.
151. Foote, *Civil War*, I, p. 702.
152. Fox, *Regimental Losses*, p. 544.
153. Freeman, *R. E. Lee*, II, p. 402.
154. Fuller, *Grant and Lee*, p. 286.
155. Gallagher, *Civil War*, p. 52.
156. Hattaway & Jones, *How the North Won*, p. 243.
157. Heidler & Heidler, *Encyclopedia*, pp. 374, 779.
158. Johnson and Buel, *Battles and Leaders*, II, pp. 598–603.
159. Livermore, *Numbers & Losses*, pp. 92–93.
160. Lowe, "Field Fortifications," p. 65.
161. McPherson, *Atlas*, p. 80.
162. McWhiney & Jamieson, *Attack*, pp. 8, 19.
163. Nolan, "Demolishing the Myth," p. 33.
164. Phisterer, *Statistics*, p. 214.
165. Thomas, *Lee*, p. 262.
166. Weigley, *American Way of War*, p. 111.
167. Woodworth, *Davis & Lee*, p. 192.
168. Fox, *Regimental Losses*, p. 544.
169. Foote, *Civil War*, I, p. 702.

170. Fox, *Regimental Losses*, p. 550.

171. Freeman, *Lieutenants*, II, p. 225.

172. Freeman, *R. E. Lee*, II, p. 402.

173. Weigley, *American Way of War*, p. 111.

174. Alexander, *Lost Victories*, pp. 280–81.

175. Beringer et al., *Why the South*, pp. 239, 460.

176. Bradford, *Oxford Atlas*, p. 77.

177. Cobb, *American Battlefields*, p. 201.

178. Current, *Encyclopedia*, Vol. 2, p. 640.

179. Donald et al., *Civil War*, p. 223.

180. Eicher, *Longest Night*, p. 405.

181. Esposito, *West Point Atlas*, I, Map 73.

182. Foote, *Civil War*, II, p. 44. Foote stated that the original Confederate loss figure of 5,309 was later reduced to 4,201 when it was discovered that over a thousand supposedly missing or wounded Rebels had gone on Christmas holiday immediately after the battle. Ibid.

183. Fox, *Regimental Losses*, pp. 544, 550.

184. Freeman, *Lieutenants*, II, p. 385.

185. Freeman, *R. E. Lee*, II, p. 471.

186. Fuller, *Lee and Grant*, pp. 273, 286.

187. Gallagher, *Civil War*, p. 60.

188. Hattaway & Jones, *How the North Won*, p. 307.

189. Heidler & Heidler, *Encyclopedia*, p. 779.

190. Johnson and Buel, *Battles and Leaders*, III, pp. 145, 147.

191. Jones, *Right Hand*, p. 51.

192. Livermore, *Numbers & Losses*, p. 96.

193. Lowe, "Field Fortifications," p. 65.

194. McWhiney & Jamieson, *Attack*, pp. 8, 19.

195. Nichols, *Reynolds*, p. 153.

196. Phisterer, *Statistics*, p. 215.

197. Thomas, *Lee*, p. 272.

198. Weigley, *American Way of War*, p. 113.

199. Fox, *Regimental Losses*, pp. 544, 550.

200. Heidler & Heidler, *Encyclopedia*, p. 1112.

201. Alexander, *Fighting for the Confederacy*, p. 217.

202. Alexander, *Lost Victories*, p. 322.

203. Beringer et al., *Why the South*, p. 460.
204. Bradford, *Oxford Atlas*, p. 82.
205. Cobb, *American Battlefields*, p. 208.
206. Current, *Encyclopedia*, Vol. 1, pp. 282, 338.
207. Eicher, *Longest Night*, p. 488.
208. Esposito, *West Point Atlas*, I, Map 91.
209. Fox, *Regimental Losses*, pp. 544, 550.
210. Freeman, *Lieutenants*, II, p. 648.
211. Fuller, *Grant and Lee*, p. 273.
212. Gallagher, *Civil War*, p. 69.
213. Hattaway & Jones, *How the North Won*, p. 384.
214. Heidler & Heidler, *Encyclopedia*, p. 398.
215. Hess, "Spades," p. 21.
216. Johnson and Buel, *Battles and Leaders*, III, pp. 237–38.
217. Livermore, *Numbers & Losses*, pp. 98–99.
218. Lowe, "Field Fortifications," p. 65.
219. McPherson, *Atlas*, p. 115.
220. McWhiney & Jamieson, *Attack*, pp. 8, 19.
221. Nichols, *Reynolds*, p. 178.
222. Nolan, "Demolishing the Myth," p. 33.
223. Phisterer, *Statistics*, p. 215.
224. Weigley, *American Way of War*, p. 114.
225. Carhart, *Lost Triumph*, p. 113.
226. Current, *Encyclopedia*, Vol. 2, p. 209.
227. Fox, *Regimental Losses*, pp. 545, 550.
228. Heidler & Heidler, *Encyclopedia*, p. 274.
229. Phisterer, *Statistics*, p. 215.
230. Trudeau, Noah Andre, *Gettysburg: A Testing of Courage* (New York: Harper-Collins, 2002) [hereafter Trudeau, *Gettysburg*], p. 32.
231. Fox, *Regimental Losses*, pp. 545, 550.
232. Heidler & Heidler, *Encyclopedia*, p. 2132.
233. Phisterer, *Statistics*, p. 215.
234. Fox, *Regimental Losses*, pp. 545, 550.
235. Ibid.
236. Heidler & Heidler, *Encyclopedia*, p. 925.
237. Alexander, *Fighting for the Confederacy*, p. 275.

238. Beringer et al., *Why the South*, pp. 261–62, 460.

239. Black, *Seventy Battles*, p. 212.

240. Boritt, *Why the Confederacy Lost*, p. 68.

241. Bradford, *Oxford Atlas*, p. 85.

242. Civil War Times, *Great Battles*, pp. 312–15.

243. Cobb, *American Battlefields*, p. 218.

244. Current, *Encyclopedia*, Vol. 1, p. 338; Vol. 2, p. 683.

245. Donald et al., *Civil War*, p. 357.

246. Eicher, *Longest Night*, p. 550.

247. Esposito, *West Point Atlas*, I, Map 99. Esposito stated that incomplete Confederate returns showed 20,451 casualties but that "their actual casualties appear to have been nearer 28,000, or one-third their force." Ibid.

248. Foote, *Civil War*, II, pp. 576, 578. Foote stated the number of casualties that Lee reported, including 5,150 captured or missing, and then pointed out that Union prisoner-of-war records showed that 12,227 named Confederates had been captured between July 1 and 5, 1863, Lee had recently ordered a halt to counting minor wounds, and a few of his units had made no casualty reports. Thus, Foote concludes that Lee's casualties were at least 25,000 and quite possibly far greater, perhaps Livermore's 28,063. See the footnotes below on Johnson & Buel's and on Livermore's numbers for Gettysburg.

249. Fox, *Regimental Losses*, pp. 545, 550.

250. Freeman, *Lieutenants*, III, p. 190.

251. Fuller, *Lee and Grant*, pp. 273, 286.

252. Hattaway & Jones, *How the North Won*, p. 409.

253. Heidler & Heidler, *Encyclopedia*, pp. 374, 836.

254. Johnson and Buel, *Battles and Leaders*, III, pp. 437, 439. The editors pointed out that Union records included names of 12,227 Confederate prisoners taken at Gettysburg while Confederate unit records reflect only 5,150 captured or missing. Perhaps this 7,000-soldier discrepancy caused Livermore's alleged double-counting. If his wounded number was 6,000 too high, perhaps his missing number was 6,000 or so too low. Part of the problem is that many Rebels were both wounded and captured and thus may have been counted in either, neither, or both categories by different statisticians. See next footnote.

255. Livermore, *Numbers & Losses*, pp. 102–3. Livermore's Gettysburg calculations were criticized by Joseph B. Mitchell in his "Confederate Losses at Gettysburg:

Debunking Livermore," *Blue & Gray Magazine*, VI, No. 4 (April 1989), pp. 38–40. Mitchell argued that it "is patently obvious" that Livermore double-counted about 6,000 Confederate wounded at Gettysburg and concluded that each side had about 24,000 casualties there. Mitchell's major argument is that Livermore based his calculation of wounded personnel on an over-estimated size of Lee's forces. But see the prior footnote and the footnote above on Shelby Foote's numbers for Gettysburg; both sources reveal a 7,000-man undercount of Confederate missing.

256. McPherson, *Atlas*, p. 123.
257. McWhiney & Jamieson, *Attack*, pp. 8, 19.
258. Nichols, *Reynolds*, p. 214.
259. Nofi, Albert A., *The Gettysburg Campaign, June and July, 1863* (New York: Wieser & Wieser, Inc., 1986)[hereafter Nofi, *Gettysburg*], p. 167.
260. Nolan, "Demolishing the Myth," p. 33.
261. OR, Ser. I, XXVII, Part I, p. 187 and Part II, p. 345.
262. Phisterer, *Statistics*, p. 215.
263. Thomas, *Lee*, p. 304.
264. Trudeau, *Gettysburg*, p. 529.
265. Weigley, *American Way of War*, p. 117.
266. Lowe, "Field Fortifications," p. 65.
267. Nichols, *Reynolds*, p. 214.
268. Nofi, *Gettysburg*, p. 162.
269. Carhart, *Lost Triumph*, pp. 253–54.
270. Alexander, "Ten Days," pp. 20–21.
271. Fox, *Regimental Losses*, pp. 545, 550. Confederate numbers are incomplete.
272. Ibid., p. 545.
273. Berkoff, "Botched Battle," pp. 70–71.
274. Current, *Encyclopedia*, Vol. 1, p. 221.
275. Fox, *Regimental Losses*, pp. 545, 551.
276. Heidler & Heidler, *Encyclopedia*, p. 286.
277. McPherson, *Atlas*, p. 138.
278. Fox, *Regimental Losses*, pp. 546, 551.
279. Ibid.
280. Current, *Encyclopedia*, Vol. 2, p. 880.
281. Heidler & Heidler, *Encyclopedia*, p. 1605.
282. McPherson, *Atlas*, p. 138.

283. Weigley, *American Way of War*, p. 118.
284. Welsh, "Dual Disasters," p. 49.
285. Current, *Encyclopedia*, Vol. 3, p. 1043.
286. Foote, *Civil War*, II, p. 877.
287. Fox, *Regimental Losses*, pp. 546, 551.
288. Fuller, *Grant and Lee*, p. 287.
289. Heidler & Heidler, *Encyclopedia*, p. 1334.
290. Livermore, *Numbers & Losses*, pp. 108–9.
291. Phisterer, *Statistics*, p. 215.
292. Foote, *Civil War*, II, p. 877.

MEMOIRS, LETTERS, PAPERS, AND OTHER PRIMARY DOCUMENTS

Alexander, Edward Porter. *Fighting for the Confederacy: The Personal Recollections of General Edward Porter Alexander*. Edited by Gary W. Gallagher. Chapel Hill: University of North Carolina Press, 1989.

———. *The Military Memoirs of a Confederate*. New York: Charles Scribner's Sons, 1907.

Badeau, Adam. *Military History of Ulysses S. Grant, from April, 1861, to April, 1865*. 3 vols. New York: D. Appleton and Company, 1868.

Basler, Roy P., ed. *The Collected Works of Abraham Lincoln*. 8 vols. New Brunswick: Rutgers University Press, 1953.

Benson, Susan Williams, ed. *Confederate Scout-Sniper: The Civil War Memoir of Barry Benson*. Athens and London: University of Georgia Press, 1992.

Blackford, William Willis. *War Years with Jeb Stuart*. Baton Rouge and London: Louisiana State University Press, 1945. 1993 Reprint.

Cadwallader, Sylvanus. *Three Years with Grant*. New York: Alfred A. Knopf, 1956. Published version of 1896 manuscript entitled inaccurately *Four Years with Grant*.

Cox, Jacob Dolson. *Military Reminiscences of the Civil War*. 2 vols. New York: Charles Scribner's Sons, 1900.

Dana, Charles A. *Recollections of the Civil War*. New York: Collier Books, 1893, 1963.

Davis, Jefferson. *The Rise and Fall of the Confederate Government.* 2 vols. New York: Da Capo Press, Inc., 1990. Reprint of 1881 edition.

Douglas, Henry Kyd. *I Rode with Stonewall: Being Chiefly the War Experiences of the Youngest Member of Jackson's Staff from the John Brown Raid to the Hanging of Mrs. Surratt.* St. Simons Island, Georgia: Mockingbird Books, Inc., 1961. Reprint of Raleigh: The University of North Carolina Press, 1940.

Dowdey, Clifford and Manarin, Louis H., eds. *The Wartime Papers of R. E. Lee.* New York: Bramhall House, 1961.

Freeman, Douglas Southall and McWhiney, Grady, eds. *Lee's Dispatches: Unpublished Letters of General Robert E. Lee, C.S.A., to Jefferson Davis and the War Department of the Confederate States of America 1862–65.* Baton Rouge and London: Louisiana State University Press, 1957, 1994. Update of Freeman's original 1914 edition.

Gaff, Alan D. *On Many a Bloody Field: Four Years in the Iron Brigade.* Bloomington and Indianapolis: Indiana University Press, 1996.

Gibbon, John. *Personal Recollections of the Civil War.* New York and London: G. P. Putnam's Sons, 1928.

Gordon, John B. *Reminiscences of the Civil War.* Baton Rouge and London, Louisiana State University Press, 1993. Reprint of New York: Charles Scribner's Sons, 1903.

Grant, Ulysses S. *Memoirs and Selected Letters: Personal Memoirs of U. S. Grant, Selected Letters 1839–1865.* Reprint. New York: Literary Classics of the United States, Inc., 1990.

Hotchkiss, Jedediah. *Make Me a Map of the Valley: The Civil War Journal of Stonewall Jackson's Topographer.* Edited by Archie P. McDonald. Dallas: Southern Methodist University Press, 1973, 1989.

Johnson, Robert Underwood and Buel, Clarence Clough, eds. *Battles and Leaders of the Civil War.* 4 vols. New York: Thomas Yoseloff, Inc., 1956. Reprint of Secaucus, New Jersey: Castle, 1887–88.

Jones, J. B. *A Rebel War Clerk's Diary at the Confederate States Capital.* 2 vols. Philadelphia: J. B. Lippincott & Co., 1866. 1982 reprint.

Jones, J. William. *Personal Reminiscences of General Robert E. Lee.* Richmond: United States Historical Society Press, 1989. Reprint.

Longstreet, James. *From Manassas to Appomattox: Memoirs of the Civil War in America.* New York: Smithmark Publishers, Inc., 1994.

Nicolay, John G. *The Outbreak of Rebellion*. New York: Charles Scribner's Sons, 1881. Reprint of Harrisburg: The Archive Society, 1992.

Porter, Horace. *Campaigning with Grant*. New York: Smithmark Publishers, Inc., 1994. Reprint.

Rhodes, Robert Hunt, ed. *All for the Union: The Civil War Diary and Letters of Elisha Hunt Rhodes*. New York: Orion Books, 1991. Originally published by Andrew Mowbray Incorporated in 1985.

Sears, Stephen W., ed. *The Civil War Papers of George B. McClellan: Selected Correspondence 1860–1865*. New York: Ticknor & Fields, 1989.

Sherman, William Tecumseh. *Memoirs of General W. T. Sherman*. New York: Literary Classics of the United States, Inc., 1990. Reprint of 1885 second edition.

Simon, John Y., ed. *The Papers of Ulysses Grant*. 28 vols. Carbondale and Edwardsville: Southern Illinois University Press, 1967–2006.

Stoddard, William O., Jr. *William O. Stoddard: Lincoln's Third Secretary*. New York: Exposition Press, 1955.

Taylor, Walter H. *General Lee: His Campaigns in Virginia 1861–1865 with Personal Reminiscences*. Lincoln and London: University of Nebraska Press, 1994. Reprint of Norfolk: Nusbaum Books, 1906.

Tower, R. Lockwood, ed. *Lee's Adjutant: The Wartime Letters of Colonel Walter Herron Taylor, 1862–1865*. Columbia: University of South Carolina Press, 1995.

The War of Rebellion: A Compilation of the Official Records of the Union and Confederate Armies. 128 vols. Washington, Government Printing Office, 1880–1901.

Watkins, Sam. R. *"Co. Aytch," Maury Grays, First Tennessee Regiment; or, A Side Show of the Big Show*. Wilmington, N.C.: Broadfoot Publishing Company, 1987. Reprint of 1952 edition and of Nashville: Cumberland Presbyterian Publishing House, 1882.

Welles, Gideon. *Diary of Gideon Welles*. 3 vols. Boston and New York: Houghton Mifflin Company, 1911.

Wiggins, Sarah Woolfolk, ed. *The Journals of Josiah Gorgas 1857–1878*. Tuscaloosa and London: The University of Alabama Press, 1995.

Woodward, C. Vann, ed. *Mary Chestnut's Civil War*. New Haven and London: Yale University Press, 1981.

STATISTICAL ANALYSES

Fox, William F. *Regimental Losses in the American Civil War, 1861–1865: A Treatise on the Extent and Nature of the Mortuary Losses in the Union Regiments, with*

Full and Exhaustive Statistics Compiled from the Official Records on File in the State Military Bureaus and at Washington. Dayton, Morningside House, Inc., 1985. Reprint of Albany: Brandow Printing Company, 1898.

Livermore, Thomas L. *Numbers & Losses in the Civil War in America: 1861–1865.* Millwood, New York: Kraus Reprint Co., 1977. Reprint of Bloomington: Indiana University Press, 1957.

Phisterer, Frederick. *Statistical Record: A Treasury of Information about the U.S. Civil War.* Carlisle, Pennsylvania: John Kallmann, Publishers, 1996. Reprint of *Statistical Record of the Armies of the United States* (1883), a supplementary volume to Scribner's Campaigns of the Civil War series.

ATLASES

Bradford, James C. *Oxford Atlas of American Military History.* Oxford: Oxford University Press, 2003.

Cobb, Hubbard. *American Battlefields: A Complete Guide to the Historic Conflicts in Words, Maps, and Photos.* New York: Macmillan, 1995.

Davis, George B.; Perry, Leslie J., and Kirkley, Joseph W. *Atlas to Accompany the Official Records of the Union and Confederate Armies.* Washington: Government Printing Office, 1891–95.

Esposito, Vincent J., ed. *The West Point Atlas of American Wars.* 2 vols. New York, Washington, London: Frederick A. Praeger, Inc., 1959.

Greene, A. Wilson and Gallagher, Gary W. *National Geographic Guide to the Civil War Battlefield Parks.* Washington, D.C.: The National Geographic Society, 1992.

McPherson, James M., ed. *The Atlas of the Civil War.* New York: Macmillan, 1994.

Symonds, Craig L. *Gettysburg: A Battlefield Atlas.* Baltimore: The Nautical & Aviation Publishing Company of America, 1992.

CHRONOLOGIES

Bishop, Chris and Drury, Ian. *1400 Days: The Civil War Day by Day.* New York: Gallery Books, 1990.

Bowman, John S., ed. *The Civil War Almanac.* New York: World Almanac Publications, 1983.

Mosocco, Ronald A. *The Chronological Tracking of the American Civil War Per the Official Records of the War of the Rebellion.* Williamsburg: James River Publications, 1994.

ENCYCLOPEDIAS

Chambers, John Whiteclay, II. *The Oxford Companion to American Military History*. Oxford: Oxford University Press, 1999.

Current, Richard N., ed. *Encyclopedia of the Confederacy*. 4 vols. New York: Simon & Schuster, 1993.

Faust, Patricia L., ed. *Historical Times Illustrated Encyclopedia of the Civil War*. New York: HarperPerennial, 1991.

Heidler, David S. and Heidler, Jeanne T., eds. *Encyclopedia of the American Civil War: A Political, Social, and Military History*. New York and London: W. W. Norton & Company, 2002.

Wagner, Margaret E.; Gallagher, Gary W.; and Finkelman, Paul, ed. *The Library of Congress Civil War Desk Reference*. New York: Simon & Schuster, 2002.

OTHER BOOKS AND PUBLICATIONS

Abbazia, Patrick. *The Chickamauga Campaign, December 1862–November 1863*. New York: Wieser & Wieser, Inc., 1988.

Alexander, Bevin. *How Great Generals Win*. New York & London: W. W. Norton & Co., 1993.

_____. *Lost Victories: The Military Genius of Stonewall Jackson*. New York: Henry Holt and Company, 1992.

_____. *Robert E. Lee's Civil War*. Avon, Massachusetts: Adams Media Corporation, 1998.

Ambrose, Stephen E. *Halleck: Lincoln's Chief of Staff*. Baton Rouge and London: Louisiana State University Press, 1962, 1990.

Arnold, James R. *The Armies of U. S. Grant*. London: Arms and Armour Press, 1995.

_____. *Grant Wins the War: Decision at Vicksburg*. New York: John Wiley & Sons, Inc., 1997.

Barry, John M. *Rising Tide: The Great Mississippi Flood of 1927 and How It Changed America*. New York: Simon & Schuster, 1997.

Bearss, Edwin Cole. *Unvexed to the Sea: The Campaign for Vicksburg*. 3 vols. Dayton: Morningside House, Inc., 1991. Reprint of 1986 edition.

Beecham, R. K. *Gettysburg: The Pivotal Battle of the Civil War*. Stamford, Connecticut: Longmeadow Press, 1994. Reprint of Chicago: A. C. McClurg, 1911.

Beringer, Richard E.; Hattaway, Herman; Jones, Archer; and Still, William N., Jr. *Why the South Lost the Civil War*. Athens: University of Georgia Press, 1986.

Bevins, Alexander. *Robert E. Lee's Civil War*. Avon, Massachusetts: Adams Media Corporation, 1998.

Black, Jeremy, ed. *The Seventy Great Battles in History*. London: Thanes & Hutson Ltd., 2005.

Black, Robert C., III. *The Railroads of the Confederacy*. Chapel Hill and London: University of North Carolina Press, 1998.

Bonekemper, Edward H., III. *How Robert E. Lee Lost the Civil War*. Fredericksburg, Virginia: Sergeant Kirkland's Press, 1998.

_____. *McClellan and Failure: A Civil War Study of Fear, Incompetence and Worse*. Jefferson, North Carolina: McFarland & Company, 2007.

_____. *A Victor, Not a Butcher: Ulysses S. Grant's Overlooked Military Genius*. Washington: Regnery Press, 2004.

Boritt, Gabor S., ed. *Lincoln's Generals*. New York and Oxford, Oxford University Press, 1994.

_____. *Lincoln, the War President*. New York and Oxford: Oxford University Press, 1992.

_____, ed. *Why the Confederacy Lost*. New York and Oxford: Oxford University Press, 1992.

Botkin, B. A., ed. *A Civil War Treasury of Tales, Legends and Folklore*. New York: Promontory Press, 1960.

Bowers, John. *Stonewall Jackson: Portrait of a Soldier*. New York: William Morrow and Company, Inc., 1989.

Bridges, Hal. *Lee's Maverick General: Daniel Harvey Hill*. Lincoln and London: University of Nebraska Press, 1991. Reprint of New York: McGraw-Hill, c1961.

Buell, Thomas B. *The Warrior Generals: Combat Leadership in the Civil War*. New York: Crown Publishers, Inc., 1997.

Bushong, Millard Kessler. *Old Jube: A Biography of General Jubal A. Early*. Shippensburg, Pennsylvania: White Mane Publishing Company, Inc., 1955, 1990.

Cannan, John, ed. *War in the East: Chancellorsville to Gettysburg, 1863*. New York: Gallery Books, 1990.

Carhart, Tom. *Lost Triumph: Lee's Real Plan at Gettysburg and Why It Failed*. New York: G. P. Putnam's Sons, 2005.

Carmichael, Peter S. *Lee's Young Artillerist: William R. J. Pegram*. Charlottesville: University Press of Virginia, 1995.

Casdorph, Paul D. *Lee and Jackson: Confederate Chieftains*. New York: Paragon House, 1992.

Castel, Albert E. *Decision in the West: The Atlanta Campaign of 1864*. Lawrence: University Press of Kansas, 1992.

Catton, Bruce. *The American Heritage New History of the Civil War*. New York: Penguin Books USA, Inc., 1996.

_____. *The Army of the Potomac: Glory Road*. Garden City, New York: Doubleday & Company, Inc., 1952.

_____. *The Army of the Potomac: Mr. Lincoln's Army*. Garden City, New York: Doubleday & Company, Inc., 1951, 1962.

_____. *The Army of the Potomac: A Stillness at Appomattox*. Garden City, New York: Doubleday & Company, Inc., 1953.

_____. *Grant Moves South*. Boston: Little, Brown and Company, 1960.

_____. *Grant Takes Command*. Boston: Little, Brown and Company, 1969.

_____. *Terrible Swift Sword*. Garden City, New York: Doubleday & Company, Inc., 1963.

_____. *This Hallowed Ground: The Story of the Union Side of the Civil War*. Garden City, New York: Doubleday & Company, Inc., 1956, 1962.

_____. *U. S. Grant and the American Military Tradition*. Boston: Little, Brown and Company, 1954.

Civil War Times Illustrated. *Great Battles of the Civil War*. New York: W. H. Smith, Inc., 1984.

Clark, Champ, ed. *Gettysburg: The Confederate High Tide*. (The Civil War Series) Alexandria, Virginia: Time-Life Books, Inc., 1985.

Clark, John E., Jr. *Railroads in the Civil War: The Impact of Management on Victory and Defeat*. Baton Rouge: Louisiana State University Press, 2001.

Coburn, Mark. *Terrible Innocence: General Sherman at War*. New York: Hippocrene Books, 1993.

Coddington, Edwin B. *The Gettysburg Campaign: A Study in Command*. New York: Charles Scribner's Sons, 1968, 1979.

Commager, Henry Steele, ed. *The Blue and the Gray. Two Volumes in One. The Story of the Civil War as Told by Participants*. New York: The Fairfax Press, 1982. Reprint of Indianapolis: Bobbs-Merrill, c. 1950.

Congressional Quarterly, Inc. *Presidential Elections, 1789–1996*. Washington: Congressional Quarterly, Inc., 1997.

Connelly, Thomas Lawrence. *Army of the Heartland: The Army of Tennessee, 1861–1862*. Baton Rouge and London: Louisiana State University Press, 1967.

_____. *Autumn of Glory: The Army of Tennessee, 1862–1865.* Baton Rouge and London: Louisiana State University Press, 1971, 1991.

_____. *The Marble Man: Robert E. Lee and His Image in American Society.* New York: Alfred A. Knopf, 1977.

_____ and Bellows, Barbara R. *God and General Longstreet: The Lost Cause and the Southern Mind.* Baton Rouge: Louisiana State University Press, 1982.

_____ and Jones, Archer. *The Politics of Command: Factions and Ideas in Confederate Strategy.* Baton Rouge: Louisiana State University Press, 1973.

Current, Richard N., ed. *Encyclopedia of the Confederacy.* 4 vols. New York: Simon & Schuster, 1993.

Cooling, Benjamin Franklin. *Forts Henry and Donelson: The Key to the Confederate Heartland.* Knoxville: The University of Tennessee Press, 1987.

Cozzens, Peter. *The Darkest Days of the War: The Battles of Iuka and Corinth.* Chapel Hill and London: The University of North Carolina Press, 1997.

_____. *The Shipwreck of Their Hopes: The Battles for Chattanooga.* Urbana and Chicago: University of Illinois Press, 1994.

Davis, Burke. *The Long Surrender.* New York: Vintage Books, 1985.

Davis, Burke. *They Called Him Stonewall: A Life of Lt. General T. J. Jackson, C.S.A.* New York: Wings Books, 1988. Reprint of New York: Rinehart, 1954.

Davis, Kenneth C. *Don't Know Much about the Civil War: Everything You Need to Know about America's Greatest Conflict but Never Learned.* New York: William Morrow and Company, Inc., 1996.

Davis, William C. *Brother against Brother: The War Begins.* (The Civil War Series) Alexandria, Virginia: Time-Life Books, Inc., 1983.

Davis, William C. *The Cause Lost: Myths and Realities of the Confederacy.* Lawrence: University Press of Kansas, 1996.

_____. *Jefferson Davis: The Man and His Hour.* Baton Rouge, Louisiana State University Press, 1991.

_____. *The Orphan Brigade: The Kentucky Confederates Who Couldn't Go Home.* Mechanicsburg, Pennsylvania: Stackpole Books, 1993.

Dew, Charles B. *Apostles of Disunion: Southern Secession Commissioners and the Causes of the Civil War.* Charlottesville: University Press of Virginia, 2001.

Donald, David Herbert, ed. *Why the North Won the Civil War.* New York: Macmillan Publishing Co., 1962.

Donald, David Herbert. *Lincoln.* New York: Simon & Schuster, 1995.

Donald, David Herbert; Baker, Jean Harvey; and Holt, Michael F. *The Civil War and Reconstruction*. New York and London: W. W. Norton & Company, 2001.

Dowdey, Clifford. *Lee*. Gettysburg: Stan Clark Military Books, 1991. Reprint of 1965 edition.

_____. *Lee's Last Campaign: The Story of Lee and His Men Against Grant—1864*. Wilmington, North Carolina: Broadfoot Publishing Company, 1988. Reprint of New York: Little, Brown and Company, 1960.

Eckert, Ralph Lowell. *John Brown Gordon: Soldier, Southerner, American*. Baton Rouge and London: Louisiana State University Press, 1989.

Eicher, David J. *The Civil War in Books: An Analytical Bibliography*. Urbana and Chicago: University of Illinois Press, 1997.

_____. *The Longest Night: A Military History of the Civil War*. New York: Simon & Schuster, 2002.

Engle, Stephen D. *The American Civil War: The War in the West 1861–July 1863*. Oxford: Osprey Publishing, 2001.

Faust, Patricia L., ed. *Historical Times Illustrated Encyclopedia of the Civil War*. New York: HarperPerennial, 1991.

Feis, William B. *Grant's Secret Service: The Intelligence War from Belmont to Appomattox*. Lincoln, Nebraska and London: University of Nebraska Press, 2002.

Fellman, Michael. *Citizen Sherman: A Life of William Tecumseh Sherman*. New York: Random House, 1995.

Fishel, Edwin C. *The Secret War for the Union: The Untold Story of Military Intelligence in the Civil War*. Boston and New York: Houghton Mifflin, 1996.

Flood, Charles Bracelen. *Grant and Sherman: The Friendship That Won the Civil War*. New York: Farrar, Straus and Giroux, 2005.

Foote, Shelby, ed. *Chickamauga and Other Civil War Stories*. New York: Dell Publishing, 1993.

_____. *The Civil War: A Narrative*. 3 vols. New York: Random House, 1958–1974.

Frassanito, William A. *Grant and Lee: The Virginia Campaigns 1864–1865*. New York: Charles Scribner's Sons, 1983, 1986.

Freeman, Douglas Southall. *Lee's Lieutenants: A Study in Command*. 3 vols. New York: Charles Scribner's Sons, 1942–44 (1972 reprint).

_____. *R. E. Lee*. 4 vols. New York and London: Charles Scribner's Sons, 1934–35.

Fuller, J. F. C. *The Generalship of Ulysses S. Grant*. Bloomington: Indiana University Press, 1958. Reprint of 1929 edition.

_____. *Grant and Lee: A Study in Personality and Generalship*. Bloomington: Indiana University Press, 1957. Reprint of 1933 edition.

Furgurson, Ernest B. *Ashes of Glory: Richmond at War*. New York: Alfred A. Knopf, 1996.

_____. *Chancellorsville 1863: The Souls of the Brave*. New York: Alfred A. Knopf, 1992.

_____. *Not War But Murder: Cold Harbor 1864*. New York: Alfred A. Knopf, 2000.

Gallagher, Gary W. *The American Civil War: The War in the East 1861–May 1863*. Oxford: Osprey Publishing, 2001.

_____. *Lee and His Generals in War and Memory*. Baton Rouge: Louisiana State University, 1998.

_____, ed. *Lee the Soldier*. Lincoln and London, University of Nebraska Press, 1996.

_____, ed. *The Spotsylvania Campaign*. Chapel Hill and London: University of North Carolina Press, 1998.

_____, ed. *The Third Day at Gettysburg & Beyond*. Chapel Hill and London: The University of North Carolina Press, 1994.

_____, ed. *The Wilderness Campaign*. Chapel Hill and London: University of North Carolina Press, 1997.

Gienapp, William E., ed. *The Civil War and Reconstruction: A Documentary Collection*. New York and London: W. W. Norton & Company, 2001.

Glatthaar, Joseph T. *The American Civil War: The War in the West 1863–1865*. Oxford: Osprey Publishing, 2001.

_____. *Partners in Command: The Relationships between Leaders in the Civil War*. New York: Macmillan, Inc., 1994.

Goodwin, Doris Kearns. *Team of Rivals: The Political Genius of Abraham Lincoln*. New York: Simon & Schuster, 2005.

Goss, Thomas J. *The War within the Union High Command: Politics and Generalship During the Civil War*. Lawrence: University Press of Kansas, 2003.

Gott, Kendall D. *Where the South Lost the War: An Analysis of the Fort Henry-Fort Donelson Campaign, February 1862*. Mechanicsburg, Pennsylvania: Stackpole Books, 2003.

Grant, Susan-Mary and Parish, Peter J., eds. *Legacy of Disunion: The Enduring Significance of the American Civil War*. Baton Rouge: Louisiana State University Press, 2003.

Griffith, Paddy. *Battle Tactics of the Civil War*. New Haven and London: Yale University Press, 1996.

Groom, Winston. *Shrouds of Glory. From Atlanta to Nashville: The Last Great Campaign of the Civil War*. New York: The Atlantic Monthly Press, 1995.

Guernsey, Alfred H. and Alden, Henry M., eds., *Harper's Pictorial History of the Civil War*. New York: The Fairfax Press, 1977. Reprint of *Harper's Pictorial History of the Great Rebellion in the United States*. New York: Harper & Brothers, 1866.

Hagerman, Edward. *The American Civil War and the Origins of Modern Warfare: Ideas, Organization, and Field Command*. Bloomington and Indianapolis: Indiana University Press, 1992.

Harman, Troy D. *Lee's Real Plan at Gettysburg*. Mechanicsburg, Pennsylvania: Stackpole Books, 2003.

Harsh, Joseph L. *Confederate Tide Rising: Robert E. Lee and the Making of Southern Strategy, 1861–1862*. Kent, Ohio and London: The Kent State University Press, 1998.

Hassler, Warren W., Jr. *Commanders of the Army of the Potomac*. Baton Rouge: Louisiana State University Press, 1962.

Hattaway, Herman and Jones, Archer. *How the North Won: A Military History of the Civil War*. Urbana and Chicago: University of Illinois Press, 1991. Reprint of 1983 edition.

Heleniak, Roman J. and Hewitt, Lawrence L., ed. *The Confederate High Command & Related Topics: The 1988 Deep Delta Civil War Symposium*. Shippensburg, Pennsylvania: White Mane Publishing Co., Inc., 1990.

Henderson, G. F. R. *Stonewall Jackson and the American Civil War*. New York: Da Capo Press, Inc., 1988. Reprint of New York: Grossett & Dunlap, 1943.

Hendrickson, Robert. *Sumter: The First Day of the Civil War*. Chelsea, Michigan: Scarborough House, 1990.

Hennessy, John J. *Return to Bull Run: The Campaign and Battle of Second Manassas*. New York: Simon & Schuster, 1993.

Hughes, Nathaniel Cheairs, Jr. *General William J. Hardee: Old Reliable*. Baton Rouge and London: Louisiana State University Press, 1965.

Hurst, Jack. *Nathan Bedford Forrest: A Biography*. New York: Alfred A. Knopf, 1993.

Johnson, Clint. *Civil War Blunders*. Winston-Salem: John F. Blair, 1997.

Jones, Archer. *Civil War Command & Strategy: The Process of Victory and Defeat*. New York, The Free Press, 1992.

_____. *Confederate Strategy from Shiloh to Vicksburg*. Baton Rouge and London: Louisiana State University Press, 1991.

Jones, R. Steven. *The Right Hand of Command: Use & Disuse of Personal Staffs in the Civil War*. Mechanicsburg, Pennsylvania: Stackpole Books, 2000.

Jones, Terry L. *Lee's Tigers: The Louisiana Infantry in the Army of Northern Virginia*. Baton Rouge and London: Louisiana State University Press, 1987.

Jordan, David M. *"Happiness Is Not My Companion": The Life of General G. K. Warren*. Bloomington: Indiana University Press, 2001.

_____. *Winfield Scott Hancock: A Soldier's Life*. Bloomington: Indiana University Press, 1996.

Judge, Joseph. *Season of Fire: The Confederate Strike on Washington*. Berryville, Virginia: Rockbridge Publishing Co., 1994.

Katcher, Philip. *The Army of Robert E. Lee*. London: Arms and Armour Press, 1994.

Keegan, John. *The Face of Battle*. New York: Dorset Press, 1986. (originally New York: The Viking Press, 1976).

_____. *Fields of Battle: The Wars for North America*. New York: Alfred A. Knopf, 1996.

_____. *The Mask of Command*. New York: Viking, 1987.

Kegel, James A. *North with Lee and Jackson: The Lost Story of Gettysburg*. Mechanicsburg, Pa.: Stackpole Books, 1996.

Kennett, Lee. *Marching Through Georgia: The Story of Soldiers and Civilians During Sherman's Campaign*. New York: HarperCollins, 1995.

Ketchum, Richard M. *The American Heritage Picture History of the Civil War*. 2 vols. New York: American Heritage Publishing Co., Inc., 1960.

Kiper, Richard L. *Major General John Alexander McClernand: Politician in Uniform*. Kent, Ohio and London: Kent State University Press, 1999.

Konstam, Angus. *Seven Days Battles 1862: Lee's Defense of Richmond*. Westport, Connecticut and London: Praeger, 2004.

Krick, Robert K. *The American Civil War: The War in the East 1863–1865*. Oxford: Osprey Publishing, 2001.

Lamers, William M. *The Edge of Glory: A Biography of General William S. Rosecrans, U.S.A.* Baton Rouge: Louisiana State University Press, 1999. Reprint and expansion of New York: Harcourt, Brace & World, 1961.

Lawson, Melinda. *Patriot Fires: Forging a New American Nationalism in the Civil War North*. Lawrence: University Press of Kansas, 2002.

Lee, Fitzhugh. *General Lee: A Biography of Robert E. Lee*. New York: Da Capo Press, 1994. Reprint of Wilmington, North Carolina: Broadfoot Publishing Company, 1989 and New York: D. Appleton and Company, 1894.

Levine, Bruce. *Confederate Emancipation: Southern Plans to Free and Arm Slaves During the Civil War.* Oxford: Oxford University Press, 2006.

Lewis, Lloyd. *Captain Sam Grant.* Boston: Little, Brown and Company, 1950.

Lewis, Thomas A. *The Guns of Cedar Creek.* New York: Harper & Row, 1988.

Long, David E. *The Jewel of Liberty: Abraham Lincoln's Re-election and the End of Slavery.* New York: Da Capo Press, 1997. Reprint of Mechanicsburg, Pennsylvania: Stackpole Books, 1994.

Longacre, Edward G. *General John Buford: A Military Biography.* Conshohocken, Pennsylvania: Combined Books, Inc., 1995.

_____. *General Ulysses S. Grant: The Soldier and the Man.* New York: Da Capo Press, 2006.

_____. *Grant's Cavalryman: The Life and Wars of General James H. Wilson.* Mechanicsburg, Pennsylvania: Stackpole Press, 1996. Originally *From Union Stars to Top Hat*, 1972.

Lossing, Benson. *A History of the Civil War, 1861–65, and the Causes That Led up to the Great Conflict.* New York: The War Memorial Association, 1912.

Lowry, Don. *Fate of the Country: The Civil War from June–September 1864.* New York: Hippocrene Books, 1992.

_____. *No Turning Back: The Beginning of the End of the Civil War: March–June, 1864.* New York: Hippocrene Books, 1992.

Luvaas, Jay and Nelson, Harold W., ed. *The U.S. Army War College Guide to the Battle of Antietam: The Maryland Campaign of 1862.* Carlisle, Pennsylvania: South Mountain Press, Inc., 1987.

_____. *The U.S. Army War College Guide to the Battle of Gettysburg.* Carlisle, Pennsylvania: South Mountain Press, Inc., 1986.

Marvel, William. *Lee's Last Retreat: The Flight to Appomattox.* Chapel Hill and London: University of North Carolina Press, 2002.

Matloff, Maurice, ed. *American Military History.* Washington, D.C.: U.S. Army Center of Military History, 1985.

Marszalek, John F. *Sherman: A Soldier's Passion for Order.* New York: Macmillan, Inc., 1993.

_____. *The Shiloh Campaign, March–April 1862.* New York: Wieser & Wieser, Inc., 1987.

_____. *The Vicksburg Campaign, April, 1862–July, 1863.* New York: Wieser & Wieser, Inc., 1990.

Marvel, William. *Lee's Last Retreat: The Flight to Appomattox*. Chapel Hill and London: University of North Carolina Press, 2002.

McDonough, James Lee. *Chattanooga: A Death Grip on the Confederacy*. Knoxville: The University of Tennessee Press, 1984.

McFeely, William. *Grant: A Biography*. New York and London: W. W. Norton & Company, 1981.

McKenzie, John D. *Uncertain Glory: Lee's Generalship Re-Examined*. New York: Hippocrene Books, 1997.

McMurry, Richard M. *Two Great Rebel Armies: An Essay in Confederate Military History*. Chapel Hill and London: The University of North Carolina Press, 1989.

McPherson, James M. *Battle Cry of Freedom: The Civil War Era*. New York: Ballantine Books, 1988.

_____. *Crossroads of Freedom: Antietam*. Oxford: Oxford University Press, 2002.

_____. *This Mighty Scourge: Perspectives on the Civil War*. Oxford: Oxford University Press, 2007.

McWhiney, Grady, ed. *Grant, Lee, Lincoln and the Radicals: Essays on Civil War Leadership*. New York: Harper & Row, 1966 (Reprint of Chicago: Northwestern University Press, 1964).

McWhiney, Grady and Jamieson, Perry D. *Attack and Die: Civil War Military Tactics and the Southern Heritage*. Tuscaloosa: The University of Alabama Press, 1982.

Meade, Robert Douthat. *Judah P. Benjamin: Confederate Statesman*. Baton Rouge: Louisiana State University Press, 1943, 2001.

Meredith, Roy. *The Face of Robert E. Lee in Life and Legend*. New York: The Fairfax Press, 1981.

Miers, Earl Schenck. *The Web of Victory: Grant at Vicksburg*. Baton Rouge: Louisiana State University Press, 1984. Reprint of New York: Alfred Knopf, 1955.

_____. *The Last Campaign: Grant Saves the Union*. Philadelphia and New York: J. B. Lippincott Company, 1972.

Miller, William J. *Mapping for Stonewall: The Civil War Service of Jed Hotchkiss*. Washington: Elliott & Clark Publishing, 1993.

Mitchell, Joseph B. *Decisive Battles of the Civil War*. New York: Ballantine Books, 1955.

Morris, Roy, Jr. *Sheridan: The Life and Wars of General Phil Sheridan*. New York: Crown Publishers, Inc., 1992.

Murphin, James V. *The Gleam of Bayonets: The Battle of Antietam and the Maryland Campaign of 1862*. Baton Rouge and London: Louisiana State University Press, 1965.

Nagel, Paul C. *The Lees of Virginia: Seven Generations of an American Family*. New York and Oxford: Oxford University Press, 1990.

Neely, Mark E., Jr.; Holzer, Harold; and Boritt, Gabor S. *The Confederate Image: Prints of the Lost Cause*. Chapel Hill and London: The University of North Carolina Press, 1987.

Nevins, Alan. *Ordeal of the Union*. 8 vols. New York and London: Charles Scribner's Sons, 1947–50.

Newell, Clayton R. *Lee vs. McClellan: The First Campaign*. Washington, D.C.: Regnery Publishing, Inc., 1996.

Nichols, Edward J. *Toward Gettysburg: A Biography of General John F. Reynolds*. State College: Penn State University Press, 1958.

Nicolay, Helen. *The Boys' Life of Ulysses S. Grant*. New York: The Century Co., 1909.

Nofi, Albert A. *The Gettysburg Campaign, June and July, 1863*. New York: Wieser & Wieser, Inc., 1986.

Nolan, Alan T. *Lee Considered: General Robert E. Lee and Civil War History*. Chapel Hill and London: University of North Carolina Press, 1991.

Osborne, Charles C. *Jubal: The Life and Times of General Jubal A. Early, CSA, Defender of the Lost Cause*. Baton Rouge and London: Louisiana State University Press, 1992.

Perret, Geoffrey. *A Country Made by War: From the Revolution to Vietnam—the Story of America's Rise to Power*. New York: Random House, 1989.

_____. *Ulysses S. Grant: Soldier & President*. New York: Random House, 1997.

Pfanz, Donald C. *Richard S. Ewell: A Soldier's Life*. Chapel Hill and London: University of North Carolina Press, 1998.

Pfanz, Harry W. *Gettysburg—Culp's Hill & Cemetery Hill*. Chapel Hill & London: The University of North Carolina Press, 1993.

_____. *Gettysburg: The Second Day*. Chapel Hill and London, The University of North Carolina Press, 1987.

Phisterer, Frederick. *Statistical Record of the Armies of the United States*. Edison, New Jersey: Castle Books, 2002. Reprint of 1883 book.

Piston, William Garrett. *Lee's Tarnished Lieutenant: James Longstreet and His Place in Southern History*. Athens and London: The University of Georgia Press, 1987.

Pollard, Edward A. *The Lost Cause. A New Southern History of the War of the Confederates*. New York: Gramercy Books, 1994. Reprint of New York: E. B. Treat & Company, 1866.

Priest, John M. *Antietam: The Soldiers' Battle*. Shippensburg, Pennsylvania: White Mane Publishing Co., Inc., 1989.

Rhea, Gordon C. *The Battle of the Wilderness May 5–6, 1864*. Baton Rouge and London: Louisiana State University Press, 1994.

_____. *The Battles for Spotsylvania Court House and the Road to Yellow Tavern, May 7–12, 1864*. Baton Rouge and London: Louisiana State University Press, 1997.

_____. *Cold Harbor: Grant and Lee May 26–June 3, 1864*. Baton Rouge: Louisiana State University Press, 2002.

_____. *To the North Anna River: Lee and Grant May 13–25, 1864*. Baton Rouge: Louisiana State University Press, 2000.

Robertson, James I., Jr. *General A. P. Hill: The Story of a Confederate Warrior*. New York: Random House, 1987.

_____. *The Stonewall Brigade*. Baton Rouge and London: Louisiana State University Press, 1963 (1991 Reprint).

_____. *Stonewall Jackson: the Man, the Soldier, the Legend*. New York: Macmillan Publishing USA, 1997.

Roland, Charles P. *An American Iliad: The Story of the Civil War*. Lexington: University Press of Kentucky, 1991.

Ross, Ishbel. *The General's Wife: The Life of Mrs. Ulysses S. Grant*. New York: Dodd, Mead and Company, 1959.

Rowland, Thomas J. *George B. McClellan and Civil War History in the Shadow of Grant and Sherman*. Kent, Ohio and London: The Kent State University Press, 1998.

Royster, Charles. *The Destructive War: William Tecumseh Sherman, Stonewall Jackson, and the Americans*. New York: Vintage Books, 1993.

Savage, Douglas. *The Court Martial of Robert E. Lee: A Historical Novel*. Conshohocken, Pennsylvania, Combined Books, Inc., 1993.

Scott, Robert Garth. *Into the Wilderness with the Army of the Potomac*. Bloomington: Indiana University Press. 1985.

Sears, Stephen W. *Chancellorsville*. Boston and New York: Houghton Mifflin Company, 1996.

_____. *Controversies & Commanders: Dispatches from the Army of the Potomac*. Boston and New York: Houghton Mifflin Company, 1999.

_____, ed. *The Civil War: The Best of American Heritage.* New York: American Heritage Press, 1991.

_____. *George B. McClellan: The Young Napoleon.* New York: Ticknor & Fields, 1988.

_____. *Landscape Turned Red: The Battle of Antietam.* New York: Book-of-the-Month Club, Inc., 1994.

_____. *To the Gates of Richmond: The Peninsula Campaign.* New York: Ticknor & Fields, 1992.

Shaara, Michael. *The Killer Angels.* New York: Ballantine Books, 1974.

Simpson, Brooks D. *Ulysses S. Grant: Triumph Over Adversity, 1822–1865.* Boston and New York: Houghton Mifflin Company, 2000.

Simpson, Harold B. *Lee's Grenadier Guard.* Vol. 2 of *Hood's Texas Brigade.* Fort Worth: Landmark Publishing, Inc., 1970.

Smith, Gene. *Lee and Grant: A Dual Biography.* New York: Promontory Press, 1984.

Smith, Jean Edward. *Grant.* New York: Simon & Schuster, 2001.

Sommers, Richard J. *Richmond Redeemed: The Siege at Petersburg.* Garden City: Doubleday & Company, 1981.

Stackpole, Edward J. *They Met at Gettysburg.* New York: Bonanza Books, 1956.

Swinton, William. *Campaigns of the Army of the Potomac.* New York: Richardson, 1866.

Steere, Edward. *The Wilderness Campaign.* New York: Bonanza Books, 1960.

Stern, Philip Van Doren. *Robert E. Lee: The Man and the Soldier.* New York: Bonanza Books, 1963.

Stewart, George R. *Pickett's Charge: A Microhistory of the Final Attack at Gettysburg, July 3, 1863.* Boston: Houghton Mifflin Co., 1959.

Stoddard, William O., Jr. *William O. Stoddard: Lincoln's Third Secretary.* New York: Exposition Press, 1955.

Swinton, William. *Campaigns of the Army of the Potomac.* New York: Richardson, 1866.

Tanner, Robert G. *Stonewall in the Valley: Thomas J. "Stonewall" Jackson's Shenandoah Valley Campaign Spring 1862.* Mechanicsburg, Pennsylvania: Stackpole Books, 1996.

Thomas, Emory M. *Robert E. Lee: A Biography.* New York and London: W. W. Norton & Company, 1995.

Tidwell, William A.; Hall, James O.; and Gaddy, David Winfred. *Come Retribution: The Confederate Secret Service and the Assassination of Lincoln.* Jackson and London: University Press of Mississippi, 1988.

Time-Life Books Editors. *Voices of the Civil War: Second Manassas.* Alexandria, Virginia: Time-Life Books, 1995.

Trudeau, Noah Andre. *Bloody Roads South: The Wilderness to Cold Harbor, May–June 1864.* Boston, Toronto, London: Little, Brown and Co., 1989.

_____. *Gettysburg: A Testing of Courage.* New York: HarperCollins, 2002.

_____. *The Last Citadel: Petersburg, Virginia June 1864–April 1865.* Baton Rouge: Louisiana State University Press, 1991.

_____. *Out of the Storm: The End of the Civil War, April–June 1865.* Boston, New York, Toronto, London: Little, Brown and Company, 1994.

Vandiver, Frank E. *Mighty Stonewall.* College Station: Texas A&M University Press, 1989. Reprint of 1957 edition.

Virginia Civil War Trails. *Lee vs. Grant: The 1964 Campaign.* Richmond, undated.

Wallace, Willard M. *Soul of the Lion: A Biography of General Joshua L. Chamberlain.* Gettysburg: Stan Clark Military Books, 1991. Reprint of Edinburgh, New York and Toronto: Thomas Nelson & Sons, 1960.

Walsh, George. *"Whip the Rebellion": Ulysses S. Grant's Rise to Command.* New York: Tom Doherty Associates, LLC, 2005.

Ward, Geoffrey C.; Burns, Ric, and Burns, Ken. *The Civil War: An Illustrated History.* New York: Alfred A. Knopf, Inc., 1990.

Warner, Ezra J. *Generals in Blue: Lives of the Union Commanders.* Baton Rouge and London: Louisiana State University Press, 1964.

_____. *Generals in Gray: Lives of the Confederate Commanders.* Baton Rouge and London: Louisiana State University Press, 1959.

Waugh, John C. *The Class of 1846: From West Point to Appomattox: Stonewall Jackson, George McClellan and Their Brothers.* New York: Warner Books, Inc., 1994.

_____. *Reelecting Lincoln: The Battle for the 1864 Presidency.* New York: Crown Publishers, Inc., 1997.

Weber, Thomas. *The Northern Railroads in the Civil War, 1861–1865.* Bloomington and Indianapolis: Indiana University Press, 1999. Reprint of 1952 edition.

Weigley, Russell F. *The American Way of War: A History of United States Military Strategy and Policy.* New York: Macmillan Publishing Co., Inc., 1973.

_____. *A Great Civil War: A Military and Political History, 1861–1865.* Bloomington and Indianapolis, Indiana University Press, 2000.

Weir, William. *Fatal Victories.* Hamden, Connecticut: Archon Books, 1993.

Welles, Gideon. *Diary of Gideon Welles.* 3 vols. Boston and New York: Houghton Mifflin Company, 1911.

Werstein, Irving. *Abraham Lincoln Versus Jefferson Davis*. New York: Thomas Y. Crowell Company, 1959.

Wert, Jeffrey D. *A Brotherhood of Valor: The Common Soldiers of the Stonewall Brigade, C.S.A., and the Iron Brigade, U.S.A*. New York: Simon & Schuster, 1999.

_____. *Custer: The Controversial Life of George Armstrong Custer*. New York: Simon & Schuster, 1996.

_____. *General James Longstreet: The Confederacy's Most Controversial Soldier—A Biography*. New York: Simon & Schuster, 1993.

_____. *From Winchester to Cedar Creek: The Shenandoah Campaign of 1864*. Carlisle, Pennsylvania: South Mountain Press, Inc., 1987.

_____. *Mosby's Rangers*. New York: Simon & Schuster, 1990.

_____. *On Fields of Fury: From the Wilderness to the Crater: An Eyewitness History*. New York: HarperCollins Publishers, 1991.

Wheeler, Richard. *Lee's Terrible Swift Sword: From Antietam to Chancellorsville, An Eyewitness History*. New York: HarperCollins Publishers, Inc., 1992.

_____. *On Fields of Fury: From the Wilderness to the Crater: An Eyewitness History*. New York: HarperCollins Publishers, 1991.

Wicker, Tom. *Unto This Hour*. New York: The Viking Press, 1984.

Wiley, Bell Irvin. *The Life of Billy Yank: The Common Soldier of the Union*. Baton Rouge and London: Louisiana State University Press, 1952, 1991.

_____. *The Life of Johnny Reb: The Common Soldier of the Confederacy*. Baton Rouge and London: Louisiana State University Press, 1943, 1991.

_____. *The Road to Appomattox*. Baton Rouge and London: Louisiana State University Press, 1994. Reprint of Memphis: Memphis State College Press, 1956.

Wilkinson, Warren. *Mother, May You Never See the Sights I Have Seen: The Fifty-seventh Massachusetts Veteran Volunteers in the Army of the Potomac, 1864–1865*. New York: Harper & Row, 1990.

Williams, Kenneth P. *Grant Rises in the West*. 2 vols. Lincoln: University of Nebraska Press, 1997. Originally vols. 3 and 4 of *Lincoln Finds a General: A Military Study of the Civil War*, New York: Macmillan, 1952.

_____. *Lincoln Finds a General: A Military Study of the Civil War*. Vol. 1. Bloomington: Indiana University Press, 1985. Reprint of 1949 edition.

_____. *Lincoln Finds a General: A Military Study of the Civil War*. Vols. 2 and 5 (Prelude to Chattanooga). New York: The Macmillan Company, 1959. Reprint of 1949 edition.

Williams, T. Harry. *Lincoln and His Generals*. New York: Alfred A. Knopf, Inc., 1952.

_____. *McClellan, Sherman and Grant*. New Brunswick: Rutgers University Press, 1962.

Wills, Brian Steel. *A Battle from the Start: The Life of Nathan Bedford Forrest*. New York: HarperPerennial, 1992.

Wilson, Harold S. *Confederate Industry: Manufacturers and Quartermasters in the Civil War*. Jackson: University of Mississippi Press, 2002.

Winders, Richard Bruce. *Polk's Army: The American Military Experience in the Mexican War*. College Station: Texas A&M University Press, 1997.

Winik, Jay. *April 1865: The Month That Saved America*. New York: HarperCollins, 2001.

Woodworth, Steven E., ed. *Civil War Generals in Defeat*. Lawrence: University of Kansas Press, 1999.

_____, ed. *Davis and Lee at War*. Lawrence: University of Kansas Press, 1995.

_____, ed. *Grant's Lieutenants from Cairo to Vicksburg*. Lawrence: University of Kansas Press, 2001.

_____. *Jefferson Davis and His Generals: The Failure of Confederate Command in the West*. Lawrence: University Press of Kansas, 1990.

_____. *Nothing But Victory: The Army of the Tennessee, 1861–1865*. New York: Alfred A. Knopf, 2005.

PERIODICAL ARTICLES

Alexander, Ted. "McCausland's Raid and the Burning of Chambersburg," *Blue & Gray Magazine*, XI, Issue 6, pp. 10–18, 46–61.

_____. "Ten Days in July: The Pursuit to the Potomac," *North & South*, Vol. 2, No. 6 (Aug. 1999), pp. 10–34.

Allen, Stacy D. "Corinth, Mississippi: Crossroads of the Western Confederacy," *Blue & Gray Magazine*, XIX, Issue 6 (Summer 2002), pp. 6–24, 36–51.

_____. "Shiloh! The Campaign and First Day's Battle," *Blue & Gray Magazine*, XIV, No. 3 (Feb. 1997), pp. 6–27, 46–64.

_____. "Shiloh! The Second Day's Battle and Aftermath," *Blue & Gray Magazine*, XIV, No. 4 (April 1997), pp. 6–27, 45–55.

Anderson, Kevin. "Grant's Lifelong Struggle with Alcohol: Examining the Controversy Surrounding Grant and Alcohol," *Columbiad: A Quarterly Review of the War Between the States*, Vol. 2, No. 4 (Winter 1999), pp. 16–26.

Arnold, James R. "Grant Earns a License to Win," *Columbiad: A Quarterly Review of the War between the States*, Vol. 1, No. 2 (Summer 1997), pp. 31–41.

"The Battles at Spotsylvania Court House, Virginia May 8–21, 1864," *Blue & Gray Magazine*, I, Issue 6 (June–July 1984), pp. 35–48.

Barton, Dick. "Charge at Big Black River," *America's Civil War*, Vol. 12, No. 4 (Sept. 1999), pp. 54–61.

Bauer, Dan. "Who Knows the Truth about the Big Bender: Did U. S. Grant Leave His Army at Vicksburg in 1863 to Go on a Drinking Binge?," *Civil War Times Illustrated*, XXVII, No. 8 (Dec. 1988), pp. 34–43.

Bauer, Daniel. "Did a Food Shortage Force Lee to Fight?: An Investigation into Lee's Claim That He had to Attack at Gettysburg because His Army Lacked Sufficient Rations to Do Anything Else," *Columbiad: A Quarterly Review of the War Between the States*, Vol. I, No. 4 (Winter 1998), pp. 57–74.

Bearss, Ed. "The Vicksburg Campaign: Grant Marches West: The Battles of Champion Hill and Big Black Bridge," *Blue & Gray Magazine*, XVIII, Issue 5 (June 2001), pp. 6–24, 44–52.

_____. "The Vicksburg Campaign: Grant Moves Inland," *Blue & Gray Magazine*, XVIII, Issue 1 (October 2000), pp. 6–22, 46–52, 65.

Berg, Gordon. "Opening the Cracker Line," *America's Civil War*, Vol. 19, No. 2 (May 2006), pp. 46–52.

Bergeron, Arthur W., Jr. "The Battle of Mobile Bay and the Campaign for Mobile, Alabama, 1864–65," *Blue & Gray Magazine*, XIX, Issue 4 (April 2002), pp. 6–20, 46–54.

_____. "Three-day Tussle at Hatcher's Run," *America's Civil War*, Vol. 16, No. 1 (March 2003), pp. 30–37.

Berkoff, Todd S. "Botched Battle at Bristoe," *America's Civil War*, Vol. 16, No. 4 (Sept. 2003), pp. 22–29, 70–71.

Bolte, Philip L. "An Earlier 'Bridge Too Far,'" *North & South*, Vol. 3, No. 6 (Aug. 2000), pp. 26–32.

Bonekemper, Edward H., III. "Slavery, Not States' Rights, Inspired Secession," *Washington Times*, Aug. 23, 2003, p. B3.

_____. "Lincoln's 1864 Victory Was Closer Than It Looked," *Washington Times*, July 15, 2000, p. B3.

Bounds, Steve and Milbourn, Curtis. "The Battle of Mansfield," *North & South*, Vol. 6, No. 2 (February 2003), pp. 26–40.

Bradley, Mark L. "Last Stand in the Carolinas: The Battle of Bentonville, March 19–21, 1865," *Blue & Gray Magazine*, XIII, Issue 2 (December 1995), pp. 8–22, 56–69.

_____. "Old Reliable's Finest Hour: The Battle of Averasboro, North Carolina, March 15–16, 1865," *Blue & Gray Magazine*, XVI, No. 1 (Oct. 1998), pp. 6–20, 52–57.

Brennan, Patrick. "Hell on Horseshoe Ridge," *North & South*, Vol. 7, No. 2 (March 2004), pp. 22–44.

_____. "It Wasn't Stuart's Fault," *North & South*, Vol. 6, No. 5 (July 2003), pp. 22–37.

_____. "Thunder on the Plains of Brandy," *North & South*, Vol. 5, No. 3 (April 2002), pp. 14–34.

Broome, Doyle D., Jr. "Daring Rear-guard Defense," *America's Civil War*, Vol. 6, No. 5 (Nov. 1993), pp. 34–40.

Brown, Kent Masterson, "A Golden Bridge: Lee's Williamsport Defense Lines and His Escape Across the Potomac," *North & South*, Vol. 2, No. 6 (Aug. 1999), pp. 56–65.

Bruce, George A. "Strategy of the Civil War," *Papers of the Military Historical Society of Massachusetts*, 13, 1913, pp. 392–483.

Calkins, Chris M. "The Battle of Five Forks: Final Push for the South Side," *Blue & Gray Magazine*, IX, Issue 4 (April 1992), pp. 8–22, 41–52.

_____. "Final Bloodshed at Appomattox," *America's Civil War*, Vol. 14, No. 2 (May 2001), pp. 34–40.

_____. "Hurtling Toward the End," *America's Civil War*, Vol. 17, No. 1 (March 2004), pp. 38–44.

Campbell, Eric A. "Slept in the Mud, Stood in the Mud, Kneeled in the Mud," *America's Civil War*, Vol. 15, No. 6 (January 2003), pp. 50–55.

Case, David. "The Battle That Saved Washington," *Civil War Times Illustrated*, XXXVII, No. 7 (Feb. 1999), pp. 46–56.

Castel, Albert. "The Historian and the General: Thomas L. Connelly versus Robert E. Lee," *Civil War History* 16 (1970), pp. 50–63.

_____. "Why the North Won and the South Lost," *Civil War Times Illustrated* XXXIX, No. 2 (May 2000), pp. 56–60.

Cheeks, Robert C. "Carnage in a Cornfield," *America's Civil War*, Vol. 5, No. 2 (July 1992), pp. 30–37.

_____. "Failure on the Heights," *America's Civil War*, 5 (November 1992), pp. 42–49.

Chiles, Paul. "Artillery Hell! The Guns of Antietam," *Blue & Gray Magazine*, XVI, Issue 2 (Dec. 1998), pp. 6–18, 24–25, 41–59.

Clark, John E., Jr. "Reinforcing Rosecrans by Rail: The Movement of the Federal Eleventh and Twelfth Corps from Virginia Was a Wonder of Strategy, Logistics, and Engineering," *Columbiad: A Quarterly Review of the War between the States*, Vol. 3, No. 3 (Fall 1999), pp. 74–95.

"Common Soldier: Dr. John Kennerly Farris, Confederate Surgeon, Army of Tennessee," *Blue & Gray Magazine*, XVII, Issue 2 (December 1999), pp. 46–47.

Connelly, Thomas Lawrence. "Robert E. Lee and the Western Confederacy: A Criticism of Lee's Strategic Ability," *Civil War History*, Vol. 15 (June 1969), pp. 116–32.

———. "The Image and the General: Robert E. Lee in American Historiography," *Civil War History*, Vol. 19 (March 1973), pp. 50–64.

"Controversy: Was Butler 'Bottled Up'?," *Blue & Gray Magazine*, VII, No. 1 (Oct. 1989), pp. 27–29.

Cooling, Benjamin Franklin. "Forts Henry & Donelson: Union Victory on the Twin Rivers," *Blue & Gray Magazine*, IX, Issue 3 (Feb. 1992), pp. 10–20, 45–53.

———. "Monocacy: The Battle That Saved Washington," *Blue & Gray Magazine*, X, Issue 2 (Dec. 1992), pp. 8–18, 48–60.

Cozzens, Peter. "Moving into Dead Men's Shoes: The Fight for Battery Robinett at the Battle of Corinth, Mississippi," *Civil War Times Illustrated*, XXXVI, No. 2 (May 1997), pp. 24–33, 47–49.

Crawford, Mark J. "Dinwiddie Court House: Beginning of the End," *America's Civil War*, Vol. 12, No. 1 (March 1999), pp. 50–56.

Daniel, Larry J. "The South Almost Won by Not Losing: A Rebuttal," *North and South*, Vol. 1, No. 3 (Feb. 1998), pp. 44–51.

Davis, Stephen. "Atlanta Campaign. Hood Fights Desperately. The Battles for Atlanta: Events from July 10 to September 2, 1864," *Blue & Gray Magazine*, VI, Issue 6 (August 1989), pp. 8–39, 45–62.

Delcour, Melissa, "Lightning Strike in the Valley," *Military History*, Vol. 22, No. 3 (June 2005), pp. 26–32, 78.

Dew, Charles B. "Apostles of Secession," *North & South*, Vol. 4, No. 4 (April 2001), pp. 24–38.

Dolzall, Gary W. "Enemies Front and Rear," *America's Civil War*, Vol. 16, No. 2 (May 2003), pp. 38–45.

———. "Muddy, Soggy Race to Campbell's Station," *America's Civil War*, Vol. 15, No. 3 (July 2002), pp. 26–32, 80.

———. "O. O. Howard's Long Road to Redemption," *America's Civil War*, Vol. 14, No. 5 (Nov. 2001), pp. 38–44.

Durham, Roger S. "The Man Who Shot John Sedgwick: The Tale of Charles D. Grace—A Sharpshooter in the Doles-Cook Brigade, CSA," *Blue & Gray Magazine*, XIII, Issue 2 (Dec. 1995), pp. 24–29.

_____. "Savannah: Mr. Lincoln's Christmas Present," *Blue & Gray Magazine*, VIII, Issue 3 (Feb. 1991), pp. 8–18, 42–53.

Elmore, Tom, "The Burning of Columbia, South Carolina, February 17, 1865, *Blue & Gray Magazine* XXI, Issue 2 (Winter 2004), pp. 6–27.

Epperson, James F. "Grant Story Flawed"[letter to editor], *Columbiad: A Quarterly Review of the War between the States*, Vol. 3, No. 2 (Summer 1999), pp. 8–9.

_____. "The Chance Battle in the Wilderness," *Columbiad: A Quarterly Review of the War between the States*, Vol. 2, No. 1 (Spring 1998), pp.77–96.

Evans, E. Chris. "'I Almost Tremble at Her Fate': When Sherman came to Columbia, South Carolina, secession's hotbed became a bed of coals," *Civil War Times Illustrated*, XXXVII, No. 5 (Oct. 1998), pp. 46–51, 60–67.

_____. "Return to Jackson: Finishing Stroke to the Vicksburg Campaign, July 5–25, 1863," *Blue & Gray Magazine*, XII, Issue 6 (Aug. 1995), pp. 8–22, 50–63.

Feis, William B. "Charles S. Bell: Union Scout," *North & South*, Vol. 4, No. 5 (June 2001), pp. 26–37.

_____. "'He Don't Care a Damn for What the Enemy Does out of His Sight': A Perspective on U. S. Grant and Military Intelligence," *North & South*, Vol. 1, No. 2 (Jan. 1998), pp. 68–81.

Fleming, Martin K. "The Northwestern Virginia Campaign of 1861: McClellan's Rising Star—Lee's Dismal Debut," *Blue & Gray Magazine*, X, Issue 6 (August 1993), pp. 10–17, 48–54, 59–65.

Fonvielle, Chris. "The Last Rays of Departing Hope: The Fall of Wilmington, Including the Campaigns against Fort Fisher," *Blue & Gray Magazine*, XII, Issue 2 (Dec. 1994), pp. 10–21, 48–62.

Freeman, Kirk. "Big Black River," *Military Heritage*, Vol. 2, No. 3 (Dec. 2000), pp. 76–85.

Furqueron, James R. "The 'Best Hated Man' in the Army, Part II," *North & South*, Vol. 4, No. 5 (June 2001), pp. 66–79.

Gallagher, Gary W. "Brandy Station: The Civil War's Bloodiest Arena of Mounted Combat," *Blue & Gray Magazine*, VIII, Issue 1 (October 1990), pp. 8–22, 44–53.

Garavaglia, Louis A. "Sherman's March and the Georgia Arsenals," *North & South*, Vol. 6, No. 1 (Dec. 2002), pp. 12–22.

Gilbert, Thomas D. "Mr. Grant Goes to Washington," *Blue & Gray Magazine*, XII, Issue 4 (April 1995), pp. 33–37.

Glynn, Gary. "Black Thursday for Rebels," *America's Civil War*, Vol. 4, No. 5 (Jan. 1992), pp. 22–29.

Goodman, Al W., Jr. "Decision in the West (Part IV): Between Hell and the Deep Sea: Pemberton's Debacle at Big Black River Bridge," *North & South*, Vol. 1, No. 5 (June 1998), pp. 74–9.

_____. "Grant's Mississippi Gamble," *America's Civil War*, Vol. 7, No. 3 (July 1994), pp. 50–56.

"Grant and Lee, 1864: From the North Anna to the Crossing of the James," *Blue & Gray Magazine*, XI, Issue 4 (April 1994), pp. 11–22, 44–58.

Greene, A. Wilson. "April 2, 1865: Day of Decision at Petersburg," *Blue & Gray Magazine*, XVIII, Issue 3 (Feb. 2001), pp. 6–24, 42–53.

Guttman, Jon. "Jeb Stuart's Last Ride," *America's Civil War*, Vol. 7, No. 2 (May 1994), pp. 34–40, 79–80.

Haggerty, Charles. "George Who?," *Civil War Times Illustrated*, XLI, No. 4 (Aug. 2002), pp. 20–28.

Handlin, Oscar. "Why Lee Attacked," *The Atlantic Monthly*, CXCV (March 1955), pp. 65–66.

Hardy, Michael C. "'A Day of Carnage & Blood'," *America's Civil War*, Vol. 18, No. 1 (March 2005), pp. 38–44.

Harman, Troy D. "The Unchanging Plan," *Civil War Times*, XLII, No. 3 (Aug. 2003), pp. 42–47.

Harsh, Joseph L. "'As Stupid a Fellow as I Am . . .': On the Real Military Genius of Robert E. Lee," *North & South*, Vol. 3, No. 5 (June 2000), pp. 60–71.

Hart, B. H. Liddell. "Lee: A Psychological Problem," *Saturday Review*, XI (December 15, 1934), pp. 365ff.

_____. "Why Lee Lost Gettysburg," *Saturday Review*, XI (March 23, 1935), pp. 561ff.

Hattaway, Herman. "The Changing Face of Battle," *North & South*, Vol. 4, No. 6 (Aug. 2001), pp. 34–43.

_____. "Dress Rehearsal for Hell: In early 1864, Mississippi was a proving ground for the 'total war' that would make Sherman infamous—and victorious," *Civil War Times Illustrated*, XXXVII, No. 5 (Oct. 1998), pp. 32–39, 74–75.

Hennessy, John, "The Second Battle of Manassas: Lee Suppresses the 'Miscreant' Pope," *Blue & Gray Magazine*, IX, Issue 6 (Aug. 1992), pp. 10–34, 46–58.

Hess, Earl J. "'Set Your Spades to Work': Field Fortifications in the Chancellorsville Campaign," *North & South*, Vol. 9, No. 1 (March 2006), pp. 12–23.

Himmer, Robert. "July 1, 1863: George Gordon Meade's Lost Afternoon Re-examined," *North & South*, Vol. 9, No. 1 (March 2006), pp. 52–64.

Hinze, David C. "'At All Hazards': Ulysses S. Grant's Instructions to Benjamin M. Prentiss Left Little Doubt as to the Importance of the Hornets' Nest at Shiloh," *Columbiad: A Quarterly Review of the War between the States*, Vol. 3, No. 3 (Fall 1999), pp. 19–38.

Hintz, Kalina Ingham. "When the General Fell: The Monumental Death of John F. Reynolds," *Blue & Gray Magazine*, XXII, No. 2 (Spring 2005), pp. 24–28.

Holsworth, Jerry W. "Uncommon Valor: Hood's Texas Brigade in the Maryland Campaign," *Blue & Gray Magazine*, XIII (August 1996), pp. 6–20, 50–55.

Holsworth, Jerry W. "VMI at the Battle of New Market and, Sigel's Defeat in the Shenandoah Valley," *Blue & Gray Magazine*, XVI, Issue 4 (April 1999), pp. 6–24, 40–52.

Howey, Allan W. "The Widow-Makers," *Civil War Times Illustrated*, XXXVIII, No. 5 (Oct. 1999), pp. 48–51, 60.

Hudson, Leonne. "Valor at Wilson's Wharf," *Civil War Times Illustrated*, XXXVII, No. 1 (March 1998), pp. 46–52.

Jamieson, Perry D. "Background to Bloodshed," *North & South*, Vol. 4, No. 6 (Aug. 2001), pp. 24–31.

Johnston, Terry A., Jr. "Failure before Knoxville: Longstreet's Attack on Fort Sanders, November 29, 1863," *North & South*, Vol. 2, No. 7 (Sept. 1999), pp. 56–75.

Joinson, Carla. "War at the Table: The South's Struggle for Food," *Columbiad*, 1, No. 2 (Summer 1997), pp. 21–30.

Jones, Archer. "What Should We Think about Lee's Thinking?," *Columbiad*, 1, No. 2 (Summer 1997), pp. 73–85.

Kelly, Dennis. "Atlanta Campaign. Mountains to Pass, A River to Cross: The Battle of Kennesaw Mountain and Related Actions from June 10 to July 9, 1864," *Blue & Gray Magazine*, VI, Issue 5 (June 1989), pp. 8–30, 46–58.

Kendall, Drew J. "'Murder' at Malvern Hill," *Military History*, Vol. 19, No. 3 (Aug. 2002), pp. 42–48.

Kennett, Lee B. "'Hell' or 'High Old Times,'" *America's Civil War*, Vol. 17, No. 6 (Jan. 2005), pp. 46–52.

King, Curtis S. "Reconsider, Hell!," *MHQ: The Quarterly Journal of Military History*, Vol. 13, No. 4 (Summer 2000), pp. 88–95.

Krick, Robert K. "Lee's Greatest Victory," *American Heritage*, 41, No. 2 (March 12, 1990), pp. 66–79.

Krolick, Marshall D. "Gettysburg: The First Day, July 1, 1863," *Blue & Gray Magazine*, V, Issue 2 (Nov. 1987), pp. 8–20.

Kross, Gary. "At the Time Impracticable: Dick Ewell's Decision on the First Day at Gettysburg with Excerpts from Campbell Brown's Journal," *Blue & Gray Magazine*, XII, Issue 3 (Feb. 1995), pp. 53–58.

_____. "Attack from the West," *Blue & Gray Magazine*, XVII, Issue 5 (June 2000), pp. 6–22, 44–50 at pp. 11–17.

_____. "Fight Like the Devil to Hold Your Own: General John Buford's Cavalry at Gettysburg on July 1, 1863," *Blue & Gray Magazine*, XII, Issue 3 (Feb. 1995), pp. 9–22.

_____. "Picketts's Charge! Including Supporting Actions on Culp's Hill," *Blue & Gray Magazine*, XVI, Issue 5 (June 1999), pp. 6–21, 38–51.

_____. "That One Error Fills Him with Faults: Gen. Alfred Iverson and His Brigade at Gettysburg," *Blue & Gray Magazine*, XII, Issue 3 (February 1995), 22, 52–53.

Leonard, Phillip A. B. "Forty-seven Days. Constant bombardment, life in bomb shelters, scarce food and water, and rapidly accumulating filth were the price of resistance for the resolute Confederate citizens of besieged Vicksburg, Mississippi," *Civil War Times Illustrated*, XXXIV, No. 4 (Aug. 2000), pp. 40–9, 68–69.

Leyden, John G. "Grant Wins Last Battle by Finishing Memoirs," *Washington Times*, March 23, 2002, p. B3.

Long, David E. "Cover-up at Cold Harbor," *Civil War Times Illustrated*, XXXVI, No. 3 (June 1997), pp. 50–59.

Lowe, David W. "Field Fortifications in the Civil War," *North & South*, Vol. 4, No. 6 (Aug. 2001), pp. 58–73.

Malone, Jeff. "Melee in the Underbrush," *America's Civil War*, Vol. 5, No. 5 (Nov. 1992), pp. 26–32.

Marshall-Cornwall, James. *Grant as Military Commander*. New York: Barnes & Noble Books, 1995. Reprint of 1970 edition.

Marvel, William. "Many Have Offered Excuses for the Confederate Retreat to Appomattox, Perhaps Beginning with Robert E. Lee," *America's Civil War*, Vol. 14, No. 3 (July 2001), pp. 62–70.

_____. "Retreat to Appomattox," *Blue & Gray Magazine*, XXXVIII, Issue 4 (April 2001), pp. 6–24, 46–54.

_____. "Thorn in the Flesh," *Civil War Times Illustrated*, XLI, No. 3 (June 2002), pp. 42–49, 60–62.

Matter, William D. "The Battles of Spotsylvania Court House, Virginia, May 18–21, 1864," *Blue & Gray Magazine*, I, Issue 6 (June–July 1984), pp. 35–48.

McGehee, Larry. "U. S. Grant Had a Career of Many Hills and Valleys," *Potomac News & Manassas Journal & Messenger* [Virginia], Sept. 8, 2001, p. A6.

McMurry, Richard M. "Atlanta Campaign. Rocky Face to the Dallas Line: The Battles of May 1864," *Blue & Gray Magazine*, VI, Issue 4 (April 1989), pp. 10–23, 46–62.

McPherson, James M. "To Conquer a Peace?: Lee's Goals in the Gettysburg Campaign," *Civil War Times*, XLVII, No. 2 (March/April 2007), pp. 26–33 at p.28.

_____. "The Unheroic Hero," *The New York Review of Books*, XLVI, No. 2 (February 4, 1999), pp. 16–19.

Mertz, Gregory A. "No Turning Back: The Battle of the Wilderness," *Blue & Gray Magazine*, XII, Issue 4 (April 1995), pp. 8–23, 47–53; Issue 5 (June 1995), pp. 8–20, 48–50.

_____. "Upton's Attack and the Defense of Doles' Salient, Spotsylvania Court House, May 10, 1864," *Blue & Gray Magazine*, XVIII, Issue 6 (Summer 2001), pp. 6–25, 46–52.

Mewborn, Horace. "Jeb Stuart's Ride around the Army of the Potomac, June 12–15, 1862," *Blue & Gray Magazine*, XV, Issue 6 (Aug. 1998), pp. 6–21, 46–54.

Meyers, Christopher C. "'Two Generals Cannot Command This Army': John A. McClernand and the Politics of Command in Grant's Army of the Tennessee," *Columbiad: A Quarterly Review of the War between the States*, Vol. 2, No. 1 (Spring 1998), pp. 27–41.

Miller, J. Michael. "Strike Them a Blow: Lee and Grant at the North Anna River," *Blue & Gray Magazine*, X, Issue 4 (April 1993), pp. 12–22, 44–55.

Mitchell, Joseph B. "Confederate Losses at Gettysburg: Debunking Livermore," *Blue & Gray Magazine*, VI, No. 4 (April 1989), pp. 38–40.

Morgan, Michael. "Digging to Victory," *America's Civil War*, Vol. 16, No. 3 (July 2003), pp. 22–9.

Murphy, Brian John. "Grant versus Lee," *Civil War Times*, XLIII, No. 1 (April 2004), pp. 42–49, 63–66.

_____. "The Secret War between Grant & Halleck," *Civil War Times*, XLV, No. 6 (August 2006), pp. 44–49.

Naisawald, L. VanLoan. "'Old Jubilee' Saves Lynchburg," *America's Civil War*, Vol. 16, No. 2 (May 2003), pp. 30–36, 72.

Nofi, Albert A. "Calculating Combatants," *North & South*, Vol. 4, No. 2 (January 2001), pp. 68–69.

Nolan, Alan T. "Demolishing the Myth: Evaluating Lee's Generalship," *North & South*, Vol. 3, No. 5 (June 2000), pp. 29–36.

_____ and Storch, Marc. "The Iron Brigade Earns Its Name," *Blue & Gray Magazine*, XXI, Issue 6 (Holiday 2004), pp. 6–20, 47–50.

Nosworthy, Brent. "Breechloaders Level the Playing Field," *Military History Quarterly*, Vol. 18, No. 3 (Spring 2006), pp. 80–83.

O'Beirne, Kevin M. "Into the Valley of the Shadow of Death: The Corcoran Legion at Cold Harbor," *North & South*, Vol. 3, No. 4 (April 2000), pp. 68–81.

_____. "A 'Perfect' but Flawed Campaign," *Military Heritage*, Vol. 2, No. 5 (April 2001), p. 65.

O'Reilly, Frank A. "Lee's Incomplete Victory: Battle of Fredericksburg," *America's Civil War*, Vol. 14, No. 5 (Nov. 2001), pp. 30–37.

Owens, Richard H. "An Astonishing Career," *Military Heritage*, Vol. 3, No. 2 (Oct. 2001), pp. 64–73.

Poggiali, Leonard. "Conditional Surrender: The Death of U. S. Grant, and the Cottage on Mount McGregor," *Blue & Gray Magazine*, X, Issue 3 (Feb. 1993), pp. 60–65.

_____. "Lost Opportunity in the Wilderness," *Columbiad: A Quarterly Review of the War Between the States*, Vol. 3, No. 2 (Summer 1999), pp. 21–37.

Popchock, Barry. "Daring Night Assault," *America's Civil War*, IV, No. 6 (March 1992), pp. 30–37.

Popowski, Howard J. "'We've Met Once before…in Mexico,'" *Blue & Gray Magazine*, I, Issue 6 (June–July 1984), pp. 9–13.

Poulter, Keith. "Decision in the West: The Vicksburg Campaign, Part 1: The Entering Wedge," *North & South*, Vol. 1, No. 2 (Jan. 1998), pp. 18–25.

_____. "Decision in the West: The Vicksburg Campaign, Part II: Running the Batteries," *North & South*, Vol. 1, No. 3 (Feb. 1998), pp. 68–75.

_____. "Decision in the West: The Vicksburg Campaign, Part III," *North & South*, Vol. 1, No. 4 (April 1998), pp. 77–83.

_____. "Stop Insulting Robert E. Lee!," *North & South*, Vol. 1, No. 5 (1998), p. 6.

Powell, Dave. "The 96th Illinois and the Battles for Horseshoe Ridge, 1863 and 1895," *North & South*, Vol. 8, No. 2 (March 2005), pp. 48–59.

Powles, James M. "New Jersey's Western Warriors," *America's Civil War*, Vol. 14, No. 4 (Sept. 2001), pp. 46–52.

Rafuse, Ethan S. "Not since George Washington," *Civil War Times*, XLIII, No. 1 (April 2004), pp. 28–33.

"Reconsidering Grant and Lee: Reputations of Civil War Generals Shifting," Associated Press, http://www.cnn.com/2003/SHOWBIZ/books/01/08/wkd.Grant.vs.Lee.ap/index.html.

Rhea, Gordon C. "'Butcher' Grant and the Overland Campaign," *North & South*, Vol. 4, No. 1 (Nov. 2000), pp. 44–55.

_____. "Butchery at Bethesda Church," *America's Civil War*, Vol. 14, No. 6 (Jan. 2002), pp. 48–54, 80.

_____. "Cold Harbor: Anatomy of a Battle," *North & South*, Vol. 5, No. 2 (Feb. 2002), pp. 40–62.

_____. "'The Hottest Place I Ever Was In': The Battle of Haw's Shop, May 28, 1864," *North & South*, Vol. 4, No. 4 (April 2001), pp. 42–57.

_____. "Last Union Attack at Spotsylvania: The belief that one more hard blow would shatter the Confederate line at Spotsylvania may have been one of Ulysses S. Grant's greatest miscalculations.," *Columbiad: A Quarterly Review of the War between the States*, Vol. 3, No. 4 (Winter 2000), pp. 111–39.

_____. "Mule Shoe Redemption," *America's Civil War*, Vol. 17, No. 2 (May 2004), pp. 46–53, 72.

_____. "'They Fought Confounded Plucky': The Battle of Harris Farm, May 19, 1864," *North & South*, Vol. 3, No. 1 (Nov. 1999), pp. 48–66.

_____. "Robert E. Lee, Prescience , and the Overland Campaign," *North & South*, Vol. 3, No. 5 (June 2000), pp. 40–50

_____; Rollins, Richard; Sears, Stephen, and John Y. "What Was Wrong with the Army of the Potomac?," *North & South*, Vol. 4, No. 3 (March 2001), pp. 12–18.

_____. "Spotsylvania: The Battles at Spotsylvania Court House, Virginia, May 8–21, 1864," *Blue & Gray Magazine*, I, Issue 6 (June–July 1984), pp. 35–48.

Riggs, Derald T. "Commander in Chief Abe Lincoln," *America's Civil War*, Vol. 13, No. 3 (July 2000), pp. 34–40.

Roberts, Donald J. II. "Belmont: Grant's First Battle," *Military Heritage*, Vol. 2, No. 6 (June 2001), pp. 40–49.

Rogan, George. "Salem Church: Final Federal Assault at Chancellorsville," *America's Civil War*, Vol. 11, No. 6 (Jan. 1999), pp. 42–48.

Roland, Charles P. "Lee's Invasion Strategy," *North & South*, Vol. 1, No. 6 (1998), pp. 34–38.

Rollins, Richard. "Robert E. Lee and the Hand of God," *North & South*, Vol. 6, No. 2 (Feb. 2003), pp. 12–25.

Roth, Dave. "Grierson's Raid: A Cavalry Raid at Its Best, April 17–May 2, 1863," *Blue & Gray Magazine*, X, Issue 5 (June 1993), pp. 12–24, 48–65.

Scaife, William R. "Sherman's March to the Sea: Events from September 3 to December 21, 1864, Including the Occupation of Atlanta, More Battles with the Unpredictable John Bell Hood, the Burning of Atlanta, 'Marching Through Georgia,' and the Fall of Savannah," *Blue & Gray Magazine*, VII, Issue 2 (Dec. 1989), pp. 10–42.

Schiller, Herbert M. "Beast in a Bottle: Bermuda Hundred Campaign, May 1864," *Blue & Gray Magazine*, VII, Issue 1 (Oct. 1989), pp. 8–26.

Schiller, Laurence D. "The Taste of Northern Steel: The Evolution of Federal Cavalry Tactics 1861–1865," *North & South*, Vol. 2, No. 2 (Jan. 1999), pp. 30–45, 80–84.

Sears, Stephen W. "All the Trumpets Sounded. Bruce Catton: An Appreciation," *North & South*, Vol. 3, No. 1 (November 1999), pp. 24–32.

_____. "The Dahlgren Papers Revisited," *Columbiad: A Quarterly Review of the War between the States*, Vol. 3, No. 2 (Summer 1999), pp. 63–87.

_____. "Glendale: Opportunity Squandered," *North & South*, Vol. 5, No. 1 (Dec. 2001), pp. 12–24.

_____. "Gouverneur Kemble Warren and Little Phil," *North & South*, Vol. 1, No. 5 (June 1998), pp. 56–72.

_____. "The Lee of Gettysburg," *North & South*, Vol. 6, No. 5 (July 2003), pp. 12–19.

_____. "McClellan at Antietam," *Hallowed Ground*, Vol. 6, No. 1 (Spring 2005), pp. 30–33.

_____. "'We Should Assume the Aggressive': Origins of the Gettysburg Campaign," *North & South*, Vol. 5, No. 4 (May 2002), pp. 58–66.

Selcer, Richard F. "A Legend Is Born," *Civil War Times*, XLV, No. 10 (Jan. 2007), pp. 22–31.

Skoch, George F. "Miracle of the Rails," *Civil War Times Illustrated*, XXXI, No. 4 (Sept.–Oct. 1992), pp. 22–24, 56–59.

Smith, David M. "Too Little Too Late at Vicksburg," *America's Civil War*, Vol. 13, No. 2 (May 2000), pp. 38–44.

Smith, Gene. "The Destruction of Fighting Joe Hooker," *Battles and Leaders* (Supplement to American Heritage) (Washington: Library of Congress, 1995), pp. 10–17.

Smith, Robert Barr, "Killing Zone at Burnside's Bridge," *Military History*, Vol. 21, No. 2 (June 2004), pp. 34–40.

Smith, Timothy B. "The Forgotten Battle of Davis' Bridge," *North & South*, Vol. 2, No. 5 (June 1999), pp. 68–79.

_____. "Myths of Shiloh," *America's Civil War*, Vol. 19, No. 2 (May 2006), pp. 30–36, 71.

Suderow, Bryce A. "Glory Denied: The First Battle of Deep Bottom, July 27th–29th, 1864," *North & South*, Vol. 3, No. 7 (Sept. 2000), pp. 17–32.

_____. "'Nothing But a Miracle Could Save Us': Second Battle of Deep Bottom, Virginia, August 14–20, 1864," *North & South*, Vol. 4, No. 2 (Jan. 2001), pp. 12–32.

_____. "War Along the James," *North & South*, Vol. 6, No. 3 (April 2003), pp. 12–23.

Suhr, Robert Collins. "Attack Written Deep and Crimson," *America's Civil War*, Vol. 4, No. 3 (Sept. 1991), pp. 46–52.

_____. "Old Brains' Barren Triumph," *America's Civil War*, Vol. 14, No. 2 (May 2001), pp. 42–49.

_____. "Saving the Day at Shiloh," *America's Civil War*, XII, No. 6 (January 2000), pp. 34–41.

_____. "Small but Savage Battle of Iuka," *America's Civil War*, XII, No. 2 (May 1999), pp. 42–49.

Swain, Robert L., "Generals at Odds," *Military History*, Vol. 23, No. 5 (July/Aug. 2006), pp. 38–45.

Swift, Gloria Baker and Stephens, Gail. "Honor Redeemed: Lew Wallace's Military Career and the Battle of Monocacy," *North & South*, Vol. 4, No. 2 (Jan. 2001), pp. 34–46.

Sword, Wiley. "The Battle above the Clouds," *Blue & Gray Magazine*, XVIII, Issue 2 (Dec. 2000), pp. 6–20, 43–56.

Symonds, Craig L.; John Y.; Poulter, Keith; Newton, Steven H.; Sears, Stephen W., and Woodworth, Steven E. "Who Were the Worst Ten Generals?", *North & South*, Vol. 7, No. 3 (May 2004), pp. 12–25.

Thomas, Emory. "'Damn the Torpedoes...': The Battle for Mobile Bay," *Civil War Times Illustrated*, XVI, No. 1 (April 1977), pp. 4–10, 43–45.

Thompson, Robert N. "The Folly and Horror of Cold Harbor," *Military History*, Vol. 23, No. 8 (Nov. 2006), pp. 38–45.

Tomasak, Peter. "'Glory to God! We Are Saved'… Night Assault at Gettysburg," *North & South*, Vol. 1, No. 5 (1998), pp. 32–44.

Trinque, Bruce A. "Battle Fought on Paper," *America's Civil War*, Vol. 6, No. 2 (May 1993), pp. 30–36.

Trudeau, Noah Andre. "Climax at Vicksburg," *North & South*, Vol. 1, No. 5 (June 1998), pp. 80–89.

_____. "'A Frightful and Frightening Place'," *Civil War Times Illustrated*, XXXVIII, No. 2, pp. 42–56.

_____. "That 'Unerring Volcanic Firearm'," *Military History Quarterly*, Vol. 7, No. 4 (Summer 1995).

Welch, Richard F. "Gettysburg Finale," *America's Civil War* (July 1993), pp. 50–57.

Welsh, William E. "Dual Disasters on the Rappahannock," *America's Civil War*, Vol. 16, No. 5 (Nov. 2003), pp. 42–49.

Wert, Jeffry D. "All-out War," *Civil War Times*, LXIII, No. 1 (April 2004), pp. 34–40.

_____. "Closing the Back Door: The Shenandoah Valley Campaign of 1864," *Hallowed Ground*, Winter 2004, pp. 25–30.

_____. "'No Retreat Was Ever Possible'," *Civil War Times Illustrated*, XXXIX, No. 2 (May 2000), pp. 32–37.

Wheelan, Joseph. "Polk's Manifest Destiny," *The History Channel Magazine*, Vol. 4, No. 1 (Jan./Feb. 2006), pp. 41–45.

Williams, T. Harry. "Freeman: Historian of the Civil War: An Appraisal," *Journal of Southern History*, XXI (February 1955), pp. 91–100.

Wilson, John. "Miracle at Missionary Ridge," *America's Civil War*, XII, No. 7 (misprinted as 6) (March 2000), pp. 42–49.

Winschel, Terrence J. "Grant's March through Louisiana: 'The Highest Examples of Military Energy and Perseverance'," *Blue & Gray Magazine*, XIII, Issue 5 (June 1996), pp. 8–22.

_____. "Grant's Beachhead for the Vicksburg Campaign: The Battle of Port Gibson, May 1, 1863," *Blue & Gray Magazine*, XI, Issue 3 (Feb. 1994), pp. 8–22, 48–56.

_____. "The Siege of Vicksburg," *Blue & Gray Magazine*, XX, Issue 4 (Spring 2003), pp. 6–24, 47–50.

_____. "A Tragedy of Errors: The Failure of the Confederate High Command in the Defense of Vicksburg," *North & South*, Vol. 8, No. 7 (Jan. 2006), pp. 40–49.

_____."Vicksburg: 'Thank God. The Father of Waters again goes unvexed to the sea," *America's Civil War*, Vol. 16, No. 3 (July 2003), pp. 18–19.

_____. "Vicksburg the Key," *North & South*, Vol. 7, No. 7 (Nov. 2004), pp. 58–67.

Wittenberg, Eric J. "Roadblock en Route to Washington," *America's Civil War*, Vol. 6, No. 5 (Nov. 1993), pp. 50–6, 80–82.

_____. "Sheridan's Second Raid and the Battle of Trevilian Station," *Blue & Gray Magazine*, XIX, Issue 3 (Feb. 2002), pp. 8–24, 45–50.

Woodworth, Steven E. "The Army of the Tennessee and the Elements of Military Success," *North & South*, Vol. 6, No. 4 (May 2003), pp. 44–55.

_____. "Shiloh's Harsh Training Ground," *America's Civil War*, Vol. 15, No. 2 (May 2002), pp. 34–40.

Young, Alfred C., "Numbers and Losses in the Army of Northern Virginia," *North & South*, Vol. 3, No. 3 (March 2000), pp. 14–29.

Zentner, Joe and Syrett, Mary. "Confederate Gibralter," *Military History*, Vol. 19, No. 6 (February 2003), pp. 26–32, 73.

INDEX

Note: The abbreviations (C) and (U) stand for Confederate and Union, respectively.

A

abolition of slavery, 335. *See also* Emancipation Proclamation

acoustic shadow, 140

Adams, Charles Francis, Jr., 311

Adams, Michael C. C., 91, 273, 298, 375, 430

African-Americans, 143, 282, 333, 341, 353, 382. *See also* Slaves/slavery

Alabama, 35, 37, 44, 59, 76, 157, 173, 219, 240, 242, 251–53, 269, 287, 332, 341–43, 346, 351, 428, 430

Aldie, Virginia, 176

Alexander, Bevin, 73, 92–93, 98, 107, 110, 200, 353, 358, 388, 400, 403, 408, 415–16

Alexander, Edward Porter, 74, 86–87, 90–91, 121, 166–67, 170, 173–74, 190–92, 197, 200–2, 204–6, 208, 249, 290, 314–15, 322, 324, 391, 420

Alexandria, Virginia, 5, 66, 100, 175, 266

Allegheny Mountains, 28, 30, 252

Allen, Stacy, 53, 94

Amelia Court House, Virginia, 367

American Revolution, 3

amphibious operations, 144, 215, 218, 221–22, 353–54, 386, 416

Anderson, Richard H., 116, 160, 166, 187, 299, 367

Antietam Creek, Maryland, 113–14

Antietam (Maryland) Campaign, xviii, xxv, 10, 97, 112–27, 131, 133, 138, 206, 209–10, 318, 327, 388, 391–92, 396, 399–401, 408, 429

Appomattox Court House, Virginia, 42, 349, 369, 372, 374

Appomattox River, Virginia, 286, 333, 366–67, 369

Appomattox Station, Virginia, 369

Appomattox (Virginia) Campaign, xxi, xxv, 347, 353, 366, 368, 374, 377, 380, 394, 396, 415, 418–19, 431

Arkansas, 29, 146, 150, 231, 242

Arkansas Post, Arkansas, 148, 439

Arkansas River, 148

Arlington House, Virginia, 5

Arlington, Virginia, 5, 22

Armistead, Lewis A., 89, 204

Army of the Cumberland (U), xxii, 143, 156, 247–48, 252–53, 275, 287, 325, 376, 428

Army of Georgia (U), 355

Army of the James (U), 286, 365, 367

Army of Mississippi (C), 139

Army of the Mississippi (U), 134, 138

Army of Northern Virginia (C), xiv, xviii, 2, 29, 73, 75, 91, 110, 120, 132, 170, 176, 193, 198, 200, 206, 208–11, 248, 273, 277, 282, 285, 288, 298, 310, 312, 315, 322, 329, 332, 358, 364–66, 369, 373, 375–76, 395, 398, 418–19, 424–25, 428, 432

Army of the Northwest (C), 28

"Army of Observation" (U), 239

Army of the Ohio (U), xxiii, 44, 50, 106, 143, 275, 287, 325, 332, 344, 376

Army of the Potomac (U), xiv, xviii, 2, 66, 90–91, 97, 99, 127, 156, 161, 174, 179–81, 208, 251, 253, 269, 272–75, 277, 280, 283, 285, 289, 296–98, 300, 303, 310, 314, 337, 362, 375–76, 413, 417, 420, 424–25

"Army of Relief" (C), 237

Army of Tennessee (C), xx, xxiii, 129, 135, 173, 248, 262, 264, 267, 275, 277, 283, 288, 321, 327, 329, 332, 346–47, 351–52, 376, 427–28, 435

Army of the Tennessee (U), xvii, 39, 48, 134, 136, 138, 235, 253, 274, 325, 330, 355, 376, 408, 420

Army of Virginia (U), 75, 98, 101

Army of the West (C), 139

Arnold, James R., 222, 232, 242, 410, 418

Ashland, Virginia, 71, 79

Atlanta, Georgia, xxiii, 136–37, 173, 252, 274–75, 277, 282, 284, 287–88, 321–22, 324–27, 329–31, 334–35, 338, 342–47, 353, 374, 376–77, 392, 424, 427–29

battles of, xxiii, xxv, 330

Atlanta (Georgia) campaign, xxii, xxv, 247, 262, 274, 330, 338, 420

Atlantic Ocean, 264, 345

Augusta, Georgia, 355

Averasboro, North Carolina, 358

B

Ball's Bluff (Virginia), Battle of, xxv

Baltimore, Maryland, 323–24

Baltimore & Ohio Railroad, 323

Baltimore Pike, Maryland, 323

Baltimore Pike, Pennsylvania, 189

Banks, Nathaniel P., 70–71, 98, 100, 224, 233, 240, 243, 252, 275, 278–79, 287, 412, 430

Baton Rouge, Louisiana, 218

"Battle above the Clouds" (Chattanooga, Tennessee), 259

Bauer, Daniel, 191

Bearss, Edwin C., 151, 214, 226, 234, 244, 407

Beauregard, Pierre G. T., 50, 56, 59, 62–64, 67, 76, 134–35, 158, 179, 286, 308, 315–16, 352, 354, 356, 398, 403, 408, 430–31

Beaver Dam, Virginia, 79–80, 82, 210, 400

Bell, Charles S., 240

Belmont (Missouri), Battle of, xvi, xix, xxv, 32–33, 35, 231, 251, 393, 409, 418, 431

Belmont School House Ridge, 181

Bentonville (North Carolina), Battle of, xxv, 358

Beringer, Richard E., 336

Bermuda Hundred, Virginia, 286–87, 303, 307–8, 314

Bethesda Church (Virginia), Battle of, 307, 310

Beverly's ford, Virginia, 175

Big Bayou Pierre, Mississippi, 222–24, 226

Big Black River, Mississippi, 224–26, 228, 231, 238–39
Battle of, 232–33

Big Round Top, Gettysburg, 194

Birney, David B., 340

Black River, North Carolina, 357–58

black soldiers. *See* African-Americans

Blair, Francis, 22

Bloody Angle, Spotsylvania, Virginia, 302, 405

Bloody Lane (Sunken Road), Antietam, Maryland, 114, 117

Blue Ridge Mountains, Virginia, 70, 101, 176–77, 358

Boatswain's Swamp, Virginia, 82–83

Bolivar Heights, Virginia/West Virginia, 109

Bolivar, Tennessee, 140–41, 144

Bolton Station (Bolton Depot), Mississippi, 230

Boomer, George, 231

Boonsboro, Maryland, 109, 113

Bowen, John S., 219

Bowling Green, Kentucky, 37

Boydton Plank Road (Virginia), 359, 361

Bragg, Braxton, xx–xxi, 55, 57, 63–64, 105–6, 128, 137–39, 156–60, 171, 173, 217, 248–52, 255, 257–59, 261–65, 267, 270, 283, 326–27, 332, 354–55, 357, 398, 403, 407–8, 423, 427–29

Brandy Station (Virginia), 274–75
Battle of, 175–76

Breckinridge, John C., 55, 64, 287

Bridgeport, Alabama, 252–55

Bridgeport, Mississippi, 232

Bristoe Station, Virginia, 103, 266, 268
Battle of, 266, 268

Bristoe (Virginia) Campaign, 266

Brock Road, Spotsylvania, Virginia, 293, 295, 299–300

Brown, G. Campbell, 184

Brown, John, 12

Brown's Ferry, Tennessee, 254, 257

Bruce, George, 196, 404

Bruinsburg, Mississippi, 218, 221

Buchanan, Robert C., 13–14

Buckner, Simon Bolivar, 15, 41–43, 394

Buell, Don Carlos, xvii, 43–44, 48, 50–52, 59, 61, 63–65, 94, 133, 137–38, 140, 143, 423

Buell, Thomas, 87, 106, 124, 226, 407, 412–13, 415

Buford, John, 180–81, 183–84, 188

Bulge, Battle of the, 407

Bull Run (Manassas) (Virginia), First Battle of, xvi, xxv, 24, 372, 402

Bull Run (Manassas) (Virginia), Second Battle of, xviii, xxv, 103, 392

Bull Run mountains, 101

Bureau of Military Intelligence, 337, 341

Burke (Burkeville Junction), Virginia, 367

Burns, Robert, 41

Burnside, Ambrose E., xviii, xxi, 118–21, 127–31, 133, 137, 153, 156–57, 210, 248–49, 252, 258, 263–64, 272, 280, 289, 294, 297, 302, 305, 309, 333, 365, 399, 408, 412, 427

Burnside's Bridge, Sharpsburg, Maryland, 118–19

Burton, Brian, 406, 415

Butler, Benjamin F., 277, 279–80, 286–87, 342, 353–54, 365, 412, 430

"Butternut Guerillas," 204

C

Cadwallader, Sylvanus, 236–37, 422

Cairo, Illinois, 21–22, 32, 35, 38, 241, 252

California, 13

Camp Bartow, Virginia, 31

Campbell, John A., 350

Campbell's Station, Tennessee, 264

Camp Elkwater, Virginia, 29–30

Camp Yates, Illinois, 17

Cape Fear River, North Carolina, 354–55, 358

Carlisle, Pennsylvania, 176–77, 180, 183–84

Carnifax Ferry (Virginia), Battle of, 31

Carolinas, xxv, 172, 179, 249, 252, 271, 283, 332, 349, 351–52, 354–55, 376–77, 418, 424, 426, 428

Carrick's Ford (Carrickford) (Virginia), Battle of, 24

Carter, Ann H., 4–5

Carthage, Mississippi, 151, 215–16, 219

Casdorph, Paul D., 383

Cashtown, Pennsylvania, 179–80, 183–85, 191

Cashtown Road (Chambersburg Pike), Pennsylvania, 180–81, 184–85, 187, 192–93 casualties, Civil War, 93–95, 373–75, 394–400, 418. *See also* Grant, Ulysses S., casualties in battles of; Lee, Robert E., casualties in battles of; *individual battles and campaigns*

Catherine Furnace, Virginia, 164

Catlett's Station, Virginia, 101

Catton, Bruce, 241, 251, 269, 273–74, 318, 327, 331, 384–85, 393, 409

Cedar Creek (Virginia), Battle of, 341

Cedar Mountain (Virginia), Battle of, xix, 100, 122, 125, 209

Cemetery Hill, Gettysburg, Pennsylvania, 185–87, 189, 197, 201, 203, 207

Cemetery Ridge, Gettysburg, Pennsylvania, 185, 189, 194–96, 199–200, 202–5

Cerro Gordo (Mexico), Battle of, 9

Chamberlain, Joshua L., 195, 364

Chambersburg, Pennsylvania, 177, 179, 324, 338

Chambersburg Pike (Cashtown Road), Pennsylvania, 180–81, 184–85, 187, 192–93

Champion's Hill (Mississippi), Battle of, 171, 230–31, 244, 405, 409, 431

Chancellorsville, Virginia, 160–61, 165–67

    Battle of, xx, xxv, 10, 153, 155, 162, 167–68, 170–71, 174, 176, 194, 209–10, 224, 267–68, 296, 311, 392, 396, 401, 406–7, 429

Chantilly, (Virginia), Battle of, 105, 122, 125, 209, 401

Chapultepec (Mexico), Battle of, 9

Charleston, South Carolina, 35, 45, 50, 158, 179, 228, 343, 346, 351, 355–56

Charleston, Virginia/West Virginia, 28, 31

Charlotte, North Carolina, 356

Charlottesville, Virginia, 358

Chase, Salmon P., 152

Chattahoochee River, Georgia, 288, 326, 343

Chattanooga Creek, Tennessee, 260

Chattanooga, Tennessee, xiv, xxi–xxiii, 106, 129, 136–37, 169, 173, 211, 247–60, 262, 264, 270–71, 343–44, 405, 428

    campaign of, xxv, 137–38, 251–60, 263–66, 268–70, 273, 326, 380–81, 386, 393, 397, 407, 409, 423, 427–28, 431

Chattanooga Valley, Tennessee, 259

Cheat Mountain (Virginia), Battle of, xvi, 28–30, 79

Chesapeake Bay, 99, 280, 306, 314

Chesnut, Mary, 346, 350

Chesterfield Bridge, Virginia, 305

Chicago Convention (1864), 342

Chicago (Peace) Platform (1864), 342

Chicago Times, 236

Chicago Tribune, 136

Chickahominy River, Virginia, 68, 71, 75, 77, 79–82, 84, 314, 417

Chickamauga Creek, Georgia, 250

Chickamauga (Georgia), Battle of, xxi, xxv, 137, 173, 247, 250–52, 257, 261, 265, 268, 277, 327, 402, 423, 428–29

Chickamauga Station, Georgia, 262

Chickasaw Bluffs (Mississippi), Battle of, 147

Chilton, Robert, 112

Churubusco (Mexico), Battle of, 9

Cincinnati, Ohio, 18, 152, 277

City Point, Virginia, 307, 333–34, 339–40, 369

Clarksville, Tennessee, 44, 48

Cleburne, Patrick R., 260, 262

Clinton, Mississippi, 229

Coddington, Edwin B., 187

Cold Harbor, Virginia, 308–9, 312–14, 407

    Battle of, xxii, xxv, 92, 285, 297, 308–13, 315–16, 383, 400, 404, 407, 417–18

College Hill Line, Corinth, Mississippi, 140

Colquitt, Alfred H., 163

Colston, Raleigh E., 164

Columbia Barracks, OR, 13

Columbia River, 13

Columbia, South Carolina, 356–57

Columbus, Kentucky, 21, 31–33, 35, 44, 50, 147

Comstock, Cyrus B., 314

Confederate Adjutant's Office, 353

Congress, Confederate, 127, 350, 353

Congress, United States, 19, 24, 270

Connecticut, 118, 342

Connelly, Thomas L., 106, 380, 427

conscription, Confederate, 127

Contreras (Mexico), Battle of, 9

Cooling, Benjamin Franklin, 41, 44

Cooper, Samuel, 28

Corinth, Mississippi, xvii, 50–51, 64, 134–37, 139–42, 144

    Battle of, xvii–xix, xxv, 50–51, 134, 141–43, 152, 265, 431

    Halleck's campaign against, xvii, 134–37, 141, 424

Corinth Road, 55, 64

Couch, Darius, 120

Cox, Jacob D., 28, 30–31, 120, 128, 312, 393, 420

"Cracker Line," 254, 257

"Cradle of the Confederacy," 356

Crampton's Gap, Maryland, 110, 113

Crater (Petersburg, Virginia), Battle of the, 333–34

Crittenden, Thomas L., 61

Cross Keys (Virginia), Battle of, 74

Cross Lanes, Virginia, 31

"Crossroads of the Western Confederacy," 134

Crump's Landing, Tennessee, 50, 52

CSS *Virginia*, 65

Culpeper Court House, Virginia, 179

Culpeper Mine Road, Virginia, 293

Culpeper, Virginia, 98, 100, 288

Culp's Hill, Gettysburg, Pennsylvania, 185–87, 189, 197, 199

Cumberland Island, Georgia, 4

Cumberland River, xvi, 22, 35–36, 38–39, 48

Cumberland Valley, Pennsylvania, 177

Custer, George A., 201, 372

Custis, Mary Anne Randolph, 5. *See also* Lee, Mary A. R.

D

Dallas (Georgia), Battle of, 287

Dalton, Georgia, 287, 344

Dana, Charles A., 213, 251, 269, 311, 315, 377, 399

Danville railroad (Virginia), 361

Darbytown Road, Virginia, 341–42

Davis' Bridge (Mississippi), Battle of, 142

Davis, Jefferson F., xiii, xviii, xx–xxi, xxiii, 11, 23–24, 28, 31, 33, 43, 45, 65, 67–68, 73–74, 76, 105–7, 123, 141–42, 155–58, 169, 171–72, 179, 209, 215, 228, 234, 236, 248–49, 251, 255, 257–58, 262, 264–65, 267, 279, 283, 308, 322, 326–32, 343, 346–47, 350, 352–54, 360, 366, 382, 426–27, 431, 433

cabinet of, 156, 172, 350

Davis, Varina, 68, 346

D-Day, 222

deaths in Civil War. *See* casualties, Civil War

Decatur (Atlanta) (Georgia), Battle of, 330

Deep Bottom, Virginia, 333

First Battle of, 334

Second Battle of, 337

Democratic Party, 148, 286, 287, 331, 335, 338, 342, 392

Democratic Peace (Chicago) Platform, 335, 342

Dent, Frederick F., 3, 15

Dent, Frederick T., 3

Dent, Julia Boggs, 3, 6, 13. *See also* Grant, Julia Dent

Department of the Cumberland (U), 252

Department of Mississippi and East Louisiana (C), 143

Department of the Missouri (U), 35–36

Department of the Ohio (U), 252

Department of Tennessee (U), 143

Department of the Tennessee (U), 252

Department of the West (C), 326

desertions, Confederate, 106, 127, 329, 332, 336, 343, 347, 349, 353

Detroit, Michigan, 13

Devil's Den, Gettysburg, Pennsylvania, 194–95

Dickey, T. Lyle, 237

Dinwiddie Court House (Virginia), Battle of, 362–63

District of Southeast Missouri (U), 21

District of West Tennessee (U), 38

Dodge, Grenville, 277

Donelson. *See* Fort Donelson

Doolittle, James, 270

Dowdey, Clifford, 383

draft, Confederate, 127

draft riots, 337

Drayton, Thomas F., 249

Drewry's Bluff (Virginia), Battle of, 68, 286–87

Duff, William L., 237

Dunker Church, Sharpsburg, Maryland, 116–17

E

Early, Jubal A., xxiii, 68, 100, 116, 160, 165–66, 184–88, 192, 197, 266–67, 295, 307, 313, 316, 322–26, 330, 334, 338, 340–41, 358, 367, 381, 394, 406, 428–29

Eastern (Virginia) Theater, xiv, xvii, xxiv–xxv, 65, 105, 155, 169, 245, 247, 257, 262, 265, 272, 279, 284, 349, 375–77, 394, 423, 426, 429, 433

East Tennessee & Georgia Railroad, 250

East Tennessee & Virginia Railroad, 250

East Woods, Sharpsburg, Maryland, 116

Ecelberger, Gary, 226

Eighteenth Corps (U), 307, 314, 316, 340

Eighteenth North Carolina Infantry (C), 164

Eighteenth Virginia Infantry (C), 205

election of 1864. *See* presidential election of 1864

Eleventh Connecticut Infantry, 118

Eleventh Corps (U), xxiii, 164, 181, 183–85, 253, 266

Ellison's Mill (Mechanicsville), Virginia, 92

Ely's Ford, Virginia, 159, 289

Emancipation Proclamation, 98, 106–7, 125, 143, 391

Emmitsburg, Maryland, 181

Emmitsburg Pike, Maryland, 203

Emmitsburg Road, Maryland, 194

England, 211, 390

Epperson, James F., 289, 291

Europe, 389

European intervention, possible, xviii–xix, 107, 125, 212, 392

Everlington Heights, Virginia, 417

Ewell, Richard S., 18, 67, 70, 74, 82, 174–75, 177, 179–80, 183–88, 191, 197–99, 201, 211, 289, 293, 295, 303–4, 307, 367, 404, 406

Executive Mansion, D.C., 243

Ezra Church (Georgia), Battle of, 330

F

Fairfax Court House, Fairfax, Virginia, 105

Fair Oaks/Seven Pines (Virginia), Battle of, xviii, 71, 73

Fairview Plateau, Chancellorsville, Virginia, 165

Falmouth, Virginia, 128–29

Farmville, Virginia, 367, 369

Farragut, David G., 341–42

Fayetteville, North Carolina, 355, 357

Feis, William, 226, 280, 409

Fifteenth Corps (U), 216, 219, 232, 314–15

Fifth Corps (U), 120, 195, 293, 302, 307, 314, 316, 340, 361–62, 364

First Corps (C), xx, 2, 128, 155–57, 174, 184, 191, 198, 211, 257–58, 262, 279–80, 289–91, 294

First Corps (U), 112, 116, 181, 185, 199

First Minnesota Infantry (U), 196

First Rhode Island Light Artillery (U), 402

First Texas Infantry (C), 116

Fisher's Hill (Virginia), Battle of, 340

Five Forks, Virginia, 223 ; Battle of, 311, 362–65, 416

Fleetwood Hill, Virginia, 175

Fleetwood House, Brandy Station, Virginia, 175

Fleming, Martin, 29, 406

Florida, 45, 65, 283, 304, 352

Floyd, John B., 29–30, 41, 408

Fonvielle, Chris, 354

Foote, Andrew H., xvii, 35–39, 48

Foote, Shelby, 42, 298

forage and supplies from invaded territory (living off the countryside), 226– 27, 270

Ford's Depot, Virginia, 363

Forrest, Nathan Bedford, 41, 44, 63, 147, 219, 262

Fort Anderson, North Carolina, 355

Fort Beauregard, South Carolina, 45

Fort Clark, North Carolina, 45

Fort Coburn, Mississippi, 221

Fort Donelson, Tennessee, 33, 394
    Campaign, xiv, xvi–xvii, xix–xx, xxv, 35–44, 48, 50, 87, 134, 231, 251, 265, 273, 380, 385–86, 393– 94, 405, 409, 423, 431

Fort Fisher, North Carolina, 354, 357, 413

Fort Harrison (Virginia), Battle of, 341

Fort Hatteras, North Carolina, 45

Fort Henry, Tennessee, 35
    Campaign, xiv, xvi–xvii, xix, xxv, 36–39, 43–44, 48–50, 134, 265, 385, 393, 431

Fort Hindman, Arkansas, 148

Fort Humboldt, California, 13–14

fortifications, use or non-use of, 305, 313, 359, 377

Fort McAllister, Georgia, 344

Fort Monroe, Virginia, xviii, 5, 66, 68

Fort Morgan, Alabama, 342

Fort Pemberton, Mississippi, 150

Fort Pulaski, Georgia, 45

Fort Stedman, Virginia, 360–61, 401

Fort Sumter, South Carolina, 17, 22, 42

Fort Totten, New York, 5

Fort Vancouver, Washington, 13

Fort Wade, Mississippi, 221

Fort Walker, South Carolina, 45

Forty-seventh North Carolina Infantry (C), 205

Foster, Sam, 332

Fox's Gap, Maryland, 110, 112–13

France, 106, 211, 251

Franklin (Tennessee), Battle of, 271, 332, 345, 349

Franklin, Virginia, 70

Frayser's (Frazier's) Farm (Glendale) (Virginia), Battle of, 85–86, 400

Frederick, Maryland, 107, 109–10, 179, 322–23

Fredericksburg, Virginia, 4, 66–68, 70, 128–31, 157, 159–61, 165–66, 293, 298, 301–2, 406
  Battle of, xviii–xix, xxv, 129–33, 153, 156, 172, 190, 204–6, 209–10, 296
Freeman, Douglas Southall, 83, 85, 89, 92, 122, 193, 328, 382–83, 415, 421–22
Fremantle, Arthur J. L., 210
Frémont, John C., xv, 21, 70–71, 74, 151
Front Royal, Virginia, 70
Fuller, J. F. C., 104, 152, 226, 235, 315, 380, 383, 388, 396, 401, 407, 420, 423
Furgurson, Ernest B., 383

G

Gaines Mill (Virginia), Battle of, 82–83, 92, 199, 388, 400–1
Galena, Illinois, 15, 17, 21, 134, 271
Gallagher, Gary W., 381, 410
Galt House, Louisville, Kentucky, 252
Garnett, Richard B., 199, 204
Garnett, Robert S., 23–24, 28
Gauley Bridge, Virginia, 28
Geary, John W., 255, 257
Georgetown Pike, Maryland, 323
Georgia, xiv, xxi–xxiii, 4–5, 45, 65, 156, 163, 173, 248–50, 262, 264, 270–71, 277, 279, 283, 287, 304, 320–21, 324–26, 329–30, 332, 338, 343–46, 352, 355, 376, 382, 413–14, 424, 426–28, 430

German-Americans, 287
Germanna Ford, Virginia, 159, 289
Gettysburg (Pennsylvania), Battle of, xxi, 10, 88, 92, 153, 156, 171–72, 174, 176–85, 187–92, 196–98, 201, 205–12, 240, 242, 244, 248, 265, 268, 311, 318, 327, 380, 386, 391–92, 395–96, 399, 401–4, 406, 408–10, 415, 417, 423, 429
  Campaign, xiv, xx, xxiv–xxv, 156, 177, 212, 244, 423
Gibbon, John, 199, 311, 365
Gibraltar of the West, 213
Gilmer, Jeremy F., 87
Glendale (Frayser's or Frazier's Farm) (Virginia), Battle of, 85–86, 400
Globe Tavern (Virginia), Battle of, 334, 340
Goldsboro, North Carolina, 356, 358
Gordon, John B., 295–96, 374
Gordonsville, Virginia, 98–100, 279, 290, 313
Gorgas, Josiah, 177, 212, 244, 325, 350, 357, 390
Grand Gulf, Mississippi, 151, 219, 221–27, 229, 233, 243
Grand Junction, Tennessee, 144, 147
Granger, Gordon, 261
Grant, Fred, 271
Grant, Hiram Ulysses, 1. *See also* Grant, Ulysses S.
Grant, Julia Dent, 3, 6–7, 9, 13–15, 236. *See also* Dent, Julia Boggs
Grant, Orvil, 15
Grant, Simpson, 15
Grant, Ulysses S.,

aggressiveness of, xxii, xxiv, 10, 94,
140, 142, 241, 251, 263, 265, 270,
273, 283, 302, 304, 312, 320, 375,
377, 387–88, 392–93, 404, 408,
425, 432
alcohol use by and drunkenness
allegations against, xiii, xv,
13–15, 18, 94, 151–52, 236–37,
421–22, 424
amphibious operation of, xix, 218,
221–22, 386, 416
Appomattox Campaign of, xxv,
253, 366–75, 377, 380, 380, 396,
415, 418–19, 431
Belmont (Missouri), Battle of, xvi,
xix, xxv, 32–33, 35, 231, 251,
393, 409, 418, 431
Big Black River (Mississippi), Battle
of, 232
boyhood of, xv, 1–2
Brigadier General, promotion to,
21
"butcher" allegations against, xiii,
244, 308–10, 319, 381–82, 387,
397, 399–400, 424, 431–32
Captain, promotion to, 14
casualties in battles of, xiv, xix, xxi–
xxii, xxiv, 33, 42, 44, 62, 94–95,
142, 152, 227, 233–36, 239–41,
244, 264–65, 281, 296, 304, 308,
310–12, 317, 319, 321, 335, 366–
67, 375–77, 383, 387–88, 395–
400 (*see also* Appendix 1;
casualties, Civil War; *individual
battles and campaigns*)
cavalry, use of, 59

Champion's Hill (Mississippi), Battle of, 171, 230–31, 244, 405,
409, 431
Chattanooga (Tennessee), campaign of, xxv, 137–38, 251–60,
263–66, 268–70, 273, 326, 380–
81, 386, 393, 397, 407, 409, 423,
427–28, 431
civilian jobs of, xv, 15
Cold Harbor (Virginia), Battle of,
xxii, xxv, 92, 285, 297, 308–13,
315–16, 383, 400, 404, 407, 417–
18
Colonel, appointment as, xv, 18
compared to Robert E. Lee, xv–
xxiv, 379–433
Corinth (Mississippi), Battle of,
xvii–xix, xxv, 50–51, 134, 141–
43, 152, 265, 431
Crater (Petersburg, Virginia), Battle
of, 333–34
deceptiveness of, 33, 226, 241, 243,
313–14, 333, 285–86
discretion delegated by, 288, 405
financial hardships of, xv
focus on enemy armies by, xvi, xix,
42, 136–38, 225–26, 269, 272–
73, 280, 285, 288, 386, 394, 425,
431
Fort Donelson (Tennessee), campaign of, xiv, xvi–xvii, xix–xx,
xxv, 35–44, 48, 50, 87, 134, 231,
251, 265, 273, 380, 385–86, 393–
94, 405, 409, 423, 431
Fort Henry (Tennessee) Campaign,
xiv, xvi–xvii, xix, xxv, 36–39,

43–44, 48–50, 134, 265, 385, 393, 431

general-in-chief, promotion to, xxii, 271

horse-related skills of, 1 –2 , 7

Iuka (Mississippi), Battle of, xviii–xix, 139–40, 143, 152, 265, 431

Jackson (Mississippi), battles of, 171, 229, 240, 431

Lieutenant General, promotion to, 270

logistics of, 242, 282, 386

Major General, promotion to, xvii, 42, 242

maneuverability of, 227, 241–42, 244, 265, 281, 306, 311 319, 377, 383, 406–8, 423

memoirs of, 2, 6–8, 20, 50, 60, 136, 146, 221, 233, 235, 285, 310, 340, 345, 380

Mexican War experience of, xv, 6–9, 15

Moral courage of, 419–21

national generalship of, xiii , xxiii–xxiv, 324, 376, 424

nickname "Sam" of, 2

nickname "Unconditional Surrender" of, xvii, 41–42

North Anna River (Virginia), Battle of, xxii, xxv, 305–6, 308, 333, 387, 415

orders of, 405–6

Overland (Virginia) Campaign of, xiv, xxv, 280, 285, 289, 293, 297, 310, 317–20, 376, 382, 385, 387–88, 392–93, 399, 407, 409, 414, 424–25, 430, 432

overlooking enemy threats by, 32, 51

perseverance of, 143, 264, 375, 386, 394, 417–18, 425

Petersburg (Virginia), Battles at, xxiii, xxv, 277, 286–87, 311, 313, 315, 318, 332–35, 337, 340–41, 346, 349, 358–59, 360–61, 365–66, 374–75, 396, 431–32

Petersburg/Richmond (Virginia), siege of, xiv, xxiii, 157, 277, 285, 313, 317, 321–22, 335, 341, 375, 407, 424

political common sense of, 412, 430

Port Gibson (Mississippi), Battle of, 223–24, 240, 243

presidency of, 382

presidential candidacy disclaimer of, 271

quartermaster experience of, 7

quickness of, 227, 230, 235, 241, 243–44

Raymond (Mississippi), Battle of, 227–28, 431

reinforcements, nonrequests for, 410–11

religion of, 421

resignation of army commission by, xv, 14

respect for enemy prisoners by, 263, 397

Sayler's (Sailor's) Creek (Virginia), Battle of, 367

Shiloh (Tennessee), Battle of, xvii, xix, xxv, 33–34, 47–48, 50–51, 53–54, 62–63, 67, 87, 133–35,

137, 141, 231, 251, 265, 277, 385, 393–94, 405, 414, 417, 420, 431

Spotsylvania Court House (Virginia), Battle of, xxii, xxv, 285, 297–300, 303–5, 317–18, 387, 396, 399, 405, 409, 416, 418, 431

strategic vision of, 425

strategy of, xix–xx, 9–10, 213, 240, 245, 293–97, 318, 321, 375, 381, 384–86, 406–7, 415, 423–30

supply lines abandoned by, 226–27

sympathy for wounded soldiers by, 40 , 62

tactics of, xix, 10–11, 245, 293–94, 381, 385, 400–5

Trevilian's Station (Virginia), Battle of, 313, 416

uniform of, 2

use of assigned generals by, 412–13

use of cavalry by, 416–17

use of military intelligence by, 229–30, 243, 279, 289, 322–23

use of staff by, 274–75, 288–89, 413–14

use of Union resources by, 232, 242, 281–82, 410–11

Vicksburg (Mississippi), attacks on by, xix, 237, 404–5, 410–11

Vicksburg (Mississippi) Campaign, xiv, xx, 11, 133, 156, 213–44, 251, 265, 268, 381, 386, 393, 403, 406, 410–12, 420, 423

Vicksburg (Mississippi), early attempts to capture by, xix, 143–52, 416–18

Vicksburg (Mississippi), siege of by, 179, 237–240, 422

victim of unexpected attacks, 393–94

West Point years of, 1–2

Wilderness (Virginia), Battle of the, xxii, xxv, 160–61, 166–67, 267, 280, 285, 289–91, 293, 296–97, 299, 302, 304, 312–13, 318, 375, 385–87, 396, 399, 401, 403, 408–9, 417–18, 425, 431–32.

Grapevine Bridge, Virginia, 84

Gravelly Run, Virginia, 362–63

Greenbriar, Virginia, 30

Greene, A. Wilson, 366

Greenville, Mississippi, 217

Gregg, John, 227–28, 295

Grenada, Mississippi, 145–46

Grierson, Benjamin H., 217–19, 224

Grierson's Raid, 217–18, 382, 416

Griffin, Charles, 364

Grindstone Ford, Mississippi 224

Groveton, Virginia, 103

Guinea Station, Virginia, 165

Gulf of Mexico, 251

H

Hagerstown, Maryland, 109–10, 125, 177, 323

Haines' Bluff, Mississippi, 149–50, 219

Halleck, Henry W., xvi–xvii, 35–38, 42–44, 48–51, 64–65, 94, 98–99, 133–42, 144–45, 148, 152, 225, 227, 233, 251–54, 265, 269, 275, 301–2, 307, 313, 323, 325, 337–38, 340, 355, 409, 424

Halleck Line, Corinth, Mississippi, 140

Hampton Roads, Virginia, 65, 314, 397
  Peace Conference, 350

Hampton, Wade, 87, 172, 206, 313

Hancock, Winfield Scott, 167, 183, 185, 188–90, 195–96, 293–95, 302, 305, 309, 314, 316, 334, 337, 365

Hankinson's Ferry, Mississippi, 224–25

Hanover Station, Virginia, 71, 76

Hanovertown, Virginia, 306–7

Hardee, William J., 55, 63–64, 327–28, 330, 332, 344–45, 351, 358

"Hardscrabble," 15

Hard Times, Louisiana, 219

Harmon, Troy D., 207

Harper's Ferry, Virginia/West Virginia, 12, 24, 66, 71, 109–10, 113–14, 119–20, 122–23, 125, 339–40

Harrisburg, Pennsylvania, 105, 158, 179

Harris Farm (Virginia), Battle of, 303

Harrison, Thomas, 179

Harrison's Landing, Virginia, 76, 80, 90, 92, 97, 99–100, 417

Harsh, Joseph L., 388

Hartranft, John F., 360

Hatcher's Run, Virginia, 359, 362–64

Hatchie River, Mississippi, 141–42

Hatch, Ozias M., 127

Hattaway, Herman, 44, 58, 241, 376, 384

Hatteras, North Carolina, 45

Haw's Shop (Virginia), Battle of, 307

Hazel Grove, Chancellorsville, Virginia, 165–66

Helena, Arkansas, 146, 150

Herr's Ridge, Gettysburg, Pennsylvania, 181, 183, 185

Hess, Earl, 168

Heth, Henry, 180–81, 196, 302

Higgerson's Field, Virginia, 293

Hill, Ambrose P., 76, 79–80, 82, 85, 88, 99–100, 119–20, 125, 129, 164, 174, 184, 186–87, 177, 179–81, 195–96, 198, 201, 266, 289, 293–95, 304–5, 366

Hill, Daniel H. "Harvey," 76, 79–80, 84, 88–90, 92, 99, 109–10, 112–13, 116–17, 123, 210

Hitchcock, Ethan Allen, 43

Hoke, Robert F., 308

Holly Springs, Mississippi, 142, 145–48, 152

Holmes, Theophilus H., 84–85, 249

Hood, John Bell, xxiii, 12, 112, 116, 120–21, 170, 185, 191, 194, 326–32, 334, 338, 343–46, 349, 376–77, 398, 403, 427–28

Hornets' Nest, Shiloh, Tennessee, 56–58

Horseshoe Ridge, Chickamauga, Tennessee, 250

Hotchkiss, Jedediah, 82, 166, 335

Hovey, Alvin P., 231

Howard, Oliver O., 164, 181, 183, 254–55, 344, 355, 412

Huger, Benjamin, 84–86, 89, 412

Humphreys, Andrew A., 130, 311, 361, 365

Hundley's Corner, Virginia, 79–80

Hunt, Henry J., 202

Hunter, David, 151, 287, 313, 322, 338–39

Hurdle, R. W., 35

Hurlbut, Stephen A., 53, 56, 60, 141, 217

I

Illinois, xv, 11, 15, 17–19, 21, 53, 127, 146, 223, 342

Imboden, John D., 205

Indiana, 253, 260, 342

Indianapolis, Indiana, 252

Ingalls, Rufus, 2

inter-theater troop transfers, xxi, xxiii, 137–38, 155, 157, 247–249, 265, 275, 278, 313, 333–34, 350, 356, 358, 423

Iowa, 57, 233

Irish Brigade (U), 117

Iron Brigade (U), 103, 181

Iuka, Mississippi, 139

    Battle of, xviii–xix, 139–40, 143, 152, 265, 431

Iverson, Alfred Jr., 183

Ives, Joseph C., 74

J

Jackson, Andrew, 4

Jackson, Mississippi, 171, 217–18, 224, 226, 228–31, 240, 242, 244, 270, 431

    battles of, 171, 229, 240, 431

Jackson Road, Mississippi, 231

Jackson, Tennessee, 140–41, 143–44, 147

Jackson, Thomas J. "Stonewall," 24, 66–68, 70–71, 73–77, 79–86, 88, 91, 98–101, 103–4, 107, 109, 113, 116–17, 123, 128–29, 133, 160–61, 163–65, 168–69, 171, 174, 186, 194, 268, 305, 388, 401, 407, 416

James River Canal, Virginia, 313

James River, Virginia, xxiii, 65, 67–68, 76–77, 81, 84, 87–88, 90, 92, 97, 99, 277, 280, 286, 307–8, 310, 313–16, 333–34, 337, 339, 369, 386, 396

    crossing of, 285, 313–16, 407, 417

Jamieson, Perry D., 7, 265, 397, 399

Jefferson Barracks, Missouri, 3

Jericho Mill, Virginia, 305

Jetersville, Virginia, 367

Johnson, Bushrod R., 362

Johnson, Edward, 184, 187, 197, 328

Johnston, Albert Sydney, 12, 28, 38, 50–51, 56, 62, 94

Johnston, Joseph E., xviii, 24, 67–68, 71, 73–74, 76, 157, 159, 226, 228–30, 232, 234–40, 244, 257, 264, 275, 277–79, 281, 283, 288, 304, 322, 324–32, 352, 355, 357–58, 360, 367, 376, 403, 428–31

Johnston, Samuel L., 193

Jones, Archer, 44, 123, 173, 208, 241, 384, 401, 426–27

Jones, J. B., 43, 244

Jones, John R., 125

Jones, R. Stephen, 405–6, 414

Jones, William E., 175

Jonesboro (Georgia), Battle of, 330

K

Kanawha River, Virginia/West
 Virginia, 31
Kanawha Valley, Virginia/West
 Virginia, 29–30
Katcher, Philip, 404
Kautz, August V., 340
Keegan, John, 384
Kelly's Ford, Virginia, 159, 175, 266
Kennesaw Mountain (Georgia), Battle
 of, 288, 326
Kentucky, xvi–xvii, xix, 21–22, 31–32,
 37, 43–44, 50, 57, 136–40, 143, 147,
 237, 241, 253, 423
Kernstown (Virginia), Battle of, 66
Kershaw, Joseph B., 334, 341
Kilpatrick, Hugh Judson, 344, 355
King George III, 391
Kinston, North Carolina, 357
Knefler, Fred, 260
Knoxville, Tennessee, xxi, 137, 248–49,
 258–59, 262–65
Kolb's Farm, Georgia, 327
Konstam, Angus, 89
Kross, Gary, 187, 205, 406

L

Lagow, Clark, 216
LaGrange, Tennessee, 217
Lake Ontario, 13
Lake Providence, Louisiana, 150

Laurel Hill (West Virginia/Virginia),
 Battle of, 24
Law, Evander M., 110, 193, 304, 382
Ledlie, James H., 305, 333
Lee, Ann Carter, 5
Lee family reputation, 3–4
Lee, Fitzhugh, 161, 361–64, 404
Lee, Henry III "Light-Horse Harry,"
 3–5
Lee, Henry IV "Black-Horse Harry," 4
Lee, Mary A. R., 5
Lee, Matilda, 3
Lee, Robert E.,
 aggressiveness of, xiv, xxiv, 74,
  92–93, 105, 107, 155, 157, 170,
  177, 210–11, 266, 282–83, 320,
  365, 387–94, 400–1, 403–4, 412,
  426, 433
 Antietam (Maryland) Campaign
  of, xviii, xxv, 10, 97, 112–27, 131,
  133, 138, 206, 209–10, 318, 327,
  388, 391–92, 396, 399–401, 408,
  429
 Appomattox Campaign of, xxi, xxv,
  347, 353, 366, 368, 374, 377, 380,
  394, 396, 415, 418–19, 431
 boyhood of, xv, 1 , 3
 Brigadier General, commission as,
  23
 Bristoe (Virginia) Campaign of,
  266
 Bull Run (Manassas) (Virginia),
  Second Battle of, xviii–xix, xxv,
  97, 102–3, 105, 122, 125, 133,
  194, 209–10, 401, 407

casualties in battles of, xiv, xviii–xx, xxiv, 47, 91–92, 95, 105, 107, 113, 123–25, 127, 131–32, 153, 169, 210–11, 244, 279, 304, 308, 311–12, 317, 319–20, 334, 375–77, 386–89, 394–400, 403, 412, 424 (*see also* Appendix 1; Casualties, Civil War; *individual battles and campaigns*)

Chancellorsville (Virginia), Campaign of, xx, xxv, 10, 153, 155, 162, 167–68, 170–71, 174, 176, 194, 209–10, 224, 267–68, 296, 311, 392, 396, 401, 406–7, 429

Cold Harbor (Virginia), Battle of, xxii, xxv, 92, 285, 297, 308–13, 315–16, 383, 400, 404, 407, 417–18

Colonel, appointment as, 9

compared to Ulysses S. Grant, xv–xxiv, 379–433

Crater (Petersburg, Virginia), Battle of, 333–34

declination of command in other theaters by, 264 , 268

Fredericksburg (Virginia), Battle of, xviii–xix, xxv, 129–33, 153, 156, 172, 190, 204–6, 209–10, 296

General, promotion to xvi

Gettysburg (Pennsylvania), Battle of, xxi, 10, 88, 92, 153, 156, 171–72, 174, 176–85, 187–92, 196–98, 201, 205–12, 240, 242, 244, 248, 265, 268, 311, 318, 327, 380, 386, 391–92, 395–96, 399, 401–4, 406, 408–10, 415, 417, 423, 429

Gettysburg (Pennsylvania), Battle report of, 190

Gettysburg (Pennsylvania), Campaign of, xiv, xx, xxiv–xxv, 156, 177, 212, 244, 423

health of, 160, 248–49

loss of battlefield control by, 30, 77–90, 194–95, 305, 401, 403, 409–10

Malvern Hill (Virginia), Battle of, 84, 87–88, 90, 92, 133, 211, 314, 388, 392, 396, 400–1, 406

Maryland Campaign of (*see* Antietam (Maryland) Campaign)

Mechanicsville (Virginia), Battle of, 77, 79–81, 92, 290, 401

Mexican War experience of, xv, 6, 9

military advisor to Jefferson Davis, xvii, 65, 427

Mine Run (Virginia) Campaign of, 267–68

moral courage of, 421

nicknames of, 4, 74

North Anna River (Virginia), Battle of, xxii, xxv, 305–6, 308, 333, 387, 415

Oak Grove (Virginia), Battle of, 75

one theater general (*see* Lee, Robert E., Virginia myopia of)

orders of, 29–30, 79, 81, 86, 175–79, 186–87, 212, 400, 405–6 (*see also* Lee, Robert E., vague orders of)

Overland (Virginia) Campaign of, xiv, xxv, 280, 285, 289, 293, 297, 310, 317–20, 376, 382, 385, 387–88, 392–93, 399, 407, 409, 414, 424–25, 430, 432

oversight of subordinates, 28–29, 66, 79–84, 86, 91–92, 191–97, 204, 412–16

perseverance of, 417–18

Petersburg (Virginia), Battles at, xxiii, xxv, 277, 286–87, 311, 313, 315, 318, 332–35, 337, 340–41, 346, 349, 358–59, 360–61, 365–66, 374–75, 396, 431–32

Petersburg/Richmond (Virginia), siege of, xiv, xxiii, 157, 277, 285, 313, 317, 321–22, 335, 341, 375, 407, 424

political common sense of, 430–31

pre-Civil War career of, xv

reinforcement requests of xvi, 104–5 , 169–70, 177, 278–79, 303, 316–20, 411, 423–24

religion of, 421

resignation letters of, 248, 347, 366, 373, 418–19

resignation of U.S. Army commission of, xvi, 23, 426

Savage's Station (Virginia), Battle of, 84–85, 91

Sayler's (Sailor's) Creek (Virginia), Battle of, 367

Seven Days' (Virginia), Battle of, xix, xxv, 29, 47, 76–78, 80, 87, 90–93, 95, 122, 125, 133, 185,

196, 199, 206, 209–10, 217–18, 239, 253, 296, 305, 311, 327, 392, 396, 399, 401, 404, 408, 410, 415, 417, 429

Seven Pines/Fair Oaks (Virginia), Battle of, ix, xviii, 71–73

slaves owned by, 5

southeastern command of, xvi–xvii, 45, 64

South Mountain (Maryland), Battle of, 109–10, 113, 123, 125, 209

Spotsylvania Court House (Virginia), Battle of, xxii, xxv, 285, 297–300, 303–5, 317–18, 387, 396, 399, 405, 409, 416, 418, 431

strategy of, xv, xxi, xxiv, 9, 66, 73, 90–92, 122–23, 168–72, 174, 206–12, 282–83, 318, 389–90, 431–33

superintendent of West Point, 12

surrender of, xiv, 415

tactics of, xiv, xxi, xxiv, 9, 89–92, 116, 122–23, 170, 174, 189, 197–98, 206–12, 290, 295, 300–6, 359, 384, 390, 400–5, 431–32

temperance of, 421–22

transfer of troops, opposition to by (*see* Lee, Robert E., Virginia myopia of)

Trevilian's Station (Virginia), Battle of, 313, 416

use of assigned generals by, 174, 267, 412–13

use of cavalry by, 416

use of resources by, 212, 412

use of staff by, 81, 274, 405, 413–16

vague orders of, 176–77, 186, 212, 400, 405–6

Virginia myopia of, xxii–xxiii, 127, 155–56, 169–70, 233–34, 237, 243–44, 248, 255–56, 261–62, 267, 281–82, 320, 352, 355, 375, 421–33

western Virginia Campaign of, xvi, 23, 27–28

West Point cadet years of, 1, 4

Wilderness (Virginia), Battle of the, xxii, xxv, 160–61, 166–67, 267, 280, 285, 289–91, 293, 296–97, 299, 302, 304, 312–13, 318, 375, 385–87, 396, 399, 401, 403, 408–9, 417–18, 425, 431–32

Lee, Stephen D., 120

Lee, William H. F. "Rooney," 30, 175

Leesburg, Virginia, 106

Letcher, John, 23

Lewis' Farm (Virginia), Battle of, 361

Lick Creek, Shiloh, Tennessee, 55, 59

Lincoln, Abraham, xiii, xvi, xxi–xxiv, 17, 22, 24, 35, 42–43, 49, 64–68, 70–71, 74–75, 92, 95, 97–98, 106–7, 124–25, 127–29, 131, 136–37, 143, 145, 148, 151–52, 156, 206, 211, 213, 237–38, 242–43, 251–52, 263–65, 270–74, 277–79, 281–86, 294, 319–22, 325, 331, 335–44, 347, 350, 354, 369, 374–77, 384, 390–93, 396, 411, 418–19, 423–25, 430, 432–33

cabinet of, 24, 68, 98, 335

General Orders No. 1 of, 35, 65

Special Orders No. 1 of, 65

Lincoln, Mary Todd, 272

Little Bayou Pierre, Mississippi, 223–24

Little Round Top, Gettysburg, Pennsylvania, 189, 193–95, 203

living off country, 227, 270

Locust Church (Virginia), Battle of, 267

Logan, John A., 19, 213, 216, 227, 274

London *Times*, 389

Long Bridge, Virginia, 314

Longstreet, James, xx–xxiii, 2, 13, 71, 73–74, 76, 79, 85–86, 88, 100, 103–4, 107, 109–10, 112–13, 117, 123, 127–28, 155–58, 168–72, 174–75, 177, 179, 184–85, 189–94, 196–200, 202, 204, 211, 248–51, 255, 257–58, 261–62, 264–65, 273, 279–80, 282, 289–91, 294–95, 299, 304, 371–72, 417, 423, 428–29

Lookout Creek, Tennessee, 259

Lookout Mountain, Tennessee, 255, 257, 259–60

Battle of, 259–60, 263

Lookout Valley, Tennessee, 254–55, 257, 260

Loring, William Wing, 28–29, 232, 234, 249

Lost Cause, Myth of the, xiii, 374, 380, 395, 432

Loudon Heights, Virginia, 109

Louisiana, 6, 143, 151, 211, 217–19, 222, 242, 252, 287

Louisiana Tigers (C), 116

Louisville, Kentucky, 252

Lowe, David, 116, 168, 341, 359

Lowry, Don, 294

Luray, Virginia, 70

Lutheran Seminary, Gettysburg, Pennsylvania, 196

Lynchburg, Virginia, 313, 316, 322, 325, 367

Lyon, Nathaniel, 18

M

Magruder, John B., 79, 84–85, 89, 91, 249, 412

Maine, 303

Malvern Hill, Virginia, 314
　　Battle of, 84, 87–88, 90, 92, 133, 211, 314, 388, 392, 396, 400–1, 406

Manassas (Bull Run) (Virginia),
　　First Battle of, xvi, xxv, 24–25, 372
　　Second Battle of, xviii–xix, xxv, 97, 102–3, 105, 122, 125, 133, 194, 209–10, 401, 407

Manassas Junction, Virginia, 24, 65–66, 103, 266

Manassas, Virginia, 66, 103, 106, 110, 112, 133

Manigault, Arthur M., 329

Mansfield, Joseph K. F., 116

Mansfield (Sabine Crossroads), Louisiana, Battle of, 287

March through the Carolinas (Sherman's), xxv, 351–52, 355–56, 418

March to the Sea (Sherman's), xxv, 332, 343–45, 351, 355–56, 385, 412

Marvel, William, 353, 374

Marye's Heights, Fredericksburg, Virginia, 130–31, 133

Maryland, xviii, 5, 71, 97, 105–7, 109–10, 119, 122, 125, 138, 158, 177, 179, 181, 206, 253, 322–23, 330, 339

Maryland Campaign. *See* Antietam (Maryland) Campaign

Maryland Heights, Maryland, 109

Mason-Dixon Line, 177

Massachusetts, 116, 286–87, 303, 381

Massanutten Mountain, Virginia, 70

McClellan, George B., xv–xvi, xviii, 13, 18, 24, 43, 47–49, 64–68, 70–71, 73–77, 79–81, 84, 86–88, 90–92, 95, 97–102, 104, 109–10, 112–14, 117–27, 129, 131, 151, 206, 210, 242, 272, 283, 297, 299, 335, 338, 342, 384, 392, 399, 407–9, 411, 416–17, 419, 423, 430

McClernand, John A., 19, 36–40, 53, 55–56, 60, 145–46, 148, 151, 213, 215, 219, 221–25, 227, 229–30, 235–36, 385, 430

McCook, Alexander M., 61

McDowell, Irvin, 24, 66–68, 70–71, 272, 399

McDowell, Virginia, 70

McFeely, William S., 48, 385

McLaws, Lafayette, 89, 109–10, 113, 116, 160, 166, 185, 191–95, 249

McLean, Wilmer, 372

McMurry, Richard, 379, 408, 429

McPherson, James B., 63, 141, 150–51, 213, 216, 219, 222–31, 236, 274, 325, 338, 412

McPherson, James M., 208, 212, 242, 319, 389, 395, 397, 419, 422

McPherson's Farm, Gettysburg, Pennsylvania, 181

McPherson's Ridge, Gettysburg, Pennsylvania, 181

McWhiney, Grady, 7, 265, 397, 399, 437

Meade, George G., 160, 172, 177, 179–81, 183, 185, 188–91, 196, 199–200, 206–7, 210, 248–49, 265–67, 272, 274–75, 277, 280, 289, 291, 293, 297, 299–301, 306–7, 309–10, 323, 333, 342, 360, 362–65, 375, 399, 405–6, 408–9, 423–25

Meadow Bridge, Virginia, 79

Mechanicsville Bridge, Virginia, 79

Mechanicsville, Virginia, 79–80, 82–83
    Battle of, 77, 79–81, 92, 290, 401

Memphis & Charleston Railroad, 35, 134, 139

Memphis and Ohio Railroad, 37

Memphis, Tennessee, 33, 37, 135, 138, 144–46, 148–49, 214, 418

Meridian, Mississippi, 218, 271
    Campaign, 218, 270–71, 412

Mertz, Gregory A., 375

Mexican War, xv, 1, 3, 6–11, 15, 20, 43, 88, 411, 419
    casualties, 9, 88

Mexico, 6, 10–11, 18, 20, 88, 144, 241, 251, 270

Mexico City, Mexico, xv, 8–11,
    Battle of, xv, 7

Middleburg, Maryland, 109

Middleburg, Virginia, 176

Middle Theater, xvii, xxii–xxv, 67, 106, 157, 173, 212, 245, 247–51, 283–84, 393, 426, 429

Middletown, Maryland, 323

Midwest, 38, 145, 181, 242

Miles, Dixon S., 113

Miller's cornfield, Antietam/Sharpsburg, Maryland, 114, 116–17, 124, 133

Milliken's Bend, Mississippi River, 151, 214–15

Mine Run (Virginia), Campaign of, 267–68

Missing order. *See* Special Orders No. 191 of Lee

Missionary Ridge, Chattanooga, Tennessee, xxii, 259–60, 270, 407

Mississippi, xvii, xviii–xx, 35, 44, 50, 57, 129, 134–35, 137, 142–43, 145–46, 151, 156–58, 171–72, 216–19, 223, 225, 234, 236, 240, 242, 257, 270, 342, 382, 416, 426

Mississippi Central Railroad, 144–45

Mississippi River, xix, 20–21, 35, 138, 143–46, 148–51, 159, 171, 173, 211, 213–14, 216–19, 221–22, 226, 228, 233, 236, 238, 241–42, 252, 349, 416, 418, 427, 430

Mississippi Valley, xiii, xvii, xx, xxii, 27, 31, 45, 50, 67, 137, 143, 155–56, 173, 242, 244

Mississippi Valley (Western) Theater, xvii, xxiv, 67, 173, 244, 257, 426, 429, 431. *See also* Trans-Mississippi

Missouri, xvi, 5, 13, 18, 20–21, 32, 35, 231, 237

Mobile, Alabama, 158, 251, 269, 275, 287, 338, 341–42, 353, 423

Mobile Bay, Alabama, 321, 342, 347

Mobile & Ohio Railroad, 134, 217

Moccasin Bend, Tennessee River, Tennessee, 254

Molino del Rey (Mexico), Battle of, 9

Monocacy Creek, Maryland, 323

Monocacy, Maryland, 323, 339 Battle of, 323–24

Monterey (Mexico), Battle of, 7, 28

Morehead City, North Carolina, 358

Mount Crawford, Virginia, 358

"Mule Shoe," Spotsylvania, Virginia, 300–3

Mumma Farm, Sharpsburg, Maryland, 114, 117

Mummasberg Road, Gettysburg, Pennsylvania, 183

Murfreesboro (Stones River) (Tennessee), Battle of, xxv, 137

Murphy, Brian John, 8, 409

Murray, Williamson, 405, 425

Muscle Shoals, Alabama, 37

N

Napoleon, 226, 234, 242, 391

Nashville, Tennessee, 35, 39–40, 44, 48–50, 139, 252, 271, 277, 332, 345–46, 349

Battle of, 49, 139, 332

National Road, Maryland, 323

Native Americans, 382

Nelson, William, 51–53

Nelson's Crossing, Virginia, 307

Nevins, Alan, 242

New Bern, North Carolina, 352, 358

New Carthage, Louisiana, 151, 215–16, 219

New Market, Virginia, Battle of, 287

New Orleans, Louisiana, 251

Newton, John, 199

New York, 5, 13, 117–18, 303, 342

New York Times, 151, 381

Nineteenth Corps (U), 323

Ninth Corps (U), 119, 121, 157, 249, 280, 289, 294, 316, 360, 365, 427

Nolan, Alan T., 380, 388–89

Norfolk, Virginia, 68, 76

North Anna River, Virginia, Battle of, xxii, xxv, 305–6, 308, 333, 387, 415

North Carolina, xxv, 45, 157, 163–64, 172, 179, 203, 205, 252, 286, 332, 351–54, 356–59, 367, 428

Northern Neck, Virginia, 4

North Woods, Sharpsburg, Maryland, 114

O

Oak Grove, Virginia, Battle of, 75

Ohio, 1–2, 18, 173, 253

Ohio, Army of the, xxiii, 44, 50, 106, 143, 252, 325, 332, 344

Ohio Railroad, 37, 134, 217, 323

Ohio River, xvi, 1, 21–22, 25, 38, 275, 376

Opequon Creek, Virginia, Battle of, 340

Orange and Alexandria Railroad, Virginia, 175, 266

Orange Court House, Virginia, 99–100, 249, 290

Orange Plank Road, Virginia, 163, 165, 291, 294–95

Orange Turnpike, Virginia, 163, 291–93, 295

Orchard Knob, Chattanooga, Tennessee, 259–61

Ord, Edward O.C., 139–40, 142, 340, 360–61, 365–67, 371

Oregon, 342

Outer Banks, North Carolina, 45

Overland (Virginia) Campaign, xiv, xxv, 280, 285, 289, 293, 297, 310, 317–20, 376, 382, 385, 387–88, 392–93, 399, 407, 409, 414, 424–25, 430, 432

Owens, Richard, 413

Owl Creek, Shiloh, Tennessee, 55

Oxford, Mississippi, 145–47

Ox Hill, Virginia, 105

P

Paducah, Kentucky, xvi, 21–22, 32, 36

Palo Alto, Mexico, Battle of, 7, 270

Pamunkey River, Virginia, 76–77, 306–7, 314

Panama, 13

Parke, John G., 365

Patterson, Robert, 24

Patton, George, 407

Peace (Chicago) Platform, 335, 342

Peace Conference, 350

Peace Democrats, 335

Peach Orchard, Gettysburg, Pennsylvania, 194–95

Peach Tree Creek (Georgia), Battle of, 330

Pemberton, John C., 65, 67, 143, 145–47, 150, 157, 171, 179, 215, 217–19, 223–24, 226–32, 234, 238–39, 326, 394, 403, 408

Pender, William Dorsey, 168, 180, 185

Pendleton, William Nelson, 125, 192, 381

Peninsula Campaign, xviii, xxv, 65–67, 69

Pennsylvania, xx, 105, 109, 155, 172–74, 176, 179, 191, 209, 242, 324, 333, 338, 342

Pennsylvania Volunteers, 333

Perkins's Plantation, Louisiana, 215

Perret, Geoffrey, 385, 400

Perryville (Kentucky), Battle of, xxv

Petersburg, Virginia, xiv, xxv, 157, 285, 308, 316, 319, 321–22, 325, 329, 339, 357, 374–75, 396, 407, 424, 431–32

battles at, xxiii, xxv, 277, 286–87, 311, 313, 315, 318, 332–35, 337, 340–41, 346, 349, 358–59, 360–61, 365–66, 374–75, 396, 431–32

Petersburg/Richmond (Virginia), siege of, xiv, xxiii, 157, 277, 285, 313, 317, 321–22, 335, 341, 375, 407, 424

Pettigrew, James J., 205

Philadelphia, Pennsylvania, 158

Philippi, West Virginia, 28

Pickett, George E., 200, 202, 204–5, 361–65

Pickett's Charge, Gettysburg, 199–200, 401

Pennsylvania, xx, 105, 109, 155, 172–74, 176, 179, 191, 209, 242, 324, 333, 338, 342

Pillow, Gideon J., 21, 41, 408

Pittsburg Landing, Tennessee, xvii, 50–53, 58–59, 64, 233

Plank Road, 163, 165, 291, 293–95, 359, 361. *See* Orange Plank Road

Pleasonton, Alfred, 175, 180

Plum Run, Gettysburg, Pennsylvania, 195

Point Lookout, Maryland, 323

Point Pleasant, Ohio, 1

Polk, James K., 6, 8

Polk, Leonidas, 21, 32–35, 44, 50, 55, 64, 251

Pollard, Edward A., 381

Pontoon bridge, world's longest, 314

Pope, John, xvii–xviii, 43, 75, 98–101, 103–5, 133, 272, 399, 407–8

Porter, David Dixon, 148, 150, 214–16, 221, 239, 354

Porter, Fitz John, 77–83, 86, 89–90, 120–21

Porter, Horace, 299, 314, 343, 365, 382, 405, 413–14

Port Gibson, Mississippi, 222, 240, 243 Battle of, 223–24

Port Hudson, Louisiana, 143, 150, 211–13, 222, 224, 228, 233, 240, 244

Port Republic (Virginia), Battle of, 74

Port Royal, South Carolina, 45

Potomac River, 5, 71, 77, 109–10, 113, 122, 123, 190, 206, 280

Powhite Creek, Virginia, 82

Prentiss, Benjamin M., 51, 53, 55–58, 60

presidential election of 1864, xxiii, 159, 282, 286, 322, 325, 331, 335–36, 343, 376, 392, 396, 432

Presidio, San Francisco, CA, 13

Price, Sterling, 139

prisoner exchanges, 98–99, 336, 341

Q

"Quaker cannons," 66, 69–69

"Quinine Brigade," 217

R

Raleigh, North Carolina, 164

Ramseur, Stephen D., 163

Rapidan River, Virginia, 99, 101, 159–60, 167, 266–67, 279–80, 289–91, 297, 318, 331

Rappahannock River, Virginia, 101, 128–29, 131, 159, 167, 266, 396

Rappahannock Station, Virginia, 266–67, 401

Rawlins, John A., 21, 36, 422

Raymond, Mississippi, 227–28, 431

Reams Station, Virginia, 334

Red River (Louisiana) campaigns, 224, 279, 287

Reed, Charles Ellington, 273

Reno, Jesse L., 112

Resaca de Palma (Mexico), Battle of, 7

Resaca, (Georgia), Battle of, 287

Reynolds, John F., 181–84, 188, 199

Rhea, Gordon C., 272, 281, 293, 297, 306–7, 309–11, 318, 320, 387, 396, 400, 418, 424–25

Rhode Island, 130, 208, 286, 402

Rhodes, Elisha Hunt, 130, 208, 286, 297, 303, 311, 353, 360–62, 402

Richmond and Danville Railroad, Virginia, 367

Richmond Dispatch, 95

Richmond Examiner, 25, 74

Richmond, Louisiana, 151

Richmond and Petersburg Railroad, Virginia, 313, 315–16, 334, 340, 358, 361

Richmond, Virginia, xiv, xvi, xviii, xxiii, 18, 23–25, 27–28, 30, 47, 62, 65–68, 70–71, 73–77, 79, 81, 84, 88, 90–91, 95, 97–100, 105, 128, 151, 157, 160–61, 169, 171–72, 177, 179, 209, 215, 224, 234, 244, 248–49, 262, 264, 277, 279–80, 283, 285–88, 297, 305, 308–11, 313–17, 319–22, 324, 332–35, 340–41, 346, 349–58, 361, 366–67, 371, 375, 380, 382, 389, 392, 396, 399, 407, 416, 423–24, 428, 432

Richmond Whig, 95

Rich Mountain (Virginia), Battle of, 23, 28

Riddell's Shop, Virginia, 314

River Queen, 350

Roanoke River, Virginia, 357

Robertson, James, 80, 83, 88

"Rock of Chickamauga," 250. *See also* Thomas, George H.

Rodes, Robert E., 161, 164, 183–84, 188, 197

Rohrbach Bridge, Sharpsburg, Maryland, 118

Ropes, John C., 381

Rosecrans, William S., xxi, 31, 138–43, 152, 156–57, 217, 248, 250, 252–53, 409, 428

Rosser, Thomas L., 363–64

Rossville Gap, Tennessee, 263

Round Tops, Gettysburg, Pennsylvania, 177, 189, 194–95

Ruggles, Daniel, 58

Rusling, James F., 420

Russia, 389, 391, 403, 414

Rust, Albert, 29–30

S

Sabine Crossroads, Mansfield, Louisiana, Battle of, 287

Sackets Harbor, New York, 13

Salem Church, Spotsylvania, Virginia,
  166
Salem, Virginia, 101
"Sam" Grant, 2, 18. *See also* Grant,
  Ulysses S.
Santa Anna, 10
Saunders' Field, Wilderness, Virginia,
  292–93
Savage's Station, Virginia, Battle of,
  84–85, 91
Savannah, Georgia, 45, 158, 338, 343–
  47, 349, 351–52, 355
Savannah River, Georgia, 45
Savannah, Tennessee, 50–51, 61
Sayler's (Sailor's) Creek, Virginia, Bat-
  tle of, 367
Schofield, John M., 325, 329, 332, 354,
  356–58
Schurz, Carl, 183–84
Scott, Winfield, xv–xvi, 7–11, 22, 24
Sears, Stephen, 200, 384
Second Corps (C), 128, 174, 177, 183–
  84, 197–98, 267, 293, 303–4, 307,
  313, 322, 394
Second Corps (U), 84, 189, 195, 295,
  316, 361–62, 365, 367
Second Manassas, Virginia, Battle of,
  xviii, xix, xxv, 97, 102–3, 105, 122,
  125, 133, 194, 209, 401, 407
Second Maryland Infantry (U), 118
Second U.S. Cavalry (U), 12
Seddon, James A., 132, 157–58, 169,
  171, 229, 248, 298, 328
Sedgwick, John, 166–67, 293, 365
Seminary Ridge, Gettysburg, Pennsyl-
  vania, 185, 191, 195–96, 202, 204–5

Seven Days', Battle of, xix, xxv, 29, 47,
  76–78, 80, 87, 90–93, 95, 122, 125,
  133, 185, 196, 199, 206, 209–10,
  217–18, 239, 253, 296, 305, 311,
  327, 392, 396, 399, 401, 404, 408,
  410, 415, 417, 429
  compared to Shiloh, 93–95
Seven Pines/Fair Oaks, Virginia, Battle
  of, ix, xviii, 71–73
Seventeenth Corps (U), 216
Seward, William, 272, 342
Shad bake at Hatcher's Run, Virginia,
  363–64
Sharpsburg, Maryland, 113–14, 118–
  23, 125, 131, 177
  Battle of, 118–23, 131. *See* Antietam
    (Maryland) Campaign
Shenandoah Mountains, Virginia, 70,
  358
Shenandoah River, Virginia, 74,
  109
Shenandoah Valley, Virginia, 24,
  66–67, 70–71, 74, 98, 125, 129, 277,
  287, 303–4, 313, 321–23, 338–41,
  347, 358, 361, 396, 402
Shenandoah Valley (Virginia)
  Campaigns, xx, xxii, 29, 73–75, 79,
  81
Sheridan, Phillip H., 262, 270, 274,
  300, 306, 308, 313, 334, 338–41,
  358, 360–65, 367, 369, 372, 405–6,
  416
Sherman, William Tecumseh, 2, 38, 43,
  50–51, 53–56, 60, 63, 137, 144–48,
  150, 152, 213, 216, 219, 221–22,
  225, 227–30, 232–33, 236, 238–40,

247, 253, 257–60, 270–71, 281–83, 287–88, 298, 312, 318, 338, 342–47, 360, 392, 405–6, 408, 412–13, 419, 428

March through the Carolinas, xxv, 349, 351–58, 377, 418, 428

March to the Sea, xxii–xxiii, 262, 274–78, 320–22, 324–26, 329–32, 334–38, 342–47, 376, 382, 385, 392, 412, 424, 428

Shields, James, 74

Shiloh, Tennessee, xvii, 50–51

Battle of, xvii, xix, xxv, 33–34, 47–48, 50–51, 53–54, 62–63, 67, 87, 133–35, 137, 141, 231, 251, 265, 277, 385, 393–94, 405, 414, 417, 420, 431

Battle of compared to Seven Days' Battle, 93–95

Shunpike Road, Shiloh, Tennessee, 52

Sickles, Daniel E., 164, 189, 194–96

Sigel, Franz, 277, 279, 287, 412, 430

Simpson, Brooks, 385–86

Simpson, Harold, 310

Sixth Corps (U), 112, 166, 189, 195, 286, 293

Sixth Virginia Cavalry, 101

Slash Church, Virginia, 79

slaves/slavery, 5, 98, 125, 143, 335, 350, 353, 390, 392, 394

Slocum, Henry W., 185, 344, 355, 358

Smith, Charles F., 22, 53, 133, 139

Smith, Edmund Kirby, 12, 138, 350

Smith, Gustavus W., 73

Smith, Jean Edward, 7, 10, 19, 21, 36–38, 63, 280, 297, 313–14, 385–86, 394, 405, 407

Smith, William F. "Baldy," 253–54, 263, 274, 307–8, 365

Smith, William Sooy, 270–71

Smithfield, North Carolina, 358

Smithland, Kentucky, xvi, 22, 32

Snake Creek, Shiloh, Tennessee, 52, 55

Snavely Ford, Sharpsburg, Maryland, 118–19

Snodgrass Hill, Chickamauga, Georgia, 250

South Carolina, 22, 35, 45, 50, 65, 179, 228, 304, 345–46, 352, 355–56

South Mountain (Maryland), Battle of, 109–10, 113, 125, 209

South Side Railroad, Virginia, 342, 359, 363, 365

Special Orders No. 191 (of Lee), 107, 109

Spencer rifles, 181, 275, 341, 401–2

Spotsylvania Court House, Virginia, Battle of, xxii, xxv, 285, 297–300, 303–5, 317–18, 387, 396, 399, 405, 409, 416, 418, 431

Springfield, Illinois, 17, 146

Spring Hill, Tennessee, 332

Stanton, Edwin M., 43, 48–49, 66, 76, 98, 145, 252–53, 274, 315, 323, 340, 430

Staunton, Virginia, 28, 70, 174

Steele, Frederick, 217

Stephens, Alexander, 350

Stewart, Alexander P., 57

St. Louis, Missouri, 3, 15, 18, 35, 42

Stoneman, George, 160

Stones River (Murfreesboro), Tennessee, Battle of, xxv, 137

Stratford Hall, Virginia, 4

Streight, Abel D., 219

Stuart, James Ewell Brown "Jeb," 75–76, 101. 103–4, 110, 160–61, 164–66, 174–78, 180, 183–84, 189, 201, 211, 300, 404, 406, 416–17

Sudley Springs, Virginia, 103

Sumner, Edwin V., 84–85

Sunken Road, Sharpsburg, Maryland, 117

Surrender Negotiations (Grant and Lee), 369–73

Susquehanna River, 105

Sutherland Station, Virginia, 365

Swinton, William, 381

T

Tallahatchie River, Georgia, 145, 150

Taneytown, Maryland, 183, 189

Taylor, Walter H., 82, 186, 267, 367, 374, 379

Taylor, Zachary, xv, 7–8, 10, 411

Telegraph Road, Virginia, 305

Tennessee, xvi–xvii, xix, xxi–xxiii, xxv, 22, 35–39, 43–44, 46–48, 50–52, 55, 57, 59, 61, 106, 128–29, 134–40, 143–44, 147, 156–59, 171, 173, 179, 211, 217, 219, 228, 235, 237, 241, 248–54, 259, 262, 264, 266–67, 271, 274–75, 279, 281, 283, 287–88, 321, 325, 327–29, 332, 344–47, 349, 352–52, 354–55, 376, 408, 424, 426–28, 430, 432

Tennessee Campaign (Hood's), xxv

Tennessee River, xvi, 22, 35–37, 39, 43–44, 48, 50–52, 55, 61, 139, 143, 254, 259, 344

Tenth Corps (U), 340

Terry, Alfred H., 354

Texas, xv, 6, 12, 22, 110, 116, 241–42, 251, 295, 332

Texas Brigade (C), 294–95

Third Arkansas Infantry (C), 29

Third Cavalry Division (U), 355

Third Corps (C), 174, 195, 198, 267, 293

Third Corps (U), 164, 189, 194

Thirteenth Corps (U), 215

Thirteenth North Carolina Infantry (C), 205

Thirty-seventh Massachusetts Infantry (U), 402

Thomas, George H., 134, 250, 253–54, 259–61, 263, 270, 321, 325, 344–46, 349, 351

Thompson, Robert N., 274

Thoroughfare Gap, Virginia, 101–4

Tilghman, Lloyd, 36–37

Timeline of Civil War, xxv

Totopotomoy Creek/River, Virginia, 307–8, 312

Trans-Mississippi, 144, 228

Trans-Mississippi Army (C), 350

Traveller, 166

Trevilian's Station, Virginia, Battle of, 313, 416

Trimble, Isaac R., 187

troop transfers, 249, 358, 423. *See also* inter-theater troop transfers.

Trudeau, Noah Andre, 243

Tullahoma (Tennessee), Campaign of, xxv, 156, 248, 268, 427

Tunnel Hill/Mountain, Chattanooga, Tennessee, 260

Tupelo, Mississippi, 135–36

Turner's Gap, Maryland, 110, 112–13

Twelfth Corps (U), xxiii, 116, 185, 195, 253, 266

Twelfth Massachusetts Infantry (U), 116

Twentieth Maine Infantry (U), 195

Twenty-first Illinois Volunteers (U), 17–19, 21

Twenty-fourth Corps (U), 365

Twenty-third Corps (U), 354

U

"Unconditional Surrender" Grant, xvii, 41–42

Union Party, 335

United States Ford, Virginia, 306

Upton, Emory, 300–1

U.S. Army Field Manual, 212

U.S. Military Academy, 2–3, 18. *See also* West Point

USS *Chattanooga*, 254

USS *Diligence*, 237

USS *Essex*, 36

USS *Lexington*, 60

USS *Louisville*, 224

USS *Merrimac*, 65

USS *Monitor*, 65, 68

USS *Tyler*, 60

V

Valley Campaigns, 66–67, 70, 304, 338, 340, 439. *See also* Shenandoah Valley (Virginia) Campaigns

Van Dorn, Earl, 139–43, 146, 249

Vera Cruz, Mexico, Battle of, xv, 8–10

Vermont Brigade (U), 203

Vicksburg and Jackson Railroad, 226–30

Vicksburg, Mississippi, xx–xxi, 136–37, 156, 158–59, 169, 171–73, 208, 212–13, 259, 269–71, 273, 279, 326, 346, 380, 385, 403, 416–18, 423, 427, 430–31

attacks on, xix, 237, 404–5, 410–11

Campaign, xiv, xx, 11, 133, 156, 213–44, 251, 265, 268, 381, 386, 393, 403, 406, 410–12, 420, 423

early attempts to capture, xix, 143–52, 416–18

siege of, xix, 179, 237–240 , 422

Vietnam War, 385

Virginia, xiv, xvi–xviii, xx–xxi, xxiii, 2–5, 12, 22–24, 27–31, 46–47, 65–68, 70, 75, 79, 91, 97–99, 101, 106, 110, 114, 120, 123–25, 128–29, 132, 155, 157–58, 169–72, 174, 176–77, 179, 193, 198, 200, 202–6, 208–11, 226, 238, 247–48, 250, 252–53, 257–58, 265–68, 272–74, 277, 279–85, 287–88, 293, 298, 304,

307, 310, 312–13, 315, 320–22, 329,
331–32, 349–50, 352, 355–56, 358,
364–66, 369, 373, 375–76, 382, 386,
395, 398, 402, 406–7, 418, 423, 425–
29, 432–33
Virginia's Constitutional Convention,
22–23
Virginia Legislature, 350
Virginia Military Institute, 287
Virginia Militia (C), 23
Virginia Peninsula, xviii, 47, 65, 68–71,
77, 81, 84, 105, 179, 408. *See also*
Peninsula Campaign

W

Walker, John G., 109, 113, 116
Wallace, Lewis "Lew," 33, 39–40,
52–53, 61, 63, 323–24, 414
Wallace, William H. L., 56, 60
Warren, Gouverneur K., 293, 300,
302–3, 305, 307, 314, 340, 361–65
Washburn, Cadwallader C., 151
Washburne, Elihu B., 17–18, 21, 49,
151, 270, 336
Washington, D.C., xvii, xxiii, 4–5, 12,
18, 22, 24, 48–49, 65–67, 70–71,
100–1, 105, 128, 133, 138, 145, 152,
172, 179, 190, 213, 237, 243, 251,
258, 270–71, 274–75, 294, 307, 314,
322–24, 340, 402, 412, 428
Washington, George, xv, 3, 5, 270
Washington, John A., 30
Watkins, Sam R., 135, 262, 329
Waugh, John, 317

Wauhatchie, Tennessee, Battle of, 255,
257
Waynesboro, Virginia, 358
weaponry, 10, 90, 128, 401–2
Webster, Joseph D., 40–41, 58–59
Weigley, Russell F., 64, 90, 124–25, 134,
137, 144, 205, 241–42, 388, 430, 432
Weldon, North Carolina, 339
Weldon and Petersburg Railroad, 334,
339–40
Weldon Railroad (Globe Tavern), Vir-
ginia, 334, 339–40, 342, 358
Wert, Jeffry, 373, 425
Western and Atlantic Railroad, 343
Western Department (U), 138
Western Theaters, 65. *See also* Middle
Theater and Mississippi Valley The-
ater
Western Virginia Campaign, 27–31,
406
West Point (U.S. Military Academy),
New York, 1–2, 4–5, 12, 18–19, 237,
329
West Virginia, xvi, 28, 30, 253, 313
West Woods, Sharpsburg, Maryland,
114
Wheatfield, Gettysburg, Pennsylvania,
194–96
Wheeler, Joseph, 262
Wheeling, Virginia/West Virginia, 28
White House, D.C., 272, 277, 331. *See
also* Executive Mansion
White House Landing, Virginia, 76, 81,
84, 306–8, 314
White Oak Creek, Virginia, 85

White Oak Road, Virginia, 362
White Oak Swamp, Virginia, 85
White's Ferry, Maryland-Virginia, 106
Wilcox, Cadmus, 199
Wilcox's Landing, Virginia, 314
Wilderness, Virginia, xxii, xxv, 160–61, 166–67, 267, 280, 285, 289–91, 293, 296–97, 299, 302, 304, 312–13, 318, 375, 385–87, 396, 399, 401, 403, 408–9, 417–18, 425, 431–32
Wiley, Bell I., 389
Willard Hotel, D.C., 271
Williamsburg (Virginia), Battle of, 68
Williams, Kenneth P., 238
Williamsport, Maryland, 71, 125, 206
Williams, T. Harry, 41, 138, 212, 226, 380, 384, 393, 413, 416, 420, 425, 431
Willis, Edward, 307
Willoughby Run, Pennsylvania, 181
Wilmington, North Carolina, 349, 352–58, 418
Wilmington & Weldon Railroad, 358
Wilson, James H., 236, 291
Winchester, Virginia, 177, 340–41; Third Battle of, 340
Windmill Point, Virginia, 314
Wing, Henry, 294
Winschel, Terence J., 222
Wisconsin, 233, 270
Wise, Henry A., 29–30
Wittenberg, Eric J., 416
Woodworth, Steven E., 408, 420
Wool, John E., 66

Wright, Ambrose, 199, 302, 305, 308, 311, 365–66

Y

Yallabusha River, Mississippi, 146
Yates, Richard, 18–20, 223
Yazoo Pass, Mississippi, 243
Yazoo River, Mississippi, 147, 149–50, 219, 227, 233, 237
Yellow Tavern, Virginia, 300, 318, 387
York, Pennsylvania, 177
York River, Virginia, 65, 67, 76–77, 314
Yorktown, Virginia, 67–68
Young's Point, Louisiana, 148–49